JOSE MANUEL AZCONA PASTOR

Possible Paradises

Basque Emigration to Latin America

FOREWORD BY WILLIAM A. DOUGLASS
TRANSLATION BY ROLAND VAZQUEZ

University of Nevada Press
Reno   Las Vegas

The Basque Series

Series Editor: William A. Douglass

Translation and production support was provided by a grant from Euskal Fundazioa.

University of Nevada Press,
Reno, Nevada 89557 USA
www.unpress.nevada.edu
Copyright © 2004 by University of Nevada Press
All rights reserved
Manufactured in the United States of America

The paper used in this book meets the requirements of American National Standard for Information Sciences-Permanence of Paper for Printed Library Materials, ANSI z39.48-:1984- Binding materials were selected for strength and durability.

This book has been reproduced as a digital reprint

Library of Congress Cataloging-in-Publication Data

Azcona Pastor, Jose Manuel.

Possible paradises : Basque emigration to Latin America / by Jose Manuel Azcona Pastor ; foreword by William A. Douglass ; translation by Roland Vasquez.

p. cm. - (The Basque Series)

Includes bibliographical references (p.) and index.

ISBN 978-0-874:17-444-1 (hardcover: alk. paper)

1. Basques-America-History.
2. Basque Americans-History.
3. Immigrants-America-History.
4. America-Emigration and immigration-History. 5. Pafs Vasco (Spain)-Emigration and immigration-History. I. Title. II. Series.

E29.B35 A98 2002

980' .0049992-dc2:1   2002000077

ISBN 978-1-943859-91-7 (paperback: alk. paper)

Contents

List of Illustrations	vii
Foreword	xi
Preface	xvii
Acknowledgments	xix
Chapter One	
The Basque Country at the Time of Columbus	1
Chapter Two	
Mastery of the Land	24
Chapter Three	
Colonial Commerce	74
Chapter Four	
Basque Americans	123
Chapter Five	
The Overseas Destinations	162
Chapter Six	
The Human Deluge to Rio de la Plata	227
Chapter Seven	
Foundations of the Recent Exodus	294
Chapter Eight	
The Bureaucracy, the Dreamed-of Voyage, and the Typology of the Emigrant	359
Chapter Nine	
Dramatic Exile	392

Chapter Ten

    The Future of the Basque-American Communities   406

Appendix 1   415

Appendix 2   421

Notes   473

Bibliography   507

Index   523

Possible Paradises

The Basque Series

Illustrations

CHART

5.1 Destinations of Emigrants from Baztan to the Americas in the Twentieth Century — 176

GRAPHS

4.1 Spanish Emigration to the Americas, 1765-1800 — 136
4.2 American Donations in Pesos for Religious Buildings in the Basque Country, 1541-1980 — 155
4.3 American Donations in Pesos for Furnishings in the Basque Country, 1541-1980 — 157
4.4 American Donations in Pesos for Religious and Pious Foundations in the Basque Country, 1541-1980 — 159
4.5 American Donations in Pesos and Shipments to the Basque Country, 1541-1980 — 161

PHOTOGRAPHS

(following page 122)

- Scene from a ship bound for Río de la Plata, ca. 1900s
- Los Pirineos Bakery street vendor, ca. 1950s
- Basque dairyman in Buenos Aires, Argentina, ca. 1940s
- Departing farewell, ca. 1900s
- Basque street dairymen vendors, Buenos Aires, Argentina, ca. 1900-1950
- The establishment of Argentine dairy business of J. E. Uriburu, ca. 1900s
- Immigrant arrivals in Argentina
- Hotel de los Emigrantes, ca. early 1900s
- Advertisement for Basque dairies, ca. 1900-1950
- Port of Buenos Aires for unloading goods, ca. 1920s
- South American garment industry with immigrant laborers
- Dining room at Hotel de los Emigrantes, Buenos Aires
- Passenger ship *Isabel de Borbon*, 1928
- Passenger carriages at the Hotel de los Emigrantes, ca. 1870-1880
- Immigrant fisherman, Venezuela, ca. 1890
- Disembarkation of passengers and goods, ca. 1870-1880
- Hotel de los Emigrantes, Buenos Aires

Immigration inspectors
Arrivals in Río de la Plata
Immigrants waiting for meals
Interior view of Hotel de los Emigrantes

TABLES

y 1	Introduction of Slaves into the Americas by Basque Merchants, 1586-1599	93
3.2	Basques in Positions of Power in the Viceroyalty of Peru, 1735-1803	102
4.1	Spanish Emigration to the Americas by Region, 1493-1600	130
4.2	Destination of Spanish Emigration to the Americas, 1493-1600	133
4.3	Europeans in the Mexico City Census, 1689	134
5.1	Principal Basque Family Networks in Central America in the 18th Century	181
5.2	Basque Families in Colombia after the Spanish Civil War	204
6.1	Population in the Basses-Pyrenees and France, 1801-1936	235
6.2	Urban and Rural Population Distribution in the Basses-Pyrenees and France, 1846-1936	236
6.3	Marriages in the Basses-Pyrenees and France, 1801-1900	238
6.4	Mortality Rates in the Basses-Pyrenees and France, 1801-1900	239
6.5	Surplus Births in the Basses-Pyrenees, 1800-1910	239
6.6	Migratory Surplus in the Basses-Pyrenees, 1836-1901	240
6.7	Emigration from Iparralde to America, 1831-1841	241
6.8	Emigration from Iparralde to America by Occupation	242
6.9	Rural Depopulation of Iparralde between 1856 and 1892	243
6.10	Basque Businesses in Montevideo, 1860-1878	247
6.11	Resident Population Loss in Five Bizkaian Towns	250
7.1	Population of Europe, Selected Countries, 1800-1900	298
8.1	Origins of Navarrese Emigrants to Río de la Plata, 1830-1900	379
8.2	Origins of Bizkaian Emigrants to Río de la Plata, 1800-1900	383
8.3	Origins of Gipuzkoan Emigrants to Río de la Plata, 1852-1900	386
8.4	Main Shipping Companies Operating in Gasteiz, 1880-1895	389
8.5	Port of Embarkation of Basques, 1830-1900	390
8.6	Companies Transporting Emigrants to Argentina, 1890	391
9.1	Principal Shelters of Basque Exiles in France and Belgium, 1937	395

APPENDIX TABLES

1.1	Basque Crew Members on Magellan's Voyage of Circumnavigation	415
1.2	Privateering Recruiters and Vessels in Atlantic Spain, 17th Century	416
1.3	Basque Positions and Titles in the Bourbon Court, 1721-1799	417

2.1	Iron and Steel Exports from the Basque Country to the Americas, 1511-1699	421
2.2	Iron and Steel Exports from the Basque Country to the Americas, 1700-1799	425
2.3	Basque Companies Trading in Iron and Metal Manufactures in Sevilla, 1596-1693	428
2.4	Ships of the Company of Caracas, 1728-1785	431
2.5	Basque Members of Club of the Vizcayans in the Consulate of Mexico, 1700s	432
2.6	Number of Members of the Royal Basque Society, 1765-1793	433
2.7	Number of Members of the Royal Basque Society in the Americas, 1765-1793	434
2.8	Number of Members of the Royal Basque Society in the Main Cities of the Viceroyalty of Nueva Espana, 1765-1793	435
2.9	Number of Members of the Royal Basque Society in the Main Cities of the Viceroyalty of Peru, 1765-1793	436
2.10	Provincial and Local Origin of Basque Emigration to America, First Half of the 18th Century	437
2.11	Destination of Basque Emigration to America, First Half of the 18th Century	440
2.12	Sample of American Donations Destined for Religious Buildings in the Basque Country, 1526-1814	441
2.13	Sample of American Donations Destined for Social Welfare Buildings in the Basque Country, 1526-1929	444
2.14	Sample of American Donations Destined for the Promotion of Schools in the Basque Country, 1609-1930	445
2.15	Sample of American Donations Destined for Infrastructure and Services in the Basque Country, 1638-1892	447
2.16	Sample of American Donations Destined As Furnishings in the Basque Country, 1591-1850	449
2.17	Sample of American Donations Destined for Pious and Charitable Purposes in the Basque Country and Navarre, 1553-1901	454
2.18	Noble Descent and Institutional Activity of Central American Basques, First Generation	459
2.19	Noble Lineage and Institutional Activity of Central American Basques, Second Generation	460
2.20	Occupations of Basques in Puerto Rico in the 19th Century	462
2.21	Basque Workers, Barracas al Norte, 1855 (Buenos Aires)	464
2.22	Basque Workers, Barracas al Norte, 1869 (Buenos Aires)	465
2.23	Basque Emigrants Indebted for Their Passage, Uruguay	467

Foreword

WILLIAM A. DOUGLASS

In 1969 I received funding from the National Institute of Mental Health to initiate anthropological field research among the Basques of the eastern Nevada town of Elko, the first such grant support for the fledgling Basque Studies Program of the University of Nevada, Reno. Conducting the field research was relatively straightforward, contextualizing its results was another matter. At the time, little had been published about the Basque experience in North America. It therefore seemed appropriate to collaborate with Jon Bilbao, a historian by training, on an introduction that would situate the Elko study within the broader historical and geographical framework of Basque emigration to Nevada.

We quickly determined that respecting state, and even national, borders was an entirely artificial exercise. It became apparent that to understand why a Basque emigrant settled in Elko it was necessary to know why he rejected Boise, Idaho. The logical progression was then to question why an Elko or Boise Basque eschewed Buenos Aires as his choice of destination. In short, once we had placed our feet on the path the journey took us several years to complete, and our itinerary embraced five centuries of history and two continents.

In 1975 we published our book *Amerikanuak: Basques in the New World*. By then our "introduction" had become a much larger study, which both subsumed and transcended our original intent. The Elko Basques certainly inform the pages of our book (particularly chapter 7), but they are largely lost from specific view within its labyrinth. Jon and I never regarded *Amerikanuak* to be anything more than an initial foray into its vastly complicated subject matter. Nor did we believe that it was a balanced one. We had lived in Elko for a summer, sharing the lives of the boarders at the Star Hotel and, in my case, of the herders in the sheep camps of the Copper Mountains near Jarbidge. We subsequently interviewed more than one hundred Basques throughout the American West, applied a questionnaire to dozens more, and conducted archival research in the county and city records of several states. In short, both our field and archival research in the United States was extensive.

The same cannot be said for our Latin American efforts. In the spring of 1971 we conducted "parachute" research that, over about a six-week period, took us to eight countries. We visited Mexico City, Bogotá, Lima, and Buenos Aires together, interviewing local Basques and examining the records of their ethnic organizations. Jon covered Santiago, Montevideo, and Sao Paulo on his own, while I traveled to

Necochea, Argentina (to experience the Basque presence in a more rural Argentine setting), and Caracas by myself. Neither of us experienced firsthand Castro's Cuba, although Jon had published a book on Basque activities on that island during the first part of the sixteenth century. He had lived in Batista's Cuba for a number of years and therefore had many memories of its recent Basque presence. Back in Reno we combined our data with the, at the time, few published sources on Basque emigration to Latin America and produced a counterweight of sorts to our more profound investigations of Basques in the American West.

Amerikanuak has become a kind of classic in its own right, probably because there was nothing else quite like it available. To our chagrin, in a sense the book seemed to stifle rather than stimulate additional research. For several would-be investigators of the North American Basque immigrant experience (though certainly not all), *Amerikanuak* dampened enthusiasm ("it's been done"). For others it served as a foundational text that was more to be respected than questioned.

Regarding the situation in Latin America, the book simply failed to stimulate much interest at all. In part there was the language difficulty, because the Spanish edition did not appear for eleven years (in 1986). However, the relative scholarly neglect of the Basque immigrant experience in Latin America was more deep-seated and deserves consideration.

One of the anomalies characteristic of Basque-American studies is the wealth of research on Basques in the United States compared, until quite recently, with the paucity of such efforts regarding them in several Latin American countries. This is true despite the extensive Basque presence, numbering literally in the millions of persons throughout the five centuries of Latin American history, whereas Basques entered the United States in significant numbers beginning only in the middle of the nineteenth century and today their descendants number only somewhere between 50,000 and 75,000 individuals. Nor have U.S. Basques attained the social, political, and economic prominence of Latin American ones. Why, then, the relative scholarly neglect of the latter—at least at the time we were writing *Amerikanuak*?

To my mind the answer lies in the differing colonial (and subsequent) histories of the two respective New World regions. While one European power or another colonized all of the Americas, the British colonial link never served as a conduit for transferring Old World Basques to the New World. It was not until after the American Revolution that Basques began to enter the United States—both as part of the California Gold Rush and in the emigrant ranks of Europe's "huddled masses" (which included a significant contingent of southern and central Europeans).

The Spanish and French colonial experiences presented Basques with a profoundly different playing field. All Old World Basques were citizens of one of these two continental powers and, therefore, enjoyed access to their overseas empires. Indeed, the opportunities were both considerable and varied, since the ranks of the New World colonial elite tended to be dominated by Old World–born individuals.

Fluent in the dominant language (Spanish or French) and functional in the dominant culture (Hispanic or French), the aspiring Basque emigrant during the colonial era could move back and forth between the Old and New World with relative ease.

At the same time, the individual colonies were administrative extensions of the metropole. That is, prior to various nineteenth-century independence movements in Latin America, the several Spanish colonies were integrated parts of a Spanish empire rather than qualitatively different extensions of Spain itself. For a Basque to reside in Lima or Buenos Aires was pretty much akin to a move to Seville or Cadiz (indeed there were Basque merchant families with members in various New World capitals, southern Spain, and the Basque Country itself vertically integrated into a single family enterprise).

Consequently, there was little incentive for colonial historians to think in terms of, say, "Basques in Peru." Rather, Basques were part of either the *peninsulares* (Old World–born persons) or the New World–born *criollos* (persons of European descent) contesting political and economic power within colonial venues. Hence, the "Basqueness" of a particular viceroy or a prominent prelate, such as Juan de Zumárraga, was rarely noted, let alone investigated.

I would further argue that for a few generations after independence the subject of New World history was studiously avoided by Spanish historians out of a sense of offended national honor. The colonial period was equally distasteful (and therefore to be avoided) to many Latin American historians or became the subject of considerable revisionism, which emphasized the triumphs of *criollos qua* residents of the New World rather than as European descendants.

Finally, when considering the post-colonial emigrations to any New World destination there is a tendency to ignore that of the "Mother Country." Hence, in the vast literature regarding U.S. immigration the English immigrant is relatively neglected. It is the non-Anglo, with his/her "foreign" ways and tongues that provide the sum and substance of the immigrant story—at least in its huddled-masses, rags-to-riches variation. The same is true of the post-colonial emigration of Spaniards (including Spanish Basques) to Latin American destinations. While they numbered in the millions they adapted easily, "fitted in," and hence called little attention to themselves. Again, there was relative scholarly neglect of their story. We know considerably more, for instance, about Italian than Spanish immigration in Argentina (let alone the Old World–regional composition of the latter).

Since the appearance of *Amerikanuak* a historical accident has rescued studies of the Basque emigrant experience from relative obscurity, while shining considerable light upon its Latin American dimension. Reference is to the quincentennial anniversary in 1992 of Columbus's first voyage. As several European and American governments prepared for the commemoration, considerable emphasis was placed upon a better understanding of the importance of that foundational link established half a millennium earlier between the Old World and New. For obvious reasons, there was enhanced interest in Spain—sponsor of the voyage and the quintessential colonizer of the Americas.

As a consequence, over a several year period it became relatively easy to acquire funding for Iberian emigration studies. Beginning about 1990 there has been a plethora of monographs and conferences on one or another of its aspects. Included in the number of publications was a book by a young historian, José Manuel Azcona, entitled *Los paraísos posibles* (*Possible Paradises*), a study of Basque immigration in Argentina and Uruguay.

Based upon his doctoral dissertation research, in most respects the book represented a significant improvement over *Amerikanuak* in our understanding of the Basque presence of southern South America. Consequently, I solicited the right to translate it from the Spanish original for inclusion in the Basque Book Series of the University of Nevada Press. However, it became apparent that *Los paraísos posibles* itself was quickly becoming dated as the avalanche of new publications on its topic continued. Consequently, Professor Azcona agreed to rewrite, indeed expand, his work to incorporate the latest findings while encompassing Basque emigration throughout Latin America. The present text is the result of his fine efforts. In my view it represents a qualitative advance of the arguments presented in *Amerikanuak* over a quarter of a century ago regarding the Basque presence in Latin America, while introducing significant new ones.

Finally, the present text represents, to my mind, the culmination of a certain approach to Basque emigration. Taken in tandem with *Amerikanuak*'s treatment of the North American Basque experience and work in progress regarding the Basque presence in Oceania and the Philippines, with *Possible Paradises* we have pretty much fleshed out the *mappemonde* of the subject. That is, we now know that Basques circumnavigated the globe (Elcano), saved souls (Zumárraga), opened the Pacific sea route to Asia (Legazpi and Urdaneta), liberated continents (Bolívar), and governed nation-states (Urquiza). We also know that they hunted whales and fished cod during the sixteenth century off Labrador, were a piratical scourge on the American run during the seventeenth and eighteenth, herded sheep on the pampas and in the American West beginning in the nineteenth, and cut sugarcane in tropical Australia during the twentieth. To be sure, there is always more to be done—gaps and lacunae in the record yet to be filled in—however, at this point, we are unlikely to turn up any new mother lodes of previously unmined information. The broad outline for the Hispanic world is now complete in Azcona's new synthesis.

As we go forward from here I would sound two notes—one cautionary and the other optimistic. In rescuing Basque emigration from the obscurity created, historically, by its French and Spanish overlays, we must be cautious not to commit a kind of reverse sin. That is, we must be extremely cautious to contextualize our analysis so as not to attribute to our protagonists questionable ethnic attitudes and motives that might not square with *their* reality. In evaluating the life of a Zumárraga, for example, it would be as egregious to treat him *solely* in terms of his "Basqueness" as to regard him as *only* a loyal "Spaniard." Similarly, the Basque claim upon the liberator Bolívar, a second-generation American-born *criollo*, is both real and tenuous and must be understood in both terms.

Opportunity also abounds, since we are now in a position to redefine the historian's task regarding Basque emigration. Until our Basque *mappemonde* was in place we had to send out explorers to chart the details, knowing that the exercise was largely static and descriptive. However, once completed, that cartographic product allows us to then explore rapidly shifting intellectual realms. It is not so much that the world as defined by the historic record changes, rather our understanding of it does. Depending upon the new *questions* that we pose to our data we access many new worlds, maybe an inexhaustible supply.

Preface

Traditional Basque historiography has not devoted much attention to the phenomenon of immigration to the Americas until recently. Other issues were the object of its attention and thorough study: the *foral* question, the Carlist wars, nationalism, and, more recently, the processes of industrialization that radically transformed the territory's economic structures and its inhabitants' behavioral norms.

Around 1992, however, the date of the official commemoration of the quincentenary of the European discovery of America, monographic studies began to proliferate that have helped to clarify the important connections established between the Basque Country and the Americas from 1492 until the present. We now have at least an interesting perspective of all the dreams and events from these more than five hundred years of colonial adventure and exodus. Nevertheless, much has been written in an apologetic tone that does not appropriately describe the real situation experienced by the diaspora from the Basque Country. During such a lengthy span of time, and under institutionally distinct perspectives (the Spanish Empire from 1492 to 1830 and the American republics from that point to the present), the Basques have experienced different situations in their transatlantic travels. Thus, the immigrant protagonists of the story that follows have been functionaries, clerics, colonists, armed conquistadors, and peasants. Sometimes they have maintained cordial relations with other ethnic collectivities; at others they have been beset with disputes. Some Basques have reached the heights of power, while others have not transcended a languid, monotonous peasant life. Among so many immigrants, we will find varied forms of social interaction, different types of occupations, and, of course, distinct political tendencies. Moreover, the goals and life circumstances of our protagonists will differ, depending on the country in question.

This book begins by analyzing those Basques who distinguished themselves on the first expeditions. It then studies colonial commerce and its repercussion on Basque soil, followed by consideration of the lived circumstances of the diaspora in each territory of the New World. The text then proceeds to examine the dramatic reasons for the recent exodus and exile after the Spanish Civil War, and closes with a look at the future prospects of the present-day Basque-American communities.

Care has been taken to study the emigrants from both slopes of the Pyrenees because, although the Basques form an ethnic community with similar interests, they live in two distinct states, Spain and France. The former are from the provinces of Bizkaia, Araba, Gipuzkoa, and Navarre; the latter from the provinces of Basse Navarre, Labourd, and Soule, which compose Iparralde (literally, "the Northern Section"). The sum total will be referred to, interchangeably, as Euskal Herria or the Basque Country.[1]

Acknowledgments

I would like to express my most heartfelt gratitude to William A. Douglass and to the Center for Basque Studies of the University of Nevada, Reno, for having initiated translation and publication of this work. I am also indebted to Euskal Fundazioa for its generous support of translation and production costs.

Chapter One

The Basque Country at the Time of Columbus

At the time of the European discovery of America by Admiral Christopher Columbus in 1492, the territories of the Iberian Peninsula were still not completely integrated under a single crown. Rather, the peninsula was divided into various kingdoms with distinct jurisdictions and institutions. The Basque Country (Araba, Bizkaia, Gipuzkoa, and Navarre, as well as Labourd, Basse Navarre, and Soule) found itself subject to different political dominions. For example, Navarre—which would not be incorporated into the kingdom of Castile until 1512—was governed in the form of an independent kingdom by the Foix-Albret dynasty of French origin.

As a consequence of the Hundred Years' War, England had set itself on the peremptory and obligatory path of abandoning France. Thus, Labourd and Soule had passed to French jurisdiction, while Basse Navarre was incorporated into the Kingdom of Navarre. On the Iberian Peninsula, the Province of Gipuzkoa, the County of Araba, and the Seigneury of Bizkaia were connected to the Kingdom of Castile, following the earlier refusal, between 1200 and 1332, of the first two historic territories to profess loyalty to the King of Navarre.[1]

At the same time, the Kingdom of Navarre became a political jewel desired by both Castile and France. Until 1483, Louis XI was sure of having influence in Navarrese affairs as a result of his close family ties with King Francisco de Foix. But that year the young monarch died without leaving heirs, and the Navarrese Crown passed into the hands of Catherine, his unmarried sister. At this conjuncture, the Catholic Monarchs, Ferdinand and Isabella, tried to undermine French influence in Navarre by arranging a marriage between Catherine and their son Juan. To reinforce their marriage proposal, they deployed an expeditionary army in Araba. In an attempt to counteract this armed contingent and exert pressure on Navarre, France also stationed troops in Bayonne. With the situation thus, Louis XI died and his son Charles VIII assumed the French throne. Charles's regents advised him that reaffirming French power and some years of peace were necessary. The French therefore decided to withdraw their military pressure on Navarre.

Meanwhile, the queen mother, Magdalena of Navarre, decided that Catherine would not marry Juan. Magdalena cited the great difference in age between the two, although the political reality was that she felt that Navarrese interests were more closely connected to those of France. She, therefore, preferred that Catherine marry Jean d'Albret, the French prince. At this moment, the Catholic Monarchs found themselves faced with a clear dilemma: either provoke a war with France in order to annex Navarre or concentrate their efforts on the wars in the south of the peninsula in order to do away definitively with the last Arab redoubts. They chose the latter, although they did continue to exert diplomatic pressure on Navarrese territory until 1512. That year, Castilian troops conquered Navarre by arms, impelling it into their orbit as part of their expansionist policy. In 1514, this territory was fully integrated into the Crown of Castile. Nevertheless, the Catholic Monarchs promised to respect all the institutions, uses, and customs of the Old Kingdom of Navarre. Thus, from then on, a viceroy would be the representative of the Crown in Navarre, while the *forua*, Cortes, money, legislation, and (as mentioned) the Navarrese uses and customs remained in effect. Likewise, the fiscal system and self-taxation were also maintained. In exchange, Navarre would render tribute to the Castilian Crown. Spanish territorial unity had been realized, and the first European imperial nation-state was further strengthened with the incorporation of Navarre into its domain.[2]

Land and Sea Commerce

The common characteristic of Basque society throughout the ancien régime, differentiating it from the rest of Europe, was the juridical equality of all those under the aegis of the *foral* system. The best example of this situation was the Foru Berria of 1526 (Fuero of Bizkaia). Confirmed by Emperor Charles V, it consolidated the "universal nobility" of the Basques. Regardless of the modesty of their origins, Basques of the day could therefore aspire to all types of privileges and honorary posts. This circumstance would confer some particular features upon Basque participation in the American colonial and commercial enterprise. The Basques would enjoy the privileges reserved for the nobility of all the monarchy's territories, including the American ones. In addition, it made their noble status compatible with the devotion to business and commercial work. The legislatures of Bizkaia, Gipuzkoa, and Araba developed legislative power with full attributes, sanctioning or vetoing laws emanating from the Crown through the right of *pase foral*. Government of the seigneury and provinces resided in the deputations and municipalities, elected by the legislatures, and in the monarch's delegate in each historic territory (magistrates and, in Navarre, the viceroy). Administration of justice fell to the common institutions under the central government's jurisdiction, although the juridical norm was consonant with Basque foral law. In the case of Bizkaia, a room of the Chancellery of Valladolid was reserved one day a week to resolve the matters that were not settled in its own territory.

In spite of the foregoing, it is no less certain that the central authorities of the

Spanish monarchy undermined the foral laws, and the Basque and Navarrese authorities yielded to the designs of Madrid more often than is acknowledged. Thus, for example, in maritime service, the *foral* exemptions never functioned. Not only were the captains and high commanders Basques by birth, but Basque coastal towns provided numerous naval troops. In addition, on more than a few occasions, the Crown of Castile forced Basques to lend the government funds and provide it with infantry soldiers.

Regarding economic activities, around 1492 the Basques articulated their economy around the primary sector, artisanship, and commerce. As was characteristic of the period, cereal grains and vineyards predominated in its agriculture. In addition, horticultural products and fruit trees, cultivated in small quantities, made a rich contribution to the daily diet. But the fruits of the harvests were not sufficient everywhere to feed the entire population; this circumstance fostered commercial exchange between the coastal mountain zones and the flat, rich plains that sometimes produced a surplus of cereal grains. Animal husbandry was balanced by farming and forestry in some Basque regions; in others it appears to have been the primary economic activity. Nevertheless, beginning in the thirteenth century, this sector had come to compete with other productive activities.

Fishing and mining had already become common pursuits by the median centuries of the Middle Ages. Like hunting, river fishing provided an ideal complement for the diets of Basques of the time and for family subsistence, while the offshore fishery provided a specific profession along the entire Basque coast. The latter offered a great variety of species: sea bass, mojarra, gilthead, conger, horse mackerel, chub mackerel, eel, sea bream, anchovy, sardine. However, it was deep-sea pursuits, particularly for whales, for which the Basques soon became known in the European ports. The prominent role of whaling in the Gipuzkoan and Bizkaian medieval economy is reflected in the fact that the municipal coats of arms of many coastal *villas*—Getaria, Motriko, Ondarroa, Lekeitio, Bermeo, Hondarribia—include the effigy of the precious cetacean. This makes sense because whaling, which took Basque crews to the coasts of Terranova, was the most enriching and risky of all maritime pursuits of the epoch. In large measure, this fishing activity was closely related to the precarious yields of Basque and Navarrese soil, with the exception of the south of both Navarre (La Ribera) and Araba, where primary-sector production was clearly intense. In the mountainous terrain of the rest of the Basque Country, agriculture had never been the basis for sustaining the Basque people.

Iron extraction was the core of Basque mining concentrated in Gipuzkoa (Mutiloa, Zerain, Legazpia, and Arrasate) and, especially, Bizkaia (Somorrostro and Enkarterriak). The great abundance of iron fostered charcoal production in the mountains, as well as the development of the ironworks and the manufacture of derivative products. And, although the majority of European nations produced iron for their local necessities (tools, wheels, nails, and so forth), other types of industry, such as armaments, construction, or shipbuilding, required high-quality iron. It was precisely this mineral that Bilbao and its district could offer. Because it did not contain phosphorus, Basque iron was more malleable and less fragile. It is enough to recall that the English called the finely tempered swords, and the bars with shackles used to hold the ankles of ship prisoners, "bilbos." England was the principal importer. Between 1490 and 1492 alone, it bought just under 4,500 tons of iron, 3,000 of which came from the Basque Country. Until the thirteenth century, Basque foundries were located in the mountains, next to the mines. Iron was produced through the use of large quantities of charcoal produced in the forests.

Nevertheless, during the thirteenth century, iron production was organized on a preindustrial scale. The foundries were subsequently moved to the vicinity of the rivers in order to employ hydraulic energy, and output increased markedly. This early industrialization was developed largely thanks to both the quality and the quantity of Basque iron products. Around the beginning of the fifteenth century, the Basques were famous throughout Europe for their ironworking capacity—so much so that when the French decided to create their own foundries, they contracted Basque technicians to direct them. In addition to arms, the Basque ironworkers made all types of farm tools and shipbuilding materials. According to some estimates, one-third of Basque iron production was used in ship construction, one-third in making farm tools and arms, and one-third exported in the form of ingot.

The fact that the Kingdom of Castile was largely dependent on Basque iron at the end of the fifteenth century is clear evidence of the industry's prominence. In 1480, Queen Isabella even asked the Basque authorities to induce their foundries to abandon their tasks in order to manufacture arms for the fort of Sicily and the fleet combating the Turks. This request was repeated in 1488 and again in 1489. Iron was so fundamental to the Bizkaian economy that, at the dawn of the modern era, it came to serve as a unit of value. Production also received special protection in the *foral* ordinances, confirmed by the Catholic Monarchs in 1483, who protected the industry and promoted its development. Bear in mind that Basque iron also had two particular added advantages: (1) It came from mines with surface veins that were easily extractable, and (2) due to the geographic situation of this mining district, the iron was easily transportable by sea.[3] These two advantages enhanced the renown of the ductile, easily malleable, and resistant Basque iron. The favorable circumstances would underpin the impressive accumulation of capital during the entire modern era; in the latter half of the nineteenth century, it came to be one of the pillars of the fascinating Basque industrial revolution.

In the mid-fifteenth century, commerce began to surpass whaling as the main activity of Basque seamen. Ships were already being built to transport the readily marketable merchandise. Bilbao, the quintessential commercial port, completely eclipsed the whaling and fishing ones of Bermeo and Lekeitio. Mercantile contacts followed. They were developed due to circumstances specific to the Basque Country: scarcity of certain foodstuffs, surplus of iron, privileged geographic situation. Improvement of the transportation infrastructure and the international political situation played a critical role as well. Commerce was the primordial activity of the period. Provisions needed by the population therefore reached the Basque coast. And it was Basque merchants and outfitters who maintained both their own commercial relationships abroad and the maritime ones of the territories of the Crown of Castile. Castilian wool and wheat, Basque iron, and Andalusian oil and wine constituted the bulk of the exported articles traded for Flemish or English cloth and French wine. In this scheme, the port of Bilbao served as the prototypical springboard for Spanish exports to the rest of Europe.

Commerce with Flanders experienced its greatest period of growth between 1480 and 1500. It was Basque shipping that carried the bulk of the wool, iron, oil, fruit, and wine destined for Brussels; cloth was the principal return article. The Basques had founded a Confraternity of the Basque Nation there; its existence clearly reveals the strong rootedness of Basque sailors and merchants in Flemish business circles. A variety of products were transported to England (to Bristol, Plymouth, Portsmouth, and Southampton) in Bizkaian and, more frequently, Gipuzkoan ships. Iron came from Enkarterri; swords from Bilbao, well known for their quality; and wool from Castile. On occasion, Andalusian oil, French wine, Castilian grain, and Navarrese grain and wool were also transported. From England, cloth and sometimes vegetables and grain were imported. The Basques' commercial relationship with France was very intense from the mouth of the Bidasoa to Calais; that is, in the regions of Gascony, Brittany, and Normandy. Iron, wool, salted meat and fish, and hides made up the bulk of Basque-French commercial transactions.

Basque merchants were also active in the Mediterranean. They arrived there after sailing along the Iberian coast, and thereby also traded in Portugal and Andalusia. In effect, taking advantage of the interruption in other fleets caused by the Hundred Years' War, Basque merchants began to provide transport to the countries that frequented the commercial routes of the Mediterranean, in direct competition with established Italian cities. In the mid-fifteenth century, a great part of the commerce of Provence came to depend upon Basque ships. Likewise, the Basques became involved in salt transport from Ibiza for Genoa, Sicily, and Apulia, and in Sevillan wheat, Catalan herring, and Andalusian and Portuguese hides.

Although with a lower trade volume, the merchants of the Basque Country intervened directly in overland Iberian mercantile transactions. They attended the most important fairs and markets that were held in the various peninsular kingdoms; their presence at the fairs of Medina del Campo, which took place at the end of the fifteenth century, is documented.[4]

The Basque Dockyards

There are indications that Basque dockyards of proven technical merit have been in existence since the Middle Ages. The mining commerce described to this point, whaling, and fishing (in general) were commercial and mercantile activities that forcefully developed the Gipuzkoan and Bizkaian shipbuilding industry. Therefore, the Basques, along with the Portuguese, were considered the best shipbuilders in Europe at the start of the modern era. In almost all the Basque coastal ports, shipyards were very active thanks to the rich timber supply from nearby forests and high demand for vessels due to the commercial boom. Thus, in Bilbao, shipyards were located in Areatza and Deusto, on the right bank of the Nervión River. The Manzana repair dock, the Basurto de Acha shipyard, that of San Mamés, that of Ayeta in Zorroza, and that of San Nicolás de Ugarte y Portu occupied the river's fifteenth-century left bank; others, in which small-tonnage vessels for transporting iron from Enkarterri were built, stood next to the Kadagua and Galindos Rivers. As for Gipuzkoa, there were shipyards on the Oiartzun River, in the *villa* and port of Errenderia, upriver from Aginaga, Urdaiaga, and Mapil on the Oria, as well as in Pasaia.

The entire Cantabrian coast was like one big shipyard, a continuous dockyard. Frequently, the merchant ships built there were sold in the ports of destination, favoring the growth of the early Basque ship industry and the very commercial structure that itself profited from the availability of this important product. Thus, in 1481, fifty vessels were prepared for urgent shipment to Naples to collaborate in the pacification of the Italian kingdoms. In 1488, in fulfillment of the treaty signed between the Catholic Monarchs and the Navarrese Alain d'Albret, a squadron was formed in Bizkaia to fight against French monarch Charles VIII's fleet at Saint Aubin. And in 1492, during the War of Granada, Bizkaian and Gipuzkoan ships and captains (Arriarán and Martínez Díaz de Mena from Bilbao, and Pedro de Urrezti from Ondarroa, among others) were part of a squadron in the Strait of Gibraltar that contained Muslim attacks at the end of the Reconquest.

But Basque ships were devoted not only to mercantile and commercial ventures. Their presence is also documented on diplomatic missions: carrying the Castilian ambassador of Henry IV to England in 1465, or participating in the voyage of the Archduchess Juana to Flanders at the end of that century. Basque maritime collaboration in the Castilian War of Succession following the death of Henry IV of Castile was noteworthy. In 1474, Tristán de Leguizamón was appointed head armorer of the Armada of Vizcaya. Composed of thirty ships, it successfully faced the French Admiral Colón, a corsair in the service of Louis XI of France. The available sources also indicate the presence of Bizkaian caravels and naos in the combat against the Portuguese along the coast of Gibraltar in 1475, as well as in the archipelago of Cape Verde one year later.

At the end of the fifteenth century, therefore, on the eve of the modern era, when word reached Europe of a new continent beyond the ocean, Basques found themselves in an advantageous situation. They enjoyed unique political privilege due to the *foral* code. Furthermore, they were able to provide human capital accustomed to the arts of navigation and skilled in adventure and risk. Social peace, moreover, had reached the Basque territories.[5] In spite of everything, although the Basque population numbered some 200,000 around the year 1500, the population density of the Basque regions, especially the number of inhabitants per square kilometer in Bizkaia (30), meant that these territories greatly exceeded the Spanish mean at the time of 20 inhabitants per square kilometer.

And the Basques had an abundance of naos and caravels, as well as iron, equipment, and arms. These regions had a surplus population obligated to search for fortune outside of its homeland. For this combination of reasons, through the able exploitation of all their political, economic, social, and human advantages, Basques assured themselves a prominent role in the colonial undertaking in the New World. From then on, America was the destination that many of them yearned after and pursued as sailors, soldiers, clerics, merchants, judges, secretaries, administrators, colonists, and simply adventurers.

Andalusia, America's Waiting Room

Basque participation was so important in the incipient colonial enterprise that, as early as 1540, Basque residents in Sevilla founded the Confraternity of the Basque Nation in the Convent of Saint Francis, in the Barrio de la Mar next to city hall. It would serve as a model for those that would later arise in Mexico, Lima, and Madrid. The confraternity provided religious, welfare, and social services. Its members were primarily individuals involved in mercantile business.[6]

The Basques had previously created the College of Basque Pilots of Cádiz, whose founding date is not known. There is proof, however, that its ordinances were confirmed by the Catholic Monarchs at the end of the fifteenth century. Established as a guild, the members had to contribute a portion of their earnings, as had been done from ancient times in the confraternities of seamen of Basque coastal towns. This was used to create a fund destined for charitable works, cultural activities, and the needs of the association itself, especially the maintenance of the Chapel of the Virgin of Distress that the College established in the early Cathedral of Cádiz.[7]

Sevilla, the first base of the Catholic Monarchs, connected to the ocean by the Guadalquivir River, was especially attractive to the Basque seamen. Moreover, the fertile plains surrounding the city produced abundant wheat, wine, and oil, products in great demand in the Basque Country. These were the reasons for the birth of a successful Basque-Andalusian commercial relationship, established on the shores of Betis, whereby these products were traded for northern iron and wood. Sporadic mercantile contacts were followed by the creation of Basque firms that increased considerably in number after the Indies market opened up. Thus, little by little, the Basques living in Sevilla began occupying Castro Street. Called the "Street of the Vizcaínos," it was strategically located on the banks of the river, next to the cathedral, on whose front steps a wide variety of mercantile transactions were carried out. The Basque integration into the social life of Sevilla translated into a presence of Bizkaians, Arabans, Gipuzkoans, and Navarrese in a wide range of bureaucratic, financial, ecclesiastic, and, of course, commercial positions. There was no lack of men who had attained the habit of one of the military orders existing on the reconquered peninsula, especially the Order of Santiago. Shipowners and captains from the Basque yards were also numerous. Others occupied posts of responsibility in Sevilla's municipal government, thus confirming the social recognition received there by Basques of the day.

Basque activity in Cádiz, in turn, increased notably after the city in 1494 was declared the only port from which ships could leave for the New World, and when the Spanish transatlantic commercial focus moved there in 1680. The process culminated with the transfer of the Casa de Contratación, or House of Trade, to Cádiz in 1717. Nevertheless, the Basque colony had already become sufficiently established in the city. For example, the colony collaborated in the defense of Cádiz at the end of the sixteenth century during the siege of the Anglo-Dutch army. It also participated in the foundation of the Confraternity of the Most Holy Christ of Humility and Patience, with its seat in the Church of Saint Augustine; the coats of arms of Bizkaia, Gipuzkoa, Araba, and Navarre were placed in the church's chapel. The majority of the Basques in Cádiz came from Bilbao, Donostia, Deusto, Lekeitio, Getaria, Portugalete, Santurtzi, Azpeitia, Elorrio, Gasteiz, Oñati, Urdunia, and Balmaseda. They tended to be single and, after reaching a certain economic level, would marry either Andalusian women or the daughters of other transplanted native Basques. Their wills discuss in detail the composition of their fortunes, accumulated throughout a lifetime of commerce and mercantile transit. Part of their capital was reinvested into the shipbuilding sector. The great majority of their wealth, however, was devoted to buying land (for its high profitability and as a basis for the creation of an estate, a prerequisite for a noble title), second residences, jewels, paintings, and movable goods in general. There was no lack of foundation of entails and chaplainship (contributions for masses and other church services) in their hometowns. Nor did they forget their native lands, granting legacies destined for beneficent, hospital, religious, and cultural projects.

Attempts to exploit the American route from the Basque Country were frustrated in 1494 when the Castilian Crown designated Cádiz as the sole port from which the ships for the New World could leave. This circumstance, however, did not result in exclusion of Basque participation in the Indies run. On the contrary. Basque maritime interests, involved in Mediterranean and African commerce for quite a time, remained well settled, thanks, precisely, to the consolidation of their activities carried out in Lower Andalusia.[8]

Fascination with the New World

A Basque population with high birth rates, poor agriculture, and a civil legislation known as the *mayorazgo*, which reserved the family patrimony to a single heir, were among the leading factors in driving the Basques seaward in search of other lands in which to settle. The Reconquest was, in large measure, the solution to these problems. In effect, Christian military control of the regions being recovered from the Muslim invaders opened ample and promising future prospects for the surplus Basque population. It is not strange that in the early Middle Ages there is a plethora of last names of Basque origin in all corners of peninsular geography; this is even so in the Canary Islands, in whose conquest their presence is documented. Andalusia was no exception. Many Basques traded their native region for the more fertile areas of Córdoba, Jaén, Sevilla, or Cádiz when these cities were won for Castile by Ferdinand III "The Saint" and his son Alfonso X "the Wise."

On October 12, 1492, the lookout for the forecastle, Juan Rodríguez Bermejo, nicknamed "the one from Triana," cried "land" in the early morning, thus changing what began like any other day in the waters of the Atlantic. It had all begun much earlier, in an Old Castile immersed in the fight against the last Muslim redoubt on the peninsula. Christopher Columbus, a Genovese navigator,[9] promoting a maritime expedition to the Indies via the Atlantic Ocean, visited the Castilian court in the spring of 1485 in search of sufficient economic backing to execute his plan. Nevertheless, as the Portuguese kingdom had done months earlier, the Catholic Monarchs, heeding the council of the Crown's scientists, rejected Columbus's project. Other urgent matters, such as the definitive conquest of the Kingdom of Granada, required resolution. The monarchs did leave a door open to the hopes of the Genoa native, however. Years passed, with Columbus traveling the peninsula in search of backers to support his revolutionary project. As a result of his continual sojourns throughout Castilian lands, he met influential people that believed in him, both clerics and courtesans. They would prove very helpful in gaining him access to the Catholic Monarchs in the future. One was Alonso de Quintanilla, the kingdom's head accountant, member of the Royal Council, and an advocate of maritime trade. It was this royal functionary who put Columbus in contact with Pedro González de Mendoza, archbishop of Toledo and cardinal. Luis de Santángel, the monarch's ecclesiastic scribe, quickly established a friendship with the discoverer. His intervention would be decisive in the first months of 1492. Juan Cabrero, the personal valet of Ferdinand the Catholic, was also a great help around this time, as were the Aragonese treasurer, Gabriel Sánchez, and the queen's confessor, Fra Juan Pérez.

Thanks to the mediation of Fra Juan Pérez, Queen Isabella agreed to receive Columbus in her camp at Santa Fe in December 1491. There, the Italian navigator explained the details of his expedition and elaborated his conditions to the sovereign. But the royal technical committee summoned for the occasion again rejected Columbus's project. The outlandish privileges sought by the Genoa native must have weighed on the mind of the monarchs as much as the scientific judgment. His requests would have been completely unacceptable for monarchs that had proposed to do away with the seignorial system. During the first days of 1492, however, Boabdil the Younger surrendered Granada to Ferdinand and Isabella. Peninsular unification, the longtime dream of the Catholic Monarchs, was then a reality. The moment was right for a Christopher Columbus wishing to approach the monarchs once again. The queen summoned him to further discuss the Atlantic project. The kingdom's most eminent men of science were present. Given several discrepancies, they ultimately decided to submit an unfavorable report. In accordance with this decision, the monarchs dismissed a Columbus that was already thinking about how to present his proposal to the French court.

When he had barely traveled six kilometers from the camp at Santa Fe, in the village of Pinos del Puente, a constable summoned Columbus to return to the queen's presence. Chroniclers attribute this sudden change of the sovereign's attitude to the direct intervention of Luis de Santángel. But, apparently, all of Columbus's protectors acted jointly before both monarchs to convince them to resume the conversations. Santángel argued before the queen that, although the risk of the Columbian project was great, the costs were reasonable for an undertaking that could serve to exalt God and the Church, and aggrandize the kingdoms of Castile. The only stumbling block remaining, and not the least important, was the financial one. Bear in mind that the Castilian Crown was financially strapped due to the War of Granada in which the last Muslims were expelled from Spain. But the converted former Jew and royal scribe Santángel promised to lend the Crown the 1,140,000 *maravedíes* requested by the Genoa native. Now, all that remained was to transcribe the conditions that the two sides would promise to respect. Fra Juan Pérez and Juan de Coloma, the representatives of Christopher Columbus and the Crown of Castile, respectively, systematically prepared and drew up the conditions of Columbus's contract, known as the Capitulaciones de Santa Fe. Both parties signed it on April 17, 1492.

There is not unanimity among historians regarding the juridical nature of the Capitulaciones de Santa Fe. Some researchers (García Gallo and Morales Padrón) think that it was a question of a favor insofar as it was a free concession and, therefore, revocable whenever the monarchs considered it opportune to do so. In contrast, others (Altolaguirre, Madariaga, Lalinde, Rumeu, and Manzano) believe that the document signed in 1492 was a properly arranged contract imposing obligations and duties upon both signatories.

The document in question consists of a preamble and five clauses clearly stipulating all the political and economic privileges and benefits that the Genovese would receive. Thus, Columbus achieved his objectives: the status of admiral, of a lifetime and hereditary nature, on the ocean and on all the islands or mainlands that might be discovered or gained for Castile. He also demanded the title of viceroy and governor of the new territories, as well as the power to intervene in making political appointments.[10]

Likewise, Columbus was granted the power to resolve, either personally or through the mediation of his officials, all the disputes regarding New World mercantile and commercial traffic. And at an economic level, the discoverer was recognized and empowered to

1. take for himself one-tenth of all the gains found within the borders of his admiralty, free of any taxes, and
2. contribute, if he so desired, one-eighth of the costs of any future armada, receiving one-eighth of the profits in return.

Satisfied by all that he had received,[11] Columbus left for the port of Palos, the place chosen for organizing the expedition. Among the many reasons that this *villa* was designated as the starting point of Columbus's undertaking, the following stand out: the existing obligation that weighed on the city to provide the Crown with two caravels for twelve months; its good fleet and expert sailors; Cádiz's preoccupation with the departure of Jews after the 1492 decree of expulsion; and Columbus's personal interest, as he had "some acquaintances and friends" there, according to Las Casas. On May 23, Columbus gathered the authorities and the townspeople to publicly inform them of the orders of the monarchs in a royal provision requiring them to supply him with two caravels that had to be outfitted as punishment for certain crimes committed by its inhabitants in the past. In Moguer he read another royal provision ordering the local powers to lend him all their support. The reaction was the same in both places: lack of interest. Nevertheless, he obtained the vessels, two caravels and a nao. Palos contributed one caravel, the other was prepared in Moguer, and the nao arrived from Puerto de Santa María.

The *Santa María*, nicknamed "La Gallega," was a nao of one hundred tons, surely built in the Basque shipyards and property of the Bizkaian Juan de la Cosa.[12] It was a tubby vessel, heavy, with rounded sails, and therefore not very apt for a voyage of discovery. In spite of everything, Columbus chose it as the flagship of his fleet. It was shipwrecked off the coast of Haiti on December 25, 1492, and with its remains the fort Navidad ("Christmas"), the first Spanish-American establishment, was built.

The *Pinta*, the fastest of the three vessels, was a caravel owned by Cristóbal Quintero and provided by the inhabitants of Palos de la Frontera. It is not known if Columbus leased or commandeered it, although the fact that its owner joined the expedition unwillingly suggests that it was requisitioned. Commanded by Martín Alonso Pinzón, its tonnage (probably between fifty and sixty) and the reason for its name are both unknown. It bore rounded sails and had a larger crew—so many that it greatly bothered the admiral that its captain was always out front in the tense hours between October 10 and 12.

The *Niña*, the other caravel, was built on Moguer's banks. It was obtained through a contract with Juan Niño. Its official name was the *Santa Clara*, in honor of the patroness of Moguer. It weighed about sixty tons and had a Latin rigging that was transformed into a rounded one in the Canary Islands. Of the three vessels, it was Columbus's favorite. He moved to it when the *Santa María* was shipwrecked, also using it on his second and third ocean crossings.

More difficult to obtain than the ships were the crew. No one wanted to embark on an expedition considered by many chimerical. It would be Martín Alonso Pinzón, and his brothers Vicente Yañez and Francisco Martín, that overcame the hostilities toward Columbus's project by enlisting in the crew. They received the positions of captain of the *Pinta*, captain of the *Niña*, and master of the *Pinta*, respectively. To these were added the influential clan of the Niños, always faithful to Columbus since his arrival in Andalusian lands. Juan, owner and master of the *Niña*; Peralonso, pilot of the *Santa María*; and Francisco, who enlisted as a cabin boy, would join the expedition from this family. Encouraged by the participation of such respected figures, the number of recruits increased until, according to researcher estimates, it reached about ninety. In addition to the aforementioned, among those occupying important positions were the Bizkaian Juan de la Cosa, shipmaster of the *Santa María*; Cristóbal García Sarmiento, pilot of the *Niña*; Sancho Ruiz de Gama, pilot of the *Pinta*; and Juan Quintero, boatswain of the *Pinta*. In addition to the top-ranking officers, the following also embarked: royal officials; a doctor; a surgeon; a pharmacist; caulkers and coopers; the scribe Rodrigo de Escobedo, whose mission consisted of writing up the chronicle of the discovered lands; Diego de Arana, the armada's bailiff and cousin of Beatriz Enríquez de Arana, the admiral's lover; and the interpreter Luis de Torres, who spoke Arabic and Hebrew. No cleric's presence is recorded among the crew. Four criminals were incorporated, however: Bartolomé Torres, who had assassinated the town crier of Palos, and three accomplices that had assisted in his unsuccessful escape.

Except for the Portuguese Juan Arias and perhaps two other sailors of the same nationality, and three Italians, one each from Genoa, Calabria, and Venice, the participants were Spaniards. Most came from Lower Andalusia, from the districts of Tinto and Odiel, and Basques were strongly represented. The Bizkaian boatswain Juan de Lequeitio, nicknamed "Chanchu," and Domingo de Lequeitio, also a Bizkaian boatswain; the cabin boy from Natxitua (Bizkaia), Martín de Urtubia; the caulker from Erandio (Bizkaia), Lope Aresti; the coopers from Lekeitio and Ispazter (Bizkaia), Pérez Vizcaíno and Domingo de Anchía, respectively; as well as shipmaster Juan de la Cosa and the expedition's bailiff, Diego de Arana, from Córdoba of Basque origin, were part of the *Santa María*'s crew. On the *Niña*, in turn, the Bizkaian Juan Ruiz de la Peña and the Gipuzkoans from Deba, Juan Martínez de Açogue, Pedro Arraes, and his son Juan, joined. Lastly, Juan Quintero from Algorta (Bizkaia) and the Gipuzkoan Ojer de Berástegui embarked on the *Pinta*.

The Adventure That Changed the Geography of the World

On August 2, 1492, when men, ships, and supplies were ready, Christopher Columbus ordered his whole crew to embark. They set sail for the Canary Islands in order to make a brief call to store water and prepare for the long ocean crossing. The admiral's plans were foiled on August 6, however, when the *Pinta*'s rudder broke. The fleet was thus forced to remain in port for one month, repairing the caravel and substituting the Latin sails of the *Niña* with other, more rounded ones to gain additional security. Overcoming the setback and supplied with water, firewood, meat, and other provisions, on September 2 the three vessels once again took to sea. They headed westward, managing to follow the 28th parallel. According to the cartography of the day, Cipango and the easternmost lands of Asia were to be found at this latitude. At the same time, the admiral warned the crew that he did not expect to find land before traversing 750 leagues from the Canary Islands. Beginning on September 9, in case his predictions were wrong or to confuse the pilots, Columbus decided to keep two accounts of the distance traveled by the ships: one secret and accurate; the other, public, showing fewer leagues than really covered.

A more southern route would have been more favorable for navigation given the advantageous position of the trade winds and sea currents. Nevertheless, the southerly trajectory, later chosen for the second trip, was prohibited to Columbus by the sovereigns in order to respect the Treaty of Tordesillas of 1494.[13] The Genoa native therefore opted for the parallel of the Canary Islands, the most convenient latitude that he could follow, making use of the trade winds from the northwest.

In spite of everything, pushed by the trade winds and with fair weather, on September 16 the fleet entered the Sargasso Sea. On the twenty-first, they lost the trade winds and were becalmed; on the twenty-fifth, Martín Alonso Pinzón thought he sighted land, but it was only a cloud. The slow pace of navigation, and the fact that no sign of civilization appeared, brought out the first symptoms of unrest among the crew. Columbus himself, who set the distance between the island of Hierro and Cipango at 750 leagues, began to be worried in early October. His concern was understandable, as on the third the fleet had greatly exceeded the navigator's calculations, with neither Cipango nor its adjacent islands in sight. On October 6, the pilots recorded in their respective logs a distance of 800 leagues traveled from the Canary Islands, a figure that rose to 966 in Columbus's secret tally. In view of the situation, that very day Martín Alonso Pinzón proposed to the admiral that they abandon the course of the 28th parallel and point the ships southwest, a suggestion adamantly rejected by the Genoa native. The Bizkaian crew members of the *Santa María* were displeased with the decision to press forward. After calling an emergency meeting, they went to the admiral and threatened to throw him overboard. The beleaguered Christopher Columbus urgently sought help from the captains of the caravels. And, for the moment, only the diligent actions of the Pinzón brothers prevented mutiny. The Bizkaians of the flagship were loath to submit. In fact, they did so only because of lack of support from the rest of the sailors. Moreover, the prospect of being judged in a war court upon their return seems to have further calmed the spirits of the Basque insurrectionists.

After this incident, which underscored the strong personality of the Basque element on the Columbian expedition, the Genoa native (following the advice of the Pinzón brothers) decided to amend his course to the previously rejected west-southwest one. It seems likely that Columbus was trying to soothe the souls on board with this concession. Nevertheless, the tension mounted over the following days. On the night of October 9 to 10, mutiny was rife throughout the fleet. They had already traveled more than 1,000 royal leagues—the crew were aware of only 900—and there were no special signs of ever reaching the final destination. The Basque sailors therefore decided to protest again. This time the whole crew (even captains and pilots) supported the rebels. The admiral again sought the help of the Pinzón brothers who, in an attempt to reconcile the positions of Columbus and the crew, offered the Solomonic ploy of sailing on for three more days. If they did not reach the stipulated destination within that time, they would return to Spain. Order prevailed once again and the crossing proceeded. On the morning of October 12, the lookout of the *Pinta*, Juan Rodríguez Bermejo, known as "the one from Triana," spied land. Columbus, claiming to have seen lights a few hours earlier, was awarded primacy, and thus the prize of 10,000 *maravedíes* conceded by the monarchs.

According to Columbus's map, the expedition had reached one of the islands bordering the Asian continent. In reality, they had discovered the American island of Guanahaní somewhere in present Bahamas. That same day, Christopher Columbus took possession of it for the Crown of Castile in the name of the Catholic Monarchs. The royal scribe, Rodrigo de Escobedo, legalized and certified the claim. The territory conquered and recognized was christened San Salvador. In any case, the Genoa native's plan had resulted, albeit unintentionally, in the incorporation into the Spanish realm of a new island of a land previously unknown.

On October 14, the admiral and his fleet left San Salvador in search of the much yearned for Cipango. In the days that passed until the twenty-sixth of the month, Santa María de la Concepción (Cayo Rum), Fernandina (Long Island), Isabela (Crooked Island), and Arenas (Mucaras) would be discovered. Columbus thought he was in Asian lands. Already on the seventeenth, he spoke of Indians and India in his diary. When he established contact with the natives, Columbus questioned them about the origin of their shining gold adornments. They indicated to the south and southwest, toward two large islands that they called Colba (Cuba) and Bohío (Hispaniola). In Columbus's judgment, the first of these had to be the Cipango he dreamed of. He arrived before nightfall on the twenty-seventh. The crew disembarked on the northern coast, someplace between Cape Lucrecia and the periphery of Camagüey, in a place that Columbus called Puerto de Mares. The admiral christened this island with the name Juana, in honor of Prince Juan. Thinking himself in Cathay, an Asiatic province belonging to the dominions of the Great Khan, he sent a delegation inland in search of the famous Asian king, bearing presents and a letter of greeting from the Catholic Monarchs. Within a few days, however, the emissaries returned. They had found no sign of gold, spices, the Great Khan, or the opulent cities that, according to medieval tradition and travelers' tales, should have been there.

Completely disconcerted, Columbus set sail on November 12 on a southeasterly course. He planned to reach Cipango, but beforehand wanted to visit the island of Babeque to the east, rich in gold according to the natives. He discovered the innumerable islands that he would name Mar de Nuestra Señora. On the twenty-second, since the fleet was navigating with tremendous difficulties, Martín Alonso Pinzón was sent ahead with the *Pinta*, while the admiral chose to return to Cuba. From there, he sailed in pursuit of the island that the natives called Bohío, which he would call Hispaniola. On December 5, he passed the westernmost point of Cuba, Cape Maisí, which he named Alpha and Omega believing it to be the easternmost extreme of Asia. The following day, he sailed the northern coast of Hispaniola, naming all the geographical features that he came across. The expeditionaries crossed the Tortuga Channel and set up camp in the Bay of Saint Thomas from December 20 to 23. There they received messengers from Guacanagarí, the cacique, and a multitude of natives that spoke of a district rich in gold that they called Cibao.

On the twenty-fourth, the expedition left the port of Saint Thomas on a course for the community of the cacique. At midnight, off the cape of Haiti, the *Santa María* ran aground on a sandbar due to the negligence of its master, Juan de la Cosa, who had left the helm in the hands of an inexperienced cabin boy. The ship was lost but the crew and cargo were saved. The fort of Navidad was built with the scraps. It was the first Spanish establishment in the New World. Thirty-nine men stayed behind under the command of Diego de Arana, among them the Bizkaians that had been part of the complement of the ill-fated ship. On January 4, Columbus left Hispaniola on a course for Castile. On the sixth, he met Martín Alonso Pinzón, who was returning from the supposed Cibao with some gold. Ten days later, after stocking up on water on the island of Matinimó, they began their return to Spain together. The elements were favorable for the sailors until February 12, when, having reached the coast of the Azores, a strong storm separated the two caravels. The *Niña*, commanded by Columbus, barely managed to reach the estuary of the Tagus in Lisbon on March 4. There, they had to cast anchor in order to repair the damages caused by the storm. On the thirteenth, the vessel left Portugal for Palos, which it would reach in two days. Hours later the *Pinta*, which had reached the port of Baiona (Galicia) at the end of February, arrived as well. The first Columbian adventure was over.

Columbus's Subsequent Expeditions

After traveling for thirty-two weeks, Columbus's first, mythic voyage had been a success. Once he was back in Castile, the admiral, swollen with pride and grandeur, wrote a long, detailed letter to the Catholic Monarchs describing his voyage. This letter was answered by one from the Court, inviting the Genoa native to appear before the monarchs. The meeting took place in Barcelona. Columbus reached the Court accompanied by six Indians who brought some small samples of gold; he also bore other objects from the recently discovered lands, including cages with parrots. These animals were obviously unknown in the Spain of the day. The royal reception was so enthusiastic and receptive that, on April 28, 1493, the Catholic Monarchs placed their seal on the titles and concessions of the Capitulaciones de Santa Fe. Columbus was thereby granted permission to carry and display his own coat of arms.

The international repercussions of the voyage were spectacular. The European chancelleries took an immediate interest in Columbus's undertaking. But the Catholic Monarchs were particularly worried about the interest shown in his voyage by neighboring Portugal. Remember that, in the last quarter of the fifteenth century, the court in Lisbon had begun a triumphant and successful commercial, mercantile, and colonizing push into Africa. The Portuguese conquest of Brazil has to be placed in this contesting of politico-economic power and intense competition between Spain and Portugal. It would not be until the Treaty of Tordesillas in 1494, sanctioned by the Vatican for the purpose of mediating between Portugal and Castile, that order was imposed on this expansion and conquest of America. And this exploration had economic and political repercussions not only for the Spanish and Portuguese states but also (and especially) for merchants of the two countries. Recall that this was the first international division of the world.[14]

On the second voyage, the admiral would pay special attention to the provisions necessary to make his expedition successful. He was already aware that reliance upon the sea for food en route and improvisation of a supply once arrived were great mistakes. Thus, all types of foodstuffs were loaded for maintaining the colonists that the expeditionaries planned to establish at the destination. Likewise, they took seeds, plants, and domestic animals. There were problems when the time came to choose the future new settlers, given the overwhelming number of volunteers that showed up at Cádiz's port. They were all men: noblemen and soldiers, peasants and artisans, hoping for quick riches, as well as fame and glory. As on the first voyage, men of Basque stock accompanied Columbus among his sailors. These included the following:

1. Juan de la Cosa, who embarked with Columbus as cartographer
2. Lope de Olano, Francisco de Garay, and Martín de Zamudio—three protagonists of notable American feats
3. Sebastián de Olano, Juan Ortiz de Matienzo, Fernando de Guevara, Luis de Arteaga, Bartolomé Salcedo, Miguel de Muncharaz, Luis de Lizarzu, Juan de Azúa, Pedro de Arana, Gabriel Butrón, Hernando de Berrio, Juan Ezquerra, Juan de Oñate, Diego de Arciaga, Pedro Vizcaíno, Juan de Barruti, Juan de Zamudio, and Juan Ibarra de Ibañez[15]

On September 25, 1493, the great, well-armed colonizing expedition composed of three naos and thirteen caravels set sail from Cádiz. Columbus headed for the Indies on October 13, following a more southerly course than the one chosen a year earlier. After twenty-one days of sailing, the fleet sighted the first island of the arc of the Lesser Antilles, an archipelago that it sailed between November 3 and 17. On the nineteenth, the explorers reached the large island that the natives called Borinquen. Giving it the name San Juan Bautista (Puerto Rico), they supplied themselves with water there before concluding their voyage in Hispaniola on November 22. One week later, on the twenty-ninth, Columbus reached the fort of Navidad. The spectacle before his eyes was wrenching. The fort was nothing but a heap of ruins. The thirty-nine men that composed its detachment had been killed by Caonabó and Mayrení, caciques of the Taino and Caribbean tribes that maintained their lifestyle by war. The explanation of the cacique Guacanagarí provided partial clarification: The differences arising within the garrison, the men's difficulty in acclimating to the surroundings, greed for gold and women, and the Spaniards' violation of the natives had combined to trigger the tragedy. In effect, the bailiff Diego de Arana's lack of leadership resulted in the disorder and dispersion of the men under his command, a circumstance that led the group to its tragic end. And although there is no dependable and scientifically rigorous data as to what happened in that first Spanish settlement, the group of Basques might have formed a dissident faction, facilitated by their common mother tongue and ethnic solidarity.[16] But this is clearly only conjecture.

If this were not enough, the caciques Caonabó and Guarionex rebelled against the Spaniards. Their uprising was harshly repressed by the admiral. He forced them to submit, imposing a high tribute of gold dust. The monarchs were informed of his action, and felt obligated to send an inquisitorial judge, Juan de Aguado, in order to investigate and later recount what had happened in Hispaniola. Columbus thought it wise to return to Spain and defend himself personally against his detractors' accusations before the monarchs. Thus, in the Burgos Palace of Cordón, Ferdinand and Isabella heard of the events in the Indies from the admiral's mouth. In spite of all, the monarchs authorized the Genoa native to undertake a new overseas crossing while bestowing all privileges and favors upon him.

As has just been seen, the troubles of Admiral Columbus began very soon in the New World. Greed, desire for glory, personal discord, and the tensions of the inclemencies and discomforts of the initial conquests were causes of Columbus's exasperations and the royal lawsuits against him. These suits would last until the eighteenth century, with his descendants as defendants.

But, returning to the tale of Columbus's voyages, it must be stressed that the organization of the third voyage was more complicated than the previous two. In good measure, this was due to the ominous accounts coming from Hispaniola. It was not easy to raise either the 330 settlers desired or the 4 million *maravedíes* that the undertaking would cost. The ships (seven caravels and one nao) were prepared in Sevilla and took four months to equip. In spite of everything, on May 30, 1498, Columbus's third fleet sailed from Sanlúcar de Barrameda. It included the Basques Lope de Olano, Pedro de Araba, Pedro de Ledesma, Martín Arriarán, and Bernardo de Ibarra.

The course plotted by the admiral took the fleet directly to the island of Trinidad, whose coast it reached on July 31. For thirteen subsequent days the explorers devoted themselves to sailing and exploring the Gulf of Paria. There, they discovered the mouth of the Orinoco River, whose immense flow dilutes the ocean's salt content. The explorers noticed this dilution, which led Columbus to think that such a bountiful flow could only run off a continent. Nevertheless, health problems impeded him from landing and thereby verifying the continental discovery.

Afterwards, he set a course for Hispaniola. There, in his three years of absence, Bartolomé Columbus (brother of Christopher) had overseen the first colonial achievements:

1. He pacified the island.
2. He imposed agricultural servitude on the Indians.
3. In 1496, the city of Santo Domingo was founded, shifting the colonizing focus to the southern part of the island, near the gold mines of San Cristóbal.
4. Evangelization yielded important results through the work of the Franciscans Juan Borgoña and Ramón Pane.

But not all the news was positive. The *alcalde mayor* of the island, Francisco Roldán, had led a rebellion backed by a discontented group that did not accept submission to the Columbus family. The Bizkaians Adrián de Múxica, Pedro Gámiz, and Domingo de Escobar were some of the Basques that joined the uproar. The iron-handed discipline imposed by the provincial governor, Bartolomé Columbus, attacks against the Indians, deprivations, hard work, and even hunger were not the liberties and easy wealth of which the mutineers had dreamed. The arrival of Columbus did nothing to solve the problem. The demands remained: surrender ships for the rebels' return to Spain, satisfaction of payments owed them, concession of slaves to work the land, and restoration of their belongings. Columbus informed the Catholic Monarchs about these developments and, in general, about the grave situation on Hispaniola.

This would not be the last problem that the Columbuses had to face. On August 23, 1500, the Genoa native found himself quelling a new rebellion on the island, far from the colony. The fuse of the insurgency had been lit by the Gipuzkoan Hernando de Guevara's marriage to an Indian princess. This wedding—the first mixed marriage in the New World—was not to Roldán's liking. The *alcalde mayor* ordered Guevara to forsake the native woman. The Basque refused and was jailed in the stronghold of Santo Domingo. His compatriots, again led by Adrián de Múxica, sparked the explosion of the second rebellion on Hispaniola. While combating this band of revolutionaries, Columbus received the order from Governor Francisco de Bobadilla to embark for Spain as a detainee, along with his brother Bartolomé. Bobadilla seized all of their possessions and initiated judicial proceedings that took them directly to Spain for judgment. On November 20, they reached Cádiz, where the monarchs ordered their release; they were pardoned, and their sentences repealed. In December, a humiliated Columbus requested the restoration of his privileges from the monarchs, as well as an exemplary punishment for Bobadilla.

After the bitter denouement of his third voyage, the discoverer remained in Castile enjoying his noble grandeur, lacking motivation to undertake new crossings. Nevertheless, a royal order dated 1501 obligated him to set sail for the Indies for the purpose of preempting the Portuguese in the discovery and possession of eastern islands and lands.

The four caravels that composed the fourth and final expedition of the Genovese admiral—the *Santa María, Capitana, Gallega,* and *Vizcaína* (the last of them the property of the Getaria [Gipuzkoa] outfitter Juan de Orquina)—were prepared in Sevilla in 1502. One hundred forty men composed the complement of Columbus's fourth crossing. Once more, a considerable number of Basque sailors (around 15 percent of the crew members) appeared among them.[17] On April 13, 1502, the fleet left Sevilla, and on June 15 they sighted the island of Guadalupe. Columbus's clear purpose was to follow the route to the Gulf of Paria, in order to map the Venezuelan coast and find a logical course leading to the legendary Spice Islands. After various attempts (at least preliminary),[18] the explorers ended up running aground on the present-day island of Jamaica. And an exploratory mission remained there for a full year waiting for assistance to come from Hispaniola. On June 28, 1504, a vessel from Santo Domingo saved the ill-fated expedition. The exploratory odyssey of Christopher Columbus came to a definitive end on November 7, the day he reached the port of Sanlúcar de Barrameda.

On November 26, 1504, Queen Isabella of Castile would die in Medina del Campo. Beginning that very day, Admiral Christopher Columbus was relegated from any matter related to the recently discovered Indies. His various ailments would keep him in Sevilla until the spring of 1505, when he headed out to Segovia and then Valladolid. He would die there on May 20, 1505, without knowing that he had discovered a new continent, America, and without knowing that he had achieved the most important and significant feat of the modern era.

The First Repercussions of the Discovery in the Basque Country

As has been stated, in 1503 the Catholic Monarchs conceded Sevilla the commercial monopoly of traffic with America through the House of Trade. In 1529, the Spanish Emperor Charles V authorized the ports of Bilbao, Donostia, La Coruña, Baiona (Galicia), Avilés, and Laredo to trade freely with America, the only condition being that ships put in to Sevilla on the return trip in order to pay the well-known taxes.

This situation, to a certain extent privileged, favored a traffic of very important people and merchandise from the outset. It also fueled boom activity in Basque ironworks and dockyards. The residents of Iparralde also benefited from this measure, since the vessels from Saint-Jean-de-Luz were registered as Bizkaian and, therefore, had the rights and privileges (and also obligations) of the Spanish Basque ships.

Beginning in 1520, two new American plants, beans and corn, were added to the traditional cultigens of Basque agriculture. The result for Basque culture was two new foods: *talo*, or cornbread, and *lapikoko*, a type of bean stew. The potato, also of American origin, reached the Basque Country in the second half of the sixteenth century. The spreading cultivation of these three crops increased the agricultural land of the Basque Country. These plants were more dependable in their productive cycle (especially corn) than millet, the principal crop of the Basque regions up to that point.

The reason for such agrarian development lies in the structural crisis of the rural Basque economy of the day. The high yields that corn offered compared to other, traditional plants (millet, barley, rye, and oats) explain why it replaced them so quickly. Moreover, corn changed the system of crop rotation. It almost completely eliminated fallowing through more intensive land use, thus permitting simultaneous exploitation of all cultivable lands. In sum, corn was the ideal remedy for the food shortage suffered for ages by the coastal Basque regions. It increased their level of self-sufficiency, thereby lowering their dependence on external food supplies.

The commercial structure was thus modified. Imports of subsistence goods were reduced in favor of other, more profitable, articles that promoted capital accumulation in the mercantile sector.[19]

But the influence of the New World in the Basque Country was most felt in the traditional economy. In effect, the industrial and rural sectors were driven by the stimulus of the overseas Spanish voyages of conquest and colonization of the newly discovered territories. Ironworkers, shipbuilders, and assemblers experienced unprecedented development of their industries. The rural Basque population was able to increase the cultivable surface of its *baserriak*, or farmsteads, thanks to the introduction of vegetable species from America.

Iron, as previously indicated, constituted one of the Basque economy's principal commodities of exchange. Its importance was reflected in the large number of foundries that had operated from ancient times in both Bizkaia and Gipuzkoa along the riverbanks near the prime sources of ore and fuel (wood). The Foru Berria (Fuero of Bizkaia) had already granted exclusive mineral exporting rights to the natives of the region, and the monarchy reserved the Spanish and American markets for iron from the Basque foundries. In this context, the sector's boom was possible only because of the increased demand resulting from changes taking place in agriculture and architecture, development of the ship industry, improvement in ground transport, needs stemming from war, and arms production. In the international market, the Basque Country and its iron industry enjoyed a privileged position for a long time due to the extraordinary quality of its ore and the ease of its extraction, distribution, and transport.[20]

Prior to the discovery of America, Basque iron already enjoyed considerable success in European markets. The appearance of new markets in America would take the Basque iron industry to new levels, especially given that demand would increase in the imperial state itself. The Spanish crown had a great need for iron products: arms, nails, farm equipment, and civil and military technology. This demand translated into a considerable increase in the number of ironworks in both Gipuzkoa and Bizkaia; in the sixteenth century, they came to number a not inconsequential three hundred. In sum, the Basque iron industry was relevant in the European metallurgical context until the end of the sixteenth century and the beginning of the seventeenth. During these years, Bizkaian and Gipuzkoan production reached eight to ten thousand tons annually, which came to represent almost 16 percent of all European production. And, from early colonial times, iron materials produced in the Basque Country found an excellent market in the Indies. It makes sense that the *Recopilación de las leyes de los reynos de Indias*, in one of whose chapters it was ordered "that they not be allowed to transport iron if it is not from Vizcaya," guaranteed that provision to the New World be restricted to Basque mineral and its derivatives alone.

In close relation with the iron industry, ship construction was notably driven by the trips to and from the New World. Even before 1492, given the excellent quality of their products, Bizkaian and Gipuzkoan shipyards were in great demand. They furnished both the monarchy and private merchants with vessels for the fleets that sailed on the American run. The Crown itself contributed to the expansion of the sector through the concession of numerous and diverse protectionist decrees and measures. In effect, Queen Isabella of Castile was already subsidizing the construction of ships over 660 tons in 1498, and in 1502 she offered Basque assemblers 50,000 *maravedíes* and a guarantee of cargo for six months for all the ships that they could build of more than 1,500 tons. That Bizkaian and Gipuzkoan natives accepted the challenge of tripling the tonnage capacity of their ships within four years clearly suggests complex shipbuilding technology and a society sophisticated in its economic, labor, professional, and administrative aspects. The Spanish Hapsburg monarchy then continued to facilitate the expansion of the Basque shipbuilding sector. It decreed ordinances that obligated the use of nationally built ships for traffic with the Indies, while prohibiting foreign participation in colonial commerce.[21]

The armory was, after the foundry and the shipyard, the third sector that experienced a noteworthy expansion with the colonial expeditions. Since ancient times the Basque regions had supplied the peninsular kingdoms with all types of steel blades and armor. The skilled ironworkers produced arms of excellent quality, as well as tools, equipment, and other utensils destined first for the internal market and later for overseas. The swords, knives, machetes, crossbows, darts, halberds, and armor from Bizkaia, Araba, Gipuzkoa, and Navarre had such prestige that the Catholic Monarchs issued official dispositions to get Basque armorers to destine their entire production for the royal armed forces. This arms tradition continued in the Basque Country during the modern era, especially in the Gipuzkoan *villas* of Soraluze, Arrasate, Oñati, and Eibar, and the Bizkaian ones of Ermua, Durango, and Elorrio.

Many were the Basque armorers that devoted their best production to satisfying the military demand of the Spanish Crown, whose requests grew. Thus, it makes sense that with the opening of the overseas colonial market the Basque arms industry made great progress. The Basque regions were able to stock the armies and royal fleets for the Indies with all types of arms without having to resort to foreign import. Moreover, the Basque Country had overwhelming advantages in expanding this sector beginning in the sixteenth century. In effect, apart from the existence of many masters of recognized prestige in the trade,[22] the proximity of the foundries, the abundance of some species of trees like walnut (highly valued in the production of stocks for muskets and hackbuts) and ash (excellent for lances and picks), the possibility of shipping output quickly by sea, and the Basque associative tradition across economic sectors were some of the factors explaining the boom in the Basque arms industry.

In sum, the discovery and subsequent colonization of the New World had immediate, substantial consequences for the demography and economy of the Basque

Country. The conquest of the New World by Spain, and the incursions of France in the Caribbean and in North America (the future United States and Canada), substantially widened the horizons of the Basques from both sides of the Pyrenees. They did not hesitate to set sail in search of better opportunities and greater material riches. Although in the pages to follow a full, detailed account of the Basque migratory process to America will be provided, it is worth mentioning here that emigration was considerable during the colonial centuries. But it wasn't only voluntary departures to the recently discovered continent that unbalanced the Basque sociodemographic panorama during the modern era. Military demands to maintain Spanish imperial power also greatly affected Basque demography. The new lands further extended a Spanish empire that was already large. In addition to its New World holdings, the empire included possessions in Asia and Africa, Mediterranean islands, and parts of Italy and the Low Countries. These territories made Spain the main political power in the Europe of the fifteenth, sixteenth, and seventeenth centuries. And, frequently, the territories had to be defended against smaller nations, eager to expand their possessions at the slightest sign of Spanish weakness. Consequently, the Basques participated actively in the formation of regiments when the situation and the monarchy so required. The situation was such that, by the mid-seventeenth century, Bizkaia made several public calls seeking to repatriate Bizkaians living in "the Indies, Flanders, Italy, and other provinces" in the face of its lack of inhabitants "due to the many people that ordinarily leave to serve His Majesty in his armies and navies." It is in this context that statements like "of four parts of the people of Vizcaya, three are women, due to the many men that leave and never return" may be understood.

Chapter Two

Mastery of the Land

In the Footsteps of Columbus

As has been shown thus far, the Basques played a critical role in the Columbian project of the discovery and colonization of the New World. In the crews of Columbus there were always a great number of "Vizcayans"[1] listed as masters, boatswains, captains, pilots, sailors, coopers, caulkers, carpenters, or simple cabin boys. To those already cited, the following took part in subsequent voyages: Francisco de Garay, one of the first Basque explorers and colonizers, the pilot Alonso Sánchez Cotillos, the sailors Martín de Alzate and Martín de Arriarán, the royal secretary Bernardo de Ibarra, and the master Juan de Ajanguiz. Some of them, as already mentioned, paid for their zeal for adventure and wealth with their lives. Others followed Columbus through the unknown Atlantic and Caribbean waters. And, more than a few decided to return to the Basque Country after the often negative and disappointing experience of America.

These Basque pioneers found themselves in the midst of the collective efforts of the colonization of the New World during the first years of the American adventure. One example is the plan established by the Bizkaian Luis de Arriaga in 1501 and approved by Queen Isabella to populate Hispaniola with two hundred families from Bizkaia. The colonists' mission was to found four settlements of fifty members each. In exchange, they would receive a hacienda on the condition that they remain in their respective settlements for five years and pay their taxes to the Crown. Although this plan was never carried out, it was undoubtedly the first large-scale scheme of Iberian migration to America. In 1533, Emperor Charles V demonstrated an intense interest in the colonization of America with Basque natives by sending sixty peasants with their families to Santo Domingo in order to found a city.

During and after Columbus's fourth voyage, several trips of discovery and exploration were conducted around the American continental lands. The lack of news about the admiral and his fleet, and the later disillusion with which the Crown of Castile received news of Columbus's progress in the New World, were the main reasons that the Catholic Monarchs, beginning in 1495, authorized whoever so requested to go discover new lands and greater wealth, although this measure openly contradicted the privilege granted to Columbus in the Capitulaciones de Santa Fe. Through a royal provision, dated April 10 of that year, the Catholic Monarchs allowed complete freedom of navigation to the Indies to whomever so desired, to explore the economic potential of those lands. The decree discussed the various obligations of the new adventurers—to set sail from and put into port exclusively in Cádiz, to pay one-tenth of whatever they obtained in their commerce, to surrender one-fourth of the gold that they acquired, and to transport anything that the Crown might order free of charge. It also introduced a series of resolutions to set in motion migratory policies attractive to future settlers—freedom to travel to the Indies, property rights once there, maintenance by the Crown for one year, one-third of the gold that they discovered and payment to the treasury of only one-tenth of what they found or confiscated. In short, it was a question of modifying both the activity of discovery and the management of exploitation of the New World, which were privatized at the same time that the Crown began reexerting its will and expanding its sovereignty beyond limit.[2] These legislative measures were unsuccessful from the beginning, however, as Columbus returned to the peninsula in 1496 after his second expedition and managed to get his privileges and payments reconfirmed and the royal provision repealed on June 2, 1497.

Nevertheless, two years later, in 1499, the sum of adverse circumstances in the Indies made the Crown realize that the favors granted to Columbus were becoming detrimental to its interests. The admiral and his brothers demonstrated their incapacity to colonize the new territories peacefully, and the discoveries were paralyzed. Moreover, neighboring Portugal already had a clear idea about its path to the East Indies. In view of the situation, the Catholic Monarchs did not hesitate to again authorize private expeditions to the New World. It remains unknown whether or not the Crown intended to suspend Columbus from his duties with this legislative measure. In any case, it is clear that from 1499 to the creation of the Casa de Contratación (House of Trade) in 1503, this measure authorized a series of maritime expeditions called "lesser journeys," "Andalusian journeys," and "journeys of discovery and salvage," in which the Basques again participated actively.

The geographical scope of these expeditions was the Caribbean Sea, between the northern coasts of South America, the arc of the Lesser Antilles, and the south coast of the Greater Antilles. Juridically, all the explorations were organized, directed, and financed privately through agreements with the Crown. All of the known contracts of this type had the same major points: they authorized "going by the Ocean to discover islands and mainlands," with the exception of those belonging to Portugal or already discovered by Columbus; expenses would be paid by the sponsors or their associates; explorers were granted ownership of everything they discovered and the right to disembark in Spain free of taxes except for one-fifth of the profits, which would be for the king and queen and supervised by a royal delegate on board each ship; explorers were prohibited from bringing in wood from Brazil because it was considered a government monopoly; and they were granted tax exemptions for all of the merchandise that they brought to trade. The protagonists of these lesser expeditions were sailors and men who were accustomed to maritime tasks and expert in the sailing arts, mostly—as in prior journeys—natives of Atlantic Andalusia. Given that a great number of Basques had settled in that region much earlier, and had achieved high socioeconomic status, it is logical to surmise that some of them participated in the organization, financing, and ranks of the private fleets that set out for the New World. These expeditions were composed of few ships—sometimes only one caravel. On the basis of the practical knowledge acquired by Basque pilots and sailors prior to 1492 and Columbus's voyage, the theory that the Basque natives living in Lower Andalusia participated in these lesser journeys gains credibility.

Alonso de Ojeda, Americo Vespucci, and the Bizkaian Juan de la Cosa were the first to leave, following the route of Columbus in 1499. Their expedition was a complete disaster, fraught with casualties and no profits—they managed to bring back only a few pearls and emeralds, Indians captured in the Bahamas, and the prohibited wood from Brazil. Nevertheless, they discovered the stretch of coast between Cape Orange and the mouth of the Demerara River to Trinidad and the entire northern coast of present-day Venezuela, acquiring the conviction that this stretch belonged to a single continent. In addition, as a result of this journey, in 1500 Juan de la Cosa drew up his famous *Carta de Marear o Mapamundi*, the first map in which America appears.

A few months later, Pero Alonso Niño and his partner Cristóbal Guerra obtained a license to explore, but at a minimum distance of fifty leagues from Columbus's previous discoveries. After raising the necessary resources, they managed to charter a caravel and assemble a crew of thirty-three men, some of them of Basque origin. Their substantial profits (they managed to bring back a great quantity of pearls "as if they were straw") provided the incentive for future expeditions.

At the end of 1499, the Pinzón family recruited Basque sailors living in Andalusia to fill out the crew for four caravels that they chartered to try their luck in the Indies. Like the expedition of Ojeda, Vespucci, and Juan de la Cosa, the attempt ended in failure. It did not yield any profits and two ships with all of their crew were lost. The journey was a geographic success, however; this was the first expedition to cross the equator and discover present-day Brazil and the mouth of the Amazon River. Their route was followed by Diego de Lepe and Gonzalo de Vedya's January 1500 expedition and Alonso Vélez de Mendoza and Luis Guerra's June 1500 foray, both yielding the same results.

Juan de la Cosa again set out for the Indies in February 1501, this time with the Sevillan Rodrigo de Bastidas. The economic disasters of the previous voyages caused distrust among the investors, and the expedition's departure therefore had been delayed several months. Nevertheless, Juan de la Cosa finally found twenty investors in Sevilla to finance the small armada, most probably some of them Basque. Two ships were thus manned with full crews, among them Vasco Nuñez de Balboa (the future discoverer of the South Sea) and the pilot Andrés Morales. The great value of the journey, as for all of those in which the Basque cartographer participated, was its geographic nature; the present-day Caribbean coasts of Colombia and part of those of Panama were discovered. In addition, until the expedition was economically fruitful, the monarchs made Bastidas travel to Alcalá de Henares to show them the wealth obtained, in order to promote the expedition's success and provide incentive for other private ventures in the Indies.

Alonso de Ojeda struck another deal with Ferdinand and Isabella on June 8, 1501. The presence of the English in the area of Spanish influence that Ojeda claimed to have discovered on his previous journey forced the Crown to expedite its discoveries on the mainland, settle, and take possession of the lands discovered to that point. Ojeda's goal was clear: establish a seat that would serve as a base from which to continue his exploration and proceed inland. Associated with the Gipuzkoan merchant Juan de Vergara, Ojeda's four-ship, 150-man expedition set sail in January 1502. One of the caravels, the *Santa Ana*, was captained by Hernando Guevara, the Gipuzkoan whose mixed marriage had caused the second revolt on Hispaniola during Columbus's third voyage. The many hardships encountered on the way—adverse climate, dispersion of the fleet, lack of provisions, and infighting—did not prevent the expedition from founding the first European colony on the continent in May of that year. Called "Santa Cruz," according to some historians it was located on Honda Bay, on the Guajira peninsula in the far northwest of Colombia.

After the discovery expeditions, large-scale explorations and conquest of the mainland began. Inhabitants of the Basque Country were again protagonists. Thousands of Bizkaians, Arabans, Gipuzkoans, and Navarrese left their established occupations and homes to start a New World Basque odyssey that would continue for five centuries. Many Basques seized the opportunities that the recently discovered lands offered. Zeal for wealth, desire for fame and glory, and simple necessity were some of the things that drove the Basques to the far reaches of the then unknown American continent. There, where the monarchy needed enterprising people, the Basques were quick to respond. Thus, after Columbus's undertaking of discovery, they successfully completed the first trip around the world, played a prominent role in the first expeditions to the Pacific Ocean, and demonstrated great skill in cosmography and navigation. They explored eastern Colombia, much of Mexico and California, the endless Amazon, and the Río de la Plata. They played important roles in revolts and rebellions, were assigned to govern and manage the lands of the Crown, participated in the foundation of numerous American cities, and conquered the islands of the Pacific, which they named "the Philippines" in honor of their master and king, Philip II. They colonized vast territories, demonstrated the fallacy of El Dorado, advanced the discovery of mining deposits and operations, increased livestock wealth, and contributed to the infinite expansion of the Crown. They built and supplied vessels, tools, equipment, and various war materials for the maritime and military expeditions in the New World, frequently risking their fortunes. They served as bishops, archbishops, and apostles of the Christian faith, evangelized and instructed thousands of indigenous people, and were unflinching pioneers of Indian rights. They introduced the use of printing in the New World, supported the publication of the first books, and designed great, beautiful cathedrals and other buildings that still stand. They wrote distinguished civil, military, and religious histories of the New World, and undertook varied and lucrative commercial ventures. Many perished in the process. Others, the great majority, went unnoticed. And the strongest and most gifted accomplished great feats, achieving glory and their place in history. This was the anonymity and grandeur of the enterprising men committed to fashioning the New World, which they did with enthusiasm from their varied personal circumstances. They were the Basque heroes of the New World.[3]

Navigators, Explorers, and Conquistadors

The majority of the Basque natives that arrived in the Americas as part of the first wave of the Spanish undertaking were sailors and soldiers that joined forces with other Spaniards to carry out the transatlantic project of colonization, territorial expansion, and development during the sixteenth, seventeenth, and eighteenth centuries. As already noted, Basque participation was significant in all fields of collective action ordered by the Spanish monarchy and performed by the residents of their kingdoms.[4]

Since the end of the fifteenth century, the traditional naval and mercantile countries sought the quickest way to access the valued spices of the Orient. As is well known, the sea route around America was discovered by Ferdinand Magellan and Juan Sebastián Elcano in 1519. As early as 1508, however, the main Castilian investors, tempted by the great profits obtained by their Portuguese rivals in the Orient, attempted to enter this lucrative market. The extent of success of the Portuguese undertakings in some ports of India pointed to the potential for greater profits; it provided an excellent incentive to finance expeditions in search of new routes to Asia. Thus motivated, in 1508 the Board of Navigators met in Burgos and decided to underwrite the first voyage in search of the Spice Islands, captained by Juan Díaz de Solís and Vicente Yáñez Pinzón. At the same time, they agreed to send two other expeditions to the lands of Veragua and Urabá, a region between Colombia and Panama that, it was rumored, held vast deposits of gold. The command of these fell to Diego de Nicuesa and Alonso de Ojeda, respectively. The Bizkaians Lope de Olano and Juan de la Cosa participated, the former as lieutenant and the latter as royal pilot.

The main goal of Díaz de Solís and Yáñez Pinzón's expedition was to find direct passage to the Orient from the point that Columbus had touched land on his fourth voyage, but in the opposite direction—toward the north of what would later be recognized as the isthmus of Central America. As such a venture would require knowledge of the terrain of the route followed by the fourth voyage of Columbus, a select crew had to be recruited. The Bizkaian Pedro de Ledesma was included as the pilot of the caravel *Magdalena*, a small vessel built and purchased in Portugalete (Bizkaia) for a frustrated voyage to the Spice Islands in 1506. The results were disappointing for the Castilian business interests, as the expedition did not manage to find the hoped-for passage to the Orient.

The second venture was two-pronged. Diego de Nicuesa was ordered to head for the coast of Panama, while Alonso de Ojeda plotted a course for the northwestern coast of Colombia. Both sailors had managed to put together a magnificent fleet, equipped thanks to the economic support of several Basques living in Hispaniola. Nicuesa left the Caribbean island in 1509 with four ships and a crew of seven hundred men, and explored the coast from Venezuela to the Gulf of Darien. Ojeda set sail for the Port of Calamar in Cartagena. He eradicated an indigenous population there against the advice of Juan de la Cosa, who lost his life in the battle. Following this event, the latter expedition divided. After suffering several hardships, Alonso de Ojeda decided to return to Hispaniola. The rest of the expedition, commanded by the still-novice Francisco Pizarro, sailed with the *bachiller* of Basque roots, Martín de Enciso, to Darien, where "a lot of gold had been seen." This was on the advice of Balboa, who had boarded as a stowaway among Enciso's crew. The crew founded the city of Santa María de la Antigua de Darien (the present-day Colombian city of Acandí), establishing the first Castilian seat of government on the continent. Balboa and Martín Sánchez de Zamudio, also Basque, were named mayor and alderman of the new city by its first settlers. Around that time, Diego de Nicuesa had arrived at Darien with his fleet. There, Nicuesa had a confrontation with his Bizkaian lieutenant, Lope de Olano, because of the latter's conspiracy plot. Olano was arrested, but released shortly thereafter by Diego Macax, also Basque, while Nicuesa founded the city of Portobelo in Panama. The repeated correspondence between Olano and his relative Sánchez de Zamudio (originally from Bilbao), and other Basques living in the nearby settlements at the time, probably played a role in the former's release. In any event, what is certain is that the group of Basques freed Olano, captured Nicuesa, and put him on a ship sailing for Hispaniola. That these events pertain to a narrative of ethnic Basque collective action in the New World is clearly reflected in the writings of the chronicler Fernández de Oviedo, who states that "Lope de Olano was Vizcayan [i.e., Basque], knew that in Darien, Martín de Zamudio was one of the mayors . . . and this mayor . . . was a relative of Lope de Olano. And there were also other Vizcayans, those connected to him and other Basques of his language to whom he wrote that the governor was holding him prisoner and mistreating him, and turning many of them against Diego de Nicuesa."[5]

While expeditions continued to search in vain for the route to the Spice Islands, the conquest of Cuba was being planned in Hispaniola. In 1509, King Ferdinand ordered Diego Columbus to investigate the island's potential gold reserves and to prepare an assault on it. In 1511, the governor named Diego Velázquez de Cuellar to carry out this mission. Velázquez surrounded himself with a contingent of three hundred men, including Juan de Aguirre, Pedro de Rentería, and other Basques. In spite of native resistance, they managed to conquer the island territory completely after advancing westward from the easternmost region closest to Hispaniola. The process of colonization began quickly and included a relevant number of Bizkaians, Gipuzkoans, Arabans, and Navarrese. The possible benefits of the Basque presence in the New World were recognized even by the monarch when he affirmed in a letter to the governor of Santo Domingo, dated 1511:

> I have been displeased upon hearing about the great need of people, service, and Indians on that island, and by this post I am ordering the House of Trade officials in Sevilla that from now on they do not harass the people who want to go over there, as they have done until now. On the contrary, let them disregard what can be disregarded without harm, let them procure as many workers as possible, and to this effect, let them announce everywhere that the kingdom needs the many mines that are being discovered over there as well as the great wealth [of the island]. Furthermore, I order them to inquire in the mountains of Gipuzkoa, where there are many people without means to make a living, and let them procure as many workers as possible to go to those parts.[6]

The region of the Antilles became the center of attention of the first Basque immigrants to the New World. According to Labayru,[7] in 1514 many citizens of the Basque Country could be found in this region, including Juan de Azúa, Juan Vizcaíno, Pedro de Arana, Gabriel Butrón, Hernando de Berrio (court clerk), Juan Ezquerra, Cristóbal Vizcaíno, Inés Machín, Juan de Bergara (pharmacist), Juan de Oñate, Diego de Arriaga, Pedro de Bergara (sexton), Juan de Barrutia (master), Gonzalo Vizcaíno, Juan de Ochoa, Francisco de Barrena, Juan de Aguirre, Miguel de Bergara, Pedro Vizcaíno, the licentiate Matienzo, Diego de Ayala, Juan de Urueba, and Juan de Zamudio (mayor and governor of Hispaniola). But not only men went to the Americas from the Basque region during that period. Labayru also notes that a significant shipment of arms from Bizkaia was sent to Francisco de Garay, who amassed a great fortune by financing agriculture, livestock, and mining in Santo Domingo and Jamaica and later invested in provisioning various expeditions of discovery and exploration of the American mainland.

The conquest of Cuba was followed by the annexation of Puerto Rico and the occupation of Jamaica. The Crown thereby assured itself of complete dominance in the Antilles, which was rich in pearls and gold. Nevertheless, the dream of the spices remained unrealized and the precious metal was running out. It therefore became necessary to accelerate the process of conquest and discovery. The Caribbean islands served as an excellent military and commercial base from which to undertake exploratory journeys of the South and Central American mainland in order to find the longed-for passage.

Around 1510, Vasco Nuñez de Balboa was in the region called Castilla de Oro, on the Panamanian coast, with about two hundred Spaniards, when he heard from the indigenous people that a great sea and a land rich in gold existed to the south. It was not until well into 1513, however, that he decided to set sail in search of the South Sea, which would turn out to be the Pacific Ocean. From Antigua the crew traveled parallel to the coast to the port of Caretas, where they entered straits and had to overcome many physical obstacles in their path. Twenty days later the Europeans beheld the Pacific Ocean for the first time. During the expedition of Balboa, some Basques stood out, such as Antonio de Baracaldo, Pedro de Orduña, the merchant and ship owner from Bilbao Pedro de Arbolancha, and the Araban Pascual de Andagoya, one of the future founders of Panama City and its first alderman. In the opinion of some scholars, others were also on the isthmus at the time—the Bizkaians Lorenzo de Galarza, Rodrigo de Motrico, the licentiate Hernando de Celaya, Juan de Basurto, Pedro de Jaúregui, Juan de Castañeda, Diego de Esquivel, Juan de Avendaño, Martín de Cote, and the Gipuzkoan Rodrigo de Lazcano. They all remained for more than two months on the beaches of the Pacific, after which they undertook the return trip to Antigua.

In spite of the accomplishments of Balboa's advance scouts and his main crew, around 1519 the desire to find the route connecting the West with the East through the Atlantic remained utopian. To the extent that the American continent was showing its true face, for the Europeans its profile collided head-on with the geographical mind-set of the epoch. It was considered inconceivable that such a land mass could extend from pole to pole without a single break, without a channel permitting passage to the yearned for lands of the Orient. In this regard, in February of 1518 the Portuguese Ferdinand Magellan proposed to Emperor Charles V that a new route be opened to the Spice Islands following the coast of South America. The monarch's decision was probably greatly influenced by the advice of Magellan's Bizkaian companions: Sancho de Matienzo, treasurer of the House of Trade, and the chronicler Domingo de Ochandiano. The emperor and Magellan agreed on the conditions of the expedition in Valladolid, barely a month before the explorer's arrival at the court. The preparation of this mission of discovery was entrusted to Nicolás de Artieta. It was made up of five vessels, christened *Trinidad*, the flagship bought right in Bilbao, *San Antonio, Concepción, Santiago,* and *Victoria* (which appears to have been built in the shipyards of Zarautz around 1515). As was frequent in that period, Artieta bought a great part of the equipment that would be used by the fleet: armor, artillery, gunpowder, crossbows, firearms, mortars, falcons, lances, and pikes, as well as naval tools and equipment such as anvils, harpoons, cords, files, and drills. The recruiting of the crew presented some problems, but the organizers managed to enlist 265 men from Portugal, France, England, the Low Countries, Castile, and of course the Basque Country. The Basque personnel are listed in table 1.1 in appendix 1.

The ships set sail from the port of Sanlúcar de Barrameda on November 20, 1519, toward the Spice Islands. After taking on fresh water in Tenerife and then again in Brazil, the explorers headed south. Hugging the South American coast, they arrived at the great estuary of the Río de la Plata, which they believed to be their long sought strait. Upon discovering their error, they pointed their vessels south toward previously unnavigated waters. The harshness of winter in the Southern Hemisphere, however, forced the fleet to take refuge in a natural port that they called San Julián after the saint's day. Soon some of the crew members felt the first symptoms of discontent and malaise as a result of the despotic, authoritarian attitude of Magellan. Nevertheless, the commander took advantage of the disorganization of the rebels to recover and reaffirm his command, execute the leaders of the mutiny, and condemn another forty crew members to death, among them Juan Sebastián Elcano. All were pardoned, however, given the obvious need for hands to continue the expedition, especially after the loss of the ship *Santiago*.

Once the conspiracy was aborted and the austral winter passed, the four vessels again set out in August 1520. At the end of October, they established contact with the Patagonian Indians, thus named by Magellan because of their large legs. Shortly thereafter, the expedition entered the strait that they called Todos los Santos, or All Saints, and that is presently named the Strait of Magellan in honor of the Portuguese navigator. Given that the passage was discovered, part of the crew expressed a desire to head home. This suggestion was resolutely rejected by the armada captain, resulting in the desertion of the vessel *San Antonio*, which set sail for the Iberian Peninsula. The expedition continued onward with the remaining ships and entered the narrow sea passage. After thirty-eight days of navigation through reefs, rocks, and deep waters—and helped in good measure by the visual references provided by the Patagonian Indians through fires lit along the coast (for which the sailors named it Tierra del Fuego, or Land of Fire)—the three vessels that survived the rough seas finally reached the Pacific Ocean.

Three months later they landed at the archipelago of the Mariana Islands, and then the Philippines. After some attempts to Christianize the natives, the Europeans were attacked, and Magellan lost his life in the course of one of the skirmishes. The survivors quickly set sail to the south, toward the Spice Islands. They had to burn the *Concepción* due to the shrinking number of crew members and pilots after their battles with the natives. Elcano assumed command of the *Victoria* and was named treasurer of the armada in this restructuring.

In July of 1521, the explorers reached Borneo and, in November, the Spice Islands. There, they gathered a large quantity of spices and learned of Portuguese plans to intercept the Spanish fleet once it reached the Cape of Good Hope. The expedition therefore speeded up, although the *Trinidad*, leaking water, and its fifty-four frightened crewmen remained at the mercy of the Portuguese. In February of 1522, Elcano entered the Indian Ocean. After several days the explorers managed, with great difficulty, to sail around the southernmost cape of Africa, and crossed the equator in early June. They found themselves in desperate conditions, and more than twenty-two crewmen died. Among these were the Basques Lorenzo de Iruña, Juan de Santelices, Martín de Inchaurraga, and Lope Navarro.

Driven by their hunger, the survivors managed to reach Cape Verde and get provisions at the Portuguese settlement on the island of Santiago. The Portuguese authorities ordered the capture of the Spaniards, however. Elcano was forced to give the urgent order to weigh anchor. Thirteen crewmen were stranded, captured, and imprisoned as a result, among them the Gipuzkoans Pedro de Tolosa and Roldán de Argote, and the Bizkaian Pedro Chindurza. On September 6, 1522, the *Victoria*, leaking from all of its joints, cast anchor in Sanlúcar de Barrameda. Almost three years had passed since its departure on a voyage that saw it traverse nearly 14,500 leagues. Only eighteen exhausted men had successfully concluded the first circumnavigation of the earth. In addition to Elcano, Juan de Acurio from Bermeo, Juan de Arratia from Bilbao, and Juan de Zubileta from Barakaldo returned. Emperor Charles V recognized the feat of the Getaria native by awarding him the motto "Primus Circumdedisti Me" for his coat of arms and a yearly pension of five hundred ducats. (The pension was never paid because of the economic hardships suffered by the Crown at that time.)

At the same time that Elcano was undertaking the first trip around the world, the Emperor Charles V was trying to extend his political control over the majority of the territories of South and Central America. For some time the Crown had been hearing suggestive news coming from the coast of the mainland to the west of Cuba. Juan Díaz de Solís and Vicente Yáñez Pinzón had already visited the Mexican coast for the first time, exploring the accessible shore of the Yucatán Peninsula in previous years. Then, in 1512, Juan Ponce de León and his Basque pilot Juan Pérez de Ortubia discovered Florida and sailed along its coast until the 38th parallel. In 1517, the governor of Cuba, Diego de Velázquez, sent two ships owned by the Bizkaian Lope Ochoa de Salcedo westward to explore the Yucatán. The journey was largely unsuccessful, given the hostility of the natives. Nevertheless, news of the existence of a fertile, flourishing country on the other side of the Caribbean motivated the authorities to promote a new expedition. Under the command of Juan de Grijalba, it sailed along the Yucatán coast and the Gulf of Mexico for six months. In some places, the explorers found peaceful Indians who freely gave them large quantities of gold. In others, however, they could not even disembark due to well-armed warriors who did not hesitate to attack the invaders. Some crew members, such as the Gipuzkoan Juan de Guetaria, were even killed. In spite of the losses, the net result was positive. The expedition gathered 20,000 pesos in gold, contact was made with a region outside of Mayan influence, the diversity and variety of lands and peoples were learned, and the evidence of geographic continuity proved that it could not be another island. All of these factors decisively influenced the organization of a new expedition commanded by the Extremaduran Hernán Cortés. Its mission was to collect as much gold as possible and find deposits of the precious metal. Few thought that it would be the beginning of the real conquest, that of the mainland.

The final preparations of the conquering expedition were carried out in the city of Havana. It set sail from there in February 1519 after being equipped with food, rescue supplies, and arms and equipment. The fleet was composed of eleven ships, 518 soldiers, 109 crewmen, sixteen horses, thirty-two Bizkaian crossbows, thirteen firearms made in Gipuzkoa, four falcons, ten bronze cannons, and a variety of munitions. The number of Basques that accompanied Hernán Cortés in 1519 and Pánfilo Narváez one year later[8] was very significant according to the names in the documentation. The following Basques participated in the conquest of Mexico: Juan Arguena, Martín López, Pedro de Anaya, Antón de Arizabala, Juan de Arriaga, Juan Pérez de Arteaga, Pedro de Berrio, Sebastián de Zubieta, Pedro de Carranza, Andrés de Eibar, Juan de Fuenterrabía, Cristóbal Martín de Gamboa, Diego de Arisnea, Heredia el Viejo, Martín de Ircio, Pedro de Ircio, Hernando de Lezama, Martín Ruíz de Monjaraz, Gregorio de Monjaraz, Juan de Montano, Juan de Lizana, Rodrigo Guipúzcoano, Martín Ramos, Juan Espinosa, Pedro de Orduña, Alonso de Motrico, Diego de Olarte, Gonzalo de Ochoa, Diego de Sopuerta, Andrés del Arnés de Sopuerta, Juan de San Sebastián, Pedro de Urbieta, Juan Ruiz de Viana, Alonso de Zuazo, Juan de Guetaria, Ramos Martín, Juan de Aguirre, Hernando de Argueta, Miguel Arriaga, Domingo de Arteaga, Juan de Azpeitia, Juan Díaz de Azpeitia, Francisco de Berrio, Hernando de Elgueta, Gaspar de Guernica, Diego de Guinea, Juan de Guevara, Juan Bono de Guecho, Juan de Vizcaíno, Guillén de Laloa, Hernando de Lezama, Juan de Lezcano, Diego de Motrico, Francisco Martín, Juan de Ochoa de Lexalde, Diego de Ordaz, Diego de Orduña, Francisco de Orduña, Francisco de Orozco, Ochoa de Verazu, Alonso de Orduña, Juan de Orozco Melgar, Diego de Olarte, Ochoa de Asúa, Juan de Ochoa, Martín de San Juan, Juan de Susmiaga, Antonio de Sánchez, Santiago Vizcaíno, Anton de Torraeta, Gonzalo de Urriola, Juan de Ugarte de la Cruz, Pedro Vizcaíno, Alonso de Vergara, Juan de Vergara, Pedro de Vergara, Martín de Vergara, Miguel de Veraza, Juan de Zamudio (on Cortés's ship), Juan de Zamudio (on Narváez's ship), and Juan de Zubia.[9]

This list does not include the sailors who were crew members of the vessels in Cortés's fleet. There is strong evidence that those of Basque origin were numerous. The documentary sources affirm that in 1519 the Bizkaian naval outfitter Martín López accompanied Cortés and, because of his shipbuilding knowledge, the commander had assigned him to build two brigs to ensure that Montezuma could be successfully transported through the lagoon of the city of Mexico. Some time later, after Cortés' retreat, Martín López also participated in the construction of a fleet of thirteen brigs of various sizes in Tlaxcala, which were carried, still unassembled, to the lagoon in the city of Mexico to participate in the siege of the Aztec capital. In addition to Martín López, other Basques also accompanied Cortés on his expeditions to the mainland: the caulker Juan de Bilbao, the carpenters Juan Martínez de Aroa, Juanes de Zuaxo, Juanes de Marquina, and Miguel de Urbieta, the sailors Juan de Balzola, Pedro de Ochoa, Juan de Escarza, Juanes de Arrieta, Martín de Aspiruntza, and Domingo de Elejalde, the boatswain Martín Pérez de Lezcano, and the Bizkaian cosmographer and sailor Ortuño Jimenez.

A number of these Basques participated and stood out in some of the battles that took place during the conquest of the Aztec Empire, which permitted them to ascend in rank. One, Hernando de Lezama, was named captain under Cortés during the siege of Mexico. The same honor fell to Andrés de Monjaraz, from Durango, who was assigned as the personal guard of Montezuma and died during the battle of Mexico. Juan de Montano, from Portugalete, was ensign to Pedro Alvarado during the assault on the Mexican capital, while Fernando de Salcedo was bestowed the rank of captain by Cortés. After the conquest of Mexico, some of them managed to improve their professional status by trading their pikes, mortars, and hackbuts for a calmer life in the royal administration. This was the case with the artillery captain under the command of Narváez, Francisco de Orozco, who became the alderman of the *villa* of Tepeaca upon its founding. Years later, he was assigned the mission of settling the province of Oaxaca. Antón de Arriaga also occupied a relevant post in the administration of Nueva España as the solicitor of the Aztec capital after having taken part in the conquest of the cities of Mexico, Pánuco, Michoacán, and Zacatula. Another notable was Juan Pérez de Arteaga, captain under Cortés and one of the settlers of Puebla de los Angeles and a member of its first town council. In addition, Pedro de Carranza was the alderman of the city of Mexico in 1527, and Hernán Cortés named Pedro de Ircio, from Enkarterri, as the mayor of Tepeaca in 1520. Cortés also designated Juan Ochoa de Lexalde, from Araba, as the first bailiff of the *villa* of Veracruz and inspector of weights and measures in the city of Tacuba. The Bizkaian Juan de Orduña was named alderman of Tepeaca in 1520 and, four years later, secretary of Mexico's city council. As some scholars have shown, aside from the Extremaduran-Andalusian group that surrounded Cortés, no ensemble of colonists was as numerous as the Basque contingent.[10]

The conquest of Tenochtitlán permitted the Spanish Crown to really enjoy the true wealth of the Americas for the first time. But the adventurers were convinced that lands even more profitable for the monarchy existed beyond the borders of the city of Mexico. Once the central core of the Aztec Empire was conquered in 1521, therefore, a rapid process of expansion was set in motion in two directions. One was to discover the seaward route to the Orient that, with time, would yield the greatest profits; the other was to explore northward in search of the great wealth spoken of by the first native Mexicans.

The discovery mission to the north of Nueva España, begun in 1529, was supervised by Nuño de Guzmán, the most ruthless of the Mexican conquistadors according to historians. Juan de Tolosa, the brothers Cristóbal and Juan de Oñate, Juan de Villalba from Gasteiz, Domingo de Arteaga, Jerónimo Pérez de Arceniega, Martín de Rentería, Miguel de Ibarra, and Jerónimo de Orozco were among the troops that made up the expedition. The initial objective of the campaign commanded by Guzmán and captained by the Oñate brothers was the pacification of the Indians living in what is presently the state of Jalisco. The adventurers were opening a route to the north of this region and south of Zacatecas. They suffered everything from diseases to attempted mutinies, and were repeatedly faced with Indian attacks. In spite of the hardships, they managed to found the *villa* of San Miguel de Culiacán in the north of the present-day state of Sinaloa. Among its first settlers were the Bizkaians Pedro de Guernica, Juan Vizcaíno, and Pedro de Armentia.

A short time earlier, Cristóbal de Oñate had gone to explore the western Sierra Madre, in the territory of the current state of Durango. After an intense pacification effort, he, his brother Juan, and Miguel de Ibarra (from Eibar) founded the *villa* of Espíritu Santo de Guadalajara. Eventually, it would become the center of future northward expeditions. Around the same time, Juan de Tolosa, one of Oñate's men, discovered silver in Zacatecas during a self-financed expedition. He founded the city of that name, and began what would later be one of the most important mining districts in the New World. Some historians have pointed out that, beginning with the discovery of the famous Zacatecas mines in 1546, Basque miners quickly invaded the hills of northwest Nueva España, settling many cities such as San Martín, Fresnillo, Indé, and Santa Barbara.[11] Diego de Ibarra, Tolosa's associate, also participated. As the first mayor of Zacatecas, he oversaw the campaign to attract many family members and friends from the Basque Country to work in the rich silver deposits. In 1550, Ibarra was placed in charge of continuing the expansion of Nueva España northward. He turned this task over, however, to his young nephew Francisco de Ibarra. Accompanied by Juan de Tolosa, between 1554 and 1574 Ibarra conquered the lands that he called Nueva Vizcaya (Royal Provision of July 24, 1562), comprising the present states of Durango, Chihuahua, Coahuila, Sinaloa, and Sonora, as well as some areas of Zacatecas, San Luis de Potosí, and Nuevo León. Ibarra also founded the city of Durango, named after his own birthplace in Bizkaia. He achieved the rank of governor and declared that the Foru Berria would be the law of all territory he managed to conquer. Thus, all of its inhabitants would be considered noblemen and would be exempt from payment of royal taxes. (This declaration was proclaimed invalid by the Crown.) Until his death in 1575, Francisco de Ibarra consolidated his triumphs in Nueva Vizcaya, converting it into the launchpad for later northward exploration. He continued his advance exploration, in the process founding the *villa* of San Sebastián.

Northern Nueva España was not the only theater of operations for Spanish explorers during the first half of the sixteenth century. As early as 1522, the Araban Pascual de Andagoya had already discovered the route that Francisco Pizarro would follow and extend to Incan Peru. At that time, the territorial overseer, Andagoya, acquired substantial information that spoke of the existence of an important Indian chief and a wealthy, gold-filled region south of Panama. He sensed the great profits that could be made by undertaking an ambitious expedition to southwest America, along the Pacific coast. He did not hesitate to invest in a fleet and seek the permission of Governor Pedrarias Dávila to explore the province of Birú (the present valley of Tolima) in Colombia. There, he received the first word of what was called Peru, which led him to redirect his expedition further southward. Several hardships and an unfortunate accident prevented him from continuing the mission, however, and thereby becoming the recognized discoverer of Peru.

Nevertheless, the path for the conquest of not only Peru, but also Colombia, had been found. The inroads made by the territorial overseer from Araba into Colombia had demonstrated the existence of a land almost unparalleled in richness. It is not surprising that the expeditions of discovery and confiscation accelerated the foundation of the Spanish colonial seat in what would later be Nueva Granada. As might be expected, numerous natives of the Basque Country, residing for years in the Antilles, Panama, and Nueva España, participated from the outset, seeking the fulfillment of the economic, social, and professional aspirations that had brought them from their birthplaces to the New World. One example was the presence of the captains Berrio, Viana, Heredia, Amaya, and Bascona in the fleet led by German explorer Ambrosio Alfinger in service to the Spanish Crown in 1529. Others with Basque last names, such as Aguirre, Baracaldo, Carranza, Duarte, Inza, Montoya, Navarro, Ochoa, Olano, Orozco, Salazar, Soraluce, Ugarte, and Zegarra, were among those included in Jiménez de Quesada's expedition. Others, named Arce, Ayala, Guevara, Navarro, Ortíz, Salazar, and Vascuña traveled with Nicolás de Federman; Avendaño, Esquivel, and Orozco were with Belelcázar; Gamboa, Lara, Salazar, Tolosa, and Vizcaíno sailed with Jerónimo Lebrón; Amaya, Berrio (who years later would explore the Meta River to its confluence with the Orinoco), Mayorga, Perea, Velandia, and Vergara accompanied Luis de Lugo on his trip.

Basques also stood out in the settling of cities in Colombian territory. Thus, Pascual de Andagoya founded the port of Buenaventura in 1540. A few years earlier, in 1532, the Araban Pedro de Heredia (who had already been the governor of Santo Domingo and Nueva Andalucía) settled Cartagena in the region in which Juan de la Cosa had died years earlier. In addition, along with his brother Alonso de Heredia, he would found Maritue, Tolú, and Mompós. Diego de Ospina founded Neiva; Pedro de Ursúa y Armendariz (later assassinated by his compatriot Lope de Aguirre),

Pamplona and Tudela de Muzo; Juan de Lemus y Aguirre, Tuluá; Andrés López de Galazar, Ibargüe; Alonso de Olaya, Villeta; Captain Francisco Martínez de Ospina, Remedios de Antioquía; Juan de Otalora, Villa de Leiva; and Alvaro de Guzmán, Buga. And, of course, Basques participated actively in the administration and organization of the colony as governors, inspectors, magistrates, mayors, aldermen, judges, and attorneys. Bernardo de Prado Beltrán de Guevara, Pedro de Velasco y Zuñiga, Francisco Martínez de Ospina, and Juan de Villabona y Zubiaurre were among such participants.

The reports given by Andagoya about the mythic, fabulous lands that were believed to exist in Peru must have also notably influenced the spirits of Francisco Pizarro, Diego de Almagro, and Hernando de Luque; already in 1524, this group made the first attempt to explore the wealthy territories of the Inca Empire. Two ships and 120 men, including a Basque ensign named Salcedo and Captain Pedro Vizcaíno, left Panama following the route used by Andagoya. Nevertheless, adverse weather, the lack of provisions, and native attacks (in one of which Pedro Vizcaíno was killed) forced the fleet to return to the isthmus in 1525 and reorganize. One year later, the second discovery expedition set sail. Its ships skillfully sailed along the Pacific coast of present-day Colombia to the point where Andagoya's expedition ended. There, the ghost of hunger reappeared, bringing with it discouragement. It was the moment to return and rethink the project of conquest. Nevertheless, Pizarro decided to continue and sent Almagro in search of reinforcements. Only thirteen men—"the Famous Ones"—voluntarily agreed to the Extremaduran's plans; among them were the Bizkaians Domingo de Soraluce and Rafael de Ribera. This group of conquistadors made one last effort from the island of Gorgona, advancing to the south. The Spaniards' attempt would prove decisive. They encountered an Indian boat whose equipment led them to suspect that it belonged to a highly evolved, wealthy, sophisticated culture. Reconnaissance of the coast also yielded economic fruits, and would open the doors to future conquest. First, however, they would have to relay news of their discoveries and obtain the Crown's official support to continue the expedition.

With the signing of the Capitulations of Toledo in 1529, the final assault on Peru began.[12] In 1531 an armada left Panama with this goal. Several Basques were among the men of Pizarro's expedition, and others were among those who later colonized the lands and cities of the Inca Empire. Shortly after the Spanish army moved inland into Incan territory, the *villa* of San Miguel, now called Piura, was founded. Several Basques were present at the founding ceremony: Antonio Navarro, García de Salcedo, and Domingo de Solaluce, its first aldermen, Navy captain Juan de Avendaño, and Rodrigo de Lazcano. Later, in 1532, after leaving a garrison of fifty men in this city, Pizarro set sail for Cajamarca in search of the Inca Atahualpa; the Basque interpreter Hernando de Aldana accompanied him. The division of the bountiful spoils there reveals the participation of other Basque natives in the conquering mission of Peru, among whom were the noblemen Juan de Salcedo, Gómez de Carranza, Lópe Vélez de Guevara, Pedro de Aguirre, and Nicolás Azpeitia, and the soldiers Pedro de Bergara, Pedro Navarro, Antonio de Bergara, Juan Pérez de Tudela, Gaspar de Marquina, Francisco Martínez de Zárate, Juan de Bergara, and Martín de Marquina. In 1533, Pizarro proceeded to carry out the foundation of Cuzco as a Spanish city by establishing colonial administration. The notary Antonio Navarro signed the foundational affidavit. The notary, the overseer García de Salcedo, and the officials of the king, Francisco de Castañada and Tomás de Echandía, took up residency in the new *villa*. Pedro González de Ayala, Francisco Pérez de Lazcano, Domingo de Solaluce, Juan de Ureña, Juan Villafranca de Lezcano, Francisco de Zamudio, and Iñigo Ortíz de Zuñiga are also documented as among the first group of conquistadors that founded the city of Trujillo in December of 1534. In addition, Juan López de Recalde, Pedro de Castañeda, García de Salcedo, Juan de Berrio, Francisco de Isasaga, Luis García San Mamés, Jerónimo Zurbano, the *bachiller* Guevara, and Juan Larrañaga are listed among the first settlers of Lima.

The association between Pizarro and Almagro to conquer and colonize Peru had been highly beneficial until that moment. The vagueness that delimited the jurisdiction of the two expeditions, however—Nueva Castilla for Pizarro and Nueva Toledo for Almagro—created discord between their respective partisans, especially as a result of the occupation of Cuzco, the capital of the Inca Empire. In order to resolve this conflict, the bishop of Panama, Fra Tomás de Berlanga, intervened. His mediation was of little help. The die had already been cast for the civil war of Peru. In 1537, after an unsuccessful expedition southward and a consultation with his Basque captains, Lope de Idiaquez, Rodrigo de Salcedo, and Vasco de Guevara, Almagro decided to enter Cuzco, where he captured the brothers Hernando and Gonzalo Pizarro. Francisco Pizarro requested reinforcements from Lima; among those who answered his call were the Gipuzkoan Captain of Hackbuteers Pedro de Bergara, nicknamed "El Flamenco," and Captain of the Lancers Diego de Urbina, a native of Orduña, Bizkaia. With the reinforcements that arrived from the north, Pizarro was able to set out for Cuzco with an army that also included Alonso Pérez Esquivel, Alberto de Orduña, Alonso de Mendoza, and a Gipuzkoan named Anduiza. The clash between the two armies took place in Salinas, on the outskirts of the Incan capital in April of 1538. The battle ended in favor of Pizarro. According to the chroniclers of the epoch, Almagro's men came mostly from the north of the Iberian Peninsula; the phrase "most of his supporters were Vizcayans" was frequent in writings. Proof can be found in the numerous names of Basque origin among Almagro's men who died in the Battle of Salinas: Juan de Urrutia, Pedro de Salazar, Esteban Franco de Miravalles, Alonso de Ariza, Pedro de Leguizamón, and Juan de Armentia. Among the prisoners taken were Lope de Idiaquez, Vasco de Guevara, Juan Ortíz de Zárate, and Juan de Rada. Diego de Almagro was also captured and condemned to death in a trial that confirmed the charges that he captured

Cuzco without the king's authorization and caused a civil war. His Basque defense attorney, Juan de Balsa, was unable to help him. But his death only served to inspire the "Almagrists" to unite behind his mestizo son of the same name. The tension resurfaced between the two factions due to mutual suspicions and intensive spy work. The Crown, recognizing the reality of Nueva Castilla, the excesses and disputes between the conquistadors, and the border tensions, endowed Cristóbal Vaca de Castro with the power to settle such quarrels. He would not arrive in time to prevent the conspiracy plotted by the "Almagrists," however. With the cry of "long live the king, the tyrant is dead!" Juan de Rada, Martín de Bilbao, the Navarrese Juan Sojo, Sebastián de Arbolancha, Bartolomé de Enciso, Pedro Navarro, and other soldiers hailing from the Basque Country entered the house of Pizarro—where other Basques who were partisans of the governor, such as Antonio Navarro, García de Salcedo, Francisco de Ampuero, and Alonso Pérez de Esquivel, could be found—and killed the old Extremaduran conquistador.

As had occurred in other American foci of penetration (Santo Domingo, Panama, and Mexico), Peru became a central base for the discovery and conquest of nearby territories, including Ecuador and Chile. The Bizkaian Miguel de Ibarra is documented to have taken part in the conquest of the former, and a city was named after him. Diego de Almagro the younger, obsessed with discovering, conquering, and colonizing his own territory—Nueva Toledo—had sought the proper authorization from Emperor Charles V to organize an expedition to the south of Nueva Castilla. Almagro's request was granted by the emperor in 1535. The only condition imposed by the monarch was that Almagro would both finance the expensive undertaking (which cost more than one million gold pesos) and attend to the selection and organization of his army (which was composed of 560 Spaniards). After making the necessary preparations, the explorers left Cuzco in a series of groups that would reunite in upper Peru (present-day Bolivia). Among the first explorers of Chile were Martín de Cote, Francisco Galdemes, Francisco de Isásaga, Domingo de la Orta, and Juan de Larrañaga, all from Bilbao, Ortún Jiménez de Bertendona, also from Bizkaia, and the Gipuzkoans Pedro de Zárate and Gaspar de Bergara.[13] They carried out the first stage in northwest Argentina (Jujuy, Salta, Catamarca), crossing the Andes through San Francisco Pass and reaching the Copiapó Valley. There, the Navarrese Juan de Rada, representative and trusted advisor of Almagro, and the Basque by adoption, Rodrigo Ordoñez, joined the expedition. The group later crossed the Aconcagua River (also called the Chile River) and arrived at the welcoming Maipo Valley. This offered little potential for profit, however, and was inhabited by bellicose Mapuche Indians. The exhaustion of the troops, fruitless search for spoils, geographic and climatic impediments, strong indigenous opposition, official confirmation of his governance, and the possibility that Cuzco might fall under his, rather than Pizarro's, jurisdiction all made Almagro decide to return to Peru. His men crossed the Atacama Desert along the coast to Arequipa, and from there continued to Cuzco.

With Almagro's failure in Chile and death in the Peruvian civil war, Pedro de Valdivia was authorized to continue the discovery expeditions to the south of Nueva Toledo. As the lieutenant governor of the unconquered territories, Valdivia, also from Extremadura, set off for Chile at the beginning of 1540, having exhausted his personal fortune in the preparation. The group was composed of twelve people, including the young Lope de Ayala and Inés Suarez (the conquistador's lover), and just under one thousand indigenous porters. Other explorers, captains, and soldiers gradually joined them in nearby regions. Among these were the following Basques: Rodrigo de Araya (with his sixteen men), Pedro de Miranda, Francisco de Aguirre (with his twenty-five Spanish men), Gaspar de Bergara and twenty more soldiers, the veterans who had been with the elder Almagro in 1535—Francisco Galdames, Ortún Jiménez de Bertendona, Gaspar de Bergara, and Pedro de Zárate, the Gipuzkoans Francisco de Arteaga, Santiago de Azoca, and Antonio de Olea, the Bizkaians Pedro de Gamboa, Martín de Ibarrola, Domingo de Oribe, and Martín de Ortuño, the Navarrese Santiago Bazán, and the Arabans Lope de Landa and Juan de Zurbano. All told, the little army came to number about one hundred fifty.[14]

After crossing the Atacama Desert, the expedition arrived at Copiapó Valley. Valdivia founded a fort there in reaction to the indigenous resistance and reaffirmed his conviction to reach the southern straits to secure the boundaries of his extensive control. The Spanish army proceeded to Coquimbo. There, in 1544, Valdivia discovered the ideal location to found a settlement, called La Serena, to serve as a way station between Chile and Peru. He then continued southward to find an appropriate setting to establish the capital city of the territory. He located it on the shores of the Mapocho River. There, in 1541, he founded the city of Santiago del Nuevo Extremo, the present-day Santiago. The design of the city was assigned to the Basque master builder Pedro de Gamboa. On March 7, the city hall was completed. Santiago's first presidency fell to Captain Francisco de Aguirre. Documentation cites the following Basques among the first settlers of the new Andean city: Jerónimo de Vera, Lope de Landa, Francisco de Arteaga, Rodrigo de Araya, Martín de Ibarrola, Lope de Ayala, Gabriel de Salazar, Juan de Vera, Gaspar de Bergara, Santiago de Azócar from Azkoitia, the Navarrese Pedro de Miranda, Salvador de Montoya from Soraluze, Domingo de Oribe, Martín de Ortuño, and Pascual de Ibaceta.[15] The violent nature of the indigenous Indians, however, made it impossible for the small Spanish army to continue conquering Chile. They had to seek reinforcements from Peru that arrived shortly thereafter (1543) at the port of Valparaíso under the command of the Gipuzkoan Martínez de Bergara. The campaigns to pacify the dreaded Araucanians then began. These would last until well into the nineteenth century and several Basques, including the poet Alonso de Ercilla y Zúñiga, the author of *La Araucana*, took part. Other activities of note were the struggles against the English and Dutch pirates that inhabited the waters of the Pacific and the exploratory missions of the lands and coasts of southern Chile. Some natives of the Basque Country, such as the accountant Goizueta and the sailor Sarmiento de Gamboa, played important roles.

The Basque presence in Venezuela is documented as early as 1510. News of rich deposits of pearls in the region of Cabaguá prompted the arrival of naval outfitters Sancho Ortiz de Urrutia, Juan de Urrutia, and Domingo Zubizarreta, among others. Also on the Venezuelan coast at that time were Sancho de Lizaur, the royal overseer Juan López de Arrechulueta, the royal treasurer Martín de Ochandiano, and the Franciscan friar Antonio de Bilbao. In 1531, the latter was the guardian of the monastery of Cabaguá; his mission of "keeping the appetite for wealth in check" would soon acquire great importance. In 1515, the Bizkaian Bono de Quexo carried out the first exploration of the island of Trinidad, where he captured a large number of natives that he later sold on the island of San Juan. Captains Vasconia and Hernando de Beteta also explored this region. Between 1529 and 1533, the Bizkaian Iñigo de Vasconia accompanied the German Alfinger on his exploratory mission. In 1538, Gonzalo Martel de Ayala was named captain of the expedition that Jorge de Espira would direct to San Juan de los Llanos. In 1540, Martín de Arteaga and Sebastián de Amescua stood out in the expedition commanded by Felipe de Hutton in search of El Dorado, the mythical kingdom of gold in the New World. From 1526 to 1528, Francisco Fajardo organized the first settlement of Caracas; he was accompanied by the Basques Pedro de Alegría and Martín López. This attempt failed, however, and not until 1567 was the future capital of Venezuela established. That year Juan de Losada founded Santiago de León de Caracas. Diego Henares de Lezama, from Barakaldo, Sancho de Villar, from Oñati, Alonso Andrea from Ledesma, Francisco de Agorreta, Tomé de Ledesma, Francisco Maldonado de Armendáriz, and Juan de Amézaga, one of the first mayors, were all present at the foundation ceremony.

After the creation of the Venezuelan capital, Basques arrived in Caracas throughout the sixteenth century. Tomás de Aguirre, attorney general of the city since 1590, Antonio Arriaga, the pilot Martín de Arriaga, his brother Pedro de Arriaga, Felipe de Arrupe, the cleric Martín de Artuaga, the schoolmaster Juan de Arteaga, Francisco de Axpe, Prudencio de Avendaño, the lieutenant and city's judge Juan de Ayarde, the teacher Simón de Basauri, the naval outfitter Sebastián de Bengoechea, Juan de Echevarría, the alderman-for-life Bartolomé de Emasabel, Luis de Gamarra, Diego de Guevara, Diego de Henares, Juan de Ibarra, Juan de Ibaibarriaga, Diego de Leguizamón, Antonio Pérez de Mallea, Martín de Ozaeta, Juan de Sarría, Alonso de Uría, Sancho de Urqueta, Sancho de Urquiza, Juan de Bergara, Francisco de Villar, Antón de Zabala, and Sancho de Zuazo are just a few examples.

Simón Bolívar "the elder," the fifth paternal grandfather of Simón Bolívar "The Liberator" and architect of American independence, arrived from his native town of Bolibar, Bizkaia. He arrived in Santo Domingo from his Bizkaian ancestral homeland as a government clerk and secretary of the Royal Tribunal, later going to Caracas as the attorney general and alderman-for-life. In 1590, he established a boarding school of Spanish grammar that later would be directed by Juan de Arteaga and Simón de Basauri, also Bizkaians. The city's coat of arms would emerge from this boarding school, which would be the cornerstone for the future University of Caracas. The elder Bolívar was also a confirmed slave owner and managed to get three thousand black Guinean slaves sent to Venezuela. The slave trade soon began to have great economic importance. Like Bolívar, many other Basques participated actively.[16] Captains Juan de Urquiza, master of the island of Margarita, and Esteban de Iriziar were sentenced in 1589 for their collaboration with Dutch traffickers who smuggled black slaves. Clearly, not all the Basques of Venezuela engaged in slave trade as their main source of income. Many others sought their fortune in different enterprises and soon saw the necessity for colonizing the territory. Captain Antonio de Berrio, founder of Santo Tomé de Guyana, in 1593, and Juan Pérez de Tolosa, who brought social order to Venezuela, are noteworthy examples. Both focused their efforts on attracting immigrants, mostly of Basque origin, to their respective areas of influence. Their efforts yielded little success, however, as the majority of the immigrants died before reaching their respective enclaves.

Río de la Plata was the last great American continental region added to the area of Spanish influence in the sixteenth century. It was the zone furthest from the Caribbean and the regular Indies sea routes, it was sparsely populated, and its geography formed a plain inclined toward the south Atlantic. Although its coast had been explored in 1519, the region was developed slowly compared to Lima. The exploration and ensuing conquest of the Río de la Plata region undoubtedly occurred more for strategic reasons—the search for the Spice Islands and the need to demarcate the domains agreed upon by Spain and Portugal in the Treaty of Tordesillas—than because of the attractiveness of the land itself. The appearance of myths and legends, such as the treasure of Atahualpa, El Dorado, and the Land of the Caesars, was equally decisive in the discovery process, which would extend from the coast toward the interior up to the Andes, motivated by the attractiveness of its valuable ore deposits.

The exploration of the territory of the region was carried out on two fronts. One came from Peru and Chile. It was led by Francisco de Aguirre who, after crossing the Andean chain, progressed eastward through the lands of the present Argentine provinces of Tucumán and Mendoza. The other came from the estuary of the Río de la Plata. It was carried out by the group led by the Granadan of Araban origin, Pedro González de Mendoza. In May 1534, Mendoza received royal support to undertake, at his own expense, a voyage to the Río de la Plata region. He would be territorial overseer, governor, and captain general of these lands. He was responsible for building three forts and reaching the legendary dominions of the mythical "White King," said to live at the 25th southern parallel. As was customary, the possibility of profits and the obligation of beginning the evangelization process were also notarized.

Mendoza landed at Río de la Plata with eleven ships and 1,300 men and cast anchor at the mouth of the Riachuelo River, founding the port of Nuestra Señora Santa María del Buen Aire in February 1536. Captain Juan de Ayolas, from Enkarterri, the Gipuzkoan Domingo Martínez de Irala, Jerónimo Ochoa de Eizaguirre, Andrés de Arzamendia, Juan de Estigarribia, Galaz de Medrano, and Fernando de Gasteiz accompanied him. The area was not attractive for a Spanish base, however; the natives were hostile, the infertile land was inadequate for cultivation and animal husbandry, and provisions were scarce. The plight of the Argentine colony was so critical in its founding days that the chroniclers emphasized that the settlers were forced into cannibalism in what "was the harshest hunger ever witnessed among Christians."

All these factors, plus Mendoza's terminal illness, caused the expedition's captain general to order Juan de Ayolas and Domingo Martínez de Irala to continue the mission to the Sierra de la Plata up the Paraná and Paraguay Rivers. Thus, three ships and 160 men sent by Ayolas crossed Guaraní territory and founded Fort Candelaria in February 1537. There they received news of riches to the west; abandoning the riverine channel, they proceeded further into the interior and crossed the Chaco region until they arrived at present-day Bolivia, where they obtained great spoils. The Bergaran Irala remained behind with thirty men awaiting their return in vain, as Ayolas was killed by the Payagua Indians. During one of his reconnaissance missions, Martínez de Irala found the group that Pedro González de Mendoza had ordered to support Ayolas's mission in January 1537, which was under the command of the Navarrese Juan de Salazar. Together they traveled through Paraguay and, in August, Salazar founded Fort Asunción. Martínez de Irala would formally name Asunción a city in September 1541; it would become the axis of the true continental penetration and the capital of Paraguay.

In November 1538, the overseer Alonso Cabrera and Royal Treasurer Adame de Olaberriaga, a native of Azkoitia, arrived in Asunción sent by the Spanish court. They brought a document signed by the monarch authorizing the conquistadors to appoint their own governor and captain general. Martínez de Irala, nicknamed "Captain Bergara," was elected, thus beginning his seventeen-year career in administration. His first important declaration was to order the depopulation and abandonment of the enclaves of Santa María del Buen Aire, Buena Esperanza, and Corpus Christi, and the transfer of their residents to Asunción. The crises suffered in these enclaves due to the lack of settlers, hunger, indigenous attacks, and transportation difficulties made it wise to gather the inhabitants into a single urban unit that, endowed with institutions and services, could serve as the base for future conquests. The present Paraguay thus became the principle nucleus of interior expansion and control of the majority of the Río de la Plata basin.

New governor and territorial overseer Alvar Núñez Cabeza de Vaca thus traveled to Asunción in March 1542. He would not hesitate to clash with Martínez de Irala.

Several Basques arrived with the new royal functionary, including Tristán de Irazabal, Diego de Orúe, and Lope de Ugarte; they were soldiers who would later serve under the Gipuzkoan from Bergara. Obsessed with finding the legendary Sierra de la Plata and silver in Potosí, Cabeza de Vaca ordered an exploratory mission to be captained by Martínez de Irala. The recently arrived Orúe, Irazabal, and Ugarte, as well as Father Lezcano, Juan de Zaldizar, and the Donostian Diego de Olavarrieta were among those who took part. They went up the Paraguay River to San Fernando Port, moving inland to Gran Chaco in January 1548, and reaching Sierra de la Plata shortly thereafter. The explorers were completely disappointed and astonished, however, to find the region had already been conquered. After the discovery of a vein of silver in Potosí in 1545, the precious metal had attracted numerous settlers, conquistadors, and adventurers to the Bolivian lands from all corners of Europe. This was the case of the Araban Alonso de Mendoza. In 1548, he founded the city of La Paz, Bolivia's current capital, and incorporated all of its territory into the viceroyalty of Peru.

After the failure of the Chaco expedition, Martínez de Irala and his men returned to Asunción. They were determined to develop an intense colonial network there that would permit them to extend their influence to the surrounding territories and consolidate the Spanish presence in the region. The plan, which would guarantee peaceful relations with the Indians through mesticization and definitively reject the system of *encomiendas*, was not supported by some settlers like the Bizkaian Miguel de Urrutia. Nonetheless, Martínez de Irala managed to pacify Paraguay with such measures, allowing him to greatly widen the geographical scope of his rule. Upon his death in 1556, he was succeeded by his sons-in-law Gonzalo de Mendoza and Francisco Ortíz de Bergara, both also originally from the Basque Country. In 1564, the Bizkaian from Orduña, Juan Ortíz de Zárate, was named by the viceroy of Peru as the governor of Paraguay and territorial overseer of Río de la Plata. He would not assume his new offices until well into 1574, however. He served for only one year, and his tenure was characterized by the continuation of Martínez de Irala's colonizing projects. He brought in large quantities of livestock of all species and the largest contingent of settlers to that point; some of the settlers, such as Pedro de Aráuz, Domingo de Ibarra, and García de Aguirre, were natives of the Basque Country. Ortíz de Zárate would die in 1575 after having founded four settlements in these territories and naming his nephew, Domingo Ortíz de Zárate y Mendieta, as his successor.

The elder Ortíz de Zárate's death would open a conflictive parenthesis in the colony that was quickly closed in 1578 by the Bizkaian Juan de Garay. His appointment as captain general and governor of Asunción and the province of Río de la Plata that year brought a stability and security to the region unknown since the times of Martínez de Irala. Seeing the clear need for a single port to connect Chile and Peru that would not require passage through Panama, Francisco de Aguirre, Juan de Matienzo, and Jaime de Razquin firmly advised Garay to refound and repopulate the former city of Buenos Aires. Thus, after founding Villa Rica del Espíritu Santo and Santo Domingo de Jeréz to the north of Asunción in 1579, and organizing an expedition to pacify the rebellious Guaraní Indians of Upper Paraná, the younger Ortíz de Zárate set out on this new objective[17] with the intention of giving individual character to a territory that had depended upon initiatives from both Peru and Chile. Nevertheless, the new colony needed settlers to ensure even moderate success, and he did not hesitate to publicize promised wages and land to whoever would join. Several families of Creole, Indian, and Spanish colonists answered the call—enough to organize two expeditions. One was overland; the other, along the Paraná River, quickly crossed that region. The definitive founding of the colony took place on June 11, 1580, half a league to the north of the earlier settlement, with the full name of Santísima Trinidad y Puerto de Santa María de Buenos Aires. After announcing the refoundation of the city, Garay distributed the property promised to the colonists and named the first city council. The city that had served as a springboard to initiate the conquest of Río de la Plata in 1536 appeared as a corollary of the efforts of more than forty years. Of the ten Spaniards who accompanied Garay in founding Buenos Aires, four were natives of the Basque Country: Rodrigo Ortíz de Zárate, Diego de Olavarrieta, Juan de Basualdo, and Miguel Navarro. In addition, the names of the more than sixty Creoles who participated in resettling the colony show that a good number of them were descendants of the first Basque conquistadors who arrived in Río de la Plata: Luis Gaytán, Pedro de Izarra, Domingo de Irala, Pedro Gaytán, Miguel de Urso, Pedro de Sayas Espeluca, Cristóbal Altamirano, Fernández de Zárate, Fernández de Enciso, Rodrigo de Ibarrola, Domingo de Aramendia, Ochoa Marqués, Juan de Garay "el Mozo," and Hernando de Mendoza.[18]

His main objective fulfilled, in 1581 Garay returned to Santa Fe to crush an indigenous rebellion. After order was restored, he was attracted, like the rest of the Spanish conquistadors, by the legends of the imaginary Land of the Caesars in the Argentine Patagonia. He undertook a long expedition in which he managed only to reach the present-day coast of the Mar de la Plata. Two years later, Garay was killed at the confluence of the Coronada and Carcarañá Rivers by Querandi Indians. After his death, the territorial overseer Vera de Aragón and his wife Juana Ortíz de Zárate assumed the leadership of Río de la Plata. There was hardly anything left to do. After founding Concepción de Bermejo (1585) and Corrientes (1588), both retired from politics. The majority of the discovery and foundation of Río de la Plata had ended.

At the time that Juan Ortíz de Zárate was named governor of Paraguay in Río de la Plata (1564), in Nueva España Viceroy Luis de Velasco, under orders from Philip II, decided to undertake a risky expedition of conquest and incorporation of the Poniente Islands, in the Philippines, to ensure the return route (to the Americas) across the Pacific. This scientific, geographic, missionary, and, of course, military mission was assigned to Fra Andrés de Urdaneta, an Augustinian cosmographer born in Ordizia, Gipuzkoa. Because of his previous experience, he was considered capable of finding the appropriate return course from the Philippine archipelago to Nueva España through the Pacific.[19] At Urdaneta's request, however, command of the fleet fell to another Gipuzkoan, Miguel López de Legazpi, from Zumarraga. The squadron that the two Basques organized was made up of four vessels. Two were large naos: the captain ship *San Pedro*, the flagship *San Pablo*; the other two were small pataches, the *San Juan* and the *San Lucas*. The crew was composed of about three hundred men, of whom the following are documented as having been Basque natives: the master of the nao *San Pedro*, Martín de Ibarra; the boatswain of that ship, Francisco de Astigarribia; the pilot Amador de Arriarán; the color guard Andrés de Ibarra; the artillery captain Goiti Alonso de Arellano; the sailor Juan de Camuz; the captain of the guard and grandson of Legazpi, Felipe de Salcedo; the secretary Juan de Lazcano; the blacksmith Pedro de Guevara; the treasurer Guido de Labezares, from Bizkaia; Pierres Plum from Iparralde; the commission merchant of the Royal Treasury and nephew of Urdanieta, Andrés de Mirandaola; the Donostian accountant, Andrés de Cauchela; the soldiers Cristóbal Angulo, Juan de Aguirre, Pedro de Arana, and Alberto de Orozco; the court clerk, Asensio de Aguirre; and the Augustinians Fra Andrés de Aguirre, Fra Pedro de Gamboa, and Fra Martín de Rada—the last of these, also a scientist, from Navarre.

On November 21, 1564, the fleet set sail from the Mexican port of Navidad. Two months later, they landed and took possession of Meyit Island and the coral archipelago known as Los Jardines. In February 1565, the explorers reached Leyte Island, which they renamed San Pedro. There, they established the first peaceful contacts with the natives. From there they conducted secondary excursions through several of the smaller islands of the Philippine archipelago: Guam, Samar, Comiguinin, Bohol, and Butuan. Legazpi followed a similar pattern: search for a port, friendly contact with the indigenous population followed by evangelization under the direction of Urdaneta, occupation of each island at which they landed, monopolization of all provisions, exploration of the inland and the coast, and, in some instances, settlement. With the occupation of these enclaves, the initial phase of the conquest ended and the way was paved for the occupation of the ominous Cebu, where Magellan and his crew had been killed in 1521. In April 1565, Legazpi disembarked there. In May, the crew began to map the triangular periphery of what would be the first Spanish settlement in the Philippines, San Miguel, later called Ciudad del Santísimo Nombre de Jesús. After some notable skirmishes with the natives—during one of which the Basque Pedro de Arana was killed—the Gipuzkoan managed to get the indigenous population to accept the sovereignty of Philip II and the law of God. With control of Cebu clearly established, in June 1565 Urdaneta set his sights on discovering the return route to Nueva España that he had promised. He took four months to cross the Pacific and land at Acapulco. Nevertheless, the return trip to the Americas via a northern route, with its prevailing easterlies, through the South Sea was a notable accomplishment.

Once the new navigation route was plotted, the Gipuzkoan Augustinian Felipe de Salcedo, the grandson of Legazpi, immediately began preparing the next trip to the Philippines with reinforcements and provisions for the explorers that had remained behind. In May 1566, a crew including Juan de Goiri from Bilbao, Santiago de Guernica, Juan Martínez, Juan de Salcedo, and other Basques left Mexico for Cebu. Their participation was noteworthy in the many assaults on the island that were carried out between 1566 and 1568 by Portuguese fleets determined to wrest commercial dominance from the Spanish, as well as in the ultimate conquest of the Philippine archipelago begun by Legazpi in 1569. By the middle of the year, Legazpi left Cebu manned by a strong detachment and set sail to Panay Island; the Basque captains Juan Salcedo and Luis de Haya undertook that island's pacification. Meanwhile, Captain Ibarra, also Basque, took possession of Masbate Island. He also explored Mindoro Island, considered an essential passageway for the conquest of Luzon Island. This undertaking fell to the Bizkaian Juan Goiri. In June 1571, Legazpi would found the city of Manila, the present-day capital of the archipelago, on Luzon. From then on, several ships, an abundance of food supplies, and numerous colonists, soldiers, and missionaries assigned to speed up the construction, colonization, and evangelization of the city would arrive in this distant enclave. Some came from the Basque Country, which they had left much earlier for Nueva España, and then the recently conquered Philippines. This was the case of the families of Goiti, Aguirre, and Legazpi himself.

The last years of the sixteenth century and the beginning of the seventeenth witnessed the finishing touches of the processes of discovery and conquest of the New World territories begun by Christopher Columbus a century earlier. Exploration toward the north of Nueva España continued, with the intention of expanding the realm of the Spanish Crown as much as possible. The expeditions, led by various Basques that stand out for their zeal for adventure and wealth, reached the coast of California. The Gipuzkoan Creole, Juan de Oñate, was a good example. After the failures of his fellow Zacatecan townsman from Oiartzun, Francisco de Urdiñola, in 1595 Oñate received a license from the Crown to explore and colonize the region that would later become the state of New Mexico. Unlike earlier expeditions, Oñate's group was made up of colonists accompanied by livestock, mainly sheep, with which they populated the vast plains of the region. The expedition left for the Rio Grande where, after overcoming indigenous resistance, they founded the colony of San Juan de los Caballeros. Shortly thereafter they proceeded toward the city of El Paso, where the explorers separated. One of Oñate's nephews, Vicente de Zaldívar, advanced with his men through Texas and Oklahoma; Oñate continued to southern Kansas and the western Great Plains in search of Quivira, the mythic city of gold. Unsuccessful, he returned to New Mexico. There, he organized a second expedition during 1604 and 1605. This one would explore Arizona and the lower sections of the Colorado River, reaching the Pacific via southern California.

Also at the end of the sixteenth century and the beginning of the seventeenth, Viceroy Gaspar de Zúñiga commissioned the Extremaduran of Basque origin, Sebastián Vizcaíno, to lead the search for a passage—the supposed strait of Anián—that would unite the Atlantic and Pacific Oceans to the north of Nueva España. Vizcaíno explored Baja California, installing a settlement at the bay that he called La Paz during his search. Nevertheless, indigenous hostility and the lack of provisions forced his group to return to Acapulco. He would set sail from that port in 1602 to undertake a detailed study of the Californian coast, from Cabo San Lucas to beyond San Francisco, as documented in the various nautical maps that he drew and published. He christened a variety of places and geographic features on his journey that have kept their names throughout the centuries, including Monterrey, La Paz, San Diego, Santa Barbara, Bahía Vizcaíno, and Desierto de Vizcaíno.

The material covered to this point, although brief, has provided a general vision of the relevance of the natives of Gipuzkoa, Bizkaia, Araba, and Navarre in the discovery and conquest of the New World. As argued at the beginning of the chapter, the Basques participated willingly in all of the enterprises in which their presence was sought by the Spanish monarchy. They often acted collectively, as they represented an ethnic group and were seen as such by the Crown's other settlers. They frequently used Euskara, their native language, to provide greater group strength and unity. Nevertheless, the observable clanlike spirit demonstrated by the Basques could camouflage the fact that they were often highly individualistic and competitive among themselves. Not infrequently, they resolutely defied the established powers through their leading roles in desertions, rebellions, mutinies, and various conspiracies, in addition to the dark chapters in the history of the New World. The Gipuzkoan Lope de Aguirre is the clearest example of the rebels that existed in the Indies.[20]

Lope de Aguirre had been born to a noble family on the remote farmstead of Araotz (in Oñati, Gipuzkoa) around 1511. While we completely lack information about his youth, his presence in Peru in 1534 is documented. It would not be until 1560, however, that he would come to play the sad leading role that would enter him in the annals of history with the nickname "the Wrath of God."[21] The marquis of Cañete organized an expedition that year in search of the fabulous mythic riches of El Dorado. The Gipuzkoans Lope de Aguirre, Nicolás de Zozoya, Captain Juan de Iturriaga, and Martín Díaz de Armendariz, and the Bizkaians Martín Pérez de Zarrondo, Juan de Aguirre, Gonzalo de Huarte, Pedro de Munguía, Simón de Somorrostro, Francisco de Arana, and Diego Sánchez de Bilbao accompanied him. Aguirre's mestiza daughter Elvira, and his Gipuzkoan maid, María de Arriola, rounded out the list of Basque names that participated in this adventure. Soon after leaving the port of Lamas in September 1560, conspiratorial plans were hatched by Aguirre and the "Vizcayans" in the expedition—the "Marañones"—against their leader Pedro de Ursúa that would culminate in the assassination of the latter in January 1561. Aguirre and his Marañones proclaimed the Castilian Fernando de Guzmán "King of Peru," and renounced their citizenship in the Kingdoms of Spain. After a period of anarchy during which those opposing Aguirre were assassinated, the conspirators were forced to abandon Peru. In their flight, they had to cross the Andes and go down the Amazon River, also known as the Marañon River (whence came the name of the group).

After suffering several misfortunes—hostile terrain, mutinies, assassinations—Aguirre and his men managed to reach the Atlantic coast. They arrived at Margarita Island, Venezuela. There, upon debunking the myth of El Dorado, the Marañones carried out a rebellious campaign against the Spanish Crown. They captured the governor of the island and declared it free from Spanish sovereignty. Aguirre sent a letter to Philip II from this Caribbean enclave informing the monarch of the reasons for his opposition to the Crown's governing practices in the Americas. It was also there that Aguirre conceived the utopian plan to conquer Peru and proclaim the first independent kingdom in the Americas. The failure of the "Marañonist" cause, however, was absolute when the Crown authorities ordered a powerful fleet to surround the insurrectionists at Margarita Island. All was lost. Abandoned by his men and with little hope of being granted a pardon by the king, Aguirre stabbed his own daughter to death so that she would not suffer the dishonor of being the descendant of a traitor. On December 16, 1561, Aguirre's trial began. No one came to defend him, he was declared a traitor, and all of his possessions were confiscated. That same year, Lope de Aguirre would die at the hands of two of his Marañon hackbuteers. It seems clear that common ethnic roots were not always a guarantee of Basque solidarity in the New World.

This well-known and perhaps even dramatic case has been chosen to show that the proverbial solidarity among ethnic Basques was not always real. Nevertheless, the coming pages will show several demonstrations of solidarity and unity among the Basque colonists. As with any collectivity or people, both types of behavior can be observed among the Basques.

Privateering Licenses: Pirates, Corsairs, Buccaneers, and Freebooters

Shortly after the discovery of the Americas and during the first years of its conquest, at the beginning of the sixteenth century, an old form of getting rich was transferred to this new geographic space with its own, unique nuances and well-defined characteristics. Reference is to piracy. There were many reasons for the appearance of this old practice in the New World. The most significant was the great wealth of the Americas, especially gold and silver, and the existence of impoverished groups in Europe that viewed piracy as a practical way of achieving their socioeconomic aspirations. Moreover, the European powers could attack the Spanish overseas empire through this activity.[22]

The first reason given was the fundamental incentive. The capture of indigenous treasures and later appearance of silver mines controlled by the Spanish Crown during the conquest attracted an entire legion of disinherited in Europe. Had the Americas been poor in precious metals, piracy surely would have faded, regardless of the composition of its ranks. The Indies, however, were seen through French, Dutch, and English eyes as a land of immense wealth cornered by the King of Spain for himself. The lack of objective information about the New World led the Europeans to imagine it as a paradise of Dorados in which riches hung from the trees and pervaded the earth, the sky, and the sea. In this context, the abundance of pirate ships in American waters during that period makes perfect sense.

With the economic motive that drove piracy well defined, it is also clear that there were those who embraced this exotic profession because they liked adventure, searched for freedom, were defending religious principles and their monarchs, aspired to increase their social status, or simply wanted to escape their creditors and even their spouses.[23] It is also clear that piracy was mostly stocked from the ranks of the underprivileged, poor, and miserable. European demographic development only served to dangerously increase the number of dispossessed, representing a real threat to Old World governments. Neither commercial capitalism, religious wars, nor battles for hegemony could absorb them all. Some western European monarchs therefore sent dissidents out to sea to live off of the wealthiest powers of the era, Spain and Portugal, by stealing their goods.

Finally, it is appropriate to consider what the American seas offered the pirates. The Caribbean extended for 2,700,000 square kilometers, with more than a thousand islands, islets, and keys, most of them uninhabited. These provided excellent hideouts for those wishing to conceal themselves after carrying out missions of plunder. The Pacific was an open ocean with an easy escape toward the Orient, where refuge could always be sought when the Spanish warships pursued the so-called seadogs.

American piracy[24] was born with the clear French objective of breaking the Spanish monopoly in the Americas, in an attempt to deprive the Hapsburgs of an important source of income with which to finance their wars against France. Ill-defined privateering soon became authentic piracy, isolated and without government support, when periods of peace with Spain occurred. French piracy then broadened with inclusion of large numbers of Huguenots, driven by a great anti-Catholic fervor. The difficulty in finding Spanish merchant ships on the high seas led pirates to attack Indian settlements. Usually small and sparsely populated, these easily fell into the hands of the skilled crews of sea robbers, although the spoils were usually sparse. French piracy began to decline in the decade of the 1550s, and would have disappeared if not for the appearance of American silver. Around the mid-sixteenth century the large mines of Mexico and Peru were opened; in the decade of the 1560s Spain began to transport the precious metal to Europe by sea. This not only revived French piracy, but attracted the attention of English smugglers. Sponsored by their monarch, they did not hesitate to fly the black flag with skull and crossbones and join their French colleagues in attacking and plundering Indian settlements and the Spanish silver fleets. Spain was hard-pressed to defend itself from the combined attacks of the French and English pirates. Only with the fortification of key American sites and the strong, armed escort of the Spanish silver fleets could it manage to do so.

At the height of the 1590s, however, other adventurers honored the New World with their presence: the Dutch "sea beggars." They joined forces against the Spanish power in the fray, pursuing merchants, exploiting salt mines, attacking fortifications, and spying on the fleets. The Dutch offensive even joined the buccaneers, a strange breed of Caribbean pirates that had appeared in San Cristóbal at the end of the seventeenth century and set the stage for freebooting. This was the golden era of American piracy during which the now famous names of El Olonés and Henry Morgan stood out. The taking of Panama by the latter in 1671 marked the heyday of the sea thieves. Spain took advantage of a pause in the practice to launch its corsairs on a large scale. England had managed to establish some colonies in North America by that time, and needed a stable law of the sea to conduct its own maritime commerce. It therefore signed a peace agreement with Spain and ordered its Jamaican governors to suspend all corsair privileges and repress piracy. The freebooters then took refuge on the island of Tortuga and in Santo Domingo, where they were gradually domesticated; during the last quarter of the seventeenth century, freebooting lost its importance, and its practitioners converted into an auxiliary arm of the French and, occasionally, English navies. In 1697 Louis XIV, favoring a politics of mutual understanding with Spain in the hope of placing a French monarch on the Spanish throne, also ordered the repression of piracy. Paradoxically, this moment of decline coincided with the financing and apogee of Spanish privateering, which, with the help of all the European monarchs, especially the British, pursued and executed the last pirates of the Antilles. At that point, the black flags disappeared and with them the last pirates in American waters.[25]

The Spanish Crown applied the same model of defense that had been put in practice for ages throughout Europe to confront piratical actions: the privilege of privateering.[26] In spite of the initial hostile reaction of the Catholic Monarchs, who considered privateering a piratical activity, in 1489 Ferdinand the Catholic permitted interested Bizkaians and Gipuzkoans to carry it out without restriction, particularly in Italian waters. Later, during the reign of Emperor Charles V and the Hapsburg monarchs, the practice was openly reestablished as a means of defense, given that Spanish merchants in the Indies began to fall into the hands of pirates and corsairs in the service of foreign powers.[27] The Spanish Crown wanted its corsairs to defend the coasts of Spain and its colonies in the face of enemy corsairs and pirates, thereby ensuring the safety of commercial traffic. Attacking enemy commerce was another important objective. The Crown hoped that the corsairs would collaborate with the royal armadas in the missions of discovery, communications, towing, and transport. One objective not fulfilled was the incorporation of their ranks into the Royal Armada. In fact, given the better economic opportunities, many sailors left the armada to participate in privateering ventures. Lastly, privateering would increase Spanish naval power without cost to the Royal Treasury since privateers were paid one-fifth of the spoils that they seized on the high seas. In summary, the Spanish monarchy tried to use privateering as another weapon in its complex military, political, and economic struggle against the Low Countries, France, England, and Portugal during the seventeenth century.

The preeminent corsair region of Spain and the monarchy was the Basque Country, especially the province of Gipuzkoa. There were various reasons for this. First, the relative poverty of the terrain and a crisis in the iron industry in Gipuzkoa by the seventeenth century offered a favorable context for privateering. Second, commerce, a main activity of Basque sailors since ancient times, was based on export of wool to Flanders and iron to other countries. At the height of this commerce, an important group of merchants traveled the European seas selling their goods and services. But, in the sixteenth century, the merchants of Bilbao managed to gain control of their own commerce, which would permit them to monopolize both this activity and the shipping of Castilian wool to Europe. This commercial activity eclipsed that of other ports, such as Santander and Donostia. In these circumstances, many merchants from the latter were forced to look for new forms of investment. Of all the possibilities, privateering was one of the most lucrative, and Donostia became the main privateering port on the Iberian Peninsula. Finally, some authors (such as Teófilo Guiard) attribute the birth of Basque privateering to the attacks of pirates and enemy corsairs that weakened Bizkaian and Gipuzkoan commerce, thereby forcing natives of these provinces to themselves become privateers. Others (such as Aingeru Zabala) link its appearance to the beginning of the wars that naturally deflected part of commercial investment into privateering. Both explanations are equally valid to clarify why it arose in the Basque Country; neither, however, explains why, although Bilbao was a richer city and with more sea traffic, Donostia was the most important privateering port in northern Spain and the second most important in the Spanish Empire after Dunkerque.[28] The appearance of privateering should therefore be seen in the context of seventeenth-century Gipuzkoa's conjunctural and structural crisis.

Whatever forces gave rise to privateering in the Basque Country, between 1622 and 1697 (the peak years of Spanish privateering), Donostia had one hundred forty-one licensed outfitters and two hundred seventy-one corsair vessels. This was a large number, representing 30 percent and 38 percent of the outfitters and ships, respectively. In addition, numerous foreign outfitters—French, English, Flemish, and Irish—and sailors from neighboring regions lived in Donostia's inns between expeditions, meaning that privateering substantially improved the local economy.[29] Hondarribia was the second leading Iberian port in number of both outfitters, forty-eight, and corsair vessels, seventy-one. Mutual investments by its main outfitters and those of San Sebastián were constant. Although it did not have a good sea outlet, the protected port of Pasaia was one of the most attractive for corsairs from Donostia and Hondarribia; a high percentage of the ships used Pasaia as their base of operations. Don Alonso de Idiaquez, the first superintendent of the Northern Squadron, had his home and his ships there, stimulating the increase of outfitters and vessels to eighteen and thirty-five, respectively. Other Gipuzkoan privateering ports of lesser importance were Orio, Zarautz, and Getaria.

As a consequence of its economic and commercial importance, the Seigneury of Bizkaia had fewer armaments than Gipuzkoa: seventy-seven ships belonging to fifty-nine licensed outfitters. Bilbao lodged fifty vessels in its docks, thirty-one of them belonging to inhabitants of the city. Muskiz and Somorrostro had eleven corsair vessels in their ports, while Bermeo, Lekeitio, and Ondarroa combined to arm nine ships for privateering. Despite the lack of documented numbers, it is also known that the *villas* of Ea and Gaminiz armed corsair vessels. Nevertheless, Bizkaian privateering activity was clearly relatively unimportant compared to that of Gipuzkoa. (See table 1.2 in appendix 1.)

The social origin of the Basque corsairs was varied.[30] Although not numerous, they had to hold a title of nobility to ensure their commercial profits; they also longed for other, more substantial, rewards such as specific habits of military orders or credentials as sea or war captains. Among them, the marquis of Valparaíso, the viceroy and captain general of the Kingdom of Navarre, and King Charles II stood out; the latter armed a frigate in 1684 to encourage the outfitters who resisted joining the Spanish privateering squadrons. The majority of the Basque privateering outfitters had their origins in lower nobility. Despite their noble status, residents of the Basque Country did not discount devoting themselves to commerce and even manual labor, activities considered lowly in other regions. Thus, the upper strata of Basque nobility—the *parientes mayores*—largely came from among the most important privateering outfitters of the Iberian Peninsula. One of these was Alonso de Idiaquez, admiral (1637), fleet admiral (1638), and superintendent of the Northern Squadron. He used privateering as a means of social mobility. In 1624, he received the habit of Knight of Santiago, which entitled him to seek, although in vain, the title of viscount and the position of captain general of Gipuzkoa. Other outfitters of diverse social origin used privateering for social ascent. The Gipuzkoan Agustín de Diústegui, possibly a member of the lower nobility, was named Knight of Santiago; in 1658, he set out for the Americas and was named Coast Guard in Campeche, and in 1664 he commanded the Squadron of Barlovento. Finally, Francisco de Zárraga

Beográn, from Donostia, pursued a good career in the Spanish administration, albeit one insufficient for acquiring the prestigious habit of Santiago. The majority of outfitters sprang from among the lower social strata of universal nobility. This group was characterized by a fair level of wealth and armament of small or midsized privateering vessels. Their greatest aspiration was to be named sea and war captains in order to serve in the Royal Armada and enjoy its privileges and wages. Many had to be satisfied with the simple title of sea captain, however. Among these, the Gipuzkoan Antonio de Beroiz stood out; throughout his long career he managed to arm about sixty corsair vessels.

There was no lack of merchants who, for a variety of reasons, decided to expand their businesses through privateering or used it to protect their other interests from the predators of the sea and occasionally even to avenge the seizure of some of their goods. The privileges granted this group were more extensive in Bilbao than in Donostia, which is only logical given the greater importance of the former port in the wool trade. Two residents of Bilbao were distinguished examples: Guillermo Franquelin, who armed two vessels and sought a license to go to the Cape Verde Islands and then to the Indies, and Lorenzo de Echevarri. Outfitters who came from the lower classes were the exception. More frequently, cities, or institutions related to their economic life, armed Coast Guard vessels to pursue enemy corsairs, thus facilitating commerce and fishing. For example, Donostia had already sought permission to arm various patches to pursue French pirates in 1622, and in 1691 the consulate of Bilbao chartered two frigates to guard the port and escort arriving merchants.[31]

The outfitters were, of course, not the only ones involved in privateering activity. In the strict sense, the real corsairs were sailors and soldiers that embarked in the armed ships in search of spoils, often risking their lives in the process. These crewmen were mostly from the area, although there were also several foreign sailors among the ranks of the Basque corsairs, often potential enemies,[32] such as Flemish, French, and Irish. According to the Basque corsair Captain Pedro de Alcega, "in the provinces of Gipuzkoa, Bizkaia, and Cuatro Villas (Santander), there are over five or six thousand sailors with equipment and rope, the proudest and bravest that there are in the world."[33] The financial benefits of privateering attracted many people who quickly became sailors ready to serve on the ships having such permits. As Captain Pedro de Alcega affirmed, most of the crewmen were originally from the Basque Country. The 1686 petition requesting that each ship of the Compañía Guipuzcoana (Company of Caracas) have "a Basque chaplain, because most of the people on board do not understand the Castilian language," also confirms this fact.[34]

A large number of those cited in the preceding pages went to the Americas and worked in the main zones of contraband. They were especially prevalent around the coasts of Cuba, where the English trafficked; Santo Domingo, preferred by French pirates; Puerto Rico, also frequented by the English; Honduras and Panama, a meeting place for all nations; and Colombia and Venezuela, often patrolled by Dutch corsair ships. The technique of combat of the Basque corsairs was the same used by pirate vessels: intimidate enemies into surrendering their ships. If this was unsuccessful, they pursued and boarded enemy vessels, often after forcing them to run aground in shallow waters. According to the ordinances, the prisoners had to be taken to a Spanish port and surrendered to the authorities, to be tried for piracy. In no case could the corsairs take justice into their own hands, although it is clear that the Spanish-American authorities frequently looked the other way after bloody executions. The scuttles of the captured ship were closed to take it to an Iberian port, preferably the one from which the corsair came. The spoils could not be divided, hidden, or sold. They had to be surrendered in full to the port's intendant to begin this process. After thoroughly examining the confiscated merchandise to discover if there were goods belonging to Spaniards or subjects of allied countries (in which case these had to be returned), he declared whatever had been in the pirates' and smugglers' possession for more than twenty-four hours "good spoils." The merchandise was sold at a public auction, as were the captured ship and its arms, and the corsairs were paid the one-fifth of the net profit owed them (discounting the amount deducted for sales rights that had to be paid to the Crown for any transaction).[35] In general, the process of selling merchandise captured at sea was extremely slow; the outfitters protested against it repeatedly, as it was detrimental to their interests. They invested significant amounts in deposits, armament, and the salaries of officials and crewmen. They wanted to be reimbursed as soon as possible with the profits from the spoils. Sometimes the complaints of the corsairs were transformed into street disturbances and illegal seizures, with which part of the outfitters' investments were immediately recovered.

In spite of its historic prevalence in Europe and, of course, among natives of the Basque Country, Spanish-American privateering did not have its own characteristics until the last quarter of the seventeenth century. Until that time, it was subordinated and connected to Spain's general privateering, whose regulation also applied to the Americas. Around the middle of the century a great controversy broke out regarding the continuity of privateering in the Americas, ending with its complete prohibition. Nevertheless, the pro-privateering stances of the overseer from Donostia, Miguel de Mecoalde, and other leading officials of Basque privateering must have greatly influenced Philip IV, since the privileges were reestablished in 1655. The destabilization of Caribbean sea trade after the English conquest of Jamaica that year made the reestablishment of privateering in the Americas advisable. To this end, the ordinances of 1674 were proclaimed, regulating various points relating to the spoils, their division, and the treatment of prisoners. The occupation of corsair was reevaluated and its salaries adjusted to make them comparable to those offered in the Armada.

The War of the Spanish Succession was also a good moment for privateering and the many Basques who devoted their fortunes and lives to it. The English, French, and Dutch, Spain's adversaries, took advantage of the war to carry out pseudo-legal smuggling operations in the Antilles (Puerto Rico, Cuba, and Santo Domingo), and on the mainland (Cumaná and La Guaira). The Spanish corsair reponse was tremendous. To this were added the Royal Coast Guard that operated from the main Caribbean ports, and ships of private companies to which the Crown entrusted coastal surveillance in the areas of mercantile transactions. The Company of Caracas, formed by decree on September 25, 1728, began this type of approved privateering by taking control of the mainland coasts between the Orinoco and Ríohacha. To do this, it could send two large ships to Venezuela yearly, both equipped for war with forty or fifty cannons, and have various smaller, armed ships with privateering privileges to watch out-of-the-way routes and spots. The first corsair ships of the Company of Caracas, the frigates *San Ignacio* and *Santa Rosa*, set sail from Pasaia in 1730 and were soon tested. That same year, the boarding longboats of the *San Ignacio*, commanded by the Donostian Captain Ignacio de Noblesa, seized the Dutch sloop *Tufan Elida* and its valuable cargo of flour, spirits, oil, gunpowder, arms, and cloth that was auctioned off for 1,278 pesos and 6 reales. In 1731, the same Gipuzkoan ship made off with the valuable contraband merchandise carried by the Dutch frigate *The Young Gentleman*. In August of the same year, the *San Ignacio* seized the Dutch sloop *The Rising* in port with its bays full of cacao and tobacco, and in September it captured the sloop *Young William* in Patanemo, in whose compartments were stored large quantities of cloths, tobacco, flour, and cacao.[36]

The Clergy and the Church in the Americas

For the Castilian Crown, converting the conquest and colonization of the New World into a missionary enterprise responded not only to the task of evangelism around the globe, to which it was committed, in line with the religious spirit of the epoch; the Crown was also legitimizing its own sovereignty on the American continent. The papal bulls of 1493 of commission and donation issued by Alexander VI constituted the legal argument for Spain's annexation of the newly discovered territories. Thus, from the outset, the Spanish Crown had an evangelizing obligation in the very process of occupying the new lands. The American Church was converted into a national one that fused the interests of altar and throne, cross and sword, Bishop of Rome and King of Spain.[37] This process gradually took shape over the course of three centuries. As mentioned, the papal concession was initiated with the bulls, which juridically strengthened Spanish sovereignty overseas.[38] Some years later, in 1501, Alexander VI granted the Castilian monarchs the right to collect the tithes in the Americas and to administer them to guarantee the maintenance of worship, clerical personnel, and church construction (Bull *Eximiae Devotionis*,

November 16). It would not be until 1508, however, that the Spanish Crown's desire to control the American Church was achieved: the concession of universal patronage over the Indies, a privilege that it already enjoyed much earlier over the Canary Island archipelago and, beginning in 1492, over the Kingdom of Granada. By virtue of the Bull *Universalis Ecclesiae* (August 5, 1508), Pope Julius II transferred the Royal Patronage, or the right to name all ecclesiastical posts, bishops, and benefices in the New World, to the Catholic Monarchs. This was as compensation for the zeal expended in the diffusion of the Faith, and in exchange for the promise to maintain the cult, promote the evangelical enterprise in the newly discovered lands, and build churches, cathedrals, hospitals, and social service centers. Such concessions were expanded in the years that followed, including the right to create the first permanent diocese in the New World—Santo Domingo, Concepción, and San Juan, Puerto Rico—(Bull *Romanus Pontifex*, 1511), and Pope Leo X's 1518 concession of the power to set and alter the borders of the American dioceses to Emperor Charles V according to the conditions. Under the Bull *Exponi Nobis* of June 9, 1522, Charles V received the right to decide the number of religious personnel that could go to the Americas and the power to veto however many he wanted without first consulting the religious orders affected. Shortly thereafter, in 1524, the Council of the Indies was founded. From then on, it assumed complete jurisdiction over religious matters for the royal delegation. In 1538, Emperor Charles V introduced the *placet regio*, a type of royal pass or visa through which each bull, memo, or communiqué of the Holy See could be publicized and enacted only after having been studied and accepted by the Council of the Indies. This measure was consolidated the following year; the Crown received control of the correspondence of the American prelates with the Apostolic See, an effective measure with which to control the relations between the Roman shepherd and his overseas flocks.

Philip II continued this policy of state control of American ecclesiastical affairs. The Catholic monarch par excellence soon well understood that to efficiently carry out his program of reforms in the Americas it would be necessary to have greater control over the cult and the clergy. In the opinion of the "Prudent King," American issues were exclusively the domain of the Crown of Castile by expressed desire of those occupying the papacy, who considered Philip vicar and delegate within his patrimonial domains. Although the personnel to evangelize the overseas kingdoms were already in place, during the reign of Phillip II a strict inspection of the missionary activity and conduct, as well as individual backgrounds of regular clergy members, was conducted. The monarch saw no effort as too great to preserve the Faith from the "heretical plagues," and the counter-reformist influences in the ecclesiastical politics of the Americas. He did not hesitate to establish the Inquisition in the Americas—1570 in Lima, 1571 in Mexico City, and 1610 in Cartagena, Colombia—to confront sorcerers, Illuminati, Erasmists, Lutherans, Anglicans (especially captured English corsairs), and, beginning in 1580, Portuguese Jews. Philip II also assumed command of the mission of spreading the dogmatic and pastoral provisions of the Council of Trent (1545–1563), to the point of making them the law of the kingdom.

Once the legal framework for the relations between Church and State was designed and the diocesan map for future American Church action was worked out,[39] the missionary mandate only had to be put into practice; this was the primary objective and juridical foundation of the overseas Spanish presence. The first obstacle that the Church-State agreement had to overcome was how to operationalize the evangelizing commitment in the Americas. Two very different proposals were the basis for the resulting debate. On one hand, there were those who argued that the Americas should be a place to reestablish the Church of the first Christians: simple and free from European vices accumulated throughout centuries. Defenders of this project believed isolation of the native American nuclei absolutely necessary to carry out a pure evangelizing process, free from the harmful habits and bad examples brought by the European colonists. Humanists, reformed mendicant orders, utopian thinkers, and intellectuals influenced by Erasmist theories and Franciscan mysticism supported this dream of the Church. In spite of serious attempts to put this isolationist theory into practice,[40] the theses advocating indigenous evangelization in contact with the rest of colonial society triumphed in the long run.

A large number of ecclesiastics, both priests and monks, were devoted to this missionary activity, although it was the monks that played the leading role in the evangelization of the Americas. The spiritual maintenance of the first Spanish immigrants and those established in the New World was left to the diocesan priests. The religious orders were the real craftsmen of the indigenous catechization in the Americas. During the entire Spanish-American epoch, members of the Carthusians, Benedictines, Trinitarians, Camillians, Minims, Oratorians, and Servites crossed the ocean hoping to save souls and establish themselves in the recently discovered lands; however, the majority of American evangelization was done by the Franciscans, Dominicans, Mercedarians, Augustinians, and Jesuits,[41] most of whom came from Spain and other European countries.[42] The Basque Country was no exception, and a large number of clerics that swelled the ranks of the evangelical orders of the Americas left from there.

The Basque clergymen were part of American missionary activity from the beginning of the colonization of the New World. They served in a variety of pastoral and ecclesiastical roles; they wore miters, occupied cathedrae, founded schools, hospices, and hospitals, occupied university chairs, were chroniclers, censors, and inquisitors of the Holy Office. It can be stated without question that no ecclesiastical sector or activity lacked Basques. The Basque clergy was generally well integrated into the heart of the Basque community.[43] Their autonomy was due to only a remote presence of the ecclesiastical hierarchy in the Basque Country, mostly limited to an annual visit, and the absence of economic resources with which to finance it. This situation favored the development of a clergy in touch with the lifestyles of the popular classes and willing to emigrate if assured ecclesiastical work. In addition, the Basque Church had penetrated the various social classes equally and deeply, and each observed its doctrinal strictures with respect. The life of the community was full of demonstrations of piety, and religion occupied a privileged position in the scale of social values for the Basques. Religious vocations flourished as a result. Service to the Church was also one of the most common opportunities in noble Basque families in the modern era for all sons after the first born, and constituted the obligatory fate of the illegitimate sons of the most noteworthy Basque figures.

Basque friars had to employ missionary methods very different from those used to that point to achieve their catechistic ends in the Americas. The vastness of the territories, the variety of political organization within the different aboriginal groups, their cultural variation and linguistic diversity, and the sheer length of the evangelizing process forced them to tailor their missionary methodology to the conditions. For example, the friars had to learn native languages to better diffuse their religious doctrines. The preparation of sermon books, catechisms, and tomes printed in indigenous tongues favored not only pastoral work, but also the diffusion of printed materials in general. The congregation imparting religious instruction in the Americas was bolstered by the founding of academies and schools. The new beliefs were often taught via a diversity of graphic materials (stamps, maps) and rote rules of memorization. Instruction also incorporated other materials, all of them transmitting the social mores of Western society. The Basque missionaries did not reject any resource that might assist in the goal of conversion. Thus, they used murals in their convent portals and engraved decorations in their churches and chapels to reveal proper religious motifs; such visual images must have been more effective than the long written paragraphs that were surely largely unintelligible for the natives. Similarly, the preachers encouraged the natives' "good" qualities as a means of gaining their trust. They created centers where the natives demonstrated their talents in music, painting, and sculpture, for which they were awarded prizes. And, when the occasion called for it, the friars did not hesitate to repress and punish those who continued to hold pagan beliefs. To the extent that they were able, they tried to alter practices such as polygamy and consanguine marriage, deeply rooted in the indigenous communities.

The delicacy of the treatment, the understanding of indigenous customs, the ordered life of the colonists settled in the Americas, and the gentleness of the precepts dictated by the Church—fasting, Lent, and so on—were thought to assist in the transformation of the indigenous world.[44] Unfortunately, this was not always so, and frequently the new Christians had to be watched to prevent them from falling back into idolatry, an unmistakable sign of feigned conversion. Nevertheless, during the modern era, the Basque missionaries destined for the Americas implemented these new forms of their ministerial practice; some of them managed to climb the ladder of the American Church hierarchy.[45] Thus, in the sixteenth century, the venerable José Anchieta—a Canary Islander of Gipuzkoan origin on his father's side—combined missionary and educational duties in dependencies of the Portuguese Crown. He founded a school in the town of Piratininga, and worked in Santos and in the Mission of San Pablo. Today a Brazilian city in the state of Espíritu Santo honors the famous missionary of Basque origin, Anchieta, by bearing his name.

In Nueva España, the first bishop of Chiapas was Fra Juan de Arteaga y Avendaño (1541), who died shortly after being replaced by Fra Bartolomé de Las Casas. Years later, the Gipuzkoan Dominican Andrés de Ubilla was bishop of this same diocese. The Bizkaian Francisco de Mendiola occupied the seat of Guadalajara until his death in 1576. In 1593, the Gipuzkoan Franciscan Martín de la Ascensión (Loinaz and/or Aguirre could have been his civil surnames) was assigned to the convent of Churubusco, in Veracruz, where he taught theology and philosophy. In the early decades of the seventeenth century, Julián de Cortazar, from Durango, served as bishop of Tucumán. There, he promoted the construction of sanctuaries, schools, and a boarding school, and undertook renovation of the cathedral. Some years later, he was promoted to the bishopric of Santa Fe (Bogota). In 1630, the Augustinian Antonio de Conderina, from Bilbao, was appointed to the American see of Santa Marta in Nueva Granada. In those years the Creole nun of Bergaran origin, Sor Juana Inés de la Cruz, also stood out in Mexico for her intellectual prowess and the quality of her poetry. Among the most relevant Basque men of the Church in eighteenth-century Mexico, it is worth citing Mateo Cayetano de Urrutia y Guerrero, Joaquín Antonio de Velarde y Murga, José Ignacio de Arancibia y Ormaegui (a native of Lekeitio), and the Araban layman Domingo de Aberasturi, who worked in the hospice of San Jacinto in Mexico City. In addition, Juan José de Eguiara y Eguren was a Creole of Bizkaian origin whose family had settled in Nueva España several generations earlier. After occupying the positions of synodic examiner of the archbishopric, censor of the Holy Office, and deputy of the Seminary Council, he wrote the foundational statutes for the College of Saint Ignatius—also called College of the Vizcayans—founded by agreement of the Confraternity of Aránzazu in 1732. Juan Márquez de Castañiza, bishop of Durango (Mexico), also belonged to the Mexican clergy and episcopate.

The Augustinian Andrés de Salazar, originally from the noble estate of the Tower of Muñatones in Somorrostro (Bizkaia), worked in Peru. He landed at the port of Callao in 1573 with an expedition of fourteen clerics, the Bizkaian Juan Martínez de Ormaechea among them. Salazar stood out in his mastery of indigenous languages, which brought him the chair of "General Language of the Indians" in Lima. He died in a shipwreck in 1622, leaving behind an important corpus. Francisco de Urquizu, a Bizkaian from Elorrio, the Franciscan teacher Martín de Aróstegui, and the Mercedarian teacher Gabriel de Landa also stood out in the viceroyalty of Peru. Landa's process of beatification was begun by the Basque Antonio de Vidaurre, the prior of the Mercedarians of Lima. Several Basques occupied important positions throughout the eighteenth century: Antonio Ibañez de la Rentería, a presbyter and doctor of theology from Bizkaia; Antonio de Soloaga, archbishop of Lima in 1711; Sebastián de Lartaun, a Gipuzkoan who led the bishopric of Cuzco and had the support of his countrymen, the Bizkaian Iñigo de Rentería and the Gipuzkoan Pedro Arteaga de Mendiola, both justices of the High Court, in his disputes with the archbishop of Lima and future saint, the Basque Toribio de Mogrovejo; the Araban Diego de Montoya, bishop of Trujillo (a see occupied years later by the Navarrese Martíñez de Compañón); and the Bizkaian martyr from Orduña, Mario Herran.

In the last third of the eighteenth century, the Bizkaian Juan Diego de Zamácola y Jáuregui arrived in Peru. His brother, Simón Bernardo de Zamácola, was a royal clerk, Oñacino alderman, and author of the publicized project to create a new port in the estuary of Bilbao; Simón Bernardo's activity in favor of obligatory military service in the Basque Country caused the famous rebellion known as the Zamacolada. Although Juan Diego did not occupy any relevant ecclesiastical posts, he did leave a deep mark in Peru, performing his mission in the parish of Cayma, very near Arequipa. Born in the town of Dima in 1746, he sponsored the initiatives to build a free school for children, a hall for town meetings, and a prison, and various proposals aimed at avoiding the absenteeism of the local landowners. He also proposed economic measures to promote wealth and other plans; a canal to increase the area under irrigation, the exploitation of mineral deposits on the Charcani ridge, and the first testing of mineral waters were among the most noteworthy. Throughout his long life he also presented a varied program of reforms to improve the standard of living of his Peruvian parishioners. A true member of the community, concerned about its problems and eager for its progress, a chronicler of its events and prolific writer, he disagreed with the winds of independence that blew throughout all Spanish America at that time. He belonged to the Real Sociedad Bascongada de Amigos del País (Royal Basque Society of the Friends of the Country), beginning in 1788 as an honorary member. He died in 1823 and was buried according to his wishes in the church of Cayma, to whose service he had dedicated forty-five years of his life.

The venerable Franciscan lay brother, Pedro de Bardeci, a native of Orduña (Bizkaia), died around 1700 in Chile. In Venezuela, another Bizkaian, Manuel Jiménez Bretón, was elected to the see of León in Caracas in 1748; he died, however, before occupying the post. The Araban Discalced Carmelite Juan Antonio de Viana y Sáenz de Villaverde, Censor of the Holy Office and prior of his order in Madrid, was named bishop of Caracas, a post that he held until 1798.

At the end of the sixteenth century the Franciscan Martín Ignacio de Loyola arrived in Río de la Plata and occupied the episcopal see of the region. A synod of the diocese was held in Asunción during his term to determine the organizational bases of its church and missions. Years later, in the seventeenth century, the Bizkaian Franciscan Gabriel de Guillétegui y Ubilla served as commissary general in Peru; he was later named bishop of La Paz and Asunción (Paraguay). Although it was late, perhaps the most distinguished work done in the viceroyalty of Río de la Plata was that of the members of the Society of Jesus in the Jesuit *reducciones* of Alto Paraná during the eighteenth century.[46] Their peculiar system of evangelization had led the followers of Saint Ignatius of Loyola to found *reducciones* in this region, in which the natives lived as a community and free from corrupting European influence.[47] At the beginning, the Jesuit presence was not well received by the native Guaranís; some Jesuits, such as the Gipuzkoans Juan de Lizardi and Cristóbal de Mendoza, were martyred. Then pastoral work of the Society's army began to yield the desired fruits, with creation of seventeen *reducciones* within the borders of Uruguay and thirteen in Paraguay at the beginning of the 1700s. The largest and most important were those of Concepción (5,653 inhabitants), San Carlos (5,355 inhabitants), Encarnación (4,700 inhabitants), San Nicolás (4,699 inhabitants), San Javier (4,117 inhabitants), and Loreto (4,060 inhabitants). Several Basques—Diego de Boroa, Pedro de Ortíz de Zárate, Pedro de Ledesma, José Francisco de Arce, Juan Lascamburu, Juan de Azpilicueta, Ignacio de Tolosa, José de Anchieta—stood out in their missionary work in the *reducciones* of Paraguay. Among them, the work done in 1750 in this region by José Cardiel y Laguna deserves special mention. Although born in La Rioja, he moved to Gasteiz with his family at a young age. There, he completed all of his schooling and enrolled in the Society of Jesus. In 1750, after having traveled throughout much of Argentina, he was sent to the *reducción* of Saint Ignatius of Guazú. There, the news of the signing of the Treaty of Borders between Spain and Portugal reached him via the colony of Sacramento. The abusive terms of the treaty incited an indigenous resistance largely promoted and supported by Jesuit missionaries such as Cardiel y Laguna. His diplomatic activity in favor of indigenous interests was unsuccessful, and he was forced to transfer the Indians of the *reducción* to their native areas, in Portuguese territory. From then until his death, he worked to spread news of the historical reality that he had lived in Paraguay and of the Society's innocence in the Guaraní revolt.

Undoubtedly, the Spanish Church in the Americas frequently behaved controversially. In spite of the Church's imperfections and often questionable treatment of the natives, however, it clearly attempted to uphold the principles of humanity, charity, and justice that guided Christian doctrine. The discovery and conquest of the New World meant an unending series of abuses and annoyances for the native population. The clerics that arrived at Santo Domingo were sympathetic to the plight of the natives. Thus, on Christmas 1511, the Dominican Fra Antonio de Montesinos used the pulpit to condemn the Spaniards' reproachable treatment of the natives. His criticisms reached such an extreme that he threatened to deny confession and absolution to those who mistreated the Indians. The echo of these events reached Spain, where reform measures were soon taken. Thus, during the Council of Burgos of

1512, several theologians and jurists composed a legal corpus, the Laws of Burgos, which, among other issues, established the liberty and organization of Indian society; it also advocated good treatment of the natives, the construction of churches, and the spread of the Christian doctrine. In 1513, four new decrees were added to the existing ones, each designed to augment the protection of the natives. In addition, the office of Protector of Indians was created, harsh penalties were instituted for those that disobeyed the Laws of Burgos, freedom was proclaimed for those Indians illegally enslaved, and forced Indian labor in the mines was prohibited.[48]

The constant protests of the missionary orders in reaction to the Spanish colonists' lack of respect for the royal ordinances clearly confirm that abuse of the indigenous population continued. The circumstances motivated the Crown to promote the New Laws of 1542 (by then Fra Bartolomé de Las Casas had already written his *Brevísima relación de la destrucción de las Indias*). These laws contemplated the abolition of the right to enslave and exact personal servitude and a ban on the distribution of more Indians to the Spaniards. Thus, although the knowledge and the enactment of these laws in the Americas provoked the most heated protests by colonists and *encomenderos*, it is clear that both Church and State had managed to endow the Americas with a legal framework that guaranteed the integrity and respect of the indigenous population. The efforts of two renowned Basques stood out in the formation of the juridico-doctrinal corpus in favor of the defense of the natives: the Dominican Francisco de Vitoria, one of the most important Spanish theologians and jurists of the sixteenth century, and the Franciscan Juan de Zumarraga, the first archbishop of the American Church.[49]

Francisco de Vitoria was probably born in the Araban capital around 1480. He held the most important chair of the University of Salamanca for many years. During that time he wrote and published his *Relectiones theologicae*, which cover a wide range of theological and political issues, including his theories about international law. Vitoria was always a strong opponent of the abuses of the conquest. He harshly condemned Pizarro's campaign in 1534 and the death of the Inca Atahualpa, and in the *Relectiones de Indios* he forcefully reproached the conduct of the Spaniards that confiscated Indian land. He believed that colonization was legitimate only if its primary goal was the well-being and prosperity of the natives, and not the profit of the colonizers. This position collided head-on with the mentality of the day. It was not kindly received by Emperor Charles V, who did not hesitate to request that the Dominican superiors call for the Araban friar's obedience.

The Franciscan Juan de Zumárraga had been born in Durango (Bizkaia) around 1476. A man well versed in theology and philosophy, he was named the bishop of Mexico and Protector of Indians in 1527 by Emperor Charles V. Later, between 1536 and 1543, he served as the president of the High Court of the Holy Office in Nueva España, a period during which he instituted 152 litigations against blasphemy, the Lutherans, the Judaizers, idolatry, sacrifices, witchcraft, superstition, bigamy, moral transgressions, and crimes against orthodoxy. In 1547, he would occupy the post of archbishop of Mexico. What Francisco de Vitoria taught in Salamanca about the rights of foreigners in American lands, Juan de Zumárraga tried to put into practice in the jurisdiction of his archbishopric, doing his best to protect the natives from the Spanish colonial predation in Nueva España. In spite of his defects,[50] the friar from Durango took pains to preserve the dignity of the Indian and helped to implant a Christian humanism in Mexico. The introduction of the first printing press and the first bilingual work (titled *Breve y más compendiosa doctrina cristiana en lengua mexicana y castellana*), intended to improve the Indians' comprehension of religious texts, were both products of his efforts. Because he was a Basque speaker, Zumárraga very quickly understood the indispensability of the vernacular languages as vehicles for dialogue and communication with the natives. He recommended that the clerics of his diocese learn the languages spoken in Mexico and spread the Christian doctrine in the most common ones. The Franciscan from Durango also promoted the construction of schools and hospitals for the Indians, supported female instructors, organized the first libraries, and established the first university.

Father Vitoria in Spain and Fra Juan de Zumárraga in Mexico were not the only Basque religious figures that stood out in the defense of native dignity. The licentiate Alonso de Zuazo, judge of Santo Domingo between 1517 and 1527, was noteworthy in his protection of natives, as were the Gipuzkoan Pedro de Rentería and the Bizkaian Francisco Marroquín, from Enkarterri. Marroquín served in the missionary evangelization in Guatemala beginning in 1530 and came to occupy the bishopric of the capital city. During his episcopate he proposed to recruit missionaries in Castile, suppress the traffic of slaves, and establish indigenous *reducciones*. He promoted the construction of roads, fostered horse breeding, and advocated the creation of hospitals and schools and the learning of native languages.

Lastly, the Araban Franciscan Jerónimo de Mendieta was a noteworthy Basque figure in American ecclesiastical history. A great missionary, he wrote a work in five volumes, *Historia eclesiástica indiana*, that analyzed the Spanish settlements in Mexico and the evangelizing process in Nueva España in detail, thereby contributing an important anthropological document of the region. He had arrived in the Americas in 1554 and from that moment worked as a missionary in Tlaxcala, Toluca, Xochimilco, Tlatelolco, and Tepeaca. He served as secretary of the prelate in the Franciscan province of Santo Evangelio, learned the native languages, supported the foundation of *reducciones*, and tried to restore a Christianity based on charity and justice. All of his work supported the native population, which he proclaimed had to be respected as human beings worthy of cultural and religious promotion.[51] He died during a dysentery epidemic in 1604.

In addition to advancing Christianity on the new continent, the missionary work of Spain in the Americas contributed to the significant development of Spanish-American culture and arts. The catechizing methods used by the missionary clergy of the Americas were employed toward that end. During the entire colonial period—especially throughout the sixteenth century—the ecclesiastics assumed an almost exclusive responsibility for the diffusion of art and culture. This was so pervasive that current historians no longer make a distinction between the evangelical work and cultural activity of all of the religious orders in the instruction of language, literacy, music, art, and education.[52] The contribution of the Basque clergy was noteworthy in these endeavors.

Education, understood as the ideal vehicle for native acculturation to the Spanish lifestyle and comprehension of the truths of Christian doctrine, constituted one of the main preoccupations of both the Church and the monarchy. Almost invariably, a school center for natives and children of settlers governed by ecclesiastics accompanied each urban foundation. In addition to the Christian faith, the students were taught to read, write, and do simple crafts. The first school in the New World, dating from 1505, was built in Santo Domingo. From then on, numerous centers of instruction—primary, secondary, trade, and university—were founded throughout the vast terrain. With them proliferated libraries and the taste for reading, which stimulated the importation of books to the Americas and, later, the introduction of the printing press. The Bizkaian Juan de Zumárraga, with simple evangelizing ends, was its original promoter. In time, however, printing became the ideal mechanism for the diffusion of chronicles, writings, and memoirs about the missionary practice and the discovery and conquest of the New World, many of great artistic value. Such is the case of the *Historia eclesiástica indiana* of Jerónimo de Mendieta, the *Extirpación de la idolatría del Perú* of Pablo José de Arriaga, and the *Historia del descubrimiento y conquista del Perú* of the Gipuzkoan Agustín de Zarate.

The Basque ecclesiastic missionaries also made use of the theater for their evangelizing objectives. The Jesuits in particular exploited this genre to spread the Christian doctrine and faith in the form of short farces, allegories, and sacramental plays written with didactic intentions. The same can be said of the use of music for religious ends; abundant references document the construction of rudimentary organs in churches and cathedrals, the use of string and wind instruments, and monodic and vocal choral works in which the natives performed.

The Basques also knew how to diffuse European architecture in the Americas. Late Gothic and silver filigree were the styles used by the Araban Claudio de Arciniega in Mexico. He worked on the construction of the cathedral of the Aztec capital for almost twenty years, and planned the cathedral of Puebla and the church of Michoacán. Around the same time, the Bizkaian Juan de Veramendi, another of the great architects of the sixteenth century in the New World, worked in the viceroyalty of Peru. Veramendi's greatest work was the construction of the cathedral of Cuzco in 1560. Other Basque architects who designed cathedral buildings, public squares, town halls, and diverse monuments in Renaissance and Baroque styles included Cristóbal de Aulestia in Mérida (Yucatán); Diego de Aguirre, Matías Maestro,

Agustín de Gavira, Juan de Egoaguirre, and Juan Iñigo de Eraso in Lima; Francisco de Ibarra in Callao; Miguel de Arregui in Cuzco; and Fra Mariano de Garay in Cayma.[53] The main novelty brought to the New World by these Basque master workers and architects was the construction of edifices with two elements of the European tradition until then unknown in the American territory: the dome and the arch.

Sculpture and painting also served evangelism. As in so many other aspects of the acculturation process, the Basque missionaries and artists who immigrated to the New World with the new creed imposed new aesthetic standards on its doctrinal contents. Iñigo de Loyola, in Cuzco, was among the Basques noteworthy in such endeavors. The Gipuzkoan Echave family developed their own school of painting of Basque origin in Mexico, although it was influenced by Italian mannerism. Other Basque painters in the Americas were Sebastián de Arteaga and José de Ibarra in Mexico and Nicolás de Goríbar in Quito.

In sum, the cultural current established between Spain and its overseas possessions was the ideal vehicle to bring ideological, artistic, and cultural tendencies from the Old World to the new continent. The methods of missionary work, and the rapid establishment of schools, professional and art academies, educational centers, libraries, and universities created the necessary environment to produce a legion of artists, chroniclers, writers, professors, thinkers, humanists, and intellectuals who played key roles in the diffusion of ideas and the arts in the Americas. The time of plenty, or the cultural confirmation in Spanish America, did not really begin until the mid-sixteenth century. In the preceding period, the expeditions of discovery and conquest, the problems of colonization of vast territories, the sparse Spanish immigration to the Americas, and the foundation of few urban centers delayed cultural development. But, as these problems were corrected, European civilization continued to spread unceasingly—to a greater or lesser extent—throughout the Americas, configuring activities that have left their mark on the history of humanity.

Officials, Governors, and Functionaries

One of the most characteristic features of Basque society, which also differentiated it from the rest of the kingdoms of the Iberian Peninsula during the modern era, was, without doubt, that of universal collective nobility, already discussed. Belonging to the nobility, even the lowest level, provided the residents of the Basque Country the enjoyment of privileges inherent in such status throughout the territories of the Spanish Crown. It also created an incredible advantage for Basques aspiring to occupy administrative positions, whether civil or ecclesiastical. It is worth repeating that in a noble community such as the Basque Country, in which a very particular form of civil legislation—the *mayorazgo*—was also applied, those excluded from the family inheritance were forced to seek their fortune elsewhere. They frequently chose a military, administrative, or ecclesiastical career in the hope of satisfying their desires for economic well-being and social triumph. Thus, many Basques in the modern era chose administration as their destiny. They were especially well equipped to prosper in it, as a result of their mastery of the Spanish language, written and oral, and their excellent calligraphy. These were precisely the qualities that converted many disinherited Basques into the best secretaries and functionaries of the Spanish monarchy. Of course, only the most well-off could travel to Salamanca to study language and letters.

The existing literary references of the epoch attest to the fact that, during the reign of Emperor Charles V, the secretarial posts were frequently filled by Basques.[54] Under Philip II, the development of the state bureaucratic apparatus, without which the reorganization of the administration would have been inconceivable, was dramatic. And it would have been impossible to manage this system without the efficient secretaries that served as the connection between the monarch and state advisors. The power and influence of the corps of secretaries stirred the appetites of those hoping for success at the court. The Catholic Monarch initially governed with only one secretary, but soon decided to divide the responsibilities among several people. After the fall of Antonio Pérez, matters of state were thus entrusted to the Basque Juan de Idiaquez. Idiaquez demonstrated irreproachable efficiency and professionalism in performing his functions.[55] Other Basques of great worth in the service of Philip II were Antonio de Eraso and Francisco de Arrieta.

Philip III's ascendancy to the throne brought with it a radical change in the system of Spanish governance. The monarch bestowed power upon the court favorite. But the rise of the court favorites meant the decline of the secretaries, who, although they continued to be important functionaries, no longer had easy access to the monarch. In the epoch of Philip III, the Basques Esteban de Ibarra, Cristóbal de Ipiñarrieta, and Antonio de Aróstegui, among others, occupied secretariats. During the reign of Philip IV, Tomás de Zuazo, Bartolomé de Legaso, and Francisco de Arrieta also served in such positions. Then, with the last of the Hapsburg monarchs, the secretaries once again acquired great importance. Thus, in 1682, José de Veitia Linaje was named secretary of state, a post later occupied by Juan de Larrea (1695) and Juan Antonio López Zárate (1697), also Basques.[56]

With the Bourbons, the administrative secretaries were reduced to mere assistants of the monarch, with no authority to make decisions. Nevertheless, the concentration of power in the figure of the king, the centralization of the state administration, and, definitively, the profound transformation to which all of the bureaucratic machinery was subjected forced an increase in the number of administrative secretaries, and they became real ministers.[57] Men with Basque surnames intermittently occupied both these important posts and others that composed the Spanish monarchy's administrative corps. The names in table 1.3 in appendix 1 represent only a small sample of this trend.

The condition of nobility, often linked to a juridical degree acquired in the most prestigious Spanish universities, also facilitated access to important positions in the American administration for a good number of Bizkaians, Gipuzkoans, Arabans, and Navarrese. Moreover, several Basques were rewarded with positions in Spain, usually in the Council of Castile and the Council of the Indies, after occupying posts in the Spanish-American administration. At least the cases of Simón de Anda, Francisco Antonio González de Echávarri, and Francisco Leandro de Viana, cited in table 1.3 in appendix 1, attest to this.

In all the American territories, Basques performed varied functions in the complex web of Spanish administration.[58] Thus, in Venezuela, Juan Pérez de Tolosa was the governor of Caracas at the time of its foundation; Diego de Henares de Lezama, from Barakaldo, designed the first map of the Venezuelan capital; Sancho de Villar was one of the city's first mayors; Juan de Amézaga served as its secretary of the interior. Moreover, Bartolomé de Emasabel, Diego de Leguizamón, Sancho de Urquieta, Tomás de Aguirre, and Alonso de Uría worked actively in the city hall. At the end of the sixteenth century, a Bizkaian from Zenarruza-Markina settled in Venezuela—Simón Bolívar, ancestor of the future Spanish-American liberator. In 1589, he was the attorney general of the Court and the first alderman-for-life of Caracas, and years later he was named general accountant of the Royal Treasury (1593). In 1592, he founded a boarding school of Castilian grammar, in which Juan de Arteaga and Simón de Basauri, also Basques, served as professors. The Bizkaian Alonso Andrea de Ledesma, a decorated soldier in the Royal Army, who would defend Caracas from the attack of the corsair Amias Preston (1595) with his life, arrived in Venezuela with Bolívar. During the seventeenth century, Tomás de Aguirre was the mayor of Caracas and Bernabé de Oñate Mendizabal was treasurer of the king in Venezuela. Sancho de Alquiza was the governor and captain general, posts that were also held by the Araban Francisco Ruiz de Aguirre y Ruiz de Zurbano in the provinces of Dorado, island of Trinidad, and La Guatena. In the eighteenth century, just over three thousand Basques disembarked in Venezuela, according to figures provided by some authors. Of these, almost six hundred—Lardizabal, Zuloaga, and Arriaga, among others—were captains general, and twenty-seven were employed in the administration of the treasury—Muxica in Caracas, Arraiz y Zabala in Maracaibo, Echeverría in Guiana, Arteaga in Mérida, Ezonda in Marinas, Eguino in Maracay, Oráa in La Guaira, Uriz y Huarte in Tocuyo, Iriondo y Michelena in Barquisimeto, Goicoechea in Trujillo, Garmendia in El Pao, Juan Bautista de Zarandia in Caracas, Eyaralar in Puerto Cabello, Oroquieta in Valencia, Mendía in Turmero, Eguiño in Aragua, Larragoiti in San Felipe, Elizalde in Calabozo, and Castillobeiti in Orituco. Another arriving at that time was the justice of the High Court of Caracas (1789), the Araban José Bernardo de Asteguieta y Díaz de Sarralde.

In addition to founding urban centers and colonizing Río de la Plata in the sixteenth century, the Basques participated in both the administration and organization of the territory. Domingo Martínez de Irala, Juan Ortíz de Zárate, Juan de Garay, Martín Ruíz de Gamboa, Francisco Argañaraz y Murguía, Martín Ordoñez de Loyola, Rodrigo Ortíz de Zárate, Diego de Olabarrieta, Juan de Basualdo, Miguel Navarro, Luis Gaytán, Domingo de Irala, Pedro Izarra, José Fernández de Enciso, Rodrigo de Ibarrola, Domingo de Aramendía, Ochoa Marqués, Miguel de Urso, Cristóbal Altamirano, Hernando de Mendoza, and Juan Ramírez de Velasco were all good examples. In the seventeenth century, the list increased with the names of Alonso Pérez de Salazar, Ventura de Múgica, Jacinto de Lariz, Pedro Baigorri, José Martínez Salazar Robles, José de Garro, Manuel Velasco y Tejada, Juan José de Mutiloa y Andueza, and Alonso de Arce. In the eighteenth century, Miguel de Salcedo, Domingo Ortíz de Rozas, José de Andonaegui, the Creole of Basque origin Juan José Vértiz y Salcedo, and the Araban Martín de Alzaga administered and governed the region of Río de la Plata; the last of these occupied various posts in the city hall of Buenos Aires and was an active participant in the recapture of the city in 1806 and its defense against English attacks. Bruno Mauricio de Zabala and José Joaquin de Viana y Saenz de Villaverde also stood out. The former, born in Buenos Aires in 1682, achieved the rank of captain early thanks to his participation in the wars of Flanders and the War of the Spanish Succession in 1700. This also got him named captain general and governor of Río de la Plata. In 1717, Viana repelled the Portuguese attack carried out from Colonia del Sacramento; in 1724, he established a garrison in Montevideo to protect Spanish territory from Portuguese threats. In 1725, he began the task of converting the city's military headquarters, sending for Spanish colonists—many of them from the Basque Country—to whom he distributed parcels of land. In 1730, the seat became a municipality, making Zabala its founder and directly tying his name to the colonization of the Banda Oriental of Uruguay and its separation from the jurisdiction of Río de la Plata. José Joaquin de Viana y Sáenz de Villaverde, the second example cited, founded the *villa* of San Fernando de Maldonado in Uruguay in 1755. Viana contributed eficaciously to the development and protection of the Banda Oriental during his tenure. He established military posts in the interior of the country, such as those of San José and Casupá, and distributed strategically situated lands among the more noteworthy residents for defensive purposes.

The Basque presence in Chilean lands dated from the time of the conquest and expanded with the advance of the colonization process of the sixteenth century. At that time, Diego de Arana, the president of the High Court of Santiago (from Bilbao), Francisco de Axpe, and the Gipuzkoan Martín García Oñaz arrived in this Andean territory; the last was named governor of Chile in 1592, and the city of San Luis was founded during his rule. One century later, in 1692, the Gipuzkoan José de Garro would arrive in these lands as president and captain general. In the eighteenth century, three Arabans stood out in the Chilean government. The first of these was José Antonio Manso de Velasco y Sánchez de Samaniego. He was named governor and captain general in 1736. He occupied his post for eight years, during which the *villas* of San Felipe de Aconcagua, Talca, Rancagua, Copiapó, Cuico, and San Fernando were either built or refounded. In 1744 he culminated his career by being named the viceroy of Peru. He was succeeded by Ortíz de Rozas, under whose command the University of San Felipe and the Mint were founded. The second example is Luis Gonzaga de Araba y Sáenz de Navarrete, from Gasteiz. In 1789, he was named governor of the city and port of Valparaíso, and in 1795 he was appointed to the same post in the *villa* of Concepción. He was promoted to colonel, brigadier, and captain general and governor of the Yucatán in Nueva España, a position that he would never occupy as a result of being distracted by the Chilean pro-independence uprising. Lastly, Ignacio José de Rezabal y Ugarte, also from Gasteiz, became captain general of Chile in 1795, succeeding the charismatic President Ambrosio O'Higgins in the post. His university training provided him access to the American administration. Thus, in 1777, he was named justice of the High Court of Chile, in 1780 he became chancellor of the High Court of Lima, and in 1783 occupied the same office in Cuzco. In 1795, he took the post of regent of the High Court of Santiago, one that propelled him to captaincy general of Chile that same year. He was a member of the Royal Basque Society and wrote various works.

In the viceroyalty of Peru, the Bizkaian Lorenzo Aldana was the governor of the city of Lima in the sixteenth century. In the ensuing century, Juan de Villela occupied the post of justice of the High Court of the city of Los Reyes; the sailor Martín de Oronzúa held the position of head bailiff of the *villa* of San Felipe de Austria; and Martín de Arriola was justice of the High Courts of Charcas and Lima. Some authors have detected the presence of more than fifty Araban settlers in eighteenth-century Peru, many of them serving as justices, mayors, attorneys general, and governors. Several stood out: Manuel Sáenz y Martínez de Arlucea, treasurer of the Royal Banks of Lima beginning in 1741 and magistrate of Pasajes in 1750; Joaquín Antonio Pérez de Uriondo y Martínez de Murguía, justice of the High Court of Charcas in 1743 and superintendent of the Potosí mines; and Gregorio de Viana y Sáenz de Villaverde, magistrate of Canas and Canchis in 1759. Around that time, Luis Guendica y Mendieta was named governor of the citadel of Callao; Pablo Antonio de Olavide y Jaúregui and Antonio Hermenegildo Querejazu occupied the post of chief justice of the High Court of Lima in succession; and the Donostian sailor José Manuel Goicoa was sent to the Command Headquarters of Lima and later to that of Montevideo.

Among the Basques serving in administrative positions in Colombia during the sixteenth century was the Araban Pedro de Heredia. He was governor of Santo Domingo and Nueva Andalucía in 1533 and founder of the cities of Cartagena, Mompós, and Maritue. Francisco de Gamarra, Juan de la Puerta de Salazar, and Alvaro de Mendoza were governors of Popayán, the territory conquered by the Bizkaian Francisco de Salcedo. Bernardino de Múgica y Guevara would govern the provinces of Saldaña, Páez, and Pijao; Lope de Orozco, that of Santa Marta. The Navarrese Jerónimo de Inza and the Bizkaians Pedro de Ayala and Martín de Arriaga presided over the city halls of Santa Fe (Bogota), Cali, and Cartago, respectively. The Gipuzkoan Andrés Díaz Venero de Leyva was the first president of the High Court of Santa Fe (1564), and the Bizkaian Juan de Torrezábal was among the fourteen viceroys of Nueva Granada. At the beginning of the eighteenth century, Bilbao native Andrés de Barrenechea y Campo governed San Francisco de Quito; Cristóbal Vélez y Ladrón de Guevara served as the magistrate of Chita and the governor of Santa Marta; the Araban merchant, Diego de Zárate y Murga, was the magistrate of San Francisco de Quito; Nicolás Vélez de Guevara y Suescun managed the royal tobacco monopoly in Cartagena (Colombia); and the Bizkaian sailors Miguel de Lastarria Dendagorta and Cosme de Carranza commanded the squadron of the naval station of Cartagena.

The presence of the Bizkaians Francisco de Orduña Barriaga, Domingo de Zubizarreta, Juan de Verástegui, and Juan Martínez Landecho is documented in the sixteenth century in Guatemala; the last of these was the fourth president of the local High Court, a post from which he would be dismissed. In addition, around 1650, the Bizkaian Juan de Zuazo y Otalora was named captain general of the province of Comayagua, at the same time that the lawyer from Durango, Juan Bautista de Urquiola, was appointed justice of the High Court of Guatemala. Other distinguished Basques in Guatemalan society and administration were Bartolomé de Amézqueta, professor and rector of the university, and Jacobo de Villaurrutia, one of the founders of the Royal Basque Society in Guatemala. The trustee Pedro de Zabaleta, the alderman Florentín de Aitamarren, Juan López de Larburu, Jacobo de Alcayaga, Felipe de Ulaiz, and José de Arría, and the councilmen Juan López de Arburu and Pedro de Arratia were also members of its city hall in the seventeenth century.

But the majority of the Basques who arrived in the Americas between 1500 and 1800 were concentrated in the viceroyalty of Nueva España.[59] During this period, Mexico was an important administrative, ecclesiastical, and commercial center, fields in which the Basques had excelled for a long time. Thus, it is not strange that numerous Bizkaians, Arabans, Gipuzkoans, and Navarrese stood out in all of these facets established in the territory conquered by Hernán Cortés for the Spanish monarchy in 1521. In the seventeenth century, Agustín de Zabala was field marshal in Zacatecas (1624). At the same time, Martín de Zabala—from Elorrio and possibly the brother of Agustín—was promoted to the post of governor and captain general of Nuevo Reino de León, with the mission of pacifying and populating the territory. In 1625, Philip IV named the Gipuzkoan Francisco de Villarreal advisor of the Head Accountant's Office of the Mexican Treasury; in 1635, he designated the Araban Lope Díez de Armendaríz as the viceroy of Mexico. Around the middle of that century, the brothers Juan and Martín Castaños y Beisagasti, both sailors with important posts in the Royal Armada, and the Bizkaian Diego de Largacha, a general from Veracruz, were prominent. The Araban Pedro Martínez de Murguía y Ortíz de Guinea was named governor of the province of Nueva Vizcaya in 1689; at that time, Juan Antonio de Urrutia y Arana distinguished himself in Mexican public service as alderman and head judicial administrator. In the eighteenth century, the Arabans Domingo Ignacio de Vitoria y Pagazaurtundua—head judicial magistrate and general administrator of the marquisate of the Valley of Oaxaca—and Francisco Leandro de Viana y Saenz de Villaverde—chancellor and justice of the High Court of Mexico and magistrate of the Council of the Indies—were stationed in Nueva España. Another individual worth mentioning, also Araban, was José Antonio Fernández de Jáuregui y Urrutia; he was named governor and captain general of Nuevo León by the Crown in 1734. One year later, in 1735, Francisco Antonio González de Echavarry y Ugarte, from Gasteiz, was named judge of the High Court of Mexico City; he occupied this position for over thirty years, after which he was appointed as its governor and captain general. At the end of the eighteenth century, the Gipuzkoan José Joaquín de Arrillaga, governor of Alta California; Felipe Goicoechea, governor of Baja California; Diego de Borica y Retegui, provincial governor, interim governor of Nueva Vizcaya, and governor of California; Jacobo Ugarte y Loyola, provincial governor; and the Creole of Bizkaian origin Andrés de Mendívil, who occupied the position of postmaster general, all served in Mexico. The last Mexican viceroys were also of Basque origin: Miguel José de Azanza, Félix Berenguer de Marquina, José de Iturrigaray, the Gipuzkoan Pedro de Garibay, and the Araban Juan José Ruiz de Apodaca y Eliza.

In sum, a legion of Bizkaians, Gipuzkoans, Arabans, and Navarrese covered a wide bureaucratic spectrum in the administrations of both the Old and New Worlds. Their work was fundamental to judicial practice and law enforcement of the Spanish imperial government in the Americas. Many of them—the immense majority—were more closely committed than most to the social, political, administrative, and ecclesiastical transformation of their newly adopted homelands. And, as it could not be otherwise, they also served directly in the Crown's economic activities relating to the New World.

Chapter Three

Colonial Commerce

The Indies Monopoly

After the phase of discovery and conquest, America became enormously important for the historical development of Europe. Aside from the social, political, or religious consequences or effects of the progressive incorporation of the new continent into the European mentality, America considerably increased the supply for the European market. Converted from the outset into the permanent colony of the growing transatlantic European economy, America supplied merchants with an abundance of important, valuable raw materials at that time: dyeing substances, medicinal plants, cinnamon, sugar, tobacco, cacao, hides, precious woods, pearls, emeralds, silver and gold, and many other, lesser products. At the same time that materials from America increased, the new continent stimulated a strong demand for European goods that promoted the production of exports of various kinds: food products, livestock, arms, tools, textiles, sacred objects and art, books, and paper. And, of course, there was the lucrative slave trade and the dazzling attraction of American precious metals. Conscious of the economic role that the newly discovered lands were going to play, the Castilian monarchs did not hesitate in establishing a rigid monopoly on the organizational, technical, and control system that made the Guadalquivir the most important port complex in Atlantic commerce and Sevilla the critical link in the relations between Europe and America for two centuries.[1]

The initial monopolistic model to imitate was the Casa da Inda of Lisbon.[2] Nevertheless, the quick proof that the new Indies would constitute more than a limited series of coastal installations, such as those established by the Kingdom of Portugal in Africa and Asia, prompted the Spanish Crown to leave ample room for individual initiatives after the very first discovery contracts. Thus, the Spanish monopoly was based on two restrictions: (1) concentrating at a single port all of the organizational elements for implementing the monopoly, in order to facilitate the control of the new possessions, traffic, and tax collection; and (2) reserving the right to trade and live in America to the subjects of the Crown of Castile, thereby forbidding the presence of foreigners and ethnic or religious dissidents.

In this regard, the city of Sevilla was designated the seat of the Spanish monopoly in America. In spite of its lack of direct participation in the first voyage of discovery, already by Columbus's second expedition it would acquire a relevant role, while the ports of Huelva were rejected as having limited economic suitability. Sevilla's advantages at the end of the fifteenth and beginning of the sixteenth centuries clearly outweighed its disadvantages. There were concrete nautical reasons; according to Pierre Chaunu, the trip to America from the Gulf of Cádiz would save 15 percent of the time and 20 percent of the cost compared to the same trip from Galicia. There were strategic arguments; as an interior riverine port, Sevilla would offer more security from possible enemy corsair attacks. Historical and economic conditions also influenced the decision. Sevilla was able to guarantee the basic supplying of America without high re-export costs. It boasted a noteworthy maritime and commercial tradition. And, the city's direct dependence on the Castilian Crown had configured its favorably consolidated administrative structure.[3]

With the discovery fever and the volume of commercial transactions with America progressively increasing at the beginning of the sixteenth century, the Spanish Crown had to apply severe measures of political, economic, social, and fiscal control to avoid the emigration of dangerous people to the New World to ensure the political and religious security of the state. Control of the flow of arms and subversive literature that could assail the Castilian Catholic monarchy was also vital. The interest of the Crown in using a single port was therefore logical, and it soon took the shape of a monopolistic administration. In 1503, the Catholic Monarchs ordered the creation of a Casa de Contratación, or House of Trade, in Sevilla. Initially formed to manage the new discoveries, the office soon became the key instrument of Spanish economic monopoly. It controlled the fleets, shipments, and personnel involved in the commerce and colonization of America. Thus, upon its foundation, all of the ships that went to America had to set sail from and put into port at Sevilla, where they were subject to the fiscal and administrative control of the House of Trade. Among the customs functions and measures regulating maritime traffic that the House of Trade exercised were inspection and concession of licenses to ships after three rigorous visits on board; meticulous inspections of both the crews and cargoes; organization of the fleets; control of emigrants and of goods of those deceased in America; charge and administration of ship taxes (the *avería, almojarifazgo, quinto, cruzada,* and *alcabala,* among others); and close scrutiny of the gold and silver from America, and its coining in the Mint House in Sevilla. The office was originally staffed with three functionaries—a commission merchant, an accountant, and a treasurer. Their number grew, however, as the scope of the office's powers was extended and the administrative and bureaucratic requirements multiplied as a result of the expansion and incorporation of new American territories. By 1687, 110 staff members were listed in the House of Trade. Until 1597, its presidency fell to a member of the Council of the Indies.

The initial judicial powers of the House of Trade were reduced with the passage of time, however. This was first done in 1523 through the creation of the Council of the Indies, which from then on would assume the political and administrative powers of the Indies monopoly. In 1539, the birth of the Corporation of Indies' Shippers, the famous Consulate of Sevilla, further decreased such powers. Although recognized as the commercial board with exclusive jurisdiction in merchant disputes and losses, the Consulate of Sevilla stood out primarily as a powerful, restrictive association of merchants of the Indies, in charge of the consolidation, representation, and defense of commercial interests. As a result of the revenue it generated and its mercantile monopoly, the Consulate even became a financing organ of the Crown, which expanded its privileges in the lucrative Indies trade. The Consulate thereby determined the volume of the fleets, influenced the prices of goods, and inspected merchants' insurance, cargoes, and operations. In the seventeenth century, it came to impede the naming of those in charge of the fleets of the Indies and negotiated the admission of foreigners in American commerce. Vis-à-vis the Consulate or, in other words, vis-à-vis the corporation of the people of the sea wishing to promote guild activity, the Corporation and Confraternity of the Sailors and Pilots of the Passage of the Indies was the workforce that maintained the new Indies commercial traffic.[4]

In search of security and efficiency in the Atlantic crossing, the Spanish economic monopoly also organized maritime traffic in a unique way. From early on, transport between Spain and America was threatened by the raids of pirates and corsairs, mostly in service to France and England. This piratical activity in the Atlantic made sense, especially in the area along the coast of Andalusia, the Canary and Azore Islands, and, of course, the Caribbean. At the beginning of the sixteenth century, the ships that serviced the new Indies commerce were small. They often sailed alone or in improvised convoys, usually without a military escort, which made them easy spoils for the "sea dogs." Defense was urgent, and steps were soon taken. In 1512, the House of Trade ordered two caravels to the Canaries to protect the vessels coming from America against Huguenot French corsairs. Then, in 1521, a squadron of three to five ships was ordered to patrol the area between the Spanish coast and the Canary Islands. In 1528, an armada was organized to protect the Iberian coast and ships coming from America. Such defensive measures were increasingly taken in the decade of the 1530s as a consequence of the war with France and rising piracy. Navigation in convoys, protected by ships of the Royal Armada, was well established among the Spanish merchants. By 1540, it was already considered obligatory to sail the Atlantic in groups of at least ten vessels and under the protection of warships that increased in size and armaments with time.

This fleet system was developed until 1561. That year, a royal decree ordered that each year two convoys for Nueva España and the American mainland be chartered in Sevilla, Cádiz, and Sanlúcar de Barrameda. In April 1564, after several experiences that served to perfect this system, the first Indies fleet set sail for Veracruz, in Nueva España, and the port of Nombre de Dios, in Panama. It was escorted by eight war galleons. This modus operandi was consolidated in 1566 to channel and defend traffic to America. Soon, a distinction would be made between "fleets" and "galleons," based on the fact that the ships destined for the continent were protected on their return trips to Spain—when they would be carrying Peruvian gold and silver—by "fleets" of eight galleons, while those from Nueva España were only accompanied by two (thus, "galleons").[5] The system of fleets in itself functioned well, although the escort ships sometimes carried merchandise in the bays and even in the cannons. Nonetheless, the enemies of Spain found it very difficult to capture or destroy such fleets.[6] The Spanish Crown was thereby able to control the Atlantic while ensuring relatively efficient imperial communication with the Americas, albeit at a high cost. But the system of fleets was not Spain's last word on the defense of its commerce. It also added naval patrols—the Ocean Armada, the Armada of the Indian Guard, the Windward Armada, and the Coast Guard Squadron—that unremittingly watched the American coasts to protect Spanish commerce from the threat of the corsairs and other pirates.

Once organized, controlled, and protected, Indies commerce spread with great vitality by supplying the American market with high-priced consumer goods and receiving mineral wealth from Nueva España and Peru in exchange.[7] Nevertheless, after a century of almost uninterrupted expansion, Spanish commercial traffic with America declined. The great increase from 1562 to 1592 was followed by a leveling off from 1593 to 1622, and a great decrease from 1623 to 1650; it would not recover for a full century. Even with this, the Spanish monopoly (really in Andalusia, centered on Sevilla) lasted for the majority of the seventeenth century. At its end, however, the Andalusian capital suffered a great deal of adversity, which weakened its hegemonic position in colonial mercantile traffic. Its population was decimated by a plague epidemic and fell from a high of 150,000 in 1588 to 85,000 one century later. Its merchants suffered the crushing burden of royal taxes and the resulting indebtedness. Moreover, its geographic location became a serious problem. Sevilla was an interior port whose access was problematic for newer, heavier transatlantic vessels. From the beginning of the eighteenth century, navigation through the Guadalquivir therefore became extremely difficult for the Indies fleets. But, Sevilla's loss was Cádiz's gain. As a seaport, the so-called "little cup of silver" was a more accessible seat for the commercial convoys. In addition, foreign merchants, excluded from Indies colonial commerce from the beginning, preferred Cádiz. They wanted to avoid the Sevillan administration and considered Cádiz's bay more favorable for smuggling than an interior port. Finally, Cádiz had advantageous customs tariffs that whetted the appetite of foreign commercial investors. Thus, Cádiz's economic ascent at the expense of rival Sevilla was determined. People, like commerce, moved to Cádiz. Its population increased from 2,000 in 1660 to 40,000 in 1700. The Spanish monarchy had to yield to the evidence of this shift of economic power, and in 1717 the House of Trade was moved to Cádiz.[8]

The Indies Run

Since ancient times commercial activity was one of the fundamental pillars of the Basque economic framework. But the opening of the New World immeasurably stimulated that economy by considerably increasing demand for its two main products: iron from the foundries and ships from the yards.

As already stated, beginning in 1503, Spanish colonial commerce was channeled exclusively through the House of Trade, first in Sevilla and then in Cádiz. The "Indies run," as the transatlantic journey was called,[9] had to leave from and return to a single Spanish port. All merchants wishing to establish commercial relations with the New World were therefore required to direct their ships and goods through the monopoly's central seat. The Basques were not an exception to this legal norm of the Spanish Crown, and they did not hesitate to augment their former presence, first in Sevilla and then in Cádiz. As usual, they offered their extensive mercantile experience, their skilled sailors, and the basic products of their region. In spite of the measures adopted by Emperor Charles V in 1529 to liberalize commerce,[10] this channeling of trade through a single port was the only means by which private merchants could protect their interests. But a physical presence in the main Andalusian centers was insufficient. Control of the Indies run would go to those who filled the positions of highest responsibility in all the organizations connected to New World traffic—the Council of the Indies, the House of Trade, and the Corporation of Indies' Shippers—as well as the high positions in the state administration. Timely, direct influence in urban centers such as Sevilla and Cádiz through control of the city halls and ecclesiastical councils was also of vital importance, as was control of the financial resources.

A quick check of the lists of people that occupied the principal posts of the administrative framework of the House of Trade in the sixteenth, seventeenth, and eighteenth centuries—treasurers, chief justices, judges, district attorneys, accountants, and commission merchants—researched by some of the most prestigious scholars of the subject,[11] clearly demonstrates that the Basque population residing in Andalusia held a disproportionately high number of such positions. Thus, among others, Domingo Ochandiano, Andrés Munibe, José de Veitia Linaje, and Francisco Alberro were treasurers. Martín de Oña, Bernabé de Otálora, Pedro Uribe, Manuel de Murguía, and Alberto de Isasi were among the chief justices. Bernardo Díaz de Argandoña was the best-known district attorney of the office.[12] His work was often decisive when it came to protecting the economic interests of the Basque community in Andalusia in relation to the other Spanish merchants and businessmen that participated in the Indies run. In 1593, for example, to the benefit of the Basque shipyards, Basques convinced Philip II to prohibit ships built in Sevilla, Cádiz, Puerto de Santa María, and Huelva from forming part of the convoys to Nueva España and the American continent.

Natives of the Basque Country—by expressed desire of the House of Trade sometimes and royal decree at others—also occupied many positions of responsibility at sea, such as captains, generals, and admirals in the Indies run.[13] Thus, the Gipuzkoans Diego de Alcega (1585) and his brother Juan (nephews of the former archbishop of Sevilla, Don Cristóbal de Rojas y Sandoval) and Martín Pérez de Olazabal (1589) stood out in the sixteenth-century fleet of Nueva España. Throughout the seventeenth century, the following Basques captained this squadron: Alonso de Chaves Galindo (1603), Juan Fuertes de Portu (1604), Juan Gutierrez Garibay (1605 and 1610), López Díaz de Armendariz (marquis of Cadeira) (1607, 1611, 1617–1622, and 1634), Antonio de Oquendo (1612, 1614, and 1625), Carlos de Ibarra (1619 and 1635–1637), Alonso de Múxica (1627 and 1630), Miguel de Chazarreta (1627 and 1630), Martín de Orbea (1639), Pedro de Ursúa (1642), Diego de Egües (1656), and Fernández de Saldivar (1683). A lesser number of Basques took part in the fleet for the American continent. Nevertheless, Captains Miguel de Eraso (1587), Juan de Urbina Apaloa (1589), Juan Gutiérrez Garibay (1597, 1600, and 1602), Martín de Chavarrieta (1620), Juan de Isarraga (1646), and Antonio de Isasi (1646) distinguished themselves by their participation. In addition, several other Basques served as generals of the Royal Armada: Antonio de Oquendo from Donostia (1623 and 1635), Carlos de Ibarra from Eibar (1635–1637), Tomás de Larraspuru from Azkoitia, who specialized in the pursuit of buccaneers and corsairs on the Indies run (1630 and 1632), Juan de Echabarri (1650), Martín de Castaños, Manuel Emparan, and José Manuel Goicoa. At least eight captains general, six admirals, and a large number of other officers with names of Basque origin also appear on the officers' lists that made up part of the Windward Armada between 1640 and 1750.[14] The same can be said about the Armada of the South Seas, in which Basque surnames were common among high officials, including Martín Oriondo, Martín de Famalbide, Diego Sorricoleta, Juan de Urdanegui, Juan de Mengolea, Juan Pérez de Luzurriaga, Domingo de Iturri Gaztelu, and Dionisio López de Artunduaga.[15]

Beginning in 1524, the House of Trade of Sevilla was subordinated to the powerful, new Royal and Supreme Council of the Indies.[16] Its importance and prestige, obvious from its title, conferred power upon its officers. From its foundation to the early eighteenth century, a large number of natives of Bizkaia, Araba, Gipuzkoa, and Navarre held some of the highest positions in the Council of the Indies. Among its advisors were the following Basques: Juan González de Urquieta, Luis de Oyanguren (1662–1668), Diego de Ibarra (1676), Pedro Gamarra Urquizu (1675–1678), Jerónimo de Eguía (1680–1682), José de Veitia y Linaje (1677–1685), José Arredondo (1687–1691), Juan de Larrea (1697–1706), Francisco Colón de Larriátegui (1697–1699), Antonio Aranguren y Zubiate (1699–1701), and Mateo Ibañez de Mendoza (1700). Juan López de Zubizarreta (1567–1590), Tomás de Ayardi (1578–1603), Martín de Aróstegui (1587–1590), Juan de Oriar (1638), Juan de Subiza (1638–1649), Manuel de Plaza y Lazárraga (1645–1647), and José de Manurga y

Vera (1654–1683) served as accountants. Ulloa de Luyando (1558–1559), Francisco Eraso (1559–1570), his brother Antonio Eraso (1571–1586), Antonio González de Legarda (1626–1628), Gregorio de Leguía (1650–1659), Juan de Veitia Linaje (1677–1682), Francisco de Amolaz (1684–1691), Antonio Ortíz de Otálora (1684–1691), Juan de Larrea (1691–1694), and Manuel Apérregui (1700) were secretaries. Dr. Verástegui (1550–1551), Jerónimo de Ulloa (1562–1567), Lope de Gamboa (1567–1571), and Pedro de Gamarra y Arriaga (1699–1702) were among the noteworthy attorneys general.[17]

As was already mentioned, the other great managing organization of Spanish commercial traffic to America was the Consulate of Sevilla, created through a royal provision dated August 23, 1543. With time, it became the authentic managing organ of mercantile traffic with the Indies, relegating the House of Trade to the role of simple intermediary between the merchants and the Crown. The wide range of functions that the Consulate performed amply justified the efforts of members of the Basque community in Andalusia to procure control of it at all costs. Thus, from 1636 onward, some native of the Basque Country almost always occupied the posts of prior and consul of this organization. Lorenzo López Eceiza (1685–1692), Antonio de Legorburu (1693–1695), and Ramón Torrezar (1696–1703) are good examples.

In addition, posts within the municipal and ecclesiastical institutions of both Sevilla and Cádiz were objects of desire to Basques involved in the Indies run. Especially in the time of the Hapsburgs, the possession of one of a number of posts in the city halls and ecclesiastical council "was an honor for him who obtained it since they were fully aristocratic and could have also been a good business for his personal income and the rights that he administrated."[18] These municipal councils exercised authority over an extensive jurisdiction in which they approved selection of certain positions, named castle wardens, collected certain taxes, and demanded the rendering of services when the Crown called for them. Men of the Basque community in Sevilla came to occupy some of the highest municipal positions—head prosecutor, assistant prosecutor, head bailiff, police chief, mayor, *venticuatros* (equivalents of present-day councilmen), jurors, and clerks. Thus, for example, Domingo Echevarria (1662), Juan Fernández Orizco (1665), Pedro Olarte (1702), Pedro Ibañez (1711), Juan M. Vivero (1767), and Jimeno de Bertendoa (1774) were *venticuatros;* Lorenzo Ignacio Ibarburu y Galdona (1719) was police chief of Sevilla; Juan M. Uriortúa served as head prosecutor in 1779, assisted by Ramón Larumbe and Martín Uztáriz. Basques were also notably present in the municipal administration of Cádiz, as the House of Trade and the Consulate were moved there with all of their dependencies and, therefore, the center of mercantile power of the Indies run. In the eighteenth century, Juan Vicente Arteaga y Ochoa, Juan A. Uztáriz, Carlos Olarte, Miguel Iribarren, and Bartolomé de Alsasua were aldermen-for-life on Cádiz's municipal council; Juan M. Aguirre, Ignacio Zubirtuaga, Agustín Villota,

Joaquín Zuloaga, Juan Sorozábal, Juan Francisco de Leceta, Pedro M. Basoa, and Cristóbal Javier Iztúriz, among other Basques, were elected aldermen; and Manuel Díaz Saravia was one of many that served as deputy of commoners.

The Gipuzkoan Cristóbal de Rojas y Sandoval occupied the highest office of the Archdiocese of Sevilla in the sixteenth century. The canon and chancellor Andrés Ibarburu y Galdona and the master of ceremonies Adrián Elosu formed a part of the cathedral council in the seventeenth century, as did the archdeacon José Antonio Bizarrón and the canon Francisco José Olazabal in the eighteenth century.

Finally, it was also Basques, in close collaboration with foreign businessmen, who spearheaded the first banking initiatives in sixteenth-century Atlantic Andalusia. Juan Iñiguez, Domingo de Lizarraga, Pedro de Morga, Pedro Arriarán, Jimeno de Bertendona, and Juan de Arregui were among the noteworthy pioneers. These financial projects failed completely, however. The infrequency of the fleets from America and the Crown's seizure of the shipments, as well as the constant bankruptcies of Philip II's Royal Treasury, were the main impediments to prosperity of the banking sector in Andalusia. Even with all this, a group with great economic power—primarily merchants, industrialists, and shipowners—consolidated their position in the seventeenth century as buyers of precious metals. Their agenda consisted of purchasing the silver brought from America by individuals, refining it, and transforming it into legal tender in the Mint House. This was a risky business that could bring either great fortune or complete bankruptcy, as demonstrated by the cases of the Bizkaians Juan Ochoa Iurretauría in 1640 and Pedro Galdona in 1709, respectively. Significant evidence of the Basque primacy in this dangerous activity is that in the second half of the seventeenth century the number of buyers of gold and silver was reduced to six, all of them natives of the Basque Country: Juan Ochoa Iurretauría, Pedro Galdona, the Arriolas, Pedro Aramburu, Juan Cruz Gainza, and Lorenzo Ibarburu.

Whales and Cod

It has been frequently affirmed—and not without reason—that the commercial nature of the Basques has always stood out because of their constant foresight, exercised for centuries. The 1700s provided the clearest demonstration: commercial activities carried out by the natives of the seven Basque provinces reached their apogee. As already indicated, commerce has been one of the traditional occupations of the maritime Basque people. Already in the early Middle Ages, this activity was becoming a natural element in the economic structure of the Basque Country. By the late Middle Ages, it became one of the basic components of the Basque economy. In addition to generating significant amounts of income in itself, commerce permitted the development of the industrial sector. Its strategic position—a horseback ride from France to Castile, between Aragón and the Cantabrian—would make the Basque Country a prime crossroads of international mercantile transactions.

First there was whale hunting and cod fishing. Although these activities were practiced in medieval times, they reached their peak between 1500 and 1700. Great strides were made in whaling in the provinces of Bizkaia and Gipuzkoa in the southern Basque Country (i.e., Hegoalde) between 1520 and 1600, but the practice declined in the seventeenth century. The French Basque territory (Iparralde), however, experienced an increase in the scope of its fishing during the seventeenth and eighteenth centuries. The whale was native to the Basque coast from ancient times. Originally, only beached whales were exploited; later, they were captured at sea using small rowing vessels. As the years passed, and techniques, materials, and experience evolved, the Basques increased the number of kills and moved to more western coasts—Cantabria, Asturias, Galicia—to head out in search of the prized cetaceans on their migratory route into the Gulf of Bizkaia, driven by the dominant warm currents. The prolonged campaigns were complete successes, generating an industry on a grand scale. The whale was seen as an inexhaustible source of wealth. Every part was used: the blubber, after conversion into whale oil, was used as a lamp oil and a lubricant; the meat, as food; the tongue, from which a pure oil was obtained, was practical for greasing clocks; the hide; the baleen, when well treated, became combs and diverse utensils, such as frames for the finest women's corsets. Soap was also obtained, and if the whale had ambergris in its stomach, this was used for making medicines, perfumes, and cosmetics. Even the skeleton was used as a construction material.

The profitability of this activity was evident. Whale hunting thus became a highly organized enterprise from early on. And Basque whalers gained a reputation as experienced sailors skilled in the use of the harpoon and boning knife. Their mastery in the art of hunting and navigation was recognized in the most important ports of Europe, cities in which the Basques were already firmly established in the fifteenth century, performing a wide variety of commercial roles: wool and iron exporters, transporters, mercenaries, fishermen, and pirates. It was precisely in these seats that natives of the Basque Country received news of the voyages undertaken by the Venetian John Cabot (1497) and the Portuguese Corterreal brothers along the Canadian coasts. A virgin fishing area was brought to the attention of the Old World. The Basques—accompanied by British, Portuguese, Dutch, and Bretons—did not hesitate to head for the northern seas in search of the green cod so frequently talked about on the docks of Europe. And thus they reached the waters of Iceland and Greenland, from there navigating toward the Canadian coast. There, as had been asserted, they found precious schools of fish incomparable in magnitude to any known at that time. In addition to being abundant, the cod was of the finest quality. And, it was during this search for cod that the Basque sailors encountered the first whales of Terranova.

From the beginning of the sixteenth century, the Basques maintained strong trade relationships with the American continent. In the 1530s the whaling campaigns began to reach an industrial level far superior to that carried out on the Iberian Atlantic coast. The Basques of Iparralde, excluded from the commercial activities of the Indies run, were especially interested in this enterprise. Thus, in 1520, Pierre de Lhande sought permission from the Council of Bayonne to set sail for Terranova in search of cod and whales. One year later, in 1521, Michel de Segure and Mathieu de Biran also sought the necessary permits for setting out on the same course. In 1527, Bartolomé de Montauser, from Bayonne, left for the Canadian coast; in 1549, Jacques de Ibaceta did the same with the priest Andrés de Ariz. In 1542, the resident of Saint-Jean-de-Luz, Angertor Denisquet, captained the ship *Saint-Espirit* to Terranova with its bay full of barrels and the desire to fill them with whale oil. Such frenetic whale hunting by the continental Basques reached its peak on the coast of Canada around 1598. They had also made Bilbao their base of operations and preeminent business center. The presence of a massive number of Labourdine whaling masters and captains in the consular archives of Bilbao attest to this: Pedro de Susi, Perocho de Urtubai, Miguel de Echeto, Martín Zabaleta, Pedro Sanz, Joanes de Larralde, Joanes de Gasteluzar, Miguel de Amézaga, Miguel de Suarade, Joanes de Arestegui, Joanes de Araneder, Marticot de Echevarri, Martín Sáez de Arexmendi, Joanes de Echevarri, Joanes de Arrazu, Esteban de Iriarte, Joanes de Farga, Sabat de Lasala, Juan Gais, Pelen Dugarana, Miquelón de Ansogarlo, Juanot de Arreche, Martín Sáez de Lizardi, Joanes de Aranybar, Marticot de Garalde, Beltrán de la Ronda, Juan Loco, Martín de Larraegui, Pietre Sáez de Agorreta, Oyer de Arriaregari, Martín Sáez de Ibaneta, Marticot de Inorai, Juaneto de Arrese, Joanes de Irigoyen, Basco de Mendi, Sabat de Larregui, Joanot de Arrazabal, Martín de Iparraguire, Joanes de Zuricarai, Joanes de Bidarte, Martín de Miranda, Miguel de Oyarzábal, Joanes de Ugarte, Ogero de Challa, and Joanes de Oyhagaray.[19]

The whaling enthusiasm soon moved to the peninsular Basque coast, where numerous Gipuzkoans and Bizkaians achieved great success in the Terranovan whaling business during the sixteenth and seventeenth centuries. Among the most noteworthy were Martín Cardel, Domingo de Albistur, Pablo de Aramburu, Francisco de Illareta, Martín Sáez de Echave, Domingo de Mendaro, Miguel de Iturain, Joanes de Lizarza, Miguel Eguzquiza, Martín Ruiz de Echave, José Pérez de Hoa, Domingo de Gorocica, Martín de Zaldivia, Cristóbal Arias, Juan de Anzonegui, Martín Ochoa de Irazabal, Martín Davile de Aguirre, Juan de Ochoa, Domingo de Sarasu, Juan de Espilla, Andrés de Alzola, Pedro Ochoa Arriola, Esteban Lete, Domingo Gauchegui, Miguel de Irasa, Ramón de Arrieta, Juan Zubieta, Juan Martínez de Careaga, Rodrigo Legarra, García de Uribe, Martín Pérez de Idiaquez, Domingo López Izarra, Miguel Cerain, Juan Armendia, Juan Bolívar, Juan Igarza, Antonio de Erauso, and Miguel de Erauso.

The royal legislation regarding whaling activity oscillated between permissiveness and prohibition in that period, always according to the needs of the Crown. It is clear, however, that the captures reached extremely high levels and the yields were substantial, both of which favored the uninterrupted continuation of this activity until the eighteenth century. From the permanent bases in Canada where the catch was processed—whales boned and their oil gathered, and cod washed, dried, and salted—and, after sailing two thousand nautical miles, the ships completed their voyage and arrived at the main Spanish ports (Santander, Alicante, Cádiz, and Bilbao). But it was via the Nervión River that one-fourth of all the fish consumed in the kingdom would be introduced, a total estimated at about 400,000 quintals yearly (40 million kilos, 88 million pounds). The ships that carried both the cod and the precious whale products to Bilbao anchored at the docks of Olabeaga, from where various barges transported them to Bilbao's Arenal for storage and later redistribution among the numerous authorized consignee firms that existed at the time. The great majority of these were managed by noteworthy people of the city that combined their status (occasionally noble) with their business interests. As is known, commerce was highly esteemed among the residents of the Basque Country. The following list is a small sample of the merchants from Bilbao and the merchandise that they were consigned in the eighteenth century:[20]

Business Firm	Products
Juan Abasolo	Flax, whale baleen, liquor, lard, cod
J. Fernando Aldayturriaga	Pressed wood, whale baleen, wines, cinnamon
Nicolás Arana	Linens, hides, whale oil, sugar, cacao, cloves, cheeses
Juan Archer	Cod, liquor, capers
Daniel Arthum	Cod
Lorenzo Barrow	Cod, cured meats, ciders, wheat
Pedro Beckwelt	Cod, salmon, bait, fat, sugar, molasses, cacao, wax, rum, wood, tinplate, flour
Widow and Sons of Brodiers	Fishing tackle, tar, resin, hardware, cod, salmon, molasses, cacao, liquor, beer, grains
Browne and Laules	Salmon, cod, lard, slag, hides
Darrigues and Lavigne	Cod, salmon, herring, fat, lard, preserves, cacao, sugar, cloves, hardware, tin, books
Dubrocq Brothers	Utensils, hardware, cod, salmon, pepper, beer, lard, lampreys
Juan Bautista Echevarria	Whale baleen, cheeses
José Eguia	Burlaps, cod, salmon, cheeses, linseed oil, white lead
Gardoqui and Sons	Cod, salmon, slag, sardines, wines, cacao, sugar, rice

Business Firm	Products
Gomez and Barrena	Cod, cheeses
Ventura Gomez de la Torre	Cod, starch, herring, fat, bait, sugar, cacao, pepper, cheeses, sails, wheat
Gonzalo del Rico	Linens, cloths, utensils, cod, smoked salmon, herring, lard, wines, cheeses, sails, fruit, cacao, pepper, books
Hody and Bowy	Linens, cloth, sugar, cacao, oil, cod, raisins, green herring, tin, copper
Juan Iraurgui	Cod, salmon, fat, almonds, raisins, olives, brooms, ceramics, cacao
Juan Larralde	Linens, watches, sugar, tobacco, cloves, pepper, salt, cod, bait, lard, cookies, wines
Pedro Larrauri	Cod, slag, liquor
Miguel Leoz y Ripa	Whale oil, cheeses, liquor
Linch, Kelly, and Moroni	Drugstore goods, bottles, hides, salt, logwood, cod, bass, salmon, herring, cured meats, fat, lard, cheeses, sails, wood, copper, tin, flour
Francisco Ignacio Orueta	Cod, salmon, lampreys, fat, lard, cacao, pepper, cinnamon, tinplate
Juan de la Pedrueza	Cod, salmon, fish pâté, lard, hides
Domingo Recacoechea	Drugstore goods, sugar, cacao, wax, copper, shot, cod
José Rojas	Cod, sardines, fat, liquor, cinnamon, linens
Enrique Santaulary	Wine, cod, slag
Sarachaga Brothers	Cod, salmon, lard, sugar, cloves, hazelnuts
Juan Smith	Cod, hides, lard, cured meats, chacolí
Juan Villavaso and Co.	Cod, salmon, lard, ceramics, bottles, linens, charcoal
Antonio Zubillaga	Linens, whale baleen, paper, books, utensils, watches

Basque North American commercial cod fishing and whaling, so healthy and prosperous for years, radically changed beginning in the late seventeenth century.[21] Until then, the Spanish Crown had not seen the necessity of legalizing the navigation, fishing, and seasonal stay in Terranova of its citizens through capture or declaration of sovereignty in relation to the rest of the European powers, as these practices had been common and long developed by its Bizkaian and Gipuzkoan subjects. Louis XIV's France, to the contrary, hastened to take possession of Terranova. This circumstance restricted the fishing activity of the Gipuzkoans and Bizkaians from then on, and caused the fortunes of the fishermen from Iparralde to prosper. Basque sailors and whalers became subject to endless politico-administrative obstacles. They could be easily spared, however. Sometimes, this was thanks to the diplomats of Charles II. At others, it was due to the Bizkaian and Gipuzkoan ability to fish under the French flag in American waters or their frequent financing of French expeditions, both facilitated by the tradition of camaraderie between the Basque seamen from the two sides of the border.

But the situation of Basque cod and whale merchants worsened beginning in 1713 with the signing of the Treaty of Utrecht. The treaty put an end to the War of Spanish Succession and recognized Philip V as the new Spanish monarch, and France transferred sovereignty of Terranova to England. Thus, beginning in 1715, the British authorities refused the Basques fishing rights in those waters. The untenable situation provoked heated protests and complaints from the Basque seamen against the new Bourbon monarch. He was forced to intervene in numerous forums during the eighteenth century. It was a question of respecting a customary right—one that neither the laws nor the British government would consider. All the negotiations for recovering this ancestral right of open access to the fishing waters of Terranova, exhaustively recognized in the Treaty of Utrecht, were in vain. Bizkaia and Gipuzkoa, noteworthy fishing pioneers on the banks of the Canadian coast and in commerce with North America, were thereby displaced from this lucrative activity. The Basque attempts to outwit the British obstacles to fishing were useless. They were forced to supply themselves through French or English merchants. They also had to frequent other waters for whaling, those of the North Sea. The supply of salted fish depended on French and English ports until 1763. That year, the French government definitively ceded control of Canada to the English, giving Great Britain exclusive control of the European cod market. The merchants of Bilbao were then directly supplied from North America, especially the ports of Boston, Jersey, and Salem.

The situation did not improve in the decades of the 1770s and 1780s. The revolt of the American colonies against the English Crown interdicted commercial cod traffic with European ports. At that time, Bilbao saw its mercantile relations with Boston, Salem, Virginia, and Charleston interrupted due to systematic blockades by the British Navy. Beginning in 1783, once the American War of Independence was finished, the networks were revived, but without Basques abandoning the Baltic routes that would serve as a complement to North American commerce until the end of the century.

The Iron That Forged Colonial America

Like the rest of the socioeconomic indicators of the Basque Country, the iron industry—based on the traditional extraction of the Bizkaian mineral—experienced a period of strong consolidation and great prosperity. The profound transformations in this sector, always closely related to foreign demand and the political circumstances of the moment, were determined by the historic development of both Bizkaia and Gipuzkoa.

Two reasons stand out for the moderate recovery experienced by the Basque iron industry at the beginning of the modern era. On one hand, the structural changes in the Basque economy during the late Middle Ages—increase of agricultural production and growth in the ship industry—generated a rising demand for farm tools and iron equipment in general. On the other, the appearance of modern nation-states arose from the development of armies and a political climate in which a nation's ability to maneuver depended in good measure on its capacity for war. Thus, from the reign of the Catholic Monarchs to the imperial raids of the Hapsburgs, the necessity for armaments soared for a Spanish monarchy wishing to successfully wage its numerous military campaigns. The discovery of America, the rise of an unlimited colonial market, the arrival of abundant shipments of precious metals, as well as the development of plans for construction, industrialization, and navigation in the New World constituted the final call that the Basque iron industry needed for its inception, boom, and consolidation. Other factors were also influential: the development of the means of both land and sea transport in America; the growing demand for military equipment with which to carry out the process of conquest; and demand for construction materials and farm tools, indispensable in the colonizing undertaken after 1492. For developing the American economy, iron, processed or raw, became an article of prime necessity. The mining sector generated the greatest demand for iron products, given the need for quicksilver, hand tools, fuel, hydraulic rams, ore grinders, and other such goods. Also, with the new textile industries created in the New World, thanks to the stimulus of the Crown and the Indies authorities, the demand for hardware and special iron utensils took off. The naval factories also became very important in the time of the Hapsburgs. And thus, the most important American shipyards (Havana, Panama, Cartagena, and Guayaquil) demanded a great deal of equipment and tools from Spain. These came mostly from the Basque Country. Lastly, the sugar refineries that were being opened in the New World, prototypes of the extraordinary agro-industrial plants developed in America starting at the end of the sixteenth century, also needed a variety of tools in great quantity to function, as well as carts, hardware, and replacement parts for mills. In this context, the Basque foundries discovered an excellent, inexhaustible market in the Americas.

Thus, the favorable conjuncture of events in the creation of the American market propelled the development of the Basque foundries and, in the long run, defined their later leap into modern industrialization. For almost a millennium, they had been the basic unit of local industry. They arose with a clear export mission, the only way to compensate for the trade deficit of a land that needed to import grain and other subsistence products. Their work methods experienced an important change in the fifteenth century, moving from traditional charcoal to hydraulic energy. Thus, the harshest tasks of human labor were gradually taken over by the rivers. This substantial technical development, combined with the convenience of the supply of iron ore, transport and distribution of metal manufactures, the high quality of its rich vein of ore and the resulting goods, and the privileged geographic location, placed Basque iron production in an advantageous position with respect to the rest of the European producers during the early centuries of the modern era. It makes sense that the Spanish Crown protected this rich source of income to such an extent, and reserved Bizkaian and Gipuzkoan iron for the Spanish and American markets. The Crown also conceded a special customs rate that allowed the Basque Provinces to freely import the consumer goods that its population demanded.

Table 2.1 in appendix 2 provides the official figures for the important volume of Basque iron and steel products exported to America in the sixteenth and seventeenth centuries. Examining the table, one can conclude that until 1600 the global volume of Basque iron that manufactures shipped to the New World via the port of Sevilla remained at significant levels, reaching 30,000 quintals (3 million kilos, 6,600,000 pounds) in 1596. Nevertheless, from the early decades of the seventeenth century on, excepting deviations in 1605 and 1608, the quantity of exports decreased steadily. According to some authors, the explanation rests in the lacunae in existing documentation and the intensification of illegal commerce that evaded detection and, therefore, quantification. This must be the case, if it is recognized that Atlantic mercantile traffic peaked precisely during these early decades of the seventeenth century. Nevertheless, what is certain is that around that time, Basque iron production, technically outdated and threatened by foreign competition in both America and Spain, had partly stopped focusing on external trade. Although the export levels from 1643, 1646, and 1647 stand out in the 1640s, exceeding 8,000 quintals (800,000 kilos, 1,760,000 pounds), it would not be until 1668 that Basque manufactures shipped abroad would regain the importance that they had at the end of the sixteenth century. Beginning with that year, a notable improvement is evident: more than 83,000 quintals in the decade of the 1670s, 68,000 in the 1680s, and over 132,000 (13,200,000 kilos, 29,040,000 pounds) in the last ten years of the century.[22]

As can also be appreciated in light of the data shown in table 2.1 in appendix 2, iron—processed and raw—occupied a privileged position in the overall calculation of Basque metal exports to America. This material was of primary necessity in the complex colonial economic framework. On the other hand, thanks to the agricultural development occurring in America from the beginning of the sixteenth century, especially in the regions of Nueva España, the Caribbean, and some areas of the viceroyalty of Peru, the New World became an excellent market for tools and other equipment made in the foundries of the Basque Country. The large shipments that were sent to those lands, especially beginning in the second half of the seventeenth century, make sense in this context. Lastly, it is worth noting that the export of nails to America from Basque workshops was moderate. Such manufactures, also considered critical due to their multiple potential uses, were preferentially bought in Flanders, especially from the first quarter of the 1600s on.

But the outlook for commerce in iron would change substantially beginning in the early years of the eighteenth century. The War of Spanish Succession of 1700, and the sharp drop in prices of Basque iron and steel products in European markets, represented the low point of an industrial depression for Bizkaian and Gipuzkoan foundries that had begun to show its first signs in the mid-1600s. From then on, Basque industries had to face strong foreign competition. Sweden, Belgium, and Italy began to introduce their metallurgic products into the Spanish Empire through several Iberian ports. Basque iron entered a state of decline from which it would recover due only to the revolutionary technical transformations at the end of the nineteenth century.[23] Thus, and in reference to the American market, the traditional monopoly enjoyed by the Basque Country was reduced to the commerce of semiprocessed iron in its distinct varieties—jimmies, grating, platinum, thin and thick pieces, irons, squares, wheelbarrow bodies—and of farm tools and material used in the naval and armament industries of the New World. In other words, the Basque traffic in iron would be limited from then on to the commercialization of metallic goods of lesser mercantile value, although those in greatest demand, a fact always kept in mind by ship outfitters and captains when the time came to calculate freight cost and load value. In addition to the wide range of high-quality products from Sweden, Denmark, Italy, Flanders, France, and Germany, the Basque iron industry also had to compete with other Spanish industrial complexes. Especially beginning in the 1760s, such national rivals fought to make headway in both the Spanish and colonial markets. Thus, for example, after the War of Spanish Succession (1700–1713) the iron and steel factories of Liérganes and La Cavada (Cantabria) underwent a phase of strong expansion that would last until 1759. The workshops of Sevilla and Toledo began to make tools and arms of a caliber comparable to those forged in Bilbao, Durango, or Bergara. And at the end of 1725, Philip V launched what would be the fifth Spanish foundry and the eighth blast furnace of Spain near Ronda (Málaga). Moreover, by that time, other highly profitable industrial complexes in Eugui (Navarre), El Ferrol, and Gerona had arisen.

In view of the situation, the Basque colony living in Sevilla, conscious of the threat to its longstanding monopoly, undertook actions in the Consulate of Sevilla to ensure the prohibitions on foreign iron imports throughout the kingdom, including America. They also insisted that the Basque Provinces had enough iron goods to satisfy the New World's demands. And they underscored the grave damage that both national and foreign competition were causing to their metal manufactures, which was the main export of the Basque Country. These protests achieved the desired results to some degree. In 1702, the Crown reaffirmed the prohibitions decreed in 1675 with regard to the entry of foreign iron and its derivatives into America. Nevertheless, Philip V's interventions in 1725 and 1739 on behalf of the Basque commission and the Association of Basques of Sevilla against the commercialization of non-Basque iron in America clearly shows that the disrespect for the law protecting Basque foundries continued in the eighteenth century. Thus, both foreign European manufactures and those made in various workshops in Spain continued to be strong competition for Basque metal products during the 1700s.

But, in spite of this competition and the adverse combination of crises, the Basque foundries experienced a moderate pace of growth that was reflected in their export volume, as seen in table 2.2 in appendix 2. This was possible due to the British demand—until the 1760s—and the recovery of a good part of the national and colonial markets. The export of iron and steel products to England was considerable in the first half of the eighteenth century: more than 40,000 quintals (4 million kilos, or 8,800,000 pounds) in the decade of the 1720s and around 25,000 in the 1750s. Nonetheless, beginning in 1760, the English market lost importance because the British Isles began to prefer Swedish and Russian iron. The recovery of the national market was more important, given its stimulation by demographic growth and Bourbon policies worried about the restoration of the navy and the transformation of the army. On the American scene, the reformism of the 1800s allowed the institution of a true and coherent economic policy that especially affected the mining industry and its subsidiary sectors. It makes sense that in that century mining would require large quantities of semiprocessed iron, equipment, and nails that the merchants procured in the overseas market and that the Basque workshops made. The construction industries and shipyards were also beneficiaries of Bourbon reformist policies, and agricultural production experienced a general increase. As a consequence of their development, all these activities needed large quantities of metal manufactures that the Basque foundries were in charge of providing, trying to respond to the challenge of increasing demand and foreign competition.

The Basque colony residing first in Sevilla and, from 1717 on, in Cádiz, was in charge of providing an outlet for Basque iron and steel production destined for colonial America. These exports were channeled through the so-called iron or volume companies, founded by those Basque merchants and businessmen that from the beginning of the Indies run had established their residency in the seats of the Spanish commercial monopoly. Generally constituted for a set, relatively short period of time—from three to nine years, and never more than fifteen—these companies were formed by several partners that shared the costs and profits of all transactions. The most common arrangement was one whereby two partners oversaw the company's management: one from Sevilla or Cádiz and the other from the Basque Country. The one living in Andalusia rented the house, store, or warehouse—usually on Castro Street (Sevilla), better known at that time as the "Street of the Vizcayans"—where the headquarters of the company would be established; received the goods shipped from the Basque Country from the partner there; saw to their storage and incorporated them into the company stock; made purchases at the best prices for clients in and near the city; and, most importantly, carried out the loading for the destination in the Americas, either directly or through intermediaries. He ensured the shipments and took care of the books to answer to the other members of the company. For this task, the administrator collected a salary and a per diem. The partner in the Basque Country was entrusted with representing the enterprise and buying goods from the iron merchants at the best prices possible. He also saw to the loading, insured the goods shipped to Andalusia, and did the company's bookkeeping for the transactions that had to be billed to his counterpart in Sevilla. For his work, he received a commission of between 2 and 4 percent. Table 2.3 in appendix 2 lists some of the most noteworthy Basque metallurgical export companies that operated in Sevilla during the time of the Hapsburgs.

But if the commerce in iron and its derivatives was highly profitable for the partners in the iron companies, it clearly was not the only vehicle used by some Basques in Sevilla and Cádiz to amass tremendous fortunes. Although iron commerce was always profitable, Basque businessmen became wealthy from the diversity of their transactions and due to their intervention in multiple sectors of commerce and the economy in general. Thus, the members of the iron companies frequently participated directly in the mercantile traffic of the Americas by shipping other goods that were as profitable, or more so, as metal manufactures. Such was the case of Juan de Irauzqui and Martín de Ibarra, who, in addition to maintaining a partnership with Martín Lope de Isasi and Pedro de Eizaguirre for iron commerce, founded a risk insurance company for ships and merchandise. Juan de Munibe and Juan Martínez de Loyola made a fortune buying logwood in America, which they then placed on the market in Sevilla. Various lots of wine, oil, and tar sent to America were noted on the stock balance sheet drafted upon the closing of the iron company formed by Andrés de Arrizabalaga, Juan de Isasi, Martín Lope de Isasi, and Pedro de Ochoa. The same year, Andrés de Arrizabalaga sent goods destined for the fortifications of Florida on the ship *Espíritu Santo* valued at 3,255,478 *maravedíes;* they consisted of iron, tools, and various merchandise including 500 *arrobas* of oil and 150 casks of sherry from the 1579 harvest. Also, Martín de Arespacochaga, aside from the iron company that he managed with his brother Francisco in Sevilla, ran another for commerce in indigo and blackberry with Francisco de Zuazo in Guatemala. Lastly, the Gipuzkoan Juan García de Arregui spent a good part of his time buying shipments of cloth from Segovia, which he sent to the Americas.

There was no lack of those devoted to the lucrative business of introducing slaves into the new continent. Although it was in the last third of the fifteenth century that Sevilla, along with Lisbon, would constitute the most important slave market on the Iberian Peninsula, this traffic would peak in the sixteenth century; this was an epoch in which Sevilla served as a magnet for all mercantile activities. Not only the merchants of the Consulate but the general population of Sevilla participated in the slave trade. As can be seen in table 3.1, the Basque businessmen were not an exception to the norm.

The Privileged Companies

The arrival of the eighteenth century witnessed a new dynasty on the Spanish throne, the Bourbons, with the coronation of Philip V in May 1701. The new royal house ushered in a period of reforms—social, political, religious, administrative, cultural, and economic—that would reach its peak during the reign of Charles III, the monarch of the Enlightenment par excellence; it would last throughout the entire age of Enlightenment.[24]

Rebuilding Spain administratively was the point of departure of this new reformist policy whose principal objective was fomentation of central authority and state expansion. Thus, like their French relatives, the Spanish Bourbons aspired to build an economically rich and politically powerful kingdom. In short, stimulation of the country's productive forces and promotion of its material prosperity would contribute—in the judgment of the new dynasty—to the fortification of monarchic absolutism within the country and the development of a more aggressive international policy.

Within the monarchy's commitment to regeneration, the essential motor of growth was the promotion of commerce and, particularly, regulation of mercantile relations with the American colonies. As mercantilists of the Enlightenment, the Spanish leaders were convinced that only a favorable trade balance would facilitate the steady flow of American precious metals into the country. They were also aware that this would be impossible without the creation of some exclusive markets, and saw colonial commerce as the most suitable means in their power to achieve the proposed objectives. The Spanish Bourbons viewed recapture of this commerce from foreign control and its conversion into a key instrument in the broader economic reconstruction as their most pressing necessity.

Since the early years of the seventeenth century, America had been the stage on which other European powers became established. Before then, Portuguese and Spaniards had managed to preserve the territorial integrity of their respective overseas possessions through force. But the impossibility of completely settling such a vast territory made a good part of America appear to be a no-man's-land for the rest of the European powers. The old papal titles were worthless in a reformed Europe that did not obey the Holy See—England, Denmark, and Holland—or, like France, put national interests and matters of state before such obedience. Thus, between 1598 and 1618, and at the same time that a period of international peace was curiously unfolding in Europe, an ambitious commercial process emerged. It projected

TABLE 3.1 *Introduction of Slaves into the Americas by Basque Merchants, 1586–1599*

Year	Merchant	Slaves	Destination	Ship
1586	A. de Urquizu	2	Mainland	S. Salvador
1586	J. de Zaldivar	8	Peru	San Juan
1589	A. de Urquizu	15	—	—
1590	L. de Aldas	2	Honduras	N.S. Rosario
1592	J. Jaúregui	1	Cartagena	San Gabriel
1593	M. Jaúregui	1	Mainland	El Angel
1594	J. de Ibarra	1	Nueva España	Buen Jesús
1594	J. de Olano	2	Margarita Is.	N.S. Guía
1594	J. de Uribe	4	Mainland	San Juan
1594	J. Iturrieta	3	Cartagena	S. Salvador
1594	A. de Larreátegui	1	Nueva España	La Concepción
1594	J. Pérez Zubiaurre	1	Nueva España	S. Gregorio
1594	I. de Atienza	1	Margarita Is.	S. Francisco
1594	J. Aristizabal	1	Nueva España	La Trinidad
1595	F. Zulueta	1	Nueva España	Sta. Catalina
1596	M. de Luzuriaga	2	Cartagena	La Asunción
1596	Lope de Munibe	1	Peru	La Magdalena
1597	D. de Aréchaga	1	Nueva España	Sta. Catalina
1598	P. López Verástegui	1	Cartagena	N.S. Rosario
1598	Pedro Iturralde	2	Cartagena	Jesús, Mª, José
1598	D. de Zárate	1	Portobelo	—
1599	J. de Loyola	1	Nueva España	La Trinidad

Source: García Fuentes, 1991, 66.

into all corners of the world governed by mercantilist norms and the old concept of world equilibrium, in which the colonial enclaves played a fundamental role. Imbued with this political economic ideal, Holland, England, Portugal, and France burst on the Spanish-American scene through smuggling and piracy. The result was the loss of exclusive Spanish continental hegemony in the Americas. Facing this prospect, the Bourbon monarchy considered political changes and reforms that would straighten the course of the Spanish colonial economic imperative. From 1700 on, rationalizing and intensifying the export of American riches and propping up the old structure of the commercial monopoly were the new Spanish Enlightenment leaders' goals for America. The first changes were put into practice after the end of the War of Spanish Succession in 1713. Thus, the definitive transfer of the House of Trade and the Consulate from Sevilla to Cádiz in 1717 was followed in 1720 by the publication of the *Project for Galleons and Fleets, of Peru and Nueva España, and for the registered and dispatch ships that might sail for both kingdoms.*[25]

But, beyond a doubt, the great reform of the early eighteenth century was the creation of privileged commercial or trade companies. A novel mercantile policy was put into practice in Spain with the new century. Patterned after that instituted by the major European colonial powers (England, Holland, and France), it attempted to reconcile the interests of private merchants with more general national ones. The system chosen consisted in the concession of licenses for the establishment of companies of commerce and sailing. In turn, these licenses promoted the participation of the emerging bourgeoisie in American commerce and permitted them to participate directly in the profits of the monopoly. The monarchy also tried to promote a more intensive utilization of the Empire's resources, incorporating territories insufficiently supplied by the traditional system of fleets and galleons in this commerce.[26] The new model for overseas commerce was based on establishing a company through stock offerings that the Crown endowed with exclusive rights in a delimited colonial territory, sometimes underdeveloped or peripheral. Such companies occasionally even assumed the functions of state power within these territories. Their commercial agents therefore directly intervened in both political and military issues thanks to the corsairing privileges conceded by the monarch. But the most significant novelty was that the ships of these mercantile companies were permitted to navigate directly to America from their base ports, bypassing Cádiz. This type of commercial company thus sprang up in Spain during the first half of the eighteenth century. And, in large measure, it would be Basques that spurred almost all of them. A review of the histories of the mercantile companies arising in the 1700s confirms this point.

The first experience in this new field of relations with America was inaugurated in 1714 with the creation of the Company of Honduras. Founded by the Araban Diego de Murga, the marquis of Montesacro, it controlled the trade monopoly in mahogany and dyeing woods from Central America until 1717. The company was definitively liquidated that year after successfully concluding its first and only voyage. Although the results were modest, the Araban initiative left clear that the formation of stockholder companies was feasible in Spain, if they were suitably regulated through royal decrees and granted privileges in order to improve efficiency.

In 1728, the Real Compañía Guipúzcoana de Caracas (Royal Guipuzcoan Company of Caracas) began operations. It was the product of the Province of Gipuzkoa's desire to create within its territory a shareholding company that engaged in traffic with Venezuela. The merchants from Donostia understood well that region's economic potential. The Bizkaian Pedro de Olavarriaga's reports for the viceroy of Nueva Granada left no room for doubt. "It can be assured," wrote Olavarriaga, "that the province of Venezuela would be one of the best and most fertile of all the West Indies if it were cultivated, but the laziness of its natives is so great that in the midst of this abundance they barely find enough to survive."[27] The author based his report on abundant data about the number of cacao trees that could be planted, the potential annual yield of tobacco, and other similar calculations. He also included an open criticism of Spain for the lack of ships that it sent to this region, which left the field open to foreign intrusions.

Facing this situation, and in view of the frugality with which cacao reached Spain from Caracas, the Crown welcomed the application presented by the Province of Gipuzkoa. The Consulate of Donostia sent the then-secretary of the legislature of Gipuzkoa, Felipe de Aguirre, to the court to determine the Crown's conditions for creation of the future company. Within a few weeks, his brilliant negotiations and the invaluable help of his fellow Gipuzkoan Miguel Antonio de Zuaznabar bore the desired fruits. Philip V granted Gipuzkoa a royal decree on September 25, 1728, establishing a company that would supply the province of Venezuela with Spanish products and then transport precious cacao from Caracas to Spain. The company would also have to protect the Venezuelan coast to prevent the smuggling that the English and Dutch regularly carried out there from bases in the Antilles, to the great detriment of Spanish colonial commerce. Although the royal decree granted by Philip V in 1728 did not initially specify the new company's trade monopoly with Venezuela, the Gipuzkoans did not discourage the efforts to put it into practice. Thus, in autumn 1728 the regulations that would govern the destiny of the organization were written up. Working capital of one and a half million pesos was viewed as necessary, since the initial outlay—acquisition of ships for commerce, costs for sailors and coast guard, purchase of goods to sell in the colony, and other expenses—was large. Both the Province of Gipuzkoa and its consulate therefore began a campaign to attract investors. They did not manage to reach their goal, but did raise 706,300 pesos, which turned out to be enough to begin the commercial venture with Venezuela.

The new company displayed a very complete organizational structure. It established a directorship in Donostia composed of five members, plus one secretary and three inspectors responsible for ensuring the reliability of the accounts that were presented to the shareholders' board. In Madrid, Zuaznabar himself would be the commissioner to the court; Santiago de Irisarri, a resident of Cádiz, was designated the company's commission merchant there; and the Bizkaian Pedro de Olavarriaga would occupy the head commissionership in Venezuela.

The undertakings of the Company of Caracas were positive from the outset. Its first ships, the *San Joaquín*, *San Ignacio*, and *Santa Barbara*, set sail for the Americas in 1730. By 1734, a significant distribution of dividends was approved. But if the company was profitable for the shareholders' board, it was no less so for the coffers of the Bourbon Royal Treasury. The Company of Caracas had to pay substantial fees to this institution for the commercial privileges that it enjoyed. Nevertheless, in exchange for the services the Company of Caracas provided to both Philip V's treasury and his defense policy, the Crown granted it more than a few favors. Thus, in July 1742, during the war with the English, the monarch suppressed section 5 of the royal decree of the constitution of the commercial company. The company therefore retained a monopoly on commerce with Caracas. Two years later, in 1744, Philip V permitted the vessels of the Company of Caracas to return directly to their port of origin without having to pass through Cádiz first. The captains of the company's ships were also granted privateering privileges, allowing them to capture English and Dutch smuggling ships that endangered Spanish commerce in Venezuelan waters. In addition, in 1749, the Company of Caracas was granted an increase in its zone of commercial influence to incorporate the regions of Maracaibo, Barinas, and Orinoco. Furthermore, in 1765 the king authorized the company to ship slaves to Venezuela. And, in 1766, the Province of Gipuzkoa was notified of the monarch's desire to support the construction of a large dike in the port of Pasaia.

Services and favors were exchanged between the Crown and the Company of Caracas throughout its whole history. This relationship would progressively languish from 1778 on as a consequence of the Regulations of Free Trade decreed by the government of Charles III. The monopoly of the Company of Caracas in Venezuela would then be replaced by another commercial monopoly, this time in the Philippines. (See table 2.4 in appendix 2 for a list of the ships of the Royal Guipuzcoan Company of Caracas.)

The success of the Company of Caracas stimulated the formation of other similar enterprises. Some did not get beyond the idea phase, however, as in the case of the proposal by the Board of Merchants of Bilbao in 1736 for the creation of the Company of Buenos Aires.[28] From the beginning of the eighteenth century, Río de la Plata was a region that offered great enticements for those in search of wealth or wishing to prosper in the Americas. The members of the Consulate of Bilbao were not an exception, and from the early 1730s they expressed their interest in linking their city's port with Buenos Aires. They gave a variety of reasons for establishing a shareholder company for commerce with Río de la Plata. The population increase experienced by Buenos Aires, Tucumán, and Asunción was the most solid basis for instituting a regular supply system to the area. In addition, in the judgment of the Bilbao merchants the Río de la Plata region had great economic potential, largely due to its livestock production. Moreover, the Royal Treasury would make a profit if the creation of a trading company forestalled the smuggling that both England and Portugal engaged in on a regular basis from Colonia del Sacramento (Uruguay).

Based on these assumptions, the Consulate of Bilbao named José de Zavala y Miranda as its representative in the court, thereby granting him full power to attempt to get a royal decree that would permit the creation of a trading company in Bilbao. But Zavala's actions were not successful. The mercantile initiative in Bilbao collided with the interests of Lima and Cádiz merchants. And, in its inability to control the commerce of Buenos Aires, the Consulate of Lima had established internal customs to prevent Peruvian silver from being rerouted to Río de la Plata. The Consulate of Cádiz also completely rejected any attempt at forming a privileged company that would further reduce the monopoly it had held since 1717. In this situation, José de Zavala unilaterally decided to introduce changes in the initial Bilbao project. Also hoping to overcome the distrust in Lima, he gave assurances that the future company would transport goods only to satisfy the needs of the provinces of Río de la Plata, Tucumán, and Paraguay. In addition, in order to avoid the opposition of Cádiz and stimulate its commercial interest in the Río de la Plata region, he indicated in his report that Buenos Aires was the place in America that consumed the least amount of Andalusian fruit. But Zavala introduced another novelty: Bilbao's commerce with Honduras, which the Crown seemed more inclined to accept on the condition that such traffic be carried out from the port of Castro-Urdiales (Cantabria).

As is logical, this last consideration was a primary reason that Zavala's report was rejected by the Consulate of Bilbao, which did not hesitate to remove him from his position. The Consulate then opted to name another ambassador to the court, responsible for defending a new mercantile project in Madrid. Also oriented toward Río de la Plata, this commercial initiative expressly specified that all goods would be loaded and unloaded in Bilbao. It was presented to the marquis of Ensenada in 1745. Like the previous one, however, it was never implemented, as it was also opposed by Lima and Cádiz. In spite of the failure of the attempts to open the Nervión to direct traffic with Spanish colonial America through a privileged company, the desires of some members of the Basque colony residing in Madrid to capture part of that trade would not fade. They would use the route of Cádiz and settle for a mercantile company that was not privileged and, therefore, more modest. Thus, in 1752, the Company of Buenos Aires was born, fruit of the agreement signed between the Gipuzkoan José de Aguirre Acharan, the Navarrese Pedro de Astruarena e Iturralde and Francisco de Mendinueta.

Another of the privileged shareholding companies born in the eighteenth century as the result of Basque mercantile commitment to developing its activity in the American colonies was the Royal Company of Honduras. Created by a royal decree in 1740, its central base was established in Cuba, from where it exercised the monopoly of commerce of the Caribbean island until the company's definitive liquidation in 1765. Its commercial transactions were diverse. During its first ten years, it was in charge of constructing vessels for the Royal Armada. Later, and through the expressed desire of the monarch Ferdinand VI, the Havana-based company focused its activity on the acquisition and transport of various shipments of tobacco to Spain. And, during the last third of the 1700s, it specialized in buying and selling Cuban sugar there, as well as providing the regular supply of slaves for the island. Its main promoter and first director was the shareholder of the Company of Caracas, Martín de Aróstegui. And like the Caracan company, its main defender in the court was Miguel Antonio de Zuaznabar. Many stockholders of the Caracas company were therefore logically engaged in the Havanan company as active partners.

In spite of the respective mercantile successes of the privileged stock companies, their commercial trajectory declined progressively throughout the second half of the eighteenth century. The liberalizing economic policy undertaken by Charles III in 1765 marked the end of the closed economic system and, consequently, of the monopolies exercised in this sector. Initially, and with the aim of not provoking greater opposition on the part of the fleet merchants that had their interests focused on the main nerve centers of the Empire, the economic policy was applied to marginal areas devoid of silver production; nevertheless, as the results corroborated the success of the policy, it was gradually extended throughout the American territory.

As already stated, the mercantile reforms of Charles III began in 1765 with the publication of the Royal Instruction of October 16, authorizing direct commerce with the Americas through individual ships from nine Spanish ports—Santander, Gijón, La Coruña, Sevilla, Cádiz, Malaga, Cartagena, Alicante, and Barcelona—to five Caribbean islands—Cuba, Santo Domingo, Puerto Rico, Trinidad, and Margarita. This was a trial measure, hence its application in a limited area. But once the economic results were confirmed as satisfactory, consecutive decrees dated 1778 extended this authorization to other Spanish ports—Alfaques de Tortosa, Almeria, Palma de Mallorca, Santa Cruz de Tenerife, Vigo, San Sebastián (1788), and Valencia (1791)—and to other American regions—Guatemala, Cartagena (Colombia), Santa Marta, Portobelo, Chagre, Nueva España, and Venezuela (1789).

In this new liberalizing economic conjuncture—the opening of new ports for commerce with the Americas and suppression of numerous rights that encumbered this mercantile traffic—the privileged companies in which the natives of the Basque Provinces had participated no longer had a reason for being. Even so, in 1785 Charles III still put his seal of approval on a royal decree authorizing the creation of a new mercantile company for commerce with Asia, the Royal Company of the Philippines, an ambitious project in which the Basques had had special interest from the beginning of the 1700s. As has been documented, after the Company of Caracas was launched in 1728, other plans for the creation of companies with different destinations through stock issues soon appeared. One plan presented by four Basque merchants living in Cádiz was to send ships to Manila to traffic in various types of Asian products. But, although this commercial proposal was approved by Philip V, Manuel de Arriola, Francisco de Arteaga, Juan Martínez de Albinagorta, and Juan de Leaequi could not carry out their proposals. Less than a year after the monarch had granted them the necessary permit, the contents of the royal decree approving the creation of the proposed company were changed. The successful mercantile transactions begun by the Company of Caracas led the king to harbor hopes that commerce with the Philippines would also be undertaken through a great stockholder company, and not by backing the four merchants cited. A new royal decree dated 1733 established the basis on which a commercial company with the Philippines would be directed, although one was never founded.

It would not be until March 1785, therefore, that the Royal Company of the Philippines was founded. As in the case of the Havana initiative, the new company for commerce with Asia was created on behalf of the stockholders of the Company of Caracas.[29] The Caracan company had seen its privileges abolished in 1781, and its survival was therefore uncertain. Some shareholders proposed dissolving the company to recover their investments and dividends. Nevertheless, at the last general meeting held by the Company of Caracas in 1785, the then-director of the National Bank of San Carlos, Francisco Cabarrús, from Bayonne, presented a positive vision of the company's future. After pondering the profits that it had reported and considering what such a company could mean for the state, he proposed that the Company of Caracas change its purview to linking the American and Asian markets, serving the Philippine Islands as the focal point. The idea was not rash. In the way that the initiative was posed, instead of reaching Asia through foreign mediation, American silver would go there directly through the Spanish, who would then retain the profits that others were receiving. The future company would obtain this silver in exchange for the Spanish products that would supply America and the American goods that became popular in Asian markets. Moreover, the Philippines could also supply a great many goods in high demand in Asia and Europe. After this optimistic exposition, Cabarrús specified the concessions that the future company had to seek from the monarch. These may be summarized as follows:

1. Free commerce with America on an equal basis with the rest of the merchants
2. Near exclusivity on commerce with the Philippines for twenty years, leaving their residents free to trade with India
3. Exclusive wholesale rights on spices and goods from India in a Spanish port
4. Availability of one or two ports of arrival on the return route around the Cape of Good Hope from the Philippines

In exchange for such prerogatives, the company would promise the king to develop the cultivation of sugar and various spices, saving the state almost 3 million pesos a year, maintain armed ships with privateering privileges to combat the pirates in those waters, and to build any ships ordered by the Royal Treasury. The project, which was enthusiastically accepted by the shareholders' board of the Company of Caracas, became a reality within eight months. The majority of the partners of the former Caracan company thereby reinvested their titles and profits, raising more than 16 million reales. The new company managed to reap magnificent dividends in its first years. English and Dutch piracy, however, as well as the wars of the Napoleonic epoch, inevitably ruined an enterprise whose fixed costs had been established by the extravagant expectations of the ministerial dreamers. In 1834, it folded once and for all in the wake of constant difficulties.

In sum, it has been shown that Basque participation was decisive in the creation of privileged companies for colonial commerce in the 1800s. And this was so even though the Basque ports were not formally authorized to contract directly with America.

Enlightenment Colonial Commerce and Its Scope

The eighteenth century, commonly considered the greatest mercantile century in the history of the Spanish Empire, witnessed commercial deployment of the Basques. But this presence in the American economy was not new for the natives of the Basque Country. As is well known, Basque men of the sea, businessmen, and merchants have been represented in the annals of history since the first phases of the overseas adventure. Whether from Sevilla, Cádiz, or the other side of the ocean, many Basques were directly involved in the transactions between Spain and the colonies. And through the growth in American commerce during the 1700s, the Basque participation was even more evident. Of the 1,023 merchants licensed for traffic with the New World in the Consulate of Sevilla between 1700 and 1800, ninety-seven, or 9.5 percent, were originally from the Basque Country.[30] A similar claim can be made for Cádiz. Between 1739 and 1823 the Basque merchants registered in that consulate occupied a privileged place, constituting 21.5 percent of the total licenses issued by the authorities of Cádiz during that period.[31]

Region	Number	Percent
Basque Country	446	21.62
Andalusia	363	17.60
Cantabria	237	11.49
Navarre	205	9.94
Castile-León	202	9.79
Galicia	162	7.85
La Rioja	139	6.74
Cataluña	138	6.69
Asturias	42	2.03
Castile-La Mancha	33	1.60
Levante	29	1.40
Madrid	25	1.21
Extremadura	20	0.96
Others	14	0.67
Aragón	7	0.33
Total	2,062	100.00

If the number of sons of Basques, born in Andalusia, Madrid, or even the Americas were added to these figures, the list would be even more extensive, and the percentages considerably higher. But if the above data convincingly demonstrates a great influence of the Basques in the Consulates of Sevilla and Cádiz, the obligatory ports of American commerce, then their activity would have been equally pervasive throughout the New World. This is the argument that follows.

The Basque presence in commercial and maritime vocations is documented from the conquest's early years. It would not be until the second half of the eighteenth century, however, that the participation of the successors and continuers of those first mercantilists reached its peak in the viceroyalty of Peru. Some were able to begin their commercial travels thanks to the support of fellow countrymen, or they were already occupying key posts in the administration, serving as ministers of great responsibility or enjoying prominent social positions. Those listed in table 3.2 are only a sample of the Basques that served in these strategic positions in Peru in the second half of the eighteenth century.

But the majority of the merchants native to the Basque Country that developed their businesses in the viceroyalty of Peru cultivated their fortunes through the principles of hard work, business acumen, operational capability, and unsurpassed professionalism. In general, they were licensed in the Consulate of Lima, a guild that united—under certain conditions—whoever performed any type of mercantile activity. A quick review of the organization's leadership corps during the 1700s gives a good idea of the magnitude of the Basque element at both the heart of this institution and within Peruvian commerce:[32]

Name	Post	Years
Joaquín J. de Arrese	Consul	1773–1777
Tomás de la Bodega y Quadra	Consul	1762–1766
Jerónimo de Calatayud	Consul	1754–1757
Pedro de Elcano y Balda	Prior	1760–1761
Ignacio de Elola	Consul	1757–1759
	Prior	1765–1766
Juan B. de Sarraoa e Iriarte	Consul	1785–1788
	Prior	1795–1796
Blás Ignacio de Tellería	Consul	1797–1800
Domingo de Zaldivar y Pascual	Consul	1760–1764
Pedro del Villar y Zubiaur	Consul	1750–1753
	Prior	1762–1764

In order to exercise the right of elector and be eligible for a position in the Consulate, one was required, in addition to proving residence in Lima, to have access to a minimum capital of 12,000 pesos—in either wholesale warehouse stock or

TABLE 3.2 Basques in Positions of Power in the Viceroyalty of Peru, 1735–1803

Name	Origin	Position	Years
José A. de Arreche	Bizkaia	General overseer	1777–82
José de Gorbea y Vadillo	Bizkaia	Criminal district attorney	1784–1803
Antonio de Elexpuru y Larrínaga	Bizkaia	Secretary of correspondence to the viceroy	1761–76
Miguel de Arriaga y Gurbista	Bizkaia	General director of customs	1761–76
Juan de Echevarría y Uría	Bizkaia	General accountant of customs	1761–76
Joaquín J. de Arrese y Lardizabal	Gipuzkoa	General administrator of customs and tariffs	1782–90
Juan Domingo de Ordozgoiti	Gipuzkoa	General administrator of customs and tariffs	1791
José I. de Lecuanda y Ezcarraga	Araba	High official and accountant of customs	1791–94
		Administrator of customs	1795–97
Cristóbal de Leuro y Dudagoitia	Bizkaia	Ordering accountant of High Tribunal of Fiscal Inspection	1741–74
Francisco de Ersilbengoa y Orbezu	Bizkaia	Accountant of Public Review Board of Lima	1735–67
Estanislao de Landazuri y Bolivar	Bizkaia	Judge superintendent of Mint of Lima	1778–92
Francisco de Ocharan y Mollinedo	Gipuzkoa	Mayor of Lima	1780
		Appeals judge of Tribunal of Mining	1788
Francisco de Urrizmendi y Aramendi	Bizkaia	Head guard of port of Callao	1749–56
Mateo de Amusquibar y Ochoa de Recalde	Bizkaia	Inquisitor of the Holy Office	1744–63
Juan Ignacio de Obiaga	Gipuzkoa	Inquisitor of the Holy Office	1759–84

Source: G. Lohmann Villena, 1988, 55ff.

a commercial volume—or ownership of a seagoing vessel. It is therefore clear that Basque participation in the Consulate and in the general commerce of Peru was financially significant as well. It could be said that this ethnic group came to form a true plutocracy whose members were connected by family ties and common origin.

Among the Basque merchants that were noteworthy in eighteenth-century Peru was Domingo de Azcuénaga e Iturbe; he dealt in cloths beginning in 1749, although books could also be found among his general goods. Juan Bautista de Baquijano y Urigüen, born in Iurreta (Bizkaia) in 1701, was one of the pioneers in dissipating the existing prejudices of the epoch about the incompatibility between participation in commercial activity and nobility. In spite of his title of count of Vista Florida—granted by Ferdinand VI in 1754—he knew how to successfully manage business affairs, thus accruing a considerable fortune. He dealt in Castilian fabrics, sugar, and slaves. At his death (1759), an audit of his personal fortune placed his worth at more than 625,000 pesos.[33] In 1771, Francisco Antonio de Berchaguren y Yarzo, a native of Muskiz (Bizkaia), entered into a partnership with Francisco Antonio de la Mella y Barriola, from Balmaseda. They sold articles from Castile, clothes and general merchandise on the Arica-La Paz-Potosí run, a routing right that various wholesalers had acquired for this purpose (among them, Tomás de la Bodega y Quadra, another Bizkaian). Joaquín Cabeza de Vaca y Echeverría, from Hondarribia, also achieved commercial success in Peru. After his passage through Nueva España, where he was mayor of Mexaltepeque (Oaxaca), he established his residence in Lima in 1751. Together with fellow Basques (Bartolomé de Eguizabal and Francisco Mena), he received products from Guatemala on a regular basis, especially indigo, which he easily sold on the Peruvian and Spanish markets.

In 1749, the Gipuzkoan Pedro de Elcano y Balda, from Zarautz, entered into a partnership with two other Basques in Cádiz to establish an outfitting company that would soon make a great name for itself on the Lima market. Proof of Elcano's success was his capacity to make personal loans that brought him substantial dividends. At his death, his personal fortune was approximately 200,000 pesos. Like his fellow Gipuzkoan Elcano, Ignacio de Elola y Beobide (from Larraun) was very successful in Peruvian business thanks to trading a great variety of goods, including fabrics, linens, tacks, and nails from Bizkaia, silk from Granada, taffeta from Valencia, baize from England, wool from Soria, silk from Cataluña, thread from Córdoba, and ribbons from Brittany. Included among his goods was a total of 183 kilos of fashioned silver.

The Bizkaians Juan de Zarandona y Chavarría and Juan de Ororbiogoitia y Aguirre were among the other most important merchants in Peru during the second half of the eighteenth century. The former made his fortune through the sale of Peruvian brandy, liquor, Chilean wines, clothes from Conchucos, pastries from Arequipa, cloths from Quito, thread from Coquimbo, canvas, sacks of anise, vinegar, coffee, glass marble from Quito, cotton tablecloths, shirts from Brittany, sacks of suet, leather soles from Guayaquil, ponchos from Chiloé, and raisins and peppers from Chiapas. The variety of origins of all these goods gives an idea of the range of the Larrabetzu-born Zarandona's mercantile activity. Ororbiogoitia served as a banker and important moneylender, judging by the list of his debtors, who, at his death, owed him over 91,000 pesos. Among them were the tribunal of the Consulate of Lima, the count of Premio Real, Don José Antonio de Lavalle y Cortés and the commission merchants from Lima, and the brothers Antonio and José Matías de Elizalde.

A large number of Basques also contributed to the development of the Peruvian shipping sector. The Gipuzkoans Javier María de Aguirre y Aldazabal (owner of two ships of deep draft) and Juan Miguel de Mendiburu y Arzac (the only one with three vessels registered to his name in the port of Callao), both from Donostia, and Juan Ignacio de Otaegui y Ondemar were perhaps the most noteworthy figures.

Mining was another of the sectors in which natives of the Basque Country prospered. One example is the Bizkaian Juan de Arrieta e Iturriaga, who successfully applied the ore grinder invented by the baron of Nordenlicht. Another is Francisco de Ocharan y Mollinedo, from Enkarterri. After occupying the positions of captain of the dragoons of Angares (Huancavelica), supervisor of Customs of Callao, mayor of Lima, co-judge of appeals of the Mining Tribunal, and Lima agent of the Company of Mines and Commerce of Guatemala (1750), in 1752 he took on the responsibility of transporting quicksilver to the various mining centers in need of it. At the end of 1781, he ran the mines of Huancavelica. Upon discovering their dilapidated condition and the impossibility of turning a large profit, however, he resigned. Other Basque miners of the viceroyalty of Peru were the Bizkaians Nicolás González de Saravia y Mollinedo, Pedro Ventura de Orbegozo y Lequerica, and Manuel Antonio de Santelices y la Vía, and the Gipuzkoan Juan Domingo de Ordozgoiti.

As in Peru, the Basque presence in Río de la Plata, substantial since the first steps of the conquest of southern South America, swelled considerably beginning in the second half of the eighteenth century. A powerful colony of rich, influential soldiers and merchants originally from the Basque Country converged on that region during the epoch. But it was in the early decades of the 1700s that Buenos Aires would become truly attractive. Those lacking fortune and wishing to quickly prosper in the New World flocked to the city.[34] The transport of blacks (first through the Company of Guinea and later the British South Sea Company), Anglo-Portuguese smuggling from Colonia del Sacramento (Uruguay), and the affluence of the Spanish transatlantic ships and some French vessels spurred growth of the region's economic life. In addition, the flourishing economy of the Río de la Plata region (especially Uruguay's Banda Oriental and predominantly in the livestock sector) and the population growth in the main urban centers of the area were the reasons for reviving the commercial interests of the Basques, especially those from Bilbao.

Given the continued great successes reaped by the Company of Caracas, the merchants of the Consulate of Bilbao repeatedly solicited a mercantile monopolistic concession from the king similar to that held by Donostia. As already seen, the attempts to open the Nervión to commerce with America failed. With the idea of forming a partnership for traffic with Río de la Plata still latent, however, three Basques living in Madrid formed a mercantile company in 1752 that would operate through the traditional Cádiz route. Although the three partners possessed a certain amount of commercial experience, their most distinguishing feature was their contact with officialdom, important at a time when mercantile traffic depended on licenses granted by the administration. One of the three, Pedro de Astruarena e Iturralde, a native of Arizcun, was the nephew of the secretary of the Royal Treasury and became a member of the Board of the Treasury and the Board of Supplies. Around the middle of the century, he was the contractor of supplies and medicines for the Royal Squadron of Galleys and for the public market squares of Melilla, Alhumecas, Ceuta, and Orán, and shareholder in the companies of Havana and San Fernando de Sevilla. Astruarena was also connected to other influential Basques in the court, such as the dean of the Council of the Indies, Francisco Javier de Goyeneche. Another of the partners was the Gipuzkoan José de Aguirre Acharán. Like Astruarena, he was a member of the Board of the Treasury and the Board of Supplies; he was also director of the construction of a new supply store and owner of a soap factory in Fuencarral (Madrid), shareholder in the Company of Caracas, and, beginning in 1749, the main investor in a company founded to do business with Callao. The third partner was Francisco de Mendinueta, from Pamplona; until that time, he had been involved with Spanish-American commerce and was a contractor of army provisions. Given that the three partners lived in Madrid and their occupations kept them permanently in the city and the court, they decided to name another Basque, Nicolás de Aizpurua, as the company's representative in Cádiz.

After repeatedly perfecting their commercial project to adapt it to official requirements as much as possible, in 1754 Mendinueta presented a document according to which the new company was obliged to dispatch three thousand tons of merchandise that the Crown considered necessary for the supply of the three provinces of Río de la Plata, Tucumán, and Paraguay over the course of six years, and not introduce anything into upper Peru except the iron and steel needed for the mines. The company also promised to transport the two hundred dragoons and four hundred infantry that the king wished to send to Río de la Plata, and put two-thirds of their transport space at the disposition of small merchants for shipping their merchandise. Lastly, the Buenos Aires company proposed to take charge of the transport of three thousand black slaves, although none of the three partners had any experience in such matters.[35] The Crown accepted the complete proposal of the Basque merchants, thereby formalizing the association's charge. The company's first ship, the *San Francisco Javier*, was built in Pasaia (Gipuzkoa) in 1735, with a gross weight of 675 tons. The partners later constructed the *San Ignacio de Loyola*, weighing 459 tons, in the same Gipuzkoan port, and bought the *San Pedro* ("El Prudente"), weighing 267 tons, from some Frenchmen. The *San Juan Evangelista*, 220 tons, and the *Santa Cruz*, built in Denmark with a weight of 389 tons, completed the company's fleet.

As already mentioned, during the decade that their activity lasted, and in agreement with the consignment in the royal seat, the company transported its own merchandise and the stock of others gathered at the port of departure to sell in Buenos Aires. These goods could be from merchants in Cádiz, shipped there by dealers from elsewhere in Spain, or acquired in other countries. The various connections of the three partners with the Basque Country facilitated the shipment of its iron, to be used in the forges of Río de la Plata, or already manufactured articles such as pots, shovels, plowshares, spalling hammers, and nails. And although the main objective was trade with Río de la Plata, the company occasionally introduced some Basque ironware into Cádiz for sale to other merchants in the city. From the north, wood used for repairing its ships also arrived. The friendly contacts of the three partners in the Buenos Aires enterprise with other important merchants of Basque origin likewise gave rise to additional transactions outside of the Río de la Plata region, thereby breaching the conditions of the agreement signed by the monarchy. Thus, the shipment of liquor and wine consigned to Domingo Ignacio de Lardizabal, a resident of Nueva España, could be added to the already mentioned sale of Basque iron in Cádiz. Another project beyond the company's scope was investing in Lima through its association with the Uztariz family, of Navarrese origin but living in Cádiz. In 1762, the royal factories of Talavera de la Reina (Toledo), devoted to the production of silk fabrics and fine gold and silver textiles, had granted the family the shipment of one vessel a year to Peru, another to Nueva España, and a third to Havana. Unable to capitalize on its opportunity for lack of ships, the family firm of the Uztariz Brothers entered into an equal partnership with the Buenos Aires company. The latter would furnish its frigate *San Francisco Javier* with all its equipment, and the Uztariz Brothers would provide merchandise of equal value, which came to 918,350 silver reales. The ship set sail in 1763 with its cargo of fabrics and some wax items and spices and returned two years later with hides, copper, and cacao.

In spite of the great profits obtained in its first years of commercial operation, fortune did not smile on the Company of Buenos Aires. One of the noteworthy causes of its misfortune was the inexperience of the three partners in black slave trade and the difficulty of organizing it from Spain. Their lack of preparation forced them to resort to foreign commission merchants, who were difficult to control from Madrid. The three partners' lack of knowledge about Río de la Plata also made choosing appropriate goods for local needs and tastes difficult. The several thousand gold nails for coaches and the over six hundred stamps with the image of San Emigdio recorded in the company's 1766 balance sheet were proof of this. In addition, the exclusive commercial charter of the company, so irritating to the port merchants, allowed it to increase the price of the hides and the total of its cargo, but did not give it a big advantage as a seller of overseas products; it had to compete with the low prices of the goods smuggled from Colonia del Sacramento. Furthermore, the taste for privileged companies, so fashionable in the early decades of the eighteenth century, gave way to a less restrictive line of thinking in the last third of the century. Without underestimating the importance of the large companies for the development of certain colonial regions, the Crown showed itself less inclined to grant them commercial monopolies. Lastly, the incomprehensible opposition in Buenos Aires to the monopolistic objectives of the Basque undertaking, the war against England and Portugal, and the creation of sea couriers to Montevideo would usher in a new mercantile era in Río de la Plata in 1767. The Regulations of Free Trade of 1778 only served to further intensify the Buenos Aires port traffic, generating a new wave of Basque immigration into the region. Thus, the Anchorenas, Alzagas, Ugartes, Letamendis, Sarraetas, Aranas, and many others joined the families of Basques with deep roots there. Together, they formed an economically prosperous and politically influential collectivity.

In Nueva España, the age of Enlightenment was a time in which the Basque presence would reach very high levels, both quantitatively and qualitatively, in all facets but especially in economic activities. Throughout the 1700s, Mexico experienced unprecedented economic expansion, primarily as a consequence of a renaissance in the mining sector, the noteworthy population increase occurring at the time throughout the viceroyalty, and the reforms carried out by the Bourbon dynasty, which only confirmed the economic potential of Nueva España. It makes sense that, in view of this promising outlook, numerous Basques risked crossing the ocean in search of better fortune and settled in Mexico at that time.

Commercial activity was among those chosen by the Bizkaians, Arabans, Gipuzkoans, Navarrese, and natives of Iparralde that emigrated to Mexico in the eighteenth century. Everyone concurred that this sector could yield excellent profits with low risk. The relevance of Basque natives in mercantile endeavors was such that, along with their rivals of the "Club of the Cantabrians," the "Club of the Vizcayans" came to occupy the relevant posts of the Consulate of Merchants of Mexico (see table 2.5 in appendix 2).

The presence of Basques in the commerce of Nueva España was sustained for decades. Many were initiated into their mercantile careers as apprentices or, occasionally, as clerks for some family member or countryman, later establishing their own businesses. The Basque mercantile activity in Mexico, like in the rest of the colonies, was based on family, friendship, and marriage relations. These were all critical for ensuring both commercial and sociopolitical control. Perhaps the best examples of this familial mercantile system in Nueva España during the age of Enlightenment were Francisco Fagoaga and Juan de Castañiza. The commercial firms founded by both entrepreneurs, having possibly the greatest economic breadth in

Mexico City, are models for understanding the behaviors of Basque merchants residing there.

A native of the valley of Oiartzun (Gipuzkoa), Fagoaga had moved to Mexico in the first third of the eighteenth century, founding one of the most important families in colonial commerce. Fagoaga married Josefa de Arosqueta, the only child and heiress of the Lekeitio native Juan Bautista de Arosqueta. He was then able to combine his mining businesses (he had bought the post of gold and silver sorter for 6,000 pesos) with the mercantile activities of his father-in-law. Later, he summoned his nephew Manuel de Aldaco to Mexico to manage his silver bank and marry one of his daughters.

Juan de Castañiza, a Bizkaian from Enkarterri, established himself in Mexico in the mid-eighteenth century. His import company dealing in Spanish goods was so successful that it brought him considerable wealth. Like Fagoaga, in 1763 he sent for his nephew, Antonio Bassoco, to manage his company. After Castañiza's death, the mercantile firm did not disappear; his oldest son, Ignacio María de Castañiza y Agüero, inherited the haciendas and marquisate of his father, while one daughter, María Teresa, married her cousin Antonio Bassoco. But mercantile consolidations through the practice of endogamy went further in this case, when a brother-in-law of Bassoco married a daughter of Fagoaga, thereby managing to gain access to the silver production sector.

Although commerce was their main activity in eighteenth-century Mexico, the natives of the Basque Country did not ignore other opportunities. They embraced a wide range of commercial interests that would permit them to make up for the losses suffered in some of their lines, should the need arise. The exploitation of mines was thus another important source of profits that the Basques did not ignore. That the number of Mexican mines reached three thousand by the end of the eighteenth century illustrates this activity's significance to the colony. In 1786, Charles III named a native of Iparralde, Fausto de Elhuyart, director general of the Tribunal of Aztec Mining. Even earlier, however, in 1761, Francisco de Gamboa published *Commentaries on the Mining Ordinances* to divulge technical aspects of extracting precious metals.

As a result of their privileged economic position, the Basques of Nueva España began forming a part of the ranks of the local nobility as in no other place in America. Castañiza himself obtained a marquisate that his firstborn would inherit, the Bassocos and Fagoagas also obtained noble titles that they left to their successors, as well as a massive number of Bizkaians, Gipuzkoans, and Arabans, such as the marquis of Jaral, Miguel de Berrio y Saldivar; the count of the House of Loja, Francisco José de Landeta y Urtuzuastegui; the count of Miraflores, Pedro de Garrastegui y Oleaga; the marquis of Monserrate, Francisco Javier Vasconcelos Berruecos y Cuelleno; the marquises of San Juan de Raya, Vicente Manuel de Sardaneta y Legazpi and his wife; the marquis of Reunion of Nueva España, Francisco Javier de Venegas;

the marquis of Sonora, José de Galvez, secretary of state, inspector general of Nueva España, and universal minister of the Indies; and the count of the Valley of Orizaba, Rodrigo de Vivero y Aberrucia. If the families of the Villaurrutias and the Iturbides are added, it is clear that the Basque presence in the Mexico of the 1800s was extraordinarily important.

For Cuba, and especially Havana, the eighteenth century was also an epoch of vertical economic growth. Havana already possessed the largest shipyard in the Spanish Empire in the first half of the century, and a large part of Spanish commerce with America passed through it in both directions. The city was also an exporter of tobacco, and sent large quantities of white sugar and hides to Europe. Moreover, in the sugar sector, Cuba would experience a production takeoff of global dimensions at the end of the 1700s. This economic boom largely resulted from both the intensive harnessing of the island's national resources and its exceptional geographic situation. But, in addition, from a very early date the Crown had been investing millions of pesos in military equipment and resources to make Havana unassailable. The city was heavily armed, walled, and equipped with four large castles and at least three smaller forts. Thus, Cuba's military importance and economic possibilities were combined in a way that generated a production-oriented, service economy, creating a socially aggressive urban oligarchy of soldiers and merchants.[36]

These conditions alone explain the fact that the natives of the Basque Country—sailors, merchants, soldiers, and producers par excellence—migrated in numbers to the island; Cuba's eighteenth century could be characterized, especially qualitatively, as a period of Basque preeminence. The formation of the Royal Company of Havana in 1739 undoubtedly marked the watershed of this presence. The company was basically created through Basque capital and monopolized the extensive Havanan foreign commerce: the annuity from both tobacco and the shipyards. As in other regions of the New World, the reinforcement of economic relations by marital alliances was a common practice for the Basques of Cuba; they thus came to constitute a truly decisive pressure group in the island's social, economic, and cultural life in the second half of the eighteenth century. The case of the Gipuzkoan Domingo de Lizundia y Odria de Echeverría, marquis of Real Agrado and treasurer of the Royal Tobacco Income, perfectly illustrates this policy of class and region-based endogamy. His daughter married the Araban brigadier Matías de Armona y Murga, who soon reached the rank of marshal (the army was the decisive governing power). Lizundia's brother José, a member of the Council of His Majesty in the Head Accountants' Office and administrator general of royal income, married into another of the most influential and rich Basque families in Cuba: that of the Bizkaian José de Beitia y Rentería, marquis of Real Socorro. These are illustrations of the intertwining of economic and family interests at the highest levels of the royal bureaucracy, army, American nobility, commerce, maritime transport, communication, sugar, and tobacco.

The means by which the highest Basque officials of the Spanish colonial army made the transition from military positions to productive and commercial Cuban life are interesting. For example, Colonel Silvestre Abarca y Aznar, a native of Lumbier (Navarre) went to Cuba in 1763 with the brigadier of the army engineering corps, Agustín Cramer Mañecas (also from Navarre), to repair the damages done by the English to the forts of Havana. Both formed a part of the Basque and Navarrese elite that dominated the Cuban economy of the second half of the eighteenth century, and this was one of the reasons that they were appointed to construct the warehouse of the Royal Tobacco Trading Post in 1770 (it would remain one of Havana's main buildings until the early twentieth century). In 1768, Brigadier Cramer Mañecas, a shareholder in the Royal Company of Commerce of Barcelona, published the most important treatise of the period on the promotion of commercial activity in Cuba; in 1777, he wrote an important study on commerce and navigation in the province of Guiana. Among the many soldiers devoted to mercantile practice, the following were also noteworthy: the Gipuzkoans Sebastián de Arratibel Zafinea; Gabriel Francisco de Ercaizti Goizueta, honorary treasurer of the Army; Francisco Isaac de Mendiola y Múgica, honorary commissary of war; Juan Ignacio Urriza, intendant of both the Army and the Royal Treasury, and superintendent of the latter's tobacco branch; and the Araban Domingo Ugarte Zubiate, captain of a regiment of the infantry of Havana. Ugarte married María Jesús Arostegui, the daughter of one of the founders of the Royal Company of Commerce of Havana, Martín de Arostegui Larrea.

Dozens of other prominent Basques typified this rich period in Cuban history. Thus, the Gipuzkoan Sebastián de Lasa e Irala and his son carried out noteworthy work in the introduction of new types of sugar cane into Cuba. Gabriel de Azcárate Lascurain, also originally from Gipuzkoa, had an active commercial life, devoting himself almost exclusively to the black slave trade. Azcárate married his two daughters off to other known slave traders, both of Basque origins. What most calls attention to this family is that it engendered a liberal family of high cultural level in its third generation. Its most outstanding figure was Nicolás de Azcárate Escobedo, who devoted his life and the money he inherited from his grandfather to fight slavery. The younger Azcárate founded an association in which all of the members promised not to possess slaves. In addition, he was a lawyer who occupied the post of public defender of slaves in Havana without receiving a salary.

In sum, it can be said that in the eighteenth century the Basques stood at the peak of Cuban society. They dominated its economy as a result of the combination of their capacity for action, an elaborate family and region-based strategy, and a modern concept of the economy. Only the Catalonian wave, beginning in the last third of the eighteenth century and accelerating in the early nineteenth, was able to neutralize Basque dominance. At that time, the Navarrese Bernardo de Goicoa, general director of the Royal Company of Commerce of Havana, wrote a report with the aim of restoring free trade that augured the Catalonian penetration in American commerce. In the first quarter of the nineteenth century, his premonition became a reality.

Affecting Basque commerce within the North American economic sphere in the eighteenth century were great political transformations that obliged the maritime and commercial leaders of the period to maintain permanent vigilance over the zone.[37] At the beginning of the century and as a consequence of the internationalization of the Spanish conflict of succession and the resulting Treaty of Utrecht (1713), the waters of the north were declared English domain almost in their entirety. These included those of Terranova, where the Basques had long developed their main fishing activity in cod and whales. This circumstance had important implications for the economy of Bizkaia and Gipuzkoa. While the French were able to continue fishing in those waters on the basis of their control of an important portion of Canada, the subjects of Philip V were totally excluded from doing the same. The possible alternatives were either to continue fishing, but under the French flag, or to replace true production with pure commerce, importing the cod captured by others. In Gipuzkoa, the negative effects of the prohibition of fishing the northern waters were mitigated to an extent by a concession to the Company of Caracas allowing it to direct ships, men, and resources elsewhere in the Atlantic. The Seigneury of Bizkaia, however, lacking such privileged concessions, had to choose the commercial recourse of dealing for cod first with the French, then with the English, and then directly with the North American ports after the United States' Declaration of Independence in 1776.

But cod and whale products were not the only trade conducted between Bilbao and the Americas that pioneered the process of independence in the New World. For some time, both sides of the Atlantic also conducted significant commerce in tobacco. This business, a highly profitable one at the end of the eighteenth century, was immediately regulated by the administration, however. The traffic of this high-demand American product to Bizkaia was unregulated, although the surplus had to be sold exclusively in a trading post opened for that purpose in Bilbao. The precious plant was imported from Virginia via one or two ships a year, enough to supply the city and even to trade with Castile.

Basque Colonial Associationism

The Basques were clearly present in all American societies, even if their numbers varied significantly. Their presence was modest but influential in Costa Rica and Guatemala, for example, and considerable in Mexico, noteworthy in Cuba, Peru, Chile, Colombia, and, beginning in the eighteenth century, in Venezuela and Río de la Plata. Almost all these places experienced the same settling process that corresponded to the Spanish Crown's project for the Americas: conquest, Christianization, administration, and economic exploitation. It was thus that the first Basque soldiers and clerics arrived, followed by the bureaucrats and merchants. Along with them, many sailors, pursers, commission merchants, and freight loaders were obliged to live in American port cities for several years.

A good number of Basques came to excel and gain notoriety in the communities in which they lived while performing such jobs. This often caused conflict with a rival economic or social community, jealous of the Basque high level of success and their recognized solidarity. The Basque is characterized by a series of features in colonial writings, among which the following stand out: the notion of group; the love of their common land of origin as well as the language and its frequent use; the spirit of solidarity, support, and mutual aid; their sense of justice; the defense of freedom; their brusqueness, sometimes bordering on violence; ambition and cornering of important positions; business initiative; hard work; loyalty; and sense of responsibility.

The associative tendency of the Basques of America—to consolidate their elite standing, and as a method of defense in relation to other communities—materialized in the New World. Numerous associations of mutual aid, brotherhoods, and confraternities were founded during the seventeenth and eighteenth centuries in the style of those of Sevilla and Cádiz in the mid-1500s. They would be the seeds of future organizations created throughout the American republics at the end of the nineteenth century. The Brotherhood of Aránzazu of Lima, the Confraternity of Aránzazu of Mexico, and the College of the Vizcayans of Nueva España were all fruit of this ethnically based associative practice.

The first attempt to establish a fraternal society in the viceroyalty of Peru dates from 1612.[38] That year, a group of Basques—among whom were the accountant of the Tribunal of Fiscal Inspection, Domingo de Garro, Juan Pérez de Gordejuela, Pedro de Echegaray, Lope de Munibe, Miguel de Munibe, Juan Ortíz de Bedia, Diego de Mallea, Andrés de Zabala, Pedro de Ormaechea, Andrés López de Arcaya, Martín Pérez de Urasandi, Diego de Olarte, Juan de Cortabarría, Juan de Urrutia, Juan Martínez de Arraona, Matías de Rezola, and Pedro de Urdarribia—all of them prominent Lima merchants, raised 10,000 pesos to buy the chapel of Encarnación de Nuestra Señora y Anunciación de Nuestro Señor in the city's Church of San Francisco, property of General Luis de Mendoza y Ribera. Although the transaction was made official on March 18, 1612, the brotherhood would not formally be founded until 1635. That year, a meeting that brought together over a hundred Basques—forty-nine Bizkaians, thirty-three Gipuzkoans, nine Navarrese, seven Arabans, and six Cantabrians—approved the statutes of the association, whose ultimate aim would be the union and confederation of natives of these territories to perform charitable works. It was also stipulated in the brotherhood's founding article that funerals would be held for deceased members, and they would be buried in the church's crypt; prisons would also be visited in an attempt to help the prisoners both legally and economically; they would also welcome and house newly arrived Basque immigrants; they would attempt to find husbands for orphaned girls and endowments for those who devoted themselves to the church; and they were able to name their own chaplains. The members of the brotherhood, their descendants, and Basque natives that were not members would be the beneficiaries of all these charitable activities. Nobody would be admitted if they accepted Judaism or Islam, were pursued by the Holy Office, had married a mulatta, Indian, or black, or engaged in dishonest and harmful activities.

The chapel acquired was furnished with three altars: the image of the Virgin of Aránzazu was worshipped in the center with a lavish mantle of pearls and diamonds; to its right, another smaller retable remembered the Virgin of Begoña, patroness of Bizkaia; on the opposite side, there was a retable dedicated to the Guardian Angel. Juan de Urrutia, from Tolosa, the majordomo of the brotherhood on repeated occasions and a noted Lima merchant, ordered an exact copy of the image worshipped in Oñati (Gipuzkoa). The sculpture reached Lima in 1646, and was immediately placed in its position in the chapel of the Church of San Francisco. The inaugural ceremony was officiated by Fra Ignacio de Ibarra of Azkoitia and presided by the viceroy of Peru himself, García Sarmiento de Sotomayor.

The Brotherhood of Aránzazu of Lima fulfilled its religious and charitable functions for many years thanks to the generosity of its members, most of whom were among Lima's commercial elite. Nevertheless, it declined in the second half of the nineteenth century when the institution, which still had 378 members in 1857, came under the jurisdiction of the Public Social Service of Lima.

In 1681, the Basque colony settled in Mexico City also decided, with complete autonomy and without requesting the required permits from the ecclesiastical authority, to create a primarily religious-based brotherhood dedicated to Our Lady of Aránzazu. It was installed in a chapel of the city's Franciscan convent. Fifteen years later, in January 1696, the ordinances for converting the association into a confraternity were approved. An inventory done in the chapel of the Basques in Mexico in 1710 gives an idea of the wealth of both the brotherhood and its members: the statue of the Virgin of Aránzazu dominated the main altar and was dressed in a garment that had 180 emeralds; her veil had 74 diamonds, and her arms were covered with pearl bracelets; there were five sumptuous smaller altars with twelve life-sized marble statues dressed in Chinese silks; the mirrors of the altars were made of crystal cut in Venice; and it had fifteen silver lamps and eight chalices, two of which were gold.

As already stated, the Mexican Basque community gathered in the Franciscan chapel without the approval of the ecclesiastical authorities until 1696. That year, its members proposed the association's official recognition as a confraternity (*cofradía*), thereby elevating the lesser status that it had as a brotherhood (*hermandad*); this recognition was achieved a few months later, after the presentation of a completed application to the city's archbishop and the conclusion of a period of great tension during which the ecclesiastical hierarchy went so far as to recommend the excommunication of all the Basques in the association. Its definitive recognition came in 1729, when the Confraternity of Our Lady of Aránzazu was approved by the Council of the Indies. It was combined with the Association of Saint Ignatius of Madrid by royal disposition, from then on possessing all of the immunities and privileges that had been enjoyed by the association.

The confraternity undertook a wide range of social and charitable activities without great regard to the nationality of the beneficiaries. Thus, its patronage of a large number of charities ranged from dowries for the marriage of orphaned girls or religious work to solemn burials for the dead. The confraternity, which managed an important amount of capital, also filled the functions of a financial institution, extending mortgage loans to its members for their mining, farming, and commercial investments. Social and philanthropic interests were therefore interwoven with its economic functions; these latter were of great importance given the lack of banks and credit institutions at that time. The confraternity listed among its ranks a large number of members prominent in ecclesiastical, economic, political, and cultural spheres throughout the viceroyalty of Mexico. Among the noteworthy confreres were Juan José Eguiara y Eguren, Francisco Javier de Gamboa, José Francisco de Uribe, Francisco Fagoaga Iragorri, Juan de Castañiza, Francisco Fagoaga Arosqueta, Antonio de Bassoco, General Francisco de Echeveste, Manuel de Aldaco, the marquis of Guardiola José Padilla Estrada, Ambrosio de Meabe, Miguel de Amozarrain, José de Gárate, Pedro Negrete, José Dávalos Espinosa, and archbishop of Mexico Juan Antonio de Vizarrón y Eguiarreta.

They all shared a great concern for female education, especially for those women from the most disfranchised classes. Their contribution, through the College of Saint Ignatius (better known as the College of the Vizcayans) stood out in a framework in which the educational institutions dedicated to women in Mexico City were limited to convents of nuns in seclusion and only a few public schools. Thus, the foundation of a school-hospice for poor girls, maidens, and widows of Basque origin, and in which kindergartners and young children would also be taught, was approved at the confraternity's meeting on November 1, 1732. The first funds for creating the school-hospice were collected immediately. Many Basques contributed to the consummation of this noble project. The gradual scale of cash donations, from the 6,000 pesos from Archbishop Juan Antonio Vizarrón to the one and a half reales from a Basque nun, reflects the range of both fortunes and generosity found among the Basques of Mexico City.

The Basque confreres began the work of building the College of the Vizcayans in 1734 without waiting for royal authorization. But it would not be until 1767, after the bureaucratic obstacles were overcome, that Charles III and Pope Clement XIII approved the opening of the center and its statutes. These statutes, written by Francisco Javier de Gamboa, dealt with three issues: the purpose of the institution, according to the Ignatian motto of "to the greater glory of God"; the educational ideals reaffirmed in the promotion of religious and moral values; and the patronage of the school that would depend solely upon the Confraternity of Our Lady of Aránzazu. The lay character of the foundation and the noninterference of the ecclesiastical and political powers were also stressed. The beautiful architectonic building that housed the school and residence, and that remains the object of admiration in the area surrounded by the Mexico City streets of San Ignacio, Aldaco, Echeveste, and Meave, cost more than one million pesos. Bequeathals and charities were immediately created for a large number of girls; these continued into the nineteenth century and still function today.

The College of the Vizcayans opened its door to seventy girls. In 1795, there were between two hundred sixty and three hundred female students, all of recognized nobility in their moral behavior. Lacking economic resources, most entered as beneficiary pensioners of the institution. School life was completely regulated according to a quasi-monastic schedule that began at five-thirty in the morning. It was interrupted by two hours of siesta, and concluded at nine o'clock at night. Three hours a day were allotted to reading, writing, arithmetic, and Christian doctrine.

The center's library contained the works of Spanish and Spanish-American authors. The predominant themes were theology, moral and Christian doctrine, the lives of the saints, asceticism and mysticism, and there were copies of the Sacred Scriptures and catechisms. The *Spiritual Exercises* of Saint Ignatius of Loyola, the *Mirror of Youth* and the *Devotion to the Holy Trinity* of the Jesuit Juan Antonio de Oviedo, widely read in Nueva España, and the *Treaty of Victory* of Melchor Cano could be found there. There were also other works of the beatified Juan de Avila, Fra Luis de Granada, the Jesuit Eusebio de Nieremberg, Father Torrubia, Cayetano Cabrera y Quintero, and Juan de Palafoz y Mendoza. Also read were the hagiographies contained in the *Christian Year*, the books dedicated to San Francisco de Borja, San Luis de Gonzaga, and especially, because of the reputation that he gained as a matchmaker, Saint Anthony of Padua. The Marian theme was represented by the works of San Alfonso María de Ligorio, the collections of devotional sermons and books, but especially the *Mystical City of God* of María Jesús de Agreda, which was one of the most widely read works in the female institutions of the viceroyalty. Along the same line was *The Deception of Clerics and the Souls That Deal with Virtue*, a work by María de la Antigua. The school had a history of the Church, the popes, and chronicles of the religious orders. There were also works of classic literature like the New Testament Epistles, and those of Cicero, and Latin, Spanish, and Spanish-American poets. Musical instruction was also a well-planned activity in the school's curriculum. Among others studies were the *Art and General Compendium of the Gregorian Chant* by Francisco Marcos y Mavas; *Book for Self-Instruction and with Bass for Accompaniment* and *Beginner for All Explanations to Sing Solfeggio in All Keys*, works by Master Jerusalem, the teacher of the chapel of Mexico City's cathedral and father of two of the students. In the nineteenth century, *The Philharmonic Instructor* of J. Antonio Gómez, the *Complete Method for Singing* by Miguel Beristain, the *Solfeggio of Solfeggios* by Danhauser, and other general works were purchased.

The end-of-the-century pro-independence winds were gaining force among the members of the confraternity and some of the former schoolgirls, such as Josefa Ortiz, one of the most ardent conspirators of Mexican emancipation. In April 1813, the then-rector of the Confraternity of Aránzazu, the Araban Tomás Ramón de Ibarrola, warned that "the detestable system of insurrection in the comments directed against the European Spaniards" was spreading among the schoolgirls. The sentiment, however, was not common, and it determined the configuration of the two factions that carried the banners of Nuestra Señora de los Remedios (pro-Crown) and Nuestra Señora de Guadalupe (pro-independence). In 1821, the College of the Vizcayans changed its description from royal to national, reflecting the political change, but the school was able to continue with the name of College of Peace in spite of the difficulties, and still functions today in Mexico City. On the other hand, the Confraternity of Our Lady of Aránzazu was dissolved in 1860 during the presidency of Benito Juarez.

The Fruits of the Enlightenment

The eighteenth century was the time in which the ideas presented by the European rationalists the previous century gained official acceptance. This was when the Enlightenment movement, through a renewed ideological arsenal (reason, progress, nature, happiness), penetrated the bourgeois class. In the end many nobles and representatives of reigning dynasties were imbued with its principles. It was ultimately rooted in cultural progress and social and economic reform. In short, the Enlightenment firmly advocated the happiness of humankind, an ideal its partisans believed feasible only if the cultural and reformist crusade undertaken by the intellectuals triumphed.[39] Following the old Platonic model, these partisans hoped to find the executive champions of their ideas in the sovereigns. This would be the function of *despotismo ilustrado*, an absolutist system that, inspired by the ideas of the Enlightenment, would pursue the cultural, social, and economic modernization policies dreamed of by the progressive intellectuals in all classes. In spite of the European monarchs' inclination to put it in practice, however, various factors obstructed the Enlightenment reformist campaign. One was the entrenched privileges of the dominant classes, which were directly opposed to the new reformist ideas. Another could be found in the very structure of the absolutist regime, which was more interested in reinforcing its authority and expanding its administration and territory than in the proclaimed happiness of its subjects. A third was the immobility of the ecclesiastical authorities. Although the impact of the Enlightenment was significant and the movement was responsible for a good number of initiatives and accomplishments in economic and cultural matters, the weight of religious tradition and the scant development of the social sectors interested in change would clearly be decisive in obstructing greater proliferation of the new ideal.

Spain participated fully in the European Enlightenment movement. The country would combine (with national nuances, of course) all the characteristics considered common to the ensemble. Beginning with the authentic precursors of imperial modernity in Europe, like Benito Jerónimo Feijóo, Gaspar Melchor de Jovellanos, Pedro Rodríguez Campomanes, Pablo de Olavide, and Gregorio Mayans, for the first time in the history of Spain a culture based on legends and myths was rejected, and greater reliance was placed on science and the scientific development of society. Avoiding the permanent conflicts with religion and its tribunals, and confronting the indifference, when not hostility, of the university, the eighteenth-century men of the Enlightenment tried to advance the first truly modern social and economic projects. All the Spanish regions were incorporated into the Enlightenment movement, each with its own rhythms and characteristics. Like the rest of Europe, and given that the new ideas did not find sympathy in either the monastic cloisters or the university halls, the scientific and philosophical orientations of the Enlightenment were channeled through the *tertulias* held by magnates and high-level functionaries in some prominent cities. Participants discussed foreign works of physics, philosophy, and medicine, and even conducted simple scientific experiments.

Azkoitia (Gipuzkoa) was one of the places where the idea of the Enlightenment took hold. Manuel Ignacio de Altuna, who spread the ideas of his close friend, the French philosopher Rousseau, in Spain, was mayor of the *villa*. Some of the most important ancestral estates of Gipuzkoa, such as those of Idiaquez, Insausti, Eguía, Balda, and Floriega, were located in Azkoitia. Javier María de Munibe, eighth count of Peñaflorida, one of the most distinguished figures of the eighteenth-century Basque bourgeoisie and a firm defender of the theories of the Enlightenment, also lived there. An anxious and active minority of modernists began gathering in his Azkoitia palace in 1748; they met regularly to widen and improve their knowledge: on Monday nights, they discussed only mathematics; on Tuesdays, physics; on Wednesdays, they read history and translations of their academic brethren; on Thursdays, they organized a small concert; and on Fridays they talked about current events.

Beginning with these informal but rigorous meetings of notables, the idea formed among the *tertulia* participants to create an economic association or academy of agriculture, science and applied arts, and commerce capable of promoting the progress of the Basque Country. Thus, in April 1765, a royal ordinance decreed by Charles III approved the birth of what would be the Real Sociedad Bascongada de Amigos del País (RSBAP, Royal Basque Society of the Friends of the Country).

Its objectives were "to cultivate the inclination and taste of the Basque Nation for Sciences, Humanities, and Arts; to correct and refine its customs, banish leisure, ignorance and their sad consequences, and to strengthen the union of the three provinces of Araba, Bizkaia, and Gipuzkoa." The new institution, which would be the first in a series of similar associations whose foundation would be spurred by nobility and bourgeoisie throughout the Iberian Peninsula, was to be organized in sections or departments: agriculture, industry, commerce, applied arts and sciences, politics, and fine arts. Members would thus try to promote and spread the main techniques and advances in Europe in each of these sectors. From the political point of view, the Royal Basque Society thus represented the moderate advance of Spanish Enlightenment thought, being debated amid criticisms of its doctrinaire enemies and tremendous social indifference. The Society did not constitute a club of free thinkers, nor was it distinguished by political formulas or social advances. It represented a movement that, without breaking with tradition, would try to make the renovationist winds compatible with religious and dogmatic obedience; with the maintenance of *foral* prerogatives and the predominance of agricultural over business interests; with loyalty to the monarchy and the adoption of industrial advances. When, beginning in 1770, the Crown encouraged the organization of agricultural and economic associations throughout the kingdom, the Royal Basque Society would be the model.

But the practical measures carried out by the Royal Basque Society were more important than its theoretical, philosophical ideas. Among its contributions to agricultural modernization were rationalized fields, until then unknown; the promotion of livestock, introduction of new breeds; the analysis of soils; and visits to neighboring countries in search of the best cultivation techniques. In addition to creating new iron manufactures, the Society would substantially improve the methods of processing in the foundries; the organization of competitions, in which the iron merchants with the greatest productivity were awarded prizes, clearly shows the importance that the Society conferred upon the industrial sector. But its concerns extended beyond strictly economic matters and into a wide range of social welfare. In this sense, the unusual importance given to hygiene stands out. Thus, the Society developed rules to subject the construction of houses to minimum hygienic standards, spread vaccination against smallpox, and promote the benefits of mineral waters, especially those of Zestoa (Bizkaia). The foundation of the House of Mercy of Vitoria and statistical and survey works are some of its other noteworthy accomplishments. Nor did the Society neglect education and the diffusion of the scientific and philosophical knowledge that had inspired its foundation. It quickly opened the so-called Schools of Primary Education in Gasteiz, Bilbao, Loyola, Bergara, and Donostia. The rudiments of language (both Spanish and Basque), calligraphy, writing, mathematics, and drawing were taught in these schools. But its greatest accomplishment in the field of education was the creation of the Royal

Patriotic Seminary, a means of spreading higher knowledge among young people both in the Basque Country and overseas. Its teaching program insisted from the beginning upon the study of such subjects as physics, chemistry, commerce, mathematics, metallurgy, and natural sciences, without forgetting the humanities, music, and foreign languages.

Even though they were not the only channels of diffusion, it was through the Royal Basque Society and its seminary that Enlightenment ideas spread into colonial America.[40] The expansion of the Society through the territories of the New World began in the early 1770s. In its first stage (1765–1770), the pace of the institution's social acceptance was slow and the Basque Country was its principal realm of influence. Beginning in 1770, however, it spread progressively throughout America and was characterized by the geographic diversification of its members and the strong rate of growth in its membership. (See table 2.6 in appendix 2.) In the mid-1880s, this growth stabilized at significant levels.

The spread of the Royal Basque Society through American lands continued on a course parallel to that in Spain. Due to the vastness of the territory, however, such growth was even more spectacular and was characterized by large-scale surges in membership that were very localized in time and space. (See table 2.7 in appendix 2.)

According to scholars,[41] various factors facilitated this noteworthy, rapid spread of the sphere of influence of the Royal Basque Society in America. It was not by chance that this spread took place shortly after the foundation of the commissions of the society in Madrid, Cádiz, and Sevilla. The centralizing character of the state's administrative apparatus and public business sector that controlled the kingdom's purse strings and the commercial traffic with America possessed by the two Andalusian cities pointed to such expansion. Moreover, the minimal obligations that the American members assumed upon joining the institution must have been another positive factor. Almost all of them were honorary members of the Society. In exchange for keeping members informed and sending them periodic publications, therefore, the Society received their promise to promote the organization and pay their dues. There was no doubt that this process of expansion also notably influenced the work performed by the Consulates of Bilbao and Donostia, given the Society's significant level of commercial penetration on the new continent. The decisive elements fostering the large-scale enlistment of members in America, however, were the networks of family and friendship relationships woven by the Basque immigrants in America; and the role played by the confraternities, associations, and brotherhoods around which the Basque colony in America was organized. In this sense, the key elements in the expansion process of the Royal Basque Society throughout America were the Confraternity of Our Lady of Aránzazu of Mexico, its counterpart in Lima, and the Association of Saint Ignatius of Loyola of Madrid. It makes sense that these were the three cities in which the largest number of members of the Royal Basque Society in the diaspora lived.

In any event, the combination of factors cited gave rise to the founding of numerous economic associations in America following the example of the Royal Basque Society. Already in 1771, the fraternal institution had been obliged to delegate its power to individuals in Mexico City, which in little time became the most powerful center of all those founded on the American continent. Pedro de Aguirre Albisua and Bartolomé de Alsasua were responsible for promoting the ideal of the Enlightenment of the Royal Basque Society in Nueva España at that time. It would not be until 1772, however, that the seeds sown by the Society began to bear fruit in this viceroyalty. That year, the Society sent its member Martín de Aguirre Burualde to America to find enterprising members to support its Enlightenment agenda. The first he managed to recruit for the reformist ideal of the members of Irurac Bat[42] was the justice of the Royal High Court of Mexico, the Araban Francisco Leandro de Viana. From then on, both were commissioned to proselytize new members for the Society. Within a few months, Aguirre was replaced by Ambrosio Meabe, a Bizkaian very involved in the mining sector of Nueva España who had managed the business of the powerful Fagoaga family. Between Viana and Meabe, they completed the task assigned them, managing to recruit over two hundred members in 1773. In the following years, the number of memberships increased progressively until it reached its high point of 530 in 1787, only to decline notably later (see table 2.8 in appendix 2). Merchants, miners, *hacendistas*, intellectuals, royal functionaries, clerics, and soldiers living in almost all the provinces of Nueva España (Guanajuato, Mexico City, Michoacán, Oaxaca, Puebla, and Guadalajara) were the main occupations of the members. Marquis Castañiza, Count Bassoco, the Fagoaga family, Sebastián de Eguía, José Ramón de Goya, Ambrosio de Meabe, Fausto de Elhuyart, Francisco Javier Gamboa, Colonel Juan de Amestoy, Bishop Santiago Echevarría, Viceroy Antonio Bucarelli y Ursúa, Justices Antonio de Urizar and Antonio de Villaurrutia, and Joaquín de Plaza y Ubilla, chancellor and commissioner of the Society, were the leading exponents of the Enlightenment in Mexico.[43]

In the viceroyalty of Nueva España, in the captaincy general of Cuba, recruitment of members for the Society began in 1773.[44] The impulse was provided by the Basque *hacendados:* Joaquín de Aristarain, Martín de Arosllozu, Francisco José de Basabe, count of the House of Montalvo, Antonio José Beitia, Ignacio Echagoyen, Martín de Echevarría, Francisco Javier de Garaicoechea, Andrés Jáuregui, Domingo de Lizundia, José Ilincheta, and, above all, Francisco Arango Parreño, the most important figure of the Cuban Enlightenment. And it was during the tenure of the Bizkaian Governor Luis de las Casas y Aragorri that the first long-term Cuban newspaper began publication and the Economic Association of Havana was constituted (1792), five years after an institution of the same name was founded in Santiago, Cuba (1787).

As for the Philippines,[45] where the majority of the members resided in the capital, Manila, it is curious to note that even though the first member, the Araban Captain General Simón de Anda y López de Armentia, joined in the year 1769, the large-scale incorporation of new members did not begin until 1780. In this captaincy general, Simón de Anda himself and the Augustine monk Manuel Rebollo, from Valladolid, promoted the foundation of the Economic Association of Friends of the Country (1781).

The Royal Basque Society's expansion through the viceroyalty of Peru occurred much later than in Nueva España and did not attain significant membership until 1783, although the pace of affiliation increased from then on. The advocates of the Peruvian Enlightenment were the Araban Juan Eguino y López de Arregui and the Bizkaian Domingo de Larrea y Amez, both Lima merchants. As with the rest of the Economic Associations of Friends of the Country in America, Peru's had a large number of merchants, high-level functionaries, clerics, aristocrats, and intellectuals, the majority of them also members of the Confraternity of Our Lady of Aránzazu of Lima. Among the long list, the following names are worth citing: Pedro José de Zárate, the marquis of Monterrico, the Navarrese Antonio de Elizalde y Arretea, count of Premio Real, the erudite Bizkaian José de Baquijano, the Gipuzkoan Blás Ignacio de Tellería y Tapia, the miners Santiago de Urquiza Sánchez de Alba and Juan Fermín Errea y Eugui, the Navarrese bishop Baltasar Jaime Martínez Compañón y Martínez Bujanda, the cleric Juan Domingo de Zamácola y Jáuregui (brother of Simón Bernardo de Zamácola, a leading figure in the Seigneury of Bizkaia during the first third of the nineteenth century and after whom the famous "Zamacolada" was named), and the Navarrese viceroy Manuel de Guirior y Portal de Huarte and his successor Agustín de Jáuregui y Aldecoa, natives of Aoiz and the Valley of Baztán, respectively. (See table 2.9 in appendix 2.) Their spirit of the Enlightenment led them to found the Academic Association of the Lovers of Lima in 1791 and promote its ideals through their official organ of expression, the *Mercurio Peruano*.

Although it was in the viceroyalties of Nueva España and Peru that the Royal Basque Society had its largest numbers of members, there was also significant membership in other American territories with important Basque colonies. Thus, in Nueva Granada there were Royal Basque Societies in Santa Fé de Bogota (1801), Cartagena (Colombia), Mompox (1784), Caracas (1810), and Quito (1791). And in the viceroyalty of Río de la Plata, the Buenos Aires and Charca chapters totaled just under two hundred fifty members between 1765 and 1793. Among the benefits of the American expansion were valuable memoirs about medicine and seeds and timely information about agriculture and industry, as well as financial contributions.

Lastly, relations with America suffered from the bad luck that befell the original program of the Royal Basque Society. In the early 1780s, as a result of the failure of the Bourbon economic reform, conflicts involving participation of the Basque ports in the free trade policy (1778), and the tariffs on Basque products outside its provinces' borders decreed by the state administration, the support received by the

Society from both the commercial institutions and *foral* organizations began to decline. The network of institutional contacts and supports in America withered as well. Influence reached its low point during the period following the critical years of the War against the French Convention (1793–1795), when the Society tried repeatedly to reestablish the contacts with their American members. But they no longer possessed the same capacity for convocation, influence, and integration, and the efforts were in vain. The impossibility of recovering the colonial support was an aggravating factor in the crisis that confronted the institution between 1796 and 1808, and which it was ultimately unable to overcome.

Scene from a ship bound for Río de la Plata, ca. 1900s. Courtesy Archivo General de la Nación, Buenos Aires, Argentina

Top: Los Pirineos Bakery street vendor, ca. 1950s. *Bottom:* Basque dairyman in Buenos Aires, Argentina, ca. 1940s. Both photos courtesy Archivo General de la Nación, Buenos Aires, Argentina

Departing farewell, ca. 1900s. Courtesy Archivo General de la Nación, Buenos Aires, Argentina

Top: Basque street dairymen vendors, Buenos Aires, Argentina, ca. 1900–1950.
Bottom: The establishment of Argentine dairy business of J. E. Uriburu, ca. 1900s.
Both photos courtesy Archivo General de la Nación, Buenos Aires, Argentina

Top: Immigrant arrivals in Argentina, n.d. *Bottom:* Hotel de los Emigrantes, ca. early 1900s. Both photos courtesy Archivo General de la Nación, Buenos Aires, Argentina

Top: Advertisement for Basque dairies, ca. 1900–1950. *Bottom:* Port of Buenos Aires for unloading goods, ca. 1920s. Both photos courtesy Archivo General de la Nación, Buenos Aires, Argentina

Facing page, top: South American garment industry with immigrant laborers. *Facing page, bottom:* Dining room at Hotel de los Emigrantes, Buenos Aires, n.d. Both photos courtesy Archivo General de la Nación, Buenos Aires, Argentina

Top: Passenger ship *Isabel de Borbón*, 1928. *Bottom:* Passenger carriages at the Hotel de los Emigrantes, ca. 1870–1880. Both photos courtesy Ministerio de Trabajo y Seguridad Social de España

Top: Immigrant fisherman, Venezuela, ca. 1890. *Bottom:* Disembarkation of passengers and goods, ca. 1870–1880. Both photos courtesy Ministerio de Trabajo y Seguridad Social de España

Top: Hotel de los Emigrantes, Buenos Aires, n.d. *Bottom:* Immigration inspectors, n.d. Both photos courtesy Archivo General de la Nación, Buenos Aires, Argentina

Arrivals in Río de la Plata, n.d. Courtesy Archivo General de la Nación, Buenos Aires, Argentina

Top: Immigrant arrivals waiting for meals, n.d. *Bottom:* Interior view of Hotel de los Emigrantes, n.d. Both photos courtesy Archivo General de la Nación, Buenos Aires, Argentina

Chapter Four

Basque Americans

Royal Dirigisme

There is no doubt that the discovery and conquest of the New World offered subjects of the Spanish monarchy an unsurpassable opportunity to expand their professional, economic, social, and residential opportunities when the immense American colonial territory was incorporated into the Castilian Crown. The opening of this vast area also meant the end of the ethnic and cultural isolation that the American indigenous world had enjoyed until then, as well as the configuration of a new, multi-racial society. The first step in this process was the invasion of Castilian conquerors, first in the Antilles (1493–1521), and then on the continent. Subsequently, there was a constant flow of European population that would last for five centuries, marked by stages with their own rhythms and characteristics.[1]

To regulate this migratory movement, the Crown, as in so many other spheres of American life, wavered between the theoretical ideals—shaped by numerous dispositions to control the Hispanic population in America—and the necessity of ensuring an effective Spanish presence in distant lands. It is therefore logical that passage to the Americas was always controlled by the state. From the outset, the sovereigns claimed control of all ocean expeditions, demanding that all such undertakings receive prior royal authorization in order to know "the people that go, and of what importance and occupation is each one of them."[2] Facing an unknown reality, the Catholic Monarchs felt forced to improvise a migratory and colonizing policy to address both the agreements with explorers and the type of people to whom fell the task of exploiting the recently discovered territories. Thus, after some futile attempts to convert the Americas into a penal colony whereby Spain could cleanse itself socially, there emerged little by little a migratory policy encouraged by the Crown itself. It established families of colonists in America devoted to a great variety of farming and other occupations in order to build a worthy future.

The creation of the Casa de Contratación (House of Trade) in 1503 was the catalyst of the legal system that regulated the passage and settling of immigrants in America. The most important measure adopted in this period was the requirement for all passengers to obtain a permit from that office before embarking for America. This so-called "License of Passengers to America" was made up of personal dossiers. To be complete, it had to include (a) an application duly filled out by the potential emigrant; (b) notarization of the same; (c) a copy of the royal decree authorizing the emigration; (d) concession of the boarding license by the functionaries of the House of Trade; (e) "proof" regarding the *limpieza de sangre* (i.e., freedom from Jewish or Moorish ancestry) of the applicant, which had to include declarations from three witnesses and could be accompanied by a certificate of baptism; (f) if the emigrant was married and traveling alone, documentation of his wife's consent to the voyage with an expressed declaration;[3] (g) a short note effectively indicating that the emigrant had boarded; (h) a marginal accounting verifying that he had paid for the boarding license; and (i) in order to facilitate the concession of the authorization to travel to America, attached letters from family members already settled in America sending for the applicant. The following data were also added: the applicant's age, sex, and profession, and a brief physical description that included the functionary's first impression, and, in general, body stature and color of complexion or hair, supplemented by some distinguishing physical feature, often a facial one, physical defect, scar, or sign of some disease.[4] Such iron-handed administrative control was instituted both to prevent spontaneous or clandestine emigration and to shape the type of settler that would go out the Americas according to the Crown's taste.

But the monarchy's regulated dispositions also included a long list of prohibitions created to spare the New World from the traditional ills that afflicted Spanish society. Thus, the first ones excluded from the American colonization process were Moors and Jews, "declared enemies of the faith," who were expelled from the peninsula between 1492 and 1502. They were followed by the so-called "new Christians"—converted Moors and Jews that were unable to document Christian ancestral roots more than two hundred years old—because they were suspect of the same crime against the faith. Exclusion for religious reasons was extended to those guilty of heresy, those condemned by the Inquisition, and even those punished by the Holy Office (although they had already fulfilled their penalties), and their children and grandchildren. According to strictly ethnic and cultural criteria, prohibitions from going to the Americas also affected the Gypsy population. According to the view of the epoch, this group did not fit the prototype of the honorable settler, Old Christian, and stable lifestyle that could serve as an example for the Native American. Non-Spaniards were also prohibited from settling overseas. This made complete sense, given the principle defended by the Spanish Crown from early on that the Americas belonged to it alone. America therefore had to remain closed to the rest of the nations of the world, especially enemies and all those who did not faithfully follow the Catholic Church of Rome.

Nevertheless, legislation did not represent an insurmountable obstacle to going and settling in the Americas. The introduction of the Tribunal of the Holy Office into American lands to control the activities of those barred is the best evidence of this. Non-Spaniards were frequently authorized to travel to America, subject to naturalization, for business or evangelical motives. In addition, a monarchy with financial pressures was always disposed to grant personal exemptions—nontransferable and valid for two years—in certain cases for compensation. Apparently, the easiest way for non-Spaniards wishing to travel to America was to buy a royal license. The sanctions imposed on unauthorized non-Spaniards were very severe. Those who embarked without licenses would be punished with four years in prison; ships' captains and officials transporting non-Spaniards or other unlicensed passengers were threatened with the death penalty (Royal Decree of November 26, 1607); those non-Spaniards found in America would have their possessions confiscated and be expelled (Royal Decree of September 26, 1560); and those found aboard ships on the Indies run could be immediately executed without previously consulting the monarchy.[5]

However, as already stated, the policy was not always applied to the letter of the law. Some authors have identified at least fifteen non-Spaniards living on Hispaniola in 1503 that were authorized to continue there in light of their service to the Crown.[6] Years later, Ferdinand the Catholic granted non-Spaniards permission to do business in the Americas if they were naturalized in Castile and associated with Spanish merchants. The requirement for naturalization was to be married to a Spanish woman and have proven residence in Sevilla, Cádiz, or Jerez for fifteen or twenty years. Emperor Charles V opened the Indies run and American territory to the subjects of all those states under his imperial sovereignty. Philip II applied a more permissive policy to non-Spaniards. During his reign, he lowered to ten the number of years of residence in Spain required for naturalization eligibility. In addition, on more than a few occasions the clandestine non-Spanish presence in America was legalized after the payment of indemnizations or compensations, so necessary for a state in a permanent state of war.

Another issue regulated in the legislation was female emigration. Although authorizations were sometimes conceded in order to promote the transport of single women to compensate for the imbalance in predominantly male colonial society, most women were prohibited from traveling to America. During the reign of Philip II, as a result of denunciations of some female conduct considered licentious and inappropriate, travel of all single women not accompanied by their closest male relatives was restricted. It was hoped that the New World would thereby be spared the ills present in Spain. Thus, in the same way an attempt was made to keep religious undesirables, delinquents, vagrants, and others branded as unacceptable out of the Americas, the Crown also sought to protect the overseas territories from conduct of morally "distracted" women judged damaging to a well-ordered society. Married women did not possess juridical status, and thus could not apply for emigration on their own. They could therefore undertake the transatlantic voyage only if they were accompanied by their spouses, or after the authorities from the House of Trade had been duly informed that the husband, already in the New World, had summoned his wife.[7]

Nevertheless, such restrictive measures did not yield the desired results. The

House of Trade observed the legislation especially closely in the case of Muslims, Jews, Gypsies, and Protestants. Its attitude toward non-Spaniards and other emigrants, on the other hand, was more permissive. The paths of evasion and even roguishness were the order of the day in the transport of people to America. Thus, several means of outwitting the law were added to the exceptions that already existed for non-Spaniards. Enlisting as a sailor or soldier was the ideal ruse to conceal the emigrant's intention to settle on American soil, which was accomplished through desertion once the transatlantic voyage was over. Signing up as a servant in the retinue of some important person or using the Canary Islands as a secret catapult to the Americas were also common. There were those who made their fortune through the sale of the official documents necessary for obtaining the boarding license, or who lodged stowaways in the bays and holds of their ships in exchange for significant sums of money.

In summary, the law was not always or fully observed in practice. Consequently, America soon stopped being the ideal society initially imagined and designed. The New World was not free of non-Spaniards, exiles, suspected heretics, delinquents, the poor, idlers, and women of licentious conduct. The Americas thus appeared in the eyes of some of the people of the time as "a refuge and shelter for Spain's desperate, church for revolutionaries, safe-conduct for killers, stage for swindlers, general lure for free women, common deception for many and particular remedy for few" (Miguel de Cervantes Saavedra).[8]

The migratory directives themselves changed to reflect the political, social, and economic conjuncture of the Spanish monarchy.[9] The sixteenth century was thus a favorable period for the departure of emigrants as a necessity for the conquest and exploitation of the New World, on one hand, and to relieve the manifest demographic pressure that existed in large areas of the peninsula, on the other. With the opening of the Americas, the Castilian Crown wanted to maintain a stable and equilibrated population in its new possessions, capable of guaranteeing Spanish domination of the natives. There was no better way of doing this than promoting the emigration of men, women, and families from a country in which the population density had reached high levels. This was especially true between 1530 and 1591, as a result of vigorous economic growth.[10] In response to these two variables, numerous measures were adopted to stimulate emigration to the Americas. Already in the time of Ferdinand the Catholic (1511), the agents of the House of Trade of Sevilla were exhorted to extenuate the legal requisites for the sake of increasing the migratory flow. They were also urged to send agents to the northern provinces of the peninsula where, in the opinion of the Crown, there were "more than enough people to be able to go to work in the recently discovered Indies."[11] The authorization of recruitment campaigns for the undertakings of conquest and colonization decreed in the times of Emperor Charles V and Philip II had the same ends. Under these reigns, the already mentioned vigorous population and economic growth occurred.

Nevertheless, the demographic climate worsened considerably at the end of the 1500s. A mortality crisis caused by epidemics and wars characterized the peninsula throughout most of the seventeenth century. Calls for limits on the flow of American emigration as a remedy were heard from a wide range of social groups. Thus, between 1592 and 1598, numerous attorneys counseled the king that,

> it may be of use to order [moderation in the transport of] people that leave these kingdoms, attentive that, outside of them, no resource is as lacking as people, and to expressly order that they do not go to the Indies for some years if they are not clergy to preach and spread the doctrine, and officials and ministers to govern the lands, and their servants and families, taking great care that the rest do not go, because those kingdoms cannot be populated without depopulating these ones.[12]

Such opinions would find an outlet in the legal dispositions that called for a closer watch over clandestine emigration. The reason given by the legislators was "the lack that [the emigrants] create in these kingdoms, in the populations, farming and cultivation of the lands as well as for war."[13]

After the demographic crisis of the 1600s, the eighteenth century saw a reversal of a positive view of emigration to the Americas. This period was marked by the "populationist" policy instituted by the Bourbons. For Enlightenment believers of the 1700s, "the population of the country is one of the simplest standards for judging the goodness of its constitution. When depopulation increases, the State is on the road to ruin; and the country that increases its population, even if it is the poorest, is surely better governed." They added that "the true force and opulence of a State depends on the number and vigor of the individuals that compose it."[14] This summarizes the demographic thought of the period. On one hand, the political, economic, and social power of the state identified with the number of its servants; on the other, the number depended on state action. In this context, it makes sense that emigration would stop being considered an exclusively private matter and become something that the Crown would invest in. This was especially true given that the New World was a primary source of income for the Bourbon monarchy. This circumstance collided head on with the fact that during the eighteenth century the laws regulating emigration to America tended to become more restrictive, limiting access to the licensees and endlessly repeating the penalties that awaited those that dared to make the trip without the necessary documents. This was intended to reshape the profile of the emigrant to meet the needs of the colonial economy: qualified artisans, merchants, and bureaucratic personnel. In any case, the government clearly promoted the revitalization of the Indies run, stimulated private participation in overseas commerce through the privileged companies, opened sea routes that circumvented the monopoly of Cádiz, and decentralized commercial traffic thanks to the Free Trade decrees of 1765 and 1778. It also financed the transport of large contingents of troops and spent a significant amount of money on establishing settlers in the main strategic commercial American seats (Montevideo, Antilles, Patagonia).

In sum, colonial emigration to the New World was a voluntary movement, although it was led by the Crown from the start through the promotion of settlement policies and restrictive legislation. The object was to guarantee Spanish domination of the Americas through a stable and equilibrated population. The results mobilized large human contingents hoping to achieve their golden dreams in America. But they also severely impaired Spain's demographic strength at the time.[15]

The Basque and Navarrese Migratory Current in the General Spanish Context

Starting in the sixteenth century, migratory waves to America were frequent. Natives of all the historical regions of Spain took part in them, although to differing degrees. The populations of the Basque Country and Navarre nourished this migratory flow, with pulses and characteristics similar to those in Spain's other regions. Thanks to the boarding licenses, it has been possible to calculate fairly reliably the volume of Spanish emigration to America, especially in the sixteenth century, as well as determine its Iberian origins. Nevertheless, all researchers agree that, in spite of its documentary importance, this source does not exactly correspond to the reality of the colonial period. Clandestine and illegal embarkations in the sixteenth and seventeenth centuries were often denounced. And it is known that licenses were frequently falsified, especially in the city of Sevilla. Furthermore, administrative difficulties with comprehensive registration surged in the 1700s once free trade was decreed. Given these limitations, the current lacunae in research on migration in the modern era are understandable.[16] Consequently, there is no uniform set of criteria among specialists regarding the magnitude of the migratory current to the Americas for this period. Thus, the data contributed by the historians varies significantly.

The most reliable estimates, although they are sometimes debated, are those proposed by Magnus Mörner.[17] Using data based on the number and tonnage of the ships that crossed the Atlantic, the median number of passengers that these ships transported to America, and the median percentage of the crew members that were registered as sailors as the only means to pay for the trip, but deserted upon reaching their destination, Mörner established an annual mean of 3,018 immigrants to the Americas for the period 1506–1650. Domínguez Ortiz[18] calculates that around 5,000 immigrants landed in America per year during the same period. In any case, aside from the differences in estimates, all the demographers appear to agree that this migratory current was generally less intense than that occurring between 1880 and 1914.[19] Given the impossibility of calculating the exact volume of the population that went to the Americas during this period, and the serious documentary limitations and lacunae in the existing sources,[20] it is necessary to rely on data that, although incomplete, offer a global and approximate vision of the Spanish migratory process to America between 1500 and 1800. Among such works, those of Professor Peter Boyd-Bowman[21] are undoubtedly the most reliable base for serious, rigorous study of sixteenth-century Spanish immigration in America.

In his commitment to discover the ethnic makeup of emigration from Spain to America, Boyd-Bowman identified the origin of 53,359 people settled in the New World between 1493 and 1600. The distribution of these settlers by place of origin permits an initial approximation of the regional heterogeneity of Spain's population and colonization of the Americas in the 1500s, as shown in table 4.1.

The participation percentage of the Iberian regions contributing to the migratory flow to America is shown in the last column of the table. The first thing to be noted is the undeniable primacy of Andalusia in migration to the Indies during the 1500s, with a percentage (36.9 percent) much higher than the rest of the regions. It is followed in importance by Old Castile (including León), whose contribution (19.8 percent), nevertheless declined throughout the last third of the century. Extremadura maintained extraordinary stability throughout the sixteenth century, supplying 16.5 percent, or about one-sixth of the total volume of emigration. This profile was the opposite of that of its neighbor to the north, New Castile, whose figures, 15.6 percent, grew continuously. In total, Castile—including Andalusia—came to represent almost 90 percent of the Spanish emigration documented in the sixteenth century. The participation of the other territories of the Spanish monarchy was therefore limited. Thus, while Galicia and the Mediterranean Levant barely exceeded 1 percent (1.2 percent and 1.3 percent, respectively), Asturias, the Canaries, and the Crown of Aragón did not even reach that level (0.6 percent, 0.3 percent, and 0.6 percent, respectively).

The contribution of the Basque Country and Navarre was around 4.4 percent, although the evolution during the years studied by Professor Boyd-Bowman shows a marked difference among the stages. Thus, between 1493 and 1519, the Basque and Navarrese share represented 4.8 percent of the total sample; between 1520 and 1539, 5 percent; and between 1540 and 1559, 5.2 percent. This last period marked the apex of Basque migratory flow to the Americas. In the period 1560–1579, their participation would be reduced to 3.5 percent; between 1580 and 1600, it would remain stable at 3.8 percent. By province, it was the Seigneury of Bizkaia that provided the largest population contingent destined for America, followed by Gipuzkoa, Araba, and, at a considerable distance, Navarre. However, students of Basque and Navarrese migration to the New World believe it was greater than shown in the official figures. Douglass and Bilbao thus observe that such estimates do not consider the fact that Basque sailors were predominant among the crews of the Indies run and, therefore, more likely to immigrate illegally by deserting once

TABLE 4.1 Spanish Emigration to the Americas by Region, 1493–1600

Region	1493–1519	1520–39	1540–59	1560–79	1580–1600	Total	Percentage (%) of Total
Andalusia	2,172	4,247	3,269	6,547	3,994	20,229	36.9
Old Castile[1]	1,393	3,341	1,949	2,859	1,354	10,869	19.8
Extremadura	769	2,204	1,416	3,295	1,351	9,035	16.5
New Castile	483	1,587	1,303	3,343	1,825	8,541	15.6
Basque Country[2]	267	671	477	627	364	2,406	4.4
Non-Spaniards	141	557	332	263	229	1,522	2.8
Levant[3]	69	253	112	209	102	745	1.3
Galicia	111	193	73	179	111	667	1.2
Aragón	32	101	40	99	83	355	0.6
Asturias	36	77	49	90	71	323	0.6
Canary Islands	8	31	24	75	24	162	0.3
Total	5,481	13,262	9,044	17,586	9,508	54,881	100.0

1. Including León.
2. Including Navarre.
3. Including Murcia.

Source: P. Boyd-Bowman, 1985.

they reached American ports. Nor do the official figures take into account the high number of Basques and Navarrese that, like the emigrants to the Americas, left their respective native provinces during the 1500s to serve the Crown in the administration, navy, and army in Spain and its European and colonial territories. Furthermore, any estimate must consider the fact that a large number of Basques who listed Andalusia as their home could have gone to America after registering as residents of Sevilla, Cádiz, Huelva, and Jerez.

In any case, sixteenth-century Basque and Navarrese emigration was very substantial and strained their demographic potential. The population of the Basque Country and Navarre had the lowest growth rate (0.16 percent) of all the Spanish monarchy's continental territories between 1530 and 1591 for a reason.[22] Like that from the rest of Spain, Basque emigration was primarily a male phenomenon. By mid-century, with the Antillean phase of conquest complete and Spanish domination in America consolidated, however, the situation began to change. The Crown demanded that married emigrants be accompanied by their wives, and reinforced conjugal union in America. This fundamentally affected young male bachelors between sixteen and twenty-five years old, especially during the period of conquest and initial colonization. Then, in the second half of the century, the mean age would increase notably with the promotion of family-based emigration.[23]

Basque and Navarrese emigration was marked by its social diversity. As occurred in the other Spanish territories in the time of the Hapsburgs, emigration in the Basque Country was always composed of a significant number of both higher and lesser nobility. This group comprised those lacking desirable opportunities for social mobility within their own class due to their unfavorable (disinherited) position within the family structure of their respective households. Merchants, artisans, and liberal professionals (especially doctors and lawyers) also constituted a large contingent. Numerous bureaucrats and functionaries were sent from Bizkaia, Gipuzkoa, Araba, and Navarre to the New World to meet the necessities of colonial administration. Nor was there a lack of Basque clerics—mostly regular—that left their ancestral homes for the Americas to engage in evangelical work, the main argument for Spanish domination in America at the time. Their numbers, however, fluctuated throughout the modern era and were directly related to the spiritual needs of the colonies and the official policy practiced in them.

In contrast, as the research data suggests, participation of the Basque rural world in the migratory flow to the Americas was minimal. This makes sense, given the inability of Basque farmers and peasants to meet the high costs of crossing the Atlantic. They were also unable to evade payment through the common strategies already mentioned: enlistment as soldiers or sailors, registration as servants for noteworthy people, or simply as stowaways, with the obvious danger that this supposed. These sectors of the population were therefore largely excluded from the migratory flow to the colonies.

As for the specific American destinations of the emigration of the 1500s, Nueva España, Peru, Nueva Granada, the Antilles, Río de la Plata, and Central America were the American regions that received the largest contingents of Spanish migrants (in that order; see table 4.2). The general data supplied by Boyd-Bowman for all of Spain can be extrapolated to the Basque case in this matter, given that sixteenth-century emigration was directed by the Crown according to the military, economic, and administrative needs of the colonial territories.

If the available information about Spanish immigration in the Indies in the seventeenth century is not as complete as might be wished, the data for the beginning of the new century is worse. With Professor Boyd-Bowman's global study covering only until 1599, dependable studies of the seventeenth-century migratory process to America are scarce. Nevertheless, a reading and analysis of the available sources (mostly regional and local) suggests that seventeenth-century migration displayed tendencies similar to those described for the 1500s. In sum, a mostly male, unmarried, young sector of the population whose social roots were as diverse as in the previous century continued to nourish the emigrant pool, although a high percentage (47 percent) corresponding to the category of servants is now evident. These individuals chose Nueva España, Peru, and, to a lesser degree, Central America and the Antilles as the places to settle and aspire to success in the New World. Given the scarcity of documentation, and awaiting publication of new research providing rigorous, scientific data about seventeenth-century immigration in America, its study can be extrapolated from the population census conducted in Mexico City in 1689.[24] Although limited to only one city and susceptible to incorrect generalization, this document has the advantage of profiling the region of origin of a significant sample of 1,182 European settlers and their main occupations. It can be considered a valid source because the capital of the viceroyalty of Nueva España was the main seat of settlement for Spanish immigrants at the time. The information offered by this census is shown in table 4.3.

The decline of the traditional sources of emigrants seems confirmed by the information in table 4.3. While Andalusia maintained its primacy (28.2 percent), albeit with a decreasing percentage, the supply by both Castiles and Extremadura (13.2 percent and 2.7 percent, respectively) sank to a minimum in comparison to previous periods. The northern regions filled the resulting void, with a predominance of Basques and Navarrese (18.4 percent), Cantabrians (11.9 percent), and, to a lesser extent, Galicians (6.4 percent) and Asturians (2.5 percent). As in the sixteenth century, the Crown of Aragón hardly participated in the migratory process. The census also reflects a significant presence of non-Spaniards living in Mexico: 114 people, or 9.6 percent of Mexico's European population in 1689. This leads to the conclusion that during the seventeenth century, royal authorizations permitting non-Spanish immigrants to settle were still frequent (as in the 1500s), whether through recourse to naturalization or privilege, or in exchange for financial com-

TABLE 4.2 Destination of Spanish Emigration to the Americas, 1493–1600

Region	1493–1519	1520–39	1540–59	1560–79	1580–1600	Total
Nueva España[1]	743	5,001	2,057	7,577	2,868	18,246
Peru[2]	92	1,522	4,067	4,661	4,002	14,344
Nueva Granada[3]	590	2,251	1,398	2,681	952	7,872
Antilles	1,254	1,675	472	1,458	490	5,349
Río de la Plata[4]	—	1,088	600	733	169	2,590
Central America	—	604	181	954	255	1,994
Total	2,679	12,141	8,775	18,064	8,736	50,395

1. Including Florida and the North America frontier.
2. Including Charcas, Quito, and Chile.
3. Including Panama and Venezuela.
4. Including Tucumán and Paraguay.
Source: P. Boyd-Bowman, 1985.

pensation. In regard to the socioprofessional distribution of the 1,182 settlers registered, the large number of merchants (53 percent), functionaries (10.4 percent), and artisans (6 percent) stands out.

In sum, this document appears to confirm a shift in the migratory pattern of the seventeenth century. Thus, the decline of the southern regions was succeeded by the increase in northern representation, especially Basque and Navarrese.

Confirming the considerable number of Bizkaians, Gipuzkoans, Arabans, and Navarrese that left their respective places of origin for the Americas in the seventeenth century are documents from around mid-century that note that these provinces suffered a great lack of population "due to the many that commonly leave to serve His Majesty in the armies and armadas, and those from the port are especially lacking." Other observers around the same time, perhaps exaggerating, estimated that three-quarters of the Bizkaian population were women "due to the many men that leave and do not return." According to such sources, the drastic Basque depopulation coincided precisely with a period in which the high cost of transport, the insecurity of navigation (as already stated, the 1600s was the great century of piracy), and the restrictive criteria of the Crown should have combined to cause a decrease in emigration to the New World. Nevertheless, as some authors have maintained,[25] these same factors could easily have encouraged illegal voyages to the Americas, numerous in that century, judging by the repetition and intensification of the punishments imposed from above upon clandestine immigrants. If the relative ease with which Basque natives averted official procedures in their maritime and commercial activities is also taken into account (beginning in 1582, the Crown gave

TABLE 4.3 Europeans in the Mexico City Census, 1689

Origin	No./%	Occupation/No.
Andalusia	333/28.2	Merchant/628
Basque Country & Navarre	218/18.4	Bureaucrat/124
Castile[1]	156/13.2	Dependent/113
Cantabria	141/11.9	Other[4]/99
Non-Spaniards	114/9.6	No information/79
Galicia	76/6.4	Artisan/72
La Rioja	37/3.1	No occupation/59
Extremadura	32/2.7	Church/8
Asturias	30/2.5	—
Aragon[2]	29/2.4	—
Canary Islands	12/1.0	—
Others[3]	4/0.3	—

1. Both Castiles, León, and La Mancha.
2. Including Catalonia and the Levant (Valencia, Murcia, and Cartagena).
3. Ceuta and Gibraltar.
4. Professionals, *encomenderos*, painters, brokers, students, administrators, foremen, cattle breeders, *hacendados*, landlords, butchers, muleteers, comedians, etc.

Source: J. I. Rubio Mañé, 1966.

preference to Bizkaian ships on the Indies run and to Bizkaians wishing to travel to America as masters), the disproportionate presence of Basques and Navarrese in the Mexico City population censuses can be easily explained. Although the causes that slowed the departure of Basque emigrants in the colonial epoch will be discussed in detail below, it can be mentioned in advance that the decline in naval construction, foundry activity, fishing, and navigation suffered by the Basque Country during the seventeenth century could have easily influenced the increase of the Basque flow to America in the 1600s.

The Basque and Navarrese contingent in the Spanish migratory process of the 1600s was a prelude to the massive levels that it would reach in the following century. The opportunities open in the field of administration thanks to the Bourbon reforms, but especially the opening of new commercial and mining centers, surely served as a powerful attraction for the relocation of many natives of the Basque Country and Navarre, whether temporary or permanent. But these circumstances will be discussed in more depth below, when the causes that slowed the departure of these emigrants are analyzed. For now, they will be cited only to introduce the reader to the quantitative aspects of eighteenth-century emigration to America and analysis of why this was especially stocked with functionaries, soldiers and merchants, professional groups, and, as in the preceding periods, some clerics and a few adventurers disposed to "make the Americas."

As with sixteenth- and seventeenth-century material, the current state of research on Spanish emigration in the 1700s is deficient. Nevertheless, the most recent studies published,[26] while of limited focus in both time and regional scope, represent a substantial advance. It is accurate to say that eighteenth-century emigration was transformed in volume, region of origin, and internal structure. In other words, a reduction in the volume of migration, a transfer in the core of the geographic weighting, and a significant difference in the composition by age, civil status, and socioprofessional condition of the emigrants are noticeable.[27] Moreover, although significant, eighteenth-century emigration was not constant in its flow between 1765 and 1800, the years for which rigorous, continuous data do exist.

The oscillations reflected in figure 4.1 respond to concrete circumstances on both sides of the Atlantic. Thus, one noteworthy drop-off in migratory flow corresponds to the years of the American War of Independence (1779–1783). Another significant decline in emigration is evident beginning in 1796, coinciding with war between Spain and England. As for the rest, the moderation of the peaks (never more than 550 licenses annually) and the stability of these high levels in non-war years can be observed. In spite of ups and downs, the available quantitative data demonstrate the general decline in Spanish emigration to the Americas in the eighteenth century. Nevertheless, that the figures analyzed so far take into account only the departures made from the city of Cádiz permits one to venture that the migratory flow had to be greater than reflected in the official figures. This was a period in which, outside of Cádiz's monopoly, authorization was granted to other Spanish ports for travel to the Americas. Moreover, during the eighteenth century, America became more attractive for other reasons as well: new territorial expansion, wide-ranging internal colonization, significant growth in commercial traffic, and greater ease in incorporating the distinct Spanish regions into the Indies run. It is just as clear, however, that eighteenth-century Spain, in full demographic and economic expansion, did not possess all the elements necessary to generate a large-scale emigration stimulated by the traditional push factors.[28]

Unfortunately, it is not possible to rigorously establish the real rhythm of Spanish emigration to the New World for the entire eighteenth century. Until now, estimates of the volume of migration to America in the 1700s has been based on the data available for the second half of the century. The starting point has been researchers' detailed analysis of the boarding licenses in Cádiz during the period 1765–1800 (located in Sevilla's General Archive of the Indies).[29] The first feature worth mentioning is the predominantly male character of eighteenth-century emigration: 86 percent male versus 14 percent female, logical in light of the very structure of Spanish society and the greater freedom of men to emigrate, on both a per-

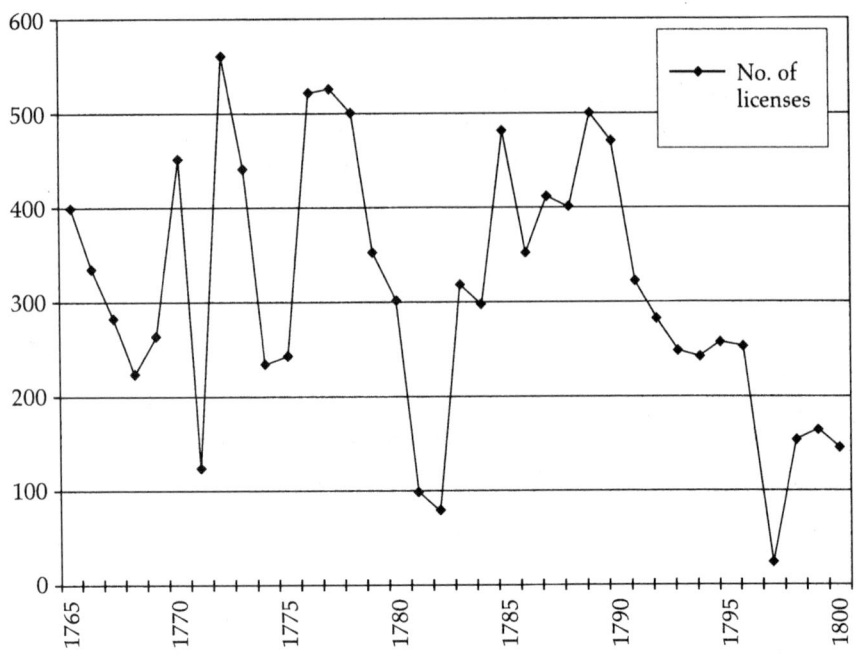

Fig. 4.1 Spanish Emigration to the Americas, 1765–1800. Source: R. Márquez Macías, 1995, 131.

sonal and juridical level. Regarding the civil status of this segment of the emigratory population, what stands out is that single men (82 percent) predominated over married (18 percent). In contrast, there was a greater percentage of married women (50 percent) than of single (43 percent) or widowed (7 percent) females. In regard to age, large segments of both sexes were clustered between fifteen and thirty years old—the height of youth and productivity.

In regard to the geographic distribution of the emigrants of the 1700s, the following list is very enlightening:[30]

Region	No./Percent
Andalusia	939/23.55
Non-Spanish	778/19.51
Basque Country-Navarre	615/15.43
Castile-León	289/7.25
Galicia	245/6.14
Cantabria	207/5.19
Catalonia	196/4.91
Asturias	151/3.79

Region	No./Percent
La Rioja	145/3.64
Madrid	112/2.81
Castile-La Mancha	95/2.38
Aragón	84/2.11
Valencia	55/1.38
Balearic Islands	27/0.68
Extremadura	26/0.65
Murcia	24/0.60
Total	3,988/100.00

Andalusia retained preeminence in the migratory current with almost one-fourth (23.55 percent) of the emigrants. The combination of the Basque Country and Navarre, with over 15 percent of the total, was situated in second place, followed by other northern regions such as Galicia (6.14 percent), Cantabria (5.19 percent), and Asturias (3.79 percent), all of them with high levels of emigration. This tendency confirms the shift of emigration to the north of the peninsula—a trend already evident in the seventeenth century. A decrease in absolute terms of the southern regions is thus also confirmed; in the case of Extremadura (0.65 percent), it is practically total. Lastly, the sample cited certifies that almost 20 percent of those authorized to emigrate to America were non-Spaniards. Considering the expressed prohibitions since the sixteenth century, such an elevated percentage is striking. Nevertheless, the already traditional illegal seats were stimulated in this century by an international conjuncture that facilitated the arrival of Frenchmen through the favoritism under the Bourbon alliance, Englishmen thanks to the Treaty of Utrecht (1713), and Portuguese thanks to their strategic border settlement of Colonia del Sacramento.[31]

Discriminating the emigrants by profession, the sector grouped under the label of servants (wet nurses, housekeepers, attendants, valets, ladies-in-waiting, pages, footmen, majordomos/stewards/butlers, porters, etc.) stands out (37 percent). Regarding the rest, merchants represented a percentage (23 percent) never attained previously, and soldiers likewise made up a very high percentage (19 percent); these contrast with the moderate numbers of bureaucrats (9 percent) and clergy (7 percent).[32] Thus, the elevated percentage of merchants indicates the new character of emigration with the presence of a specific group connected to the economic retooling of the New World and the recovery of control over the Indies run. The also substantial number of soldiers and functionaries reinforces a sense of the Bourbon Crown's attention to preserving its colonial domain through greater control by the authorities at home and planned defense in the Americas against enemy powers. The decreased volume of ecclesiastic migration reflects the reduction of the missionary and evangelizing needs in an area already Christianized, on one hand, and the increasing capacity of the Creole clergy to attend to the American congregation, on the other.[33]

The American destinations also experienced changes in emigration volume in the eighteenth century. While the viceroyalty of Nueva España maintained its attractiveness, receiving 43 percent of the emigrants, Peru suffered a profound regression compared to previous periods, and captured only about 14 percent of the immigration during the century. In contrast, other areas, such as Río de la Plata and the viceroyalty of Nueva Granada, were fortified with the arrival of abundant immigrant contingents. After a long stagnancy since the mid-sixteenth century, the Antilles experienced an intense resurgence. Within each of these regions, the urban centers, especially the capital cities, were the primary receptors. Almost all the emigrating professional groups chose the large business and administrative centers for residency, whether temporary or permanent, and for climbing the social ladder.[34]

Given that eighteenth-century emigration research is still poorly developed and incomplete for all of Spain, analysis of the emigration from Basque territory is even more difficult. There is simply a lack of rigorous, concrete studies of the colonial diaspora of the Basque Country and Navarre. This demographic process, although documented to have moved important quantities of people to American destinations, was probably even greater than customarily reflected in the statistics. Initiated by transatlantic registry ships and increased by the institution of free trade, the greater freedom of navigation and commerce in the eighteenth century substantially multiplies the difficulties for historians in quantifying the Basque migratory flow to the Americas precisely in the period of its greatest growth in the whole colonial period.

According to the available information presented above, Basque and Navarrese emigration moved a substantial volume of people during the final years of the modern era. In the general Spanish calculation, it came to represent 15.43 percent of the official emigration from the port of Cádiz at that time, 12 percent higher than during the period 1580–1600. This emigration opportunity appealed especially to the younger male population, which showed a preference for Mexico, the Caribbean, Peru, and Río de la Plata upon settling in the New World. Nevertheless, although absolute figures are surely low and below the real ones, the percentage should be more highly valued in a qualitative sense. Undoubtedly, during the eighteenth century the Bourbon Crown undertook a reformist policy that particularly affected its economy and administration, both sectors in which Basque natives were particularly adept.

The monarchy's objective was rooted in two key issues. One was to revive and develop to the maximum the possibilities of commerce with America. The other was to secure the borders of the overseas empire in the face of enemy threat through a rigid bureaucratic and military organization in the colonies. To meet the economic objectives, new ports such as Bilbao, Donostia, and Pasaia were equipped for commercial traffic with the Americas, and the European model of privileged mercantile companies was installed in Spain. The Basques clearly played a preeminent role in this context, greater than that discussed in the sources. Recall that it was the Basques who laid the foundations for the creation of all these shareholders' companies. They therefore constituted, a priori, the group most active in economic relations with the New World from their native ports. Nor should it be forgotten that the Basque Country was the region to which the greatest number of commercial licenses were granted by the House of Trade of Cádiz in the eighteenth century. Moreover, the Basque businessmen came to form authentic commercial emporiums in America and gained control of the principal organs of colonial economic power. As will be seen, on many occasions these merchants beckoned their closest relatives to help them in their businesses, thereby increasing the Basque migratory flow and planting a seed for future mercantilists and a compact ethnic group at the same time. In analyzing the number of businessmen that emigrated to America, one must therefore bear in mind that they did not appear as such in the departure records, but developed such economic activities in the long run.

Regarding the bureaucratic activity of the Basque diaspora of the 1800s, the situation appears similar. The 1700s were a time of important restructuring of the colonial government according to a more practical scheme: two new viceroyalties (Nueva Granada and Río de la Plata), and various royal tribunals (Caracas and Cuzco) were created, modifying the jurisdiction of those already in existence, and the French model of intendants with political, economic, and judicial powers was instituted, thereby replacing the governors in this duty. The objective was to simplify the colonial administration while simultaneously reinforcing the borders against potential foreign intrusion. The demand for functionaries in America increased in this context. And already in the seventeenth century the Crown showed a clear predilection for designating Basques and Navarrese to the posts of the administration that required greater trustworthiness and technical preparation.[35] The examples could be multiplied, as is clear from the material presented in previous chapters.

Nevertheless, in spite of the difficulties in documentation presented by current analyses of eighteenth-century Basque migration, some recently published studies[36] allow for an improved definition of a basic typology of Basque emigration to the Americas during the first half of the 1700s. Based on the pieces of information and the boarding licenses that the Basques of the period were required to provide before setting out overseas, and using a sample of 238 emigrants, these authors conclude that, foremost, the Basque migratory contingent to America was stocked fundamentally from a very young population; 80 percent of those undertaking the American adventure were below twenty-six years of age. Regarding the distribution by sex and civil status, the clear predominance of men over women, and of single over married can be deduced from the sample analyzed. These tendencies are similar to those in all Spanish emigration. Geographically, Gipuzkoa contributed the highest number of people to the Basque migratory current (41.59 percent), followed closely by Bizkaia (39.49 percent), and, at a greater distance, Araba (18.90 percent). Eighteenth-century emigration from the Basque Country conformed, in general terms, to the guidelines of the Spanish migratory current, marked by its strong urban character. Thus, a high percentage (41 percent) of these Basque emigrants were natives of the three capitals and the most important towns and cities, as is reflected in table 2.10 in appendix 2.

Lastly, the analyzed sample leaves no doubt that the destination was the Americas, as shown in table 2.11 in appendix 2. Thus, Nueva España continued to receive the highest number of Basque emigrants in the eighteenth century (40.67 percent). Mexico City and Puebla de los Angeles were especially attractive. The affluence of the latter could be viewed as circumstantial, however, as its elected bishop, Juan Antonio Lardizabal, brought eighteen servants with him. Peru occupied second place among the destinations of eighteenth-century Basque emigration (27.11 percent), with the city of Lima receiving one-third of this contingent. It makes sense that the majority of Basque colonial emigrants headed to these two viceroyalties. As already seen, in the sixteenth- and seventeenth-century migratory process they offered better prospects for economic and social triumph, and the bulk of government appointees were destined to these two territories, accompanied, of course, by their families and servants. The other areas of the Americas received the remaining 32.20 percent, although none of them, except for the mainland, managed to surpass 5 percent. Panama, Buenos Aires, Guatemala, Santo Domingo, and Quito were preferred urban destinations of some eighteenth-century Basque emigrants.

THE OVERSEAS CALLING

That Basque emigration overseas in the colonial era was important both quantitatively and qualitatively is irrefutable. As has been shown to this point, the Basque presence in the new lands was both numerically sizeable, especially from the second third of the eighteenth century on, and qualitatively substantial. But what were the motives that catapulted such a large contingent of people from the Basque Country to the shores of the New World? The majority of researchers are correct in highlighting that colonial migration, although geographically diverse and varied, all stemmed from a single factor: the lack of financial means. The Basque and Navarrese case was not an exception. Since everyone from the participants themselves and their daily observers to present-day scholars have pointed to this variable as the general cause of the migratory movement to America in the modern era, it would be illogical to look for different causal mechanisms. The desire of Basque emigrants to improve their socioeconomic conditions was a constant. One must look for complementary circumstances behind the departure of these first colonial settlers.

The reasons given by those who left the Basque Country and Navarre for overseas are varied. Nevertheless, several authors have pointed to three motives in particular as the principal causes of Basque migration to the Americas in the sixteenth, seventeenth, and eighteenth centuries. These are (1) the inheritance system, (2) the demographic pressure, and (3) the lack of resources—all three closely interconnected.[37] One system that sheds light on the Basque migratory process in both the colonial and contemporary periods is the peculiar form, in the Basque Country and Navarre, of acquiring the inheritance of the farmstead and its land—namely, the so-called *mayorazgo*, or system of undivided inheritance. Thus, in parts of northern Araba and Navarre, as well as in Iparralde, Bizkaia, and Gipuzkoa, it was normal for each peasant to be an owner (or renter) and to maintain a single family with the fruit of his farming labors. Basque common law emphasizes this. It was thought desirable that the farmsteads, the basic social unit of the Basque rural world, should not be divided either through sale or inheritance practices. In this context, it was customary, and guaranteed by Basque *foral* law, to choose a single heir among all the descendants. Once married, to guarantee the succession of the lineage, the chosen heir sought to maintain the family farmstead and all its possessions and "belongings" undivided. Once the wedding was held and the patrimony transmitted in life ("donatio propter nuptias"), the selected heir had to settle accounts with the rest of his or her non-inheriting siblings, who also had certain claims. Those that had left the family unit prior to the *donatio* had already received a quantity of money from the parents. Their claims, therefore, had been resolved. But the unmarried children would have the right to receive an endowment from the heir only when they decided to marry or leave. Their economic and social situation was therefore unattractive, to say the least. So it makes sense that *mayorazgo* would condition and promote a constant migration, stocked by the disinherited. They saw the New World as a gateway to longed-for prosperity, which was denied them in their birthplaces.

Another main influence on Basque colonial migration was the structural demographic pressure experienced by the Basque Country and Navarre in the modern era. The high population density in the Basque Provinces during these centuries—the result of the absence of the bioclimatic disasters and epidemics that overwhelmed the rest of Spain during this period—brought the land to its human capacity. A substantial part of the residents found themselves forced to abandon their places of origin to search for other modes of survival. Other factors came into play as well: the low productivity of Basque agriculture; the absence of industry capable of absorbing the surplus rural work force; the weakness of the Basque and Navarrese livestock sector at the time; the crisis plaguing Bizkaian and Gipuzkoan shipbuilding and foundries since at least the last decades of the sixteenth century; the loss of a good part of Basque commercial cod-fishing activity in the eighteenth century, which had been responsible for the growing participation of Basque capital in the rise of the privileged mercantile companies that century; the increase in the prices of staples such as cereal grains; some epidemics; and wars at the end of the 1700s against the French Revolution. In this context, it was not surprising that

Basque and Navarrese natives would search for a way to emigrate to distant and unknown lands as a solution to their adverse destinies. America was the answer.

Economic motives, the lack of resources, the search for a better position, making a fortune, pure necessity: these were among the profound reasons that obliged numerous Bizkaians, Arabans, Gipuzkoans, and Navarrese to head for adventure in the New World. The accounts are abundant; for the sake of brevity, however, only a few significant cases will be cited. For example, the Navarrese Jerónimo de Calatayud decided to move to Nueva España in 1664 to live more comfortably than in his native Viana, in spite of having received an aunt's inheritance. The choice seems not to have been misguided; in 1675 he sent a silver lamp from Mexico to the Virgin of Codes as a sign of his newfound prosperity.[38] In 1672, Rodrigo Miguel, also from Navarre, decided to travel to the Americas "to test fortune." And it seems that he also won it; upon his return in 1689 he married Jerónima Solano, who in a statement dated 1707 acknowledged that "with the funds that said Rodrigo Miguel, my husband, brought from the Indies, the possessions that we had sold were recovered, the house repaired and furnished with jewels, and other properties bought."[39] In 1701, the Basque José de Asarta justified his trip to America by the pure economic necessity of his family and "from there [Nueva España] to attend to his parents, brothers and sisters, nieces and nephews, who are numerous." He had to sell his part of the family inheritance to pay for the trip.[40] The need for money to embark in Andalusian ports obliged some emigrants to take extreme measures. This was the case of Martín de Astrain, who stole 900 reales from his boss in the hope of winning enough to travel to the Americas and return the money. A card game was his downfall.[41]

Lack of work, want, a bad family economic situation, and debt were other reasons given by some Basque emigrants to explain their desire to cross the Atlantic. Such was the case of a carpenter from Goizueta (Navarre), Juan Martín Minondo Echenique. He went to the Americas in 1785 to help his elderly parents, "in view of the fact that there is no advancement to be found in this town due to the lack of employment in trades and day labor; with the high cost of all food, one only manages enough for his own survival."[42] In the statements required for obtaining their boarding licenses, Martín de Ordozgoiti and Juan Francisco Barjiarena confessed their desire to emigrate to the New World because of the large numbers in their households and the impossibility of meeting the needs of the large family each had to maintain.[43]

Many emigrants went to America to serve the king, either in the administration, with arms, at sea, or in the work of the Church. Although they did not form part of the so-called "official" emigration, Basques often emigrated under the pretext of service to the king. Like other emigrants, those who served the king pursued these posts to improve their personal situation, as is well documented for a large number of Bizkaians, Gipuzkoans, Arabans, and Navarrese. The conquest, defense, and administration of foreign possessions demanded an increasing number of men. And the Basques did not hesitate to lend their services where the Crown needed them both in offices and on battlefields. The same can be said of their participation in maritime occupations, in which they were authentic masters. The longtime Basque tradition of maritime commerce could well explain the high number from these provinces in colonial emigration, given that the natives of the Basque Country were present and key players in the American enterprise from the beginning. Enlistment in the army or navy frequently provided the perfect cover for emigrating to the Americas free of charge. And the Basques were no exception in this illegal emigration, which was completed by desertion upon reaching the destination.

Then, too, there were many who left the Basque Country in search of risk and adventure or eager to see the world and lifestyles different from those of their native valleys and villages. Referring to his countrymen eager to cross the Atlantic, the licenciate Navarrese Agustín de Tirapu put it this way: "they are leaving for those parts little by little and I am glad that they have such a desire because ultimately it means seeing the world."[44] The fantastic tales that arrived from the other side of the ocean about unlimited success and fabulous wealth had a lot to do with this desire for adventure. Storytellers painted pictures of a land in which the fruits of nature were granted to men with little struggle, where the land did not already have a master, and in which there was opportunity for all types of activities. And this conviction became as entrenched as the voyage that had to be endured was uncertain. News from the absent fellow citizens was the best source to motivate the vacillators and further kindle the desires of adventurers to seek their ultimate destiny.[45] One could hear these tales of wonder through family correspondence, which made clear how easily some earned their living in the New World. But emigrants became living proof of the wealth when they returned to their native village, or when they summoned their family from the Basque Country to join them in sharing in the bonanza, or when they sent large sums of money to help maintain the family and house that they missed. The existence of a prosperous family contact in America meant a point of certainty in the adventure into the unknown and meant that the most complicated step, the first one, would be easier.

Thus, the "American relative," who could open the doors of the unknown, was another reason for undertaking the voyage, leading more and more Basques to file the information required by the agents of the House of Trade. This was what propelled the Basques Pedro Martínez and Juan de Ezpeleta to abandon their farmsteads in the sixteenth century and go to Mexico and Cartagena, respectively, in order to manage the businesses of their relatives. The examples could go on forever. The context of the call was always similar: the prosperity achieved in commerce or business by the first members of the family emigrating to the New World allowed them to summon nephews or brothers from the same native province, valley, town, or village, who would be willing to help them in their lucrative daily tasks. This gave rise to family networks that also promoted very active business ties. Such connections helped consolidate the "Basque ethnic consciousness," which was translated into a collective action characterized by reciprocity.

The Basque colonial emigrants justified their departure in ways other than those already mentioned. In addition to those who traveled to the Americas for professional reasons (merchants, bureaucrats, clerics, soldiers), there were others that accompanied family members on the journey, those that went to America to take care of their relatives, to live with someone, or participate in married life according to the Crown's orders, as well as those that crossed the Atlantic in order to take care of personal business, study, escape their shady pasts, claim an inheritance, beg, or simply prosper. In sum, between 1500 and 1800 a variety of factors combined to lead numerous Basques to decide to emigrate.

But, as some authors note,[46] "push" factors were not the only ones that shaped the phenomenon of Basque migration to the Americas. In the judgment of these researchers, the attractions of the New World also played a very important role. Among these were the mythical golden lands of El Dorado and the fabulous native treasures, news of whose existence the first Spanish conquistadors and colonizers spread to the four winds. The idealized image of American destinations reached Spanish ports and traveled throughout the rest of the country with each new report of a victorious expedition and the discovery of mineral riches of incalculable worth. It makes sense that America began to appear in the eyes of potential emigrants as a land of limitless promise where treasures patiently awaited those who would sieze them. Emigrating meant being able to transform oneself from a peasant, shepherd, or poorly paid laborer into a rich cattleman, renowned *hacendado*, or wealthy merchant. And there was nothing better than the return of the rich emigrant to one's native village to vouch for this utopian vision of the New World.

Other "pull" factors promoted the Basque and Navarrese colonial exodus. The process of economic expansion in the various viceroyalties in the 1700s, especially the second half of the century, was one.[47] Nueva España was the most important point of Basque reception in America. And this was the result of Mexico City's privileged position as a leading commercial enclave, thanks to the port of Veracruz, which was directly connected to Spain, and of Acapulco, a market to which goods came from the Orient. Moreover, Mexico City was an enormously vital administrative, religious, and cultural center. Like the former Aztec capital, cities like Zacatecas and Guanajuato became important receiving centers of Basque immigrants because of the increase in their rich mining activity. The economic opportunities in Venezuela stemming from the foundation of the Royal Guipuzcoan Company of Caracas converted this province into a continuous destination of the Basque and Navarrese diaspora of the 1700s. The work of this shareholding company was not limited to the transport of goods. It also required an abundance of workers—sailors, pilots, scribes, caulkers, directors, commission merchants, secretaries, accountants, treasurers, and officials—in both the ports of origin—Donostia and

Pasaia—and in the New World destination. And of course among them were a significant number of Basques. This is proven by the fact that Venezuela was the second most frequent American destination of eighteenth-century Basque emigration. Similarly, as soon as a prosperous shipping business developed in the viceroyalty of Peru, business management boomed there. This sector thus became the main support of the local economy in which both Basques and Navarrese developed their skills and occupied the most powerful positions in the mercantile world.[48] Finally, the attraction of Buenos Aires was supported by a growing activity in the economic life of the region thanks to the African slave trade, Anglo-Portuguese smuggling out of Colonia del Sacramento, and the traffic of Spanish transatlantic vessels and some French ships. This combination of circumstances favored the consolidation of a Basque colony in Río de la Plata that would later successfully prepare the ground for massive emigration from the Basque Country beginning in 1830.

In sum, a wide range of motives caused and shaped the migratory process in the sixteenth, seventeenth, and eighteenth centuries. Sometimes one of these motives alone served to stimulate the departure of Basque emigrants. At others, a combination of them informed the desire for distant travel. For whatever reason, carried by their spirit of adventure and restlessness, fascinated by the distant and unknown, or spirited by tragic necessity, thousands of Basques reached the shores of America. They left behind family, friends, property, and customs in the firm desire to overcome adversity. But before achieving their ultimate victory—if they ever did—Basque emigrants had to confront the Atlantic crossing. It could be said that this voyage foreboded the tortuous path they would have to follow to reach the longed-for heights of success.

The Crossing

Once Basque emigrants made the decision to head for America for one reason or another, their first step was to apply for the so-called boarding license. This was done either through the Court's House of Trade and Council of the Indies or, when necessity demanded and the emigrant wanted to hide a tainted past, through the extended illegal trade of false permits.[49] The overseas adventure of the Basque diaspora thus began.[50] The steps for obtaining this license began with the request for proof of *limpieza de sangre*, or filiation. It was based on a questionnaire about the origin of one's parents and grandparents, and countersigned by various witnesses to show that the applicant and ancestors were Old Christians and "clean of any bad race and descent of Jews, Moors, those sentenced by the Holy Office, or any other sect." The application was usually accompanied by a declaration from the interested party of his or her civil status, age, profession, and physical signs of identity, as well as his or her motives for heading to the New World. If a prospective male emigrant was married and was not traveling with his wife, he also had to present a document showing her expressed consent. Sometimes, in addition to the applicant's class background (noble status, for example), there was a declaration of social standing: for example, whether one's relatives had held public or religious posts, or whether the applicant had enjoyed some social or economic privilege such as the use of the title of "Don" or the luxury of servants. A small note affirming to the authorities that the information was accurate, a copy of the royal decree that granted the possibility to emigrate, and the presentation of letters summoning the emigrant from the relatives already settled in America, if relevant, concluded the application for the license needed to embark on a course for "El Dorado."

As we have seen, the complexity of these administrative procedures stemmed from the interest of the Castilian Crown in controlling the transport of passengers as much as possible to avoid the transfer of individuals prohibited by royal order.[51] Such strict control began to decrease with time, however, and the documentation required for leaving Spain diminished in both its quality and its level of information. To begin with, those who had already been assured a job left without adding the pertinent data about their background and *limpieza de sangre,* an exemption extended to their families. Nor did married passengers or those who had previously traveled to the Americas have to provide such information. Such was also the case for the servants that accompanied state functionaries; a declaration by their master confirming that the servant was who he claimed to be and met the requirement of being unmarried, along with a cash payment, replaced forms about ancestry and proven Christianity. This therefore became a magnificent way to elude administrative control. It also explains in part the high percentage of those going to the Americas who, according to the statistics from the mid-1600s on, claimed to be servants.

The bureaucratic procedures for obtaining the boarding license could last several days. Even several months could pass between the time it was granted and the departure of the fleet. One would have to find temporary accommodations in Sevilla or Cádiz until it came time to leave; this circumstance would likely not have posed great problems for Basque emigrants, given the large, prosperous Basque colonies in both Andalusian cities that surely lent their services as connections, mediators, and, of course, hosts. At least the case of Juan de Echarren, from Puente la Reina (Navarre), attests to this. Before leaving in 1596, he resided in Sevilla in the house of a widow who provided him with lodging and several of her dead husband's shirts. With the problem of lodging resolved and the boarding license obtained, Basque emigrants still had to overcome the difficult step of negotiating the conditions of their passage with the captain of some ship. Spanish legislation does not provide an excess of data about the price of the voyage for passengers. It only ensured that no more than the sum agreed upon between captain and traveler be charged. Nevertheless, and given that the Crown covered the costs of the clerics that went to the Americas, it is possible to approximate the rate for the lay passengers. Around the beginning of the seventeenth century, this was just over fifty silver ducats for passage, accommodations, and rights to bring half a ton of baggage, a quantity that varied depending upon level of accommodation within the ship and its destination. This was a high price, to which an additional twenty ducats would have been added for the personal damages tax. In sum, more than seventy ducats.[52] To pay this, one would sometimes have to sell property, seek loans, ask parents for an advance on an inheritance, work as a servant for someone who could pay the cost, or write to relatives in America asking them to forward enough money for the trip—this last recourse becoming more frequent with time. If one did not manage to raise enough money, there was always the option of traveling as a stowaway, with its danger.

The costs did not end for Basque emigrants with payment of the journey. Before boarding the ship that would take them to the New World, they had to supply themselves with all sorts of clothes, complements, objects of daily use, and food. All of these goods could be easily acquired in Sevilla and Cádiz. Provisions tended to include hardtack, wine, salted pork and fish, dried beef, beans, peas, rice, cheese, oil, vinegar, garlic, honey, prunes, dried figs, and capers. Nor was there a lack of condiments such as cinnamon, sugar, saffron, cloves, mustard, dried parsley, and ground pepper. Fruit and vegetables were not included in the diet on board because they were perishable; neither were milk and butter, for the same reason. The food was lavish or frugal, depending upon the economic circumstances of the emigrant. The emigrant's baggage also had to include the necessities to sustain one for the full two or three months of the transatlantic voyage. Emigrants had to bring their own bedding—blankets, sheets, pillow, and a light mattress—and enough clothes for a long trip and the harshness of shipboard life. Advice to passengers was readily given. Here is a sample:

> It is wise advice that before leaving one bring some clothing that is strong and thick, more useful than fashionable, in which without worry one can sit in the passageway, stay between decks, nap on the poop, leave for land, protect oneself from the heat, shelter oneself from the water, and even to wear at night in bed; because on a ship, clothing should be more for protecting oneself than for showing off.
>
> It is wise advice that any good sea traveler bring cork slippers, thick shoes, seaworthy stockings, hunting hats, thickset shoestrings, and three or four clean shirts; the quality of the seawater and the inconvenience of the galley is such that you are likely to first have to get them all dirty before you can launder one.
>
> It is wise advice that the curious or delicate passenger provide himself with a portable mattress, thickset sheet, a small blanket and no more than one pillow; to think that one can bring a large, full bed into the galley would make some jeer and others laugh, because by day there is no place to keep it and little space to spread it out at night.[53]

And before crossing the gangplank, there was one last piece of advice to protect the body and spirit from the dangers of the sea:

> It is wise advice that the curious sea traveler manage to clean and purge the body eight or fifteen days before the voyage, be it with honey and rose water or with alexandrian rosa, or a good fistula reed (caña fistula), or with some other blessed medicament, with good enema, or with some blessed pill; because the sea is naturally more merciful to empty stomachs than to those full of bad humors.
>
> It is wise advice that any man wishing to head for sea, be it in large ship or in small, confess, take communion, and trust God as a good and faithful Christian; because the sea traveler puts his life on the line just as much as he who enters in a summoned battle.
>
> It is wise advice that before the good Christian heads for sea, he make out his will, declare his debts, settle accounts with his creditors, divide his estate, reconcile with his enemies, earn his stations of the cross, make his vows, and absolve himself with his bulls; because later at sea such a horrible storm could be encountered so that for all the treasures of this life he would not want to find himself with any scruples on his conscience.[54]

This was clearly not a very encouraging omen of what awaited Basque emigrants in the immediate future.

Most of the vessels lacked adequate space to carry both merchandise and passengers.[55] A brief description of these ships can help one to imagine how the trip unfolded. There was a main deck that housed two forecastles. The sailors were lodged in the prow, between the rigging, equipment, and tools. The stern had two floors. Underneath the quarterdeck (below the main deck) were the wheel and the binnacle, the officials' coffer and the passengers' trunks, between which were placed their mattresses for sleeping. Over the quarterdeck was the command bridge and below this was the captain's stateroom, which was also shared by noble passengers. Artillery, water pumps, sails, equipment, ladders, and the cooking stove were piled on the main deck. Underneath, the provisions for the trip shared the hold with the merchandise that the ship was transporting to America; and next to this were the rooms of officers and passengers. Further inside, in the bottom of the ship, was the ballast bay. The seawater, which had to be frequently bailed out in order to keep the ship afloat, was filtered through this.

Given the lack of space on the ships on the Indies run, the most intuitive or well-informed passengers made sure that they were the first to arrive at the port in order to stake a claim to the best places on board. Those that had some money could always bribe a crew member so that they and their belongings would be lodged in an acceptable spot on board, sheltered, if possible, from the inclement weather.

With all the passengers and their baggage on board, and the order to cast off given, the journey of Basque emigrants to their American El Dorados began. The first stretch of the voyage, along the Guadalquivir, must have been pleasant. It was when the ship entered the ocean that the difficulties began. The first of these was becoming accustomed to the constant rolling of the ship. This provoked disagreeable seasickness, which, in turn, created filth and malaise. The tasks of defending and taking care of one's belongings and provisions all day, and finding a place to spend the night, were other challenges. Moreover, Basque emigrants had to acclimate themselves to the narrowness of the ship, the bad odors from the bay (in which live animals frequently traveled), the pestilence that came from the water removed through the pumps, and the filth created by the overcrowding of passengers and crew. To remedy seasickness it was recommended to eat little and drink less. To blunt the unpleasant smells on board, it was advised to always have some type of perfume handy. One also had to adapt to the rhythm of ship's life and the schedule and work of the crew: voices of command, movement of the sails and rigging with shouting back and forth, steering of the helm, the pilot plotting a course, observation of the binnacle, bailing water, the ritual of lighting the cooking stove. In these activities, Basque travelers were only uncomfortable witnesses.

After becoming familiarized with this new medium, the emigrants must have found the first days of navigation of the Atlantic bearable, at least in terms of provisions. The water, wine, and food were still abundant and fresh. For breakfast some cold leftover from the previous day was eaten. And at lunch, the most important meal of the day, one could eat some hot food whenever, weather permitting, the cooking stove was lit and the person in charge was receptive. According to the most experienced navigators, it was therefore advisable for the passengers to be on good terms with the cook; one should bribe him, if necessary, if one wanted to bring one's pots and pans to the precious fire. As the days passed and the voyagers entered the Atlantic, the discomforts increased. The narrowness of the ships, their endless rocking, the overcrowding of the passengers on deck, and the constant bustle of the crew looking for the best winds for sailing ahead gave emigrants little freedom of action and even less of movement. The cooking stove was not lit on stormy days; as a result, no hot food whatsoever was prepared, in order to avoid the seasickness and vomiting that were nonetheless frequent.

And on these same days of undercurrents and heavy seas, the passengers had to lodge themselves however they could under the main deck, between trunks of baggage, food, and other goods, and stay there in a completely overloaded and harmful environment, bundled up to protect themselves from the humidity and the cold. In such conditions it is not difficult to imagine, as some chroniclers relate, that there were horrible plagues of mice, cockroaches, lice, and other pests. These served to propagate endless illnesses, some of them fatal:

It is the privilege of the ship that all the fleas that jump on the planks and all the lice that hatch in the clothes and all the bedbugs that are in the cracks, be common to all, go back and forth and be shared by all and live off of all; and if someone denies this privilege, thinking that they are very clean and polished, from the augury I prophesy to them that, if they put their hand on their neck and into the haversack they will find in the jerkin more lice than money in the purse.

It is the privilege of the ship that all the mice and dormice in it will be bold and brash so that they can, with no effort, rob toilet rags, thin gauze, silk sashes, handkerchiefs, old shirts, precious hair nets, and even mended gloves; and they abscond with this all to make their bed, to give birth, and so that their offspring grow, and therefore they even gnaw when they are not hungry; and do not be surprised, brother passenger, if they bite you sometimes when you are asleep.[56]

Sometimes, the danger of piracy and, frequently, that of storms and hurricanes, were added to that of epidemics. Pirate activity gravely upset Spanish navigation to the New World from the outset. The principal objects of pirate attacks were the riches and expensive products being transported. Although both crews and passengers were secondary targets, the attackers were always mindful of those they might hold for ransom. Panic spread in the ships on the Indies run when the lookout sighted the sails of unknown boats on the endless horizon:

[We] were certain that they were thieves. I, who carried all of my things, my wife, and children—imagine how I felt. I hurried the officer to set up the artillery; . . . arms were presented. . . . Those who had money or jewels had to quickly stash these throughout the frame and joints and hiding places of the ship. All of us scattered with our arms to the most convenient posts, . . . ready to defend ourselves because the three ships were approaching us, which seemed to forebode our defeat. . . . As they continued approaching, for although there were three they were no less frightening, they recognized us and then we knew by the sails that they were friends, because they were ships from our fleet.[57]

The risk of storms and shipwrecks was also ever present during the transatlantic crossings of the Basque emigrants. Survivors would tell the tragic tale:

And the boat . . . had taken on so much water that the sailors could not overcome it, and the blankets below became soaked and without anyone realizing weighed the boat down even more; and as the damn sailors saw that the sea was raging they did not throw anything out of the boat to lighten it, but rather attempted to turn its rear, although too late, into the wind so that it would push it toward land, where they could guide it. Then a giant wave came and as the boat was low in the water it passed over and so overwhelmed the boat that the water drenched the bosoms of those on board; the friars were sitting on the chests and as the wave was large and furious, it disturbed the ship a little and hurled the chests into the water and with them many of the laymen and Fra Agustín and Fra Felipe del Castillo and Fra Pedro de los Reyes. . . . Then came another wave that set the boat square and this time Fra Dionisio and many laymen drowned. . . . All told, thirty-two people drowned, nine men of God and the rest laymen, some young and good swimmers.[58]

But in spite of the weather, piracy, epidemics, discomforts, and overcrowding, there was also time for distractions that must have relieved the monotony of such a long crossing. Thus, the Basque emigrants enjoyed participating in the games of cards and dice organized among the sailors, even though it was well known that all types of tricks and deceit were practiced. Some experienced travelers also recommended to the novices that before undertaking the sea adventure they acquire "some tasty books and a few devout hours; because," they added, "of the three practices that there are at sea, namely, gambling, talking, and reading, the most beneficial and least harmful is reading." They also suggested bringing fishing equipment to take advantage of the calm moments of navigation to "catch some fish; fishing for them will be relaxing and eating them tasty." Good weather permitted good humor to conquer the tedium and anguish of the voyage. Fake bullfights were improvised and fights were organized between fowl brought along for food. Sometimes theatrical performances, poetry readings, and guitar and singing recitals took place. As can be imagined, there was no lack of long hours of discussion and exchanges of opinions about a variety of matters, especially concerning the promise of the lands to which they were sailing. The sailors' pursuit of sharks and turtles in tropical waters must surely have fascinated Basque emigrants, who would then have the opportunity to try unfamiliar food. It is very likely that the most agreeable moments of the trip were the calls in ports of the islands of the New World. These short stops were an opportunity to rest from the constant shipboard discomforts and a chance to drink water of good quality, wash oneself, and eat fresh fruit.

Upon arriving at the first lands of the American continent, the yearning for the trip's conclusion was revived among the passengers. Many Basques—especially the women—hastened to put on the finest clothes from their trunk before disembarking in the dreamed-of Edens of the Indies. They had survived the crossing and finally reached the known safety of solid ground; for many Basques, a future full of hope began with this moment. Before disembarking, however, they were required to submit themselves to one final step: the inspection of the commissary of the Holy Office and the customs agents. Then, at last, they set foot on the golden land of El Dorado.

PILES OF MONEY

The migratory current of Basque natives to America has frequently been studied, analyzed, and interpreted by recent Basque historiography as an almost exclusively unidirectional phenomenon. Only on rare occasions has reference been made to the process of returning to the ancestral home. This omission has been due to the complexity of the Basque presence in the New World. As has been argued throughout, the Basque Provinces stocked the American continent with a great abundance of conquistadors, evangelists, colonists, administrators, soldiers of all types, and even liberators. And this does not include the thousands of anonymous immigrants that, through their constant work, participated in the formation and development of the American economies.

This complex reality explains in great part why many other aspects of the Basque and Navarrese emigratory phenomenon have been largely neglected. One of the subjects largely ignored by the historiography of the Basque Country is the connection maintained between its emigrants and their place of origin during and after their stay in America. That these contacts with their community of birth were sustained even after relocating overseas is confirmed by documents. Town governments in the Basque Country were sure to congratulate American emigrants through their relatives or local authorities for their successes in the colonial administration or in business. In passing, they would inform these native sons of the town's most urgent necessities. Likewise, when municipal elections were held annually, it was common for former American emigrants to be elected as mayors and aldermen. These were really honorary positions that placed the emigrant in a preeminent local social position. His success was thus recognized and commended by his former townsmen. In turn, the emigrant favored by fortune might confirm his overseas prosperity through his generosity, at times enormous. The desire to show off socially and the fond memory of one's hometown were evinced in donations destined for a variety of ends. Sometimes it was only small presents. In other cases emigrants sent aid for the social and charitable necessities of their hometowns. The shipment of objects was more common: in general, pieces of gold or silver destined for religious festivals or buildings. Cash gifts for financing or sponsoring a variety of architectural and urban projects were also frequent. Nor was there a lack of donations from the Indies to build works of both public and private interest.

In short, money from America was evident throughout the Basque geography. Such donations were shipped by Basque emigrants from the New World to their representatives in Sevilla or Cádiz. Following the strictly delineated notarial instructions, these intermediaries would in turn send the donations to the donor's relatives in the Basque Country. The most important transfers of American capital were thus carried out by businessmen and partners in the iron and metal manufacturing companies located in those Andalusian cities, ship captains and masters of the Indies run, officials of the House of Trade, and members of the Corporation of

Indies' Shippers (Consulate). The greatest cash transactions, however, were carried out by the Basque gold and silver buyers living in Sevilla and Cádiz. They acted like real bankers. As already stated, they were entrusted with receiving quantities of wealth arrived from the New World and distributing them in the Basque Country according to the orders of the American senders.

The Basque-Andalusian colony generally used the services of *yangüés* muleteers for the transfer of these cash contributions to their ultimate destination. The *yangüeses* were the renowned cart drivers of the era who earned their living by transporting merchandise and precious objects throughout Spain. Inventories of shipments were registered in the presence of a notary. This document included the name of the person making the transfer, specifying whether for himself or by order of a third party; the amount deposited, the type of coin, as well as if it was gold, silver, or copper; the name of the addressee and the place of destination; and, rarely, the motive for the shipment. The conditions of the transport service were also stipulated in the deposition: the muleteers promised to complete the delivery to the person indicated within thirty days of receiving the merchandise; once the delivery was made, a receipt certifying the delivery was returned to the shipper, also within one month. For their services the *yangüeses* charged 1 percent of the silver transported and 0.5 percent of the gold, a rate that remained the same until the end of the seventeenth century. For trunks and bins, they charged at the rate of twenty silver reales per *arroba*. Moreover, the muleteers pocketed an additional four silver reales for the registration, sealed paper, and affidavit, a figure that rose to six reales in 1682.[59] It was an expensive method of transport, but very reliable and secure. Not only freights of valuable goods and jewels were accepted, but clothes, presents, private correspondence, business settlements, wills, and postmortem inventories, among other items.

The quantities shipped to the Basque Country by the immigrants in America were destined for a variety of projects and investments.[60] One of the most common ends of the American donations was the construction or restoration of buildings, especially those of a religious nature: churches, hermitages, and convents. As throughout the Cantabrian region, in the Basque Provinces it is common to attribute the construction of certain religious buildings to American settlers. Almost all religious buildings received money from the New World at some point. Whether the reason was faith, gratitude, or the search for social prestige, in spite of the distance, Basque emigrants rarely forgot the church of their hometown or the main sanctuaries, hermitages, and convents of their province. Sometimes such contributions were incidental in the construction of the building. At other times, however, the donation was substantial enough to initiate important work, such as construction of towers, crypts, sacristies, and chapels, or even a completely new church. Endless examples could be cited; only a few are collected in table 2.12 in appendix 2.

This type of donation, whether driven by devotion or gratitude to the heavenly powers, or by the quest for social recognition, increased markedly from the mid-1500s to the late 1760s, with a notable exception between 1621 and 1640 and another, more moderate one, in the 1720s and 1730s (see figure 4.2).

The investment of large quantities of funds from America in the construction and improvement of social welfare buildings, such as hospitals and houses of mercy, was also common (see table 2.13 in appendix 2). Until well into the nineteenth century, both institutions were more shelters for the indigent than true health centers.

As for education, Bizkaia (especially the district of Enkarterri) was the Basque province that received the greatest number of donations from the Americas destined for the construction or equipping of schools. Almost half the total was sent there. Chronologically, two stages of substantial investment of this type are evident: the years between 1740 and 1780, and from the second half of the nineteenth century through the first third of the twentieth. The former period corresponds to the diffusion of the ideas of the Enlightenment, an intellectual movement that saw in education a vehicle to promote its cause. This investment in education had a direct antecedent in private gatherings of intellectuals of like interests and its greatest exponent in the Royal Basque Society of the Friends of the Country, whose influence in America has already been documented.[61] The second phase undoubtedly reflects the interest of nineteenth- and early-twentieth-century emigrants in creating service infrastructures and networks in their hometowns, as well as to improve the quality of life of their former townspeople. As for causes, the American donations for educational ends were numerous. Some examples are listed in table 2.14 in appendix 2.

Guided by late Enlightenment philanthropic and paternalist ideals, wealthy Basque emigrants sent large financial donations from America earmarked for the realization of a variety of improvements in local infrastructure and urban services, especially in the late nineteenth and early twentieth centuries. Their desire was to embellish, reform, or modernize their hometowns. Thus, legacies from the Americas were frequently earmarked for building or remodeling docks, cemeteries, monuments, fountains, and water systems, improving the town plazas and roads, and even construction of the incipient railways. Some money was even earmarked to assist the troops that fought against Napoleon in the War of Independence and to defray the costs of the Carlist wars. Samples are included in table 2.15 in appendix 2.

In summary, the donations from the Americas for buildings[62] and works of infrastructure were characteristically earmarked for religious edifices(the most numerous group) and, to a lesser extent, for hospitals, schools, and diverse infrastructures. As a result, the representation in figure 4.2 shows an upward trend from the mid-1500s until the middle of the 1700s. Next comes a strong localized increase in the years 1760–1780. This is followed by a marked fall and recovery, albeit with ups and downs, beginning in the second third of the nineteenth century.[63]

Donations of objects of art were another important expression of American

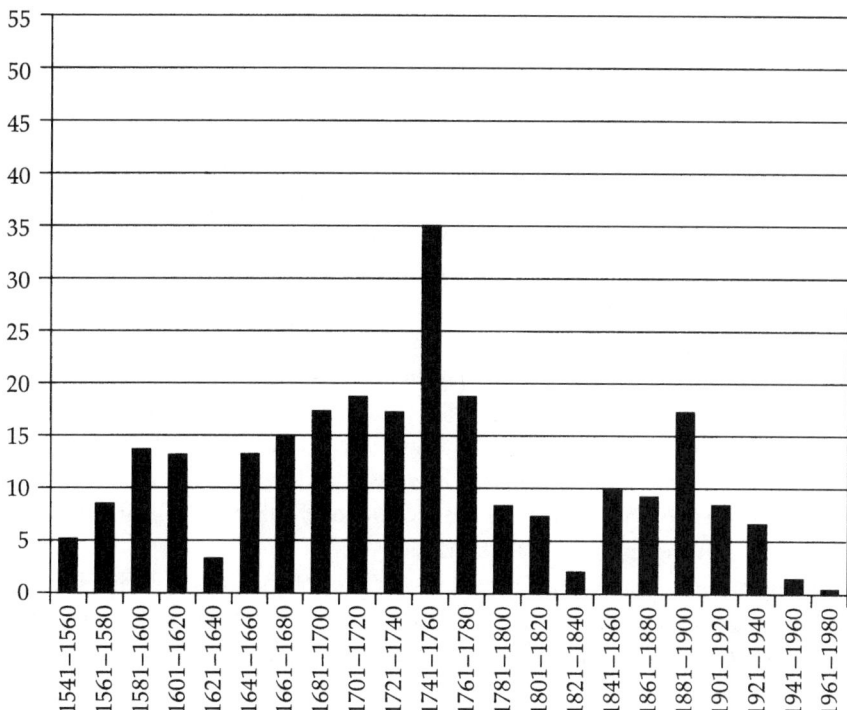

Fig. 4.2 American Donations in Pesos for Religious Buildings in the Basque Country, 1541–1980. Source: J. M. González Cembellín, 1993, 29.

wealth in the Basque Country.[64] Since the early years of the American undertaking, furnishings constituted a significant part of the shipments of both gifts and legacies from transatlantic Basque migrants. Among these donations, two general categories can be identified: pieces brought from America, and those that, although financed with money shipped from overseas, were made in Spain or the Basque Country itself. The same motives applied to this type of shipment as to those for buildings: devotion, acknowledgment, and the desire for social recognition. It was not for nothing that the inscription on the pieces from the Americas habitually included the word "devotion" and the name of the donor who desired to perpetuate his memory among his fellow townspeople through an expensive or ostentatious gift.

Gold and silver objects formed the most numerous class of movable items from America. This was true even though many pieces were lost, stolen or even frequently confiscated as a result of economic necessity, war, or the changed legislation regarding church fiscal exemptions in the nineteenth century. Thus, for example, in 1716, the rectors of the Church of Nuestra Señora de la Natividad of Elguea (Araba) had to sell a lamp that came from California to be able to pay the construction bills for the crypt; in 1741, two Mexican lamps were expropriated from the Church of Nuestra Señora de la Asunción de La Atalaya of Bermeo (Bizkaia); in 1794, Napoleon's troops took several silver pieces from Nuestra Señora de la Asunción of Hondarribia (Gipuzkoa); and the silver from the patrimony of the Virgen de Guadalupe y el Santo Cristo de Zacatecas of Ea (Bizkaia) was also surrendered in 1794 to contribute to the costs of the war against the French Revolutionary Convention.[65]

Retables composed the second most important group of furnishings of American origin existing in the Basque Country. They were built in various workshops thanks to donations made by Basque colonial emigrants. The oldest of these, dating from 1641–1650, is found in the Church of Santa María del Juncal of Irún (Gipuzkoa). Later, in 1655, various shipments from America permitted the completion of San Juan de Molinar of Gordexola (Bizkaia). In 1678, the cost of the retable of the Church of Nuestra Señora of Lacorzanilla (Araba) was defrayed with a pound of gold shipped for this purpose by the Araban Francisco Montoa y Allende Salazar, governor of Antioquia (Colombia). And, in 1698, Juan Jerónimo de Solano sent 100 pesos from Mexico City toward the construction of the main retable of the Hermitage of Los Remedios in Sesma (Navarre).

The furnishings were complemented by other pieces coming or financed from America, such as several sculptures, various paintings (especially of the Virgin of Guadalupe, devotion to whom must have extended throughout the Basque Country and Navarre), religious vestments and ornaments, tombstones, organs, and votive offerings. This type of gift became considerably more frequent in the late sixteenth century. Nevertheless, the graph of this evolution shown in figure 4.3 indicates that from the beginning of the seventeenth century, gifts of art generally declined until the mid-1700s, except for the increase experienced between 1680 and 1700. Lastly, beginning in 1760, the year in which the arrival of shipments of American furnishings again became important, the curve again exhibits a downward tendency. Examples of American furnishings existing in the artistic patrimony of the Basque Country and Navarre are listed in table 2.16 in appendix 2.[66]

Other demonstrations of financial generosity by the emigrants were aimed at religiousness, piety, and charity. Many of the financial shipments that arrived in the Basque Country from the New World were destined to help the neediest of the hometown or region of the contributor. Even so, in this category, the creation of chaplaincies stands out. It was through these pious institutions that the testator tried to ensure salvation of his soul. They consisted of the creation of an economic fund from whose interest one or more clergymen were paid for saying a set number of masses for the donor in a particular church or chapel. The management of this fund tended to fall to a patron who was a relative of the founder and expressly designated in his will. Among the main reasons for endowing the chaplaincies was the individual search for eternal salvation through the prayer of third parties. Moreover, the fact that a deceased emigrant had chosen the churches of his hometown as the place for the saying of these masses reflects a personal devotion to both

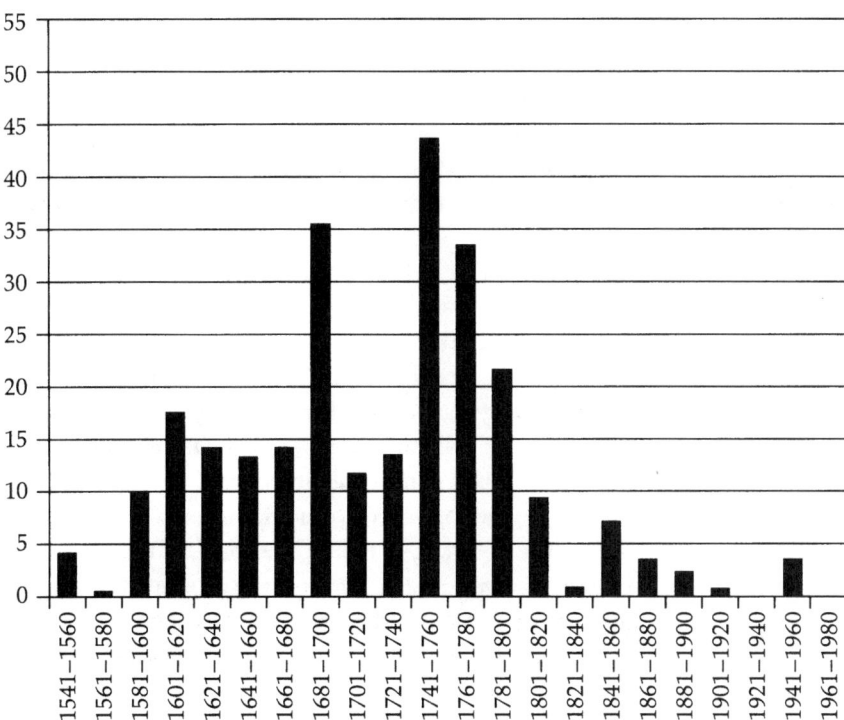

Fig. 4.3 American Donations in Pesos for Furnishings in the Basque Country, 1541–1980. Source: J. M. González Cembellín, 1993, 41.

place and its cults. In addition, the level of social recognition that characterized the donation of buildings and furnishings could be avoided in this case, given that the chaplaincies did not profit the emigrant's fellow townspeople.

Social foundations were established in the Basque Country and Navarre with donations sent by the emigrants favored by fortune in the Americas and had similar pious ends. There were numerous legacies aimed at alleviating the grave social problem of poor or orphaned girls having no option but to marry or join the Church. This issue was of surpassing importance in the social structure of the day. Two factors explain the abundance and success of this type of donation. The first is that emigration from the Basque Provinces created a significant imbalance between the sexes. The few men remaining preferred to choose the wealthiest partners when it came time to get married. The women were less well off and therefore depended upon the generosity of third parties to achieve "a suitable life" and at the same time avoid "being exposed to sin." The second factor was that, as indicated by some authors, since the norms of the Council of Trent regarding marriage were not well rooted in the Basque Country, verbal wedding vows were common. The pair could therefore begin their married life merely by giving their word. This provoked several cases of abandonment by men looking for a more advantageous union in a second marriage. In order to alleviate the serious situation posed by abandoned spouses and children, the Basque authorities frequently sought dowries for these women so that they might remarry or (if they so desired) enter a convent. This type of gift was also promoted for its favorable demographic consequences, since an advantageous marriage could prevent the emigration of some of those males wishing to go to the Americas in search of a better life.[67]

Besides being used as endowments for girls, the donations from America—especially those made during the sixteenth and seventeenth centuries—were also invested in the construction of houses and social welfare, as well as assistance for hospitals and the indigent of the donor's native district. Thus, it was common at the time for the wealthier Basque emigrants to subsidize with their estates the construction of local granaries in which wheat, other seed, and even already baked bread were provided at a reasonable cost to the neediest sectors of the rural population unable to afford them. Donations for religious educational ends were similarly abundant, especially during the seventeenth and eighteenth centuries. In some cases, they were sent to cover the costs of maintaining the master or funding a chair in grammar, Latin, philosophy, or morals. In other cases, they were destined to provide scholarships to one or more local students, usually relatives, so they could attend schools either inside or outside of the Basque Country. But, as already mentioned in relation to buildings, sponsorship of primary schools was the most common form of this kind of charity.

Sometimes other religious and pious foundations of various types were created, such as endowments for wax for churches, anniversary masses, bills for the poor and orphaned, night protection for the souls in purgatory, upkeep of holy oil or a particular venerated image, and redemption of captive souls. Examples are listed in table 2.17 in appendix 2.

As with other types of legacies, this one grew progressively from the mid-1500s on. It then diminished around the mid-1700s. A new, moderate increase of pious donations then began, which would again diminish during the 1800s. The generosity and American successes of the epoch's emigrants funded hospitals and schools during this resurgence (see figure 4.4).

As suggested by the preceding discussion, their hometown was always in the thoughts of Basque emigrants, even after long years of absence in the Americas. Their last wills and testaments fully corroborate this. But the connection maintained by the migrant Basques with their individual natal household was no less important, in spite of the distance.[68] The gifts that benefited the members of the donor's family were numerous (and complex to trace in the documentation as well), and destined for various ends. Most commonly, once the money from America was received, it was left up to the recipients to distribute it as they saw fit. They generally used it to buy land, for construction or restoration of farmsteads and urban

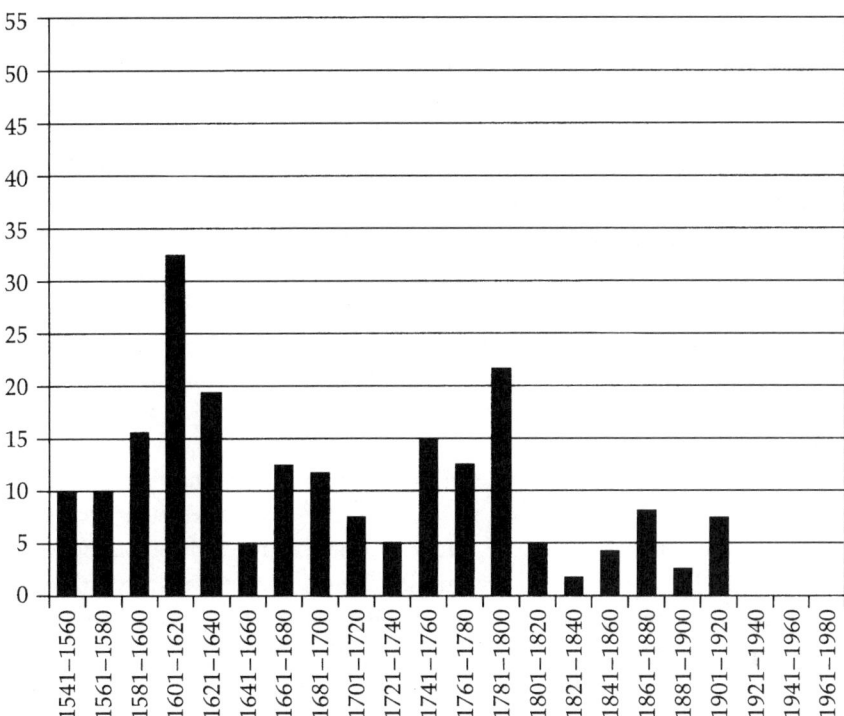

Fig. 4.4 American Donations in Pesos for Religious and Pious Foundations in the Basque Country, 1541–1980. Source: J. M. González Cembellín, 1993, 51.

mansions, or payment of the mortgages or other debts that might weigh on a family property. For example, the Navarrese Victoriano de Huici sent 6,000 reales from Chile to free the Palace of Ituren from debt. He would inherit the property in the event that he returned from the Americas. When Victoriano died in America in 1692, his illegitimate daughter living in Pamplona claimed the money. This bequest reached a resident of El Puerto de Santa María (Cádiz) via the fleet of the Indies and was delivered in person by Andrés Rodríguez Cortés. It then came into the possession of Captain Juan de Arancibar, uncle of Victoriano and resident of Cádiz. He in turn sent it via the *yangüés* muleteers to Fernando Ansorena de Garayoa, resident of Donostia (Gipuzkoa), and from there it reached Victoriano's daughter in Pamplona. Such money could be used to pay off a variety of taxes and other obligations.[69] To cite another case from a different moment in history, the Araban Isabel de Novales stated in her will that she had acquired all her money and possessions through inheritance from her son Manuel Cecilio de Valle, who had died in Guatemala in 1837 without having taken a wife. Among her property were the new house that she had had built in Retes de Tudela (Araba) and the adjacent land, which she had purchased.[70]

To summarize,[71] once money was sent from America by emigrant Basques or brought by returnees, it had four fundamental objectives: construction or restoration of buildings, religious and charitable foundations, gifts to relatives, and endowments of furnishings and art. As has been documented in the foregoing pages, most of the shipments were of a religious nature. They expressed devotion to a church or patron, thanks to the heavenly powers, or a desire for social recognition among the townspeople of the donor's place of origin. As a group, donations from America arrived in four very distinct periods. From the mid-sixteenth until the early seventeenth century, there was a rapid increase of the American shipments, in which the donations by the clergy are clearly prominent. Next, during the rest of the seventeenth century and the first half of the eighteenth century, certain fluctuations are noticeable, with a tendency toward decline; nevertheless, the donations varied according to their ends: those destined for religious buildings were on the increase, gifts of furnishings stood pat, and money for religious foundations and charity work decreased markedly. The status of each of the categories varied radically from the mid-eighteenth century on; but, in each, an expansive phase was immediately followed by a no less severe contraction. Lastly, during the nineteenth century, there was a small revival in donations, although their number did not reach that of earlier epochs. Figure 4.5 illustrates this periodicity.

Donations from America were unequally distributed in the three Basque provinces studied. Thus, Gipuzkoa received 37.38 percent, Bizkaia 36.50 percent, and Araba 26.12 percent. These percentages varied, however, depending upon the aim of the donation. Thus, in Gipuzkoa, the shipments dedicated to religious buildings stood out; in Bizkaia, those employed to build, restore, or maintain social service buildings were most notable. The furnishings of American origin benefited Bizkaia and Araba, while religious and charitable foundations were more abundant in Gipuzkoa and Araba. The extreme diversity of geographic origin of the donations stands out, but two main foci are clear: Mexico and Peru. Around the mid-eighteenth century, however, the presence of the Company of Caracas propelled gifting from Venezuela somewhat. And, after the independence of the continental colonies, only Mexico continued to be an important source of the shipments sent by Basque emigrant residents, sharing the leading role with both Cuba and Puerto Rico.

In sum, the Basques that emigrated to America throughout history maintained close and active ties to their places of origin. It makes sense that intimate memories of home and family would lead Basque emigrants—at least the wealthier—to try to make up for their absence with a contribution that would benefit their relatives and former townspeople. In socioeconomic terms, the shipments of money that came from America benefited the entire Basque Country, especially rural areas, which generated the majority of emigration. Such gifts financially endowed a good number of families. In the sociocultural aspect, Basque emigrants—either by sending money from the New World or donating it upon their return—showed a de-

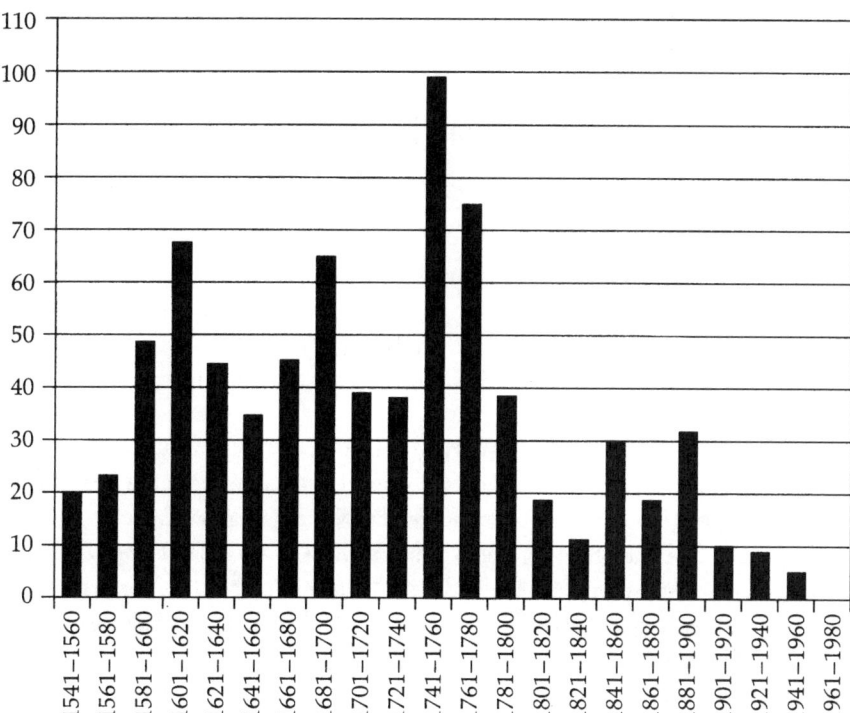

Fig. 4.5 American Donations in Pesos and Shipments to the Basque Country, 1541–1980. Source: J. M. González Cembellín, 1993, 69.

cided interest in improving the appearance and services of their hometowns. The creation of welfare funds, hospitals, primary schools, mills, fountains, roads, bridges, and other such works is the best evidence of this. Money from the emigration, therefore, was destined to the emigrant's most immediate surroundings: their family and hometown. This did not bring with it any type of risk, made the residents recognize that the absence of such emigrants was not in vain, and perpetuated the emigrants' names for generations to come.

Chapter Five

The Overseas Destinations

The Foundation of Nueva Vizcaya

To this point, the structure of Basque participation in the formation of colonial America has been shown. Now, the characteristics of the destinations of this Basque emigration will be developed.

After the occupation of Mexico City-Tenochtitlán by Hernán Cortés and his army, the Spanish troops embarked upon conquering the interior of the Aztec Empire.[1] The region of Poniente was conquered by Nuño Beltrán de Guzmán in December 1529. The lieutenant on the expedition was Cristóbal de Oñate, who was born in Gasteiz, Araba, in 1504. Under the command of Guzmán, the Basque Oñate explored the territories of Tlacotlán, Juchipila, Teul, Tlaltenango, and Nochistlán in April of 1530. He defeated an army of 6,000 Cazcan Indians in the last of these territories, leaving the difficult task of pacification to his brother Juan. From Nochistlán, Oñate marched through Juchipila, Apozol, Jalpa, and Mayahua. He then continued to Tonalá, Copala, Jalostitlán, Ixtlahuacan, Yahualica, and Teocaltiche, opening up what is today the north of Jalisco and Zacatecas. In April 1531, Oñate participated in the historic founding of San Miguel de Culiacán. In May of the same year, he explored the western Sierra Madre, penetrating into what would become the state of Durango. Without doubt, Oñate's work contributed to the enlargement of the kingdom of Nueva Galicia, with its capital in Compostela (Nayarit).

In 1532, the *villa* of Espíritu Santo was founded in Guadalajara. Its first mayor was the already-mentioned Juan de Oñate. Its alderman Miguel de Ibarra, from Eibar (Gipuzkoa), accompanied Guzmán on his expeditions. From 1532 to 1533, Cristóbal de Oñate was the lieutenant governor of the Kingdom of Nueva Galicia. In 1538, Francisco Vázquez de Coronado was the governor of Nueva Galicia and organized an expedition to conquer northern Mexico. The expedition left Compostela in February of 1540, led in its first phase by the Basque Juan de Zaldivar and Melchor Díaz. After an intense campaign that yielded few results and explored present-day Sonora, Arizona, New Mexico and parts of California, Texas, Oklahoma, and Kansas, the explorers returned to Compostela in April of 1532. In February of that year, Miguel de Ibarra became the mayor of Guadalajara. In August of 1543, with the discovery of gold mines in Xaltepec and Espíritu Santo, Cristóbal de Oñate began his duties as a mining contractor. He devoted himself completely to acquiring wealth in this field from 1545 onward.

In August of 1546, an expedition headed by Gipuzkoan native Juan de Tolosa (married to Leonor Cortés Moctezuma, the illegitimate daughter of Hernán Cortés) and Miguel de Ibarra left Guadalajara. They passed through Juchipila and set up camp at the foot of the Sierra La Bufa on September 8. There, they managed to establish a truce with the Zacatecan Indians and discovered rich deposits of very pure, valuable silver. The Basques Tolosa, Oñate, and Diego de Ibarra promptly established a company with Baltasar Temiño de Bañuelos (from Burgos) to exploit these mines. In 1548, the partners returned to La Bufa, founding the Royal Company of Our Lady of Zacatecas, which expanded significantly in 1549 and 1550. News of the mines spread rapidly to Mexico City, encouraging the construction of new roads, the discovery of new deposits, and the creation of new settlements. Michael Mathes[2] describes the adventures of these Basque mining pioneers in great detail:

> This rapid influx of population not only contributed to the opening of new roads, discovery of new deposits and settlement of new population centers, but also to the foundation of a new province. In 1552, while Diego de Ibarra organized a system of armed escorts to protect the caravans of beasts of burden loaded with silver that left for Mexico, Ginés Vázquez de Mercado, a miner from the Tepic region, explored the north of Zacatecas through Chalchihuites, San Martín, Sombrerete and the Guadiana valley, where he discovered the immense ridge of silver that presently bears his name. Wounded in a fight in Sombrerete, Vázquez de Mercado died in Teul in 1553, thereby leaving the development of the north to others.

Francisco de Ibarra, native of Durango (Bizkaia), had accompanied his uncle Diego to Nueva España as a child. Upon occupying the second viceroyalty in 1550 (shortly after Diego de Ibarra), Luis de Velasco, hero of Mixtón, knight of the Order of Santiago and influential miner from Zacatecas, married Ana, the daughter of the elder Ibarra. At the same time, he managed to have his own nephew named as a page in his father-in-law's court. Eager to increase the wealth of his territory, Velasco knighted the young Ibarra, who, paying his own expenses, would explore, colonize, and exploit the regions crossed by Vázquez de Mercado. Leaving Zacatecas in September of 1554 with Juan de Tolosa, the Franciscan missionary Brother Jerónimo de Mendoza (nephew of the previous viceroy), and thirty soldiers, Francisco de Ibarra discovered mineral deposits in Fresnillo, Sain, Sombrerete, Chalchihuites, San Martín, and Aviño. Upon his return through the valley of Guardiana, he was wounded in a skirmish with the natives. In spite of this misfortune, Brother Jerónimo was able to found the order of the Nombre de Dios. Ibarra and his contingent arrived in Zacatecas in December.

These discoveries, along with those of the mines of Guanajuato in 1554 and 1555, stimulated an even greater influx of miners. They also resulted in increased pressure on the indigenous population. In spite of the foundation of communities such as Nochistlán, Teocaltiche, Tlatenando, Teul, and Juchipila on the road from Zacatecas to Guadalajara, and the Guanajuatan towns on the one from Zacatecas to Mexico, the attacks of the Cazcans and several groups of seminomadic Chichimecs, Zacatecans, Repehuans, and Guachichils on the caravans of beasts of burden and the cattle-breeding *estancias* increased markedly. As a result, in addition to the tasks of exploring, it fell to Francisco de Ibarra to establish systems of defense against the Chichimecs.

In December of 1556, Ibarra, with Tolosa and Luis de Cortés (son of the conqueror), and accompanied by fifty soldiers, set out from Zacatecas again, and followed the route that he had established two years earlier. This time, he paid more attention to opening mines. The following year, with the assistance of Father Mendoza of San Francisco del Nombre de Dios, the Franciscans founded a second mission in San Martín. During these years, Ibarra was able to establish peaceful relations with the Chichimecs and, due to the rapid development of the region, by the order of the viceroy and a royal provision from July 24, 1562, the mining territory to the north of Zacatecas was extended to the province of Nueva Vizcaya, composed of the modern-day states of Durango, Chihuahua, Coahuila, Sinaloa, and Sonora, and parts of Zacatecas, San Luis Potosí, and Nuevo León. The first governor and captain general of the new province was Francisco de Ibarra, whose commission included specific orders to continue its exploration and development.

On July 8, 1563, the Basque Ibarra, at that time lieutenant governor, founded the *villa* of Durango. The ecclesiastic development of Nueva Vizcaya was rapid, with the creation of the Franciscan outpost in Zacatecas and the already-mentioned Durango in 1566. On November 18, 1576, Diego de Ibarra was named governor of Nueva Vizcaya, although he was not able to assume the office until 1583. Another significant Basque of the epoch was Francisco de Urdiñola, who was born in Oiartzun (Gipuzkoa) in 1522 and arrived in Nueva Vizcaya in 1576. He immediately distinguished himself in the pacification of the Guachichiles of Indé in 1579, of Saltillo in 1580, of Mazapil in 1581, and of Matehuala from 1582 to 1584. His tactics included taking hostages and prisoners, and he offered the potential of profit in times of peace. Urdiñola gained the respect of the Indian caciques. As a result, he was named captain of Saltillo in 1580, and of Mazapil in 1582. These events facilitated the foundation of the Franciscan convent of San Esteban del Saltillo by Brother Lorenzo de Gavira in 1582 and the opening of important mines in Bonanza, Mazapil, Nieves, and Concepción de Oro, bringing Urdiñola fame and power. He married Leonor López de Loys, a woman of high birth.

In 1594, Urdiñola received a citation from the Tribunal of Guadalajara ordering his detention and the seizure of his possessions under the accusation of assassinating his wife and some employees of his *estancia* in Santa Elena. As he was an officer of the Holy Order of the Inquisition, he requested that his trial be transferred to this institution. Five years of proceedings thus began, which ultimately determined that his wife had died in the spring of 1593 after twenty days of illness. On May 21, 1603, Urdiñola was appointed governor of Nueva Vizcaya by Viceroy Gaspar de Zúñiga y Acevedo, count of Monterrey. In 1604, Urdiñola reported that the province had 93 miners, 36 livestock breeders, 41 farmers, and 52 businessmen. One hundred thirty-one married and 177 unmarried residents were mentioned. On March 4, 1618, Urdiñola died on his *estancia* at the age of sixty-six.

In 1597, a son of Cristóbal de Oñate, Juan, married the daughter of Juan de Tolosa, an old associate of his father. Juan de Oñate managed to organize an expedition of 120 soldiers (some accompanied by members of their families), 9 Franciscans, 83 carriages with provisions, and 7,000 head of livestock. His nephews, Juan and Vicente de Zaldivar, sons of the lieutenant captain general of Nueva Galicia, Vicente de Zaldivar, and María de Oñate, also accompanied the expedition as brigadier and sergeant major, respectively. The colonizing expedition left Santa Bárbara on January 26, 1528. The band followed the Conchos River until its confluence with the Río Grande del Norte. They continued along the course of this channel, which they crossed at the ford called El Paso del Norte (the Northern Pass). They reached the confluence of the Chama River, managing to subject the peoples living there to the Crown. On July 11, 1598, San Juan de los Caballeros was founded. Between September 10 and November 8 of that year, Vicente de Zaldivar reached the Great Plains of Texas and Oklahoma. The two conquerors (Oñate and Zaldivar) succeeded in subduing the Acoma Pueblo, who had risen in a bloody rebellion. They thereby successfully colonized the extreme northern stretch of Spanish-occupied New Mexico and explored all the way to the plains of Kansas. Between 1604 and 1605, reconnaissance of the route from New Mexico to the Colorado River and the Gulf of California was completed. Thus, from 1540 until 1600, through great physical efforts and immense financial expenditures, and due largely to the contribution of strong family ties, a group of Basques directed the colonization and socioeconomic boom of a territory of 950,000 square kilometers. This region is formed of vast plains that extend into the horizon, with altitudes that rise from sea level to 2,500 meters. The west wind is interrupted by a sierra that reaches more than another thousand meters in height. The area ends to the east with the harshness and dryness of northern Coahuila and Tamaulipas. All of its territory enjoyed enormous mineral richness and high livestock productivity.

Among the Spaniards who went to Mexico in the sixteenth century, as indicated by the figures compiled by Peter Boyd-Bowman, there were few settlers from the north of the Iberian Peninsula.[3] As noted earlier, he found that Andalusia was the Spanish region that launched the most emigrants to America in the first century after its discovery. Thus, from 1493 to 1519, 39.9 percent of the Spaniards that went to the New World were Andalusian, compared to 4.4 percent Basques. Of the men who participated in the Mexican colonial undertaking, 30.6 percent were Andalusian, compared to 4.8 percent Basques and 0.1 percent Navarrese, and a significant core of these Basque emigrants lived in Darién in 1510. These numbers hardly changed from 1520 to 1539. Thirty-two percent of the Spanish travelers to America were Andalusians, 5.0 percent were Basques, and 0.5 percent Navarrese. In the case of Mexico, the respective percentages of the Spanish emigration were 35 percent Andalusians, 4.4 percent Basques, and 0.4 percent Navarrese. In 1540, 32.7 percent Andalusians, 4.5 percent Basques, and 0.7 percent Navarrese lived in Mexico City. In the case of Nueva Galicia, the first region to the north conquered, Basque participation was 7.05 percent. The most salient quantitative conclusion is that Basques in Mexico preferred to settle in the northern regions of the country and also demonstrated an affinity for the capital city.

From 1540 to 1559, the Andalusians sent 36.1 percent, the Basques 4.4 percent, and the Navarrese 0.6 percent of the total Spanish immigration. From 1560 to 1579, 37.4 percent of the Spanish immigrants in America were Andalusians, 2.9 percent Basques, and 0.6 percent Navarrese. In this last period, only 2.1 percent of Spanish immigrants to Mexico were Basques. Nevertheless, in Mexico City, at the end of the sixteenth century, 7 percent of the residents were of Basque origin, and 6.1 percent came from Navarre. It is significant that 9 percent of the total of the noblemen emigrating to the New World were Basques. In the period 1595 to 1598, only 3.7 percent of those that arrived in Nueva España–Mexico were Basques, as opposed to 37.7 percent Andalusians. A census of Mexico City in 1689 gives further numerical insight into the Basque presence in this country.[4] That year, there were 1,181 European-born people in the capital. Of this total, 302 (25.6 percent) were Andalusians, 162 (13.7 percent) Basques, 56 (4.7 percent) Navarrese, 37 (3.1 percent) from La Rioja, and 141 (11.1 percent) Cantabrians. All told, around 40 percent of the Spaniards settled in Mexico City at the end of the seventeenth century came from northern Spain.

In 1724, the northwest of the Iberian Peninsula continued to provide the majority of the Spanish immigrants settled in Mexico, with Basques, Santanderinos, and Burgaleses predominant among them.[5] At the beginning of the nineteenth century Humboldt described Nueva España as inhabited by men of the north of the Iberian Peninsula. According to the data presented by Jordi Nadal,[6] the Basques and Navarrese contributed 5.7 percent of the total Spanish population in Nueva España in 1530, 4.5 percent in 1591, 4.7 percent in 1768, and 5.3 percent in 1787. In comparison, the Andalusians contributed 16.2 percent in 1530, 16.1 percent in 1591, 18.4 percent in 1768, and 18.2 percent in 1787. Therefore, Basque emigration to the New World (at least in the sixteenth century) followed the basic European patterns of the time, while its Andalusian counterpart was much higher. Basque emigration will therefore have to be analyzed more qualitatively than quantitatively.

It seems probable that the successes of the Oñates, Ibarras, Urdiñolas, Zaldivars, and other Basques of the first colonial times would have attracted their fellow natives wishing to strike it rich in the New World. But the Basques in Mexico not only played an important role in the region of Nueva Vizcaya, they were also influential in Nueva España, constituting the most powerful group in Mexico City. Helped by nephews and other relatives that arrived from Spain, the capital's oligarchy was largely devoted to commerce. It thereby maintained close relations with the Old Country. Among the well-known families, the following stand out: the Fagoagas (related to Manuel de Aldaco and Ambrosio de Meabe), the Iraetas, the Icazas, and the Bassocos. The Basques had an important role in the Consulate of Mexico,[7] and they would also occupy positions of privilege at the top of the provincial government of Nueva Vizcaya throughout the entire modern era. This was the case of Martín de Alday, Manuel de San Juan y Santa Cruz, Ignacio Francisco de Barrutia, Juan José Vertiz y Ontañón, Juan Bautista de Belanzacín, José García de Salcedo, and José del Campo Soberón y Larrea.[8]

Basques were to be found in the rising local oligarchies (sometimes very poor, others very prosperous) in significant numbers.[9] Thus, the Basque presence was significant in the *villa* of Chihualima and the adjoining Real de Santa Eulalia beginning with their foundation in 1703. In the Sierra Tarahumara, Captain Juan Fernández de Letona held tight control for many years. Many relatives and countrymen worked with him, such as the already-cited Martín de Alday and his cousin, the miner and militia head José de Zubiate. José del Campo Soberón y Larrea, first count of Valle de Súchill, had mining investments in Avenito, Durango, Sombrerete, and Sinaloa. In the Bolaños mining camp, located in the north of Nueva Galicia and one of the most famous of the eighteenth century, Basque names such as Alday, Anza, Beldarrain, Berroterán, Díaz de Carpio, and Zubiate abounded. And, as has already been documented, the Basques clearly occupied a significant place in the local colonial administration.

The Passion for Mining in the Basque Community of Sonora

Men of Basque origin appeared in Sonora throughout the seventeenth century.[10] By century's end a numerous Basque-Sonoran collectivity had organized around Captain Fernández de Retama, commander of the citadel at San Francisco de los Conchos. During the incessant rebellions of the Tarahumara Indians, he fought alongside men like Andrés de Rezábal (established as a rich merchant in Sonora) and José de Zubiate. Rezábal was appointed commander of the citadel of Sinaola in 1696, a position he held until his death in 1723. During these years he was one of the richest men in the region, maintaining a significant network of contacts and heading up an important pressure group. José de Zubiate, in turn, was the cousin of Fernández de Letona and had his career in mining. He worked in Santa Rosa de Coziguriachi, then in Ostimuri, and next in Nacozari, the Apache frontier in Sonora. He would then settle in Santa Eulalia and, ultimately, in San Felipe el Real (later called Chichuchua). Zubiate made a large fortune and his heirs attained powerful positions. His wealth enabled him to earn important administrative posts. On the heels of the success of these first Basques, others settled in the region. Thus, in El Real del Aguaje, Martín de Ibarburu, who came from Andrés de Rezábal's circle, stood out. But, in addition to the Basques, other collectivities and individuals came to have influence and power in Sonora in the last years of the seventeenth century. This was the case of the Aragonese Domingo Jironza Petriz de Cruzat, who had been the governor of Nuevo México. Jironza was the first captain of the Sonora citadel in 1693. He availed himself of the friendship of the Jesuits to expand missions, and depended on the support of his nephew Juan Mateo Mange, who reached Sonora in 1693.

Jironza and Mange's promotions, however, were suddenly reversed. In 1701, Jacinto de Fuensaldaña managed to snatch the command of the citadel of Sonora away from Jironza through a royal appointment in 1699. Fuensaldaña was assisted in his maneuver by his nephew Gregorio Alvarez Tuñón y Quirós. The latter took advantage of his power and social position between 1710 and 1720 to engage in intensive commercial and mining activity, leaving the military duties in the hands of Juan Bautista de Escalante. The Basque collectivity's enmity toward Fuensaldaña and his nephew grew steadily after their subversive maneuver. The situation intensified, however, after incursions and heavy attacks by the Apaches on the Sonora frontier, and Tuñón y Quirós was accused of mismanagement and inactivity. As a result of the denouncements, the Crown sent Brigadier Pedro de Rivera as a visitor to investigate the catastrophic situation on the northern frontier. Tuñón y Quirós was suspended from his post as a result. He was replaced by Juan Bautista Anza, a young Basque settled in the province since 1718. The battle between the Basque and Aragonese factions had begun.

Juan Bautista de Anza was one of the most recognized captains in the history of Sonora. He combined his political activity with the necessities of the Jesuit missionary system. A good example of this union occurred in 1737 when a Guayma Indian declared himself a messenger of the god Montezuma, announcing the return of pre-Colombian times and the disappearance of the Spaniards. Several thousand natives rallied around his prophecies and messianic system. Anza acted quickly, however, taking the messenger prisoner and hanging him from a palm tree as an example. Another significant Basque, Agustín de Vildósola, appeared alongside Juan Bautista de Anza. Vildósola began his endeavors as a merchant in northwestern Mexico around 1719, being named captain of the militia in 1729 and sergeant major in 1731 by Anza. But he would soon fall into disgrace.

In the 1750s, the position of the Basques in Nueva Vizcaya was strengthened significantly, although in the second half of the century there were continual struggles for power between them and Cantabrians. Mexico City had over 100,000 inhabitants in the last decades of the eighteenth century, of whom 20,000 considered themselves Spaniards, whether born in the Old Country or America. This city became the heart of the economic and cultural policy of Nueva España from its foundation. Its merchants (who also participated in mining, agriculture, and livestock breeding) would be the ones that integrated the viceroyalty of Nueva España into the world economic system.[11] It would therefore be in this city that the first colonial institutions, such as the Royal Board of the Consulate of Mexico City, would proliferate.

The consulate was founded in 1591 by the Royal Decree of June 15, by petition of a group of Mexican businessmen wishing to protect their interests and promote commerce, and seeking to emancipate themselves from the House of Trade of Sevilla. It was the first consulate in Spanish America. Another institution of vital importance in the Mexican economy was the capital's city government, founded in 1527. Its mayors and aldermen controlled supply and regulated the prices of staple crops. In the second half of the eighteenth century, both public undertakings were governed by Basques and their descendants.[12]

The consulate admitted only wealthy merchants who were residents of Mexico City and capable of buying products from Europe, Asia, and other American territories. In the second half of the 1700s, an average of 130 merchants formed a part of this consulate that was divided into two factions, according to origin. The first was that of the *vizcaínos*, which encompassed the merchants of Araba, Gipuzkoa, Bizkaia, and Navarre, and their descendants born in America. They fortified their cohesion through the Confraternity of Our Lady of Aránzazu and, beginning in 1773, through membership in the Royal Basque Society of the Friends of the Country. The other faction, that of the *montañeses*, included those from Santander, Lugo, La Coruña, and Badajoz, along with their American descendants. They also reinforced their connections by worshiping Christ of Burgos. These two bands vied for control of the consulate in heated disagreements.

Beginning in 1742, elections were held: one year to choose the prior, one consul, and two deputies, and the next year one consul and three deputies. It was an attempt to reduce the friction and guarantee both groups the defense of their interests. In spite of everything, in the second half of the eighteenth century the Basques were a majority and the principal Mexican merchants came from their faction, including Antonio Bassoco, Juan de Castañiza, Juan José de Fagoaga, and Gabriel Yermo. In the second half of the century of the Enlightenment, the most zealous procurator of the consulate in the Court of Madrid was Francisco Xavier de Gamboa. Born in Guadalajara (Mexico), he was of Basque heritage. Studies that could reliably furnish the names and origins of all the consulate members are lacking. For the period between 1748 and 1826, however, it is known[13] that of the 69 members of the faction of the *vizcaínos*, 20 were priors and 38 consuls. Seventeen of these held both offices. Of these 69 Basques, 33 belonged to the Royal Basque Society and 22 of these members held a position of either prior or consul.

The majority of the consulate's members possessed commercial fortunes gained through the traffic in European, Oriental, and Spanish-American products, which serviced the internal consumption of the colony. Others, however, specialized in mining and farming ventures (Juan de Castañiza, Antonio Bassoco, and Juan José de Fagoaga). Merchants appeared who specialized in traffic with the Philippines (José David). Others preferred Iberian American commercial business. This was the case of Antonio de Icaza, connected to the oligarchies on the mainland (especially in Quito), and Pedro de Aycinena, a dealer in Oriental products and exporter of indigo in Guatemala.

The Confraternity of Aránzazu

At the end of the seventeenth century, the Basque and Navarrese residents in Mexico founded the Brotherhood of Aránzazu. This association was created in the capital of the viceroyalty in 1671, in a chapel of the Franciscan fathers that became the brotherhood's property in 1681. In 1682, a new chapel was erected and the founding statutes drawn up.[14] The foundational proceedings were as follows:

> The year 1681 some Basques moved by the zeal and love of the Holy Virgin of Aránzazu proposed to the remaining natives of the Señorío of Vizcaya, Enkarterri, Kingdom of Navarre, province of Guipúzcoa and Alava, the foundation of a chapel for the veneration of the Virgin of Aránzazu, whose sanctuary is erected in an abutment in the Pyrenees at the junction of Gipuzkoa, Araba, and Navarre and likewise serves for the burial and splendor for said Basques.[15]

To begin with, the brotherhood was open to all Basque residents in Mexico, not only those living in the capital. This institution would be presided over by a board of governors elected annually by secret vote. In 1696 (at which time it also became a confraternity), they drew up new statutes. The institution's aim was "to serve and honor the Holy Virgin Mary," although it was also founded in order to honor the dead, inspiring members to attend the burials of their deceased members. In regard to social service activity, the Confraternity of Aránzazu of Mexico proposed

1. visiting ill members,
2. serving non-member Basques, especially when they were in prison or the hospital, and
3. giving gifts to orphans.

The Confraternity of Aránzazu built a chapel bearing its name in the atrium of the convent of San Francisco el Grande. From 1681 to 1696, the brotherhood initiated the cult and the social services proposed in its statutes. From 1696 to 1732, it developed notably. The works of the cult were multiplied and social services expanded. From 1732 to 1772, the confraternity projected and inaugurated the College of the Vizcayans. For forty years, the members of Aránzazu carried out this educational mission, continuing to promote the works of the cult and social services. For the twenty-seven years between 1772 and 1799, the confraternity focused its social and apostolic labors in Europe and Asia, promoting new memberships and the Royal Basque Society. It opened free public schools in the College of the Vizcayans and sustained apostolic labors to improve the religious life of those who lacked economic means, even contributing to the evangelization of China from Mexico. During the years 1681 to 1696, this Basque-Navarrese brotherhood in Mexico worked for the construction of a new chapel. Thus, 7,142 pesos were collected from attendees for this cause at the first assembly, held on November 23, 1681.[16] Many other contributions for the project followed until they met its total budget, raising 46,030 pesos and one real.[17] This stage also marked the beginning of the social work that would continue throughout the confraternity's history. The guidelines were as follows:

1. Endowments for orphans, so that they could marry or enter into religious service
2. Contribution for the subsistence of the lay clergy through the chaplaincies

In 1696, the brotherhood was established as a confraternity. It was consolidated from that year until 1731 with acceptance of 1,275 members. Donations of the members and the acts of the cult increased in this period, and social programs benefiting women were expanded. From 1732 to 1772, it welcomed 1,247 new members. It was in this epoch that the permanent institutionalization of the education of women was developed.

The College of the Vizcayans of Mexico City

The College of the Vizcayans was born in the heart of the Confraternity of Aránzazu in 1767.[18] The Basque members had a significant precedent for such an institution in Nueva España. The College of Charity, the first educational center for the Mexican woman, existed prior to 1537. The College of Charity had been sponsored by the Confraternity of Sanctity and Charity. Its governing board ran the school throughout the colony. The aim of the College of the Vizcayans was to attend to widows lacking economic means. At the end of the eighteenth century, women made up 55 percent of the population of Mexico City. A relatively high number of them were on the verge of poverty. Widows from society's middle strata lacked basic support. Along with educating this sector of unfortunate women, the college also proposed that other paying students and "pensioners" enter its classrooms. From 1731 to 1767, the year that the Royal College of Saint Ignatius of Loyola (popularly known as the College of the Vizcayans) was opened, the confraternity lived through several years of intense preparations.[19] The building's construction was the work of the architect and member Pedro Bueno Basori, who projected it in 1733 as a splendid baroque palace. It still stands, and the institution is also active. The building is of great proportions, with seven interior patios and a capacity for 160 students. There is also a church, endowed for the Catholic cult and with a residence for chaplains. Work was completed in 1752 and the building was prepared for its inauguration. A total of 583,118 pesos had been raised for the construction. However, the members would have to wait fifteen years, the time it took to obtain the desired juridical approvals, before the definitive opening. Its splendid present facade was constructed in 1771. It was the work of the architect Lorenzo Rodriguez, who also designed the well-known Chapel of the Sanctuary of Mexico City.

The Real Sociedad Bascongada de Amigos del País

In 1763, the Real Sociedad Bascongada de Amigos del País (Royal Basque Society of the Friends of the Country) was born in Spain. It was approved by the Crown in 1770. Shortly thereafter, Martín de Aguirre Burualde, a member of the Society, went to Nueva España. Aguirre inspired Leandro de Viana (future count of Tepa), justice of the High Court of Mexico, member of Aránzazu, and its rector during 1772–1773.[20] On July 4, 1773, a circular was distributed to the Basque-Navarrese colony of Mexico City encouraging its members to join the Society. Within a few days, 171 new members joined and 10,000 pesos were collected. In 1776, the Society (with the approval of Charles III and under his protection) opened the Patriotic Seminary of Vergara. The Society sponsored a membership and fund-raising campaign in Europe and America. In Mexico, Ambrosio de Meabe promoted the Patriotic Seminary of Vergara. He raised 14,000 pesos by 1781 for its maintenance. The Society came to have 507 members in Mexico at the end of the eighteenth century, a truly extraordinary number that demonstrates the appeal and power of Basque associative tendencies there.[21]

Most Basque members of the Society were settled in Mexico City, followed distantly by Chihuahua, Pátzcuaro, Valladolid, and Puebla—fundamental nodes in the movement of Basque capital in Mexico during the second half of the eighteenth century:[22]

Distribution of Members

Place	No.
Mexico City	240
Chihuahua	32
Pátzcuaro	24
Valladolid	21
Puebla	18
Oaxaca	17
Guadalajara	16
Veracruz	16
Zacatecas	15
Fresnillo	15
Puebla de los Angeles	12
Querétaro	11
Campeche	11
Guanajuato	9
Unspecified	7
Durango	6
Sombrerete	6
Zimapán	5
Mérida	3
Santa Clara del Cobre	3
Jalapa	2
Zamora	2
Grande	2
Tezcoco	1
Zapotlán el Grande	1
Salvatierra	1
Tentitlán del Camino	1
Pachuca	1
Tuxtla	1
Santa Cruz de la Sierra	1
Teypan	1
Casamaloapan	1
Jerez de N. E.	1
Cuernavaca	1
Reynosa	1
Orizaba	1
Real del Monte	1
Total	507

Professions of Members

Profession	No.
Merchant	80
High-level functionary	58
Miner	39
High-ranking soldier	35
Religious hierarchy	27
Intellectual	16
Hacendado	14
University professor/doctor	7
Scientist	3
Architect	2
Protector of Indians	1
Medical doctor	1
Total	283

The majority of the sample (of the 283 whose professions have been traced) devoted themselves to commerce during the second half of the eighteenth century. The high-level functionaries were a strong second. This makes sense, as the tandem of commerce and public service would be fundamental for the successful development of the market. Mining, already discussed in this chapter, continued attracting eighteenth-century Basques, as it had since the earlier times of the conquest. And to defend the interests of the Basque and (more generally) Spanish merchant, a significant number of the members were in the military. The *hacendados* are found in a worthy seventh place, and the remainder of those in the table embrace the liberal and intellectual professions that mesh so well with the spirit of the Society.

The Basques that reached Mexico during the second half of the nineteenth century clearly contributed greatly to the country's economic expansion, as well as to their own profit and large private fortunes. Domingo and Pedro de Aguirre, for example, managed to accumulate a great patrimony and a no less significant financial fortune, part of which was invested in the construction of the Commercial University of Deusto, in Bilbao, and in the hospital and clinic of San Juan de Dios in Santurtzi (Bizkaia). In Puebla, the Basque colony came to acquire noteworthy levels of power, holding all key posts in the administration, local clergy, and regional commerce. The Gipuzkoan J. M. Ostolaza is one example. Together with the Navarrese Leonardo Aldama, he founded a hat factory in Tehuacán at the beginning of the twentieth century. Another is the painter J. M. Ibarrarán, who died in Tehuacán in 1910. Baltasar Uriarte (1901), Francisco Urrutia (1926), and Fernando Arruti (1934) all served as mayors. Between 1902 and 1917, Ramón Ibarra was promoted from bishop to archbishop of Puebla.

Around the 1920s, some 80,000 Spaniards were living in Mexico,[23] many of them in enviable positions. Individuals from the significant Basque colony of the time occupied notable social and economic positions. Thus, in industry, the Bizkaian Antonio de Basagoiti stood out. He was one of the promoters of the Foundry Company of Iron and Cement of Monterrey, Inc., established on May 5, 1900. The Bilbao firm Santos L. de Letona had three textile factories in Puebla de los Angeles. Other Basques were involved in coffee plantations, such as the Bizkaian Francisco de Isasi, the representative of the Descendants of José Revuelta Firm, in the state of Chiapas. The Bizkaian Nicolás Arbide (engineer) managed the public works of the state of Tapachula. Other Bizkaians, Rafael Arocena y Leandro and José María Urrutia, founded the cotton hacienda Santa Teresa. In 1923, it became the most productive of its kind.

In regard to the emigration from Navarre in particular, there is documentation of the departure of natives of Baztán.[24] In the twentieth century, their selection of destination was motivated, in large part, by the following factors:

1. The economic opportunities in the country of destination
2. The existence of relatives and former fellow townsmen in that country
3. The surmounting of set legal procedures such as the visa, work contract, and residence permit

In regard to the destination chosen by the natives of Baztán, the United States came in first place, with the majority going to California (67 percent), followed by Arizona (9 percent), Idaho (9 percent), and Nevada (8 percent). Mexico was the next most desirable place of settlement for northern Navarrese emigration, including Mexico City (the majority), Celaya, the state of Guanajuato, and Toluca, Querétaro, Torcon, and Durango. Chile was in third place, followed by Argentina and then other residual destinations: Uruguay, Venezuela, and Canada. Figure 5.1 shows the importance of American destinations.

The Navarrese emigrant tended to be a young (twenty or so years old) single man, without his own future in Baztán (he would not inherit the farmstead). Usually, he had been working in agriculture and livestock. He was called by a relative (brother, uncle) or fellow townsman. He began in America as an employee and tried to make it on his own. Sometimes he was successful and made a fortune. In many cases, he returned to Baztán to get married, or married a woman from Baztán (Chile) or a daughter of its natives (Mexico). Other times, he remained single (California, Mexico) or married a native Spanish or mestiza woman. The activities to which these Navarrese devoted themselves were

1. bread making, pastry making, fritter making, hardware,
2. flour selling,
3. livestock (sheep and cattle),

4. restaurants,
5. canneries, and
6. shoemaking.

The Basques from Iparralde reached Mexico in 1840. Some worked as silver prospectors, but the majority were merchants and storeowners. Some natives of Hasparren (Labourd) had tanneries and shoe factories. This immigration would end in 1900 largely due to Mexico's internal problems.

Local Fraternal Activity

In 1907, the Basque colony in Mexico founded the Basque Center, made up of mostly Navarrese, Bizkaians, and Gipuzkoans, with some French Basques. With the onset of the Spanish Civil War (1936–1939), the Mexican government of Lázaro Cárdenas decided to openly support the Spanish Republic. Mexico accepted a significant number of Republican exiles after the war. The Basque community in Mexico was itself divided by the conflict. A group of nationalists followed the orders of the PNV (Basque Nationalist Party). Another sector, composed fundamentally of socialists and members of the old Basque colony that had immigrated prior to 1936, opposed the nationalist agenda. Lorin Gaarder[25] details this division in Mexico City, discerning two groups within the Basque collectivity.

Group A was composed of immigrants entering the country at the end of the

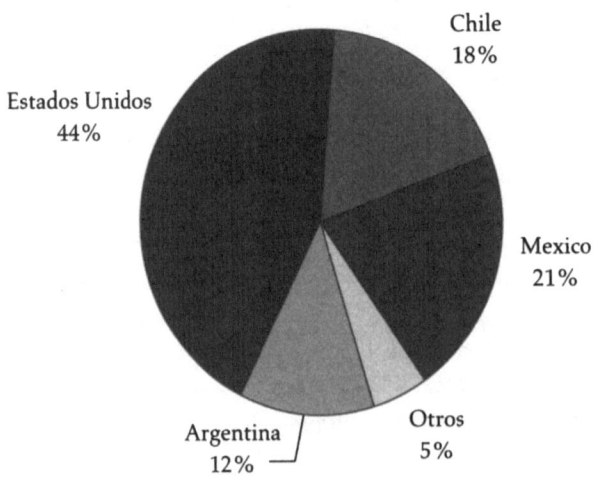

Fig. 5.1 Destinations of Emigrants from Baztán to the Americas in the Twentieth Century. Source: A. Alday-Garay, 1992.

nineteenth century or beginning of the twentieth. Of rural background, they arrived without property, capital, or technical or academic education. They immigrated in Mexico with the idea of making money after years of hard work. They maintained ties with their homeland and summoned new emigrants, normally relatives, to open new businesses.

One immigrant who stood out in this group was Braulio Iriarte, born in Elizondo (Baztán, Navarre) in 1860. He immigrated in Mexico at seventeen in 1877 with no education or professional experience. He began his career as an employee in a bakery. After years of sacrifice and saving, he came to own 80 bakeries and his own mill, El Euskaro. Founded in 1906, the mill was one of the biggest in Mexico. At the beginning of the century, Iriarte had several haciendas in Querétaro, mines in Hidalgo, and large properties in Mexico City. He also founded various financial and industrial companies, such as the Modelo Brewery, one of the largest in the country, in participation with other partners. Braulio Iriarte was president of the Mexico City Basque Center.

Group B was made up of refugees from the Spanish Civil War, proponents of nationalist ideology, who arrived between the mid-1930s and early 1940s. They did not leave the Basque Country of their own will but were forced out by Franco's persecution. The reasons for their emigration were, therefore, political rather than economic. In addition, they tended to have an academic or technical education, and some of them were even considered intellectuals.

In 1935, there was a schism among the members of the Basque Center, which thereby fractured into two different organizations:

1. *The Spanish-Basque Circle.* A clause in its statutes indicates promotion of "the love of the Basque Country and its history within the unity of Spain" as one of the objectives of the association. Its orientation was, therefore, non-nationalist but rather unitary and conservative (Carlist). Many members of the old colony described in Group A would join.
2. *The Basque Center of Mexico City* was composed of Basque nationalists and later received the exiles from Group B.

Several causes have been proposed for the rupture between the two groups of the Basque colony of Mexico. Lorin Gaarder lists and comments upon the following reasons:

The ideological divergence between the nationalists and the conservatives. If it is true that some of the members of the Spanish-Basque Circle were opposed to the Republic and Basque separatism, it is no less clear that the majority seemed not to have taken part in the dispute. This neutrality could have offended those having other ideas.

The intra-ethnic conflict among the Basques. This is one characteristic that distinguishes them from the other Spaniards, both refugees and members of the old colony. Historical and socioeconomic differences distinguish the coastal, industrial provinces of Bizkaia and Gipuzkoa from the interior, rural Navarre. In the former, the industrial revolution had generated two ideologies that broke with tradition: socialism and nationalism. The Navarrese colony gravitated towards the Spanish-Basque Circle. This could be interpreted as the reflection of an intra-ethnic division in the context of the Old World.

The resentment of the old colony toward the elitism of the refugees, who did not consider the former to be authentic Basques because they did not fight in the Spanish Civil War. Such an accusation was offensive for the old colony. The conflict between the two groups was aggravated by the presence among the new arrivals of a large number of intellectuals that proclaimed themselves the spokesmen of the Basque community.

The differing socioeconomic context of the two groups.

With the passage of time, the two associations became closer. The Spanish-Basque Circle lost its importance due to the greater allure of other associations such as the Spain Club and the Asturian Center, which had sports facilities. The Basque Center has also suffered wear and loss of functions with the passage of time, but it has remained more vital in regard to social and cultural activities. In 1972, the seat of the Basque Center was moved to its present location in the Polanco Colony, a residential area, safer, and with fewer traffic and parking problems. As of 1997, there were three functioning Basque Centers in Mexico.

Basque Family Networks and Power Elite in Central America

As has been shown repeatedly in this study, throughout America, nuclei and family networks of the power elite were structured around the Basque colonies established in the territories of greatest interest to the Spanish Crown: Mexico, Peru, Ecuador, and Bolivia. But, organizations of kinship and authority were also configured in other geographic territories initially considered "marginal." This was clearly the case in Central America. Basques there forged nuclei of control through marital and/or business alliances, as a result of geographic proximity or socioracial factors and participation in political, labor, and sociocultural associations. Education of its own intelligentsia, assuring the Basques access to the forces in power, also helped weave this web of family ties and power.

The main element of accumulation of political power would be determined by control of local offices (church assemblies, mayorships, aldermancies, judgeships, and cultural associations). Through well-planned strategies resulting from the desire to monopolize political and economic power, in Central America, as elsewhere, the Basques configured a wide vertical web through consanguine ties and agnatic relations. From this perspective, the family would serve as the basic collective entity through which the Basque colony's social structures would be sustained. The "endocracy" of the family networks and their upward mobility had a lot to do with the Basque control of a disproportionate part of the mercantile power in the Spanish-American world.

Following what has already been said, primary and secondary families merit attention. "Primary" families or groups of notables will be defined as those that have been able to configure the social and political structure of the territory in which they have been settled for three or more generations, preserving their lineage and last name through a variety of events in American history. Habitually, this has been accomplished through

1. initial accumulation of large sums of money,
2. success in business, even bearing in mind periods of bankruptcy or worsening conditions,
3. careful and successful marital connections,
4. direct control over the stem family networks and their secondary and regional dissemination,
5. capacity of their intellectuals to manage the survival of the lineage, and
6. ability of these primary families to diversify their economy and co-opt the role of the state during periods of economic crisis or power vacuum.

Secondary families are those that marry into the primary ones, thus reinforcing the power bloc and, with it, the authority and legitimacy of the principal network. In each century, one or two principal families would spring forth in Central America. Various secondary ones would spring up around these, configuring a diverse framework of interpersonal relationships in which class and elite interests coincided. This provided an exceptional capacity for mimicry and metamorphosis to adapt to the changing course of each historic epoch. This passion for the power of the kin groups in colonial, and even independent, America had its origin in the Old Country. In Spain, family and interpersonal relations were traditionally primary determinants of social ascent. This behavior reached the New World from the outset of conquest and colonization. It peaked when physical distance made protection and preservation of the lineage and last name necessary in a territory in which one had to live amid Indians, blacks, mestizos, and other castes.

The dichotomy being configured in this new society overseas between Creoles and Spaniards was often softened precisely by the intermixing of the groups through marriage (and business). And this was in large part due to the physical distance from the center of Spanish power and the resulting difficulty of enforcing the legislation that came from Madrid. Thus, the most beneficial client relationships came through alliances with the authorities in the home country, but also with the most representative elements of the Creole world. The situation thereby gave rise to true successions of political and economic power that must be situated in the long-term historical cycle.

Even with independence from Spain and the appearance of the liberal state, these families would redirect their privileged situation through the figure of the charismatic leader (notables). The result was the configuration of nations in which the landholding or commercial oligarchies were masters of collective national destinies.

As will be seen in the pages to follow, the Basque family networks described here had a determining role in the passage from one type of society (colonial) to another (the liberal state). They also formed pressure groups in Central America. As can be observed from the information in table 5.1, almost 70 percent of the principal Central American families during the century of Enlightenment were of Basque origin. As Marta Elena Casaus Arzú indicates, all of them established marital relations within their social group, at the same time extending their tentacles (beginning with Guatemala) through El Salvador, Honduras, Nicaragua, and Costa Rica. Seventeen of the families mentioned continue to form part of the present-day political and economic power in the region.

The general panorama of the Basque colony in Central America may now be considered. Guatemala, the territory examined in the greatest number of serious studies, will serve as the prime example. This will be followed by a more detailed description of the families and the power elites, both there and in Costa Rica.

The main Basque lineages were installed in Guatemala as part of its captaincy general's administrative enthusiasm to spread its influence from there into the rest of Central American territory:[26]

Aycinena e Irigoyen (1753)
Arzú y Díaz de Arcaya (1756)
Beltranena y Aycinena (1778)
Barrutia, Irisarri (1770)
Chamorro y Sotomayor (1770). Spread from Guatemala into El Salvador, Honduras, and Nicaragua.
Urruela y Angulo (1780). Branched out from Guatemala into El Salvador and Nicaragua.

Other families such as the Arribillagas, Batreses, and Arizas were based more on Guatemalan territory, although they also extended through Meso- and South America. The Arizas, for example, were located in Nicaragua, Costa Rica, and El Salvador. One element causing the Central American Basques to stick together was a

TABLE 5.1 *Principal Basque Family Networks in Central America in the 18th Century*

Name	Guatemala	El Salvador	Honduras	Nicaragua	Costa Rica
Aguirre Beltrán	X	X	—	X	X
Alejos	X	X	—	X	—
Aparicio	X	—	X	—	—
Arce	X	X	X	X	—
Ariza y Rubio	X	X	—	—	—
Ayau, Pedro	X	X	—	—	—
Aycinena e Irigoyen	X	X	X	X	—
Arzú y Díaz Arcaya	X	X	X	X	—
Barrundia Iparraguirre	X	—	—	X	—
Barrutia y Olabegoitia	X	—	X	X	—
Batres	X	X	X	—	—
Beltranena y Aycinena	X	X	X	X	—
Castilla y Portugal	X	X	X	—	—
Chamorro y Sotomayor	X	X	X	X	—
Echevarría, Francisco	X	—	—	—	X
González Saravia	X	X	—	—	—
Gutiérrez Gómez	X	—	—	X	X
Irisarri y Larrain	X	X	—	X	—
Irungaray Matheu	X	X	X	—	—
Micheo Barrenechea	X	X	—	—	—
Oliberrieta, G.	X	X	—	—	X
Oyarzábal Irigoyen	X	X	—	X	—
Piñol Salas	X	X	—	—	—
Retes Mollinedo	X	—	—	—	X
Salázar de la Peña	X	X	X	—	X
Samayoa Aguinaga	X	—	X	—	—
Sosa	X	X	—	—	—
Urruela y Angulo	X	X	—	X	—
Viteri	X	X	—	X	—
Zavala Josue	X	—	X	X	—

Source: M. E. Casaus Arzú, 1996, 297–98.

Creole family descended through the female line of Basques related to authorities in the home country. Thanks to its proliferation, it made a number of alliances possible among the Basques in the period between 1752 and 1789. This was the married couple José Tomás Delgado de Nájera y de la Tovilla and María Felipa Mencos Barón de Berrieza. From the connections with the Delgado de Nájera-Mencos family, the following eight branches of Basque origin were created:

1. Alvarez de las Asturias Arroyave
2. Arzú Díaz de Arcaya
3. Aycinena Irigoyen
4. Barrutia Echeverría
5. González Batres Arribillaga
6. González Batres Muñoz
7. Micheo Barrenechea
8. Llano Villa Urrutia

The Arribillaga family, from Irún, were military nobles that reached Guatemala in the mid-seventeenth century. The brothers Diego and Juan Arribillaga, who married the two Vasques Coronado sisters, established the lineage and entail of their name in 1656 around the hacienda of Our Lady of Guadalupe, endowed with livestock and slaves, as well as other haciendas and sugar mills.

The Batres family, one of the primary lineages of Basque origin that reached Guatemala, came from El Salvador.[27] Once in Guatemala, some family members became priests; others ended up in public administration or the army. The kin relation with the Creole nobility resulted from Juan José González Batres's marriage to Juana Arribillaga in 1723. He was mayor (*alcalde ordinario*) of Santiago, Guatemala, in 1717, 1718, 1735, and 1743, and alderman and police chief from 1742 to 1752. The Batres family was also connected to the Larraves, also from Bizkaia, who arrived at the beginning of the eighteenth century. The descendants of this branch formed part of a group of notables that signed Guatemala's act of independence.

The Ariza family settled in Guatemala through its founder, Pedro de Ariza Rubio, a soldier who moved to America in 1780. His marriage was doubly endogamous, in both origin and occupation. His wife, Rafaela Labayru Pineda, was Basque and the descendant of soldiers.

This first generation was composed of noble lineages that, through alliances of marriage, would diversify their activity at the end of the first generation with others focused on business and landowning (table 2.18 in appendix 2). Descent would become important when the time came for establishing the network. The number of children of this first generation would still be very high (from six to nine). In the case of the Batres, Arribillaga, and Ariza families, the numerous progeny, particularly female, would give rise to the following branches:

1. Batres-Arribillaga
2. Larrazábal-Arribillaga
3. Arribillaga-Castilla y Portugal
4. Batres-Díaz de Castillo
5. Arzú-Batres
6. Aguirre-Arzú
7. Cobos-Batres
8. Batres-Jauregui

The second generation, which operated during the first decade of the nineteenth century, widened the cluster of family undertakings considerably. Thus, the merchants transformed the lands into haciendas, which they would then integrate into the import and export commercial network. They also held prominent public offices, which they used to the benefit of their businesses. And this change was accompanied by a passion for university study. In addition, the desire to rise to nobility continued to be a constant ambition in this second generation. It clearly intended to validate socially the accumulated financial and bureaucratic power it wielded in liberal professions such as law, engineering, medicine, and education.[28] See table 2.19 in appendix 2 for more detail on this activity.

The number of children of this generation was reduced almost in half. Marital alliances were important enough to consolidate the practice of endogamy, which would continue to be evident in the third generation. This second generation rushed to acquire railroads and banks, and also bought enormous quantities of urban property. The family already functioned as a commercial unit in the purchase and sale of its stocks, properties, and possessions.

The possession of government bonds, banks, utilities, and transportation facilities by the third generation increased the power of the networks. As a result, this generation had a great interest in urban development. In addition, their economic control over the railroads ended up making them owners of increasingly wide zones of Guatemala. With the capital and the power to grant credit in their hands, control of the nation was easy.

The marriages of the third generation reflected more diversity, because, by the end of the nineteenth century, some were contracting matrimony with foreigners from other European groups: Neutze, Masselli, Boppel. The number of children continued to be important, but not fundamental. And, the survival of the family network from then on would depend on the institutions, Consulate of Commerce (until 1871), commercial organizations, clubs, and the political parties (conservative and liberal). Some of the richest families in Guatemala in 1821, with membership in the Consulate of Commerce from 1794 to 1871, were as follows:[29]

Aguirre
  Luis de Aguirre (prior in 1805)
  Antonio Aguirre (prior in 1858)
  Juan Fco. Aguirre (prior in 1866 and consul in 1852 and 1860)
  Pedro Ariza
Álvarez de las Asturias
  Miguel Álvarez de las Asturias
  José Mariano Romá y Asturias
Arribillaga
  Francisco Arribillaga (consul in 1813 and 1840)
  Luis Fco. Barrutia
  Xabier Barrutia (prior in 1821)
Aycinena
  José Aycinena (consul in 1798)
  Vicente Aycinena (consul in 1803)
  Pedro Aycinena Larraín (consul in 1809)
  Mariano de Aycinena Piñol (prior in 1824 and 1850)
  Mariano Aycinena (consul in 1823)
  Juan Bautista Marticorena (prior in 1807)
  Xabier Aycinena (prior in 1856)
Batres Juarros
  Manuel J. Juarros
  Manuel Larrave (consul in 1844)
Batres Nájera
  Josef Batres
  José Antonio Batres Muñoz (prior in 1813)
  Miguel Batres (prior in 1858)
Beltranena
  Pedro Josef Beltranena (prior in 1811)
  Manuel Beltranena (consul in 1855)
  Vicente Beltranena (consul in 1858)
Delgado de Nájera
  Ventura Delgado de Nájera
Echevarria
Irigoyen
  Juan Bautista de Irisarri (consul in 1796)
  José Isasi (consul in 1800 and 1816)

Micheo
> Pedro José Micheo
> Juan Pedro Oyarzábal (consul in 1807)

Urruela
> Gregorio de Urruela
> Rafael Urruela (prior in 1839)
> José Urruela (consul in 1810)
> Gregorio Urruela (prior in 1863)

The Dominican Province of San Vicente

The Dominican province of San Vicente occupied almost all of the territory of present-day Central America plus the state of Chiapas (in Mexico).[30] During the sixteenth and seventeenth centuries, 1,386 Dominicans were registered in this territory: 332 in the former and 879 in the latter. The lives of 107 extended into both. Of the total, 348 were from the Old Country, 208 were Creoles, and 11 were non-Spaniards. By regional background, the profile for the sixteenth and seventeenth centuries is the following:

1. Castile	97 (34.8 percent)
2. Andalusia	69 (24.8 percent)
3. León	29 (10.4 percent)
4. Basque Country	28 (10 percent)
5. Extremadura	16 (5.7 percent)

Of the 28 Basque Dominicans, 11 were born in the province of Araba, and of these, 8 in the capital, Gasteiz. Seventeen were from Bizkaia (one of these born in Bilbao).

In 1646, two expeditions were organized for Central America, one under the command of the procurator Fra Pedro de Velasco and the other under the Creole Fra Tomás de Cotto. Fourteen missionaries went on this last one, six of them Basque. Two were assigned to the Convent of Aránzazu, another two to Santo Domingo de Vitoria, one to that of Bilbao, and the last to that of Haro (Logroño). In 1668, another twenty-seven Dominicans set sail for Guatemala. Ten of them were Castilian, six Basque, five Andalusian, three Galician, and one each from Navarre, Aragón, and Extremadura. Another six Basque Dominicans arrived in the seventeenth century, although the exact date is unknown. This makes a total of eighteen for the seventeenth century. The other ten (of twenty-eight) went to Central America in the sixteenth century.

One of the main obstacles for the clerics to overcome when the time came to evangelize the Indians was the native language. Thus, one of the principal missionary efforts was learning the languages, as such knowledge was indispensable for effective Christianization. From the Spanish perspective, these languages were strange, with completely unfamiliar tones and sounds, and grammatical structures very different from the Romance languages. In addition, there was a gamut of native tongues, at least thirteen that were completely distinct from each other. Thus, the Basques rushed to learn the language of those they had to evangelize. At least seven of these Basque Dominicans knew one indigenous language:[31]

Name	Native Languages
Basseta, Domingo	Quiché
Castillo, Rafael del	Quiché, Cakchiquel
Cruz, Juan de la	Quiché
Gamarra, Domingo	Kekchi
Guerra, Juan	Chol, Kekchi, Pocomchi
Ochoa, Juan de	Kekchi
Ypenza, Ambrosio	Cakchiquel
Vitoria, Tomás de	Zapotec
Zárate, Pedro de	Kekchi

As for ecclesiastic posts in this region of Central America, Basques came to govern the main convents of the province (Santo Domingo de Guatemala, Ciudad Real, and Cobán), as follows:[32]

Pedro de Antezana: subprior in Guatemala in 1645; definidor in 1645.

Rafael del Castillo: prior in Quiché in 1679 and Guatemala in 1685; definidor in 1679, 1681, 1685, 1687, and 1689; provincial in 1690; procurator c. 1702.

Juan Ezquerra: prior in Cobán in 1604; definidor in 1681.

Domingo Gamarra: prior in San Salvador in 1681; definidor in 1681.

Juan Guerra: prior in Cobán (n.d.).

Pedro de Montoya: prior in Guatemala in 1590.

Antonio de Pamplona: prior in Ciudad Real in 1587 and Tecpatán (Chiapas) in 1595; vicar in Tecpatán in 1572; definidor in 1584, 1587, and 1593.

Diego de Sáenz: master of studies in Guatemala; definidor in 1678.

Felipe de Santa María: prior in Ciudad Real in 1595, in Guatemala in 1599, and in San Salvador (n.d.); definidor in 1595, 1599, and 1605; provincial (n.d.).

Tomás de Vitoria: prior in Ciudad Real in 1566 and Guatemala in 1574; vicar in Sacapulas (n.d.); definidor in 1562 and 1567; master of novices.

Ambrosio Ypenza: prior in Guatemala in 1689; definidor in 1689; and procurator c. 1686.

The group of Basques analyzed here is small in comparison to the 1,386 Dominicans located in this province. Nevertheless, qualitative analysis of this reduced Basque colony of clerics indicates their disproportionately noteworthy role.

Indigo, the Royal Consulate of Commerce, and the Economic Company of Friends of the Country of Guatemala

One of the principal exports of Central America in general, and Guatemala in particular, was indigo dye, a key material in textile manufacture. After notable prosperity in this commerce at the end of the sixteenth century and beginning of the seventeenth, there was an abrupt crisis, in part due to the decrease in indigenous labor and the decline in Guatemalan trade with Spain. Beginning with the decade 1620–1630, the production of indigo in Guatemala leveled off. Only in the last years of the seventeenth century did export grow, and it was not until the mid-eighteenth century that production enjoyed marked increases due to European demand.[33] This commercial boom brought notable prosperity to Central American businesses. It also stimulated the arrival of Spanish merchants, especially through the port of Cádiz, who wished to participate in this new opportunity. The Catalonians and the Basques stood out in this zeal for business, given that they went to Guatemala as commissaries of the Cádiz agents or as spontaneous emigrants. These were mostly young, single males that soon established marital ties within the local colonial aristocracy, as was the case of the Basque families settled there since the seventeenth century: the Arribillagas, Landivars, Varon de Berriezas, and Vidaurres.

The merchants of Guatemala City had wanted to have their own consulate of commerce since the seventeenth century. The sale of indigo had been in the hands of the large firms in the capital city. They in turn were connected with companies in Cádiz. The Spanish governor decided to break this monopoly. He moved the indigo market to San Vicente in El Salvador and named a union functionary who would be responsible for regulating quality and price. In addition, in 1782, the Crown organized the Company of Indigo Harvesters, one of whose functions was to give low-interest loans to cultivators so that they would not have to depend on the good will of the merchants. Beginning in 1784, the Spanish government authorized the creation of a variety of new consulates in Spain and the Canary Islands (1786). On October 24, 1787, a formal petition of fifty-four large Guatemalan merchants was sent to the Crown proposing the creation of a consulate for the country. The organizational proposal was similar to other such institutions, like those in Mexico City, Sevilla, and Bilbao. On December 11, 1793, the Royal Consulate of Guatemala was finally approved, terminating a history of dependence on the consulate of Mexico. The marquis of Aycinena, one of the project's main promoters, was chosen as the consulate's first prior.

The Economic Company of Friends of the Country of Guatemala was promoted by a pro-Enlightenment group led by the justice of the Royal High Court Jacobo de Villa Urrutia, who arrived in the country in 1793. On October 21, 1795, the Spanish government approved the company's statutes and operation. It would have a short life, however. It was suppressed in 1800, as part of the reaction in Spain that tended to impede Enlightenment ideas that were too close to those of revolutionary France. Nevertheless, the consulate endured, directed by active merchants who also promoted the Enlightenment. In this milieu, the already-cited Basque Villa Urrutia founded the *Guatemala Gazette*. The newspaper's first issue appeared on February 13, 1797, and it published several initiatives and concerns of the Enlightenment reformists.

Three examples of family dynasties will serve to exemplify the prosperity and fortune of the Basque immigrants in Guatemala.[34] The first saga is of the Aycinenas. The founder of this family was Juan Fermín de Aycinena e Irigoyen, who was born in Ziga (Baztán, Navarre). He initially emigrated with hardly 300 pesos to Nueva España (Mexico), where he devoted himself to commerce. In 1753 he settled in Guatemala, probably summoned by his maternal uncle Manuel de Llano, the minister-treasurer of the Royal Bank of Guatemala since 1740. On March 15, 1755, Aycinena married Ana María Carrillo y Galvez. She was a descendent of the Galvez family, which had arrived in Guatemala in the sixteenth century. She brought to the union a marriage dowry of 178,912.4 pesos, compared to the 21,000 brought by the Navarrese. In 1759 he was already *alcalde ordinario* of the city of Santiago, Guatemala, and in 1761 trustee general of the city hall, which shows his rapid social ascent. His ability in commerce and business, and the help of his wife's capital, brought him a significant fortune. He was widowed in 1768, and remarried in 1771. The new bride was María Nájera y Mendoza, of a notable Creole commercial family. With this new tie, Aycinena consolidated his power and position within the Guatemalan aristocracy. But he was widowed once more. He married for a third time, with Micaela Piñol y Muñoz, the daughter of a Catalonian merchant involved in business in Cádiz. By 1780, his fortune was so great that he pursued a title of nobility in the Court of Madrid. Charles III named him marquis of Aycinena on July 19, 1783. In this process of social ascent and recognition, he had the help of his brother-in-law Martín de Beltranena, a native of Irurita (Navarre), whom he had summoned after reaching Central America.

In 1773, an earthquake destroyed Guatemala City. Juan Fermín de Aycinena was of immeasurable help to Captain General Martín de Mayorga in constructing a new capital in its present location. As compensation, Mayorga put him in charge of supplies, materials, and work for the new construction. And he was granted concession of the *alcabala* tax for ten years, which reached one and a half million pesos. He had a large palatial house built in Nueva Guatemala. It occupied half a block on the southeastern side of the main plaza, sharing the space with the royal palace, city hall, cathedral, archbishop's palace, children's musical college, royal customhouse, and post office building. As a result of the loans that he granted to the El Salvadoran indigo harvesters, he controlled more than one-fourth of dye export during the last two decades of the eighteenth century. When Aycinena died on April 3, 1796, he was succeeded by his son, the Second Marquis Juan Vicente de Aycinena y

Carrillo. The Aycinena family firm remained at the peak of mercantile and political power. It became the main producer of indigo, coming to control the Salvadoran haciendas. Through the marriage of all the children of the dynasty's founder, "the family," as it was known at the beginning of the nineteenth century, became the most powerful and influential group in Central America. The clan went through difficult times during the wars of independence (attained by Guatemala in 1821) and afterward. But it recovered its positions during the thirty-year conservative government (1840–1871). After the liberal triumph in 1871, the Aycinena family lost part of its influence but today continues to be rich and powerful in the country.

Juan Bautista de Irisarri y Larraín was born in Aranaz (Navarre) in 1740. In 1773, he left Spain (accompanied by a friend with the last name of Parrazar) for Havana and Puerto Rico. From there, they went to Nuevo México, where Parrazar decided to settle in Oaxaca. Irisarri went to Guatemala. There, his father, Martín de Irisarri, was already in business with the Arribillaga family, influential since the country's seventeenth-century beginnings. In addition, Juan Bautista had two Navarrese friends in Guatemala: Juan Francisco de Lazoaga and Martín de Ochandorena. In 1781 he was already a merchant out on his own. In 1783 he married María de la Paz Alonso y Espinoza, who died in 1794. In the interim, the family businesses took off. In 1797, he remarried, to María Josefa de Arribillaga y Castilla de Portugal, daughter of José Agustín de Arribillaga y Montufar (fifth lord of the House of Arribillaga). The successful Navarrese businessman thereby became connected with the aristocratic circles of the Guatemalan Creole nobility. He also became related to the Aycinena family, itself connected to the Arribillagas. At that time, his company was already solid and he had the hacienda "La Soledad" (in present-day Salvadoran territory), which produced indigo, sugar cane, and livestock. He took Central American products like indigo, sugar, rice, coconut, mahogany, tar, and salt to Chile. He brought wine, oil, olives, wheat flour, raisins, and almonds to Guatemala. He became associated (under its direction) with the Aycinena company to trade via the Atlantic with Philadelphia in 1799.

Juan Bautista de Irisarri was a frequent collaborator in the *Guatemala Gazette*, in which he clearly outlined his mercantile concerns. He advocated diversifying Guatemalan commercial exchanges, opening the gates of the Pacific. He wanted an end to exclusivity in indigo commerce, whose ruin he foresaw. And he proposed the cultivation of the land, at that time abandoned, in extensive latifundia. Another of Irisarri's interesting ideas was the colonization of the port of Acajutla to create a fishing and meat salting industry that would supply Guatemala City and even allow for export. He died in 1805 without seeing his projects realized. His oldest son, Antonio José, went to Chile to consolidate his father's companies, but ended up devoting himself there to intellectual and political activities and abandoning the businesses. In contrast to the Aycinena family, the Irisarris have neither maintained their prosperity nor their family identity into the present.

Martín Barrundia Iparraguirre was born in Segura (Gipuzkoa) in 1754. He reached Guatemala around 1775, initially devoting himself to the textile industry and installing the first eighteen-thread looms. He was also a merchant, negotiator, and farmer. He owned a hacienda in the jurisdiction of Jumay, on which he planted sugar cane and raised livestock. On July 16, 1786, he married Teresa de Cepeda y Chamorro, a member of an aristocratic Creole family, with whom he had ten children. Two would be influential liberal politicians between 1821 and 1850. Although he did not reach the level of power of the Aycinenas or Irisarris, Martín de Barrundia was an important participant in Guatemala City commerce. He was alderman-for-life in Guatemala City, and member of the Royal Consulate and the Economic Company. He died in 1798. His businesses did not continue, in part, because of his sons' political activity.

The above data suggests that the Spaniards played a very important role in the Guatemalan economy during the second half of the eighteenth century and the beginning of the nineteenth; and they came to control import and export commerce with Spain. Three social groups stood out in this endeavor, by native region:

1. The Basque group, with the examples studied (Aycinenas, Irisarris, and Barrundias), and others such as Jacobo de Villa Urrutia, Simón de Larrazabal, Juan Bautista Marticorena, and José de Licendo y Goicoechea (1735–1814), who was born in Costa Rica, but was an Enlightenment teacher at San Carlos University of Guatemala and a sponsor of university reform at the end of the eighteenth century
2. The Catalonian group, such as José Piñol, Miguel Mont, and Josef Baucells
3. The Aragonese, such as Joseph López, who was a ship captain in commerce with Cádiz

The marriages between Basque and Creole families permitted the former to establish their social position and penetrate Guatemalan circles. Their enterprising and adventuresome spirit and their battle for mercantile triumph brought them success in business, sometimes awakening jealousy and hatred in the traditional families with which, nevertheless, they ended up merging.

Green Costa Rica

In colonial times, the Basques were the third largest group that settled in Costa Rica, after the Andalusians and Castilians,[35] although they never constituted a sizeable collectivity. But the importance of Basque immigration in Costa Rica must be measured qualitatively. Thus, the relationship between the particular characteristics in the socioeconomic makeup of Costa Rican society and the Basque presence is clear. As a result, the hardworking and tenacious Basque character imbued this country's peasantry in a territory lacking great mineral riches and willing native labor. Basque immigrants in Costa Rica, therefore, distinguished themselves in the farming of medium-sized properties that became the motor of national progress. By regional background, the most influential Basque families in the colonial period in Costa Rica were:[36]

Family	Place of Origin
Arlegui	Bizkaia
Armada	Bizkaia
Aspine	Bizkaia
Avellanada	Bizkaia
Ayesta	Bizkaia
Bastarrica	Bizkaia
Beracoechea	Bizkaia
Echandi	Bizkaia
Garay	Bizkaia
Ibacaya	Bizkaia
Liendo y Goicoechea	Bizkaia
Reyes	Bizkaia
Urrutia	Bizkaia
Arbarola	Gipuzkoa
Alcarazo	Gipuzkoa
Banceta	Gipuzkoa
Inza	Gipuzkoa
Laínez	Gipuzkoa
Zavaleta	Gipuzkoa
Guevara	Araba
Machado y Ugarte	Araba
Retana	Araba
Arrieta	Navarre

By percentages, the breakdown is as follows: Bizkaians, 56.5 percent; Gipuzkoans, 26.1 percent; Arabans, 13.1 percent; Navarrese, 4.3 percent.

Some interesting toponyms that testify to the Basque presence in Costa Rica have also remained from the colonial period. Thus, there is a province and a capital with the name "Heredia." Others include the cantons of Aguirre, Osa, and Esparza, and the cities of Ochoa, Esparza, and Anguciana de Gamboa. Valle de Aserri and Val del Poncal also deserve to be cited, although the latter term is no longer used. The city of Artieda was founded in 1517 by Diego de Artieda, who also built the emplacement of Esparza (in 1577) in the present-day province of Punta Arenas. In 1789, the name of Esparza was replaced by "Esparta," although the original toponym was reintroduced in 1974.[37]

Biographical profiles of two immigrants in Costa Rica will provide an idea of the prototype of the successful Basque.[38] Fra Antonio de Liendo y Goicoechea was born in 1735 in Cartago, the colonial capital of Costa Rica, to a family originally from the city of Urduña. Orphaned at age nine, at twelve he went to Guatemala City, capital of the captaincy general and intellectual and economic center of the region. Liendo studied at San Carlos University, one of the oldest and most prestigious in Spanish America (founded in 1687). He was ordained there and completed his doctorate in theology, a discipline that he would then teach at the same university. He visited Spain for religious and academic purposes, establishing connections with the political and academic circles of the reformed Spanish Enlightenment. After his return to San Carlos University, he served as a professor, transforming its pedagogy. He introduced research based on a scientific vision and concern for Central American problems, all of which made him the most important intellectual and academic figure in Central America in the colonial period.

In the twentieth century, Teodoro Olarte Sáenz expounded his reformist and progressive thoughts in the recently opened University of Costa Rica (1940). A high-profile humanist, he promoted the reform of 1957 that established mandatory interdisciplinary general studies for all university students. A philologist by training, he was the first director of the Department of Philosophy of the University of Costa Rica and one of the leading teachers in this field.

Unfortunately, there are no serious studies of Basque immigration in Central American countries aside from those just mentioned for Guatemala and Costa Rica. Although the Basques generally were not numerous, individual Basques were significant, as described in the foregoing examples in the colonial period. Remaining toponyms in these territories demonstrate this well.[39]

Nicaragua, for example, presently has a department with the name Zelaya and a town (in the central area) called Echevarría. Peter Boyd-Bowman believes that Basque and Navarrese participation in the conquest and colonization of the present-day Nicaraguan territory was 8 percent between 1520 and 1539. In Honduras, there is the Department of Olancho; in Panama, the Echandi Ridge, the Azuero Peninsula, and the Miguel de Laborda River.

As of 1997, a Basque Center in Guatemala and another in El Salvador vouch for the persistence of Basque identity in Central America.

The Pearl of the Antilles

The Basque presence in Cuba coincides with the discovery and continuation of risky feats of exploration, conquest, and colonization.[40] In 1509, Emperor Charles V ordered Diego Columbus and Pasamonte to secure Cuba, look for gold there, and arrange ports for the removal of the Indian slaves needed on the island of Hispaniola (presently Haiti and the Dominican Republic). In 1511, Diego Columbus sent Diego Velázquez de Cuellar to conquer Cuba, ordering him to colonize it. Velázquez, with a complement of three hundred men and four ships, tried to disembark on the island's eastern part. They encountered harsh resistance from the native Caribbeans. Velázquez could not penetrate the island until 1514, always depending upon the advice of his Basque confidant Juan de Aguirre in his planning. Another Basque, Pedro de Renteria, was also on Velázquez's expedition. Renteria displayed a true passion for saving the natives. He put his fortune at the disposition of the Dominican Fra Bartolomé de Las Casas to found a school to educate the native children of the coast. Cuba, like what is now the Dominican Republic, was soon converted into a base for expeditions to the mainland. For example, in 1517, three residents of Santiago (Cuba), among them Lope Ochoa de Salcedo, organized an expedition to the Yucatán (two ships and a brig) that ended in complete failure. Shortly thereafter, with the conquest of the island in hand, Hernán Cortés's expedition to Mexico (1519) was organized. It included Pánfilo de Narváez and others. Many of the Basques settled in Cuba would join these colonial adventures.

Basque merchants, with their seat in Sevilla, opened branches early on in the Spanish dominion of America (especially in Santo Domingo). For example, López Fernández de Eibar negotiated with other Basques in that city (Juan de Arechaga and Pedro de Eibar), although he also had undertakings in Cuba and Yucatán. Likewise, in 1518 Juan Ibañez de Hernani founded a company for commerce with Cuba that was ultimately unsuccessful. The Arámburu family was also frequently mentioned in the documentation of the period as commercial entrepreneurs during the first half of the sixteenth century. The silversmiths Juan and Martín de Oñate and the merchants Esteban de Guecho, Sancho de Salazar, Sebastián de Urbieta, Miguel de Aizpa, and Juan de Berne also stood out. The Basque merchants of Sevilla made their agreements with the enclaves of Santo Domingo, Cuba, and the other Caribbean islands through the shipmasters (also Basques) on the Indies run. Both masters and merchants were obligated to contract a series of debts in Sevilla. They paid these to the distributor of their merchandise in Santo Domingo or upon the return to Sevilla. Such commercial and mercantile relations continued throughout the seventeenth century. Pronounced growth in the volume of this traffic gave the island greater leadership within the Spanish colonial scheme, a trend that would accentuate during the eighteenth century.

Cuba was important between 1780 and 1819 as a frequent port of arrival and departure for fleets and ships before they crossed the Atlantic[41] or continued on to the mainland. Thus, at least since the last quarter of the eighteenth century there were connections, strong commercial connections to be precise, between Cuba and the Basque Country. These certainly continued after American independence. In addition, beginning with the decolonization of Spanish America, what remained of Spain's colonies there, Cuba and Puerto Rico, acquired an increased importance until the mid-nineteenth century. Cuba's population data suggest that its demography and commercial activity clearly benefited from the independence of the other Spanish-American colonies. Thus, its population would climb from 272,321 inhabitants in 1792, to 553,033 in 1817, to 704,487 in 1827, to one million in 1841.[42] The Basque and Navarrese element contributed significantly to this population increase. Thus, according to the boarding licenses from 1800 to 1835, these collectivities made up 9 and 4 percent, respectively, of the official immigrants. In combination they were third in population percentage, after the Catalonians (58 percent) and Asturians (14 percent).[43]

The economic growth of Cuba during the nineteenth century reflected restrictions on the commerce of the French colony of Santo Domingo, a decline of Mexican exports, and the cyclic crisis of the English Antilles. Thus, during the decades of the 1820s and 1830s, the great fortunes of prominent Basque merchants controlling the production of Cuban sugar emerged and were consolidated. All of them were slave traders as well as import-exporters. Among the main Cuban traffickers in black slaves in 1820 was a significant group with last names of Basque origin, including Julián de Zulueta y Amondo (marquis of Araba), Domingo Aldama, Joaquín Pérez de Urria, Salvador Martiartu, Francisco de Bengoechea, Martín de Zavala, José de Zangroniz and his son Juan Bautista de Zangroniz, and Bonifacio González Larrinaga and his son Jacinto Larrinaga.[44]

Julián de Zulueta had been born in Araba, the son of a peasant. He emigrated as a youth to Cuba, where he worked as a distributor. In twenty years, he became one of the richest men on the island. Among Zulueta's many businesses, he was connected to trafficking in Chinese "coolies." As homage to his origin, he named two of his sugar mills "Vizcaya" and "Alava." Loumiet d'Oloron founded two successful salt mines in the north of the country. Dufau and Labarrere established an important export business in Havana.

In the decade of 1840–1849, during which the import of blacks decreased to 52,747, José Luis Alfonso and Miguel Aldama tried (in 1844) to bring immigrants from Bizkaia to Cuba to work on one of their sugar plantations.[45] Emiliano Fernández de Pinedo establishes a clear relationship between immigration in Cuba and colonial commerce.[46] Thus, he affirms, the cultivation of the cane, thanks to the slaves, connected the Cuban economy to Río de la Plata (an area with a strong Basque presence). Part of the sustenance of the blacks consisted of cod and, especially, jerked beef, of which adults ate about two hundred grams a day. The majority of this jerked beef or salted meat was provided by Argentina and Uruguay. This demand for dried beef was what promoted and stimulated cattle raising, requiring an abundance of salt, which was clearly imported from Cádiz. The immigration boom that accompanied these activities increased the demand for wine and other, lesser products from Spain. Maritime traffic between Spain and Cuba employed ships from Santander, Cataluña, Mallorca, Valencia, Andalusia, and the Basque Country. Between 1918 and 1924,

Cuba continued as the second most common destination for Basques, as shown in the following summary of destinations of Gipuzkoans in America:[47]

Country of Immigration	No. of Immigrants
Argentina	147
Cuba	31
Mexico	14
Not given	5
Uruguay	3
Chile	2
Guatemala	1
Colombia	1
New York	1
Total	205

The Basque penchant for ethnic association prompted the organization of cultural and other types of groups in Cuba. In 1878, the Basque community of Havana organized the Basque-Navarrese Beneficent Association, whose main objective was to help the poor and pay for repatriations. It founded a funeral home with a cemetery reserved exclusively for its members. The association sponsored the festival in honor of the Virgin of Begoña, its patroness, in 1884. The activities consisted of a mass sung in Euskara with a sermon that praised the successes of the Basques, a religious procession, a parade with Basque standards, musicians, popular costumes and folk dances, and refreshments in a Basque restaurant in the area. The Havana newspapers proclaimed the Basque festival the best ever held in the city. In 1887, the association had 365 members in the capital and 228 in the Cuban provinces, in addition to a similar number of associates who lived in the Basque Country. About half of the total were of Bizkaian heritage, and the rest were natives of the other three Spanish Basque provinces. French Basques were not accepted. In 1880, Ricardo Galbis, of Basque origin and the governor of the Bank of Spain on the island of Cuba, built the first handball court in Havana. At the time, it was considered the best in the world. The most famous professional handball players of the era competed there. In 1911, the Euskaro Center of Havana opened. It would later be called the Basque Center, and would have a prestigious a cappella choir. When the Spanish Civil War broke out, nationalists and republicans were in the extreme minority; the majority of the members of the Basque Center were openly in favor of Franco.

Puerto Rico and the Dominican Republic

Numerous Basques left Hispaniola for Puerto Rico as colonizers, professionals, and simply adventurers. The latter island received the greatest number during the initial years of colonization. A significant group of Basques settled in the present-day Dominican Republic in the years prior to and during the first months of the conquest of Cuba.[48] The most significant among them were Juan de Uruena, Cristóbal de Vergara, Pedro de Arana, Pedro Arriano, and Diego de Ayala. In Puerto Rico, after its conquest by Juan Ponce de León in 1508, the colonizers Diego de Salazar, Miguel de Teso, and Luis de Añasco stood out. The first settler to establish various farming initiatives was Juan Mejia Eguiluz.[49]

Unfortunately, there are still no studies documenting the continuity of the Basque presence on these two Antillean islands. Nevertheless, toponyms suggest at least a certain consonance with general Basque colonial immigration, albeit at reduced and less significant levels than in other American regions and countries. Thus, for example, the Dominican Republic includes the province of Azua (with a capital of the same name), the province of Duarte, and the coastal town of Vizcaíno. In Puerto Rico, there is the town named Añasco, the capital Loiza, and, on the coast, Central Aguirre.

The study of Ángel López Cantos[50] brought to light the Gipuzkoan figure Gaspar de Arteaga y Aunaovidao, governor of Puerto Rico from 1670 to 1674. He was born in 1629. He came from a family with a long military tradition, and before reaching the Caribbean "had served more than thirty-two years as an ensign, infantry captain, hackbuteer and halberdier cavalry captain, lieutenant of the Commissary General of Spain, governor of the town and citadel of Bayona [Galicia], and brigadier in Galicia in the Spanish third infantry." He was in combat first in Milano and then in the War of Portugal. In 1663 he organized the students of Salamanca into an army corps. On June 23, 1670, he was awarded the post of governor of Puerto Rico for a term of five years.[51]

Gaspar de Arteaga had a violent temperament. He was extremely independent and not very cordial, even with his own family. He did not ally himself with any of the social clans or groups that fought for power in Puerto Rico. On the contrary, he tried to nullify their influence and managed to marginalize their most prominent representatives. From Havana, Arteaga's nephew, Antonio de Aguirre, encouraged him to seek friends in the following way:

> Do not let anyone not registered enter that port without registration, except whoever is so beneficial that he contributes to the resident [administrator] and more, which is very easy if one has the royal officials on your side. I recommend them to your lordship, keep them as friends, because [if you don't] you will lose needlessly and you will not gain anything. Eat and let eat is the best approach and give up trying to fix the world, for God allows it, and it is the most sound and surest thing. Your lordship will not find any place where these [prominent] men are absent, especially, as I see it, those who are best connected,

with whom you must deal, as all governors everywhere that I have been in the Indies do, for they own everything. Thus, I beg your lordship that you get along with these people, for I only desire the success of your lordship. On the contrary, I am afraid it will be the beginning of your ruin, and I am sure that if you halfway treat them with hospitality, your lordship will control them and do with them as you please. Well then, your lordship should take off the sombrero with one hand and the cape with the other and you will not regret it.[52]

Arteaga, however, disregarded this advice, and discontent with his way of governing soon emerged. The town council attacked him in 1671 in the following manner:

> Brigadier Don Gaspar de Arteaga began governing this island on August 15 of this past year of 1670, a knight of the Order of Santiago. And though we are sure that the position was appropriate to his good services, as a result of Your Majesty's justified selection, and seeing, as is well known, the great disturbances that he causes, we are persuaded that God willed his transfer for our own punishment (as He allowed Saul for the punishment of his people), or else we are forced to think that some kind of accident that befell him compels him to such excesses. Taking into account that this is the beginning of his tenure, we fear the continuation of his abuses, which our sufferings cannot suppress, because one error summons another error always, like one abyss another abyss. We shall keep Your Majesty informed, and God is our witness that this report is not prompted by ill will or vengeance, but solely by the service of God our lord, yours, and the good of the republic.[53]

The bishop Fra Bartolomé de Escañuelas swore that Arteaga was an irreligious and impious man for the following reasons:[54]

1. Because during his visit to the capital of Puerto Rico, he prohibited veteran soldiers from declaring and testifying about the customs and moral conduct of a few citizens who were their relatives.
2. Because he made certain soldiers swear their allegiance on an altar and not on the gospel in order to learn about some matters concerning smuggling.
3. Because he attended mass on Sundays and holy days in La Fortaleza (dwelling of the governors) and not in a public church.
4. Because he permitted the soldiers to live in concubinage, forbidding them to regularize their situations.

In his personal life, the governor from Gipuzkoa liked to cohabit, which, it must be added, was very common in the Puerto Rico of the 1600s. Nevertheless, the fact that the highest authority cohabited was the source of numerous criticisms. These criticisms increased until the High Court of Santo Domingo decided to initiate legal proceedings. Here are some of the charges:

That he swore many times on Christ, saying that he would destroy all of us.

That he gave the order that when the Holy Sacrament passed through the guard corps, they not present arms, as they had always done.

That no one buys or sells tobacco, even of his own harvest, because he sold it at six reales a pound and the residents bought it at one real a pound. He took the last bunch of their harvest from them to sell at his store.

That he made the fishermen pay sales taxes, which had never been paid.

That several people had told him that they would be very harsh with him during his *residencia* [offical inquiry], and that he responded that he did not care, that if they harassed him in the *residencia*, he had a rope to hang himself with.

That he said very strange things and on one occasion asserted that in Charco de las Brujas he had found a hanged man with whom he spoke, giving such bewildering reasons for this that they cannot be written and show his poor judgment.

That more than four days passed without anyone seeing him, and that the residents attributed it to wine, because it is certain that he uses it uncontrollably, and therefore sometimes says and orders one thing and then the opposite without any sense or reason. That those that are the unhappiest are the infantry, because they are sure of his orders and commands, but later he says that they lie and some are rogues and liars, and that he has never said such things.

That the order has been given that in the butcher shop they wait on mulattos before other people, regardless of how prominent they might be.

That he is friendliest with the king's black slaves, who serve him, and talks with them as if they were equals.

That he has ordered that no resident can appear at the walls, nor speak with others in secret there or elsewhere, and has given the order to the soldiers to be careful when they see such conversations.

That no man dares to deal with him in any matter because of his great temper, not even the most important people in the area.

That no one would dare to write a letter without giving it to him first so that it might pass through his hands.

That no resident can leave San Juan for his haciendas, even for three or four hours, without a stamped paper certifying that he does not owe the king anything.

That he has the plaza abandoned and most of the cannons disassembled and off their carriages.[55]

Nevertheless, no one accused Governor Gaspar de Arteaga of smuggling. In effect, neither he nor Juan Pérez de Guzmán, who occupied the same position, fell into the temptation of illegal commerce. The rest of the seventeenth-century governors did so. And as Arteaga did not engage in illegal commerce, neither did he permit the islanders to do so. He was especially harsh with the residents of the capital, and they never forgave him for this.[56]

Once the charges were known by the Council of the Indies, it had the High Court of Hispaniola order one of its ministers to go to Puerto Rico and conduct a secret investigation. This task would not be completed before Gaspar de Arteaga's death on March 7, 1674. He went through a protracted illness that he managed to conceal so as not to delight his enemies. He was buried in the pantheon of governors in the convent church of Saint Thomas of the Dominican Fathers of San Juan. As he died without confession, he was not buried without controversy. Bishop Bartolomé de Escañuelas communicated the event to the Crown. Note the cruelty:

> I sing compassion for the relief that this city and Island received, putting an end to the fatal, violent, sacrilegious, and horrible yoke that tyrannically choked it with the detestable governor. The so-called brigadier, the unworthy knight of the Order of Santiago, just died there of natural causes, on March 7 of this year. I sing to the judgment with a broken heart and with cries for the unfortunate condemnation of his soul, according to judgment based on external facts. The watchfulness, zeal, love, diligence, and efficiency of his friends and captains, of my priests and my own was not enough to persuade him, as a son of the Holy, Apostolic, and Catholic Church (if he was indeed, though seemingly he was not) to confess and receive the holy sacraments, or at least to ask for them with word or signs, or to make an act of contrition, which I personally suggested to him several times. Having heard, spoken, comprehended, and contradicted by deeds and a bit also by words—if only he had been devoid of them—he died unrepentant and a rebel, as far as it seemed externally. Thus dies whoever lives like him. I cried over him. I have related his life, in part, to Your Majesty. God did justice. Praised be His name.

The privileges granted to the Barcelonesa Company in 1756 to trade with Puerto Rico, as well as Margarita and Santo Domingo, initiated relations between Cataluña and Puerto Rico. At the end of the eighteenth century some Catalonians installed themselves as small merchants there, selling merchandise bought on the neighboring island of Saint Thomas. This group would play an important role in the development of the Puerto Rican economy in the nineteenth century.[57] With the independence of the American colonies, other groups of Spaniards came from Venezuela and Santo Domingo to settle in Puerto Rico, among them many Basques.[58] Thus, in the Puerto Rico of 1840, the merchants of Basque origin Manuel Hernaiz y Chávarri, Sobrián de Ezquiaga, Araucamendi and Brothers, and Martín J. Machicote were noteworthy. Chávarri, Anastasio Echevarría, and José María Urrutia stood out in black slave trade. Some of those cited were part of the Tariff Board, created in 1834 (José Ignacio Ezquiaga), or on the Board of Commerce (Martín J. Machicote served as prior in 1836).[59]

In addition to the contingent that the government sent, made up fundamentally of soldiers and functionaries, the group of Basques that chose to settle in Puerto Rico did so, like the other Spaniards, because of the clear economic opportunities offered by the island in the mid-nineteenth century. This was fundamentally sustained by the boom in coffee as the principal export. Puerto Rican coffee came to satisfy Cuba's demand, as well as part of Spain's. The Spanish Antilles had another attraction for the Basque immigrant: better connections via steamship lines, and the Spanish merchant marine that monopolized transportation with Europe. And, beginning in 1870, Puerto Rico had regular service to England with stopovers in Vigo and Santander. In addition, being Spanish on this island brought clear advantages. Thus, the majority of those arriving had assured employment. During the period 1882–1886, according to official statistics, soldiers sent from Spain outnumbered civilian immigrants.[60] In 1885–1886, Madrid contributed 20 percent of the Spanish exodus, the majority functionaries, soldiers, businessmen, and their families. By region, it is clear (as the following list shows) that northern Spain furnished the largest contingent:[61]

Region	No./Percent (%)
Asturias-Galicia	301/18.7
Basque Provinces-Santander	167/10.4
Cataluña	249/15.5
Balearic Islands	101/6.3
Valencia-Murcia	37/2.3
Andalusia	193/12.0
Canary Islands	154/9.6
Castile	360/22.4
Aragón	15/0.9
León-Extremadura	30/1.9
Total	1,607/100

The Basque Country and Santander contributed 10.4 percent of the total migration, in fifth place after Castile, Asturias-Galicia, Cataluña, and Andalusia.

Another complementary source for learning the Iberian origins of Spaniards is the island's 1897 census. In the district of Ponce, based on a sample that includes 76 percent of the Spaniards (excluding those belonging to the armed forces), 24.9 percent were natives of the Spanish Basque region.[62] Like the rest of the Spaniards at the end of the nineteenth century, the Basques concentrated in the urban areas of San Juan, Ponce, Mayagüez, Arecibo, and Bayamón.[63] Almost half of the Spanish colony was gathered in these places in 1899. Next, the area of coffee plantations stands out, with the municipalities of Utado, Lares, Yauco, Adjuntas, Maricao, Las Marías, and San Sebastián accounting for almost 13 percent of the Spanish colony.[64]

Commonly the immigrant was young, single, and male, and those that remained in the country married Puerto Rican women. In the urban areas, around 80 percent of the immigrants were male. In the rural areas, the figure was 85 percent. Almost all knew how to read and write. The distribution by occupation at the end of the nineteenth century and beginning of the twentieth demonstrates the involvement in commerce of the Spaniards in general and Basques in particular. Thus, in 1910, in the capital city of San Juan, 1,746 Spaniards performed the following tasks: clerks and office workers (519), merchants (283), industry and skilled labor (246), housewives (206), other (151), clerics (100), merchant marine (84), proprietors and farmers (72), professionals and artists (50), public employees (35).[65] Among the companies that employed many Spaniards were the following: Sucesión de A. Mayol and Co., which imported hardware and china; Herrero Ortega and Co., which imported hardware; Miguel Cuétara Alvarez, shoes; and those of Basque origin, Benito Zalduondo Echevarria and Zalduondo and Valle, which worked in linens. Similarly, the fusion of the Basque families Abaraca and Portilla, in mining, gave jobs to many workers of Basque origin.[66]

Given this rough sketch, it can be affirmed that nineteenth-century Basque immigration in Puerto Rico totaled 1,032 people.[67] Of this total, Araba provided 8.1 percent, or 84 immigrants; Gipuzkoa contributed 29.3 percent, or 302; and Bizkaia, 62.6 percent, or 646 of the diaspora. By sex, males predominated, with 93 percent of the total (961), versus only 7 percent females (71).[68] Estela Cifre de Loubriel's analysis shows that of the 1,032 Basques settled in Puerto Rico in the nineteenth century, 19 percent died unmarried, and 3.8 percent were nuns and priests. Therefore, only about 77 percent of the total contributed to the construction of present-day Puerto Rico through marital alliances. It is possible, however, that those who died without marrying had descendants. The percentage of illegitimate children in the period was very high.

Nineteenth-century Basque immigrants represented almost the entire spectrum of the population. Among the 1,032 individuals spoken about so far, there is everything from common soldiers to influential governors and captains general. From high court lawyers to simple scribes, from the military fortification engineer to the simple bricklayer, from the rich *hacendado* to the day laborer, and from the powerful merchant to the clerk that lived in the backroom sleeping under the counter on sacks of coffee or rice. Few Basques worked in the liberal professions, however.[69] The most common activities were commerce, the army, agriculture, the navy, and the bureaucracy. The following is a sample, with more detail given in table 2.20 in appendix 2:[70]

Occupation	No./Percent (%)
Merchants of all types and those depending on commerce	264/25.5
Soldiers, including occupation, defense, and protection personnel	154/14.9
Agricultural personnel, including landholders, peasants, majordomos, natural healers, and speculators	70/6.7
Navy, including cabin boys, pilots, and sea and port captains	34/3.3
Public employees	25/3.0
Priests and sisters of mercy	40/3.8

If a comparative study is done by Spanish regions, taking Catalonians and Canary Islanders as points of comparison, the results are as follows:

1. In the commercial branches, the Basques are first with 25.5 percent of the total. Next come the Catalonians (25 percent) and later the Canary Islanders (6.8 percent).
2. In the Army, first are the Catalonians (22.7 percent), then Basques (14.9 percent), and finally Canary Islanders (6.36 percent).
3. In the primary sector and majordomos: first come the Canary Islanders with 26 percent, second the Basques with 6.7 percent, and third the Catalonians with 4.4 percent.
4. In public administration, the Basques are first with 3 percent, the Catalonians second (1.1 percent), and the Canary Islanders last (0.6 percent).
5. In the Navy, the Basques predominate (3.3 percent); next come the Catalonians (1.9 percent) and then the Canary Islanders (1.4 percent).[71]

Basque Presence and Activity in Colombia

The Basques that went to Colombia were generally male and young. At the beginning, not many Basque women went to the country,[72] causing the newly arrived to marry native women. A great number of caulkers, pilots, carpenters, outfitters, and sailors went on the first expedition. Little by little, and as colonization progressed, public administrators arrived, and they often became business owners and merchants. They brought Euskara with them, which in the colony of Darién they spoke among themselves. In the sixteenth, seventeenth, and eighteenth centuries, 20 percent of all Spaniards in Colombia were Basques.[73] According to Peter Boyd-Bowman, between 1540 and 1559, 8.9 percent of the residents of Colombia were of Basque origin.

Slow at the end of the nineteenth century, and somewhat more pronounced in the early decades of the twentieth, the contemporary migration was of an eminently religious nature, particularly composed of Jesuit priests. The generation of Colombians between 1910 and 1940 were influenced markedly by the Basque Jesuits via the schools of Bogotá, Medellín, Cartagena, and Pasto. It was these priests that introduced handball into the country. After the Great War, civil immigration was reactivated in the decade of the 1920s, while Franciscan and Passionist priests also began to stand out in Colombian society. Before the Spanish Civil War, emigration from the Basque Country to Colombia was limited. It was fundamentally made up of businessmen, around whom the first real secular colony formed.

Between 1937 and 1945, eighty adults and forty-five children arrived. In spite of the modest number, beginning with this nucleus of professionals and industrialists, the Basque presence left its mark upon Colombia. These immigrants were devoted to teaching and public administration in the fields of economics, statistics, and finance, and to the improvement of tropical agriculture. A great part of this group of exiles has bonded definitively (socially and economically) with Colombia. Their children and grandchildren, predominantly professionals and artists, continue the Basque tradition within Colombian society. In the decade of the 1940s there was another very marked contribution to the country's economy when the Great Colombian Merchant Company was founded. In this Andean multinational company's first years, Basque sailors navigated as captains and pilots on the majority of its ships until the country was able to train its own crews. Basque families that settled in Colombia after the Civil War are listed in table 5.2.

After the Second World War, in the decades of the 1950s and 1960s, another contingent arrived.[74] Some were summoned by the established group; others were attracted by the beginnings of large-scale Colombian industrialization. Thus, from 1950 to 1980, about five hundred Basques entered Colombia. They were predominantly young, single, ambitious males with technical and industrial education, especially those from the districts of Gipuzkoa and Bizkaia.[75] Most of this contingent returned to their native country or moved to other American republics, especially Venezuela. Nevertheless, this colony contributed to the creation of the mechanical and metallurgical industries, while also importing heavy machinery and other products of Basque industry and foundries. The Basque Center of Bogotá was not founded until 1958. The notable businessman Eugenio de Gamboa y Arrupe, who disembarked in Colombia in 1916, and around whom the Basque colony was constituted, deserves mention.

The Basque exile community in Colombia, although not very numerous, as has been seen, would nevertheless be characterized by a high educational level. A few clerics that went to Colombia as a result of their tie to Basque nationalism also merit mention. This was the case of various Passionist priests and two nuns of the Sacred Heart. It was the only known example of the exile of Basque religious. The

TABLE 5.2 *Basque Families in Colombia after the Spanish Civil War*

Family	Location/Activity
Gómez-Basterra	Bogotá
Barbero-Muñoz	Bogotá
Amuchástegui-Eloizaga	Bogotá
Perea-Sasiain	Bogotá
Ibargüen[1]	Devoted to farming in Mariquita and Ibagué. Several years later, moved to Venezuela.
Larrauri	El Espinal
Díaz Sasiain	Bogotá
Espeleta-Sasiain	Bogotá
Echegaray-Barreneche	Farm work in Mariquita, El Espinal, and Ibagué. Grew rice and sesame.[2]
Gorrichu	—
Orozco	—
Juan A. Irazusta	Bogotá
León Pantaleón	Barranquilla
Jenaro Sáenz Sáenz	Bogotá
José María de Oteiza	Bogotá
Ceferino González	El Tolina. Grew sesame.
José L. Lombrana y Foncea	Mariquita region. Farming.[3]
Iñaki Garay	Bogotá

1. José Ibargüen was mayor of Zalla before his exile.
2. José María Echegaray Barreneche did not obtain an entrance permit until 1940, finally doing so thanks to his friend Félix Gamboa. Although he arrived alone, he married his girlfriend, whom he had left in his native town of Vera de Bidasoa, Navarre, by proxy. He became head of one of the most important rice-growing estates. However, at the beginning, his life in the country was lacking in comforts and filled with hard work. (See M. E. Martínez Gorroño, "El exilio vasco en Colombia," in *Emigración y redes sociales de los vascos en América* [Vitoria-Gasteiz, 1996].)
3. A lawyer by profession, after a period as a farmer, he got sick and returned to Bogotá. He must have had an impressive private library. (See Martínez Gorroño.)

Passionist priests were distributed in the three houses belonging to the order in the country: Medellín, Bucaramanga, and Bogotá. And some went on missions that were scattered in other areas, farther from the capital. The following are examples:[76]

1. Father Pacífico Apoitia was a captain of the *gudaris* in the Civil War.
2. Father José Gerrikagoitia was in the Apostolic nunciature of Guapí.

3. Father Honorio Gerrikagoitia, after the war of 1936 to 1939, was imprisoned in Galicia for several years, going from there to Colombia.
4. Father Uría was a Jesuit from Azkoitia. He lived in Bogotá, where he was a professor of philosophy of law at Javeriana University. He published some works on natural law.

Regarding the two nuns of the Sacred Heart that reached the country as exiles, one had the last name of Zabala and was the daughter of the nationalist from Bilbao, Ángel Zabala. She died in Bogotá in 1986. The other was the daughter of the Larrauri family that founded El Espinal, a small town near Girardot.[77]

The Basque collectivity connected with the liberal professions, commerce, and business were best represented by the following:[78]

1. Pedro Amuchástegui Mújica from Bilbao initially devoted himself to livestock-related work, later founding a candle factory. With time, he would work in accounting, making use of his experience with the Bank of Bilbao. He went to Colombia with his wife, Pilar Elzoizaga, and their two children, Sorne and Kepa, who currently live in the capital. Pilar is a teacher at the French School and Kepa Amuchástegui is an internationally known actor.
2. Andrés Perea Gallaga was born in Barakaldo, Bizkaia. He went to Colombia with his wife, Dominga Sasiain Aberasturi, and their three children, María Victoria, Andrés, and José. Before their exile, he had been inspector of the Treasury of the Deputation of Bizkaia and, in 1936, he was director of operations in the Basque Government, serving as a confidant in the secretariat of Heliodoro de la Torre. From this post he helped coordinate the evacuation of precious and fiduciary goods deposited in the banks under the jurisdiction of the autonomous government of President Aguirre. All these valuables were transported in the merchant ship *Torpehall*, headed for Holland. In Colombia, he was a professor at the National School of Commerce and at Javeriana University, where he obtained the chair in accounting by competition.[79] He held important technical posts in the Colombian administration.[80] He spoke fluent French, English, and German, and was the delegate of the Basque Government in Colombia for sixteen years.[81]
3. Francisco de Abrisketa Iraculis was born in Bilbao in 1913. He received a degree in economic sciences from Deusto University in 1934. He would later work in the Bank of Vizcaya until the beginning of the Civil War. During it he was named secretary of light industries of the Basque Government.[82] In May 1937 he left Euskadi on board a plane (*The Wegus*) that took him to Bayonne. From there he went to Paris, where, thanks to the Ricaurte Montoya brothers, he obtained a work contract in Colombia, where he arrived in November 1937.[83] He worked at the National University and

Javeriana University, teaching statistics and demography. He was the assessor for the Bank of the Republic.[84] He served as the delegate of the Basque Government until leaving for the United States in 1945.[85] He invited President Aguirre to visit Bogotá in 1942, where he was received with full honors.[86] Abrisketa was the first president of the Basque Center of Colombia and a great promoter of Basque culture in the country. During World War II, he was the head of espionage for the United States in Colombia. Under his supervision in this position was Luis Gómez Lekube (Cojo Gómez), from Getxo, who had his knee split by a bullet from a Colombian Caribbean coast dweller. For years this colorful character dominated, through armed violence, the impenetrable Chocó jungles that separate Colombia from Panama. He was the cousin of President Aguirre. His life as a twentieth-century buccaneer has been recounted in a biography by Kay Hummel called *A Wanted Man, el Cojo Gómez in Colombia*.[87]

4. Paulino Gómez Saiz was born in Miranda de Ebro (Burgos), but moved to Bilbao when he was two. There he married Judit Basterra Nanclares. He was president of the Socialist Youth Groups of Euskadi and joined the Socialist Party of Bilbao in 1917. During the Civil War, he was delegate of the Board of Defense of Bizkaia, delegate of Public Order in Cataluña, and director general of security and minister of governance in Negrin's cabinet, holding this last position until the end of the conflict. In Colombia, he promoted public school campaigns to teach about the importance of savings, worked in a soap factory that he himself founded, and established a pioneering frozen seafood company. He died in Bogotá in 1976.[88]

5. Juan Antonio Irazusta Munoa was Gipuzkoan and deputy of the Basque Nationalist minority in the Cortes of the Republic. After his stay in Colombia, he moved to Peru and was later consul of that country in Puerto Rico.[89]

6. Jenaro Sáenz Sáenz was from Bilbao and married to Carmen Jiménez. He was a stenographer in the Spanish Republican Congress and also served in this capacity in the Colombian parliament. He was a great promoter of cultural activities in the country.

7. Ciro Fernández de Retana was a journalist and worked for the best Colombian newspapers. After many years, he returned to his native Bilbao, where he died.

8. Gloria Azarina Muñoz was from Bilbao; she went to Colombia with her husband (Julián Barbero) and children.

9. León Pantaleón had been a teacher at the Nautical School of Bilbao. In Colombia, he settled in Barranquilla and worked as a ship's machinist.

10. Jorge Oteiza, born in Orio (Gipuzkoa), was the founder of ceramics schools

of Raquira (Department of Bogotá) and Popayán. His work is highly valued in Colombia, and his ceramic pieces have been exported throughout the world. He published the work *Aesthetic Interpretation of the Augustinian Megalithic Culture*, which deals with the remains of the pre-Colombian culture of San Agustin.

A group of renowned Basque pastry cooks settled in the neighborhood of Chapinero. These were Iñaki Garay, Orozco, and Gorrichu (from Pamplona). Lastly, José Vicente Katarain, who was the editor of the works of Gabriel García Márquez, deserves mention.

In Venezuelan Lands

In the opinion of Peter Boyd-Bowman, between 1520 and 1539, 5.4 percent of the Spanish inhabitants of Venezuela were Basques, and 1.5 percent were Navarrese. In this country, the prosperity and fortunes of the Gipuzkoan Lope de Aguirre are legendary. But little is known of the Basque participation in Venezuelan lands in the seventeenth century. Beginning in the second half of the eighteenth century, with the birth of the Royal Guipuzcoan Company of Caracas,[90] the Basque presence became significant.[91] In the following century, however, it would fall far short of the level of Basque immigration in the southern cone of South America. The Venezuelan historian A. Rojas complained in 1874 of the scarce flow of Basque emigrants to his country: "Why this decided love for the shores of Río de la Plata? Why not come to the land that their ancestors cultivated, where the variety of climates and lands, where the richness of flora and the large number of Basque descendants, attests that their American focus was here in previous periods?"[92]

The large Basque collectivity reached this country after the Spanish Civil War for political reasons. Shortly before, during the Republic, the Jesuits expelled from Spain during the Republican years found refuge in Venezuela. Many of them were nationalists and exerted their influence in support of a selective Basque immigration. The immigration would be regulated by an agreement between the Venezuelan and Basque governments. The emigrants—industrialists, doctors, engineers, and others—left France with very satisfactory work contracts. The Basques that reached Caracas met for some years at the Hotel Zuriñe. The death of the first exile prompted an initiative to form the Basque Association of Mutual Aid, a medical and funeral insurance society. The Basque Center of Caracas was founded in 1942. That same year, it changed locales and a handball court was built. In 1950, the present site was inaugurated. President José Antonio Aguirre and Jesús Galíndez participated in the activities. Following Caracas's lead, Basque centers were founded in El Tigre, Barcelona, Puerto La Cruz, Cumaná, Valencia, and other cities.

The Andes

Bolivia, the prototypical Andean country, isolated from the oceans, was the creation of Simón Bolívar, who defended its existence as a nation. The Bolivian people adopted the country's name to honor their protector. Other Basque toponyms that are signs of the Basque migratory presence include Luribay (department of La Paz), San Ignacio (department of Beni), Azurduy (department of Sucre), and another San Ignacio in the department of Santa Cruz.

The Basques went to Potosí in great numbers, protected by their ancient legal privileges as guaranteed under the *forua*. By 1602, they had already begun to distinguish themselves by their power and wealth, gaining control of the silver trade and high administrative posts. A large number of Basques were *azogueros* (bosses that oversaw the amalgamation of mercury with silver). Eighty percent of Potosí's 132 factories in 1580 were Basque-owned. Basques brought with them their mining heritage. They monopolized the most productive mines and controlled city hall. Of the twelve silver merchants of the time, eight were Basque; of the twelve municipal aldermen, six were Basque. The resentment that such privilege created among the rest of the population combined with the sharp fall in silver production beginning in 1615 to provoke a civil war between the Basques and the other "nations": Castilians, Andalusians, Extremadurans, Italians, Portuguese, and others. In 1617, in view of the situation, the viceroy annulled the election of two Basques to the magistracy, alluding to vote tampering in city government. The tension between the two bands increased. The sector opposed to the Basques adopted the name "Vicuña" because they wore hats made from the wool of these animals. The authorities supported the Basques, pursuing the Vicuñas and executing their leaders, who tended to be Andalusians. In 1618, while Luis de Valdivieso, an Andalusian, was playing handball, he struck the Basque Martín de Usurpi. Creoles and Andalusians began to knife Basques. In June 1622, the assassination of a Basque on a Potosí street provoked a civil war that lasted for two years. The brutality of this conflict was reflected in the assassination of a rich landowner who was killed by Vicuñas at the entrance of a Potosí church; they then stabbed him twice in the face as "they had said that they wanted the dagger to have blood on it."

The situation became so critical that the Basques were forced to inform Spain of the gravity of their plight. They pleaded with the king and lord of Bizkaia, Felipe IV, to remedy the situation quickly. The king sent a decree to the viceroy of Peru, ordering him to take harsh measures against the other Vicuñas. An agreement brought peace to the two opposing bands, bolstered by the marriage of the daughter of the Vicuña general Castillo with the son of Francisco Oyanume, leader of the Bizkaians. In April 1625, a general pardon was granted by the viceroy. It covered all the Vicuñas except those having committed blood crimes. By around March 1624, the Vicuñas had killed sixty-four men and wounded many more, yet they had not managed to depose the Basques from their privileged situation in the mines and city government. The violence that scourged Potosí for years left the city in ruins. In addition, the silver deposits were running out and the mines began to close. From 1620 on, the yields declined constantly.

Among the numerous writers recounting the grandeurs of Potosí was the Dominican friar Fra Reginaldo de Lizarraga, born in the Extremaduran city of Medellín in 1540. He reached Quito with his parents at the age of fifteen. In 1560, he joined the order, living in the city of Los Reyes (Lima) while he studied theology. Once Lizarraga was ordained, he traveled the northern coast of Peru. In 1579, he was summoned to Lima and then spent a year as his order's vicar in Santiago (Chile). Upon his return to Lima, in 1588, he was sent to govern the new Dominican province of San Lorenzo Mártir, founded in 1586, comprising the colonized territories of Chile, Paraguay, and Argentina. In May 1594, he fought against the English pirates that attacked the Peruvian coast. That same year, he was assigned to preach in the town of Chongos in the Jauja Valley (Peru), where he observed in abhorrence the deaths of the Indians caused by mercury in the Huancavelica mines. In 1597, he was confirmed as bishop of La Imperial (Chile), where he went in 1602. The following year he moved the seat of the bishopric from La Imperial to the city of Concepción. In 1607, he was named bishop of Asunción (Paraguay), where he died in November 1609. A tireless traveler, in his work *Description of Perú, Tucumán, Río de la Plata, and Chile*, he showed himself to be a man interested in the success of the colonial undertaking, concerned with improving agricultural and mining yields, and opinionated about the administration and treatment of the Indians.

In Ecuador, the department of Simón Bolívar encompasses 3,231 square kilometers. It is near Chimborazo Mountain, which is over 6,000 meters high. At the peak, Bolívar the Liberator wrote and recited his exalting lyric poem "Delirium." Other toponyms indicating the Basque presence in this country include the province of Azuay, the province of Bolívar, the province of Imbabura (with its capital of Ibarra), the towns of Simón Bolívar (department of Guaguas), Rosa Zárate (department of Esmeralda), Perucho y Oña (department of Simón Bolívar), San Antonio de Ibarra, Hacienda Zulueta, and Chorrera Biscaya, the Bernardo de Lecea copper mine, Loyola River, port of Bolívar, Azuay Mountains, and Minza Plains.

As Javier Ortiz de la Tabla Ducasse rightly points out, the active and early presence of Basque merchants and businessmen in early colonial Ecuador should not be disregarded.[93] Nevertheless, the importance and influence of the Basque colony must be sought in the eighteenth century, especially in Ecuadorian history from then on. That century, the Basques settled in the country thanks to important posts in the government and army, or as merchants, attracted by the prosperity of Guayaquil. This was the case of the Elizaldes, Larrabeitias, Artetas, Icazas, and others. Also deserving mention are the bureaucrats that arrived as a result of the Bourbon reforms, such as the Ascasubis, Aspiazus, and Gangotenas. The importance of the Basque presence in high government positions and as royal officials in the sixteenth and seventeenth centuries should be highlighted, as must the abundance of Basque noblemen and their considerable educational preparation. This undoubtedly explains the social and economic success of the Basque colony's members and their climb to, and continuity at, the apex of the local and regional associations.

Moreover, these high-level functionaries attracted their relatives and countrymen. They hoped to forge endogamous connections of both a social and commercial nature, with the intention of intermarrying with the Creole elites. This phenomenon intensified throughout the seventeenth century, but became especially strong in the eighteenth, when similarities of social class and commercial activity were added to the original regional marital preferences.[94]

In Peru, as has been seen, several Basques accompanied Pizarro and Almagro in their colonial adventures. Between 1520 and 1539, 5.9 percent of this territory's conquistadors were Basque. And, at the time, the Basque residents of Lima made up 11.3 percent of its population, with the Navarrese at 1.2 percent. Between 1540 and 1559, the Basques made up 4.3 percent of Peru's population. Among those that stood out in Peruvian history, the following can be described with capsule biographies:[95]

1. Pedro Ortiz de Zárate, native of Urduña (Bizkaia), and founder of the Royal High Court of Lima, entered the city on May 17, 1544. He came with his wife, Catalina de Uribe y Salazar and their oldest child, later Captain Pedro Ortiz Zárate.
2. Domingo de Alzola y Compostaeta, born in Arrasate (Gipuzkoa) around 1532, belonged to the Order of the Predicadores. He was inspector and vicar general of the Order of Santo Domingo in Peru. He moved to Mexico, where he died in 1590.
3. Agustín de Zárate reached Peru in 1543 with the post of controller. He was the author of *History of the Conquest and Discovery of Peru*, which was printed in Amberes in 1555.
4. Pedro Sarmiento de Gamboa was a great sailor and writer. Finding himself in Lima in 1564, he had to face a grave charge before the Tribunal of the Holy Inquisition for practicing necromancy.
5. Pedro José de Arriaga, a Jesuit, was born in Bergara in 1562. He was sent to Peru, where he preached the gospel to the natives. He held important posts in the order in the cities of Arequipa and Lima. He was the author of *Eradication of the Idolatry of the Indians of Peru: Spiritual Exercises*, among other works.
6. The suffragan of Cuzco, Sebastián de Lartaun, was born in the valley of Oiartzun in the Basque Country around 1519. He studied at the University of Alcalá de Henares, where he received a doctorate in theology. As canon of

the collegiate church there, he was elected bishop of Cuzco in 1570. Many matters detained him in Spain, and he could not go to Peru until three years later. Several relatives and other Basques came with him. His brother, or perhaps nephew, named Esteban, was alderman and high justice in Peru. A niece or sister married the justice and rector of San Marcos University in Lima, the licentiate Juan Fernández de Recalde. The somewhat ambiguous action of Lartaun provoked grave difficulties at the third council of Lima; incessant complaints were presented against him by his enemies from Cuzco. Before the event (council) was over, he was stricken with the illness that sent him to his grave on October 9, 1583. In the will that he made just before dying, Sebastián de Lartaun asked that the suits and complaints continue until a verdict was reached so his name might be cleared; he forgave "of good heart and will all those people that have offended and injured him in writing or speech or any other way, so that Our Lord God might forgive him his guilts and sins, and he sought forgiveness from those he had offended."

But the pastoral zeal that Lartaun exercised in his diocese must not go unmentioned. Not only did he diligently attend to the curates' needs, but he also appointed Indian overseers to assist in the service with the authority of the bishop. He also decidedly defended the mestizo clerics, and ordained some in spite of a royal prohibition. Justifying his conduct, he wrote to the king: "To speak the truth as I should, I tell his Majesty that they are the best clerics that I have in my bishopric, even though they do not know a lot because they have not pursued higher studies; but when it comes to performing the doctrine and living free of scandal and knowing the language of the Indians, they do what they should." And to reach the root of the problem, he added,

> Of course, for these kingdoms, it is important that there might be a university where scholars might be trained and the ignorant and young might learn the humanities and virtue, that with this the earth will give good fruit, and the holy Catholic faith will be better taught and sown. And, especially, if this university, in the scope that it should have, might include the native Indians, mestizos, *zambaigos* [of mixed native and African descent], and, even, the blacks; and even if only partially they are included in it [university] so they might be taught what is necessary for their salvation and to teach those of their lineage and everyone, surely this generalization, it seems, is important for the good of the world and the glory of God that it might shine in all nations. Since integrating the other nations with us makes them so servile and inept in accomplishing that for which they have been raised and have talent to accomplish, it does not seem a just and wise choice. Rather, for the

good of Christianity and the sciences, it would appear to be appropriate for them to be welcome and helped with all necessary means; so that they might bless our God and the good fortune that they have had in having your Majesty for their Lord and King, who, with such love and charity, desires their well-being and salvation and enlightened understanding. He should provide them with the means so that all might be taught, excluding no one and no generation of those that have ability and talent to be taught in the letters and virtue.

It cannot be doubted that this was the unanimous sentiment of the Third Provincial Council of Lima, where, as the metropolitan testified explicitly informing the king of everything, in all matters concerning the doctrine, "there was complete agreement." Particularly in the collective letter that the council priests sent to Philip II at the end of their terms, they insisted that schools and seminaries be established for the indigenous children, "where they might be raised with discipline and Christian policy. Because, if they are taught and raised in this way, we know that in time they will come to be not only good Christians and help their own kind be so as well, but also apt and suitable for studies and for serving the Church and even to be ministers of the Word of God in their nation."[96]

7. Fernando Arias de Ugarte was born in Bogotá, Colombia, on September 9, 1561. He was archbishop of Lima.

8. Diego de Arana was born in Abando (Bilbao). He belonged to the Peruvian army. He entered the Augustinian convent of Lima on April 7, 1560. Sent on a mission, he was later the superior of the Convent of Chuquisaca. He was elected prior of Guamacucho and sent to Catabamba. He died on August 9, 1595.

9. Antonio Salinas de Jaúregui, native of Bilbao, was a resident and general trustee of the district of the city of Cuzco at the beginning of the eighteenth century. He was an ensign in the Royal Armada.

10. Martín de Arriola Balerdi was born in Donostia. He was justice of the High Court of Charcas (upper Peru) in 1619. In 1624, he was promoted to the High Court of Lima. As governor of Huancavelica (in 1643), he reopened that country's mercury mines, considered to be unsalvageable, making them productive once again. He built the fortifications of the port of Callao and attained the post of councillor of the Indies. He died in 1653.

11. Diego Hordoño Sarricolea y Zamudio was a soldier in the port of Callao in 1628. In 1642–1643, he was alderman of the province of Arriaza and in 1665–1666 of Cajatambo. In 1662, he attained the position of admiral of the Armada of the South Seas and in 1663 he was named general in the same command.

12. Antonio de Soloaga y Gil was born in Viñaspre (Araba) in 1659. Doctor of theology, he was named archbishop of the city of Lima on February 19, 1714. He died in that city on January 22, 1722.

The group of Basques concentrated in Lima at the start of the seventeenth century was so large that its members decided to band together into a brotherhood to pay homage to the image of the Virgin of Aránzazu (and also the Virgin of Begoña). They initially met in the convent of Saint Augustine of Lima, until acquiring a chapel in the church of Saint Francis, whose proprietor was Luis de Mendoza y Ribera. In it gathered the natives of the seigneury of Bizkaia, the province of Gipuzkoa, the province of Araba, the Kingdom of Navarre, and the Cuatro Villas of the Cantabrian coast (Laredo, Castro-Urdiales, Santander, and San Vicente de la Barquera).

At the beginning of 1612 and in 1613, ordinances were established for the good governing of the association.[97] Article 1 of the new ordinances of 1635 indicates that the objective of the brotherhood was the union and confederation of the natives of the territories mentioned, "to exercise among themselves, and with those of their nation, works of compassion and charity in both life and death." Among other things, it says that the members had to be natives of the mentioned territories and their descendants had to be so through

> a male ancestor, noble, and pious men of known birth and reputation and to this effect that it is warned that no person might be admitted or buried in the chapel who is stained of Jew or Moor, punished by the Holy Office, nor married with a mulatta, Indian, or black, or that has any infamous occupation. The examination or verification that might be made concerning this must be conducted with extreme secrecy or by the majordomos of said Brotherhood, who verbally and by word, but not in writing, would make diligent verification of that which is charged to their conscience; and this diligence done thusly and not otherwise will then be written and noted in the book of the Brotherhood, for such is its purpose, together with the name of their parents and their origin.

The goal of the brotherhood was construction of a chapel-cemetery where members and legitimate women would be buried, as well as children born of legal marriages or out of wedlock (as long as they were not children of mulatta, black, or Indian women). If the deceased Basques, Navarrese, or Cantabrians were poor, the burial costs would be covered by the brotherhood.

The following were the commitments of this institution:

First: visit the sick and help them economically with alms.
Second: visit the infirm poor (to provide help and assistance and, if necessary, to take them to the hospital).

Third: visit the prisons to see if there were members of the brotherhood in order to defend them in their cases until they were free, and pay the debts of the prisoners with scrip, which they could repay when able.
Fourth: help and house the new arrivals from the mentioned provinces.
Fifth: the brothers pooled money to maintain the association and, if funds were low, these were raised from among the wealthiest.

It was also established that masses would be said for the deceased buried in the chapel on All Saints' Day. And it was agreed that if the brotherhood had enough money, it would pay for the marriage of poor orphans or provide an endowment for a nun, who might be the daughter or close relative of a member. On April 12, 1635, the brotherhood was made up of 105 brothers of the following origin: 49 from Bizkaia, 35 from Gipuzkoa, 9 from Navarre, 7 from Araba, and 5 from the Cuatro Villas. The Basque presence in Peru must have been important throughout the seventeenth century and the following one. Professor Carlos D. Malamud's study of the Navarrese Goyeneche family in Arequipa provides a good example.[98] Juan Crisóstomo de Goyeneche y Aguerrevere was born on January 26, 1741, in the Navarrese town of Irurita, in the valley of Baztán. At twenty-six, he went to the port of Callao, and then, after making contact with Viceroy Amat, was sent to Arequipa as a sergeant major. In 1770, at age twenty-nine, he married María Josefa de Barreda y Benavides (who had been born in Arequipa on October 14, 1744), the daughter of Brigadier Nicolás Barreda y Obando and María Benavides y Moscoso. Her parents, both natives of Arequipa, were well situated in the local oligarchy. She was descended on the maternal side from the noble family of Talavera de la Reina, settled in America since the beginning of the seventeenth century. From their union the following children were born: Pedro Mariano (January 22, 1772), the future justice of the High Court of Lima; José Manuel (June 13, 1776), lieutenant general of the Royal Army and first count of Guaqui; José Sebastián (January 19, 1784), who became archbishop of Lima; Juan Mariano (March 29, 1788), a merchant; and María Presentación, who remained single and in the family home.

Before his marriage, Juan de Goyeneche had already stood out as a merchant in Arequipa, acquiring lands near the city whose value increased extraordinarily. His marriage, however, clearly helped him greatly in his economic ascent and social success. He rapidly became a wealthy *hacendado* and (according to some indicators) a rich miner. In the wars of independence of the early nineteenth century, the Goyeneche family embraced the royal cause, which brought them significant problems. The family is socioeconomically representative of what could have been a good part of Basque colonial society, at least in its most noteworthy aspects. The Navarrese Goyeneche chose the colonial bureaucracy. After an advantageous marriage with the daughter of an Arequipan landowner, he came to consolidate his social and financial position. His children rapidly assimilated into the new society while maintaining the family fortune. Each one would have a specific mission to fulfill, but they would all own land, undoubtedly the most precious commodity during the ancien régime.[99]

During the nineteenth century, Basque immigration in Peru would be largely insignificant. On September 1, 1834, however, the *Mercantile Gazette* of Lima reported that, of the twelve most important shipping companies then in existence in the Peruvian capital, four belonged to Basque businessmen: Juan Francisco Izcue; the Aramburu brothers; Urien and Co.; and Dalidou Larraburu and Co.[100] Around the decade of the 1920s, there were Basque firms of great tradition in the Andean country, such as the Ezquerra Brothers, and Widow & Sons of Gabino Artadi, in Paita. The Bizkaian Vidaurrázaga, an important importer of iron and cement, lived in Arequipa.[101]

In nineteenth-century republican Peru, an incident at the Hacienda Talambo, in the north of the country, involved the Basques. Ramón Azcárate, a business partner of Manuel de Salcedo, proprietor of the hacienda, decided to bring in Basque colonists to cultivate cotton. In November 1860, thirty-five Basque families, totaling 175 individuals, lived on the property. Many spoke only Euskara. On August 4, 1863, one of the workers, Marcial Miner, had a verbal exchange with Salcedo, which became violent. Miner was supported and protected by his Basque countrymen. The fray resulted in one death, various injuries, and a diplomatic confrontation between Spain and Peru, an antecedent to the war of 1866 between the two countries.

Guaraní Paraguay

Up to 1600, a total of 3,087 Europeans had gone to Paraguay and Río de la Plata. A predominant number—1,708 or 53.3 percent—were Spaniards, although there were also Portuguese, Italians, Flemish, Germans, English, and Irish among them.[102] Of the Spaniards, 45.7 percent were Andalusian and 7.1 percent Basque. The rest came from the other regions of Spain, including the Balearic and Canary Islands. Aside from exceptional cases, Spanish immigration in Paraguay stopped completely beginning in 1600. Throughout the sixteenth century, only 1,000 to 1,200 of the 1,708 Spaniards were involved in the arduous process of actually populating and colonizing Paraguay. So these Europeans and the gradually mesticizing Guaraní population would be the precursors of the majority of the present Paraguayan population. Of the 121 Basques that entered the country in the sixteenth century, 50 were Bizkaians, 47 Gipuzkoans, and 24 Arabans.[103]

The most important of the Basques was undoubtedly Domingo Martínez de Irala. He was born in 1509 in Bergara (Gipuzkoa), thus acquiring his nickname of "Captain Vergara." He would sell his family estate in Dueñas to enroll as a simple sailor in the fleet of Pedro de Mendoza headed for Río de la Plata. He took part in the first founding of the city of Buenos Aires and that of Buena Esperanza. He was Juan de Ayolas's second in command on October 14, 1536, when, while searching for a route to the Sierra de la Plata, they discovered the Paraguay River. They finally stopped in the place they called Fuerte de la Candelaria, or La Paz, where Martínez de Irala remained as a lieutenant and representative. The lack of supplies forced him to march with Salazar and González de Mendoza, who would found Asunción on August 15, 1537. When Ayolas returned to Candelaria, he was killed by the Payagua Indians. Martínez de Irala led several expeditions looking for him, which turned punitive after learning of Ayolas's death. In November 1538, the overseer Alonso Cabrera arrived from Spain with the Azkoitian treasurer Adame de Olaberriaga. Cabrera brought a royal decree empowering the conquistadors to choose an interim governor and captain general in the event that the provincial governor died without designating a successor. The settlers chose Martínez de Irala as governor of Asunción in 1538.

This began his great administrative work that would last seventeen years. Except for this city, all the Spanish settlements in the Río de la Plata basin were undergoing a marked crisis. Lack of settlers and defense, indigenous attacks, hunger, dispersion of the enclaves, and difficult communications all threatened their survival. To resolve this problem, in 1541, the Spaniards abandoned Santa María del Buen Aire, Buena Esperanza, and Corpus Christi, concentrating their forces in Asunción. This would become the capital of the colony and only European population center in the Plata River basin until 1556. It was urgent to create a truly consolidated urban base for conquest operations and staffing of institutions and services. On September 16, 1541, the first *cabildo* of the southern cone was elected, and its laws would continue in force until 1824. It was styled after that of Gipuzkoa, and centuries later would be praised and imitated. On March 11, 1542, Alvar Núñez Cabeza de Vaca, the new governor and provincial governor, reached Asunción. He named Martínez de Irala brigadier, thereby permitting the latter to participate actively in political and military decisions. Some Basques arrived with Cabeza de Vaca, such as Tristán de Irazabal, Lope de Ugarte, and Juan López de Ugarte, who would all later serve Martínez de Irala.

The Guaraní Indians, who might have rebelled in response to the actions of the provincial governor, frequently had to be controlled. Unlike Martínez de Irala, Cabeza de Vaca did not understand the colonists' egalitarian sentiment. Some had been educated among the ranks of the Castilian *comuneros*. A conspiracy by the colonists deposed Cabeza de Vaca and entrusted the government to Martínez de Irala. The cry of liberty was heard for the first time in April 1544. The supporters of Cabeza de Vaca, however, continued causing problems. Induced by the men that arrived with Mendoza, Cabrera, and Cabeza de Vaca, and obsessed by the Río de la Plata sierra and Potosí silver, Martínez de Irala headed an exploratory expedition in 1547. He was joined by his advisor and friend Father Lezcano, Juan de Zaldivar, and the Gipuzkoans Diego de Olabarrieta (royal scribe) and Tristán de Irazabal. He ascended the waters of the Paraguay River to the port of Fernando, but this had already been conquered. In the wake of this disappointment, Martínez de Irala resigned and entrusted command to González de Mendoza. In his absence, the confrontations were repeated in Asunción, with the "Alvarists" (supporters of Cabeza de Vaca) taking power. Martínez de Irala, the only one capable of commanding, was returned to his post and adeptly put an end to these rivalries. It has been argued that the confrontations were a conflict between the Andalusian supporters of Cabeza de Vaca and the Basques, who supported Martínez de Irala. This is highly unlikely, however, given the former group's numerical advantage. It was more probably a phenomenon of simple partisanship, very common in the Spanish colonial empire. With this action began Martínez de Irala's period of political hegemony. After the failure at the Río de la Plata sierra, the expeditionaries had to figure out how to live off the land. Martínez de Irala extended his political influence and consolidated the Spanish presence by strengthening relations with the Indians through blood ties and mutual cooperation rather than imposition of the *encomienda* system. Some settlers, such as the Bizkaian Miguel de Urrutia, did not understand this benevolent attitude toward the Indians.

With peace established among the Spaniards of Paraguay, Martínez de Irala decided to penetrate the Chaco in 1553. It was another failure, known as "the bad entrance." He was compensated, however, with the arrivals between 1555 and 1556 of Mencía Calderón, widow of the third provincial governor, along with a contingent of women. There was also the first shipment of cattle. Then, too, the Bizkaian Martín de Orúe and Gipuzkoan Diego de Olabarrieta arrived with the first bishop, Pedro Fernández de la Torre, and his religious followers, bringing with them the royal title of governor and captain general for Martínez de Irala. Orúe, a royal scribe and military communard, traveled to Paraguay three times. In 1545 he participated in the deposition of Cabeza de Vaca, with whom he had arrived in 1542. In 1555, after ten years of proceedings in the Royal Court, he returned as commission merchant of the Royal Treasury with the titles for Martínez de Irala. When Ortiz de Zárate made a will, Orúe was one of those it designated as governor. He and his brother, Diego de Orúe, would leave descendants in Asunción.

Around that time, Francisco de Mendoza continued his explorations of the shores of the Paraná River. In 1553, Francisco de Aguirre, a Toledo-born Basque, would refound the city of Barco, renaming it Santiago del Estero. Martínez de Irala understood the importance of overseas transportation and sent García Rodríguez de Vergara to found a colony, Ontiveros, along the course of the Paraná. After Martínez de Irala died, but still carrying out his instructions, Ruiz Díaz de Melgarejo would found Ciudad Real del Guairá (in present-day Brazil); Nufri de Chaves, with the Gipuzkoan captain Pedro de Segura Zabala, would also establish Santa Cruz de la Sierra. The routes from the Atlantic were thus opened.

Martínez de Irala died of appendicitis on October 3, 1556. In his will, he recognized nine illegitimate mestizo children, who would prolong his lineage in the history of the Río de la Plata region and underscore his policy of union between the colonists and natives. Some of his daughters married Basques like Pedro de Segura Zavala and Pedro de la Puente. Martínez de Irala is considered the founder of Paraguay, renowned for his beneficence with the Indians, constitutional justice, the humanity of his laws, and, lastly, his decisive efforts in colonization and expansion, frequently at the expense of his own wealth. He provided Asunción with its first period of prosperity and paved the way for the birth of nations like Argentina, Uruguay, and Paraguay.

During the eighteenth century, as a result of the Bourbon reforms in the American colonies, some Basques arrived in Paraguay as functionaries, merchants, commercial clerks, and artisans. Some settled in the countryside, others in the city, and many became related by marriage to Paraguayan families rooted in the country since the days of the conquest. Such is the case of the lineages of Isasi, Goyburu, Ormaiztegui, Argaña y Villalante, Recalde, Machaín, Loizaga, Aguirre, and Goicoechea. The majority of the members of these family clans were partisans of the royalists, a fact that would result in prison and confinement for some of them.

The first French attempt at colonization in Paraguay took place in 1855 near Asunción. Three expeditions left Bordeaux with 418 members. This colony, christened Nouvelle Bordeaux, was a complete failure, and its members went to Río de la Plata. In 1872, a new attempt was made on the Agra River, as in 1871 the Paraguayan government had ceded 375,000 hectares under contract to a French concern. This colony was also unsuccessful. In spite of everything, the French colony in this country (most of them from the Basses-Pyrénées) numbered 228 people in 1886, 500 in 1889, and more than a thousand in 1910. In 1889, there were four bakeries in the country with forty-four French employees, two tile factories with forty-five workers, one locksmith with sixteen employees, two restaurants with fifteen, and two shoemakers with seventy-five.

Southern Chile: Araucanian Country

The Basque presence in Chile began with the discovery and conquest. Of those accompanying Almagro, in 1535, 178 of his expeditionaires have been identified, as have 150 of those with Valdivia in 1540. Of these 328 conquistadors, 27 were of Basque origin. Ten were Bizkaian, two Gipuzkoan, two Araban, three Navarrese, and the province of origin of the other ten is unknown.[104] But, the best known and recognized Basque inside of Chile and without was undoubtedly Alonso de Ercilla (1533–1594). He was born and died in Madrid, but his family came from Bermeo, Bizkaia, where it had an estate. A courtier, soldier, traveler, reader of classics, and poet, his life was that of a quintessential Renaissance man. He participated in several American battles and conquered Ancud (Chile), settling in the region of Corcovado. There, he composed the first fifteen stanzas of his epic poem *The Araucanian*, which he published in 1569 in Madrid. Between 1578 and 1589, Ercilla published the epic's second and third parts. In the work, he narrated the battles between the Spaniards and American Indians. From 1580 on, he was censor of books for the Council of Castile.

The seventeenth century was an epoch full of adversity for Spanish Chile, punctuated by fighting with the Araucanians mentioned by Ercilla, earthquakes, plagues, and floods that made death a daily challenge. All of Chile had a military orientation, as the famous Catalina de Erauso (better known as "the Ensign Nun") could verify. Born in Donostia of a noble family, she lived between 1592 and 1650. She was involved in religious life but escaped from the convent while serving her novitiate. Erauso decided to dress like a man to make her escape easier. Using an assumed name, she went to America in search of adventure. She joined a group of soldiers that set sail for the south of the New World, enlisting (after more than a few incarnations) in the new Chilean army that Governor Alonso de Ribera was beginning to organize in 1603. The camouflaged Basque nun attained the rank of ensign for her distinguished military performance. She always concealed her true identity, behaving like a man and just another soldier. In a duel to the death, she killed her older brother (without knowing it), who had immigrated in America when she was a child. From Chile, the Ensign Nun emigrated to Tucumán and from there to the rich and legendary city of Potosí. Upon returning to Peru, she revealed her true identity to the ecclesiastic authorities, reentering civilian life once and for all. In time, she returned to Spain, where she told about her adventures and the adversities of the war with the Araucanians. Her curious feats made her famous and her portrait was painted in Sevilla by Pacheco, at that time the father-in-law of Velázquez. Philip III granted Catalina de Erauso a yearly pension and allowed her to live in Mexico, where she died.

Basque incorporation into Chile in the seventeenth century was progressive, and was particularly notable in its Jesuit contingent, which included Navarrese and Gipuzkoans.[105] Governor José de Garro, from Gipuzkoa, deserves mention. Before occupying his post in Chile, he had already been governor of Río de la Plata in 1674. Garro guided Chile's destiny between 1682 and 1692. He was in large part responsible for the economic reconstruction and recovery of the end of the century. His brilliant action brought him the governorship of Gibraltar in 1696 and captaincy general of Gipuzkoa in 1702, the year that he died. Before him, other Basques, Francisco López de Zúñiga and Martín de Muxica, also served as governors. The latter had to repair the damage from the earthquake of May 1647 that so drastically affected the entire Chilean territory.

The eighteenth century was characterized by a period of peace and social development. The Basque presence, firmly established through the sixteenth and seventeenth centuries, would attain social prominence in the eighteenth and early nineteenth centuries. Later, it would influence the configuration of contemporary Chile beginning with the country's independence in 1818. During the century of Enlightenment, Juan Andrés Uztáriz y Vertiz Verea (1709–1718) and Agustín de Jaúregui y Aldecoa (1773–1780) were noteworthy governors. The military governor of Valparaíso, Luis de Alava y Sáez de Navarrete, and the governor of the *plaza* of Valdivia, Pedro Gregorio de Echenique y Echenique, must be cited for their role as functionaries. Ramón Javier de Vial served as the controller of the Royal Bank of Concepción in 1764. As assayer of the Royal Mint, Domingo Eyzaguirre Escutasolo inaugurated a family dynasty in 1772.

Among the intellectuals, Tomás de Azúa Iturgoyen stood out as the first rector of the Royal University of San Felipe. The work of Joaquín de Villareal was also important. A native of Berriz, he was born around 1690, and entered the Society of Jesus in 1711. As a novice, he went to Chile. In 1728, he was ordained in Concepción, one of two Araucanian seats of the Jesuit missions at the time (along with Purén). Around the mid-eighteenth century he was in Madrid. From there, he sent a report to the Council of Castile about three projects presented by the Board of Settlers of the Kingdom of Chile to found settlements in the country's inhospitable Araucanian-controlled southern territories. The Villareal report, as it became known, demonstrates his vast knowledge of those territories and the reasons and bases of the war between the Spaniards and native Araucanians. The war impeded the unification of Chilean territory and normal, fluid transportation between the cities (based in the north) and southern outposts.

Thus, considering the many resources (human and economic) allocated by the Crown in that realm with relatively limited results, Madrid's interest in Chile waned. The foundation of highly populated urban centers had been modest during the seventeenth century. But, after Villareal's proposal, this idea would be revived. The document indicated the following: [106]

1. Araucania was an empty territory that the Crown should add to its domains, with greater economic and military resources than it had been using to that point.
2. Military policy along with a policy of assimilation of the Araucanian Indians was necessary.
3. The deployment along the border proposed by Villareal not only sought the resolution of the "Araucanian conflict," but also creation of a border that would prevent invasion on the continent by another European power.
4. The shift in policy from a military to civil emphasis that affected the conflictive American regions (during the eighteenth century) found one of its most significant and emblematic supporters in Joaquín de Villareal.

Among the ecclesiastics, Bishop Manuel Alday y Aspée (1712–1788) deserves mention. He had a noteworthy involvement regarding doctrinal initiatives on the Provincial Council of Lima of 1772, which he attended as the bishop of Santiago.

The commercial scope was extremely important for the Basque colony settled in Chile. Especially during the second half of the eighteenth century, commerce was the predominant activity of the Basque group and the key that opened the doors of its success. In Concepción, Francisco de Urrutia Mendiburu stood out.[107] He maintained close and powerful connections with the merchants of Peru. Santiago Larraín Vicuña was an agent for his uncle, who lived in Peru and owned merchant ships trading in the Pacific. Juan Francisco Larraín Cerda belonged to the same stem family. In 1761, he established a shipping company with Diego Portales Irarrázaval. Using the ship christened *La Ermita*, they engaged in prolonged trade between Peru and Chile.

All these Basque merchants were characterized by their solidarity, a connecting thread linking their mercantile undertakings. In general, marital ties served to reinforce these connections. The businesses became a tight web whose threads were of the most diverse social, bureaucratic, mercantile, cultural, and landholding interests. Among the numerous cities and towns founded that characterize eighteenth-century Chile was Nueva Bilbao (presently Concepción). The new city was founded in 1794 by Santiago de Oñederra y Alvizu, who was also named its superintendent. The characteristics of the Maule River, the countryside in itself, and his seafaring vocation and passion motivated the Basque Oñederra y Alvizu to conceive of the new settlement and bring it into being. Its shipyards, endowed with the region's excellent wood, soon began to produce small ships (*faluchos*) for coastal trade to the north. In 1754, Governor Domingo Ortíz de Rozas planned the city of Illapel, which was soon abandoned. But, in 1789, Manuel de Gorostizaga revisited the idea and revived the city. Luís Manuel de Zañartu Iriarte served as alderman of Santiago for a long period in the eighteenth century. He married Carmen Errázuriz and had two daughters who, by their father's decision, were relegated to religious life. His masterpiece was the emblematic lime and stone bridge that lent character to the capital for almost a century, until a ferocious flood destroyed it in 1888.

Chile proclaimed its independence from Spain on February 12, 1818, but Basque participation had already become considerable since the creation of the Open Cabildo of September 18, 1810. Thus, at least 30 percent of those attending that meeting were of Basque ancestry.[108] And, for the first time in Chile's history, the necessity for popular sovereignty and independence from Spain was expressed. An important promoter of the idea of emancipation was José Antonio de Rojas Urtuguren, an avid encyclopedist. He returned from his travels to Spain a critic of the imperial system, as he had been able to verify the decadence of the Spanish monarchy in person. A discussion group considering controversial books (many of which had circumvented the censure of the colonial authorities) and criticizing the Spanish government and its representatives in Chile was organized around Rojas Urtuguren. In 1928, the historian Alberto Edwards interpreted the decisive (in his opinion) participation of the Basque colony in Chile's independence process in the following way:

> With good sense and a sober soul, the Basques and Navarrese also brought an almost wild spirit of liberty and backwoodedness to our aristocracy. From Independence to Irarrázaval and his autonomous commune, some of our most transcendent politicians elevate by their spiritual origin the very roots of the tree of Guernica. Unconscious yearnings for native liberties brought institutions here that a people whose masses are Andalusian or mestizo, and with Moorish habits, never knew how to understand or apply and are therefore completely foreign to these Vizcayan *forua*, tradition of their lords. It should not be forgotten that the Basque provinces were simultaneously the freest and most aristocratic nation of Spain. Their ancient liberties had resisted the victorious advance of monarchic centralism intact; all their inhabitants were juridically nobles, and even the poor dwellings of the villages boasted noble coats of arms. The aristocratic liberalism of old Chile was, at least to a certain point, a venerable medieval historical tradition, a racial inheritance.[109]

Unlike Argentina and Uruguay, Chile did not become a preferred emigratory destination after independence from Spain. Of a total of 4,001 Spanish immigrants in Chile between 1894 and 1916, 546, or 13.6 percent, were Basques. In 1907, the number of foreigners that lived in the country never exceeded 5 percent of the total population.[110] Therefore, the contemporary Basque contribution must be judged in qualitative rather than quantitative terms. In the registry of the founding members of the Basque Center of Santiago of 1922, there are 469 entries with dates of birth between 1861 and 1914. Of these, 54.2 percent came from Bizkaia (the highest number) and 1.5 percent from Araba (the lowest).[111] From 1950 to 1960, there was a noteworthy increase in Navarrese immigration from the valley of Baztán. By profession, based on a sample of 108 cases for the period 1861–1914, 51 percent worked the land. Others defined themselves as merchants (11 percent) (bakeries, tailor shops, restaurants, and arms dealers).[112] This was the case of Martín Laborde, who reached Chile around 1905, founding the shoe factory Brothers Laborde in 1917. He then summoned his brother Domingo who was already in the country, working in a factory. Later, other siblings (Juan Martín and Estefanía) and their brothers-in-law Pedro and Luís Duhalde would also form part of the company. This factory came to be among the largest in the country, with production reaching three hundred thousand pairs a year. It included living quarters and rooms to lodge and receive the newly arrived Basques. There was also a handball court.[113]

Administrative banking functions were significant within the Basque colony, and those with specialized trades (8.3 percent) devoted themselves to carpentry, gardening, house painting, and woodwork. The soap, tile, and wood industries occupied 6.5 percent, and the same percentage applied to sailors. University students accounted for 5.5 percent.[114]

The migratory path to Chile, until the beginning of the twentieth century, was most commonly by sea. The immigrant boarded at a Basque or French port, crossed the Atlantic, and arrived in Buenos Aires. If his destination was Chile, he could continue through the Strait of Magellan, disembarking in Valparaíso. He could also choose the overland route, crossing the pampa to Mendoza and, from there, directly to Santiago. Beginning in 1914, with the opening of the Panama Canal, a second access route became available. The construction of the trans-Andean railway in 1916 was an improvement over the old overland route. Air transport (common since the 1930s) considerably reduced the length of the trip, although it increased the cost.

Of a total of 171 Basque immigrants, 44.3 percent reached Chile between the end of the nineteenth century and 1930.[115] The rest would do so from then to 1990, although the largest numbers entered between 1931 and 1960, due to the Spanish Civil War (1936–1939) and the exiles that it produced. The majority arrived single (79 percent), and 60 percent of them married Basques.[116] Presently, this immigration has yielded its fruits, and a good part of Chile's commercial and industrial sectors and the liberal professions are in the hands of the Basque colony, reduced in numbers but economically powerful.[117]

The first Basque Center was not founded until 1923, when peninsular and continental Basques got together to do so. Shortly thereafter, in 1931, the ideologically nationalist Basque Youth–Euzko Gaztedija chapter was founded. In the first article of its statutes, it proclaimed that Euskadi is the homeland of the Basques, following the motto of Sabino Arana y Goiri. The Spanish Civil War divided the Basque community in Chile. Until then, the social relationship between the Basque Center and Basque Youth was generally cordial. Tensions surged with the war. The Basque Center was a social institution with no concern for politics. In addition, it had members from Iparralde and others from Spain sympathetic to General Franco. Basque Youth, on the contrary, was of a markedly nationalist character. It felt the sacrifice of its comrades in the war and sponsored actions consistent with the orientations of the Basque Government. But the situation normalized after José Antonio Aguirre's 1942 visit—the first step toward the unification of the Republic's Basque collectivity. It was the exiled Bizkaian Santiago de Zarranz who, in his position as secretary of the Basque Delegation in Chile, initiated the measures to achieve the union of the representatives of the Basque Government and the Basque Center of Santiago. The process was concluded in 1949 with the formation of Euzko Etxea, into which Basque Youth-Euzko Gaztedija was incorporated. This latter group sold its headquarters to make a contribution toward the acquisition of the new social center. In 1946, the Euzko Etxea of Valparaíso was founded. From the beginning, it had the support of the Basque Delegation. In 1991, the Navarrese Center of Chile was founded in Santiago, with Agustín Otondo y Dufurrena, from Baztán, as its first president.

It was in 1840 that the Basques of Iparralde began to head to Chile.[118] The first immigrants organized shops or small bazaars, where they sold a little of everything, including some articles imported from France. This was the case of the Harasteguy, Hinart, and Gracy shop in Temuco, and Challe's store established in Valparaíso in 1868. Poey had a store in Concepción and another in Santiago. Pra, born in Bayonne in 1835, owned the largest general stores in all of South America in Santiago and Valparaíso. Duhart, who had a retail business, soon thereafter founded large distilleries. Elissetche set up a general store in Coronel in 1860. And export firms were represented in Lantaro by Hiribarren and in Temuco by Mainguyague. That Labordian family specialized in the leather business.

Saddlemakers were represented by Esquer in Copiapó, Echeberry in Concepción, and Condeau Camachez in Santiago. Shoe factories were represented by Lacasse in Chillán, Aycaguez and Buhalde in Valparaíso and Santiago (their company dates from 1871), Etchevers in Talca, Broussain and Larronde in La Serena (their business dates from 1883), Etcheverry in La Serena, and Pimongnet in Chillán.

Two Etcheverrys and one Etchevers were hardware dealers in Chillán. Ducasse was a baker in Santiago, and Ligonzat a locksmith and coach repairman. The Lalanne brothers made sodas in Concepción. Camousseigt and Lasserre had an oil factory and a preserves factory in Santiago. Castex came from the Basses-Pyrénées in 1865 and established a pasta, soap, and candle factory in Coquimbo. Etchegaray also made soap and candles in Camalez. Duhart and Juanchuteau had twelve wine and liquor stores, and Labastie d'Orthez owned a silver mine. Basque-Béarnais hotels and restaurants were also numerous. The most representative are:

Establishment	Location
Andurandeguy	Coronel
Arrive & Arretxe	Lantaro
Mainguyague	Victoria
Lacaque de Pau	Valparaíso
Casandehore	Santiago
Chostra & Morlás	Santiago

Other activities that the Basques from Iparralde developed in Chile were (beginning in 1900) the cultivation of cereal grains and domestication of animals in the southern provinces, around Temuco, Chillán, Villarien, and Osorno.

Duhart was the French Basque most involved in promoting immigration in Chile. He was the first to establish a tannery business. He therefore needed labor, which he brought from Iparralde. In turn, with the passage of time, Duhart's employees set up businesses throughout the country. Thus, Saint-Macary, who emigrated from Escos in 1860 and first worked as a tanner in the Larralde company, owned a leather factory in 1903 with a business volume of two and a half million francs a year. In 1856, the French immigrants in Chile (almost all from the region of the Basses-Pyrénées) numbered 1,650; in 1888, 1,950; and in 1914, 10,000.

Portuguese Brazil

Very little is known about Basque immigration in Brazil. Few researchers of the Basque diaspora in America have studied Brazil; in fact, Spanish immigration there as a whole has been little studied. It is known that, in 1549, the Jesuit Juan de Azpilicueta, and in 1553 José de Anchieta, also a Jesuit, were on religious missions in Brazil, reorganizing the Society of Jesus there and evangelizing numerous natives. Like the general Spanish trend, Basque immigration appears to have been late in Brazil.[119]

Spanish emigration to Brazil predominated over its (pioneering) Italian counterpart from 1905 to 1919 in the nation as a whole, and from 1905 to 1920 in São Paulo. The year 1907 was an exception in both cases, with Italian immigration predominating. Beginning in 1905, the Italian immigrant was returning to his country, or reemigrating to Argentina or Uruguay. Italian immigration largely replaced slaves in the country, especially beginning with the abolition of the slave trade in 1888 and the great expansion of the coffee economy. Thus, the area cultivated in the state of São Paulo virtually sextupled between 1890 and 1925, going from 510,000 hectares to almost three million. Spanish immigration came, in large part, to fill the place occupied by Italian immigration until then (in the expansion of the coffee economy). Spanish immigration in general, and Basque in particular, reached Brazil at a time of little opportunity and was led, fundamentally, by peasants. In addition, there is no record of large industries belonging to Spaniards (or Basques), indicating that this diaspora was largely undiversified, unqualified, and soon diluted into Brazilian society, leaving no significant traces of its uniqueness.

The 1920 census indicates that there were 1,565,961 foreigners in Brazil. Of these, 558,405 were Italian, 433,577 Portuguese, and 219,142 Spanish. Of the Spaniards, 78.2 percent were settled in São Paulo at that time. Outside of this state, 60.2 percent of them preferred to live in the cities. Although not much information is available, in São Paulo the occupations chosen by the Spanish immigrants included quarrier, quarrier's assistant, driver, trolley conductor, worker, and day laborer. But, it is possible that the Spanish immigrant in other states was a merchant or artisan.

It is important to highlight that 78.1 percent of the Spaniards living in São Paulo in 1910 settled in the coffee-growing regions. And this means that 61 percent of all Spaniards in Brazil at the time lived in the São Paulo region, the quintessential coffee-growing area. In 1900, Spanish immigration in this state occupied three-quarters of the total immigration in Brazil. Among the foreigners arriving in São Paulo between 1908 and 1939, the Spaniards and Austrians were the most numerous: 50.9 percent and 51.8 percent of their respective total emigrations. The circulation of Spanish immigrants entering and leaving Brazil (through Argentina or Uruguay) was numerically significant. Thus, in the period between 1908 and 1926, 38,648 Spaniards arriving in Brazil came from Argentina or Uruguay (20.1 percent of the Spanish immigrants of the period). In compensation, during the same period, 44,991 Spaniards left São Paulo for Argentina or Uruguay (52 percent of the departures). Therefore, the flow clearly appears to have favored those two countries, especially Argentina.

As a general norm, as noted, the Basque immigrants reaching Brazil in the first third of the twentieth century devoted themselves to the coffee plantations, where they immediately entered into a debtor relationship with the *fazendeiro* (plantation owner). Advances and supplies of food and other means of subsistence tied them to these hacienda owners for several years.

In 1857, steamship service (Messageries Maritimes) was established between Bordeaux, Río de la Plata, and Rio de Janeiro. Of the 6,411 emigrants that left Bordeaux through this company, only 75 headed for Brazil.[120] Nevertheless, the French colony in this country numbered 592 in 1888 and 5,000 in 1915. The majority of them lived in the cities, working in commerce and industry, although there were exceptions of French Basques that established salting plants in the rural areas. Presently, and as a way of preserving the identity of the Basque immigration in Brazil, there are two Basque centers in the country.

Chapter Six

The Human Deluge to Río de la Plata

Uruguay, the Promised Land

Spain's interest in the Banda Oriental (east shore of Río de la Plata) of Uruguay had its roots in the foundation of Colonia del Sacramento by the Portuguese in 1680, directly across from Buenos Aires. The territory was virtually unpopulated, aside from a few thousand native Charrúa settled along the Atlantic side of the Uruguay River and Guaraní who lived in the converted Jesuit settlements far to the north of Río Negro. This sparseness of human population stood in sharp contrast with the abundance of cattle, introduced by Hernando Arias de Saavedra at the beginning of the seventeenth century. One century later there were millions of animals. The future Uruguay was then one immense prairie considered "lands of no profit" in spite of the great abundance of cattle. In the times of Colonia the animals roamed freely, reproducing at an astonishing rate and coopting the available rangeland. The seven cows and one bull taken to Paraguay in 1546 were the original stock from which thousands of head of cattle descended. The seven mares and seven stallions that were left by the original settlers of Buenos Aires reproduced in the same way. At the beginning of the nineteenth century, the cattle ranchers paid for the extermination of the overabundant animals, which damaged the fields. It was not uncommon to encounter droves of ten thousand wild horses. During the modern era, 800,000 hides were exported from Montevideo and Buenos Aires every year.

The first area of the Republic with cattle and horse herds appears to have been in the present-day district of Soriano. From Spain came herds of sheep and goats. Hacienda-building techniques were introduced from Jesuit missions to the districts of the northern Río Negro. The first governor of Montevideo and founder of the city, the Basque Bruno Mauricio de Zabala, took possession of the rural estates and distributed 1,600 head of sheep and cattle. He also stocked the Estancia del Rey that he had founded with 15,000 cows and 20,000 horses. Forty-four years later, when the Jesuits were expelled, they had two cattle breeding centers. One was located between Santa Lucía Grande and Chico, called Our Lady of the Forsaken. There, they had 60,000 head of livestock. The other center was between Pando and Solís Chico.

In 1757 in Uruguay, there were 102 *estancias* with 133,067 head of cattle, 124,788 mares and stallions, and 71,620 sheep. The Portuguese invasion decimated the livestock of the territory. Both the entire northern and eastern regions of Río Negro were left without a single cow. All of them were stolen and herded to Brazil. In 1819, however, with Portuguese dominance consolidated, the baron of La Laguna focused his attention on repopulating the Uruguayan countryside. In 1832 the first merino sheep, brought by Fernaux and Dample, were introduced into the country.

Spain decided to settle Montevideo in 1726 in order to isolate Colonia del Sacramento from the Portuguese Empire. In 1757, Maldonado was sent to reinforce the Atlantic coast. In the 1780s, Spain established other settlements, including Minas, Rocha, Melo, and Batoví, in the interior and on the east coast near the ill-defined border with Brazil. At the same time, the Spanish authorities accelerated the founding of settlements around the Cagancha and Santa Lucía Rivers as a defensive belt for Montevideo. Las Piedras, Canelones (Canelón), Pando, San José, Santa Lucía, Florida, and others were all located within the jurisdictional boundaries of Montevideo. They contributed to the formation of what would later be the most highly populated area of the country. On the southern coast, several spontaneous settlements, such as Víboras, Rosario, Dolores, and Mercedes, came into being.[1]

To the far north of the Río Negro were the missions of the Jesuits of the autonomous government of Yapeyú. In the few years immediately following Montevideo's founding in 1726, the missions already had about 37,000 inhabitants.[2] The city's founder, Bruno Mauricio de Zabala, had been born in Durango, Bizkaia. As a result, a good number of the first colonists whom he relied on were Basques. Zabala successfully built a network of confidants, the majority of whom were of Basque origin. Even at that very early date, an immigration process in the then-Banda Oriental of Uruguay was beginning. As will be seen, it would continue uninterrupted throughout the entire nineteenth century.[3]

Thus, the majority of the country was an open space occupied by only a few thousand indigenous people and some gauchos and Portuguese who worked hidden herds of cattle. Although Montevideo was originally founded for strategic reasons, it gradually gained importance as a hide-exporting center. Circumstances caused the revaluation of its already undeniable appeal as a natural port in the newly flourishing world of Río de la Plata. Between 1760 and 1780, the number of hides exported increased tenfold.[4] In 1785, the export of a new product—jerked beef—to Havana began. The abolition of Cádiz's commercial monopoly, and the potential for Montevideo to trade with other ports on both the American continent and the Iberian Peninsula, was facilitated by the Royal Document of Free Commerce (1778), which undoubtedly made it easier to export hides. They were the Banda Oriental's only clearly valuable commodity, if not for the authorities of the Crown, then at least for the merchants that established themselves in Montevideo in increasing numbers. The rapid reproduction of the livestock, combined with the growing Spanish demand for hides, initiated the process of the occupation of the lands, which enabled better animal husbandry and better control of exportation. What would later be the exploitation of livestock in every sense appeared at that moment. This process was characterized by a lack of complicated production techniques, given the automatic reproduction of the herds. It would later continue expanding in the form of the *estancia* system from the coast of Colonia (conquered in 1777) and Montevideo throughout most of the national territory, with the exception of significant areas.

The Basque colony established in eighteenth-century Uruguay was well aware of the aforementioned process. This is clear from a review of nearly one hundred wills of Basque colonists who had settled there. In most cases, they began working with little capital and few worldly possessions. They almost always finished their lives with enormous tracts of land and large herds of cattle. The meteoric acquisition of land and animals is also evident when one checks the high number of livestock brands and logos with Basque surnames that appear in the lists kept in the General Archive of the Nation in Montevideo. The Spanish colonial authorities demanded that proprietors submit their brands for legal approval. This was obviously done to avoid confusion and theft. The memorandum that Félix de Azara sent to Viceroy Aviles in 1801 could not have been clearer. He sought to defend the borders through the foundation of chapels and agricultural towns every twenty leagues.He also raised the possibility of systematic cattle breeding because of its high profitability.

By its very structure, the natural landscape of Río de la Plata could produce a high volume of livestock. This would become the dominant form of economic exploitation as a result of the demographic void that characterized Uruguayan territory in the times of Colonia del Sacramento. In 1797, according to the census conducted by Félix de Azara, Uruguay had but 29,985 inhabitants (almost 50,000 if the missions are taken into account). Of this total, 15,245—half of them—were settled in Montevideo, and 3,500 in Canelones. If the residents of Santa Lucía, Las Piedras, Pando, and San José, all within the jurisdiction of Montevideo, are included, 69 percent of the population at the dawn of independence was located in the capital city or its immediate vicinity. The jurisdiction of Maldonado contained 4,180 inhabitants.

In 1800 the marquis of Aviles, the progressive viceroy of Río de la Plata, issued two decrees facilitating the founding of towns and centers of colonization along the border with Brazil. This was because supporting the several unemployed families of Asturian, Galician, and Basque origin who lived in the area was expensive for the Royal Treasury. The marquis commissioned the naturalist Félix de Azara and captain Jorge Pacheco to enforce his decrees, which emphasized increasing livestock, agriculture, and commerce in a large unoccupied area of the viceroyalty. He also sought to eradicate the contraband traffic that occurred with complete impunity across the border with Brazil. Colonies and towns were founded in the present-day districts of Tacuarembó, Cerro Largo, Rivera, and Treinta y Tres by subdividing existing settlements. The goal was to promote the farming and ranching industry in the area by encouraging plowing of virgin land, the cultivation of grain, flax, and cotton, and the planting of fruit trees in the adjoining fields. This last action enabled the settlers to enclose the wild herds that they had to domesticate, facilitating their roundup. Two hatchets, one hoe, and one digging tool, called a *cavador*, were given to each settler.

Nevertheless, these steps did not achieve all of the desired results. Uruguay entered the nineteenth century with only 0.2 inhabitants per square kilometer. It was the emigration from Europe throughout the 1800s that would shape the present republic. The presence of the Basques in the northernmost districts of the country is evidenced by the trail of toponyms left by their settlements. In the district of Artigas, for example, there are towns with proper names such as Parada Artola, Tomás Gomensoro, and Javier de Viana. In connection with this same district, O. M. Arbiza studied the clearly significant presence of Basques from the time of Colonia del Sacramento, although his focus was on the nineteenth century.[5] There is a town called Villa Indart in the district of Rivera. The settlement of Peralta, in Durazno, is the namesake of one in Navarre. Algorta, in Río Negro, was named after the Bizkaian town.

Using wills and supporting documents, the author has followed the trail of Basques that began in the northern provinces of Uruguay and spread even to the south of Montevideo at the end of the eighteenth century and the beginning of the nineteenth. As with those arriving in Uruguay from other parts of Spain or Europe, the number of immigrants of this type that moved to spots outside of Montevideo was not high. Nevertheless, Basque immigration did reach a significant enough level to assist future waves. It is common to find in the wills of Basques who died in the last third of the nineteenth century far from Montevideo (but sometimes also in the capital) individuals who were born in the city, although their parents (or at least one of them) were born in a rural area of Uruguay at the beginning of the century. In turn, the grandparents of the testators were natives of the Basque Country. This convincingly demonstrates that some Basques from the first waves of immigrants chose to settle in open rural areas far away from the political center of Montevideo.

THE MIGRATORY VANGUARD

Uruguay began to receive immigrants in significant numbers beginning in the 1820s. In that decade, Basques from both sides of the Pyrenees (more so the French) began to settle in Uruguayan territories. Bordeaux, Bayonne, Pasaia, and Bilbao inaugurated what would later become a habit: serving as the waiting room for Basque immigration in America. The police records of Montevideo that have been preserved began to register immigrants beginning in 1831. Nevertheless, the existence of other, prior Basque settlements can be deduced from the reference made in these books to Basque friends and relatives that had previously arrived in Uruguay. Thus, for example, Antonio María Zubeldi, a forty-eight-year-old, single native of Oiartzun (Gipuzkoa) who had left via Bordeaux in the French brig *New Perseverance* and reached Montevideo on February 27, 1832, cited "having been called by the

Basque Yrazuyta," as his motive for entering the country. In addition, he would live with Yrazuyta, at least temporarily, in the Montevideo neighborhood of "El Cordón."[6] The same can be said of Josefa Zumarán, from Zalla (Bizkaia), a single woman who embarked in Bordeaux on the same ship as Zubeldi; she traveled to Montevideo "because she was called by her uncle Ramón de Zumarán."[7] Sergio de Arteagabeitia, a single young man of sixteen from Portugalete (Bizkaia)[8] on the same voyage, traveled to these foreign lands "called by his relative Ramón Artagabeitia to earn his livelihood." Juan Martín Ferrón, a twenty-four-year-old widower from Valcarlos (Navarre), saw the shores of Río de la Plata on the same day and from the same ship, arriving to "make his life" in the house of Domingo Ugalde.[9] The same reasons were repeated by Juan Hualde, a twenty-two-year-old bachelor also from Valcarlos, who went to join his brother Domingo Hualde.[10] And, lastly, Saturnino Balparda (from Santurtzi, Bizkaia) saw the shores of Río de la Plata for the first time on June 21, 1833, after several long, difficult days of travel on the French frigate *Caroline*. He was awaited in Montevideo by his uncle Esteban Balparda, with whom he "stayed and began to live with a view to prospering."[11]

By the 1820s there was already a relatively significant migratory current, of which little is known because the sources surviving into the present say almost nothing about it. Clearly, there existed the traditional "system of calls" as early as 1820–1830. It would be common during the rest of the nineteenth century and even into the twentieth. If an uncle or relative that had previously emigrated summoned someone from his family, it was because, logically, he had carefully assessed the economic possibilities of the area. If his economic initiatives had gone well, he would look for the support of his family, requesting by mail the company of some member to help him in his business tasks. If this occurred in 1832–1833, it was because in that decade and the preceding ones, the Basques Yrazuyta, Ramón de Zumarán, Ramon Artagabeitia, Domingo Ugalde, Domingo Hualde, and Esteban Balparda had begun a new life in the Republic of Uruguay.

These were clearly only isolated examples of what must have been common practice. What is known with certainty is that in 1832, agents of the English company Lafone and Wilson, "hooked" (recruit by persuasion) the Basques, along with Canary Islanders, to take them to Uruguay. In 1834 the numbers of settlers entering Uruguay were: Canary Islands, 640; Basque provinces, 597; Africa, 566; for a total of 1,803.[12] New, later contingents increased the numbers of Basque immigrants. The foundation of Villa del Cerro (later called Cosmópolis) in 1835 was in keeping with the aim at the time to shelter these first shipments of newly arrived colonists in a "controlled" way.

Basque immigration in Uruguay became very significant beginning in 1836. The French Basques would be the leaders in numbers, work capacity, and rapid social ascent. As a consequence, Montevideo began to grow in both its quantity of settlers and volume of construction. French store and hotel owners, English consignees, and Basque and Galician shopkeepers imposed a new rhythm of life upon the city. In 1838, agencies recruiting young emigrants to Río de la Plata were operating throughout the Basque Country. If anyone wishing to emigrate did not have enough money, they could seek instant credit in any embarkation office. In 1840, French emigration consisted mostly of the departure of Basque families. A similar assertion can be made for the Spanish Basque Country. In 1840, the deputy general of Gipuzkoa, the count of Monterron, recounted that many appeared in front of the authorities demanding passports. One year later, in front of the Legislature of Segura, the same deputy general stated the enormous danger that the large-scale emigration of its natives to Montevideo posed for the Basque Country.

Between 1835 and 1842, 33,131 Europeans disembarked in Montevideo. Of these, 6,400 French, mostly Basque and Béarnais, established businesses there in 1842. The newspaper *Le Patriote Français* placed the French population of the Uruguayan capital at 18,000 in 1841. Pierre Deffontaines estimates that 10,200 French Basques embarked for Uruguay between 1839 and 1842. The same author speaks of 14,000 individuals in the Basque colony of Montevideo that last year. The difficulty in approximating the Basque presence in Uruguay in this first phase of Basque immigration is great. The existing books that registered the arrival of the European colonists sometimes do not state the individual's nationality, or simply list it as "French" or "Spanish." The researcher must therefore, with a certain degree of error, determine the Basqueness of the immigrants by their last names and ports of departure. This procedure, the only one available in spite of all potential objections, permits a glimpse of a Basque immigration that was numerically significant as follows:[13]

Nationality	No.
Canary Islanders	4,527
French from the Basque Country	7,734
French from other provinces	983
Germans	327
Sardinians	5,598
Spaniards from Europe	9,079
Total	28,248

A comparative analysis of French and Spanish Basque immigration between 1831 and 1851 does not yield overwhelming differences. The First Carlist War occurred between 1833 and 1839; so the number of Spanish Basque emigrants must have been significant. The horrors of war, together with the resulting misery in the Basque region and the offers made by the emigrant contract agencies must have had an effect on many young Basques wishing to avoid, at any cost, a war that they did not believe in. As the Montevideo police records are far from including all those who landed on the Uruguayan shores during this period, and given the lack of other documentary sources, the predominant thesis of all the researchers (from both Río de la Plata and the Basque Country) appears the soundest one. It is believed that in the first arrivals of Basque immigrants in Uruguay, the French Basques were the most numerous and those who attained the highest levels of social triumph. This is also the theory of William Douglass and Jon Bilbao. In any case, the migratory movement of Basques to Río de la Plata was so significant in 1842 that it had already caught the attention of contemporary writers: "They bring and preserve their customs and form a small world. They have their own places for diversion, such as pool halls, cafes, etc. They generally speak both French and Spanish since their region of origin is in both countries. Many have become very rich within the space of a few years due to the great demand for the houses they build in the upper part of the city." [14]

In 1843, the Basques owned the majority of the hotels in Montevideo. In the siege that this city suffered during the Great War (1838–1851), a group of members of the liberal and business professions of French Basque origin decided to organize in defense of their interests, offering their services to the local authorities. They were called the "French Legion." In December 1842, the first two presidents general of Uruguay, José Fructuoso Rivera and Manuel Oribe, faced each other in the Battle of Arroyo Grande. The defeated Rivera barricaded himself within Montevideo. Oribe pursued him and laid siege to the city for 3,201 days (almost nine years), from February 1843 to October 1851. Oribe had the support of Buenos Aires, while Rivera was backed by France, England, and European volunteers.

In February 1843, the foreigners living in Montevideo registered to defend the city. Thus the above-mentioned French Legion was born, with abundant Basque participation. In 1845, it had 3,819 armed men. In 1846 a special corps called the "Basque Hunters" was created. All the leaders and officers were Basque. They were under the command of Juan Bautista Brie, from Saint-Jean-Pied-de-Port. But the Spanish Basques also formed a military corps, in the service of General Oribe. The Bizkaian Ramón de Artagabeitia (born in Santurtzi in 1796), who had emigrated when he was eighteen (in 1814), organized the Battalion of Volunteers. This group was joined by many Spanish Basques working for the "Oribista" cause. Lieutenant Colonel Artagabeitia initially had four hundred followers made up of "the best of the Carlist youth that the peninsula dispatched beyond the seas." This battalion was dissolved three days before the signing of the peace of October 8, 1851, that put an end to the Great War. The corps no longer had a reason for being; the war was over and the Bizkaian had to return to his private business: the maritime company that operated out of the port of Buceo (Montevideo).

In the opinion of J. Giralt, more than 15,000 Basques commanded by leaders and officers who were both Basques and Creoles participated in the Great War. The

Basque immigration was so important at the end of the 1840s that the following verse became popular:

> Quien quiera hablar en francés
> en catalán, en vascongado
> todo idioma enrevesado
> y que no sepa quién es
> y hallarse en un entremés
> en un extraño museo
> vaya hoy a Montevideo.[15]

> Whoever wants to speak in French,
> in Catalan, in Basque,
> or any other backwards language
> and does not know who he is,
> to find himself between acts in a comedy
> in a strange museum,
> let him go today to Montevideo.

In 1850, Basque emigration from Spain had also reached significant levels. It was such that, in the official bulletins, the provincial authorities reminded the captains and ship outfitters who made the American run of their obligation not to transport anyone whose passport was not in order. Figures given on French Basques emigrating to Río de la Plata for the years 1848–1850 are: in 1848, 672; in 1849, 1,012; and in 1850, 1,087.[16] The characteristics and behavior of Basque emigration from Iparralde to Uruguay in the nineteenth century are analyzed in more detail below.

It was not until the law of July 27, 1791, that France organized a general census. After the ordinance of January 16, 1882, the population would be counted every five years (see table 6.1).[17]

The distribution between urban and rural population for the period from 1846 to 1936 is shown in table 6.2.[18]

And from 1836 to 1936 the population of Basque rural cantons in France decreased as follows:

Rural Cantons	Amount of Decrease
Bidache	10,823
Espelette	8,458
Hasparren	10,304
Iholdy	9,565
Labastide-Clairence	7,915
Mauléon	14,280
Saint-Étienne-de-Baïgorry	13,007
Saint-Jean-Pied-de-Port	11,870

Rural Cantons	Amount of Decrease
Saint-Palais	16,207
Tardets	10,775
Ustaritz	8,965
Total	122,169

TABLE 6.1 *Population in the Basses-Pyrénées and France, 1801–1936*

Census Year	Basses-Pyrénées	France
1801	355,573	28,250,000
1811	383,502	—
1821	399,474	31,161,000
1831	428,401	33,218,000
1836	446,398	34,240,000
1841	451,683	34,911,000
1846	457,732	36,097,000
1851	446,997	36,472,000
1856	436,442	36,714,000
1861	436,628	37,386,000
1866	435,486	38,067,000
1872	426,700	37,653,000
1876	431,525	38,438,000
1881	434,366	39,239,000
1886	432,999	39,783,000
1891	423,572	39,946,000
1896	423,572	40,158,000
1901	426,347	40,681,000
1906	425,817	41,067,000
1911	433,318	41,479,000
1921	402,981	39,210,000
1926	444,556	40,744,000
1931	422,719	41,835,000
1936	413,411	41,907,000

Source: Based on data from H. de Charnisay, 1996, 106.

TABLE 6.2 *Urban and Rural Population Distribution in the Basses-Pyrénées and France, 1846–1936*

	Urban Population		
Year	B.-Pyrénées	France	Difference
1846	16.30	24.40	−8.10
1856	11.11	27.31	−16.20
1872	20.81	31.06	−10.23
1886	23.72	35.95	−13.23
1891	25.50	37.40	−11.90
1911	31.00	44.20	−13.20
1921	32.60	46.30	−13.70
1931	36.60	51.20	−14.60
1936	36.90	52.40	−15.50

	Rural Population		
Year	B.-Pyrénées	France	Difference
1846	83.70	75.60	+8.10
1856	84.89	72.69	+16.20
1872	79.19	68.94	+10.25
1886	76.28	64.05	+13.23
1891	74.50	62.60	+11.90
1911	69.00	55.80	+13.20
1921	67.40	53.70	+13.70
1931	63.40	48.80	+14.60
1936	63.10	47.60	+15.50

Source: Based on data from H. de Charnisay, 1996, 107.

The number of marriages for each 10,000 inhabitants (1801–1900) is shown in table 6.3. And the mortality is given in table 6.4.

In light of these statistics, it can be affirmed that during the nineteenth century the birth rate was much higher than the death rate in the Basses-Pyrénées, as seen in table 6.5.

From 1800 to 1914 there was a surplus in births of almost 200,000, of which 117,000 (59 percent) occurred from 1801 to 1850. The migratory surplus[19] from 1836 to 1901 is shown in table 6.6.

The population of the Basses-Pyrénées passed through three phases during the nineteenth century:[20]

1. From 1801 to 1846. The surplus births from these years (above the mean in France) were due to the high fecundity of the women of the region, as well as to a mortality rate well below the mean. Both elements are characteristic of a society with a young population. The very low marriage rate was due to the fact that numerous youths, with insufficient means, would remain in their parental home without being able to change their civil status. This would also explain the high number of illegitimate children around 1846. Likewise, the statistics from this period indicate that from 1836 to 1846 there was a significant level of emigration that had been evident since 1832. The authors Pierre Lhande and M. Etcheverry speak of 828 departures (a mean of 208 per year) between 1832 and 1835, and of 10,162 between 1836 and 1845, or a yearly average of 1,016.
2. From 1846 to 1872. The surplus of births decreased, falling below the mean. Compared to the previous period, the marriage rate was slightly higher, fecundity lower, and mortality higher. On one hand, the significant increase in mortality seems to prove that this emigration was recruited among the younger population. On the other, the increase in the number of marriages and the drop in fecundity indicate that the emigrants were largely young and recently married.
3. From 1872 to 1901. The surplus of births in the Department of the Basses-Pyrénées again became important, and although less than its prior level, it exceeded the country's mean. In absolute numbers, marriage, fecundity, and mortality decreased during this period. The department would continue favoring emigration with significant figures until 1841, decreasing thereafter.

But, how many residents of the French Department of the Basses-Pyrénées[21] left their homeland to emigrate to America? In the opinion of contemporaries, a significant number decided to migrate. Thus, Picamilh says that from 1832 to 1858, 35,000 emigrants from the Atlantic Pyrenees went to America, 29,000 of whom had passports. Etcheverry speaks of 61,847 overseas departures between 1832 and 1881, and of 79,262 emigrants to South America between 1832 and 1897. Butel places the number of departures for South America from 1847 to 1872 at 64,000. Chandeze believes that 61,248 passengers embarked for South America between 1857 and 1891. And Levasseur says that there were 15,474 emigrants to South America between 1880 and 1869. The most reliable data for the twentieth century has been provided by Lefebvre, who estimates that 19,146 emigrants left the department between 1897 and 1921. This therefore represents a considerable decrease relative to the figures from the nineteenth century.[22]

Barrère states that 6,912 Basque men and 1,635 Basque women (a four-to-one male-female ratio) left Iparralde for America from January 1, 1831, to December 31, 1841.[23] (See tables 6.7 and 6.8.) The Farming Association of the Basses-Pyrénées, the Farming Committee of Orthez, the Farming Chamber of Bayonne, that of Oloron, and all the bodies consulted were unanimous in deploring emigration as a cause of rural depopulation. Table 6.9 is sufficiently illustrative of this rural depopulation. In fewer than forty years, 12,393 farms had disappeared. These statistics confirm the thesis of M. Etcheverry that emigration was more prevalent among small property owners.

From 1835 to 1842, 13,765 French immigrants arrived in Uruguay, most of them from the region of the Basses-Pyrénées. France was the country with the most emigrants in Uruguay (41.58 percent) at the time. Next came Italy (32.97 percent), followed by Spain (27.70 percent). In 1850, the flow turned to Buenos Aires, which began to receive four of every five immigrants. In 1866, the French Uruguayan diaspora constituted only 16.48 percent of immigrants in the country. The Spanish was 33.54 percent and the Italian 33.13 percent. England was last with 4.51 percent.

Basque emigration from Iparralde to America began in 1825, but took place especially after 1832. It acquired real significance due to the activity of the emigration agents. The first emigrants went to Río de la Plata, especially Uruguay. This initial migratory current suffered a reversal between 1836 and 1838 due to Río de la Plata's internal political problems. But the number of departures increased again in 1840 and 1841, when whole families would sell their modest patrimonies to head to Mon-

TABLE 6.3 *Marriages in the Basses-Pyrénées and France, 1801–1900 (per 10,000 Inhabitants)*

Years	B.-Pyrénées	France	Difference
1801–10	290	320	−30
1811–20	280	310	−30
1821–30	270	310	−40
1831–40	260	290	−30
1841–50	247	274	−27
1851–60	245	255	−10
1861–70	256	258	−2
1871–80	261	254	+7
1881–90	243	239	+4
1891–1900	225	221	+4

Source: Based on data from H. de Charnisay, 1996, 111.

TABLE 6.4 *Mortality Rates in the Basses-Pyrénées and France, 1801–1900 (per 10,000 Inhabitants)*

Years	B.-Pyrénées	France	Difference
1801–10	230	280	−50
1811–20	200	260	−60
1821–30	210	240	−30
1831–40	210	247	−37
1841–50	209	233	−24
1851–60	233	237	−4
1861–70	216	225	−9
1871–80	213	236	−23
1881–90	207	221	−14
1891–1900	197	215	−18

Source: Based on data from H. de Charnisay, 1996, 111.

TABLE 6.5 *Surplus Births in the Basses-Pyrénées, 1800–1910*

Years	Surplus Births	Annual Mean
1800–1821	52,250	2,612
1822–1845	61,700	2,468
1846–1880	38,500	1,100
1881–1901	25,035	1,206
1901–1910	19,065	1,906

Source: Based on data from H. de Charnisay, 1996, 112.

tevideo, Chile, or Mexico. Nevertheless, Algeria also began to compete with the New World for two reasons:

1. The campaign of the authorities and the press indicating better salaries for French labor that went to North Africa
2. The free trip, paid for by the state shipping companies

Beginning in 1849, Buenos Aires overtook Montevideo as the main destination. From 1850 on, Río de la Plata became the main center of attraction for emigration

TABLE 6.6 *Migratory Surplus in the Basses-Pyrénées, 1836–1901*

Years	Surplus
1836–1841	4,959
1841–1846	6,711
1846–1851	14,502
1851–1856	12,093
1856–1861	3,804
1861–1866	9,723
1866–1872	9,895
1872–1876	6,374
1876–1881	7,143
1881–1886	9,301
1886–1891	13,041
1891–1896	5,802
1896–1901	4,920

Source: Based on data from H. de Charnisay, 1996, 112.

from Iparralde. This zone would receive 73 percent of the diaspora, with three of every four French Basques going to the capital of Argentina.

The discovery of new gold mines in California and the spread of steamship travel encouraged a certain number of emigrants to go to that territory from 1872 on. Around 1890, Argentina went through a serious economic crisis that would divert emigration from Iparralde toward new, burgeoning territories like California and Nevada in the United States, Canada, and Chile.

URUGUAYAN IMMIGRATION AT MID-CENTURY

In the beginning of the 1850s, Uruguay initiated an immigration process that would attempt to attract capital and abundant, cheap, and efficient labor. The Basques would play an important role in this process of massive immigration. Beginning in 1850, Basque immigration in Río de la Plata numbered thousands of people a year. It reached such a level that in 1852 the bishop of Pamplona, Severo Andriani, exhorted his parishioners to discard their favorable attitude toward emigration, which, in his own words, was already attracting numerous people. In 1855, the French government established a commission to control both emigration and emigrant re-

TABLE 6.7 *Emigration from Iparralde to America, 1831–1841*

District Population	Name	First series from January 1, 1831, to December 31, 1835		Second series from January 1, 1836, to December 31, 1841		Combined Sexes
		Male	Female	Male	Female	Total
13,868	Mauléon	254	6	665	353	1,278
13,471	Saint-Étienne	267	2	804	262	1,335
12,422	St.-Jean-Pied-de-Port	154	1	431	104	690
16,003	Saint-Palais	168	2	472	123	765
10,594	Tardets	81	3	173	69	326
10,108	Hasparren	163	4	551	97	815
7,750	Labastide-Clairence	47	1	112	37	197
9,343	Iholdy	86	36	343	144	609
11,095	Bayonne (east)	80	1	181	72	334
16,293	Bayonne (west)	155	2	485	114	756
10,821	Bidache	39	0	154	18	211
8,886	Espelette	45	1	104	32	182
12,921	Saint-Jean-de-Luz	145	3	503	91	742
9,475	Ustaritz	64	0	186	57	307
163,050	Total	1,748	62	5,164	1,573	8,547

Source: E. Barrère, *Emigration à Montévidéo*, 1842.

TABLE 6.8 *Emigration from Iparralde to America by Occupation*

District Name	Population	Peasants (47.7%)	Artisans (17.8%)	Workers (12.6%)	Some Education (5%)
Mauléon	13,868	661	211	45	2
Saint-Étienne	13,471	614	158	269	30
St.-Jean-Pied-de-Port	12,422	366	109	52	58
Saint Palais	16,003	438	154	35	13
Tardets	10,594	89	70	78	17
Hasparren	10,108	333	254	97	30
Labastide Clairence	7,750	56	35	63	5
Iholdy	9,343	355	84	157	13
Bayonne (east)	11,095	136	88	12	25
Bayonne (west)	16,293	358	79	98	105
Bidache	10,821	71	81	25	16
Espelette	8,886	90	26	19	14
St.-Jean-de-Luz	12,921	344	99	112	93
Ustaritz	9,475	170	54	15	11
Total	163,050	4,081	1,502	1,077	432

Source: E. Barrère, *Emigration à Montévidéo,* 1842.

TABLE 6.9 Rural Depopulation of Iparralde Between 1856 and 1892

Category	1856	1892	Difference
Small landowners	64,831	53,825	−11,006
Sharecroppers	13,917	11,028	−2,889
Farmers	2,876	4,378	1,502
Total	81,264	69,231	−12,393

Source: Based on data from H. de Charnisay, 1996, 117.

cruitment in the Basque Country. The members of the commission affirmed that "in some towns the farms had to be abandoned due to lack of workers." And from 1850 on the practice of keeping the family patrimony intact through the emigration to the Americas of those not lucky enough to inherit it was institutionalized in the Basque Country (both Spanish and French). Whole families went to the New World for such reasons. The disentailment measures under the debt-reduction policies of Mendizábal and Madoz, which resulted in the enclosure of the common lands, were the drop that made the migratory glass overflow.

Traditionally, the use of the commons had been an important resource in the local economy of the Basque Country. Its enclosure, combined with the active Uruguayan pro-immigration campaign, provides a coherent explanation for this first mass arrival of Basque immigrants in Uruguay in the second half of the nineteenth century. This was further strengthened by the cultural affinities between the Basque Country and the small, new Río de la Plata country. Then there was the fact that in 1726 Bruno Mauricio de Zabala (a Bikaian) founded the city of Montevideo. Various families, of Gipuzkoan origin and some related to Zabala, began colonizing that corner of the American continent in the first third of the eighteenth century. Here was the original familial nucleus of Basque expansion throughout Uruguayan territory. The expansion would continue uninterrupted throughout the nineteenth century. In the case of French Basques, once the sociocultural baseline was established by the first immigrants, affinity with them sustained the immigratory momentum through the nineteenth century. In addition, the boom of the French maritime companies, whose most important ports of departure were concentrated in Bordeaux, Bayonne, and Pauillac, serviced a constant exchange of cultural ambassadors, consuls, architects, industrialists, artists, scientists and other passengers.

This all coincided with a period of enormous French importance in the international sphere. The second half of the nineteenth century would witness the "Frenchification" of Uruguay, a country dazzled by French culture. In 1850, the traveler Xavier Marmier observed of Montevideo: "The city is constructed around the port, in the form of a peninsula that advances toward the river. Memories of France are brought back, in the flags in the stores, in the art shop windows, in the restaurants, in the cafés, as well as in the houses of the old Creole families."[24]

Between 1850 and 1870 the French stamp on the country was evident in all Montevidean architectural and social activity. Engineers and architects from France remodeled the city, working either alone or with Italian and English colleagues. They built the port area using European techniques and styles. They mapped out the new neighborhoods that would be built to the east once the Spanish colonial fortifications were destroyed. They put up new, sumptuous buildings such as the palace of the government, the new market, the university, and the Solis Theater. This influence was so prevalent in the city that in 1895 a Swiss traveler, Edouard Montet, described Montevideo as a beautiful European city, in both its general appearance and its customs, buildings, and lifestyle.

French culture found a masterful means of expanding its influence through the press. The first newspapers published in French were short-lived: *L'Echo* released only fourteen issues in 1839; *L'Epoque*, four in 1840. *Le Messager Français* existed for only two years (1840–1842); *Le Moniteur* published thirty-four issues in 1842. *Le Courrier de la Plata* produced 428 between 1847 and 1849. *Le Messager de Montevideo* existed between 1850 and 1851. *Le Patriote Français* had a printing of 2,645 issues between February 1843 and December 1850. In 1863, *Le Progres* appeared and *Le Courrier de la Plata* reappeared. With all this, it makes sense that the French Basques emigrating to Uruguay during the period in question would find favorable conditions and guidelines for integrating into Uruguayan society. From the moment that they disembarked until the time that they put their professional and social lives in order, their culture's stability in the country made it easier for them to accomplish that for which they had traveled so far: making the Americas. Upon entering Montevideo, many new arrivals had the impression that they were in another corner of their own country due to its architectural appearance, modeled with plans, cement, and bricks of French architects and artists.

In the decade of the 1860s, Basque emigration was abundant, judging by the constant calls for its control in the Basque Country. In 1860, the Deputation General of the Seigneury of Bizkaia informed emigrants of the exploitation awaiting those that left their homes. In 1862, in the face of constant disregard, Bizkaian Civil Governor Vicente Uhagón once again reminded ship outfitters and captains of the legal norms regulating the number of passengers and emigrants on the ships that usually made the crossing from the Basque Country to South America. In other words, more passengers and emigrants than permitted were always transported secretly. In 1868, the Deputation General of Tolosa released a circular in which it attested to the disagreeable spectacle of the growing emigration of both sexes to the remote regions of the New World. Uruguay was included among them. In 1868, the Basque religious authorities became concerned about the lack of spiritual attention provided to those that had emigrated to the other side of the ocean.[25] In 1869, during a visit to Uruguay, the English Reverend Murray spoke of the large Basque colony located in that republic. "I have seen," he said, "thousands of men of all ages who have come from the Basque provinces of France and Spain. They are tenacious and hardworking, they are all doing well. One can see two or three Basques stopped on the corner of every block with their hemp sandals and a small bag over their shoulders ready to be hired to transport loads."

The interest of the Uruguayan authorities in increasing the number of Basque immigrants seems clearly reflected in the report that the official consul of Uruguay in Gasteiz, Julián Quiroga, sent to his country's government on October 25, 1873. In this report, the virtues and qualities possessed by the Basques and their potential interest in being settlers in that republic were weighed and praised.[26] In Quiroga's opinion, the following were the conditions that made the Basques appropriate immigrants for the Republic of Uruguay:

1. Good knowledge of the Spanish language
2. Almost perfect capacity to perform farming and livestock tasks, which most Basques practiced since childhood
3. A strong, robust, apt constitution for hard work
4. Mastery in quarry work and stone polishing
5. Predisposition of the women to kitchen and table tasks
6. The sobriety, mildness, and excellent moral habits of the Basques

The Uruguay government promoted and stimulated immigration by any means within its reach. This immigration continued to grow, as is shown by the largely fruitless attempts to control the departure of natives of the Basque Country by its authorities between 1860 and 1875. As losers of the Second Carlist War (1872–1876), many Basques sought asylum in Uruguay. In 1887, the defeated pretender Charles VII of Bourbon was reunited in Montevido with a large group of Carlist emigrants to whom he gave an emotional speech.

THE TRAMPOLINE OF THE DIASPORA

The judgments expressed by Bizkaian Civil Governor Manuel García Aguilar in 1880 indicate how emigration followed its bullish course. The governor ordered all Bizkaian mayors to inform young people of the inconveniences of emigration to the South American republics (read: Uruguay and Argentina) that so damaged the seigneury's economy. The same occurred in 1881. In 1882, the same arguments were repeated in the face of the increasing outflow. The circular published in 1883 by the vice president of the Deputation of Bizkaia, Luis de Villabaso, in an attempt to contain the Basque diaspora headed for Uruguay, did not stem the growing tide.

In 1897, clandestine emigration continued to be the norm, causing the Basque authorities to attempt to prevent, or at least channel, the departure of hundreds of Basques for Uruguayan shores.

The growth experienced by Montevideo during the last third of the nineteenth century was prompted by the constant demand for labor, one the Basques quickly sought to fill. While the arrival of immigrants during the years prior to 1876 had always been high, their number increased beginning that year. The investments in Uruguayan real estate initiated economic processes that brought immediate multiplier effects in the work force, railway construction, telegraphs, urban infrastructural services (gas, running water), and, later, trolleys to Montevideo. As a result, a previously unknown labor pool was required. The financial services, led especially by banks with French and English capital, contributed to this economic expansion. As a consequence, Uruguay was more directly connected to the world market and able to export a greater quantity of products from its primary sector. The demand for workers caused by this process was filled in good part by Basque immigrants. These immigrants devoted themselves to commercial and industrial activity in the capital, as had become the norm. Thus, for example, Basques that established businesses in Montevideo from 1860 to 1878 (those the author has been able to collect information about),[27] invested their capital in the enterprises listed in table 6.10.

As can be verified, it was the activities related to hostelry (bars, inns, and pool halls) as well as department stores and general stores (that is, matters of buying and selling), followed by the carpentry shops, that most attracted the Basque investors. Nevertheless, in the interior of the country, Basques worked in the primary sector, as well as providing, in the case of women, much of the domestic service.

The primary activities tended to occupy some 40–45 percent of the workforce in Uruguay's rural areas. But, the difference between the more modern departments such as Flores, Soriano, and Colonia, and those less so, like Rocha and Canelones, is clear. In each of the first three, livestock breeding thrived, but an important and exceptional movement of Basque colonists appeared only in Colonia, endowing this department with a more advanced farming and ranching infrastructure. In Rocha and Canelones, where the Basque presence was less, a process of subdivision of lands became noticeable, even unto *minifundia*, surely decreasing production levels. As already indicated, in the last third of the century, throughout the Uruguayan countryside, day laborers and servants were abundant, the product of the poor functioning of the capitalist market. The constant high number of tenant farmers on the *estancias* indicates as much. In the departments in which modernization was late in arriving (Rocha, Canelones, and Cerro Largo), this number was even higher; the most common among the more legal ways of making a living for Basque day laborers were seasonal: sheepshearing and harvesting. Aside from these activities, Basque immigrants worked as day laborers in herding, fencing, grape harvesting,

TABLE 6.10 *Basque Businesses in Montevideo, 1860–1878*

Business Type	Percent
Pulpería*	10.1
Department store	8.5
General store	7.03
Blacksmith shop	6.2
Inn	5.4
Pool hall	4.6
Carpenter shop	4.6
Cafe	3.9
Liquor store	3.9
Coalyard	3.9
Brick oven	3.9
Sandalmaker	2.3
Corn storehouse	2.3
Bakery	2.3
Barbershop	2.3
Fruit and drink stand	2.3
Tailor shop	1.5
Cigarette shop	1.5
Dairy	1.5
Pottery	1.5
Jewelry maker	1.5
Money changer	1.5
Others**	17.47

* A pulpería was equivalent to a modern-day bar, although it also served as a grocery store. It was a meeting place for men like any other tavern, but where everything could be bought.
** Haberdashery, slaughterhouse, butcher shop, bookstore, grain storehouse, toy store, soap factory, hardware store, shoemaker, hotel, restaurant, broom and featherduster shop, dance academy, candymaker, and public bathhouse.
Source: Based on data from Montévidéo Police Books (AGN).

cartage, firewood cutting, and the performance of small tasks referred to as *changas* on the outskirts of the towns. The women worked as servants and cooks.

The significant number of Basque day laborers at the end of the century in both the capital city and the interior suggests that there was a labor surplus whose employment possibilities varied greatly by location. In Montevideo their occupations were connected to the urban economy, while in the interior the best possibilities for employment were limited to the sheepshearing months. For many Basque emigrants who made their life in the wide open Uruguayan countryside, this might have been their only work during the whole year. The Basque colony saw how the process of fencing in fields, beginning in 1871, with the aim of enclosing sheep, had negative repercussions on the labor market for the wage-earning immigrant workers who devoted themselves to the tasks described above.

Given the lack of opportunity some Basques settled in Uruguay apparently decided to emigrate to Argentina in 1875, 1876, and 1877 in search of a better life. The crisis that befell the country in 1890 also had negative (although only temporary) repercussions for the reception of new Basque immigrants. In general, in spite of these "bad years," the process of land acquisition followed its normal course from the 1870s to the 1890s. Analysis of the departments of Durazno, Colonia, Florida, Soriano, Salto, and Cerro Largo demonstrates this. The most systematic purchase of lands was made in the first three.

Again based on wills and testaments, the author has traced the movements of the Basque immigrants that arrived in the 1860s or 1870s. When they made out their wills, about the end of the century, these generally reflected a continuous and slow process of acquiring land throughout the last third of the 1800s. It can be observed, however, that complaints of "bad times for farming and ranching businesses" tended to appear in the mid-1870s. The same occurred at the beginning of the 1890s, although the number of cases was not very significant. Those that truly suffered from the enclosure of fields and the cyclic downward surges of Uruguay's economy appear to have been the immigrant wage earners.

Basque immigration in Uruguay in the last third of the century is difficult, if not impossible, to quantify. First, because records of immigrant entries were not kept. Second, because many persons arrived secretly, with no passport or paper to legally certify their presence in the country. All estimates (always approximate) made to date have been in Iparralde by authors who were contemporaries of the emigrants. Data is sporadic, their parameters local and often inconsistent.

In Spain, there are no figures, not even estimates, about the quantity of Spanish Basques that left their homes to go to Uruguay. The data suggested in Iparralde follow: from 1847 to 1862, twenty thousand passports were expedited for Montevideo and Buenos Aires in the Department of the Basses-Pyrénées. In many cases, a document expedited in the name of the head of the family was used to conceal the departure of others, sometimes the whole family employing the passport.

Louis Etcheverry estimates that French Basque and Béarnais emigrants between 1832 and 1884 numbered seventy-five thousand. Pierre Lhande believes that French Basque emigration between 1832 and 1907 was one hundred thousand people, an enormous figure for a region with a population of around 120,000 inhabitants at century's end. Although net population growth was the salient characteristic of the four Spanish Basque provinces during the nineteenth century, many rural towns suffered a considerable population loss. This loss is reflected in table 6.11, which includes five Bizkaian towns with a long tradition of overseas migration.

Beyond a doubt, the population decrease in these towns was due to emigration. In Echalar (Navarre), for example, the local documentation shows a total of 1,381 inhabitants in the town in 1880; 142 had gone to Argentina, 54 went to France, 37 to Cuba, 16 to Uruguay, 6 to California, and 1 to Brazil. This pattern was also common in other towns of the Basque Country.

THE MAINTENANCE OF SOCIOCULTURAL FEATURES

In 1854, a Basque religious order, the congregation of the Betharramites, became concerned about the lack of suitable church attendance among the Basque population disseminated in the Río de la Plata. In fewer than five years, this order established thirty missions in the interior of Uruguay and Argentina. In 1858, the Basques of Montevideo built their own church. During the second half of the nineteenth century, the continuous immigration of Basques in the republics of Río de la Plata and the appearance of a Basque population born in the New World accentuated the need for formal ethnic organizations. In 1876, two dozen Basques founded the Laurak Bat association in Montevideo. This center of brotherhood of Basque immigration focused on poor Basques (even providing them return passage if they wished). It also provided legal assistance to those that had been caught in the many pitfalls of Uruguayan civil life. Laurak Bat founded a school and library for children of Basque descent.

The formal ethnic organization provided the structure for the type of collective action that would be required to celebrate festivities with full pomp. Thus, in 1889, the immigrants living in Montevideo celebrated the fourth anniversary of the founding of the Laurak Bat center with a festival that lasted two days, with thirty thousand participants. The importance of the Basque colony at the time is demonstrated by the fact that in attendance were various Uruguayan government ministers and other notables of Montevideo, as well as the ambassadors from the United States, Spain, and Chile. In 1881, the Basque center began to publish a newspaper of the same name (*Laurak Bat*).

The new mentality imposed by the foreigners, among whom the Basques occupied an important place, greatly contributed to the configuration of the Uruguayan upper class. It was predominantly foreign, and included only a few native families. Replacing traditional economic models, the wealthy immigrants guided the coun-

TABLE 6.11 *Resident Population Loss in Five Bizkaian Towns*

Town Name	Population in 1860s	Population in 1920s	Population with Residence Rights	Net Population Decrease from 1860 to 1920
Billaro	912	792	865	−120
Kortezubi	808	786	879	−22
Mendata	1,153	1,006	1,119	−147
Nabarriz	655	606	647	−49
Gizaburuaga	1,419	1,116	1,297	−303

Source: C. Echegaray, 1918, 790, 797, 828, 877, 879, 899.

try toward modernization. The direct descendants of these oligarchs tended to abandon farming and sometimes industrial activities for the typical professions of the liberal classes. The legal profession, which best served the interests of the upper class, was the most prevalent. At the same time, there was a degree of intellectualism in this social group that was the product of their university education and politicization. Thus, this generation experienced clear transformation in its near-total integration into the new society. The wills and testaments consulted are quite clear that inheritance be divided equally among all children, following contemporary Uruguayan civil law. The traditional Basque system, according to which only one descendant was named as heir, was thus abandoned. All the wills studied by the author indicated the division of all property belonging to the deceased into equal parts for all children and/or heirs. If one spouse survived the other, the entire inheritance was settled upon the survivor until his or her death. The children then entered the picture as equal heirs.

Other data of interest concerns marriages. Of the 1,829 male biographies consulted, the name of the spouse or descendants is mentioned in only 670. Of these, 44.8 percent married Basque women and 55.2 percent non-Basque women. In a thorough, well-researched study, Professors Margarita Arlas and Marta Oficialdegui[28] analyze seventy-one Montevideo weddings from 1853 in which the engaged couple or the witnesses were Basque. The authors take the marriage dossiers of the city's curia as their sample. Of the total, 47 (72.13 percent) were marriages between Basques from Iparralde, with witnesses almost always of the same origin. There were two marriages between Spanish Basques (3.08 percent), and five between a French Basque and a Spanish Basque (7.69 percent). Eight unions between a Basque from either side of the Pyrenees and an individual of another nationality are documented (12.31 percent).

The migratory tendency of groups of relatives or neighbors from the same hometown seems clear. Many of the witnesses thus stated that they knew the participants in the Old Country. They said that their friendships dated from infancy, or that they had been neighbors. A member of one of the two families tends to appear among the witnesses. Others, in contrast, state that they met each other in Río de la Plata. To be more concrete, 59 percent of the parties to matrimony knew each other in their native country and came from around the area of Bayonne and Baïgorry, or the center of the Basque Pyrenees (Bigorre). Eight percent even made the trip to South America together. Twenty-three percent of the witnesses were relatives, and 12 percent of them met the participants in Montevideo. This clearly indicates strong migratory links, marked endogamy, and strong ties of friendship in the country of destination, with maintenance of customs and traditions within the ethnic group.

Many of the recent arrivals headed for the De Beauzmont Hotel on Cerrito Street (187), the Du Commerce on Piedras (89), the De París on 25 de Mayo (244), Julián Guijonets's Good Soup Inn on Andes (163), or the Nogués Inn and Cafe on Juncal (8) in search of lodging. Or, they went to some tenement house in the Old Town, where some acquaintance might have previously found lodging. For those who said that they met each other "here" (in Uruguay), the meeting places would without doubt have been one of the following:

1. Esteban Aredi's Handball Court on 18 de Julio (183)
2. Francisco Calamet's Handball Court on Rincón (212)
3. Pedro Leclairc's French Candy Store on Treinta y Tres (63)
4. Plácido Conrrard's Paris Candy Store on Treinta y Tres (88)
5. Juan Barot's French Candy Store on 25 de Agosto (47)
6. J. Martínez's De la Nobleza Vascongada Cigarette Store on Misiones (58)
7. Eugenio Echarte's Eastern Cigarette Store on Rincón (246)
8. José Suberos's Cafe and Pool Hall
9. José Devern's Cafe and Pool Hall in the Central Market
10. Martín Casenave's Solís Cafe and Pool Hall on Juncal (179)
11. Juan Etcheverry's De las Pirámides Cafe on Sarandí (244)

Regarding the participants in weddings between Iparralde natives who first met in Uruguay, the first conclusion that can be drawn is that they reached this country during the Great War (1843–1851), when the alliance between the Colorado and French governments was important.[29]

Among the French Basques in the sample by Arlas and Oficialdegui, the majority of the marriages took place among those between twenty and thirty-nine years of age (49 percent). Weddings of those in the youngest portion (twenty to twenty-nine years old) predominate, composing 43 percent of the total. Marriages between those with a noteworthy age difference (men older than 30 and women between 17 and 19) made up 10 percent of the total.[30]

The Basques in question settled in the Old Town, basically on 25 de Mayo, Sarandí, and Juncal Streets. They maintained both their residences and businesses there. And, they probably rented one or more rooms in family houses. For those immigrants with fewer resources, there was always the tenement house or a bedroom in a shared dwelling.

A sample of professions of Basques in Montevideo has been ascertained for only 182 individuals as follows:

Profession	No.	Percent
Artisanship	67	36.8
Commerce	45	24.7
Construction	39	21.4
Primary Sector	11	6.1
Shipping	12	6.6
Other	8	4.4
Total	182	100.0

As can be seen by their work activities, the Basques principally constituted craft and mercantile labor. Their settling in the city, a Montevideo where there were no machines or strong commercial and political ties to France, favored (a) the development of new craft and mercantile techniques; and (b) the perfecting of that which these Basques brought from Iparralde. In addition, the mean work activities of the Basques in the sample would have placed them in Uruguay's middle or lower middle class at mid-century. It also confirms what we already stated above: Between 1843 and 1853, the Basques from Iparralde constituted the most numerous group among all immigrants in Uruguay.[31]

In Europe, it was the norm for French Basques to marry French Basques, and Spanish Basques to marry among themselves, except in the border zones in which the mix between the two was common. There was a tendency to maintain the marital habits and customs of the native land. For the *hacendados*, economic interests were critical when the time came for finding a partner; they strongly wished to increase their patrimony as much as possible. They married the daughters of other *hacendados* and *estancieros*, or government functionaries. Many Basque immigrants, aside from the value that they placed on their future spouse's property, also looked keenly at her capacity as an administrator and daily work partner.

Cohabitation was accepted among the dispossessed classes, because the cost of the ceremony was very high for those of such limited means. In addition, being a foreigner did not create any obstacles to finding a wife. In 1829, for example, six of every ten inhabitants were women. Of the 670 cases studied in which there were children present, 15 percent reflect the Old World tradition of baptizing descendants with one's own name. Nevertheless, others baptized their children with different names, the most common being Pedro, Domingo, Martín, Margarita, and Catalina.

Basque immigration represented a significant contribution to the foundation of a modern Uruguay, which rose above the economic immobility it had inherited from the colonial period. Beyond a doubt, in a society made up of so many immigrants (like Uruguay), the Basque heritage was mixed with those of other European social groups that influenced and accentuated the Europeanization of its culture. The Basques were appreciated by Uruguayan society for their work ethic and even character. But, above all, their capacity for raising livestock, even in semiarid regions, was praised. There was little criminal activity in the Basque colony, and Basque settlers were called "spontaneous, moral, hardworking, and ready to impart their activity where the country most needed it." But, in addition, the moral rectitude of the Basques and their love of liberty were underscored. They were even labeled the "model of colonization."

The Basque success story was a pervasive image, although many of the shepherds that labored in the rural Uruguayan interior never became more than salaried sheepmen. Moreover, many shepherds preferred a seminomadic, landless life to the long-term investment of capital. Nevertheless, a relatively large number of immigrants born in the Basque Country achieved success. It was common to begin as a shepherd earning a fixed salary, working according to the *enfiteusis* system ("halves"). These tasks could be complemented with income from fencing in fields. In any case, the workers rapidly acquired a deep knowledge of the local terrain and the pastoral conditions for the livestock industry.

For many Basques (who would later be *estancieros* of note), the next step consisted of freelancing on the haciendas of their countrymen. The Basque inn, which also served as a general store, was frequently the first commercial establishment of a developing area. It was the social and economic center of a vast region, and, therefore, a place where one could stay informed about local job opportunities. The innkeeper thus found himself in an excellent situation to take advantage of any opportunity, frequently speculating in land and herds. His professional past as a fencer and shepherd automatically made him an expert investor in the livestock industry. From his work post he received timely information about the availability of pastures and local labor. It was not infrequent for Basque innkeepers to run businesses on various ranches and in sheep raising in Uruguay, becoming rich and powerful *estancieros* after years of work and sacrifice.

Nevertheless, as already noted, it is misleading to judge the reality of Basque immigration in Uruguay in the nineteenth century by the successes of the wealthiest or the palatial houses that the rich "Americans" (Amerikanuak) returning from the New World built throughout the Basque Country. Although the annals of Uruguayan history of the 1800s are full of immigrant success stories, it cannot be forgotten that thousands of Basques emigrated. Some suffered real hardship. The more than one thousand wills analyzed by the author frequently reveal truly alarming poverty. Nineteenth-century Basque immigration in Uruguay was not exclusively a history of unconditional successes. The "glorious" feats of the few hid the misery of many others.

But, in spite of everything, and although sometimes disputes have characterized the Basque colony in contemporary Uruguay, it is clear that ethnic solidarity has left its legacy. The existence of the eleven Basque centers distributed throughout the country at the end of the twentieth century indicate that. By far, all other such institutions have been outdistanced by the leadership of the two oldest extant centers in the country: Euskal-Herria and Centro Euskaro.[32]

ON THE BARD IPARRAGUIRRE

What follows is the story of an unusual Basque emigrant. The intention is to show the reader the bitter side of nineteenth-century Uruguayan migration. The general stereotype of the Basque immigrant as hardworking, trustworthy, introverted, and family- and business-oriented does not inform this example. A short biography will, therefore, provide a description of the Basque loser as well as a portrait of one of the most popular characters of the Basque Country, the composer of the well-known hymn "Gernikako Arbola."[33]

When José María de Iparraguirre met the woman who would be his wife, Ángela Querejeta, in 1858, he was a thirty-eight-year-old exile who had just returned to his native country. He had spent twelve years abroad after having fought in the forces of Carlos María Isidro of Bourbon during the First Carlist War (1833–1839). It was during his obligatory travels through France, Italy, England, and Portugal that his instrumental and singing abilities developed.

Ángela Querejeta, who was seventeen, worked in an inn in Tolosa as a maid. It was there that she met Iparraguirre, who was given to nocturnal carousing. Ángela soon fell hopelessly in love with the bard, undoubtedly due to the poet's popularity. He, in turn, responded with clear enthusiasm to that unconditional adoration, wooing the interested young woman with original ballads. Soon, the newly engaged pair made plans to marry and emigrate to Río de la Plata. Iparraguirre convinced Ángela Querejeta that they would have to wait until reaching America to wed, because the priests in the Basque Country demanded a lot of documentation before performing the ceremony, especially when the suitor had spent so much time abroad. In spite of the opposition of her parents, Ángela proclaimed herself ready to follow him wherever necessary. When Iparraguirre heard this proclamation of love, he wept.

Meanwhile, he continued his nocturnal forays, squandering all the money allotted to cover the trip's expenses. Iparraguirre fell into a state of near poverty, from which he escaped thanks to the actions of his fiancée. Meanwhile, the bard gave concerts in some Gipuzkoan towns. Between the money that he earned, that given to him by some friends, and Ángela's savings, they raised enough to pay for their trip. Querejeta thus managed to get Iparraguirre aboard a ship in Bayonne destined to depart for Río de la Plata on August 29, 1859. They married shortly after reaching Argentina. The poet's fame preceded him, and they were received in South America by a tumultuous multitude. The welcomers threw their caps in the air, shouted "long live Iparraguirre," and sang "Gernikako Arbola." Nevertheless, the singer became a manual laborer and fell to the lowest rung on the social ladder.

Thus Iparraguirre moved to Nueva Palmira (Uruguay). He visited a rich relative named Ordeñana there, hoping for help. His relative offered him the opportunity to look after some pasture and two hundred sheep, on the condition that 25 percent of the profits would go to the owner. But, at the same time, in Mercedes, Uruguay, three Basques, the doctor Durañona (from Argentina), the pharmacist Zubeldia (from Navarre), and Santiago Arizabalo (from Pasaia, Gipuzkoa), offered him money to purchase his own sheep, with the loan's repayment schedule depending on the flock's reproduction. With a complete lack of commercial insight, Iparraguirre chose Ordeñana's offer. To make matters worse, he proved an inept shepherd. The sheep were lost, easily stolen, and mixed in with those of other *estancias*. Far from suffering as a result, he began to sing *zortzikoak* (octets) with his beloved to soften the disaster. At the end of three years, after coming to blows with Ordeñana, Iparraguirre left his work in total ruin. This greatly disgusted his wife, who had recently given birth to the couple's first child, a girl.

Santiago Arizabalo gave the poet another chance, placing him in charge of a thousand sheep under an agreement by which they would divide the profits equally. In spite of the seriousness of the undertaking, Iparraguirre continued singing verses while lying down on the job. He also liked to read the newspapers that came from the Basque Country, especially when they talked about the *forua*. Meanwhile, the sheep scattered for want of care. But it did not matter to him as long as the seven black sheep in the herd were there. He composed some beautiful verses to the smallest one.

After giving up sheepherding, Iparraguirre moved his family to Montevideo. There, he was lucky enough to meet Martín Díaz (from Navarre), who lent him the money he ostensibly needed to escape his financial difficulties by opening a café. The bard rented a locale, which he christened the "Gernikako Arbola Cafe." He decorated it with paintings of the famous tree and other Basque themes. But he would be as horrible a businessman as he had been a shepherd. He treated the patrons, and few ended up paying for any of their drinks. Instead of taking care of the business, he spent the evenings in the cafe singing, accompanied by his patrons and friends. Ultimately, the bar had to close.

In 1877, the director of the Buenos Aires newspaper *El Correo Español* organized a collection to lift Iparraguirre out of poverty and pay his passage to Europe. The

Laurak Bat Association of Buenos Aires contributed a lot of money, and the campaign culminated with a benefit recital in the Colón Theater in Buenos Aires in which Iparraguirre himself performed. Two thousand pesos were raised, enough for him to embark from Buenos Aires on September 24, 1877. He reached Bordeaux on October 20.

He left behind his wife and eight children, the oldest fifteen years old. The motive for his trip to the Basque Country was the defense of the *forua*. After one year in the country, however, he was broke. It was then that friends of the poet, like Fermín Herran and Ricardo Becerro, began lobbying the Basque deputations to grant Iparraguirre a pension. In 1880, the Deputations of Bizkaia, Gipuzkoa, and Araba granted him a monthly pension of 110 pesetas, while he received 12,000 reales from his American benefactors. The bard saved half the money and used the rest to pay off his debts and buy clothes. When he died of pneumonia on April 6, 1881, he was broke again. Money had to be raised in public collections to pay for the funeral. From his departure until his death, Iparraguire sent his wife two or three letters. Ángela Querejeta would die in Mercedes on June 20, 1921, without having managed to get the Deputation of Gipuzkoa to grant her a requested lifetime pension.

THE TWENTIETH CENTURY

The new twentieth century began in a Uruguay that was in full development thanks to the efforts of the European immigrants. The borders were consolidated beginning in the 1870s; the bases of its administrative organization were settled thanks to improvements in water and land transportation; farming and ranching were modernized thanks to the breeding of livestock and the proliferation of new agro-industrial *estancias;* the port of Montevideo gave free entrance to thousands of immigrants and admitted lucrative foreign investments. The country's population exceeded one million, distributed throughout an expanse of just over 176,000 square kilometers. The capital and its department were a conglomeration of over 300,000 souls, almost half of foreign birth. Over two thousand industrial establishments spurred a powerful and growing working class. In the previous decades, Montevideo had already experienced the first signs of the "labor problem," as it was called at the time, with the first strikes and the beginnings of union organization. In the bordering departments, especially Canelones, and some areas along the coast, the cultivation of small farms called *chacras* and larger estates called *quintas* largely replaced traditional cattle raising. The cities of Salto, Paysandú, and Mercedes surpassed 10,000 residents.

Organized primary education grew, beginning with the reform sponsored by José Pedro Varela in 1875. In constant contact with Europe, the university flourished, organizing its faculties and cultural and artistic life. The generation of the 1900s made up of José Enrique Rodó, María Eugenia Vaz Ferreira, Acevedo Díaz, Carlos Reyles, Florencio Sánchez, Delmira Agustini, Julio Herrera y Reissig, and Horacio Quiroga began to give Uruguay a cultural prestige it still possesses. The old traditional bands, *Blanco* (White) and *Colorado* (Red), began to evolve slowly into modern political parties. Clubs, programs, and declarations of principles proliferated. The press, always partisan, spread throughout a country with a concern for literacy. The challenge of overcoming the trauma of a historical battle for power and lack of political stability remained. And this would not be possible without another civil war, the fourth since Uruguay became an independent state. The new conflict tremendously affected the interests of many Basque immigrants living in the Uruguayan countryside in the last years of the nineteenth century.

The revolution propelled by the leader of the National (Blanco) party, Aparicio Saravia, in 1897, established as its fundamental aim some basic voting guarantees for the population, such as the secret ballot and proportional representation throughout the country. After the assassination of President Juan Idiarte Borda, of Basque origin, Senate leader Juan Lindolfo Cuestas signed the De la Cruz Pact with the Saravist revolutionaries. The agreement reiterated the political scheme of joint participation established in the Peace of April 1872. As a result, of a total of eighteen departments, six had their chief of police from the Blanco party. With this measure, the Cuestas government inaugurated a period of peace and broad bipartisan cooperation. Its consolidation, however, required a coup d'état in 1898, given that the existing chambers of government were predicated upon the principle that executive power had to intervene directly in the electoral process and therefore could not depend on them for the reform of electoral legislation. Elections were held, and the new parliament named Cuestas for the constitutional period 1899–1903. This is how a peaceful evolution was able to continue, during which significant improvements were made to the capital's urban infrastructure, such as the beginning of construction of Montevideo's new port. The hardline Nationalists controlled the departments of Rivera, Cerro Largo, Treinta y Tres, San José, and Flores through their police chiefs.

This precarious equilibrium between the two political factions was disrupted, however, when José Batlle y Ordóñez assumed the presidency of the Republic (1903–1907 and 1911–1915). The issue of the naming of the police chiefs in the previously cited Nationalist departments was posed immediately after his election. Batlle chose two officers proposed by the Blanco group led by Acevedo Díaz, who had supported his candidacy in the General Assembly. For this, Acevedo Díaz was expelled from the National party. Aparicio Saravia, then the indisputable Nationalist leader, interpreted this action as a violation of the De la Cruz Pact, and in January 1904 he led a revolution. Saravia died in the uprising, giving victory to Batlle and spawning "Batllism" as a political current within the Colorado faction.

Military actions continued until September, along with the abuses and atrocities of any war. The instability derailed the economic trajectories of several ascendant Basque immigrants. The situation was denounced in letters from a large number of those affected—all businessmen, merchants, and rural property owners—sent from all corners of the Republic to Spain's representative in Uruguay, García Ontiveros y Serrano. All repeated the same complaint: the double payments for licenses and real estate taxes. Among the many signatures found on these letters are the following Basque ones: Antonio Maguiren, Marcelo Dobarganes, Oscar Iriarte, Lucas Sainz, and Manuel Villate in San José; Juan Oteiza and Miguel Ulíbarri in Rivera; and Fernando Yribarren, Juan Arrieta, and the widow of M. Beraza in Carmelo.

But not only the large landowners were affected by the conflicts between the Blancos and Colorados. Small commerce also suffered the consequences of the Saravist revolution due to a blockade of the ports located on the shores of the Uruguay River. Again, the protest was backed by many individuals with Basque last names.

In all revolutions it is the military levies that are most controversial, especially among the young. In April 1904, the Spanish minister in Uruguay received a letter signed in Villa Colón (Montevideo) requesting his assistance in obtaining exemption from military service for the brothers José and Ventura Estomba, natives of Ascain (Basses-Pyrénées). The two brothers had been unable to supply their nationality papers because they lacked the necessary documents that proved their Spanish citizenship. Thus, they requested of the minister that "while this verification does not arrive in this country, please intercede on behalf of said youths to avoid some sad misfortune befalling them during the time the documents are delayed in arriving." In other words, he was asked to use "his good offices" to gain exemption for the Estomba brothers from service in the Second Regiment of the Cavalry of the National Guard. Some friends of the family signed the petition: Francisco Altuna, Marcos Vera, Ignacio Villamontes, Manuel Lianiz, and Ramon Etchegaray. The same happened in the case of José Méndez, a native of Hondarribia (Gipuzkoa), who was summoned for duty in the first months of 1904, to be incorporated into the Second Battalion of Bella Vista. The testimony of his family is reflected in the following document:

Montevideo, March 29, 1904
Mr. Spanish Minister:
Please do the favor of freeing José Méndez from duty. As you well know, he is in Bella Vista, the Second Battalion. His mother is crying for him every day [because] so many days have passed and they have not freed him yet. The boy's sister who brought him the paper is also crying. They took him for the war and he will end up losing a leg or an arm, or dead, like his father, who lost a leg. Please do the favor of freeing him from duty, being that he is a foreigner. God will pay you, as it is a very great favor that we are asking you.

Nevertheless, many other Spanish immigrants decided to actively participate in the civil war, as they had in other revolutions and open armed conflicts throughout the nineteenth century. Thus, Catalans, Galicians, Andalusians, Extremadurans,

Canary Islanders, and Basques chose to join the battalions that were being formed throughout the Republic. The number of these volunteers reached such a level that, in March 1904, the Spanish Vice-Consulate in Minas (Lavalleja) had the following proclamation printed:

TO THE SPANIARDS OF SUPERIOR ORDER SO THAT IT COMES TO THE ATTENTION OF THOSE SPANIARDS LIVING IN THE DEPARTMENT, THE FOLLOWING RESOLUTION IS TRANSCRIBED:

Legation of Spain in Montevideo. It having come to the attention of this legation that battalions made up of foreigners are being organized, contracted in the Nation or outside of it, some ignorant of the true object of their contract, by the order of His Minister I remind the subjects of His Majesty living in the Eastern Republic of Uruguay, that it is their principal obligation to observe the strictest neutrality in the present political conflict, and that, those who by word, written note, or deed commit acts of hostility against the legitimately constituted government lose any right to protection, in the same way those who serve a foreign government without the permission of the King lose this protection and Spanish nationality, in virtue of article 1, last paragraph of the Constitution of the Monarchy.

THE CONSUL IN MONTEVIDEO AND THE VICE-CONSULS IN THE DEPARTMENTS WILL TRY BY ANY MEANS WITHIN THEIR REACH TO MAKE THE PRESENT NOTICE COME TO THE ATTENTION OF OUR NATIONALS.

Minas, March 26, 1904
Domingo Benedi
Vice-Consul of Spain[34]

Because of internal revolution, therefore, the 1900s did not start out well. During the first years of the century, young emigrants from all of Europe passed through Uruguay to disembark in Argentina. The bleak political outlook changed on September 24, 1904, with the signing of the Peace of Aceguá between the Blanco revolutionaries and President Batlle y Ordóñez. It was then that the Republic ceased to have a two-headed political power structure. A victorious governor, with popular support increasing daily and the backing of the conservative classes, was the supreme guarantor of internal order. With the Peace of Aceguá, all the country's social and economic forces were galvanized around the issue of growth. With a strong, unified government, the upper classes felt confident and, most importantly, so did foreign investors. The economy experienced some great changes, as the indicators of the era show; the leading meat cold-storage plant, which had stopped work as a result of the war, immediately began production and made its first exports in 1905; the Bank of the Republic was able to pay its obligations for the first time in 1907 and even made a profit, opening twenty-four new branches beginning in 1905.

This prosperity and optimism prompted the government and the socially influential to believe that the new Uruguay had to be built on new foundations, an economy based on something other than the export of traditional livestock products, which had created so many contradictions and conflicts. Many thought that the economic transformation of the rangeland needed to be carried out to its logical conclusion: the European farm. The time had also come for industrialization, the large-scale arrival of European immigrants, and the nationalization of foreign companies. The last measure, however, triggered a flight of capital that hindered development. The state was exploring a thousand paths that had never been traversed. Such possibilities appeared because peace, honorable leadership, and the force of accumulated capital came together for the first time in Uruguay's national history. The most evident symptom of the period's prosperity for contemporaries was the growth in gold reserves, a product of the extremely favorable trade balances that more than serviced growing exterior long-term foreign debt and the payment of dividends to foreign investors.

This economic prosperity coincided with a time of demographic change that first appeared in 1880–1890 and fully crystallized around 1910. The rate of population growth decreased. From 1900 to 1930, there were only two significant waves of immigrants. The source used by demographers, historians, and statisticians for the quantitative and qualitative study of Uruguay's population is the 1908 census. On October 12, 1908, the government of Claudio Williman conducted the third national census, which counted 1,042,686 inhabitants. The figure fell on the Uruguayans and their government like a bucket of cold water. The official Batllist line, reflected in the newspaper *El Día*, commented, "The data of the National Census . . . shows that our territory is depopulated, deserted. . . ."[35] In 1910 the opposition daily, *El Siglo*, said, "The most recent census has been a disagreeable revelation." The minister of His British Majesty also revealed the disillusion caused in 1909 by the government's census, and the resulting offense to national pride: "In official circles, it was privately hoped that the present census would show a much higher population. . . . The revelations provided by the census about the republic's slow population growth were very disagreeable for the governing faction, which tried to dilute the figures."[36]

Many of the contemporaries really already knew that this was a logical result, given the combination of three factors observable since 1890. The first two were a slow decrease in the birth rate and the transformation of the old "avalanches" of immigrants into mere "contributions." The third was the appearance of a completely new phenomenon: emigration of Uruguayans to the neighboring countries due to the rural occupational crisis provoked by the fencing in of the *estancias*. (Such emigration was not limited to native Uruguayans; the author's research has uncovered that, around that time, and after trying their luck in Uruguay, some Basques reemigrated, especially to Argentina.) Many others, however, decided to move to

Montevideo in search of a day's pay. Thus, the census figures show that the countryside lost population to the city, 12.7 percent of whose population had come from the interior. Montevideo became more ruralized, but at the same time more European, as Spanish and Italian immigrants arrived in significant numbers beginning in 1905. The foreigners had really already populated the country and were assuming the nationality of their adopted homeland. The nineteenth century was their work. In 1842, two out of every three people in Montevideo were foreigners, and, in 1860, one out of every two. In 1908, the city had one foreigner for every four inhabitants. Nevertheless, the immigrants, Basques among them, entered Uruguay in large numbers between 1905 and 1913, a period of great economic prosperity. In contrast to the nineteenth century, the twentieth was characterized by urban immigration, as it became more difficult to obtain property in the interior.

In the urban area, the immigrant entered various rungs of the social ladder: laborer, artisan, small businessman, and industrialist. The industrialists of the 1900s almost always had their start in the migratory waves of the nineteenth century. Starting in humble conditions, they accumulated capital through their workers' effort as well as their own. Industry was the great gate opened in 1900 thanks to the "high wage." The politicians of the time recognized the need to attract more immigrants if the country was to industrialize.

Beginning in 1907, immigration increased spectacularly. The Hotel for Immigrants was founded that year with the following expressed purpose: "The project intends to prevent these two or three thousand people that annually enter our port . . . from walking through our streets without knowing what path to pursue, and from sometimes ending up taking the steamship for only 50 centésimos to head for a Capital and an enormous country like Argentina."[37]

From 1905 to 1913, immigrants again reached the Uruguayan shores in significant numbers. It was the first wave of the twentieth century, sixteen years removed from the last one of the nineteenth. In general, these immigrants preferred to settle in the city, which, thanks to economic growth, was in need of labor. The year 1905 marked the definitive consolidation of internal peace and order. Political tranquility stimulated the economy and encouraged the emigrants headed to Río de la Plata. The 1900s were the period of the construction of a modern transportational infrastructure. The great public project that inaugurated the century, on July 18, 1901, was the port of Montevideo. The main work was finished on August 25, 1909; the French construction company came to employ 10,000 workers (among them, many Basques). In addition, construction of the railway network was resumed; between 1905 and 1913 the government, together with British companies, added 557 kilometers to those in existence, an average of 70 per year. By 1917, all the departmental capitals were connected via railway with Montevideo, where the trolley companies began the electrification and extension of their lines in 1906.

In the 1900s, Montevideo became the main industrial center of the country. The collapse of the meat-salting plants affected the coast, but not the capital, which replaced them with three cold-storage plants. The production of consumer goods grew, as did the working class. Construction was in heavy demand in the Batllist state (the present Legislative Palace and Urban Park were built at that time). It originated in the private sphere: new neighborhoods born to accompany the trolley expansion and the demographic surge, areas of upper-class chalets, like Pocitos and Carrasco. Moreover, in 1906 an unusual event occurred: the Uruguayan Industrial Union decided to promote immigration. It received a subsidy of two pesetas from President Batlle toward the feeding of each new immigrant after disembarkation.

The young people that decided to leave their homeland did not realize that there were great obstacles to social and economic mobility. Many Basques, deceived by the *ganchos* (recruiters) or by emigrants that returned from America to their hometowns wearing fine clothes, rushed with false hopes to cross the Atlantic to "make their fortune." Many of them were simply left by the wayside; others reached the middle class. Only a few, privileged individuals reached the summit, becoming part of the coveted upper class. It is more difficult for historians and researchers to trace the losers. They rarely appear in the annals of history. When they do, it is collectively, as "popular classes" or the "working class."

At this time, the majority of the immigrants reached Uruguay with a job in hand, to work in Montevideo's incipient industry, on the port construction, or as apprentices in some general store of an uncle that had immigrated previously. There quickly developed a labor glut, and working conditions in early twentieth-century Uruguay became truly inhuman. The employers demanded workdays of up to eleven or twelve hours, paid very low salaries to women and children, and imposed "work rules" with fines and harsh penalties that reduced the daily pay even more. Low levels of hygiene and security designed to reduce production costs resulted in frequent workplace accidents. It would not be until 1915 that a uniform workday of eight hours was established by law, over the objections of entrepreneurs justifying their longer schedules. The testimonies of these businessmen demonstrate the harsh reality of the Montevidean factory worker. According to Carmelo Anselmí, a proprietor of the important La Comercial cookie factory:

> In my establishment, the workers involved in production enter from 6:30 to 7 A.M., and they have a two-hour lunch break, leaving at 11 and returning at 1 P.M., quitting work once what has been prepared for the day has been finished. I have thus come to an agreement with my workers, and it is the custom of the firm in the production of my goods, that what has been prepared cannot be left for the next day given the risk of causing me damages. I therefore demand their production; due to the backup, work ends on most days between 4 and 4:30 in the afternoon, except when there is some interruption due to any

problem with the machines, ... which makes one realize that the labor of these employees is generally eight hours a day.[38]

The Center of Brickmakers, where many Basques were working, headed by Vicente Carolini, was very explicit in its response to the eight-hour law. It seems that an employee remained in the ovens for twelve hours, with two or three off to rest and eat breakfast, lunch, a snack, and dinner. This suggests that the workers lived in the establishments.

But it was in the meat-salting and cold-storage plants, the first rung frequented by the Basque immigrants, where the workdays were Kafkaesque. The companies argued that their workers were "normally" occupied for eight hours, but during the sugar harvesting season this schedule was exceeded, reaching incredible figures. Gabriel Terra described the working conditions in force in 1914–1915 in the Montevideo Cold-Storage Plant, the property of a firm from the United States that employed more than three thousand workers:

> The male and female workers belonging to the "Canning"and Painting sections state that the workday was considered as eight hours only for regulating the pay that had to be determined for each day; they were always obligated to work as many hours as necessary and, it being thus, the schedule of the workday was never under twelve hours, with twenty to thirty minutes granted so that they could eat, and this was within the establishment, due to the worry about the time.[39]

If the workers were obligated to eat inside the factories, the patrons provided the meal, but always deducting the cost directly or subletting a concession to an innkeeper. In 1915, the Montevideo Cold-Storage Plant provided the meal for their workers through an innkeeper who charged 0.24 pesos for three dishes, an amount equal to 20 percent of the daily pay of a laborer who worked eight hours. Other workers preferred to buy their meals from the owners of some "carts" that sold them within the establishment; others, in contrast, ate what their wives brought them outside. This last system was the cheapest but also the most problematic, because it required families to live near the workplace.

These conditions were no different from those in the rest of the "developed" world. However, there was an advantage in the work of the popular classes in Uruguay: the low cost of food. Since the country had an unexportable surplus of jerked beef, Uruguay could offer one of the most expensive foods in the world, and one rich in protein, at a very low price to the European immigrants and the Creole popular classes. Milk and its derivatives were, in contrast, within reach of the French worker and, to a lesser extent, the Uruguayan (here the Basque did not have problems, because he always had some fellow countryman working in the milk industry). In terms of diet, therefore, the standard of living of the worker in Uruguay was better than that of his counterpart in Europe. But the popular class was made up not only of the industrial proletariat, but also of a group more difficult to quantify: carpenters, woodworkers, apprentices, clerks, domestic servants, and others, among whom were many Basques.

The majority of those making up this social class lived in the so-called tenement houses that were the only way for the immigrant with limited resources to survive in Montevideo; thus, 68.94 percent of these houses were located in the center of the city. They were sometimes purposely built to lodge the greatest number of tenants in many rooms; common services were in the central patio, with tank or running water, kitchens, and latrines in the rear. Others had been built as large houses and were subdivided through the proprietor's ingenuity by wooden partitions. It was in these tenement houses, crowded with immigrant families that had decided to stay in the big city, that tuberculosis ran rampant. In 1908, the Uruguayan League against Tuberculosis issued a report about the 486 tenement houses in the center of the city. The report reflects how the least fortunate lived:

> The number of bedrooms was 8,400, and 23,000 people lived in them, of whom 40 percent were minors. The average is of three rooms. The space necessary for one person to live in good conditions is 40 square meters, judging now by the data that we reproduce. In a room of about 100 square meters that receives light and air through only a single door, and that is therefore dark and poorly ventilated, eight people live, two of them ill. . . . In many cases, the inhabitants cook and wash clothes in their own room in addition to other functions that would be too long to list.[40]

The Basques wishing to leave the tenement house for good would have to live outside of the city center, far from the theaters, movie houses, and shops, far from their workplaces, and, most importantly, far from the rich people that employed servants and placed orders with the artisans—that is, far from the coveted work that would take them through fire and water to the dreamed-of social mobility.

In spite of everything, the Basque immigrants that reached Uruguay at the beginning of the century attained rapid placement and a higher standard of living than that offered in their native land. The country's good economic prospects and growing industrialization, thanks to the constant work of the immigrants, enabled many of them to raise their social position. This prospect changed, beginning in 1911, but not drastically until 1913. The Moroccan crisis, the Italian-Turkish war, and social tension in several European countries, all in 1911, had unfavorable repercussions on Uruguay's economy. In May of that year, the Franco-German conflict over the African colonies began to sharpen. In September, Italy declared war on Turkey. The year 1911 also witnessed a flare-up of workers' strikes in several European countries, provoking a rapid decrease in the demand for wool products. The effects of the

Franco-German tension and the war between Italy and Turkey, in turn, were immediately felt in the field of credit, bringing problems for the rural producer, industrialist, and exporter of Uruguayan goods.

From 1912 to August 1914, the dominant empires were jolted by four grave events: the Chinese revolution of 1912; the three Balkan wars in which Turkey, Serbia, Bulgaria, Montenegro, and Romania were the chief protagonists; the continuous increase in the tension between France and Germany and Austro-Hungary; and the United States financial crisis of 1913. All these events had various repercussions in Uruguay. In short, the state's economic situation and the city of Montevideo's debt were startling. The Balkan wars, the fear of a European flare-up (already imminent), and the crisis in the United States provoked a decrease in credit worldwide. All the social classes suffered the crisis that affected Uruguay harshly, but it was the working-class immigrants recently arrived in Montevideo who most suffered the consequences. Beginning in 1912 and with growing frequency, the delegation of the Spanish government in Uruguay sent distressing reports about the Montevidean Spanish colony's desperate situation, and the need for repatriations. In 1913, the Spanish Hospital began soliciting funds to pay the food, lodging, and trip costs for the return of the poor. All the centers of the various Spanish collectivities (among them the Euskaro-Español and Euskal-Herria) supported this charity. The situation of the unfortunate was complicated when the Pinillos and Transatlántica Maritime Companies both suspended the transport that they had earmarked for repatriations. The quantity of documentation available in the archives regarding this catastrophic situation (layoffs, hunger, and poverty) of Spanish immigrants in Uruguay as well as the requests to reverse the shipping companies' decision, reflects the gravity of the situation.

SELECTIVE IMMIGRATION (1948–1959)

Exodus for political motives sometimes preceded or paralleled economic emigration. It is useful to distinguish between the two, because they involve radically different motives for leaving one's native country. Exiles were forced into expatriation for reasons of political ideology. In contrast, the economic emigrants of this third period of migration left willingly. Although they were clearly also influenced by the economic and political situation, it was predominantly a voluntary emigration. The Uruguay encountered by these individuals who made up what is called the third migratory period was completely different from that found by the immigrants of 1900 to 1932. Basque immigration, like European immigration more generally, would recede beginning in 1914, but the system of calls would continue to attract Basque youths to the eastern shores of South America.

The crisis of 1919 affected Uruguay, which closed its borders to immigration in 1932 for economic and social reasons. From 1932 to 1948, except for the few that arrived through Brazil, almost no workers entered Uruguay. The international circumstances (World War II) and the post-war situation in Spain were not favorable for undertaking the path to adventure. Beginning in 1948, the departure of Spaniards to Iberian America became voluminous. And Uruguay became a leading port of destination.

After World War II, a more favorable posture toward immigration emerged in Uruguay. The decree of February 28, 1947, that favored permanent immigration was a reflection of this. But, as in the rest of the American countries, some moral, health, political, and professional qualifications were demanded, as well as a work contract. The government's interest in attracting prepared people prompted the creation of the Immigration Advisory Commission in 1947. Consonant with these legal measures and the country's economic expansion, the commission increased the number of Spanish immigrants into Uruguay, which surpassed one thousand people in 1950 (1,618), and six thousand in 1955 (6,060). In contrast to other Iberian-American countries, like Venezuela, Argentina, and Brazil, and in spite of its need for specialized personnel, Uruguay did not sign an emigration agreement with Spain. Nevertheless, 1947–1958 was the most intense migration period from Spain to Uruguay in the twentieth century. Thus, in 1955, 10 percent of all Spaniards heading for America arrived in Montevideo.

Uruguay's economic prosperity was one of the enticements. The accumulation of foreign capital during World War II strengthened local industry, facilitating the policy of redistribution of revenue toward this sector and other urban activities. Light industry contributed to economic growth, focusing especially on Montevideo. This suggests an urban migration different from that of the first immigration period, in which Basques drawn from the rural sector predominated. Interviews of the Basque collectivity that arrived in Uruguay during this third period (1948–1959) indicate that 85 percent settled in the capital.

In addition, the motivations for abandoning one's native country were predominantly economic, although there were also ideological ones (discomfort with the Franco regime, felt persecution, etc.). Moreover, the need to have a work contract in hand before heading to Uruguay presented no problem for the Basques, as the majority had relatives or acquaintances already settled there. Like in Argentina, there were many who found jobs in Basque companies as a result of the ethnic solidarity that always existed among those resettled on the other side of the Atlantic. Thanks to the letters and work contracts from relatives, the Basques continued devoting themselves to one of the tasks that had always characterized them: dairies (called *tambos*). As Ignacio Arguiñarena stated in an interview conducted in Florida (Uruguay) on March 18, 1992:

> During the Spanish Civil War, I participated as a combatant and had the misfortune to be wounded in an arm by a stray bullet. That prevented me from working on tasks that required great physical effort. The authorities offered me

a job at the Alsasua Train Station, where I took care of the books. The salary was not enough to support my family. It was then, in 1950, when I met a man from Navarre named Urroz, who had come from Uruguay to hire employees to work in his dairies. I thought that it was a good opportunity to work and to move the family ahead, so we ultimately decided to come. The contract with that patron was for two years, and I was one of the few laborers that finished the job. I then spent four more years with him. We worked without breaks and the patron put away our salary, which we clearly did not need, because he gave us board and lodged us in his house. At the end of that time he called me and told me that I had managed to save 16,000 pesos, which came to about two million pesetas in 1955, and with that money I bought a field from the patron in which I established a dairy on my own.

The Uruguayan government needed engineers and businessmen who could build factories in the country to create wealth. The offers of employment came from all the economic sectors, and Basque departures for Uruguay multiplied. The Spanish authorities became alarmed in the face of the flow of laborers to the Consulate of Uruguay in Bilbao in search of work.

The migratory flow began to diminish in 1955. It was negligible in 1958, the year that produced a stagnation of Uruguayan economic activity in all basic sectors, coinciding with the recovery of European livestock raising, the creation of the European Economic Community, and restrictions on imports imposed by Great Britain. The new Uruguayan government implemented a less interventionist policy, opening the borders to foreign capital and investors. Foreign dependence therefore increased. The crisis of the 1960s resulted in an alarming rise in the cost of living in Uruguay, which provoked political instability. The National Liberation Movement (whose members were called the Tupamaros), one of several urban South American guerrilla forces, appeared in 1962. In 1968, a dictatorial regime was installed in Uruguay, a country with a long democratic tradition. In the face of this situation, the Basques, like the rest of the Spaniards, turned their backs on America and began to dream of a new destiny in a new destination: wealthy Europe.

The Chaco Frontier

Before the creation of the viceroyalty of Río de la Plata in 1776, as will be seen, the Basques had a noteworthy participation in the territorial consolidation of the Argentine region of Tucumán beginning at the end of the seventeenth century.[41] A clear example is the peopling of San Salvador de Jujuy, in the north of the territory, which received a large number of Basques from the time of its founding. The residents had to withstand harsh attacks by the local Indians, sometimes resulting in the deaths of both Spaniards and natives. To make the area safer, Martín Ledesma y Valderrama went from Jujuy to found the settlement of Guadalcázar (in 1625) and Fuerte de Ledesma (in 1626); both were abandoned around 1630. In 1670 and 1671, the governor of Tucumán, Ángel de Peredo, sent expeditions to punish the Mocovi and Toba. At least one Basque, Juan Amusátegui e Idiáquez, a native of Azkoitia, Gipuzkoa, participated in them. He moved to San Salvador de Jujuy in 1640, the year in which he was mayor (*alcalde ordinario*). He obtained the post of royal ensign-for-life in the city in 1655. There, he married Bartolina de Garnica y Ortiz de Zárate. Also of Basque origin, she was a member of one of the families with the best pedigrees in the region. Juan Amusátegui was promoted to brigadier as a result of his participation in the fighting against the Calchaquí Indians in the times of Governor Mercado y Villacorta, who granted him an *encomienda* of Ocloya Indians. He also participated in the Cuaco campaigns from 1683 to 1685.

José de Garro was governor of Tucumán between 1674 and 1678. He was born in Arrasate, Gipuzkoa, on January 23, 1623. At fourteen, he left his hometown "to serve in His Majesty's wars." He turned up in this capacity in the Army of Flanders as an ensign and captain in a Walloon infantry company. In 1655, he disembarked in Donostia, where he joined the Army of Cataluña as a sergeant major. In 1664, he received a furlough to go to the Court. He then joined the Army of Galicia, where he was promoted to brigadier. He later became a sergeant major in the Regiment of the Guard, beginning on December 13, 1669. Such a military career undoubtedly enabled him to become governor of Tucumán. On September 13, 1673, a title and decree of passage was presented, granting him six servants. He was dispatched on September 18, 1673, to embark on the ships of Miguel Gómez de Rivero for Buenos Aires. He came to govern Tucumán in 1674. Within a short time after taking the reins of his new post, he had to raid the natives on several occasions to pacify the area and reinforce with forty soldiers the citadel of Esteco, the most inland settlement. His pacifications could not be concluded before he became governor of Río de la Plata in 1678, a post that had been left vacant at a time in which the port of Buenos Aires was threatened by foreign ships. He managed to dislodge the Portuguese from Colonia del Sacramento, even managing to capture General Lobos, governor of Rio de Janeiro. The signing of the provisional Treaty of Lisbon in Spain in 1681 returned this city to the Portuguese, however. He was also governor and captain general of Chile, a territory in which he remained until 1692. He returned to Spain in 1693 as the commander of the *plaza* of Gibraltar, and became captain general of the province of Gipuzkoa in 1702.

The Bizkaian Martín de Jauregui was governor of Tucumán from 1691 to 1696. He went to America with four servants: Francisco Goxenola, sixteen years old, from Dima, Bizkaia; Ignacio de Sarra, twenty; Baltasar Antonio de Arana, eighteen; and Pedro de Iturbide, seventeen. The last three were from Gernika, Bizkaia. Once Jauregui assumed his post, he proceeded with the difficult task of pacifying Chaco. He also had to replace and restore the *villa* of Esteco, destroyed by an earthquake on September 13, 1693.

Juan de Zamudio succeeded Martín de Jauregui as governor of Tucumán. He had been born in Barakaldo on February 15, 1653. He left in 1666 at age thirteen with Captain Mateo de Oria, who taught him math and sailoring until he became a skilled mapmaker. His maritime knowledge landed him the task of documenting the area from Corona to Veracruz in 1667. In 1671, he was entrusted with jobs of great responsibility in the viceroyalty of Peru, where he arrived with troops to patrol the coast. He also sailed to the port of Buenos Aires several times in those years to transport missionaries of the Society of Jesus. With such merits he sought the governorship of Tucumán, which he was granted by Charles II.

He embarked from Cádiz on April 19, 1689, for his political appointment. He took two servants and three black slaves to the Americas with him. The servants were Francisco Antonio Carranza, an eighteen- or nineteen-year-old Bilbao native, and Domingo de Uribe, nineteen, from Bizkaia. One of the slaves was from Guinea, and the other two were from the Congo. The first was about twenty-four years old, and the other two were nineteen and nine or ten. After assuming his post, Zamudio, like his predecessors, began a war of pacification against the Mocovi, and therefore had to reconnoiter the frontier areas. He thus learned of the deplorable situation of the citadel of Esteco. But the most memorable feat of his command was the transfer of the episcopal seat from Santiago de Tucumán to Córdoba. This measure would further precipitate the economic and demographic decline of Santiago. And this transfer was in line with the tendency of the region's population to abandon the plains and reinforce the Spanish presence in the sub-Andean valleys. In 1701, after five years of command, Zamudio went to Buenos Aires, where he would later die.

Esteban de Urizar y Arespacochaga was born in Bizkaia on January 21, 1662. At around the age of eighteen, he was in the citadel of Cádiz, where he remained for about two years as a soldier in the Spanish infantry. He obtained a furlough there to join the Army of Milan, where he was promoted to ensign, captain, and lieutenant brigadier. In recognition of his military activity in Italy, he was appointed governor of Tucumán on December 22, 1701. Urizar embarked from Cádiz on February 5, 1702, with three servants and one black slave. For bureaucratic reasons, however, he would not assume his post until 1707. And, again, he had to suppress the raids of the Mocovi Indians and other Chaco tribes. He built an army of 1,316 soldiers (the largest ever organized in the province of Tucumán) which was joined by soldiers from Charcas, Asunción, Santa Fe, and Corrientes. In April 1710 the first offensive began; another would follow in 1711. These campaigns were successful. Urizar managed to pacify the territory and establish successful missions. Philip V granted him a lifetime sinecure. He died in Salta on May 4, 1724.

Argentina, or the Real Dream

The creation in 1776 of the independent viceroyalty of Río de la Plata, with its capital in Buenos Aires, meant that the Spanish Crown was responding to the urgent need to put an end to the politico-economic disintegration in the southern part of its colonial empire. Thus began a period of economic prosperity for the lands that make up present-day Argentina. The vigorous means employed to defend the territory of Río de la Plata from Portuguese and English attacks brought to those places all of the bureaucratic and administrative machinery that the monarchy of Charles III and (later) Charles IV was able to provide. The Enlightenment monarchs were attempting to eliminate designs on those regions that had already resulted in the Portuguese occupation of the present-day Uruguayan city of Colonia del Sacramento. In addition, the monarchy was trying to completely eradicate contraband trafficking in livestock, well organized by the Portuguese (at that time owners of the Brazilian empire). From 1776 onward, Spanish colonists increasingly settled around Buenos Aires in reaction to these developments.

By the middle of the eighteenth century, the pampas had still not been completely domesticated for either stock raising or agriculture. The Indian frontier came right up to Buenos Aires. The Indians and the desert combined to make the capital of the viceroyalty a city without territory. Enclosed within a small circumference, Buenos Aires yearned for this transfluvial "no man's land." Of high quality for exploitation by livestock, the pampas were the natural object of the city's expansion. Under this initial perspective of success and hard work, the first colonies in the recently founded and grandiose viceroyalty of Río de la Plata were beginning to emerge. Colonization of the viceroyalty in the last decades of the eighteenth century and the first ones of the nineteenth would occur in large numbers. This was especially true beginning in the 1830s. Many historians believe that Argentina, unlike the rest of Spanish America, was colonized rather than conquered during that period.

Basque participation in this colonial venture was intense from the outset. The Gipuzkoan Domingo Martínez de Irala had already established distant precedents in 1539. That year, he drafted plans for the future city of Buenos Aires. Juan de Garay, whose family was from Bizkaia, founded the city of Santa Fe in 1573. In 1580, he reestablished Buenos Aires. There was even a founding ceremony.[42] Although little information is available about the settling of that part of the colonial empire from its foundation until the establishment of the viceroyalty, the historical data suggests a high volume of Basque arrivals. In most instances, the high rate of continuity in migration among merchants, functionaries, and simple colonists at the end of the eighteenth century and the beginning of the nineteenth indicates the presence of Basque family members who had previously arrived in Buenos Aires.[43]

While "colonial immigration" had been made up predominantly of functionaries, soldiers, religious personnel, and merchants, the open immigration that followed was on a larger scale. This was due to advances in maritime transport. Open immigration also drew largely from the ranks of peasants, day laborers, steelworkers, and other such classes. If the protagonists of colonial immigration could usually depend on relatives to shelter and protect them, the "heroes" of open immigration, in their first waves, had to seek out a more diverse range of assistance. Ultimately, colonial immigration relied upon institutional protection. This will all be discussed in the pages to come. For the time being, some examples of Basques who immigrated in colonial times will suffice to provide a significant cross section. José Ignacio Sagastume Artola[44] was born in Alegria, Gipuzkoa. He arrived in Río de la Plata in the last quarter of the eighteenth century and worked there as a soldier and functionary of the Crown. José María de Sautu[45] was born in Murgía, Araba, in 1775. In 1794, at the age of nineteen, he went to Buenos Aires, where he was involved in commerce. Sautu attended to the business interests of his uncle, who lived in Spain at that time. He maintained mercantile ties with Spanish, Cuban, and Lima business agents. He was appraiser of the possessions of José Santos de Inchaurregui's estate. A person of high culture, Sautu cultivated the art of letters. He compiled a wealth of documentation and wrote about the most important historical events of the early nineteenth century. He married Josefa Castañeda and later died in Buenos Aires in 1855, survived by four children. Salvador Alberdi was born in Bizkaia in 1757.[46] In 1778, he settled in Buenos Aires. For health reasons he moved further north to San Miguel de Tucumán, where he took up residence in 1790. That year he married Josefa de Araoz, who belonged to a distinguished family. Alberdi opened a store and a boutique in Tucumán, as well as establishing several other business interests. In 1811 he was among the most powerful businessmen in the country. He died in 1822. José María de Ezcurra was born in Buenos Aires in 1791 to a Navarrese father and an Argentine mother. An *hacendado*, he managed to acquire significant landholdings that brought him a considerable fortune. He married his first cousin Isabel Fuentes y Arguibel, with whom he had eleven children. He died in Buenos Aires in 1861.[47] Juan Bautista de Udaondo,[48] a merchant, was born into a wealthy family in Bizkaia in 1796. Educated in his native country, he pursued a career in commerce. Udaondo arrived in Buenos Aires in 1816. There, he founded a maritime trading company with Manuel de Olabarria and José de Ortiz Basualdo. It sent important shipments to various ports in Europe and America. The colonial wars in which Spain was embroiled, however, caused their venture to fail and obligated them to redirect their business. Udaondo and his partners made trips to the European continent and Peru, and had the opportunity to serve General San Martín in the latter country. In 1826, Udaondo married Carmen Ortiz Basualdo and settled permanently in Buenos Aires, where he opened a large naval foundry. He died in that city on July 21, 1843.

These five examples provide a profile of the Basque immigrant that arrived in Río de la Plata at the end of the eighteenth century and the beginning of the nineteenth. Of course, not all became so wealthy and successful. Some of them did not even manage to earn enough to survive. Nevertheless, in a society in which Spaniards formed part of the upper stratum of the institutional structure, the chances of success were greatly in their favor. Moreover, those arriving during that time did not have to fight with thousands and thousands of immigrants of other nationalities in the way that would become typical beginning after the second decade of the nineteenth century. This brief period (1776–1830), although fruitful for Basque immigration in the Río de la Plata region, would play a decisive role in the events to come. It was no coincidence that most of the towns and villages of the Basque Country had fountains, churches, handball courts, and other public and institutional works financed by "Basque Americans." Many of these "Amerikanuak" had made their fortunes in Argentina. Thus, fantastic tales of quick riches in the Río de la Plata spread by word of mouth throughout the Basque Country at the beginning of the nineteenth century.

BASQUES IN BUENOS AIRES' MERCANTILE BUSINESS (1810)

At the Fourth International Conference on the History of America, César García Belsunce gave a presentation in which he reviewed the Basque population in Buenos Aires in 1810.[49] He based his analysis on the city's 1810 population census, which clearly indicated the background of the inhabitants, especially free whites. García Belsunce managed to identify a total of 264 Basque natives, 259 of them from Iberia: 227 Bizkaians, 18 Navarrese, 13 Gipuzkoans, 1 Araban, 1 Basse-Navarrese, and 4 other French Basques. The overwhelming majority of Bizkaians compared to the low number from other provinces is especially noteworthy. This could be because the census takers took the term "Vizcayan" as a general synonym for "Basque."

Basques made up 0.82 percent of the population. Men constituted 97.35 percent of the total number of Basques. This was a proportion very different than that of the whole city, where males made up 51.5 percent of the overall adult population. This male predominance was characteristic of the entrance of immigrants into Buenos Aires at the beginning of the nineteenth century. The Basques appear to have been an adult population. While the mean age of other collectivities was 22.85 years, that of the Basques was 35. In regard to civil status, what is striking is the high number of unmarried Basques. While among the free, white population over ten years old as a whole, 41.37 percent were unmarried, among the Basques the figure climbs to 51.51 percent. The relative proportions of married Basques and non-Basques is similar. The former stands at 42.05 percent, the latter at 43.99 percent. But a clear difference appears among the widowed: 8.33 percent for the non-Basques compared to 3.41 percent for the Basques. In addition, widows outnumber widowers among Basques because women traditionally did not remarry, or did so less frequently than the men. Of the total cases studied by García Belsunce, 28.56 percent of the women were widowed, compared to 2.72 percent of the men. In addition, the proportion of unmarried almost tripled among the women. Of the bachelors, 34.07 percent lived alone, 22.23 percent lived with workmates, 14.81 percent with their patrons (whether or not these had families), 12.59 percent with families (related or not), 6.67 percent with their clerks or employees, and 0.63 percent with other people (widowers, other bachelors, or a single woman). The percentages of married men and women are similar.

In terms of ages, the majority of single people were between twenty-one and thirty years old. Most married people were between forty-one and fifty. More than half, 62.38 percent, of the Basques married Americans, indicating a strong tendency of Basque immigrants to incorporate themselves into the new society. There does not seem to have been a special concern about national, ethnic, or cultural origin when the time came for choosing a mate. García Belsunce shows that in 92.3 percent of the cases, husbands were older than their wives. There was a mean difference of 12.38 years. The average number of children per marriage was 2.6, while the city's general populace had 1.8 children per couple.

THE OPEN ROAD

By the Decree of April 13, 1824, the Immigration Commission was created in Argentina.[50] Founded at the request of Bernardino Rivadavia, its mandate was to promote the entry of foreigners into the country and adequately facilitate their stay and employment in Río de la Plata. To achieve these aims, the commissioned agents in Europe proclaimed to the four winds the benefits offered in Argentina to potential immigrants.

In 1829, the Argentine government organized a special police corps, made up in large part of foreigners, in order to secure the city and port of Buenos Aires from outside attack. Many Basques served in this corps. In 1839, four thousand Frenchmen (mostly Basques) lived in the province of Buenos Aires. By 1842, the number had increased to twelve thousand. That year, the press highlighted the case of a knifing that took place when two Argentines ordered three Basques to stop speaking Euskara. One of the Basques was gravely wounded by the attackers.

Many of these pioneers initially devoted themselves to sheepherding. In 1810, between 2 and 3 million sheep grazed freely in what is today Argentine territory. They were animals of little or no quality. They inhabited second-class land. The *estancieros*, very focused on the advantages of raising cattle after the recession in colonial agriculture, hardly paid attention to them. The raising of sheep played a marginal role in the economy of Buenos Aires Province between 1800 and the end of the 1820s. During these years, the provincial elites invested their energies in cattle breeding. The scarcity of labor and the vast area of still unexploited lands, as well as the lack of capital and the existence of a safe (albeit not very active) market, inclined them toward this activity. The production of hides and meat for beef jerky rounded out the possible commercial activities of these oligarchs.

Nevertheless, at the end of the 1820s, and for the next twenty years, some *estancieros* (of foreign origin, many of them Basques) imported sheep of better stock, which they crossed with the native species. For these foreigners established in the countryside who wanted to invest their savings from years of effort and sacrifice, the wool business was enticing. To begin with, it would require less start-up capital than the cattle business and, unlike the latter, it was not monopolized by local *estancieros*. Moreover, foreign entrepreneurs could take advantage of their contacts overseas to both acquire animals of superior stock and sell the end product of their business. Excellent opportunities quickly appeared for the industry's development. The international market began to look to new territories for high-quality materials, as the traditional suppliers no longer met all its needs. Australia, South Africa, and Río de la Plata became the new suppliers of wool, a product increasingly sought by textile manufacturers in England, France, Germany, Belgium, and North America. Although existing culinary habits placed beef at the center, lamb ended up on the tables of Buenos Aires.

The presence of foreigners (Basques among them), who were familiar with cattle of much higher quality than the Creole breeds, might also have induced the crossbreeding of livestock. Between 1830 and 1835, cowhides were priced at thirteen or fourteen pesos, and those of steers reached thirty-six. A quintal of jerked beef, in which the value added by the processor exceeded that of the material itself, was sold at twenty pesos. In addition to the production of jerked beef, the cattle breeders were interested in producing hides. The European industry wanted and valued highly the hides from Río de la Plata because those of the Creole cattle were thicker than those of the thin-skinned European breeds. The land for sustaining the expansion of animal husbandry abounded in Buenos Aires Province in the first half of the nineteenth century. Large extensions of terrain were still unexploited by the whites and were under Indian dominion. But rural interests, represented by the growing number of *estancieros*, slowly gained control of the countryside. The urban oligarchy, which dominated the provincial government, would combine to create an aggressive policy of frontier expansion.

Beginning in the 1820s, a firm attitude aimed at the privatization of property began to take root. In the colonial period, in which ownership and occupation of the land did not necessarily coincide, *hacendados*, *enfiteutas* (legal tenants that split profits equally with the landowner), and squatters could peacefully share the benefits offered by the abundant open range. Livestock could thus wander without fences and in complete freedom, with no barriers to prevent them from seeking out the best pastures or fresh drinking water. But this situation would change when the richest *estancieros* discovered the advantages of securing their rights over a set area of land. They thereby managed to improve and increase cultivation, while eliminating competition. But the independent Argentine state competed to become a player. It therefore tried to foment European settlement of frontier areas within Malón Indian country.

As early as 1817 the Directorship gave away lands in frontier areas. Correspondingly, measures were taken to precisely define property limits with the creation of the Topographic Commission in 1824, at the same time as the decree of a series of laws requiring landowners to clearly delimit their properties. Around that time the provincial law of *enfiteusis* also went into effect. It stipulated that public land could not be sold, but could be rented for long periods (through twenty-year contracts). All means possible were also taken to prevent public land from falling into private hands. The government was undergoing serious financial difficulties and needed the land as a guarantee for a loan that it was negotiating with London. It was hoped that the money collected from *enfiteusis* might provide revenue for the always-empty provincial treasury.

For Rivadavia (the plan's architect) and his followers, *enfiteusis* put the land to use without losing it. These measures, however, facilitated the accumulation of land by large cattlemen and speculators. Such individuals made off with numerous lease permits and, when the opportunity arose, bought parcels at low prices. Very soon, "the pressure of the land" forced subsequent regimes to decree new measures. Between 1825 and 1837, over one million hectares were put into the hands of renters and *enfiteutas*. During the years of the administration of Juan Manuel de Rosas (1829–1852), cattle raising experienced unprecedented expansion. Abundant, cheap, and relatively safe land was therefore needed. Rosas undertook the massive transfer of public lands into private hands. Prices fell and the government had to authorize payment in treasury notes and even livestock. This process was checked in 1840, the year that the Rosas administration did not promote any legislation favoring the distribution of public land.

Overall, the concentration of public land in few hands and the boom in latifundia were the consequence of the Rosas agrarian policy. Large expanses completely devoted to livestock raising began to dominate in the province. The magnitude of the land concentration is reflected in the census of 1836. Large proprietors of over 5,000 hectares were predominant. Expanses of under 2,500 hectares made up less than 5 percent. Nineteen percent of the landowners controlled over 56 percent of the land; that is, forty-nine families owned more than one million hectares. In Baradero, Mercedes, San Antonio de Areco, and San Vicente, over 50 percent of the land was divided into expanses under 5,000 hectares, while in Lobos, Monte, Rojas, and Salto, more than 85 percent of the private holdings were larger.

Nevertheless, in spite of these high concentrations of large parcels at the end of the 1840s, Buenos Aires Province was only partially occupied and still had thousands of hectares of uncultivated public land. Moreover, another significant portion of the countryside remained under Indian control. This wholly favorable conjuncture for the sheepraising industry was capitalized upon by Basque immigrants from the outset. Familiar with the world of sheep from ancient times, the Basques of the first wave of immigration brought firsthand experience and knowledge of animal husbandry to Argentina; they would put it to immediate use with noteworthy success. Under the presidency of Bernardino Rivadavia (1825–1826) some thirty thousand Irishmen made their homes on the rangeland of Buenos Aires Province. Almost all of them devoted themselves to raising sheep. The Basques immediately joined them in this endeavor, becoming the second most active ethnic group in the sheep business. Irish shepherds dominated the northern area of Buenos Aires. Already in 1840, the Basques controlled the province's southern pastures.

The two groups, together with the Scots, arrived at the precise time that sheep breeding was experiencing one of its best moments. In these immigrants, the industry found its labor force. From the outset, a large portion of the *estancieros* of European origin used immigrants as managers and majordomos, and preferred foreign to native shepherds. The recently arrived Basques soon demonstrated that they were ideal sheepherders. Those that were not, quickly learned the skills needed to progress in all types of sheep-related work. These immigrants did not hesitate to make any effort that might start them on the road to success. In addition, many Basques—the majority—came from rural areas. They were therefore accustomed to the work so common on the sheep *estancias*. When patrons and employees were all of the same ethnic origin, as was frequently the case, there were personal connections that were further reinforced by religious, cultural, and even political ties.

In 1857, the Argentine government built the famous Hotel for Immigrants in Buenos Aires. There, immigrants were temporarily lodged by the state (including board) until they found their first job. In September of the same year, also under government protection, the Philanthropic Immigration Association was created to protect the new arrivals. And, on August 10, 1869, the Central Immigration Commission appeared. In 1874, it was renamed the General Immigration Commission. The first significant attempt to organize a colony with the participation of French Basques took place in 1853, in the province of Corrientes. There, Doctor Brougnes proposed bringing a hundred families recruited from the south of France each year. The result was not very favorable, and it would not be until 1856 that a new colony (La Esperanza) had French participation.

In 1857, President Justo José de Urquiza founded a colony of Swiss and French near Uruguay. In 1866, the Argentine government began organizing agricultural colonies of its own. In 1868, the main ones had a certain degree of French participation. Baradero had 104 French, San Carlos 95, La Esperanza 207, and San Gerónimo 23. The activity of the Argentine authorities in the matter of colonization would be reduced, from then on, to providing the immigrant with the ticket for the trip, lodging him upon his arrival, transporting him to his destination, and guaranteeing him a tax exemption once there.

One of the reasons for the growing emigration of Basques from both sides of the Pyrenees to Buenos Aires in the early decades of the nineteenth century was the area's traditional shortage of labor since colonial times, which had been general in both the cattle- and horse-breeding industries. Wool production required the combination of new skills with techniques and abilities largely unknown to Argentine workers. It was in this context that Basque immigrants would find a quick solution for their desires for success and employment. Raising sheep would require an increasingly greater number of stable workers to perform the routine tasks on the *estancia*. But it also demanded more hands during the sheepshearing season (from October to early January) than were otherwise necessary. The reader can imagine how favorably this demand was received by Basque immigrants. The expanding sheep economy constituted the clearest work opportunity for immigrants in the 1840s.

Immigrants were most commonly employed through wage labor. A worker was contracted by a patron or *hacendado* to perform a task on a permanent or temporary basis. In return, he received a salary, paid partly in cash and the rest in services: room and board during the work season. Some *estancieros* contracted Basque immigrants full-time to perform the daily tasks of the *estancia*. But it was more common for them to hire such workers seasonally and for specific tasks: lambing, docking, and, especially, shearing. It can thereby be deduced that a large number of workers changed jobs and patrons several times a year. In each shearing season, hundreds of Basques, in groups of fifteen to twenty, formed crews and rotated among the *estancias* in the area. Many other peons found seasonal work in other tasks, such as capturing or taming horses, but they were especially needed for dipping and watching the sheep, branding them, castrating lambs, and other such tasks.

During the period in question, seasonal wages were initially high, allowing the Basque immigrants to attain the desired economic autonomy within a relatively short time. Another form of work agreeable to Basque immigrants involved partnership agreements known as *aparcería*. In the initial periods of the wool fever (1820–1840) until the crisis of the late 1860s, the *estancieros* tended to sign contracts whereby the immigrant worker provided almost exclusively his labor. He was obligated to watch a flock of sheep for a stipulated period of time (three or four years). Occasionally, the immigrant began the undertaking with a small deposit to pay part of the operational costs. In addition to the grazing land, the owner of the field provided the flocks of sheep, almost always in their entirety, as well as the capitalization of the enterprise. Sometimes, if the immigrant herder owned some of the sheep, this was included in the agreement. The *estanciero* provided the shepherd with tools, supplies, and a place to live for the duration of the contract. At the end of each year the accounts were settled and the shepherd kept a portion of the profits (or losses) for himself. This fluctuated between one-half, one-third, and one-quarter, depending on the case. Included in the shepherd's earnings were the percentage of the wool that by right belonged to him, the hides and suet of the dead animals, and the lambs born that year. The *estanciero* took the rest.[51]

The Basques devoted themselves to the exploitation of the family sheep business with considerable success.[52] Although during the first stage of immigration this type of mercantile activity was less common, the system was used in later stages, on determined occasions in the 1820s and 1830s. Sheep raising was largely a family business. Only sporadically would outside workers be contracted. So these small producers were owners of the means of production. They always tried to acquire their own parcels of land, although they might work on leased range. There were also small farmers who sold some of their product in the closest town. These rural family businesses were characteristic in the 1820s and 1830s of Irish, Scottish, and Basque immigrants. All brought from their respective country the model of self-sufficient agricultural exploitation that was widely diffused in the Old World. Many Basque immigrants took advantage of the favorable circumstances presented by sheep raising to establish their own family business. The usual pattern began with a period of work as wage earners or *aparceros* in the countryside. When enough money had been saved, they bought some plots of land and the animals necessary to begin their own outfit. Labor was recruited among family members.

It is difficult to clearly establish if the Basques stood out in urban professions, or to the contrary, they devoted themselves more to rural tasks. This is because the period in question was one of continual changes, with rapidly emerging new economic structures. In an expanding province, in which it is difficult to demarcate urban from rural, and where the norm was to be settled in one environment and work in the other, distinguishing work categories is difficult. The situation becomes more complicated when, in the course of research, such ambiguous professions as "peon," "day worker," "clerk," "commerce," and even "proprietor" are found. The fact that many Basques might have stayed in Uruguay for a period before settling in Buenos Aires influenced their circumstances. First, many of them had already managed to pay the debts from the trip and even arrived in Buenos Aires with some money. Second, a good part of these immigrants were in an advantageous position relative to other possible Basque workers as a result of the professional experience that they had already gained in the neighboring country. Third, they had already overcome the culture shock of immigration before reaching Argentina. The time they lived in Uruguay thus smoothed their entry into the province of Buenos Aires. The most characteristic jobs of the Basque collectivity between 1840 and 1880 were sandalmaker, bricklayer, milkman, carpenter, cartmaker, peasant, and baker—many of which they had commonly held in the Basque Country. See tables 2.21 and 2.22 in appendix 2 for examples for different years.

Basques and Irishmen had a monopoly on raising and herding sheep. There was also a high number of Basque employees in warehouses and meat-salting plants, as reflected in statistics for the district of Barracas al Norte. There, of the 213 male Basque workers counted in the 1855 census, 19 were peons in meat-salting plants, and 18 performed their work in warehouses; 24 appear as "day laborers," 12 as "workers," and 18 as "peons" (without further clarification) that undoubtedly could have been connected with the cited occupations. In 1869, 94 were listed as peons in meat-salting plants, 8 in warehouses, 89 as simply peons, and 76 as day laborers. In 1855, the Basque immigrants living in this neighborhood were still favored by a relative labor shortage. The resulting high salaries, therefore, made rapid repayment of their trip possible. Some even saved a bit of money, with which they began farming and/or livestock businesses, or invested in Buenos Aires (city), establishing their residence there.

At the end of the 1860s, immigrant numbers kept increasing, resulting in a decline in opportunities for fast profit in the rural areas adjacent to the capital. However, the number of day laborers was high during both periods. There was a seasonal character to much employment, such as in public works, the port, and increased demand in warehouses during certain periods. This was not necessarily bad, however, since to be employed in many jobs sometimes provided greater earnings than did a fixed monthly salary.

Meanwhile, to the north of the Salado River, beginning in the 1840s, an industry clearly presented itself as the most profitable and fastest possibility for an improved standard of living: sheep raising. There were three forms of entry. Salaried workers, surely the form that predominated among the Basques, "were paid 150 pesos a month, 3 kilograms of *yerba mate*, salt, beef, and lamb at discretion. The same peon in common tasks received 10 to 20 pesos a month."[53] Between 1840 and 1845, with the same terms of employment still in effect, and excluding additional expenses or transfers of capital to Europe, the Basque shepherd could compound his earnings by acquiring about seventy head of sheep at the end of each month. The price of two pesos per head cited by Fontana for 1852 and the calculation of profit potential are consistent with the observations made by a traveler of the period: "from a shilling and sixpence to three shillings per dozen, referring to sheep of ordinary class, although the same mixed breeds can increase in price in two or three years due to the better quality of their wool. The most destitute among the recent arrivals are in the position to save twenty shillings a month."[54]

In her wonderful analysis of the socioeconomic, spiritual, and religious networks of the Basques and Navarrese in Buenos Aires from 1826 to 1865, Nora L. Siegrist de Gentile reaches interesting conclusions.[55] Thus, for example, she affirms that from 1826 to 1865 the ties between residents of the province were close within a circular world of Basques and Navarrese who managed different facets of commerce and income, as well as the earnings coming from the rural districts. Siegrist de Gentile believes that the power of kinship was all-encompassing, with all economic interests dependent on it. These family groups settled within a small radius from the center of Buenos Aires. They lived especially on Potosí (today Alsina), Defensa, Balcarce, Bolívar, Chile, México, and Independencia Streets.

When the time came to draw up a will, the executors tended to be relatives or close friends who received some money for performing the task. Everything thus remained within the ethnic circle. The group of Basques and Navarrese studied by Siegrist de Gentile were particularly devoted to Saint Roch (curer of illnesses and plagues), Saint Francis, the Third Order of Saint Francis, the Holy Sacrament, the Guardian Angel, and the Archangel Saint Raphael. This religious spirit brought these settlers and their descendants close together. In their last wishes, most sought to be buried with the habit of "the seraphic patriarch Saint Francis in the cemetery of Catholics [today Recoleta], of Buenos Aires." The donations and legacies were especially numerous for the Monastery of the Capuchin Sisters, the convents of San Francisco and Santo Domingo, and the Monastery of the Sisters of Saint Catherine. Regular transfers of funds for charitable works reached Enkarterri in Bizkaia.

The experience of the nineteenth-century Basque immigrant in the Río de la Plata region can be better understood through the analysis of a success story. The fabulous story of Pedro Luro was but one of the many that fired the imaginations of the Europeans and stimulated Basque emigration to the New World. Here is an account of Luro's life by the French writer Huret, as translated by Hammerton:

> I wish to relate in some detail the story of one of these French Basques (perhaps the most celebrated of them all), as I heard it from one of his sons. . . .
>
> Pedro Luro was born in 1820 in the little town of Gamarthe, and in 1837 he arrived in Buenos Aires with a few francs in his pocket. Entering as a labourer in a *saladero* [meat-salting plant], . . . he contrived to save enough to contemplate matrimony, but suffered the loss of his little savings by robbery. He applied himself with new energy to work; purchasing a horse and a tilt cart, he converted the latter into an omnibus and with himself as driver plied between the Plaza Montserrat and the suburb of Barracas.
>
> He then married a countrywoman, Señorita Pradere, a relative of his own, and with one of her brothers founded an *almacén* (general store) at Dolores, some three hundred kilometers to the south. But soon this store did not suffice for his activity, and leaving his wife and her brother in charge of it, he scoured the Pampa for cattle, wool, and hides. Later on, he made a proposal to a neighboring *estanciero* whom he saw planting trees on his ground, and effected a contract with him, the conditions of which are famous still in the Argentine. Luro was to plant as many trees as he liked on two hundred hectares of land, which the *estanciero* was to place at his disposal, and was to be paid at the rate of four centimes for each common tree and twenty-five for each fruit tree. . . .
>
> Calling to his aid a number of his fellow Basques, at the end of five years,

Pedro Luro had planted so many trees on these two hundred hectares that the proprietor owed him a sum not only superior to the value of the ground planted but the entire five thousand hectares comprising his *estancia* (land was sold at that time in this district at 5,000 francs per league). The *estanciero* did not care to pay Luro, with the result that the astute Basque started an action at law and converted himself into the proprietor of the 5,000 hectares.

About the year 1840, the southern part of the province of Buenos Ayres was still almost desert, the land of small value. These were the times of the Rosas tyranny, and incessant revolutions. All around the abandoned *estancias* dogs had returned to a state of savagery, and cattle wandered free in innumerable herds across these immense spaces. It happened that Luro was assisting at a *batida* (roundup) of these animals, rendered mad by being entangled in the lassos and pricked with knives in the hocks. Pondering over the value of all that flesh and fat wasted, for it was then the custom merely to secure the skin of the animal and leave its body to decay, the idea occurred to buy from the landowner all the animals of the class that were thus to be hunted and killed, at the rate of ten pesos of the old Argentine money. . . . The proprietor was highly amused at the suggestion. "I quite believe I will accept," he exclaimed, laughing, "but do you really think it would be a good business?"

It was with the only system of capture known to the *gauchos*, that is to say the lassos and the *bolas* (three balls attached by long leather thongs, which, thrown with great dexterity at the legs of an animal, entangle these and bring it to the ground), necessitating months and an enormous number of men, that he would be able to bring some thousands of cattle—and in what a sad state—to the salting factory.

All the same, Luro insisted with perfect coolness, and the contract was signed.

Now the tactics conceived by the intelligent Basque were as follows: He began by prohibiting the gauchos from scouring the country in cavalcades. During three months, only two men on horseback, going slowly, were allowed to wander about the pasture ground of these wild cattle. Little by little the animals became accustomed to the sight of them and did not fly away when they approached. When some hundreds of cattle had thus been domesticated, they were taken farther away, where others were still in a wild state, and these in turn were easily reduced to the tameness of the first.

In batches of five hundred to a thousand, Luro was soon able to herd the cattle direct to the salting factories, where he sold them at 15, 20, 25, and even 30 francs each. At the end of a year, he had thus secured no fewer than 35,000 head of cattle. He had made himself rich, and the proprietor of the *estancia* had received from him in one stroke 70,000 francs, which he had never expected, remaining enchanted with his transaction.

In 1862, Pedro Luro went still further afield, beyond Bahía Blanca, whose fort at that time constituted the frontier against the Indians. He was delayed for some time on the banks of the River Colorado, owing to the Indians having robbed him of his horses. Meanwhile, exploring the valley of the river, he quickly grasped the potentialities of the district. Returning to Buenos Ayres, he secured an interview with General Mitre, to whom he proposed to buy from the State 100 square leagues of land (250,000 hectares) at the rate of 1,000 francs per league, with a view to founding a colony of three hundred Basques in that region.

His scheme apparently approved by the President, he then set sail for Navarra Baja [sic][56] in Spain, where he recruited some fifty families, with whom he returned to the Argentine. But the Government, while agreeing to the sale of land, would not, for some unknown reason, permit the founding of the colony, so the Basques were spread over the land of their compatriot. Many of them, or their descendants, are to-day millionaires, while the land bought at the 1,000 francs the league is valued now at 200 francs the hectare, or say 500,000 francs per league.

Meanwhile, Pedro Luro continued his active commerce in skins and wool. Ere long he had constructed the largest curing factory in all the basin of the River Plate, expending millions of francs on it. Then he set himself to the exploitation of the bathing station of Mar del Plata which had been founded by Señor Peralta Ramos, one of the most fortunate of speculations, from which his heirs, continuing his work there, have benefited immensely. At his death he left to his fourteen children 375,000 hectares of land, 300,000 sheep, and 150,000 cattle, then valued at 40,000,000 francs.

Pedro Luro ... took to the Argentine more than 2,000 of his fellow Basques, whom he employed in his many agricultural and industrial establishments, providing them with cattle, letting land to them cheaply, lending them money. Almost all of these have made their fortunes. With Luro disappeared one of those types that are almost legendary, and without doubt the most famous colonist of the epic period of Argentine immigration.[57]

From another source we learn that Luro became a veritable legend on the pampas, and not only as an industrialist. Zubiaure, the stereotypic Argentine gaucho, once declared: "In this country there are only two Gauchos: myself and the Basque Luro."[58]

Luro's children enjoyed a prestigious, although sedentary, life. His oldest son became president of the Chamber of Deputies of the province of Buenos Aires. His second son was the governor of the region of the pampas that his father first brought under control. His third son was a deputy and the president of the Financial Commission of Argentina.

THE 1870–1900 PERIOD

Evidence indicating the increase in the number of Basque immigrants in Río de la Plata abounded in the local press beginning in the 1880s. The advances in navigation that made possible the embarkation of a significant contingent of passenger-emigrants had a lot to do with augmenting this diaspora in the last two decades of the 1800s. Between 1880 and 1900, many of the newly arrived found themselves in an unexpected socioeconomic situation. By that time, as has been noted, many of their Basque compatriots had already gained possession of land in the province of Buenos Aires and accumulated the capital that enabled some of them to transform family businesses into full-fledged *estancias*. The new contingents of Basque immigrants of the 1880s disembarked during the massive transformation of ranching activity described above. Given the importance that sheep raising acquired from 1880 on within the wider Argentine economy (and also that of Buenos Aires Province), the Basques maintained a special predisposition for sheep raising in these last twenty years.

But this did not prevent a good number of immigrants of Basque origin from devoting themselves to cattle breeding or the dairy industry (the famous *tambos*). The author can confirm this, having systematically consulted 616 wills (in the Archivo General de la Nación [AGN] in Buenos Aires) of those who died between 1880 and 1900. In all those wills in which the deceased claimed to own rural property in the province of Buenos Aires, there was almost always a significant number of sheep compared to a smaller number of cows. Of course, in some cases the cattle exceeded the sheep in economic importance and even number. What is more striking is that, in many of the cases studied, farming operations for flax, oats, barley, and alfalfa were claimed. This was not as common in prior periods.

This effectively establishes that the agricultural expansion experienced by the province of Buenos Aires at the end of the century affected the Basque colony. In response to the new demands, the breeding of sheep for the combined production of meat and wool became the principal activity of the Basque *estancias*, which, in turn, began to show an increasing interest in cattle. They tried to improve livestock breeds. The years from 1888 on were witness to the conversion of fifty million sheep of the merino breed into the Lincoln variety, a conversion probably unparalleled in the annals of sheep raising.

From 1880, English frozen-meat industrialists built freezer plants in the Argentine capital. They also found that there were enormous benefits in packing and exporting lamb. In any event, in 1889, or even before the boom in the sheep industry resulting from the British initiative, there were 51 million sheep in the province of Buenos Aires alone. Wool made up between 50 and 60 percent of the country's exports.

As a result of the general changes in Argentine farming, as well as mass immigrations, the value of the land increased extraordinarily. The inflated land values at the end of the nineteenth century exceeded all predictions. For example, the cost of some plots increased tenfold in one year. This increase did not affect all Basque sheepmen equally. Before the last decade of the nineteenth century, some began to work in diverse industries in order to save the capital that might allow them to return to the Basque Country relatively wealthy. As they had always intended to leave Argentina, after some years of work they were not interested in buying land. For years, they leased pasture for their sheep. Their only capital investment was in their own flocks, which could be sold relatively easily. The high price of land caused these sheepmen to find it increasingly difficult to lease reasonably priced grazing areas for their charges. At the end of the 1800s, many sheepmen not owning a hacienda apparently saw themselves constrained by the high land prices. This would drive them out of business or obligate them to move their activities to more marginal regions. In contrast, those immigrants that had bought extensive properties at relatively low prices before the increase realized astronomical profits.

These were thrifty and enterprising sheepmen who struggled for years in obscurity and isolation. Some increased their flocks and their net worth by a hundredfold or more, laying the foundations for some of the largest modern-day Argentine fortunes, while also assuring some Basques a noteworthy place among the country's aristocracy. This was the case of Andrés Inchauspe, who, by 1884, was devoting himself to commerce in Buenos Aires. Given the success of his investments, he decided to invest in land. He therefore acquired an expanse of 9,000 hectares in the Buenos Aires district of Pelmajó. He called the land "La Margarita" and decided to put it into both farming and ranching. These were among the last areas to be brought under white control after the Indians were dislodged. The purchase of these lands required an outlay of 180,000 pesos for their initial owner. This created the nucleus of what would, in time, be one of the most important farming and ranching enterprises in the province's western region. The operation was expanded after Pedro Inchauspe, the founder's oldest son, joined the enterprise.

An almost unexpected effect of the resurgence in cattle breeding was development of the dairy industry. Until around 1875, the supplying of milk to Buenos Aires was in the hands of Creoles. But then some Basque immigrants eagerly turned to this activity. The Basque was so closely identified with the dairy industry that it became "rare to see a dairyman from the country [Argentina] or any other nation."[59] The Basques reshaped the dairy industry, taking it to new heights, amassing cows at a whopping rate.[60] It was they who introduced the practice of upgrading the quality of the dairy herds. Commercializing butter production was also a Basque innovation. The first large butter plant was opened by Martín Errecaborde in 1876. Previously, the Basque dairymen had produced butter by extracting the fat from the milk and beating it by hand in simple wooden receptacles. Some progressive *estancias* had mechanical churns imported from England that were driven by wooden trestles. The Basques supplanted the English in the preparation of milk products. This was because most of the immigrants disembarked on Argentine shores were already experienced in dealing with milk and obtaining all types of transformed products from it: cheeses, butters, and curds. The first dairymen bought some cows and settled in the outskirts of Buenos Aires, creating small operations surrounded by wicker fences. They arose very early in the morning, put up to two dozen drums of milk in their carts, and immediately rushed to the city. The Buenos Aires residents soon became accustomed to awakening to the sound of Euskara intermixed with that of the clanking drums.

But there were periods in which this occupation involved serious dangers. Under the Rosas government, some gauchos killed "gringo dairymen" out of conceit. The Basque dairymen therefore approached Buenos Aires from the outskirts with revolver in holster. Sometimes, a battle ensued, with resulting injuries and even deaths. Indians also attacked the Basque livestockmen to steal their animals. The fight was on. What is certain is that, after all was said and done, some immigrants that staked their efforts and capital on the dairy business managed to amass veritable fortunes. This was the case of Juan Iriarte Ansaño, who reached Argentina from Navarre in 1877. He married María Larralda and was the founder of the first dairy in Chascomús (province of Buenos Aires). In addition to selling milk, he eventually amassed 4,950 hectares of "good lands" devoted completely to the breeding, development, and exploitation of sheep and cattle. But his was not an isolated case. At the end of the nineteenth century and beginning of the twentieth, Basque capital was so prevalent that it came to take over the Argentine milk business. From then on, Basque businesses completely controlled the dairy market. Dominating the dairy monopoly was the Unión Argentina, which belonged to a consortium made up of ten Basques who owned fifty-two farms in the province of Buenos Aires.

The immigrants of the last decades of the century that could not find opportunities in the established ranching complex or in the dairies chose to move to the pampas to work as shepherds. There, they quickly entered into a contract with a gaucho, to whom they gave respect and confidence. He showed them how to handle a lasso and the *boleadoras* (straps with leaden balls at the end that, hurled at fleeing animals, entangle their legs, bringing them to the ground). They learned how to handle a knife and the various lead-lined clubs, such as the *cachiporra* (billy club), and *macana* (cudgel), as well as the *arreador* and *rebenque* (types of whips). They soon became accustomed to the hard ranch life, the horse, and the bedroll. They had only changed places, leaving behind their Pyrenean peaks and valleys for the endlessly flat plains of the Río de la Plata. They exchanged their completely white sheep and fine small reddish cows from the Basque Country for the mud-colored, spotted sheep and speckled small-horned cows of their adopted homeland.

These immigrants, who in times past in the Basque Country had cared for a few cows in narrow defiles, became untiring herders and drovers of thousands of head of cattle on the open range. They began to introduce improvements in their tasks and form of everyday living. Some bought lambs and took care of them along with those of the proprietor's flock, as had servants in the houses of Basque peasants in the Basque Country. Little by little they increased the number of their animals until they managed to become partners with the owners of the herd. They also knew how to increase the value, quality, and quantity of cattle through more rational foraging and other techniques. One circumstance favored these "Basque gauchos," especially under the Rosas regime, but also in later periods. Sometimes, the *estancieros* of the province of Buenos Aires and those adjacent, due to strong financial pressure, had to abandon (unbranded) a part of their herds. Significant numbers of cattle thus reached the pampas, living for a time without owners or supervision until they were captured by the Basque *boleadores*.

Always preoccupied with improving sheep and cattle breeds, some of these intrepid pampeans did not hesitate accepting posts as majordomos or managers. Some became important *estancieros;* others sunk into abject poverty.

PROFILING THE DIASPORA (1900–1936)

From the records of the General Migration Administration, the author has sampled 670 Basque immigrants who arrived in Argentina during the first thirty-six years of the twentieth century. Bizkaia, with 388 (58 percent), was the province providing the most immigrants. It was followed by Gipuzkoa with 194 (28 percent), and then Araba with 88 immigrants (14 percent). The distribution of Bizkaian emigrants is as follows:

Place of Origin	No.
Lekeitio	81
Balmaseda	67
Bermeo	51
Bilbao	44
Ondarroa	38
Ibarrangelu	23
Ea	16
Markina	14
Mungia	12
Gaminiz	10
Somorrostro	9
Galdames	8
Santurtzi	6

Place of Origin	No.
Muxika	4
Elantxobe	3
Karrantza	2
Total	388

There is a clear predominance of Basque coastal villages when it came to sending emigrants to America. Bilbao, capital of the seigneury, was the urban exception; it also contributed a large number.

For Gipuzkoa, the distribution is as follows:

Place of Origin	No.
Lizartza	34
Gatzaga	31
Berastegi	24
Berrobi	20
Goiatz	16
Itsasondo	11
Oiartzun	10
Errezil	9
Elgeta	7
Oñati	6
Donostia	6
Pasaia	5
Lezo	4
Hondarribia	3
Getaria	3
Tolosa	3
Zarautz	2
Total	194

The Basque province that sent the fewest people to the Argentine shores was clearly Araba. Araban emigration came predominantly from the capital city, Vitoria-Gasteiz, as can be observed in the following:

Place of Origin	No.
Gasteiz	20
Laudio	11
Okondo	9
Foronda	9
Menagarai	9

Place of Origin	No.	(Continued)
Aramaio	8	
Añana-Gesaltza	5	
Agurain	4	
Zurbao	3	
Uribarri de Gaboa	3	
Zalduondo	3	
Gazeta	2	
Menoio	1	
Total	88	

The age profile of the emigrants clearly shows that the majority were young, single males between the ages of eleven and thirty, as reflected in the following:

Age	No./Percent (%)
1 to 10	77/11.5
11 to 20	221/33.0
21 to 30	156/23.3
31 to 40	118/17.6
Over 40	98/14.6
Total	670/100.0

Marital Status	No./Percent (%)
Single	447/66.7
Married	199/29.7
Widowed	24/3.6
Total	670/100

Regarding occupation, it was mostly the unemployed and unskilled that ventured to leave the Basque Country: 40.8 percent. Other activities declined in importance: industry and craftsmanship (16.3 percent), commerce and transport (14.8 percent), agriculture (12.1 percent), liberal professions (11.9 percent), servants (2.6 percent), religious (0.8 percent), military (0.2 percent), and state functionaries (0.1 percent).

Lastly, Bizkaian ports were more involved in embarkations than Gipuzkoan ones, perhaps because of their better infrastructure. Translated into percentages, Bizkaia serviced 97.5 percent of Basque emigration, while Gipuzkoan ports accounted only for the other 2.5 percent of the people undertaking the move to America.

Therefore, the profile of the Basque emigrant between 1900 and 1936 is as follows:

Between eleven and thirty years old
Bizkaian, 58 of every 100; Gipuzkoan, 28; Araban, 14

Emigrated from Bilbao
Single and unskilled

Among the other significant events in Argentina between 1900 and the beginning of the Spanish Civil War were the fights there between Carlists and Basque nationalists, as well as the quick diffusion of the doctrine of Sabino Arana in the lands of Río de la Plata.[61]

THE SAFEGUARD OF BASQUE IDENTITY

Since the 1850s, the massive immigration of Basques to Argentina, as well as the increasingly numerous Basque population born in the New World, favored the appearance of institutions within the Basque-Argentine colony. These institutions were generally born in Buenos Aires and appeared later in rural areas. Although the first Basque organization as such in Argentina was founded in 1877 (Laurak Bat),[62] numerous Basques had previously occupied important posts in similar Spanish and French organizations. This was the case of the Spanish Association of Mutual Aid (created in 1857), its French counterpart (same year), the French Hospital (1858), and the Spanish Hospital (1874). The respective managing bodies of these institutions had a large representation of Basques.

Among the functions carried out by these associations were the provision of medical services and construction of pantheons for the collectivity, as well as invigoration of the daily life of the immigrants through periodic gatherings. The origin of these organizations correlated with the length of their founders' and members' stay on Argentine soil and was reflective of the socioeconomic position of those Basques who had attained privileged positions in the new Argentine society. In this fashion, the middle and upper sectors of the Basque collectivity reinforced their control over the lower sectors, by strengthening ethnic ties through promotion of voluntary association. If a first-rate series of medical and welfare services arose out of the organizing of the Basque colony into mutual aid associations, the leaders of them had additional leverage. This consolidated their position as representatives of the collectivity vis-à-vis the Argentine governing class. In the case of the Basque centers as such, it would be Laurak Bat of Buenos Aires, founded in 1877, that would establish the guidelines for the birth of similar subsequent organizations.

On March 13 of that year, in a modest meeting room at 410 Cangallo Street, thirteen young Basques got together to organize an association that would reach out to the growing pool of immigrants from the Basque Country. It was agreed unanimously to form an association to be named Laurak Bat (or The Four Are One, meaning Bizkaia, Gipuzkoa, Araba, and Navarre). Its objectives were the following:

1. To organize a library containing classic Basque works
2. To create an orchestra and chorus

3. To establish correspondence with the Basque Country
4. To employ all means within its reach to preserve love for the Basque Country and its *foruak* and organize an annual protest of their abolition in 1876
5. To assist the needy Basques of Argentina, and help the poor and sick return to Europe
6. To sponsor cultural activities

By 1878, membership reached 225: 105 Gipuzkoans, 61 Bizkaians, 46 Navarrese, and 13 Arabans. One hundred twenty-four of them lived in the country's interior. The association also began to publish a newspaper of the same name in 1878. There were incessant calls in it for donations to help repatriate the needy. And when a storm swept Cantabria, leaving three hundred families homeless and poor, while drowning 39 Bizkaians and 78 Gipuzkoans, a significant amount of money was collected and aid was immediately sent to the Basque Country. In 1880, Laurak Bat promoted the construction of a handball court called the Plaza Euskara, and, in 1881, a Basque festival was held to inaugurate it. During the celebration, a seedling of the tree of Gernika was planted. That day the Coro Euskaro, or Basque choir, was organized as a group dedicated to "Basque traditions." Its goal was to organize Basque-style festivals in Buenos Aires on specific dates each year.

More evidence of the collective activity of the Basques is found in the tendency to create publications. From 1893 to 1913, various periodicals appeared in Buenos Aires. *La Basconia* (1893) would become an important source of contacts for the Basque community. It published news of Europe as well as letters and notices of those seeking to locate lost relatives. *La Basconia* was also read in the Basque Country. The newspaper *Euskal Herria* was founded in 1898, as were *Vasconia* and *Haritza*. *Irrintzi* began to publish in 1904 and *La Euskaria* in 1906.

The existence of the institutions and publications, however, does not hide the fact that the Basque community of Río de la Plata was neither unanimous nor homogeneous in its internal makeup. There was a tendency for the regional tensions and differences characteristic of the Basque Country to be reproduced in the New World. At the end of the nineteenth century, Basque groups other than Laurak Bat also appeared, demonstrating the weakening of the ties that until then had given the Basque colony a degree of cohesion. In 1895, twenty-nine members of the Buenos Aires colony from Iparralde organized the Centre Basque Français (French Basque Center) with its own building. The same year, the Navarrese in Buenos Aires created their association, the Centro Navarro (Navarrese Center), which was independent of Laurak Bat. Initially without their own locale, the Navarrese got together to commemorate their festivals in the Hotel Español.

Therefore, by the end of the nineteenth century, three independent Basque organizations existed in Buenos Aires. Moreover, in the sports competitions at the handball courts, the provincial differences were once again reproduced. A sense of brotherhood was also evident among those of the same European town or village, who got together several times a year, most notably on the day of the town's patron saint.

All the same, the great majority of the Basque immigrants would identify with the activities organized by the managing elite of the Basque centers. Their descendants born on Argentine soil, however, participated only sporadically in the events and camaraderie that their parents so enjoyed. These Argentine-Basques would frequent the institutions of other Spanish, European, and even Argentine collectivities. There appear to have been clear and pointed attempts at outreach to others by the Basques, which was not characteristic of more closed groups such as the Irish.

The social integration of the Basque colony (still preserving its habits, customs, and behavioral guidelines) into Argentine society was rapid from the start. It has already been seen how, during particular periods, Basques tended to marry men or women outside their group. Numerous statements by contemporaries refer to the speed with which the natives of the Basque Country adopted Argentine life and dress styles (especially of the gauchos). The positive acceptance and good image of the Basque throughout the country contributed to this quick assimilation. Basque immigrants quickly made these lands their new home, participating from early on in all of the country's institutions, be they political, religious, or economic. On the other hand, the geographic dispersion of the Basque colony (motivated in part by their arrival in distinct waves), and their involvement in such a wide range of occupations, accelerated the integration of the Basque immigrants in the recently founded Republic of Argentina. Nevertheless, some Basques continued to demonstrate their ethnic loyalties as well. In 1930, Laurak Bat had a thousand members, the French Basque Center, five hundred, and the Navarrese Center, three hundred.

In 1904, Martín Errecaborde, a banker from Soule, undertook the ambitious project of Euskal Echea (The Basque House). It would be a charity and educational foundation that involved the several Basque centers, thereby transcending the regional differences. Construction began in 1908, and within eight years there were already twenty-four buildings. Euskal Echea's aims were diverse:

Basque language instruction
Care of helpless and orphaned Basques
Creation of an asylum
Organization of handball matches
Provision of hospital service
Religious assistance
Repatriation of needy Basques
Schooling of Basque children
Search for lodging for Basque girls recently arrived in Argentina
Sponsorship of choral recitals

Euskal Echea had its own cemetery and supported annual memorial masses for its deceased members. This institution was maintained through the monthly contributions of its subscribers. In 1905 it had 141 contributors, and by 1907 the number had climbed to 560. In 1930, there were over two thousand. Within a short time, there were four hundred children and one hundred elderly living in Euskal Echea, cared for by an order of Basque nuns from Anglet (Labourd). The center also had a girls school and a school for boys directed by Basque Capuchins.

Sabino de Arana y Goiri's nationalist ideas quickly reached Argentina. In 1923 various patriots of Laurak Bat decided to found the Basque Nationalist Action of Argentina. This new organization had an Aranist (separatist) ideology opposed to the dominant pro-Spanish foralism in Laurak Bat. It came into being as an entity for disseminating historical information on the Basque nationalist cause. Basque Nationalist Action used culture to try to restore a sense of nationalist consciousness to the Basque people. It thereby hoped to show those Basques unfamiliar with nationalism that this doctrine was not utopian or of modern creation, but rather regarded political sovereignty as ethnically and politically maintained throughout the course of the centuries. Beginning in 1939, the organization would be called Basque Action of Argentina.

In 1929, a recreational association called Gure Echea (Our House) was founded in Buenos Aires with five hundred members and an explicit apolitical agenda. In short, it sought to be a Basque social center for the unpoliticized.

In addition to those in the federal capital, there are numerous Basque centers in the Argentine provinces. Among the most important are the following:

Laurak Bat Association of Mutual Aid was founded in Bahía Blanca, in the province of Buenos Aires, in 1899. Its present incarnation is called the Basque Union Association of Mutual Aid.

Euzko Batzokija Zazpirak Bat in Rosario, in the province of Santa Fe, was founded in 1912.

Euzkaldunak Denak Bat Association of Mutual Aid was formed in 1922 in Arrecifes, in the province of Buenos Aires.

Euskal Echea Association of Mutual Aid, in Comodoro Rivadavia, in the province of Chubut, was founded in 1923.

As of the year 2002, there are more than sixty Basque centers associated with the Federation of Basque-Argentine Entities (FEVA) in Argentina.[63]

OTHER BASQUE CONTRIBUTIONS TO THE ECONOMY OF RÍO DE LA PLATA
The first grapevines in the country were imported from Iparralde and planted in Concordia, in the Argentine province of Entre Ríos, brought by a Basque from

Irouléguy. Another Basque, Harriague d'Hasparren, was the first to produce wine in Uruguay. In 1910 his vineyards covered 200 hectares and produced from 4,000 to 5,000 barrels of wine a year.

In Argentina, in San Rafael (province of Mendoza), the viticulture was dominated by French growers and workers and came in great part from Bordeaux vines. The Basque Mignaquy founded an important trading company that specialized in wines from Bordeaux.

The Basques were also interested in sugarcane, which they cultivated in Chaco in 1889. In 1859, the Basques of Iparralde moved to Bahía Blanca, a place that in time would become one of Argentina's most important ports. In 1884, the French Basque Sansinena founded the first large cold-storage plant in the country. And in 1858, Baltasar Aguirre, also from Iparralde, introduced the first apparatus for cooking sugar in a vacuum. In Montevideo, Supervielle d'Oloron founded a bank of the same name with great success. And Ribes, from Bayonne, came to possess a fleet of ships valued at 20–25 million francs after his death.

These are but a few examples of the economic success of the Basques in Río de la Plata, as well as the commercial and mercantile relations that linked Basques on both sides of the Atlantic. The Basque immigrants in Argentina and Uruguay generated and pioneered the export of Basque products destined for the Río de la Plata area. Thoroughly imbued with native customs and traditions, these protagonists of the exodus sought to obtain in American lands the same or similar products as existed in their homeland. Thus the import of wine, sugar, handkerchiefs, and various luxury items (such as perfumes) were constantly in demand by Basques and other groups. For example, in 1889 the main products solicited from France by Río de la Plata were (in descending order): refined sugar, olive oil, tomatoes, chocolate, biscuits, wine/liquors/beer, vinegar, mineral water, cigarettes, handkerchiefs, tailoring and dressmaking articles, medicines, perfumes, chemicals and pharmaceuticals, cabinet-making materials, books, machines, and tools. In exchange, Río de la Plata exported principally hides and wool.

Chapter Seven

Foundations of the Recent Exodus

The Depopulation of the Old Continent

There is no doubt that recent Basque emigration to America must be situated within the wider, more general context of the contemporary Europe to New World diaspora between 1820 and 1940. Of course, before and after these dates, as has been shown, there were also migratory contingents from the Old World that would settle on the other side of the Atlantic. Europe was the source from which human masses flowed in this period. Ninety-five percent of the European emigrants would choose the Americas to start their new life. The Mediterranean would now cede primacy to the Atlantic in the intensity of human traffic. And white emigration would be the responsible and principal agent of this process. The first white European migrations undoubtedly coincided with the beginning of the agricultural revolution in the second half of the eighteenth century. The exodus would not take force, however, until the conclusion of the South American independence processes.

The "golden age" of these departures clearly must be situated between 1840 and 1914; the movement lost intensity beginning in 1914 and collapsed after the 1929 crisis. After World War II, the European migratory stream became a trickle. Similarly, evidence suggests that the first departures of what would later be significant migratory chains took place before 1840 (since 1815). Transoceanic emigration thus reached banner volumes. In a roughly ascending curve from 1815 to 1914, 65 million people crossed the Atlantic and, to a lesser extent, the Pacific, to settle and take root elsewhere. The phenomenon is clearly unique. The arrival of these new settlers would change the demographic course of history on both sides of the Atlantic. It would also change the populational profile of the whole American continent. The arrival of a torrent of white population transformed the receiving societies through the very imposition of the new arrivals and their intermingling with the natives.

This impulse of exodus originated in Ireland, around 1840. Beginning in 1846, as a consequence of the Great Potato Famine of that year, the departures would increase considerably and progressively. The peak year (100,000) was 1880. In total, Ireland would lose 4 million inhabitants—half its population. Initially, the Irish headed to Great Britain, especially the outskirts of London, where the great industrial takeoff of the European continent was occurring. But they would soon set out on the path for North America. British emigration in all its splendor did not begin until 1860, with its primary destination being the United States, followed by the African and Asian colonies. The maximum number of departures from this country was the 345,000 in 1913. World War I considerably reduced the flow. From 1820 to 1966, six and a half million Brits left their country, with the Scots contributing most to the total of transoceanic travelers.

The third significant wave of emigrants was the German one. The German wave reached its maximum (117,000 departures) in 1880. Its decline began in 1890 and it stopped altogether in 1900. After the Great War, however, it resumed in force. In 1923, 100,000 Germans left their country. Beginning that year, however, it would decrease, stopping with the appearance of Nazism. The principal destination chosen by Germans was North America, although to a lesser extent they also headed to Río de la Plata and Chile. In total, from 1810 to 1966, 6,800,000 Germans entered the New World.

There was also a significant migratory current from the old Russian Empire to the United States and Canada, which reached its peak in 1913 with 194,000 departures. In all, 3 million Russians emigrated between the end of the nineteenth century and World War I. One salient feature is that half of these emigrants were Jews.

Scandinavian emigration, in turn, reached its zenith in 1880 with 42,000 departures to the midwest United States and Canada; from 1820 to 1930, one and a half million Scandinavians (especially Danes) went to America. Around the same time, albeit slowly, began the emigration of the Slav minorities from the former Austro-Hungarian Empire (Poles, Czechs, Slovaks, Serbs, and Croats); they would head predominantly to North America. The maximum number of 194,000 departing emigrants occurred in 1913; from 1820 to 1945, three and a half million natives of this zone left for the New World.

Mediterranean emigration in its entirety, was significant, especially in regard to Spanish America. Although a segment also headed to the United States, the most significant sector of this group went to countries like Argentina, Brazil, Uruguay, Chile, and Mexico.

Emigration from Italy was notable from the beginning of the nineteenth century; it accelerated significantly from 1870 to 1880, reaching its high point in 1913 with 873,000 departures. After the war of 1914, it slowed and later became negligible, moderately recovering after the 1929 crash. Italy's repeated agricultural crises, delay of the industrial revolution, and low farming salaries stimulated the departure of seven and a half million nationals between 1820 and 1966, especially from Venice and the southern provinces.

Spanish emigration also became significant at the turn of the century, increasing greatly until peaking between 1880 and 1914. The high point was 1913, with 206,000 departures. Between these two dates, 2 million Spaniards left, especially Basques, Galicians, Catalans, and Asturians.

Another, less numerous but highly influential migration must be mentioned. This came from Switzerland, Belgium, the Low Countries, and France. In the French case, for example, the destinations were Canada and the United States, although the French also emigrated in lesser numbers to Río de la Plata and Mexico. In any event, between 1848 and 1939, one million people with French passports headed definitively abroad.

The contemporary Basque exodus as a whole was part of the larger general European context briefly described above. The reasons for such a population change in the Old World are addressed below.

The Effects of the Industrial Revolution

From the fall of the Napoleonic empire until the beginning of the Great War, Europe watched in astonishment as its population soared from 190 to 400 million. Many chose to make the leap to American shores. According to a calculation based on the statistics of Willcox and Carr-Saunders, the annual growth rate of the European population between 1800 and 1920 was as follows: 1800 to 1850, ten per thousand; 1850 to 1900, eleven per thousand; and 1900 to 1920, ten per thousand. Such a rhythm of increase makes talk of a veritable "demographic revolution" possible. In 1815, 20 percent of the world's total population lived in Europe; in 1914, the proportion increased to 25 percent. The figures cited do not reflect a birth rate higher than on other continents. Rather, they clearly show a steep fall in the European mortality index, as a consequence of the better sanitary and feeding conditions and a sustained rural birth rate. The death rate in western and northern Europe had already begun to decline around 1830. The same decline was apparent in southern and eastern Europe around the 1860s. This would result in a scarcity of land, while indirectly contributing to wage reduction and factory unemployment (especially between 1875 and 1900).[1]

The "brilliant years" of liberal nineteenth-century Europe would initiate a period of enormous prosperity in the advanced European countries that participated more actively in the world economy. This would have repercussions on the social welfare of nations. The idea of progress, under which the majority of governments would try to broaden their scope, would become the norm. The capitalist system consolidated and strengthened its position, with well-defined national markets appearing. The cities swelled and urban businesses of enormous dimensions were established with diverse and substantial capital. Little by little, the urban population overtook the rural. The European medical landscape would be transformed as a result of the discoveries of Pasteur and his followers. The cholera, diphtheria, and typhus bacilli were recognized. Vaccines and serums came into use. Asepsis and antisepsis came into practice and life expectancy increased. Demographic growth accelerated, infant mortality decreased, and life was prolonged by the enormous nineteenth-century advances in science and technology. Quality of life tended to improve, illness became less prevalent, and both the health and height of Europeans generally increased.

Europe had more children to export, among other reasons because fewer and fewer died at birth. The aforementioned scientific advances would also have their application in Old World agriculture, thus provoking rural mobilization. The majoritarian view in reference to the nineteenth century suggests a strong correlation between the socioeconomic transformation caused by the industrial revolution, population growth, and emigration. And the great farming and labor problems caused profound disturbances in Europe, provoking an emigration that changed the face of the earth. Table 7.1 shows the evolution of European population in the nineteenth century. Note the abundant growth in the relatively short time of one hundred years. Observe how the majority of these countries tripled their population and how, consequently, they would be potential leading contributors to the migratory flow.

The Increase in Life Expectancy

The decrease in the number of deaths in Europe and increase in the birth rate began after the Peace of Vienna, which closed the cycle of Napoleonic wars that had wreaked demographic havoc. At the beginning of the nineteenth century, only twenty-two cities in Europe exceeded 100,000 inhabitants (representing 3 percent of the total population). By 1850, forty-seven cities surpassed this figure. Five percent of Europeans lived in them. There were already nuclei of tremendous proportions. London, for example, had about one million inhabitants; Paris surpassed half a million. The population boom was much more accelerated than in the eighteenth century. The average annual growth index was around three per thousand between 1650 and 1750; between 1800 and 1850, in comparison, it was ten per thousand.

At the end of the nineteenth century, seven European cities had over a million inhabitants, one hundred forty exceeded a hundred thousand, and all these together accounted for 11.5 percent of the continent's inhabitants. The receding mortality indices show that death rates gradually declined beginning in the first years of the nineteenth century. It is therefore necessary to analyze the nineteenth-century migratory phenomenon bearing in mind the socioeconomic positions of the countries of origin as producers and suppliers of both food and employment for their native populations. Thus, uncertainty about the future and declining living conditions, provoked by the nineteenth-century crisis, weakened emigrants' ties to their native countries. The information available about the nations chosen as final destinations helped weaken the ties.

TABLE 7.1 Population of Europe, Selected Countries, 1800–1900

Country	1800 No.[1]	1800 Percent[2]	1850 No.[1]	1850 Percent[2]	1900 No.[1]	1900 Percent[2]
Russia	40	21	57	21.8	100	24
British Isles	16	9	27.5	10.5	41.5	10.6
Germany	23	13	35.1	13	56.4	14
Italy	18	9.2	25	9.2	32.5	8.4
Austria	28	15	36	13.7	50	12
France	28.2	15	35.8	13.6	40.7	10
Total	153.3	82.2	216.4	81.8	321.1	79.0

1. Number of inhabitants in millions over real territory.
2. Percentage in relation to the European population.
Source: M. Reinhard and A. Armengaud, 1966, 219.

During the nineteenth century, there was a small-scale religious diaspora; a similar one took place for political reasons. However, the mass exodus motivated by the excess number of inhabitants, undertaken by both whole family units and lone individuals, transformed the social landscape in both Europe and the New World. A portion of those who emigrated were motivated by an eagerness for wealth and planned speculation, hoping to return to their native countries "wealthy" in the shortest time possible.

Desolate Countrysides and the End of the European Agricultural Tradition

The agricultural revolution experienced by nineteenth-century Europe also played an active part in Old World transatlantic emigration. In most European countries, cultivation and pasturing area expanded throughout the nineteenth century due to new fertilizers, improved drainage in humid regions, and irrigation of arid lands. In the nineteenth century, the fields began to be intensively cultivated. When considerable population increase occurs in an agricultural society, the simplest solution for feeding the growing population is the expansion of the area cultivated to produce more food. The expansion of cultivable area into marginal areas generally acted in concert with the demographic increase.

In those regions of Old Europe in which traditional agriculture was the way of life, the departures are is easily explained. Here, population growth undoubtedly brought about mass exodus. The lag in the process of economic modernization in these regions, the difficulty of finding capital for rapid socioeconomic transformation, retrograde education, and a general cultural backwardness also contributed to making conditions ripe for emigration. In England, for example, between 1875 and 1885, the area of wheat sown decreased 20 percent. In France, to cite another typical case, the plague of phylloxera wreaked havoc on some traditional crops (for example, grapevines); this was one of the most important causes for emigration from Iparralde to Río de la Plata.[2] The Basque case is an example of the widespread European trend in which population increase was disproportional to that of new land brought under cultivation.[3]

Young countries like Australia, the United States, and Argentina would inundate the European markets (circumventing all the protectionist customs obstacles) with wheat, meat, and wool. Large-scale nineteenth-century industrial production, predominant in the more advanced nations and bringing immediate benefits, unseated agriculture in commercial importance. Agricultural production thereby definitively lost its traditional primacy in economic life.

At the same time, the "surplus" population emigrated to the cities in search of work provided by the industrial revolution, or left for the new republics of sparsely populated continents practically unknown to Europeans of the day. International migrations within Europe also occurred—for example, immigrants arrived in France from neighboring countries. The majority of those that left, however, chose America.

The Golden Era of Invention

In 1814, the Englishman George Stephenson invented the railroad. By 1830, it was already transporting wagons of passengers at 22 kilometers per hour. But what history refers to as the "railway age" would not emerge until the 1860s. In 1860, Europe had 200,000 kilometers of rails on which trains circulated at 75 km/hr. In 1880, speeds reached 100 km/hr. Little by little, the power of the locomotives would increase and the railways would be extended, connecting very distant points. Travel time was cut in a way never seen before. Railroad use became an everyday occurrence. It facilitated movement, permitted internal migration, and transported people to the embarkation ports for travel overseas. Taking a trip was transformed from an adventure full of discomforts (sometimes even dangerous) into just another part of daily life in nineteenth-century Europe.

Connected thus to the changes posed by large-scale capitalism, the railroad served distinct productive modalities. In industrialized countries, it was a vehicle for supplying primary materials and a nexus oriented to export commerce via an itinerary that passed through the mine, factory, and port. In economically dependent countries, it accelerated the outflow of food and primary materials, whose transport to ports of embarkation made their exploitation possible on an international scale, likewise facilitating the diffusion and placement of merchandise from European manufacturing centers. In addition, by bringing the diverse parts of the world into contact, the railroad would permit the exchange of news, impressions, ideas, propaganda, and so on.

In another medium, the introduction of the helix-screw propeller for large transatlantic steamships, beginning in 1860, would facilitate speeds of up to fifteen knots. Steamship lines between the New World and Europe began to abound, now able to service large intercontinental migratory movements.

The first trolley was inaugurated in Germany in 1881. Its use was soon common throughout large European and American cities. The trolley combined elements of the railroad with an electric motor. Rapid and agile in movement, it would unite urban centers with their peripheries. Although not used to connect long stretches, it became common on the internal lines of large cities as a result of the low fares and efficient service. This was especially true of American cities, rapidly expanding and increasing their urban habitat. Underground trolleys were soon also built.

In 1876, Nikolaus August Otto built the first practical internal-combustion engine, and in 1892, Rudolf Diesel introduced a much less expensive system for the locomotion of the automobile. The nineteenth-century European could travel at speeds until then unimaginable. The outdated and antiquated system of animal traction was relegated to a secondary plane.

In 1876, the Scottish-born American Alexander Graham Bell invented the telephone. In 1895, the Italian engineer Guglielmo Marconi, utilizing Hertzian waves, learned how to capture determined electrical discharges through a detecting apparatus at some kilometers of distance without any mediating cable conductor: the wireless telegraph had been born. These systems not only saved the enormous cost of the installation of telegraph wires; they also permitted telegraphic contact between two stations in movement (for example, two ships on the high seas). Little by little, the reach and power of the transmitters was perfected, and Marconi's invention was installed on all ships and its use became obligatory. The old visual alphabet of flags fell into disuse, and all European navies quickly learned the Morse system.[4] At the same time, in the second half of the nineteenth century, undersea cables were laid that connected both sides of the Atlantic in seconds. European land telegraph networks also increased their coverage. In 1850, there were only 160,000 kilometers of telegraph cable. At century's end, 6 million kilometers were already functional. In 1858, 9 million telegrams were sent; in 1908, 334 million.Until midcentury, news and information moved from one point of the world to another in mailbags. The replacement of the optic telegraph with other, more advanced models designed by Morse beginning in 1844, and the subsequent extension of the submarine cable network (1880–1910), caused profound transformations in commercial relations. Mercantile operations widened in their sphere of action, opening the most varied and distant markets to manufacturers, producers, and exporters.

In 1879, Thomas A. Edison invented the electric light, illuminating nineteenth-century Europe. A truly revolutionary apparatus, it came to be used in transport systems soon after appearing. The British railroads were the first to adopt the system of electric lighting, with great success; they were rapidly imitated by the rest of the continental railway lines. This was all due to the proliferation of electric networks and new systems of easily transportable generators. Hydroelectric energy made European and American nights brighter. The bulb, infinitely cleaner, more comfortable, and more powerful than gas or candles, eliminated these old lighting systems from everyday European and American life. These societies changed their schedules thanks to the light, being able to extend normal activities into the night.

In 1876, Charles Tellier invented and installed the first refrigeration system on a boat. The vessel was called—what else?—*Le Frigorifique* ("The Refrigerator"). There was no delay in the invention's extension to all the ships that made long trips and transported perishable products.

There is no doubt that all these advantages and innovations were exploited by the American governments interested in luring immigrants. A larger number of people could be transported more comfortably on each trip in an increasingly shorter time. Many of the transatlantic steam lines shuttled emigrants back and forth between Europe and America. More than a few nineteenth-century fortunes were owed to this commerce in emigration.[5]

The telegraph and telephone were used from America to give precise instructions to the emigration agencies, installed in Europe, about what policy to follow when the time came to contract clients (of which nationality, which number to get on each occasion, etc.). The railroads transported the "chosen" in long caravans, from the interiors of the European nations to their ports of embarkation. Once the immigrants reached America, the railroad also served to carry them from the point of arrival to those zones of the interior that the receiving republics were interested in colonizing. In the publicity that they diffused like bait, among their persuasive measures, some of these American nations included free railroad transportation, both from home to the port of departure in Europe and, after arrival in America, to the place of assigned residence.[6]

Thus, the swiftness and low cost of transportation, both land and sea, to a great degree facilitated and supported the mass arrival of immigrants in the New World. The large number of people that crossed the American borders in the nineteenth century cannot be explained in any other way. This is clear in the Basque case as the century progressed. The ports of Bordeaux, Pasaia, and Bayonne refined their navigation techniques with ships of greater tonnage and speed capable of carrying more passengers. The improvement of the communication infrastructure served to put American immigration policymakers in contact with special envoys, or "contract agents," installed in Europe. The latter got in touch with each other via telegraph or the mail system, now more efficient and rapid. In turn, in perfect harmony with the large transatlantic steamship companies, political leaders and immigration agents realized their dream of obtaining "European souls" to revitalize New World economies and societies in increasingly less time and greater numbers.

The Navigation Boom

In the mid-nineteenth century, navigation expanded dramatically. The success of the steam engine was permanent, and the accomplishments of steamships opened wide horizons to commercial transport. Builders would work tirelessly to create new types of ships able to withstand long voyages. A period of wide expansion of the use of steam in the maritime world had begun.[7] In 1813, the first regular navigation line with steamships between ports was founded in England. In 1816, this system was adopted in France. In June 1819, a 350-ton American steamer with two paddle wheels called the *Savannah* successfully completed the first Atlantic crossing. In 1838, Samuel Cunard crossed the ocean, analyzed the advantages that the new navigation methods could bring for his sea businesses, and founded the British and North American Royal Mail Steamship Company for the construction of steamers. The British ships made the Liverpool-Boston trip in about fourteen days. In 1847, the American-owned Ocean Steam Navigation Company was born. In 1852, as a consequence of a postal service contract, the Australian Royal Mail Steam Navigation Company was founded. Also in 1852, the Peninsular and Oriental Line, with service between Singapore and China, obtained the postal service concession with Australia. The Hamburg Amerika Linie began its voyages in 1856, with regular steamers between Hamburg, Southampton, and New York. The German company Norddeutscher Lloyd inaugurated its regular services with its first ship in 1858. In 1864, the French Compagnie Générale Transatlantique made its appearance. Previously (1860), the French shipping company Messageries Marítimes established a regular passenger and postal service between France and America. These last three navigation lines took charge of transporting the great majority of Basque emigrants.

Around mid-century, Isambard K. Brunel made a great technological improvement in ships. One of the grave inconveniences of long-distance steamers was the lack of coaling ports. Brunel avoided this inconvenience by constructing vessels capable of carrying large fuel supplies, with a fifteen-mile-per-hour speed that enabled them to reach Australia via the Cape of Good Hope without difficulties. These ships carried about 800 passengers in first class and 2,500 in second and third, as well as 5,000 tons of cargo. The Great Eastern Co. was founded for this purpose in 1851. From then on, the way was laid out. Navigation companies using steamships began to proliferate, and both passenger-emigrant service and mail service became increasingly more frequent and large scale.

Also from the mid-nineteenth century, Spanish-based shipping companies that made the trip from Spain to Cuba, Puerto Rico, and the Philippines or from Spain to South America began to appear. In 1854, Antonio López y López founded Antonio López and Co. He began his business with a 716-ton ship with a helix-screw propeller, *General Armero*, which made regular runs to Havana. In 1881, A. López and Co. became the Compañía Transatlántica. In 1850, Miguel Martínez de Pinillos founded the Pinillos Company, whose ships made the Antilles crossing. This company later became Pinillos, Izquierdo and Co. It established regular routes from Barcelona or Cádiz to America and the Far East, with stops in the main ports of China and the Philippines. The Pinillos business prospered especially in the routes serving Brazil, Uruguay, and Argentina. In 1880, it came to be called Compañía Marítima Frutera.

On July 1, 1885, Ybarra and Company began its business, continuing with the services and fleet of the Vasco-Andaluza, founded in 1878. From the outset, Ybarra and Company was concerned with serving the national coastal trade. The company's prestige grew rapidly. Its activity increased with the creation of regular transatlantic routes, and its scope widened with voyages to the entire American continent.

In the last years of the nineteenth century, the Naviera Vascongada, the Marítima Unión, and the Vasco-Asturiana made their appearance. The Compañía Transmediterránea's various ships constituted an important fleet, built in Barcelona and Bilbao: *Vapores Tintoré*, *Isleña Marítima*, and *Valenciana de Navegación*. It thus improved service from the peninsula to African ports. In 1897, the Spanish merchant marine, which undertook voyages to all continents, was the world's fifth largest fleet in ship numbers, capacity, and power. Around the mid-nineteenth century, it performed a unique service, transporting emigrants to American shores and the then Spanish-American colonies of Cuba, Puerto Rico, and the Philippines.

The Waiting Room of Iparralde

The 1808 French invasion of Spain created a feeling of hatred toward the invaders. Spaniards fought against Napoleon's soldiers using a system of guerrilla warfare. As a consequence, the traditional French Basque migratory path via Spain would change for another diaspora that would have the former Spanish and Portuguese colonies as their point of reference.

One critical factor was the agricultural economic crisis that scourged the Basses-Pyrénées region. The disastrous situation in which a large group of farmers found themselves in 1845 was put in evidence by the Conseil Général and prefect. A series of mediocre-to-bad harvests had occurred. Floods, damaging storms, and hail struck more than 200 towns, causing enormous losses. The prices of corn, indispensable for feeding people and animals, had risen from 9.40 to 30 francs a hectoliter. The number of emigrants thus increased considerably. Many peasants would not have been able to subsist without the cereal grains brought from Spain by mule.

The forest districts generally lost the most inhabitants, largely due to the stagnancy in wood prices, which worsened. Grape growing would experience a grave crisis in 1852, the year that the oidium fungi caused great damage. The district of Salies particularly suffered, going from 8,364 inhabitants in 1836 to 5,503 in 1856. Many grape growers left the country to practice their trade in Spain. Beginning in 1892 a new crisis would explode, this time provoked by phylloxera.

The shepherds, for their part, had the custom of burning the dry mountain pastures every year to provide fresh grass for the rams and sheep. But since these fires provoked (voluntarily or not) the destruction of the nearby woods, they were prohibited in 1830. In the face of this measure, some shepherds from Iparralde chose to migrate to America. And in this way the support occupations in sheep husbandry were lost.

The artisans suffered from the growth of industrialization, which resulted in decreased sales of handcrafted products from the Basses-Pyrénées region. In addition, to the extent that Spain underwent a strong process of industrialization, the Spanish market lost interest in goods from Iparralde.

Another longtime profitable activity in this territory was smuggling. Sometimes, it served as a supplementary economic activity; at others, it was in itself a source of personal or family wealth. There was small-scale smuggling (done by individuals) and a large-scale practice that involved caravans of 50 to 100 mules protected by men armed with rifles or carbines. The Carlist wars helped stimulate smuggling. This "colorful" form of commerce was typical in the border region of both Basque sides of the Pyrenees. Residents of the district of Saint-Étienne-de-Baïgorry lived almost exclusively off of it. At the end of the century, however, the continuous proscriptive measures and favorable customs agreements between Spain and France undermined this activity.

The South American Agricultural Love Affair

After American independence, the new Río de la Plata nations of Argentina and Uruguay, having formerly belonged to the viceroyalty of Río de la Plata, moved rapidly to populate their respective territories. In colonial times the Spanish Crown had never shown real interest in effectively settling those latitudes, distant geographically and financially uninteresting due to their lack of rich gold and silver mines. The late date of the official creation of the viceroyalty of Río de la Plata (1776) is proof of imperial indolence and negligence toward these territories.

Nevertheless, the Argentine coastal areas became somewhat relevant, from the end of the eighteenth century, as ports and inlets—especially Buenos Aires—for the products grown in the country's interior: exploitation of olives, vineyards, various cereal grains (especially wheat), and sugar cane. The existing herds of livestock, very abundant since the seventeenth century, were destined for internal consumption and minimally for export or for transport. The viceroyalty also had some handicraft industries.[8]

As we have noted, the wars of independence against Spain ruined the herds of livestock of Uruguay and Entre Rios, and in 1815 this sector found itself in open decline. The grave droughts of 1838–1839 and rising competition from Brazilian ranchers aggravated the situation even further. To counteract their bad fortune, some shepherds introduced merino sheep on their *estancias*, thus opening the doors for future wool export. Therefore, specialized farming and ranching labor that did not exist in the new republics of Argentina and Uruguay would be necessary.

Mariano Moreno (1788–1811) can be considered the first Argentine leader interested in attracting European immigrants. Moreno was secretary of the first Governing Board of the Independence. One of his first political actions was the search for Old World human stock for future emigration to the country. This politician firmly believed that one of the worst evils of his young nation was the human desertion of the interior. He thought that one of the main bulwarks of wealth was, precisely, population.[9] A belief in the need to import "European souls" was therefore fostered. There was a push to "Europeanize" the new Río de la Plata republics; the models to imitate were the nations of Europe, especially those in the north. But, to carry out such an ambitious project, elements lacking in both Argentina and Uruguay at the time were needed: human, capital, and technical resources.

To obtain these essentials, the Río de la Platan legislative bodies designed legislation to order that favored immigration. And as support for this legislative policy, an entire legion of immigration agents was sent to Europe. Often paid by the state to which they belonged, their task was to import European settlers to fill Río de la Plata's vast population vacuum. The leaders of southern South America wanted to create new, modern countries in which the foreigner would fulfill the primordial role through his work, experience, farming and ranching knowledge, and the capital he was able to bring with him to settle in America.

The foreign immigrant was to transform the mentality and work habits of Argentines and Uruguayans. Immigrants were to "Europeanize" native customs and modes of behavior. The former society, the old colonial social edifice, had to be demolished. Ideologues and planners sought to imitate powerful, refined, and industrious France and England. Immigration was identified with colonization, progress, and well-being. Thus, modern agricultural techniques were implemented in an attempt to increase national productivity and create strong, powerful countries. Likewise, efforts were made to organize a powerful bourgeoisie that would maintain the reigning liberal policy of the period and make these theoretical programs a reality.

As if this were not enough, with foreign colonization borders would be stabilized and the local indigenous population would be assimilated willingly or by force. In addition, the technological aspects of the country would be improved by mixing local blood with the European. Therefore, attempts would be made to convert the agrarian utopia into reality. And, to begin, the necessary workers would have to be recruited in the Old Continent.

The first to leave for Europe in search of settlers was Manuel Aniceto Padilla. Receiving orders from Mariano Moreno in 1810, he departed on a European mission to bring "wise men, artists, peasants, and artisans" to Argentina from northern Europe.[10] The politician Bernardino Rivadavia (1780–1845) would be the next to promote this open-door policy of attracting European immigrants.

On July 16, 1821, the Argentine legislature separated the Secretariats of Government and Treasury. Rivadavia came to occupy the former. On August 22 of that same year, executive power authorized the government to negotiate the transport of industrious European families to increase the population of the province of Buenos Aires, while granting the necessary credit for the project. As a result of this initiative, on August 24, 1821, the Buenos Aires authorities solicited the London firm of Hulle & Brothers to develop the draft of a progressive immigration law, which the company immediately provided. It was the first serious attempt by the Río de la Platan authorities to attract immigrants. Nevertheless, it was not implemented.

Again, under the law of August 19, 1822, the Argentine government was authorized to negotiate a loan of 3–4 million pesos in order to build the Buenos Aires port, as well as three new cities that would be located on the coast between Buenos Aires and Carmen de Patagones. The project also included the construction of new towns. Of course all of these colonies would have to be peopled with European settlers. Thus, on November 22, 1822, shipment of 200 European families was negotiated, and Rivadavia was empowered to introduce one thousand or more "moral and industrious" families into his country. By the decree of April 13, 1824, the Immigration Commission was created. Its motto was "to provide the agriculture, arts, and all types of industry in the country, with the hands and capacity because they cry out for them."

The commission had the power to designate as many agents in Europe as it considered necessary. These agents would be in charge of spreading news of the advantages of the Argentine regions to be colonized. Entrance of foreigners into the country was thus promoted, and attempts were made to adequately channel their settlement in Río de la Plata. To achieve these goals, the commissioned agents in Europe paraded the advantages offered to those who desired to settle in Argentina. The offer can be outlined as follows:

1. Regulation of work contracts, with corresponding and regular monthly remuneration (all legal and in order).
2. Assistance coverage to the new arrivals. The Convent of Recoletos was equipped as the primary immigrant residence.
3. Exemption from Argentine military service.
4. Preferred fiscal treatment with respect to other Argentines.
5. Freedom of worship.
6. Possibility of access to land — the *enfiteusis* system — in colonization undertakings supported and protected by the state.

The Argentine Constitution of 1853 again sought to promote immigration. Proof of this is its Article 25, which reads as follows: "The Federal Government will promote European immigration and will not be able to restrict, limit, or assess any taxes on entrance into Argentine territory on the foreigners that come with the intention of working the land, improving the industries, and introducing and teaching the sciences and the arts."

On October 19, 1876, under the presidency of Nicolás de Avellaneda, the Law of Immigration and Colonization was promulgated. Created by the Argentine Department of Immigration, its main objective was to adjudicate and regularize landownership for the newly arrived. A consequence of this law was the construction of a hotel where the newcomers were lodged. They had the right to support from the state coffers for five days from the moment they disembarked. In the event of grave illness, upkeep and medical attention would be unlimited for the duration of the convalescence. The law of 1876 also gave rise to the creation of the Office of Work. Responsible for receiving and classifying the employment needs from throughout the country, it tried to adequately distribute immigrant labor according to regional demand. It would also try to gain material advantages for the immigrant. When so requested, specialized personnel from this office would also intervene in the formalization of work contracts or in adjudicating grievances arising from them. The majority of the recent arrivals to Argentina, in addition to lacking in education, were often in need of financial resources. Beginning in 1880, the Argentine government promoted a policy of "subsidized passages" through which it paid the fares for European immigrants. From that date until the end of the century, the number of foreigners entering Argentina was spectacular.

Uruguay, in turn, launched a liberal immigration policy at a very early date. From 1828 until the end of the 1830s, Montevideo would witness significant contingents of Basques (Spanish and French), as well as Canary Islanders, Galicians, Piedmontese Italian farmers, and English technicians enter its ports. It is estimated that between 1835 and 1842, some 33,000 immigrants entered this small Río de la Plata republic, most of them Basques and Italians. The 1852 population census placed the number of inhabitants in the entire country at 131,969. Of this total, 8,585 were immigrants. From then on, the number of foreigners would increase considerably. In 1900, this new republic would have 900,000 souls, compared to the 30,000 that it had in 1800. This meant a net population increase of 870,000 people, in large part from immigration.[11]

Montevideo was the primary nucleus in which Europeans settled after the country's independence. In 1908, the city had 307,231 inhabitants, one-third of the country's total. This "macrocephaly" reflects the city's rapid growth. It absorbed additional labor thanks to an increasingly sophisticated tertiary sector, and supported, in turn, new industrial activities.

The Uruguayan legislation also soon began to display symptoms of a belief in the agrarian utopia, deciding early on to import foreigners. Article 147 of the Constitution of the Eastern Republic of Uruguay of 1830 was to the point: "The entrance of any individual into the territory of the Republic, his permanence in it and his departure with all his property is free as long as he observes the laws of the police, except if he does harm to a third party."

By government decree, on October 2, 1833, the right to introduce settlers into the country was granted to the wealthy English merchant Samuel Laffont. To this end, the immigrant *enganchador*[12] agent named a representative in Spain to promote peasant emigration from the Basque Country and Navarre. By another government decree, dated August 26, 1834, a fund of ten thousand pesos was established for passage, lodging, and upkeep expenses of European immigrants that decided on their own to go to Uruguay. That same year, "Cosmópolis," a neighborhood destined for lodging immigrants, was born in Montevideo. In 1853, a policy to lure immigrants was instituted based on the so-called farm families. Specifically, any ships carrying family nuclei intending to farm or ranch in Uruguay were exempted from all types of port and tonnage duties. In addition, this type of family immigrant group was exempted from payment of any personal taxes for four years, and for eight years it would not pay import duties on seeds, farm implements, or construction materials for houses.

The goal was to promote at all costs a migratory prototype based on the family as the fundamental populating unit. Individual immigration was rejected a priori.[13] Various legislative measures in 1855 supported this plan, and in 1856 the Office of Immigration, dependent upon the Ministry of the Treasury, was born.[14] In 1880, an Honorary Commission of Immigration and Agriculture, dependent upon the Ministry of Government, was created. It sought to form colonies by establishing farm credit and promoting agriculture in general, as well as irrigation schemes in particular.

In 1890, the so-called spontaneous immigration to Uruguay was initiated. In other words, the Uruguayan state did not participate in the immigrant's European voyage, but welcomed him upon his arrival in the country. Beginning that year, the Uruguayan authorities permitted the tax-free entrance of any goods that the immigrant wished to bring into the country. Baggage would be disembarked free of charge, and immigrants would be helped in their attempts to find a position in the field of their choice. Moreover, the state would lodge and feed the foreigners for the eight days following their arrival, and paid the cost of transportation to the place chosen to establish residence. Distance did not matter.

There is no doubt that the nations of southern South America were looking for the magic wand to make them prosper after the processes of independence of the first third of the nineteenth century. The objectives in this respect and the points of view of the Americans could not be clearer. Here is the Chilean example:[15]

> There are three main elements that must be taken into consideration in the study of this social process [that of emigration]:
>
> First, the existence of the emigrant population.
> In second place, the conditions of the country of emigration and
> Third, the distance between this country and the centers of emigration.
>
> Referring these three elements to the Chilean immigration project; with respect to the first, it is appropriate to consider whether or not there presently exists a higher number of people in Europe wishing to emigrate, and at the same time from which nationalities it would be suitable to choose to promote the peopling of Chile with good seed.
>
> In respect to the second, there will be almost no need to insist on the excellent conditions of Chile as a country for immigration, regardless of certain contrary opinions that we will discuss when the time comes.
>
> And in relation to the third, that is, the distance, we acknowledge Chile's disadvantaged situation in this respect, the practical means of extenuating these disadvantages and the precise consequences that derive from it.
>
> ... The general crisis that, at the present time, especially afflicts the nations of Europe contributes in great measure to the impoverishment of the working class and awakes in it the desire to emigrate.
>
> On the other hand, it cannot be forgotten that professional people, born and raised in the heart of these powerful European civilizations, possess tastes and goals that they wish to satisfy, aspirations and tastes clearly very legitimate, that are not in proportion to what the fruit of their work can procure them....
>
> And in this we would have to pay most careful attention to when the shipments are made on a large scale, if we do not want to suffer the disequilibrium that has, in our opinion, been produced in other countries, such as the United States. There the almost exclusive predominance of two great nationalities that were not able to import artistic taste, in the long run resulted in the lack of this precious element of civilization; and only now, due to the constant efforts of private individuals and the European war of 1870, which thrust an abundant

artistic emigration upon that nation, are we coming to see the laborious birth of the fine arts there.

... In our judgment, in addition to the book and the press, among others, there are three fundamental processes that tend to guide the transfer of the current European civilizations to the South American republics: immigration, first of all; scientific or industrial studies that the South Americans devote themselves to in Europe, whether privately or for their governments; and the contracting of professors of the Old World that brought the theoretical and practical notion of science and the arts to the New.

The statesman should take care of all three, but it is impossible to refute that the most efficient and considerable of them is immigration.

A select and abundant immigration currently is a fundamental necessity of a state in formation.

There is no element that can produce greater benefits in the new countries like this; nor is any sacrifice too great to bear to achieve it.

Great and civilized are the nations of France and England, Germany and Austria, Russia and Italy; civilized but less numerous are Spain, Portugal, Holland, Belgium, and Switzerland; numerous, but depressed in backwardness, China and Turkey, and thus it is seen, without multiplying the examples, that the importance of a nation is established and appreciated in proportion to the number and civilization of its inhabitants.

And judicious and wisely established immigration is of the utmost importance for a new state, and its enlargement and power depends on it, if the land and the climate and other conditions of the country permit the constitution of a nationality. The United States and Australia prove this truth; and to a lesser extent, Mexico and the South American republics.

While at first glance it would seem superfluous to demonstrate the utility and necessity of immigration, the fact that there are those in our country who oppose and still try to eliminate this undertaking of our public services forces us, however, to focus on it. . . .

This is not all: there is a very grave danger that because of this disequilibrium between a nation's population and that of neighboring countries', which have carefully increased their own by wisely taking advantage of the powerful European emigration, the unprepared nation risks its existence.

Therefore the transitory interests should never prevent a work as important as immigration: the future more than the present benefits from its fruits.

However slow and costly it appears at the beginning, its importance is such and its results so sure that provoking it and developing it is an unavoidable obligation of any new state.

The amount of money the treasury invests in such an undertaking contributes to the complete fulfillment of one of the highest missions of the state as a political entity: to provide the increase necessary in the national population. The public wealth spent on immigrants is the most lucrative investment that a new state can make with its capital.

To govern is to populate, an American statesman said for South America, and for Chile this problem is today the most considerable task that all national politicians have to focus on, and it will be for many years.

And it is most natural that it should be so, in view of the enormous and often insuperable difficulties against which the colonists in an untilled soil have to fight.

These very difficulties discredit the undertaking, and it is immediately possible to obtain new colonists that wish to emigrate under such conditions.

Without clear restraint and demarcation, the colony can turn into a seedbed of disputes and lawsuits, which are avoided by executing ahead of time those works and drawing up general plans for the colony, that are given to the colonists upon handing them a path right up to their house.

Roads are what attract the immigrant population and contribute little by little to forming cities. There is no greater error in the colonizing enterprise, as is well known, than to wait for population development to build roads.

The lack of roads delays peopling; while with good roads populations are born and grow with no obstacles whatsoever.

. . . The colonist chosen is a man of reflection and mature judgments, and generally has a lot to lose if he errs in his calculations upon expatriating himself. It is therefore difficult to persuade him to emigrate from one moment to the next, and for the same reason it is not possible to spend too much time pondering the inconveniences of the operations of colonization brashly ordered and carried out, without the necessary preparation. . . .

If all human undertakings always present obstacles to overcome, it is characteristic of the strong, and consequently of the Chilean tenacity and spirit, to overcome and eliminate them.

Those to whom Chile might appear as on the path of population growth are surely not discouraged, since the vast extension and enviable variety and fertility of its territories, the industrial and commercial conditions of its geographic configuration and situation, its great climatic richness that permits as much cultivation as the soil produces, the well-proven solidity of its political organization, the sobriety and the energy of a hardworking race that lives for progress and the love of the homeland, show that there the necessary elements are united to construct one of the great nationalities that with the passing of the years and the winds of progress will represent the current great European civilizations in South America.

Hopefully this very day we will manage to open a vast field to an undertaking of such proportions, and our nation will soon enjoy the great benefits of such a large, civilized population.

Thus, the fate of the agrarian utopia in Río de la Plata and the rest of the Southern Cone was determined.

Structure of the Emigration Agencies

To this point, the process by which both civil society and the authorities of Río de la Plata could create new republics based on modern farm colonies has been addressed. In Europe, news of the agrarian utopia brought to the Southern Cone an overflow of land-hungry colonists. The protagonists of these enterprises, the agents and the *ganchos*, did their job to perfection, not so much for philanthropic reasons or idealism to promote the growth and development of Uruguay, Argentina, and Chile, but to line their own pockets. In the end, one of the most significant aspects of Basque emigration to America involves this phenomenon as a mercantile business, from which some go-getters reaped personal rewards.

In the Basque Country, as elsewhere in Spain, France, and Europe, there were emigration agents starting in the late 1820s. It was in the second half of the nineteenth century, however, that emigration agencies came to form part of the urban landscape, especially in port cities.[16] From the outset, they received commissions from outfitters, ship captains, and the governments to which they were connected. The systems of embarkation and contracting of immigrants left a lot of room for speculation due to the significant number of emigration-related mercantile operations. Agents, captains, and outfitters got together to obtain immediate benefits, forming a de facto alliance of common interests to promote and exploit the migratory movement. Their methods and conduct did not always meet moral or legislative standards. The agents acted on their own or for foreign governments, or served private contractors. Their role as intermediaries enabled them to charge a set fee per emigrant embarked.

As has been noted, the centers of *enganche* were located at the ports. From there, their radius of action extended inland through subagents, who established initial contact with potential emigrants. These "secret expeditions," already common in the 1830s, were reminiscent of the former black slave trade in every way. In fact, the nineteenth-century Basque press did not tire of invoking this comparison.

The mission of the subagents consisted of traveling through their assigned territory, convincing the inhabitants of the marvelous life that awaited them if they decided to emigrate to America. The subagents took advantage of overpopulation, bad harvests, plagues, and droughts to put forth alternatives to the discouraging life in the European countryside. Habitual recruitment places were the town church's atrium, the plaza, the market, and the recreation hall.

The most common promises of these subagents were of the free concession of land and farm tools to those that chose to go to America. This propaganda was complemented by the diffusion of pamphlets throughout the rural areas and publication of appealing announcements about the diaspora in the press. Such propaganda compared the American countries to little less than earthly paradises.

The poster brought the seduction of the New World to all corners, always inviting adventure. That newspapers urged emigration under the sponsorship of the maritime companies is evidence of the fierce fight between shipping companies to secure the greatest number of clients. This is why pro-emigration publicity was so common in the press in Genoa, Marseille, Bordeaux, Bayonne, La Coruña, Pasaia, Bilbao, and Donostia.

A plethora of guides, manuals, and readers, earmarked for an easily seduced public, circulated throughout Europe. They included useful advice and information (salaries, standard of living, climate, food, uses, and customs) about the countries of destination. All this, always clearly exaggerated, generally provided the reader with a false image of American working conditions and living standards.

The policy of the American governments became a decisive complementary stimulus for the measures already mentioned. These governments provided advances for the trip, which the emigrants would pay once they were settled in America: "subsidized passages," as they were known at the time. Another ploy to attract emigrants was evident in the system that the Argentine government made fashionable beginning in 1870. The state paid for the passage to Europe of immigrants of good conduct who had amassed a degree of wealth, to induce friends and relatives to head to America. The hundred tickets issued in 1873 for various points of Europe were well worth the investment: six of the improvised "agents" themselves returned with 402 people. Sometimes, the consuls exercised recruitment, at government cost, of emigrants of the country in which they were assigned. This occurred beginning in the 1880s, years in which "offices of information for emigrants" were opened in the main European capitals.

The Uruguayan consul in Gasteiz, Julián Quiroga, is an example. In 1875, he encouraged his government to attract Basque emigrants. In principal, the propaganda would be aimed at those who were legally permitted to emigrate. But it also acted in less-favored social sectors, in which illegality always reigned. Here the most degrading forms of this traffic appeared. The politically persecuted, fugitives, sick or disabled, and children and prostitutes were embarked under trying contractual conditions. The ignorance of many of these emigrants and the lack of effective legal guarantees offered a wide-open field for speculation by the agents: peasants embarked secretly with fake passports or even no documentation whatsoever. The social discontent of these members of the diaspora placed them at the mercy of agents, outfitters, and captains.

One of the most frequent abuses consisted of charging for passage in a steamship and then embarking the passenger in a sailing ship. In other cases, advance payment for the passage did not ensure the voyage to America either. Frequently the agent, lacking scruples, paid only one-tenth of the ticket price to the captain or outfitter, so that the emigrant was forced off the ship at the first stop of the crossing. It was not uncommon to embark people headed for Montevideo, for example, in a ship for New York. There, realizing the deception, immigrants might be promised quick transport to their destination, which would never materialize or be delayed for months. The abuses committed under the apparent legality of this traffic in emigrants were not, however, checked until the early twentieth century. As will be seen in the case of the Basques, contemporaries did not tire of denouncing the tricks of these merchants of men.

The Basque Attraction and the *Ganchos*

Since the start-up of the migratory process to the Southern Cone at the beginning of the nineteenth century, the Basques were always esteemed as first-class settlers. They were thought to possess a full rosary of virtues that coincided with the ideal image of the good settler as held in Argentina, Uruguay, and Chile. The typical Basque was portrayed as a man of sane customs and a healthy life, who was also physically strong, serious, pleasant, and honest beyond a shadow of a doubt. For these reasons, the arrival of Basques from both sides of the Pyrenees was promoted from very early on.

As early as 1826, the French emigration agent Loreilhe wrote letters informing the Argentine emigration commission of the measures he took to contract emigrants from the French Basque Country. In a letter dated in Bordeaux on April 16, 1826, and directed to Manuel Pintos, president of the commission, agent Loreilhe expressed the following:

> I have, Mister President, the satisfaction of showing You all my gratitude and accepting with the best will the mission of the Commission to promote in our Departments [referring to the Atlantic Pyrenees] the emigration of the artisan and the peasant for Buenos Aires [*sic:* for Argentina]. This appointment is highly flattering for me, and even if I were only to work for glory I would be satisfied. I have great projects whose implementation would provide thousands of artisans. Having to occupy myself exclusively in this business I am going to impart a project in which I will emphasize the philanthropic and benevolent aims of the Emigration Commission with the principal articles of its regulation, and I will send it to the border departments and large cities, in which I will

have numerous correspondents. I will take care to advise you of exactly the number of individuals, their profession, age, and observations, with the advances made to each one. I will remit the accounts of upkeep and shipping expenses to you.

I wish You, Mister President, to notify me of the announcements and agreements of the Commission, which I will promptly take care of.[17]

On May 1, 1827, again from Bordeaux, the agent Loreilhe continued giving account regarding the *enganche* of Basques:

> I take note that in dealing with the outfitters you wish the shipping of the passengers to be settled in cash; it might be necessary to pay more; please speak about the matter with Mr. Mendeville [the connection between Loreilhe and the Argentine Commission].
>
> You should have been instructed by my predecessor that he already had 2,000 names registered, generally from the countryside, strong, big, and hardworking, but without resources, that needed funds for travel expenses and clothing. Some are under my supervision and I have made them considerable advances, not being able to foresee from the beginning that there would be such a long delay. I detain them and make them have patience. If it had not closed, my register would already have more than 6,000.
>
> Having taken the precaution of establishing subaltern agents in the populous southern departments, from where I can relocate many entire families that would agree, I am ready to carry out your orders as soon as you communicate them to me.[18]

On October 15, 1827, agent Loreilhe sent a letter to Mendeville, the delegate of the Argentine Commission of Emigration in Europe, in which he updated him about the situation:

> The Commission of Emigration of Buenos Aires [*sic:* of Argentina] of which you are a member, having named me its agent to facilitate the emigration of artisans and peasants, this Commission has authorized me through its office on the date December 7, 1825, to have the regulations printed; they have sent me the forms to translate them into different languages, insert them into the newspapers and distribute them in all places where the beneficial and philanthropic objectives of its government might be needed. I have punctually carried out and fulfilled its instructions.
>
> I have had the honor of writing to the president of the Commission on as many occasions as I have been able to keep him informed of my operations in this respect.[19]

To collect his expenditures, Loreilhe sent this memorandum to the Argentine Emigration Commission on December 15, 1827:

Account of the expenses and advance payments made through the account of the Emigration Commission of Buenos Aires in the Agency of Bordeaux

Items	Costs (in Francs)
For printing 10,000 prospects and regulations according to the form	1,500
For printing 600 copies of a 36-page pamphlet according to the form	2,000
Expenses in Paris, Nantes, Limoges	800
Travel expenses to the southern agency	1,000
Rent for a records office in Bordeaux, one year	1,200
Clerk for the Record and passports	1,200
Insertion into the newspapers	150
Letters and tips	1,200
Books, watermarked paper for 2,000 requests	1,100
Total as of January 1, 1827	9,150

Extract according to my books.
Bordeaux on December 15, 1827
Loreilhe

The ensuing financial efforts to attract immigrants to the Southern Cone in the nineteenth century took place in Uruguay and came from the hand of the English entrepreneur Samuel Lafone (or Laffont), as Pierre Lhande indicated in 1910,[20] and as the present author has confirmed:

> The exodus of 1832 was promoted by an English firm, "Lafone and Wilson," that tried to populate its farm establishments on the outskirts of Montevideo. It is enough to open a newspaper of the country to see long lists in both languages,[21] containing the most tempting propositions. Sometimes, it is an agent approved by the prefecture that makes a daily "business" trip to Bordeaux and takes care of contracting the emigrants and taking them to the ship. Other times, it is the intermediary who takes the steps on his own, so mysterious to the popular imagination, of the ticket acquisition and money changing.

On July 16, 1837, a mercantile contract was signed in Montevideo between the then vice president of the Uruguayan Republic, Carlos Anaya; the secretary of the treasury, Francisco Joaquín Muñoz; and Samuel Lafone. Among other clauses, the following conditions were signed by both parties for the introduction of settlers, as substantiated in documentation from the General Archive of the Nation in Montevideo:

> That neither infants, men that exceed the age of sixty-five years who are not the head of a family composed of at least two useful individuals, nor those that

might habitually suffer a physical or moral illness that renders them useless for work in industry and the arts will be acceptable to the government.

... That only for a period of six years will the colonists be exempt from the military service that by the laws of this country they might be subject to perform after they have acquired the right of citizenship. That the salary that the colonists are to earn that the government might employ to recover the debt, will be suitable and arranged between the same government and said colonists.

... The ships of Europe will bring individuals on board only at the rate of one and three quarters per ton, two from the Canary Islands and those adjacent to the continent of Africa.

... For those acceptable that the government will give to Mister Laffont a document that is worth eighty *patacones* against the public Treasury for the passage of each one that is older than fourteen years and forty for those less than this age.

... Passage will be provided neither for the infants nor for those individuals of sixty-five and over that are not head of a family of at least two useful persons. Nor for those of habitual physical illness.

... The colonists signing at their arrival the obligation to pay the public Treasury within the first twelve, eighteen, and twenty-four months for their passage, with whose act the entrepreneur will remain beyond any responsibility, they will be able to accommodate themselves where it might be most suitable for them, with right, nevertheless, of the government to employ them before others in their respective industry, recording everything that the two parties arrange.[22]

There's no doubt, then, of Samuel Lafone's intention to obtain quick and immediate profit with the business of emigration of European colonists. The official document clearly and concisely displays what is negotiated between the entrepreneur in question and the Uruguayan authorities, very interested in the arrival of immigrants. Once more, the ones that bore the brunt were the newly arrived. They had to spend long periods repaying their passages by working for compatriots, as can be seen in the case of the Basques in table 2.23 in appendix 2.

But there are more examples of profit from traffic in emigration. On November 10, 1841, in Tolosa (Gipuzkoa), José Joaquín Elormendi and Ignacio Beguiristain drew up an agreement to make money from the American enterprise:[23]

> Mr. José Joaquín Elormendi, resident of the city of Montevideo overseas, and presently having come in search of people living in this province of Guipúzcoa and *villa* of Tolosa, and José Ignacio de Beguiristain, resident of the town of Larraul, have met and agreed that the latter be transported by the former all expenses paid to said city of Montevideo, in the embarkation in which he has come in search of people, for the quantity of one thousand four hundred

copper reales, those which said José Ignacio de Beguiristain is obligated to satisfy and pay Mr. José Joaquín Elormendi, within one year from the time that he is transported to the aforementioned city of Montevideo, which in it or its surroundings he might earn with his work; and for greater security of this obligation gives for his bails Mr. Joaquín de Aristizabal, resident of the enunciated *villa* of Tolosa and Mr. José Antonio de Zuaznabar, resident of the expressed town of Larraul, who finding themselves present effectively grant said guarantee with the expression that each one did it for half of the enunciated quantity, that is, each one seven hundred copper reales only, without either of them having obligation or responsibility for a greater quantity, even if the other might die or reach a state of inability to respond for his part. And they signed in the *villa* of Tolosa, on November 10, 1841.

On October 1, 1856, the Donostia residents Celestino Albizu and Pedro Cortabarría signed a written agreement and obligation there to transport eighty-three people to Buenos Aires and Montevideo. Profit again appeared at the forefront of the operation:[24]

In the city of San Sebastián, on the fourth of October of eighteen hundred fifty and six, before me His Majesty's regular scribe, and witnesses that will express themselves, appeared Mr. Celestino Albizu, captain of the Spanish corvette named *Lasarte*, and on the other hand Mr. Pedro Cortabarría, resident of this city, and they stated that having agreed between the two that the eighty-three individuals that have made their agreements and contracts with the present Cortabarría will be passengers of the ship in question, on the voyage that it is going to make to Montevideo and Buenos Aires, they have set the amount for passage for seventy-nine of said individuals, who go as passengers in the prow, at eight hundred eighty reales each and the remaining four, who go as cabin passengers, at one thousand six hundred reales, also each. In consequence, they grant that it is Albizu that accepts as passengers to be taken to Montevideo and Buenos Aires in the ship under his command the eighty-three people whose names appear on the list submitted by the present Cortabarría, with whom all of them have made their agreements and contracts, and the mentioned Albizu confesses that on account of establishing the arrangement made regarding the said eighty-three passengers he has received from Mr. Pedro Cortabarría five thousand seven hundred eighty copper reales in good coin of gold and silver, and he therefore grants the receipt and letter of payment most firm and efficient of said quantity in favor of Mr. Cortabarría, renouncing by not appearing present the surrender of the outstanding monies, the term of two years indicated by the law for the proof of its receipt and the rest of its favor. The present Mr. Pedro Cortabarría is obligated for his part in the most solemn form to pay in the term of six months, counted from the day that the corvette *Lasarte* reaches Buenos Aires, on his own to the present Mr. Celestino Albizu or the person legitimately representing him in Buenos Aires the quantity of seventy thousand one hundred forty copper reales, that together with the five thousand seven hundred eighty reales already surrendered, as has been expressed above, forms a sum of seventy-five thousand nine hundred twenty reales, which is the total price settled and agreed upon in arrangement with Albizu for the eighty-three people that have made their agreements and contracts with Cortabarría, whose sum of seventy thousand one hundred forty copper reales the same Cortabarría will pay without any excuse or pretext in good coin of silver or gold, usual and current and in no type of paper created or to be created, nor another different sort. And if it is not fulfilled when the term of six months from the arrival of the ship to Buenos Aires passes, without necessity of citation or other judicial or extrajudicial diligence expressly renouncing it, it will be dunned by all legal vigor to pay said quantity and the costs, expenses, damages, and injuries that are caused to Mr. Celestino Albizu or his legitimate representation. And this writing was read to the parties present and was thereby affirmed and ratified by them, and its fulfillment was obligated with their present and future goods, in the most efficient way and executed according to law, with the renunciation of the laws, *forua*, benefits, and privileges that can favor them, submitting themselves if necessary to judges and justices of Buenos Aires or any other place.

Another example of the financial interests provoked by emigration comes from 1842. On January 26 of that year, Francisco Brie, a Bayonne merchant, and José de Garciarena, a resident of Ezcurra (Navarre), signed an agreement to promote the emigration of Basques from both sides of the Pyrenees to Montevideo. These were the conditions:[25]

> Art. 1. The said Mr. Brie appoints as his agent the cited Mr. Martín Garciarena, to whom he gives sufficient power for the purpose of providing passengers for Montevideo, for the expeditions of Mr. Brie and under the conditions that the former will designate him by his instructions.
>
> Art. 2. The named agent Garciarena is obligated to fulfill exactly the said instructions that may be given for this objective, and the passengers that he will provide during ten years counted from this date will be for the expeditions of said Mr. Brie.
>
> Art. 3. For each passenger that the agent Garciarena provides who embarks with the obligation in writing to pay their passage, Mr. Brie will pay said agent two *pesos fuertes*.
>
> Art. 4. So that the cited agent Garciarena gives proof of security that in this part he will proceed faithfully and that during the named term of ten

years he will not provide passengers to any merchant other than said Mr. Brie, a fine of fifty *pesos fuertes* is imposed for each one of the passengers that he is proven to have provided to another merchant.

Art. 5. On account of the care that the said agent should have in the documents that he will provide the passengers in order to ensure the cost of their passage and upkeep to Montevideo, Mr. Brie is obligated to pay to the mentioned agent Garciarena one *peso fuerte*, in addition to the two already indicated, and for each passenger, provided their documents are guaranteed with secured and certified deposits by the same agent using the bail's deposit; the payment of said extra *peso fuerte* will be understood to have been verified when from Montevideo they ship the receipt of the payment of passage for said passengers, unless they have taken care of it here.

On January 16, 1855, Juan Pablo de Altolaguirre, his affinal cousin José Prudencio de Guerrico, living in Paris, and Adolfo Vempraet, a Buenos Aires resident, reached an agreement in Oñati to ship two hundred Basque workers to Argentina to build the railroad planned in the capital.[26]

The following mercantile emigration agents and companies operated in the Navarrese Valley of Baztán between 1840 and 1880:[27]

1. Modesto Meogui and Martín José Fort became partners in 1857–1858 in the capitalistic enterprise of exporting emigrants. The former organized 47 trips, and the latter, 154. Almost all left from Bayonne.
2. Brothers Apesteguy was one of the companies that would make the most pro-emigration campaigns.
3. Juan Bautista Gortari (from Arrayoz, Navarre) preferred contracting voyages to Havana, although he also organized some to Río de la Plata.
4. Martín José Fort would hire Bartolomé Guerendiain, resident of Elizondo, to take thirty-four ships to Río de la Plata.
5. An association founded by Salvador Echegoyen and Martín Casabide contracted Agustín Sarría and Félix Casabide as representatives. Casabide, a resident of Arregui, replaced J. Ilarraz in his assignment. This crew managed to send thirty-one voyages to America—especially Río de la Plata—between 1840 and 1870.
6. Agustín Sarriá, who beginning in 1850 would negotiate with emigrants in his own company, made seventeen voyages.
7. Brie & Co. (Buenos Aires) had its most reliable collaborator in Juan de Aldaz, resident of Lecumberry. The company organized the departures from Pasaia. Aldaz chartered eleven voyages in the 1840s.
8. Nogus (Saint-Jean-de-Luz) and J. Gurochaga (Irun) contracted Miguel Machintoa, who organized nine voyages as a representative.

9. Antonio Echevarne, inhabitant of Saint-Jean-Pied-de-Port, had two representatives: Martín Sala (organized one expedition) and Juan Bautista Gorosizo (carried out the contracting of five voyages).
10. Juan Pedro Echebarnel, resident of Huarte (France), chartered three voyages.
11. Bernard Doyharçabal, from Ainhoa (France) with his own company, contracted two expeditions.

All of them sought to become wealthy through profit from emigration. Apparently such mercantile interest yielded migratory results when it came to the Basques. For in 1875, the Central Directive Immigration Commission of the Eastern Republic of Uruguay included an interesting letter in its annual report. Sent by this country's consul in Gasteiz, Julián Quiroga, the letter assessed the suitability of the Basques as immigrant-colonists. These were the contents:

It is proven by the requests made to the office, that those most accepted in the country are peasant families of the Basque provinces. It will be more efficacious to stimulate their arrival, than that of people of other nationalities, provided by the spontaneous emigration.

Together, through the arrival of Basques, with the introduction into immediate employment of the immigrants, lodging and other expenses will be avoided.

Without entering into the odious estimation of the merit or lack thereof of the diverse nationalities that make up our current immigration, given that the best rule is to accept the good where one finds it, I must state that the Basque population is the one that will be most quickly employed by the colonial companies.

Few immigrants can present these two assimilative conditions with relation to the Eastern Republic of Uruguay in such harmony as the Basques.

In continuous contact with the Castilians, and obligated by the law of official education, all more or less speak the beautiful Castilian language with perfection, habituating themselves with facility to the uses and customs of the country in which they choose to live.

Agriculture and livestock are the only two industries that are cultivated, almost exclusively, in the Basque provinces, and from this the undisputed aptitude of its natives for jobs of the field and mountain is born, to which they are devoted since childhood. Their strong and robust constitution permits them to spend the whole day on the job, with a short rest at midday.

In the tasks of the quarry, polishing of stones, and in all that embraces the vast line of public works, such as roads, bridges, railroads, etc., they have no competitors. It is enough to say about this point that during the railroad construction of the North of Spain, the contractors paid one half more to Basque peons and double to the quarriers and factory constructors.

The same happens today in Andalusia and on the railway lines of Asturias and Galicia, and it can be assured that, in general, the mere name of Basque is a first-rate recommendation. It turns out to be worthwhile, therefore, to establish an Official Agency here, represented by one of its consular agents who may be the true director and promoter of immigration.

This agent will name for himself and have under his command various other subagents, living and known in this country, that will reside in all the most appropriate places to promote emigration under the instructions of the former.

The first care of the main Agent must be to publish a pamphlet in Basque and Castilian containing the necessary news to make the situation of that country known, with statistical data about its mercantile, industrial, and agricultural wealth; the progressive increases of immigration and a table with the daily wages or salaries that artists and workers of all classes earn there. This pamphlet... must have great publicity, so that it circulates through all areas of this country and serves as the basis for the subsequent works. The agent will also have to frequently publish articles, official notices, personal advertisements, etc. in the Basque dailies, with the objective of continually calling the attention of the public to that country, even if indirectly.

The efficacy of the contract agents, *ganchos*, and *enganchadores* could not have been better with the help of precise "market studies." Greed and yearnings for wealth did the rest.

E. J. Carriarte and the Norddeutscher Lloyd

Among the holdings of the archive of the Foral Deputation of Bizkaia, there is a valuable document that clearly and directly manifests the maneuvers used by Restituto Basterra to "hook" emigrants. Basterra was a native of Zornotza and representative of the Carricarte firm of La Coruña. As a consequence of continual denouncements presented before the civil government of La Coruña by numerous swindled Bizkaians, Restituto Basterra was taken to court. But this local agent's activity will be analyzed here, not the complaints. The correspondence between him and his boss, Mr. Carriarte, general agent for the German steamer-mail company Norddeutscher Lloyd in Spain provides an approximate vision of these agents' typical mode of operation. The Basterra-Carricarte collaboration took place between 1889 and 1890.[28]

In his work *La emigración vasco-navarra*, José Cola y Goiti tells of the existence of no fewer than twenty-five emigration agents in Bordeaux in 1882. Information is not available about either the number in Bizkaia or their connections with those in the French Basque Country or elsewhere on the Cantabrian cornice. Nevertheless, the suit that the tribunals of justice brought against Basterra for swindling by overcharging some emigrants for their passages is useful. It provides insights into the methods used by this subagent in service to a well-established emigration network in La Coruña. The legality with which the migratory issue was handled in every moment is surprising, as is the legality of the people participating in it. As will be seen in the letters to follow, the association of people and capital to establish emigration agencies for financial gain was commonplace in the nineteenth-century Basque Country; although not permitted by the authorities, it was at least tolerated.

Thus our protagonist, Restituto Basterra, was recognized in the trial held against him as an emigration subagent. If he was permitted to present himself to the legal tribunals of justice with this job as a credential, it means that, in fact, this profession was recognized by society, or at least by the ordinary Spanish jurisdiction of the day. It is unnecessary to focus on the trial's details here; rather, those parts that provide information about these agents' work will be presented. Thus, the author has chosen some letters sent by head agent Carricarte from La Coruña to his employee or subagent in Bilbao, Restituto Basterra. The communications of the latter that arrived via the Official Information Office of the Argentine Republic, located in Madrid, have also been included. In Carricarte's first letter to Basterra, dated February 26, 1889, he informed him that the steamers of Norddeutscher Lloyd made a stop in La Coruña en route to Río de la Plata. The emigrant families contracted by Basterra, whose contracts were known to the Argentine Republic's Information Office in Madrid, would embark in these steamers. That is, this office, agent E. J. Carricarte, and Basterra, the subagent in Bilbao, functioned in perfect harmony. In the same letter it was suggested to the latter that "you can keep making propaganda for emigration to Buenos Aires, for which we send you a packet of announcements or prospectives." A few days later, on March 10, a note was sent from the Argentine Information Office to Basterra saying that "in no way whatsoever can I make available an advance for the passages from their domiciles to the port of embarkation." On May 10 of that same year, Basterra received another letter from the Argentine Information Office communicating the following to him:

> In answer to your letter dated the fifth of this month, it falls to me to tell you that the contract made with the Company of Norddeutscher Lloyd for its steamers to stop at the ports of Santander and Pasajes [Pasaia] is a done deal, provided that three hundred full passages are facilitated for any of them.
>
> In consequence, as soon as there is a minimum of three hundred passages for the port of Santander and it is announced twenty days in advance, a special steamer can be requested.
>
> I take advantage of this occasion to tell you that by recent disposition it has been settled that these rules be added to the applications [provided that the

application be requested by and under the responsibility of the head of the family, only men that have the required professions] in the following form:

1. Families composed of two or three people can be grouped with an equal number of single individuals.
2. Those of four or five people can go accompanied by two men traveling alone.
3. Those of six to eight people can be accompanied by one single individual.

But the heads of families must be made aware of the agreement to add outside people in their requests so that upon arriving they do not claim ignorance of signing the corresponding letters for repayment of the passage of their family and the single men that are included in their application.

Nevertheless, things would not be so easy, as can be deduced from the contents of the letter that Carricarte sent Basterra twelve days later. Migratory business with Buenos Aires was clearly declining. This location came to be viewed as unsatisfactory for shipping emigrants, and was ultimately replaced by Brazil. Here is the letter:

Dear Sir: Crossed with our previous 19th of this month that we confirm, we are graced today by a letter of the same date, the contents of which we are aware of.

As we told you in the just cited, the Management of Lloyd has given us the order not to accept families with passage subsidized for Buenos Aires, but acceding to our requests has authorized us to embark a small number of emigrants in each steamer.

Thus, we telegraph you today as follows: "You can send those receiving subsidies dispatched for March 31, being notified that the Company does not work whimsically and that when it makes a decision it does so based on sound reasons."

... In respect to emigration for Brazil, as we have told you the documentation is the same in every way to that required for Buenos Aires, which [documentation] does not have to be sent anywhere and if it deals with this agency the passenger himself will have to come a bit ahead of time, being responsible for the cost of the voyage and stay there, that the Company provides only the passage from the pier of La Coruña to the pier of his destination in the Empire of Brazil.

For each complete passage we will pay you the commission of 5 pesetas and the first departure will be the 6th of next April when the steamer *Leipzig* will touch in La Coruña.

For this emigration you can work as fast as possible; in contrast, for Buenos Aires go a bit slowly until it is possible for us to instruct you to accept all that comes your way, which we trust will be soon.

In regard to yellow fever in Rio de Janeiro, it is of no concern, as the latest news indicates the decline and confidence in the imminent disappearance of this illness.

To many emigrants who have come to this Agency to go to Buenos Aires, in virtue of not being able to take them to said place, we have made them consider embarking for Brazil, which they have accepted.

Yours sincerely. . . .

On June 9, Carricarte sent Restituto Basterra another interesting letter:

Dear Sir: We have your letters from the 5th, 6th, and 7th of the current month, and knowing their contents we send you the following telegram: "Not charging anything to emigrants we will pay you three pesetas commission per full passage. Please be so kind as to telegraph," which we confirmed receiving your answer in these terms: "Telegram received, I absolutely accept the contents, please telegraph. Nine family dispatched."

As you see we concede you a commission of three pesetas per full passage so that, continuing in your recruiting work, you might raise a good number of emigrants for the coming expeditions. You should charge them absolutely nothing at all, which you will voucher to us with a receipt from each family head, for which we send you separately a package of printed forms. The receipt will be in duplicate.

With respect to the dispatch of the documentation that Mr. Olleros refused to do, we telegraphed you as follows: "It is best to telegraph Lamas, Inspector General of Immigration, 23 Rue Clapeyron, Paris, asking him to order Olleros to dispatch his passengers," which we confirm by showing you that according to the telegram of Mr. Olleros, this man will dispatch all the documentation that you have sent him.

PS: For future embarkations kindly send us all the documentation so that we can then ship it from here directly to Mr. Olleros.

One day later, Carricarte once again insisted upon the necessity of continuing to recruit:

Dear Sir: We confirm our previous letter from yesterday and possess yours from the 8th in view of whose contents we trust that your work in that country for recruiting emigrants is yielding the results that we desire.

We urge you not to forget to make the family heads send the notes relating to not having paid anything at all, which will have to be in duplicate, shipping them to us with the documents of these people.

Awaiting your news, yours sincerely. . . .

On July 1, 1889, Basterra appears clearly defined as a contracting subagent of Carricarte:

Dear Sir: For the time being we authorize you to proceed with the jobs of propaganda and recruitment of subsidized passages for the Argentine Republic as our subagent.

Yours sincerely. . . .

On July 19 of the same year, the Information Office of the Argentine diplomatic legation, located at Desengaño Street, no. 27-2nd-left, sent an official note to Restituto Basterra:

Dear Sir: In answer to your letter of 15th of the present month, I must tell you that I cannot try to remedy the scandals of which you complain, without proof that the agent or agents to which you refer charge the emigrants a commission, for whatever the reason that they collect it, which constitutes a swindle and a violation of the most important point of the contract made in the Norddeutscher Lloyd. If you procure proof of their dealings and send them to me I will send them to the corresponding party.

The quality and type of emigrant that the director of the emigration company, E. J. Carricarte, desired is very clear from the following lines, which he again sent his subordinate on August 1, 1889:

Dear Sir: The present serves to inform you that the management of the Official Information Office of the Argentine Republic in Madrid tells us the following:

Through this office, men traveling alone are admitted on the basis of individual applications, without having to go attached to any family, but they have to be farmers, not above forty years old, presenting all required documents and the wife's consent if married.

As a consequence you already know, men traveling alone can be admitted under the conditions expressed.

On September 28, the Argentine legation again contacted the Bizkaian *gancho*:

Friend Basterra: You will receive a letter dated today from the director notifying you that in the future you can give the applications for the office to its Consul, who will dispatch them there, as it is so ordered by the Argentine Government.

(Reserved) For your Government, and so that you use all that you can, work as much as possible, as it seems that the emigration is coming to its end. Do not say anything to other agents like Mur and his group and see personally to the arrangement with the Consul. It is advice that you should take advantage of and stop being so good.

On November 21, Basterra was informed of what he had to do in his work:

Dear Sir: Your letter of the 12th of this month does not need reply as it is Mr. Olleros that has to answer your observations.

Bear in mind the following debits:

665 pesetas, cost for 3½ passages on the *Strassburg*
190 pesetas, cost for one passage on the *Karlsrhue*
122.25 pesetas, cost for commission on 40¾ subsidized passages embarked on the *Strassburg*
68.25 pesetas, cost for commission on 22¾ passages embarked on the *Karlsrhue*

With these calculations made, a balance of 1,004.25 pesetas comes out in our favor, an amount you will kindly reimburse us or deliver to Mr. Ángel Palacio from this office, thereby closing our account and your commissions with the steamer *Karlsrhue* without us having to pay any other commission on any other passenger that might embark on our steamers.

You can continue sending us passengers for payment under the same conditions that we have agreed upon.

Kindly acknowledge receipt of the present and give us consent or reparations to our letter and attached lists, sincerely yours. . . .

On December 27, doubt was cast upon Basterra's work, as he was accused of working for other *enganchadores:*

Dear Sir: Confirming our previous from yesterday and telegram as follows: "*Hanover* does not leave on the twenty-seventh. First steamer Buenos Aires *Dresden*, fifth January," and "Ducay writes saying you are his subagent. We need a telegraph if you work for him or us."

This last telegram we have directed to you in view of the fact that Mr. Ducay includes your name on the list of his subagents, and as we told you in our previous of the 21 we need to know if you work for him or for us, as we want our representatives to be absolutely unattached to any other agency.

You will also be informed by the other telegram that the first steamer that we dispatch for Buenos Aires is the *Dresden*, which will leave for this port the fifth of the coming January, and we await your news about passage for the same.

Regards. . . .

In December 1889, in harmony with his "friends from Lisbon," as far as immigration was concerned, Carricarte decided to change the ground rules of his undertaking, still in emigration:

Dear Sir: The Argentine government having suspended, as you know, the advance payment for subsidized passages for Buenos Aires, agreeing to the request of our friends from Lisbon that have emigrant contracts with the government of Brazil, we have been entrusted to represent them in the provinces of northern and northeastern Spain.

Therefore, not doubting that you will help us in our proposition, we authorize you to gather families of farmers and rural workers, which will be transported at no charge to Brazil without having to pay anything whatsoever either here or there.

The commission that we will pay you for each adult is eight pesetas.

The steamers that perform this transport are those of the Norddeutscher Lloyd, which we represent in Spain.

The climate of Santos and São Paulo, which is where they will be headed, is good and we therefore believe that your countrymen will be encouraged.

The documentation must be shipped to us, and if possible it would be helpful for them to bring a certificate from the mayor saying that the head of the family is a peasant or farm worker.

We include a note about how the families can be composed and wait for you to tell us immediately if you accept our offer, yours sincerely. . . .

The formalities of the voyage, its price, and the technical instructions were dictated in a January 6, 1890, letter from La Coruña to Bilbao, once more received by Restituto Basterra:

Dear Sir: We possess your letters of the 2nd and 4th of the current that we now answer telling you that the application for passages for Brazil is done in the following manner: children from 1 to 3 years free, from 3 to 8 one-fourth, and from 8 to 12 one-half; from that age on the full passage. The youth that you indicate cannot be admitted in any way as attached to any family, as he has been definitively excluded.

With respect to the paid passages, we have never distrusted you, and we believe it to be appropriate to work harder to give the business greater extension.

In terms of the quantity that we have handed over to the Leonato brothers, in no way is it your responsibility.

We urge you not to forget to obtain the certified occupation visas from the mayors of hamlets, who are precisely the ones that should do it, as no one has more knowledge about the individual than do they, and to make sure that all the emigrants are peasants.

On January 11, 1890, Basterra was again told to work without concern for Carricarte:

Dear Sir: In view of your letter of the 9th of the current that included the indicated copies, which for pure lack of time we have not been able to read, what we will repeat to you is that we are completely disconnected from Mr. Ducay in emigration to Brazil.

We wish you to work for our firm with the assiduity and loyalty that we recognize and to put aside other issues that have no worth whatsoever.

We have telegraphed you the following yesterday: "*Hanover* for Brazil will touch in Coruña eighteenth and not fourteenth. Telegraph the number of people you will have." And today we have also done it in the following term: "Letter received you can send us Brazil passage directly. Telegraph urgently how many *Hanover* seventeenth," which we confirm, now awaiting your news as quickly as possible.

On March 14, 1890, the "business of emigrants" for the empire of Brazil was regulated and perfectly established:

Dear Sir: We confirm to you the previous 24th . . . having to make clear to you that for the future and in virtue of the contract made, we have a steamer for Brazil every fourteen days, accepting only married couples with or without children, with no type of relatives or additional individuals, as long as all the families embark for Rio de Janeiro.

We have telegraphed you thus the 2nd of the present: "Telegraph immediately the number of passengers you have for Brazil," to which you responded saying "I suppose you received the February 25 letter where I stated that I raised 120 or 140 passengers."

In your visit and keeping in mind what you kindly told us in your cited letter with respect to advising your passengers beforehand, we have sent you the following telegram last night: "Advise definitively passage Brazil to embark Coruña 23. Passengers Buenos Aires left steamer *Berlin* that we confirm." Hoping now that your good preparations might result in the arrival to La Coruña early enough in advance and with the documents in order for the passengers that you indicate, for whom we have sought places, very pleased that you can come there as well.

The cold, calculated way in which the two men worked in a type of "fatal triangle" with the Argentine Information Office is striking. It is also surprising how Carricarte chose, at the slightest sign of worsening commercial times, to redirect his business without a second thought from Argentine to Brazilian shores. As soon as the government of Buenos Aires created obstacles for the payment of subsidized passages, Carricarte switched to activity with his "friends from Lisbon." It is obvious from his letters to Basterra that he deviated his ships full of emigrants from

Río de la Plata to Brazil, widening and protecting his business under the guarantee of the Brazilian government. In these letters, the emigrants were treated—price included—like any other merchandise transportable in the holds of a vessel streaking across the ocean for Río de la Plata. Ultimately, it seems, business was business.

Seen in that light, Carricarte's enormous interest in the mercantile aspects can be understood. Thus, he would give constant, precise instructions and norms to Mr. Basterra about the commercial policy to follow. The latter, in turn, fulfilled these instructions to the letter so that the business would be highly profitable, the spoils divided, and everyone satisfied. Basterra had a certain infrastructure (notices, pamphlets, up-to-date information from Madrid) and perhaps some subagent or another working for him. And the team was well organized. On the one hand, E. J. Carricarte acted as the general agent in Spain for Norddeutscher Lloyd. On the other, Restituto Basterra fulfilled the functions of subagent in Bilbao, although his field of action probably included not only Bizkaia but most or all of the Basque Country. Lastly, both associates received up-to-date news of the Argentine Republic's need for emigrants through that country's Madrid Information Office.

To this point, clear examples have been shown of local *enganchadores* in perfect harmony with Spanish outfitters; together with compatriots on the other side of the ocean, they made emigration a rich enterprise. American *ganchos* have also been detected; beyond the consular scope, they too tried to get rich by shipping Basque settlers. Here is a clear example, this time in Araba:

> In the place of the Valley and Brotherhood of Villanueva de Valdegovía on the fifth of April of eighteen hundred and seventy, Court de Amurrio, before me, Miguel de Angulo, . . . appear Carlos del Castillo y Sobrón, single, a native of the *villa* of Sobrón of this notarial district and twenty-eight years of age, quarrier by profession, legitimate son of Juan and Dorotea, residents in cited Sobrón; Mr. Romualdo del Castillo y Sobrón, of married status, peasant and of thirty-six years, resident in said Sobrón; and Mr. Ángel de Alonso y Angulo of this residence, cabinetmaker and age of fifty years, whose knowledge, profession, and residence, I certify, who assure their full enjoyment of the civil rights and legal capacity to exercise with complete liberty this instrument and they say: that they have contracted and agree to the following conditions:
>
> The first: that said Mr. Ángel Alonso y Angulo, representative of Mr. San Ginés outfitter in the port of Bilbao, through the former and his ships and in the next one that leaves, is to carry to the ports of Montevideo and Buenos Aires in the republics of America the named Carlos del Castillo y Sobrón. . . .[29]

The agents that came from the American continent tended to be supported and financed by the government of the republic in question, although there was no lack of those acting on their own, looking for a lucrative activity that could bring them quick, large profits:

> In the City of Vitoria, on the twenty-third of July of eighteen hundred seventy-eight, before me, Mr. José de Zumárraga, resident of the same and public notary of its district . . . appear, with the witnesses that will be expressed, Mr. Vicente Suso y Bengoa, married, of forty-eight years of age, confectioner and resident of the *villa* of Salvatierra [Agurain] of this judicial district, accompanied by Mr. Fausto Aguirre y Parrigorria, of the same status, of forty-four years of age, peasant and resident of the town of Arcaute, of this municipal district on one hand, and on the other Mr. Isidro Rico y Gómez of the same status, of thirty-nine years of age, merchant and resident of Buenos Aires, in the Argentine Republic with temporary residence in Villa de Haro . . . and they said:
>
> That Mr. Vicente Suso wishes to move to Buenos Aires with his wife Rosario Sorazábal and his daughter María Concepción de Suso y Sorazábal; and not presently possessing enough resources to pay their passage, has agreed with Mr. Isidro Rico that the latter will take him to said point with his wife and daughter in a steamship from Bordeaux to Buenos Aires provided that Mr. Suso guarantees him the payment of his passage. . . .[30]

The agents' decisive activity and powerful ability to transport hundreds of Basques to America was recognized by the contemporaries themselves. In Cola y Goiti's words:

> The influence and work of the agencies comes to be one of the most decisive, perhaps the most decisive of all the factors that promote these currents of emigration.[31]
>
> . . . What most attracts the inexpert peasants is the portraits brought of this or that friend that upon leaving their town was a young woman of crude manners and poor clothes, and appears in the portrait perfectly groomed, dressed in silk with the indispensable watch with its chain, and a beautiful fan, ultimately converted into a lady from a wealthy family, and if to this is added the painting, or the description that the *enganchador* makes in a rehearsed discourse, of what that country is, of the truth of the portraits, and another thousand inventions that his speculative imagination suggests to him. . . . And the children, remembering military service and encouraged by the prospective that he provides them, make even greater efforts to leave.[32]

Nor was the payment of the passage a problem, as has been seen, for the departure of inhabitants from the Basque Country.

CONSULATE OF THE EASTERN REPUBLIC OF URUGUAY
(MONTEVIDEO) IN VITORIA
OFFICIAL ANNOUNCEMENT
TO FARM IMMIGRANTS

By order of the Eastern Republic of Uruguay it is made known to the peasants wishing to emigrate to said state, that upon their arrival at the port of Montevideo they will encounter free lodging and upkeep for themselves and their families for the first days after disembarking; as well as employees entrusted especially to provide them free passage to the Farm Colonies already in existence or that will be founded in the future in the Interior of the Republic, in which they will easily find positions as workers, or they will be able to buy land at very low prices and payable on long installments.

In this Consulate, located on Constitution Street number 8, tickets are expedited at reduced prices for the magnificent English steamers; which leave twice a month from Bordeaux and Santander for Montevideo and Buenos Aires. The Consulate has much news referring to the mercantile and industrial state of those countries as well.

Vitoria, March 9, 1880. The Consul of Uruguay, J. Quiroga.[33]

For criticisms of the activity of these shady characters, the following statements (as well as those referred to earlier) are a good sample, the first in the form of a letter sent from Buenos Aires, and the second with the signature of the untiring anti-emigration champion, José Cola y Goiti.

Letter from an emigrant
Buenos Aires, December 18, 1887
Dear A.:
You were right in speaking so badly of Sarasqueta, whom without knowing you described as if you had known this person your entire life.

Let's begin with the departure from the port of Coruña.

This currently unpopular agent demanded all the documents from the emigrants in order to present them to the governor of the province. Many were missing some papers, a deficiency that this agent took advantage of to exploit the innocent. There is nothing as essential for the embarking as the pass of the governor, he told them. For eight duros this lack is amended, he continued brazenly.

Several of the unwary handed over this sum, but he did not give them a receipt. It happened that a Bilbao emigrant, who, as Valera would say, was passed over on the list, refused to pay him this amount if he was not given a receipt. Sarasqueta desisted from his undertaking on the persuasion that the smart Bilbao native would bring the matter to the attention of the governor of La Coruña.

They handed over payment to him without a receipt: twelve duros a young woman from Haro because she lacked permission from her mother and because she was accompanied by a disposable recruit; and eight duros for the lack of other documents, a carpenter from Haro and two youths from Laguardia (1). Some emigrants he told that they needed only the power of their mother or wife; others that they needed only the passport of the civil governor of their province.

To the 200 plus passengers that came under his responsibility he charged us one peseta for the signature of someone who did not authorize such a charge (2), and in this case our signature . . . was of no use, while that of my provincial officer demands that I be allowed free passage.

During the crossing I reached an agreement with Sarasqueta in front of two witnesses to live in the Cerrito Inn, in Buenos Aires, which he says is his, although according to the posters that he puts up in public places, it belongs to both him and his brother Pedro, partner in the aforementioned case. All right; now he wants to charge at the rate of 45 duros; and lastly from compromise to compromise, I have managed to settle the issue for a few duros more than in the agreement.

As for the placements that he promises, his personal mettle is no less questionable. He pledged his word to immediately place a married couple from Anguciana, recommended by a publicist from Vitoria, and the placement does not appear. And the same with others.

Whatever you might say about emigration is little, between Italians, Frenchmen, and Spaniards, 700 individuals enter one day, fewer another, and more than might come are needed, although this place is not as good as some believe, given the understanding that here one must work a lot. . . .

I hope that you have a Merry Christmas and happy entrances and exits of the year, since I will spend them working.

(1) The Editors keep the names of those alluded to secret, in case the legal justice system considers the letters in this matter.
(2) This is scandalously immoral. Was a grave crime committed that should be pursued at the request of our consuls, the same as could have been perpetrated on the emigrants that live under the protection of the Spanish flag?[34]

Again the tireless Colá y Goiti:

It is necessary to sound the voice of caution to the simple villagers, so that they are prepared against the scheming of these coarse and marked types, with worn faces, sour looks and poncho to the neck, unpleasant and peculiar in appearance; and to make the misguided citizens realize that they should not trust unbelievable offers, formalized by other *enganchadores*—whom we could call the cream of the crop—that disguise themselves as important people, use a pretentious coach, and have a relative in America (who nobody knows) or large properties (which nobody has seen) who come here for business (in human flesh) and take advantage of their return to take along some friends (read: colonists) away there and when it suits them well they become kidnappers.[35]

It is clear that these *enganchadores* would not have acted with such impunity except for the favorable legislation that existed in America toward European emigration in general and Basque emigration in particular. The Argentine and Uruguayan cases have already been discussed. But in Chile, for example, the same also happened, beginning in the second half of the nineteenth century. In this country, it was the government that took the initiative favoring immigration (of a markedly agricultural nature). The Chilean government opened an Emigration Office in Europe in 1882, with its seat in Paris. From the outset, it sought to attract Basque immigration, as is clear in the report published by the office itself.[36] Equally significant in their official activity were the National Agriculture Association and the Association for Factory Promotion, created in 1883. Both organisms were devoted to the transport of immigrants.[37]

In the case of Brazil, it was at the end of the nineteenth century that its authorities pressed to find European settlers. Thus, in 1887, the treasury of the state of São Paulo decided to pay those who were disposed to work on the coffee plantations transportation expenses from their country of origin.[38]

The attraction that countries like Venezuela, Mexico, the Dominican Republic, and the United States held for the Basques would occur later. In the first three cases, emigration was more directly related to exile and the favorable laws or dispositions created in regard to this. In the United States the ranching and shepherding sectors would be the driving forces for immigration, between the end of the nineteenth century and the first years of the twentieth.

In Iparralde, in the opinion of Henry de Charnisay, two thousand Basque and Béarnais natives succumbed to the deception of the *enganchador* agents during the nineteenth century. The agents received thirty francs per emigrant that paid for passage and twenty per emigrant that had to repay the price of the trip by working. The quantity was double if the emigrant left as a stowaway. Around the 1880s, the *enganchador* agents would have been able to earn from fifty to sixty thousand francs per year in Béarn and the French Basque Country. The Basses-Pyrénées had two emigration agencies in 1859:

1. The Apestéguy Firm of Bayonne had eleven subagents.
2. The Etchevarne Firm of Uhart-Cize employed two subagents. In 1861, this company had one delegate for the district of Oloron, three subagents in Bayonne and one in Uhart-Cize.

That year, the Apestéguy and Etchevarne firms sent three new representatives to the districts of Oloron, Mauléon, and Bayonne. There were twenty-five subagents. The number of agencies increased from three in 1862 to five in 1883 and six in 1886. The agencies of Bordeaux would have to be added: three in 1862, five in 1883, and six in 1886.

In 1855, the prefect tried to find a legal means to proceed against the maneuvers of these emigration agents. The Conseil Général of the Basses-Pyrénées of 1858 echoed the distinction between agents devoted to transport and those whose mission was the recruitment of peasants for America. Thus, for example, on this date, of the fifteen subagents authorized in the Basses-Pyrénées, only one (who lived in Bayonne) was occupied with transport; the rest served as recruiters. Therefore, this Conseil Général did not cease insisting, from 1858 to 1861, upon the need to intercept and if necessary detain these recruiting agents when they carried their precious merchandise to the embarkation ports. The law of 1860 prohibited any work related to the "hooking" of emigrants not permitted by the Ministry of Agriculture, Commerce, and Public Works. The Chamber of Accusation of the Imperial Court of Pau ordered the arrest of Mr. Lapagesse, emigration agent, on August 27, 1870, upon finding him guilty of having plied his trade without authorization.

The Official Norms of the Exodus

It must be established here how the freedom to emigrate or not had both strong partisans and detractors in the Spain and France of the 1800s. The current of opinion believing that the government institutions (both national and local) were endowed with sufficient power or the moral authority necessary to prohibit (if necessary) the emigration of Spaniards to America did not have many partisans. Liberal political theses were invoked instead. These defended complete individual liberty when it came to choosing one's life destiny.

It is interesting to note how the law to emigrate was recognized late in Europe. In the ancien régime before the French Revolution of 1789, free emigration between states was not permitted; it was not considered a legal act. International migrations until that time were repeatedly obstructed by the European monarchies, prohibited, limited, and checked at juridico-administrative levels. The confiscation of goods and the loss of all rights were common consequences for those that chose the diaspora. The European monarchs considered emigration a symptom of the decadence of their kingdoms. For the first time, the French Constitution of 1791 included among its legislative measures the right of the French citizens to move freely, settle, and change residence. These measures would later influence other European and American constitutional charters.

In Spain, the Royal Order of the Treasury of February 9, 1827, indicated that the Spaniard with mercantile business in America could emigrate from qualified Spanish ports on foreign ships of "friendly and allied powers," without having to obtain prior royal permission.[39]

The Royal Order of December 24, 1834, included in its second disposition the method of granting passports to those wishing to travel to the "domains of the Indies":

> That any individual that is to go to them from the Peninsula make a summary report in a government dossier in front of the police subdelegate of the district or division that corresponds to the town of his domicile, to justify that, far from trying to abandon his family, he has obtained a reliable permit or approval for the voyage, that with it he does not try to escape the proceedings of any authority, nor flee from military service, nor evade with damage to a third [party] the fulfillment of obligations or agreements in which he might find himself; that he neither has an ugly stain in virtue of that which might be considered damaging or harmful in those domains; and lastly that no reasonable impediment is against his undertaking the voyage; and that resulting thus, the corresponding passport is issued him by the same subdelegate, with expression of having filled said requirements and of there not having been any impediment whatsoever.[40]

The Royal Order of September 16, 1853, was of great importance because it would be the precursor to the rest of the Spanish laws throughout the second half of the century. It meant an end to the prohibition on emigration to South America that still weighed upon the Canary Islands. The Spanish government insisted upon avoiding "the abuses that greed tends to produce in speculators that, led by sordid interest, sometimes carry those that emigrate heaped in a narrow space and without the sanitary conditions that decorum, morality, and even humanity itself call for." In its second disposition, the document states that emigrants needed to obtain a passport. Thus, they had to affirm that they chose the voyage freely and spontaneously. Next, they had to verify permission of parent, tutor, or spouse as appropriate, and of proper age, sex, and civil status. The emigrant could not have a pending criminal charge or any legal impediment. If the candidate was between eighteen and twenty-three years old and male, he had to deposit 6,000 copper reales or provide a sworn statement of sufficient resources in order not to be considered as evading military service. The law also regulated the capacity of the ships in terms of the number of passengers, and quantity and quality of food and water for the crossing. Sanitary conditions, medical attention, the requirement of a medical kit, and price and form of payment of the passages were also discussed. And, more importantly, it provided the emigrants freedom to devote themselves to the occupation that most interested them at their destination. On November 5 of the same year of 1853, another royal order was published in which two new demands were added to the previous norm's requisites:

A document from the appropriate township stating the age, civil status, and place of birth of the interested party.

A sworn statement with three bails of recognized solvency affirming that the emigrant had obtained the corresponding license, did not find himself prosecuted and that there was no legal impediment for his absence, and that the corresponding payment had been made if he was of military age.

By the Royal Order of January 12, 1865, the Spanish government reserved the right to deny the boarding permit to Brazil "without damage of respecting the faculty of emigrating that all the Spaniards have," in response to the mistreatment that Spanish colonists received in this country.

The Royal Order of January 30, 1873, established new rules for embarkation and the number of passengers in relation to the capacity of the ship. And it prohibited the emigrants from surrendering their entire salary for the payment of transport and expenses of the voyage. Only one-third of it could be used to this end. For their part, the Royal Orders of August 8 and 21, 1874, respected the previous conditions and included the presentation of the decree of the emigrant's identity for passport acquisition.

By the Royal Order of July 18, 1881, the Ministry of Development created a "commission to study the form of containing emigration as much as possible by means of the creation of work." The immensity of the emigration and the need for legally combating it without impeding Spanish citizens' freedom of movement were made manifest.

The Royal Order of August 16, 1881, explicitly recognized that "emigration weakens the provinces of the North." The commission therefore decided to send an interrogatory to seventeen civil governors including, logically, those of Araba, Bizkaia, Gipuzkoa, and Navarre.

On May 6, 1881, two orders were proclaimed in which the legislators raised the need to know the volume and the problems posed by emigration; a "Department of Emigrations" was therefore created in the General Administration of Agriculture, and the powers of the General Administration of the Institute of Geography and Statistics were extended. The fact that this Section of Emigrations would be attached to the Ministry of Agriculture clearly shows the markedly rural character of Spanish emigration in general, and its Basque expression in particular. The first national population statistics published beginning in 1882 were owing to both organizations. But it would not be until 1885 that the first figures appeared by province.

The drawback when it came to counting the Basque exodus was that they did not include the French ports. This ultimately means that the number of Basque emigrants was greater than listed in the statistics that include only Spanish ports.

In turn, the Royal Orders of November 19, 1883, and the circular of May 8, 1888, adopted dispositions aimed at facilitating and regulating the transfer of Spaniards to the overseas provinces (Cuba, Puerto Rico, and the Philippines), although they would also repeat the conditions for transporting passengers to the South American republics and Brazil. The Royal Order of January 25, 1897, dealt with the same points as the earlier ones, although that of October 7, 1902, decreed new rules for embarking passengers overseas. The Royal Order of April 8, 1903, came to remove numerous obstacles from the migratory process. It notably simplified the process of embarkation and removed the need for passport or special governmental permit, while allowing passages to be expedited with the simple display of the personal decree.[41]

A few years later the Law of Emigration of December 21, 1907, was proclaimed. It recognized the freedom to emigrate and set protective limitations and guarantees to regulate the practice. In the Law of Emigration of 1924, the revised text of the new regulation was delineated according to the same guidelines as the precedent norm of 1907, making it easy to note the differences and innovations. A less vague and more precise definition of Basque transatlantic voyagers is offered than in 1907. Thus, all emigrants and families leaving the Iberian Peninsula to establish themselves definitively or temporarily abroad for work motives were recognized under this definition.

In the judgment of Ricardo Gutiérrez Nieto, expert in jurisprudence, the clearest amplification of the law of 1924—after all, it came seventeen years after its predecessor, and at the height of the Primo de Rivera dictatorship—was perhaps its organic content.[42] The emigration of Basque natives now came under the direct jurisdiction of the Ministry of Work, Commerce, and Industry. A General Administration of Emigration was created within this ministry. It would be in charge of effecting protective fiscal control over the Spanish exodus. To attend to this organism, a Central Board located in Madrid, a Local Board in each of the qualified embarkation ports, and a Consular Board in each of the important destinations were created.

The first two, referred to in the precedent law of 1907, had a purely consultative nature; it was necessary to consult the Central Board, however, on certain questions dealing with the risk of death or complete incapacitation of Basque emigrants due to shipwreck, fire, attack or other misfortunes, accident on board, or illness contracted during the crossing or within a month after reaching the port of destination that prevented them, in either case, from working in the chosen country.

Lastly, the Royal Order of September 16, 1924, constituted a fund denominated "Emigrant Treasury." It would be sustained through licensing fees assessed shipowners, consignees, and information offices, emigrant passage fees, fines levied for legal infractions, and subsidies and donations from associations and individuals. The fund was deposited in the Bank of Spain, where it remained at the disposition of the General Administration of Emigration for expenses, personnel, and materials necessary for the service (except for amounts not over 5,000 pesetas destined for immediate expenses). Outlays were considerable, and for various ends. Insurance and aid for those who emigrated and repatriated, their protection, and assistance for adaptation in the destinations and/or return to Spain were all paid. Various entities were funded: sanatoriums, hospitals, beneficent associations and organizations, patriotic groups, educational establishments, and other similar Spanish institutions founded in the countries of destination. All were designed to receive destitute Spaniards, elevate their cultural level, maintain their patriotic spirit, and create strong ties among them.

In spite of these legal dispositions, and some others aimed at mitigating the phenomenon, Spanish emigration continued its devastating course. There were, however, some differences, especially after the great European war of 1914–18. Many nations established barriers to emigration and regulated the human movements:

> Among said matters, what figures in the first place is discussion and approval of the future budget, in which it is indispensable to make considerable savings, in view of the abnormal situation being undergone by the country, whose profound crisis has become almost unsustainable due to the effects of the European war, as the treasury's revenue and especially the income from customs have shrunk considerably. . . .
>
> . . . the entries that refer to the promotion of immigration of course suffer reductions . . . reaching the sum of 500,000 pesos, or the half a million pesos that were destined to the same ends in the current budget. The reason that the Commission supports it is that it is not as suitable to favor immigration as before, when in the [Argentine] Republic the number of unemployed increases every day, which is an undeniable fact.[43]

Facing this new situation, both local authorities and those in Madrid understood the need to adopt new measures to better protect the Basque emigrant population. The results were not long in coming: in December 1924, in an attempt to compile both the preceding migratory legislation and the later norms published between 1908 and 1924, the Law of Reformed Emigration was created. In addition to empowering the new obligations that the law of 1907 had already imposed, the position of the consular attachés called *agregados* was established in 1924. The *agregados* specialized in serving expatriated Spaniards, having very well-defined instructions. Those worth emphasizing are the following: attending to newly arriving immigrants; collecting their complaints about and objections to their treatment while on board; informing them of the work conditions in the country in question; and taking care of the work contracts that they had signed. Likewise, their defense in the courts of the country of immigration was arranged, and the benefits of discounted repatriation rates were applied. Another of the novelties established in the application of the law referred to the specification of each agency's powers. From then on each and every one of the responsibilities, duties, and obligations of each official agency, whether already existing or newly created, was exhaustively regulated. Incompatibilities between functionaries characteristic of the 1907 law and damaging to Basque emigrants could thereby be avoided. On the other hand, all the requisites necessary for correct application of the new law in matters such as the solvency and the insurance of the emigrant, interest rate, ticket, restriction of the contract, voyage cancellation, emigrant repatriation, and conditions of transport ships were stipulated in detail.

The focus of the legislation, however, continued being the set of measures to protect third-class passengers. Such protection would even be considerably extended to include the moment of departure for America, through the entire expatriation, until the return. The interest of the public powers in continuing to offer these overseas voyagers suitable crossing conditions was reflected in the measures directly affecting transport. Thus, the following articles stand out: 39, which was designed to avoid an artificial and arbitrary increase in the prices of passage; 40, under which the transporters were obligated to contribute toward repatriation expenses; and 3, in which the measures protecting one-way voyages were extended to cover return trips. Nevertheless, the great novelty brought about by the 1924 legislation was the amplification of protective measures fundamentally meant to provide Basque emigrants a better knowledge of the countries they chose for starting a new life. From the end of World War I, the types of education needed to inform in depth those deciding to expatriate about the facts of migration were the object of frequent debate in both the Congress of Deputies and the Senate. On the one hand, there were those who advocated that such information be provided in the public schools as complementary subjects:

> I repeat once more that this [emigration] is an education problem and, therefore, the solution is in the school. . . .
>
> It is necessary for all Spaniards to acquire, from their first years, and this only a master can teach them, specific notions of geography, which they lack completely, related to the two Americas; it is necessary that . . . the master teach them what those countries are like, their language, their climate, their wealth, the conditions of life in them, the remuneration that the work has, the value of the monies, the necessities of their agriculture or of their industry; it is necessary that he who emigrates know all this before emigrating; it is necessary, in a word, that the emigrant be educated in school.[44]

Others, on the contrary, went further in their proposals. They no longer advocated instruction in the public primary schools. In their judgment, as constituted the schools could not satisfactorily prepare Basque emigrants. Rather, they believed specialized educational centers were needed. It was in these that emigrants had to be given "all that preparation necessary to go, in such conditions of execution and practice of the fundamental faculties of our spirit, for the economic struggle, not having to fear any sort of competition from the foreign nations."[45] In spite of all the different approaches that might have existed, what is sure is that the sessions of the Congress and Senate agreed that education was the only real means of avoiding the deceptions foisted for ages on the Basques and other Spanish inhabitants that crossed the Atlantic in search of new opportunities. At least the spirit of the already mentioned law of 1924 was manifested.

Migratory Legislation until 1936

If the regulations existing from the proclamation of the law of 1924 until the Spanish Civil War are examined, it can be verified how many of those suppositions and novelties defined in the second major legislation were becoming reality. Thus, there were agreements with Italy (January 20, 1926) and France (July 17, 1928) concerning cooperation between the respective emigration services for the protection of third-class passengers during the voyages of exodus to America. Article 61 of the Law of Emigration of 1924 was thus clearly and precisely concretized, although the agreements with the principal countries of reception of Basque emigration (Argentina and Uruguay) were yet to be negotiated and signed. In addition, already familiar topics such as accident insurance (January 2, 1928), subsidized repatriation (December 21, 1928), and the measures for impeding the activity of the clandestine agents and the recruiting of emigrants once and for all in the Basque Country (February 12, 1926) were addressed.

After long debate, the lamentable situation of the ignorance and illiteracy of many emigrants, amended favorably with the proclamation of Article 65 of the law of 1924, was finally concretely effected. On October 4, 1929, a royal order made 300 scholarships available for industrial and farming education. They were allocated for various young people between fourteen and eighteen years old who had failed school. Created by royal decree on August 10 of the same year, these scholarships were a direct consequence of the following words:

> As general an outcry as inspired in patriotic yearnings has been that of our consular representations in the countries of America and that of the Spanish associations established there, with regard to the lack of preparation of many of our emigrants, whose general cultural deficiency and professional special-

ization condemned them unpardonably to the most vulgar and rude, and, therefore, lower paying, occupations and jobs.[46]

The objectives of these subsidies were clarified perfectly in the prelude to the royal decree:

> A diffusion of professional skills must be the initiation of this work, through intensive teaching practices, precisely among the most needy classes . . . and organized in such a way that . . . it would yield as a result the creation of a core of learned and expert workers, nursery for new generations of farm and industrial workers, who might reap the benefits of a higher culture and more perfected specialization . . . [so as] to take the contribution of their effort to other countries, [and] will do it in better conditions of personal benefit if they themselves are solidly prepared for the struggle for work.[47]

Nevertheless, in spite of the institution of these education grants, it is clear that the spirit of Article 65 of the law of 1924 was better represented by the contents of the royal decree published on April 22, 1929. It discussed the creation of some special boards specifically geared to advise and assist Basque emigrants disposed to travel to America. These boards came to replace the former information offices and local port boards established in the 1907 regulations, which had clearly demonstrated their inefficiency. The new institutions were located in the same towns and cities of the Basque Country where the since-abandoned information centers and ticket offices had been since the beginning of the century. They were composed of the mayor (who served as president), parochial priest, municipal judge, doctor, national school master, and town hall secretary. Their principal duty was to inform those who had decided to emigrate of all the details they wanted to know regarding how to obtain documents to make the trip. They stressed the need to sign up in beneficent associations and Basque centers in the countries of destination. The boards also had to investigate the motives inducing emigrants to leave the Basque Country: if they had been persuaded or not, their professions, occupations that they intended on practicing in the Río de la Plata republics, and the references that they had in those lands. The boards were responsible for advising the future emigrants about the chances of finding work in their native provinces and the rest of Spain. Lastly, the references to ships, their destinations, and prices, formal documentation required for the overseas voyage, and data about the American job market had to be posted in a publicly visible place in board offices. The birth of these boards dealt a near-fatal blow to the scheming of emigrant recruiters. From then on, Basque emigrant protagonists had at their disposal an effective organization whose focus was to offer them more information concerning all the circumstances related to the migratory process.

The decade of the 1930s witnessed something of a boom in departures of Basque natives for the countries of Old Europe, although this trend would not develop fully until the 1950s or 1960s. Emigration to nations like France and its North African possessions, Germany, and central Europe was in its initial stages and still minor. These were frequently not places of settlement, but rather temporary points for the embarkation of Basque emigrants for American shores. In 1930, the new continent continued absorbing more than 55,000 peninsular emigrants a year. Nevertheless, to the extent that emigration to Europe was growing, the authorities understood the need to compare their migratory measures to those of the more advanced European countries of the first third of the twentieth century:

> The progressive effort in matters of emigration made by the Government of His Majesty is well-known by natives and foreigners alike, and if it is looked upon with deep satisfaction in our country, abroad it is distinguished as worthy of consideration by legislators and authorities and as a source of inspiration.
>
> But this task . . . cannot be taken to be finished. A sense of reality shows that it is susceptible to improvements that complement the institutions being created and the norms being introduced.[48]

The local information boards dealt an important blow to emigrant recruiters. Nevertheless, a door remained ajar for the activity of these clandestine agents in the Basque Country, through the issuance of the "Identity Portfolios." In order to avoid the extortion and deceit to which some unwary emigrants were subjected, and to more closely approach the European norm, on January 24, 1930, the decision was made to replace these portfolios with a special passport for those wishing to leave the Iberian Peninsula.

> With this we embrace the principles that today, rightly so, dominate in regard to the unification of procedures in the distinct countries, and falsities and frauds will be avoided by making the displacement of people difficult by requiring a document to emigrate.[49]

Thus, it was now the mayors who were the presidents of the local information boards, who were in charge of granting and arranging the passports required for Basque protagonists in their endeavor to cross the Atlantic. The last year in which the Ministry of State decided on migratory matters (before Francoism) was 1932, concretely in an order that stipulated the maximum prices authorized for third-class passages (July 6, 1932). It was precisely national conflict that caused this legislative disregard of migration. The beginning of hostilities on July 18, 1936, ushered in a new period in Spain's history and the collective subconscious of its inhabitants. From then on many Basques, goaded by hunger, human miseries, and social frustrations, had no other recourse than to emigrate. For them, laws and regulations were no longer valid. Thirty-five years of continuous effort to attain a degree of order in the unceasing migratory flow collapsed in a matter of months.

After the fratricidal battle, hundreds of thousands of people saw themselves obligated to drastically modify their lives according to the regulations imposed by the new state. In 1939, many Basques knocked on the doors of the New World in the hope of being let in and thereby healing the tremendous wounds that military defeat had opened in their lives. The laws in effect on migratory matters meant little. For them, the only possibility for improving their circumstances was onerous exile.

For God, Country, *Forua*, and King

At the end of the First Carlist War (1833–1839), without doubt, there was an extraordinary increase in departures of Basques and Navarrese to America. Nevertheless, it is prudent to recognize that the number of these departures due to natural causes and the number for political or purely military reasons is unclear. These last two motives, however, seem likely to have weighed heavily on the minds of the losers of the civil war. In 1869, the Basque writer Julio Nombela indicated that the departures of the losers numbered eight thousand between 1839 and 1840. And, although obviously not all would have crossed the Atlantic, the figure seems highly significant.

In his exhaustive study of the Valley of Baztán, Idoate Ezquieta illustrates this important outflow by studying 928 locals living between 1840 and 1879.[50] There is also evidence that the same happened in other Navarrese mountain locales, such as Uharte-Arakil and Irañeta.[51] For example, the town of Leiza had 1,724 inhabitants in 1840. Of the 121 sworn statements signed that year by the scribe José Antonio Meriotegui, 48 were emigration related.[52] Between July 27 and September 18, eighteen individuals decided to emigrate to Montevideo; on September 29, eight people formalized private agreements to go to Cuba and Mexico. The majority indicated that their motives for leaving were economic. Nevertheless, it cannot be denied that the hardships scourging the province during the First Carlist War were a highly influential factor when Navarrese (of the epoch) had to decide whether or not to emigrate. It is also significant that the mayor provided information about the moral and political conduct of all the candidates, presumably on their militancy in the band of the pretender Carlos Mª Isidro (Charles) of Bourbon in the recently concluded war.

The Second Carlist War (1872–1876) was invoked repeatedly in the press of the day to account for Navarrese emigration.[53] Thus stated the *Statistic of Emigration and Immigration of Spain in the Five-Year Period 1891–1895*. It indicated the ruin and desolation that the conflict had wreaked in agriculture and industry, addressing the pernicious influence of the emigration agents. In 1896, in a report about the construction of the Pamplona-Irun railroad, three Navarrese deputies (Ulpiano Enea, Rafael Gaztelu, and Jesús Elorz) referred to the turbulent history of Navarre in the previous eighty years. They particularly insisted on the inability to pay off local debts incurred in the wars and the poor condition in which many provincial and municipal roads had been left: "It is enough to remember that with the motive of the same [the Carlist civil wars], for a space of eleven years the fields of a great part of the province have remained uncultivated, administrative life completely disturbed, commerce stopped, all wealth in constant danger, and the whole country exposed to misery."[54]

But, as pernicious or more so, without doubt, were postwar conditions. Among those most salient were the poor harvests, grape-growing crisis, and destruction of the olive groves by frosts. Allusions to all these factors were constant in the Navarrese press. Thus, *El Heraldo de Navarra* spoke on May 3, 1897, of the precarious situation of the proletarian class in Cintruénigo, and on August 10, 1897, of that in Ablitas. *La Tradición Navarra* spoke of the very dark prospects for the proletarian class (September 4, 1898) and the difficult situation of the inhabitants of the Valley of Larraun (September 14, 1898). *El Pensamiento Navarro* mentioned the rising hunger of a local parish's residents. And the same newspapers told about the suspension of local patron saint celebrations throughout Navarre due to the poor harvests. The case of Oteiza de la Solana is illustrative: the considerable public debt incurred after the Second Carlist War due to reconstruction of buildings, vineyards, olive groves, and so on, as well as the poor harvests, had left the town in a state of constant crisis, as *El Eco de Navarra* related on December 29, 1888.

In the political terrain, there were also Navarrese Carlist militants that divided their lives between the province and America. This was the case of Francisco Martínez Alsasua,[55] who owned land in Argentina. President of the Carlist Circle of Pamplona, in 1905 he was defeated in the elections for provincial deputy of the capital district. In the election of 1907, he initially refused to head the list of candidates for the circumscription of Estella, claiming that he had to attend to his properties and businesses in Argentina. He ultimately accepted, however, winning a deputy's seat. And the same happened in 1911 and 1915, when he was reelected. After being voted into the Cortes the latter year, he spent a few months in Argentina. Other Carlist politicians with connections to America were the Pamplona city councilmen Eugenio Hernández Angostino and Martín Echarren López. The former, elected in 1913, went to Argentina in 1915; the latter, born to Navarrese parents in the city of Mar de Plata, was lieutenant mayor beginning in 1922 and founded and presided over the Spanish Traditionalist Circle of Buenos Aires. Joaquín San Julián Olaso, whose grandfather had prospered in Cuba, spent time among the ranks of the *integristas*. He was councilman between 1903 and 1907. Later, he would embrace Basque nationalism, founding the weekly *Napartarra*.

What happened in Navarre in the wake of the first Basque civil conflict also occurred in Bizkaia, Araba, and Gipuzkoa. In the case of this last province, María Pilar Pildain indicates how the First Carlist War "was an authentic bloodbath of brave youths that on one hand did not find work and on the other felt uncomfortable in the political life imposed upon them by the victors."[56] And, without doubt, the Carlist losers of the bloody battles (as those in any civil war) did not feel comfortable being dominated by the new liberal regime. Moreover, the victors imposed a distinct model of society by introducing the industrial revolution into Basque territory and filling the local landscape with factories—especially beginning in 1876.

But one must also understand that the fact that there was only one heir to a farm accentuated the anxiety of the remaining, landless siblings. America could be the solution—a solution that was linked to both the hatred of the liberals and the calamitous state of the Basque ancestral homeland after the Carlist wars (1833–1839 and 1872–1876).

In addition, the vanquished were harshly persecuted. After the Second Carlist War, the soldiers following Charles of Bourbon experienced exile. The French government ordered that the émigrés be installed in depots (concentration camps) in the departments of Vienne, Lot-et-Garonne, Charente, Maine-et-Loire, Indre-et-Loire, Loire, Lot, Sarthe, Haute-Vienne, Indre, and Dordogne. This time, Basque protagonists of the exodus did not suffer as much police persecution on the part of the French authorities as in 1839–1840.

Many decided to return to the Basque Country. In effect, Cánovas del Castillo sought to limit the time spent abroad by these Carlists, repeatedly inviting Charles of Bourbon's followers to return to Spain. Many generals, in fact, did so, some joining the national army staff. Nevertheless, many decided to emigrate to America, preferring lifelong exile to swearing loyalty to the constitution—the only thing that prevented them from receiving political pardons. Thus, colonies of Carlists surged in America again, as they had in 1839.

Melchor Ferrer[57] narrates the voyages that the pretender to the Spanish throne, Charles of Bourbon (Charles VII), made through America. He embarked in Liverpool and disembarked in Halifax. From there, he went to New Orleans, and then to Veracruz. In the Mexican locality of Boca del Monte he was recognized by the faithful Carlist supporters that had been sent to Cuba to smother the pro-independence uprising. They had fled from there (deserting, of course) to move to Mexico, where they met with Charles VII. When Charles reached Mexico City, the country's president of the time, Sebastián Lerdo de Tejada, regarded the presence of the Bourbon pretender in the city with some displeasure, but regaled him nonetheless. Those that were pleased with the arrival of the leading representative of Carlism were the monarchs who had supported Emperor Maximilian. They were very happy with Charles VII's visit. From Mexico, the pretender headed to the United States. He landed in New Orleans, and was also in Richmond, Washington, and New York, returning shortly thereafter to London.

On April 20, 1887, the Carlist pretender undertook his second voyage to America. He left from the port of Southampton in the steamer *Orinoco*. He disembarked on the island of Barbados. From there, he went to Panama; from Panama to Peru, Chile, and Uruguay. In the port of the capital of this last country, Montevideo, a multitude of followers of his cause were awaiting him. He addressed them from aboard the steamer *Senegal* with the following message on August 25, 1887:

> To the most faithful emigrant soldiers in Uruguay and the Argentine Republic.
>
> It is not possible for me to leave you without the sentiments that seize my soul sprouting from my lips. At your side I have relived these days the blessed Nation, because you carry it in your hearts, as I in mine.
>
> From Panama to the Strait of Magellan, and from Tierra del Fuego to Río de la Plata, I have traveled with respect and astonishment at the grandiose theater of the feats of your grandfathers, perpetuators of that race of giants; you maintain the Spanish name in the Spanish American Republics at the height that it deserves. There, where Balboa and Pizarro, Valdivia and Garay gave the world the spectacle of the greatest heroism that the centuries have seen, you now give that of the greatest fidelity recorded by history.
>
> Thank you, my valiant soldiers, for the consolations that I owe you. Wherever I have gone, I have heard you cited as the personification of all the traditional virtues in our nation: constancy, bravery, honor, nobility of character, religiosity. And my heart beats with pride in my chest, remembering that you were the invincible lions, so frequently admired by me on the battlefields.
>
> Not in vain God conserves for Spain this glorious reserve on the other side of the ocean. Our presence here, and the homage that you pay to the traditions of your fathers, would be sufficient to give me the security that the day of justice will arrive, in the event—which would never happen—the indomitable faith that I harbor in the restoration of our Nation might weaken.
>
> I do not bid you goodbye. I firmly hope to see you all again around me. Justice and divine compassion will signal the day.
>
> Meanwhile, continue making yourselves worthy of the hospitality that these generous and noble countries give you, as brothers that are yours, and be sure of the unperishing reminder of you that your affection carries.[58]

Once in the city, he received many visits from Spanish Carlists, including the exile Francisco Azpiroz, who had been royal chaplain in the northern campaign. Days later, Charles VII headed for Buenos Aires, where some five hundred Carlists that came up to "kiss his hand" were awaiting him. From there, he traveled to Rio de Janeiro, the city from which he set out for Bordeaux. And from Bordeaux, he went to Italy.

Having been defeated on the Iberian Peninsula, Carlism closed ranks around Carlist nuclei in South America. In 1898, in an attempt to keep its spirit alive in the New World, Francisco de Oller was named Charles of Bourbon's representative in America. From his post, he created Carlist boards in Argentina, Uruguay, Paraguay, Chile, Bolivia, Peru, and Ecuador. That same year, *The Spanish Legitimist*, a prototypical Carlist newspaper that would publish until 1912, was founded in Buenos Aires.

The emigration provoked by the Carlist wars must have been much more important than appears at first sight. It is truly difficult to follow the traces of those who "traveled" to America for political motives, because they rarely indicated—when queried by the customs agents—that the war was their real reason for settling in America. The reverse happened; aside from a few exceptions, they managed to conceal that they had just put down a rifle to board the boat for their American destination. Once they entered and settled in the young American republics, the Basque Carlists managed to act out their own identity. They formed military battalions composed entirely of Basques, mostly former Carlist soldiers, that would fight in the multiple civil wars that razed America in the nineteenth century.

One example was the Carlist Francisco Olariaga Echaide.[59] From Andoain (Gipuzkoa), he had to go to America for political reasons. He serves as an example of the trajectory followed by those who, like our "hero," were losers of one of the nineteenth-century wars.

Francisco was born into a Gipuzkoan family in which two political tendencies were in vogue in the last third of the nineteenth century: Carlism and liberalism. Although Francisco was a declared Carlist ("influenced by his confessor the parish priest of his town and because all his friends were of this persuasion"), his brother Manuel was of liberal persuasions. Another of Francisco's siblings (Josefa) was still young when the last civil war of the 1800s took place. Francisco's father, of the same first name, was born in Errenderi, educated in Donostia, and ended up settling in Andoain. Around the mid-nineteenth century, when he got married, he had a fairly successful shoeshop. His shoes, known in the area for their high quality, were sold throughout Gipuzkoa and Navarre. The elder Francisco de Olariaga had sales agents in Tolosa, Azpeitia, Donostia, and Pamplona. Between fifteen and twenty craftsmen usually worked in this shop, as well as various other subagents and apprentices. The shoes were finely crafted by hand. In the course of the nineteenth century, however, the arrival of the steam machine and the improvements in production that it brought, along with the ensuing series of industrial discoveries and inventions, revolutionized the shoe sector. Here began the drama for those that used old-fashioned methods, such as the elder Olariaga. Little by little, his shop in Andoain went into decline. After the elder Francisco de Olariaga's death, his widow Josefa Echaide Orcazaguirre moved the family ahead to the best of her ability.

The Carlist War of 1872–1876 would bring new complications. The younger

Francisco joined the cause, becoming a soldier in the underground, serving in the environs of Andalusia. His mission was to transport arms through the nearby mountains from one military position to another. He left his house at night and did not return until one or more days later. During one of these ventures he had an encounter with a civil guard from which he emerged badly wounded. As a result of this misfortune, his mother convinced him to go to America, and thereby escape the war. The eight duros needed for the trip were obtained, and Francisco Olariaga Echaide emigrated to Argentina. Years later, he would "call" other members of the family.

Draft Evasion

Ángel María Arrieta[60] argues that in the case of Araba, there must have been a high emigration of young men facing the prospect of obligatory military service that might last several years:

Without doubt numerous Basque youths, those not attracted at all by the prospect of the years in the barracks or the idea of serving the recently installed Bourbon monarchy of Alfonso XII, decided to set out for America where in the majority of the cases they would not lack the support of a relative or friend of the family.

In the case of Álava [Araba], draft evasion would be a fact demonstrable through the dossiers of dodgers from the respective town halls, it being the norm that the destination of the fleeing youth would be some point of the American continent.[61]

This is the case of the Araban Mariano Sagasti y Heredia, native of Larrea, fugitive in Argentina, for whom his brother-in-law answered:

Declaration of the brother-in-law of the presumed draft dodger. In the town of Ozaeta, on the sixteenth of February of eighteen hundred eighty-three, before his Mayor President of the Town Hall, Mr. Angel de Villar, appeared Mr. Millán de Uriarte, resident of the town of Larrea, and before me, the below-named secretary, having promised to tell the truth insofar as he might know it and be asked, previously instructed of the contents of articles 141 and following of the Law of Replacements that were read to him, about the whereabouts of his brother-in-law Mariano Sagasti y Heredia, youth number 08.00 of the current replacement, and never having been impeded from appearing, said: As he has already stated, his brother-in-law Mariano Sagasti y Heredia . . . went to the Argentine Republic and he does not know where he might be found, according to a letter that there was from another brother-in-law named Basilio, the expressed Mariano absented himself from the Province [of Buenos Aires] seventy leagues; and has again written certifying the letter so that Mariano or his brother might receive it.

That he left for said Republic six years ago, before turning fifteen, asked in what manner and with what authorization the expressed Mariano left and who lent him money for his trip, he answered that he left with a certain Andraca because his brother Basilio prepared him to leave and that he had not paid the passage nor does he know who could have given him money for his departure.

That he cannot say anything else, that he is doing errands to get him to come or send money for the buyout [from military service]. This is what he said and in it he affirmed and ratified, read what it was and in proof of it signed, which I certify.

Villar,

Millán Uriarte.[62]

On March 8, 1909, the newspaper *La Tradición Navarra* affirmed and insisted that the reasons for Navarrese emigration to America would have to be sought in the desire for adventure and the gold fever that moved the province's youths, but especially in the possibility of freeing themselves from military service.[63]

Douglass and Bilbao believe that Basques were in fact averse to fulfilling their military obligation during the nineteenth century because they were residentially very distant from the central governments of Paris and Madrid. Already in 1842, the Conseil Général of the Department of the Basses-Pyrénées began to take serious measures to check the pervasive habit among youths of not appearing for service. In 1850, the Basques of southern France alone accounted for 50 percent of the whole country's desertions.[64] As a preventive measure, the French government did not grant passports to nineteen-year-old young men for a time. It was all in vain. Glorying in their roguish abilities, these youths circumvented the law by crossing the border into Spain and embarking for the New World in Pasaia. The ships that left from Bayonne with legal passengers thus customarily docked in this port to pick up illegal emigrants before undertaking the crossing.

But evasion of military service was not exclusive to the Basques from north of the Pyrenees. It was also a custom rooted in the Spanish Basque provinces. Bayonne and Bordeaux were the ports that served for embarkation for the deserters. This evasion of military service provoked a deep frustration in the political consciousness of those who had fought for an ideal and failed. It was a more than sufficient motive for trying to abandon their dwelling. Those who lacked clear political ideals, but had the misfortune of enduring the war's disasters, also had sufficient motive for fleeing. All students of the contemporary Basque emigration to America agree that avoiding obligatory military service was one of the clearest motives for the Basques to cross the Atlantic to start a new life. Many of the protagonists of Basque migration who crossed the ocean working as sailors likely remained upon receiving word of their obligation with the state. Some probably never returned; others returned only after having lived many years on the American continent.

In any event, the evidence connects the lack of desire to perform military service in Basque collective consciousness with the ensuing emigration to America. This situation continued into the first decades of the twentieth century. The relationship can be understood thus, since it had never been common for inhabitants of the Basque Country to fulfill armed service, trying to avoid it either through finding substitutes from other provinces or paying the military institutions in cash. Moreover, if it is borne in mind that obligatory service had been imposed on Basques by Cánovas del Castillo in 1876 as the victor of the Second Carlist War, rejection of the military obligation is even more understandable.

Thus, plenty of Basques must have deserted and come to swell the ranks of emigrants settled in America. Between 1852 and 1855, there were 1,311 deserters in the French Basque provinces. The evasion of military service was just as extended among the Basques of the Spanish state. During the years 1913 and 1914 a total of 20.76 percent and 22.09 percent, respectively, of the young recruits did not appear for Spanish military service. Many of them escaped via overseas emigration. The figures of the Basque provinces along the French border were considerably higher. The ports of Bayonne and, especially, Bordeaux provided the Basques of Spain the means of departure denied them by the Spanish government. The numerous clandestine departures from both sides of the border reduce the precision of the official emigration statistics.

The problem began to preoccupy the authorities as early as the 1860s. In July 1861, the Ministry of Governance (dealing with the draft) placed its finger on the spindle for the thread of desertion by young men from the north:

[The] great number of youths from Asturias, Galicia, and other points of the Cantabrian shore that emigrate are fleeing from armed service, to the interior of the Peninsula, to foreign countries, and to our overseas possessions. . . .

With the queen aware of this matter and convinced of the need to exhaust all means within the legal orbit and in the reach of the public administration to contain this emigration in the northern provinces, a series of administrative measures was decreed to achieve such objectives, which did not have to be especially extensive, such as providing all the youths identification cards in which might be stated, apart of course from their personal descriptions, their connection or not with the armed service.[65]

The cases reviewed in the High Archive of the Navy clearly show that absence from the ranks must have been very common in the Basque Country as early as 1876, and even before. In effect, in the hundred cases examined by the author, a scheme repeatedly appears when the military authorities cited a certain youth for not having obeyed the call of those in charge of the various services. The response (by the parents or immediate family) was almost always the same. It was affirmed that the draft dodger sought was sailing or lived outside of Spain when the call came. Most of the time it was argued that the party in question lived in, had emigrated to, or was on the way to America. Thus, for example, on March 28, 1882, in the courtroom of the Municipal Justice of Elantxobe at 10 A.M., a summary discovery into the whereabouts of José Espinoza y Alegría was opened. As he did not appear in the courtroom, his father came to give his deposition and said that it was public knowledge that his son left this place eight years earlier (in 1874), "for overseas so that the Carlists would not take him to the mountain like they did with other youths"; until four years earlier, as far as the father knew, he had been sailing on some ship on the Americas run.[66]

In Bermeo in March 1882, Juan Luis Larrabaster y Esquiaga, father of Eulogio Larrabaster Calzada, appeared. Asked where his son was, he answered

> that four years ago he [Eulogio] left home to sail and within a short time he [Juan] heard that he was sick in the Argentine Republic: that a little later ran the rumor that he had died and for three and a half years he has absolutely no news of him; that he has nothing more to say; that what he has said is true under the oath that he has taken and read that this was his declaration is affirmed and ratified, saying that he is of the age of fifty-three years and does not sign because he says he does not know how, making in its place a sign of the cross, the district attorney signing it.[67]

This was the situation that characterized the fugitives and deserters that did not heed the call of army or navy authorities. Although some of the accused appear not to have been clearly aware of their military obligation (when they had to appear), on many occasions navigating in distant places probably served to "justify" their absence from the ranks.

Thanks to the *foral* legislation, and the local uses and customs, the Basques from Iparralde had devoted themselves to defending their own territory against foreign invaders in important wars. The French Revolution of 1789 suppressed the *foral* code, and from then on the Basques of this territory were obligated to perform regular military service like the rest of their compatriots.[68] The difficulty of adapting to some customs and norms of coexistence in an army whose members were of diverse backgrounds was therefore added to the long tradition of not heeding the call to arms. Moreover, this military service could last from two to seven years. It was such that the Department of the Basses-Pyrénées alone was sometimes responsible for half the individual desertions of all France.[69]

From 1821 to 1841, 1,886 youths from the Basses-Pyrénées were incorporated into service late and 231 others deserted. Beginning in 1835, the draft dodgers outside of Iparralde were cited by the army, outnumbering those within it. Thus, from

1834 to 1841, there were 430 draft dodgers from Iparralde in Montevideo. In 1842, of 1,092 youths listed to go into service, 222 were cited by the military authorities; 27 of these lived in Spain or Portugal and 131 in Montevideo. In 1843, of 993 young men listed, 194 were cited; 23 lived in Spain or Portugal and 99 in the Uruguayan capital. In 1844, of 136 dodgers, 11 lived in Spain or Portugal and 62 in Montevideo. In 1846, of 113 absentees of the call to arms, 61 were outside of the European continent. In 1853, of 3,252 calls, there were 509 absentees; of these, 196 were located in Buenos Aires or Montevideo, 37 in Spain, 73 in other colonies, and 198 within France. In 1855, of 3,264 recruits, 475 were refugees. In 1860, of the 296 draft dodgers listed, 176 lived in Montevideo or Buenos Aires. In 1866, in his three-month report to the ministry, the prefect stated that he had not found more than three men present when they were called to service in the district of Saint-Jean-Pied-de-Port. All the other youths were in America. In 1871 there were 914 draft dodgers; in 1878, 1,050.[70] These statistics also demonstrate that three of every five draft dodgers were Basques.[71]

Throughout the entire nineteenth century an intense debate was waged in France about its citizens' freedom to emigrate. What is certain is that, as so many went to America without passports, the Conseil Général decreed serious instructions in order to prevent the flight of the French Basques. It also attempted to "punish" those that had decided to leave without going through legal channels. Natives of Iparralde in the American republics without documentation thus lacked consular protection. The same year, the Conseil Général prohibited the territory's local administrations from giving passports to citizens under twenty, unless they traveled with people that took responsibility for them.

Thus, all emigrants were obligated to carry a certificate issued by the authorities of their native area stating that they had fulfilled their military obligations. This paper had to be shown at the port of embarkation. These measures did not yield the desired results, however. Measures of the "patriotic amnesty" type therefore had to be devised so that those Basques that had emigrated to America and wished to return could do so without falling into the hands of military justice.

Land Tenure and Inheritance Practices

Pierre Lhande asserts that Basque emigration was a consequence of the specific constitution of the Basque stem family. He makes the general claim that the stem family has always existed in the Basque Country, and therefore Basque emigration has always taken place. "Moreover, as the Basque valleys were not able to lodge more than a certain number of inhabitants, approximately equal to the current number, it is logical to draw the conclusion that the surplus had to go abroad." Thus, the mass nineteenth-century migration followed the tradition of previous centuries.

"Here the whole world is a proprietor," says Pierre Lhande, "and the whole country is already divided: all the fields, all the forests, all the meadows are subject to dominion, a secular dominion, a hundred times rebuilt but never partitioned."[72] Lhande did not ignore migration to the city, but urban life lacked the most indispensable elements for the Basque peasant's happiness. The city offered the peasant only "four square meters of rock and lime." For many, emigration to America was the more attractive alternative.

Chain Migration, or the Call from Relatives and Friends

Without a doubt, the call from relatives and friends already settled in America played a fundamental role as a springboard for Basque emigration to America. Those already settled in the New World whose enterprises or businesses had prospered called relatives, acquaintances, and friends hoping to share their luck or fortune, or merely commented in their letters on the possibilities for success offered by the American lands. The Navarrese transatlantic migratory chains were similar to those of the rest of the Basque territories.[73] This was the case with the emigrants from Baztán to Mexico and Chile in the twentieth century. The fundamental occupation of this group of Navarrese was the baking business and other commercial activities already under immigrant control, fruit of previous immigrations and successes in past businesses. The family chain began to function swiftly as soon as relatives and acquaintances settled in these republics. Moreover, a linked movement prompted those of the same town to settle in the same town or neighborhood overseas. And this sometimes happened for several generations. Thus, the *Statistics of Emigration and Immigration of Spain* called attention to this phenomenon:

> Those that have accepted another country always remember the place where they were born, miss the family ties and affections of their relatives; they therefore feel a necessity to call to them their kith and kin. . . . It is known that . . . those that head to the Spanish American republics of Río de la Plata come from the Spanish provinces that keep in continuous contact with those countries of . . . America, and usually know the advantages, disadvantages, and contingencies of such expeditions from the stories of relatives and friends that precede them and, sometimes, call and encourage them.[74]

Thus, of the 812 cases on record of Baztán natives that went to America in the nineteenth century, 30.6 percent (249 people) began the migratory adventure summoned by relatives already settled there, with the clear possibility of quick entrance into the labor market.

The migration chain can be explained by the significant colonies of pioneers in this process who would later attract fellow natives of the same town. Thus, for example, many emigrated from the municipalities of Burguete, Espinal, and Valle de Erro to Argentina and the western United States, but, in contrast, not to other countries. Nevertheless, emigration from Garralda (for example) headed for Mexico. In contrast, several left Sumbilla and Santesteban for Cuba. Chile was another desired country of destination where this chain emigration functioned well.

In general terms, the diaspora connected continents, countries, and regions, but also districts, towns, and even neighborhoods. The ties that most configured this chain were, undoubtedly, those of family and close kinship: brothers that called brothers or fathers that called sons. But a relationship typically close in the Basque Country and Navarre, uncle-nephew, was also highly important. The uncle in America summoned his nephew to either work with him until the latter could strike out on his own or leave him as heir and successor upon retiring from his enterprises. Many of the protagonists of these chain migratory undertakings carried a letter of recommendation and reference that had been sent to them from the other side of the Atlantic. Nevertheless, this kinship relationship did not always end well. Sometimes, the relative arrived unexpectedly; in other cases, those already settled made the new arrival go through the same hardships they had experienced after reaching America.

Love of the Homeland

To this point, the causes that motivated Basque emigration have been narrated in detail. Now, the typology of the Basque emigrants heading for overseas lands will also be discussed. But, why did the Basques emigrate in a period of time—the nineteenth century—in which their native provinces were industrializing? The latter half of the nineteenth century witnessed the industrial revolution in its most literal sense in Basque lands. It was the period of great capital accumulation, of massive iron exports to Great Britain, Belgium, and France. It was also the period of the appearance of the large Basque banks (Bilbao and Vizcaya), and of the creation of important *altos hornos* (blast furnaces), shipyards (Sota and Aznar), and significant infrastructure. This accumulation of capital and proliferation of factories, which changed the rural Basque landscape, caused the cities of the territory to experience spectacular growth. It also provoked one of the most important rural-to-urban migrations in contemporary Spanish history.

And yet the Basques, who had wealth in their own territory and factory work possibilities in their provinces, emigrated in large numbers to America. Why? In this respect, Douglass and Bilbao give explanations that appear entirely feasible. Undoubtedly, for the nineteenth-century Basque peasantry, to be *etxekojaun*, or "master of the house," was possibly the most prestigious social role. In contrast, urban inhabitants were called (somewhat pejoratively) *kalekuak*, or "those of the street." Rustic life was praised immeasurably in both popular songs and local

Basque sayings, extolling how such existence guaranteed the individual's social dignity and personal independence within the collectivity. On the other hand, city life meant work under the control of others (*kalekuak*), which resulted in a loss of autonomy and even personal independence for the Basque peasantry.[75]

Hence there appeared an implicit sentiment of contempt by the rustic man toward the factory system. Likewise, this proliferation of factories and companies throughout Basque geography came to break the traditional Basque molds and the guidelines of rural Basque behavior. The appearance of modern cities that spit out polluted air next to fields, meadows, and farmsteads provoked strange sensations in the peasants, as did the arrival of numerous factory workers to their peaceable and picturesque mountain landscapes. Furthermore, the working and living conditions in the Basque industrial nuclei of the nineteenth century and the first half of the twentieth were far from ideal. Quite the contrary. It must also be kept in mind that the few families possessing the wealth and control of the Basque capitalist system were political liberals; many peasants had fought in the ranks of Carlism, which explains their rejection of liberalism that was also laden with political connotations.

Moreover, the Basque Country had few possibilities of extending the economic base of agriculture because of a complete lack of available uninhabited lands. America, however, made it possible for the protagonists of the diaspora, after years of hard work and effort, to become members of a managing class tied to agriculture within an economic process of continuously expanding farmland. The New World presented more possibilities for economic mobility and agricultural expansion in the short and, in some cases, medium term. Thus, in spite of the good opportunities in the Basque Country to become a factory wage earner, a circumstance that attracted workers from all of Spain to this territory, the Basques continued emigrating to America.

The military and political events of the turbulent Spanish nineteenth century promoted profound anguish and personal frustration in many inhabitants of the Basque provinces, especially those that had lost the wars. For a people without political passion, the terror of the war (and the postwar) and dread of the abuses committed by both bands gave it sufficient motivation to take a chance on the migratory adventure. To this litany of political and war dramas must be added the misery caused by hunger (for example) throughout the territory in the years 1846–1847. If this were not enough, the industrial revolution displaced the rural and urban artisans on the edges of economic marginalization. Their manufactured goods could no longer compete with mass industrial production that lowered costs, popularized consumption, and fractured the traditional mode of production. Likewise, both in Araba and in Navarre to the south of Pamplona, dominated by the large property that earlier employed hundreds of people in seasonal agricultural tasks, scientific advances in agronomy diminished this demand for labor even more. Around the mid-nineteenth century, another traditional Basque activity, the traffic of livestock, especially (but not exclusively) smuggled across the international border, suffered a great turnabout. New nineteenth-century customs agreements between Spain and France largely eliminated its profitability. The connection of the two sides of the border by railroad greatly reduced transport costs.

But, without doubt, the single most important factor in Basque emigration was the relationship between the forms of inheriting the farmstead (and its farmland) and the agricultural possibilities of those that did not accede to such inheritance. This fact has already been addressed above and will not be discussed further. But it is easy to see that those second-borns, or nonheirs, the *segundones* who did not accede to the possession of land property, on many occasions chose to emigrate to America. The obsession with acquiring rural property undoubtedly acted as an important motivation for this Basque emigration.

The Myth of El Dorado

Today it is difficult to imagine the anguishes that Basques must have suffered in their risky, complicated overseas crossings of yore. Those conquistadors, soldiers, or simple colonists, conscious of what awaited them when they embarked in Sevilla, Cádiz, or even Bilbao, did not hesitate to make out their wills (those who were able to do so) before undertaking the adventure that would completely transform their lives. So much has been said about the root of the social influences and transformations that the Spaniards stamped upon America, yet the passion with which the American myth was lived in the Basque Country is seldom mentioned. But the New World also managed to endow the daily life of the Basque provinces with newly colored impressions. And, from the times of Columbus, American emigration turned into the solution and escape valve for the "second-borns" of the farmstead and its possessions. Thus, from the sixteenth century until the first third of the twentieth, hundreds of young Basques decided to go to America, obsessed by the magnificence of the stories and mythic fables that were spread throughout the Basque territory. One must bear in mind that these men's vision of the world was limited to the farmstead, its surroundings, and the neighboring town or village. Even a trip to the provincial capital was a rare event. Therefore, undertaking the crossing to the New World was a momentous upheaval.

The letters sent from the other side of the ocean by the first ones on the Indies run told great tales of the ease with which money was earned in America, the beauty of its places and peoples, and its exuberant nature and cuisine. And, protected by the right of collective nobility granted by Philip II to the Basque Provinces in the times of the overseas colonial empire, the Basques frequently went to the New World as functionaries of noble status or as colonists with privileged credentials. They thus earned fame, prestige, and notoriety in Lima, Mexico, Cuba, and Colombia. The most intrepid reached the peaks of power and cemented it through substantial marital ties. They passionately and successfully devoted themselves to commerce in its most varied branches, thanks to their high bureaucratic-administrative posts. The independence of the South American colonies beginning in 1810 brought about mass Basque emigration motivated greatly by advances in navigation and means of transport, favorable American pro-immigration laws, and the population increase in the Basque Country.

Beginning in the nineteenth century, thousands of Basques took refuge in the desire to undertake new lives overseas. The myth of El Dorado again began to function in the collective subconsciousness. This time, it was stirred by some sinister characters called *ganchos* or *enganchadores*, who, inflating the true American reality with lies, traveled the towns seducing the peasants with the favors of the other side of the Atlantic. Ultimately, for these businessmen, as well as for various captains and outfitters, migration was translated into economic terms. This emigration has always been interwoven with a finely threaded myth of the Indies, a myth that deeply pierced the Basque social structure and even induced the *bertsolariak* to devote part of their best poetry to it. That all myths have a good deal of legend was proven by the majority of Basque emigrants. In effect, from the moment they boarded the ships that took them to the supposed earthly paradises of the other side of the Atlantic, they descended into a world of thorny future realities. Ultimately, the overseas American republics never conceded success easily to anyone. It was necessary to fight for it, and only the most able managed to reach the highest pinnacles of power and wealth, which they always enjoyed showing off. The rest came to swell the "mesocracy" of a continent that, at the height of the nineteenth century, initiated independence to begin a new historical day as a young territory, anxious for modernization and progress. The offers were always attractive. But, the prices and sacrifices demanded in the fight for social triumph became, on occasion, very high. For many immigrants the price was truly exorbitant.

Chapter Eight

The Bureaucracy, the Dreamed-of Voyage, and the Typology of the Emigrant

The Requisite Documents

To emigrate legally to America, the young Basques of the nineteenth century had to carefully follow the Spanish legislation described in the preceding chapters. To obtain a passport from the civil government of their province, the candidate had to present the following documents: (1) boarding license; (2) deposit; (3) boarding obligations-contracts; (4) information from witnesses; (5) certification of good character from the mayor of one's town. The license (also called "paternal consent") conferred paternal emancipation and, at the same time, full civil rights. It was vital for procuring the passport. If the emigrant was male, inclusion of the father's (or tutor's) permission was mandatory for travel to the New World. If the emigrant was a married woman, it was the husband who granted the license and vice versa, although this latter case was infrequent. In the absence of parents, an older brother filled this function. The license was filled out in the presence of a notary. The people who granted the permission and the one (or ones) who received it were also present, as were two or three witnesses. This document was full of rich details about the work histories and social profiles of emigrants and their forebears.

A statement was also required for the passport. With this document, emigrants had to demonstrate that they were not being criminally prosecuted, nor had any legal impediment to leaving; and they had to ensure, through a solvent bondsman, judicial and financial responsibility in the face of any predicament. The process was completed in front of a notary and with witnesses. This model document was directly related to the authorities' interest in preventing young men subject to the "military replacement deposit" from fleeing to evade obligatory service. The payment of this deposit, however, cleared the emigrant with the military authorities, as the money could be used to find a "substitute." Such a deposit was not required from the young men that, having fulfilled their obligatory military service, wished to emigrate to Cuba, Puerto Rico, or the Philippines, still Spanish colonies until 1898.

With the boarding obligation or contract, the emigrant promised (was "obliged") to pay the price of the overseas' journey in cash. The "granters," or people who assumed responsibility for the reliability and punctuality of the payment of the amounts stipulated, were the emigrant's parents or siblings, depending upon the case. The granter and bondsman was often the same person, and frequently property (farmstead, land, etc.) was included as a guarantee of payment of the voyage. The act of signing the obligation took place in front of a notary, in the presence of witnesses and the captain, outfitter, or a representative from the ship. This document is of great interest for researchers of contemporary emigration; in it is registered the name of the ship, the ports of departure and arrival, and the class in which the emigrant traveled: cabin, prow, or steerage for sailing vessels and first, second, or third class for steamships in the last third of the nineteenth century. The name of the captain or outfitter and all information about the emigrant were registered. The price of the crossing and the form of payment were established. In the boarding agreement the quantity and quality of food and drinking water to be received on board were stipulated. It was also indicated if a surgeon or doctor would be on board, and data about him was included.

Regarding information about the witnesses, it is noteworthy that, at the beginning of the nineteenth century, emphasis was still placed on information of nobility and *limpieza de sangre;* this requisite became increasingly more routine, however, and a formality on the form.

In addition to the documents mentioned to this point, all of which were done in the presence of a notary, another must be mentioned. These were the so-called "certifications," done in front of the mayor or municipal judge. With these, the municipal representative indicated that the emigrants had no legal impediment of any kind to prevent them from leaving, and also vouched for their good conduct. Once all of the necessary legal documents were obtained, the emigrant had permission to receive the precious passport that made the move to America possible and that, as has been indicated, was issued by the civil governor of each province.

The Dreamed-of Voyage

Among the reasons for the massive contemporary Basque diaspora were undoubtedly the spread of maritime traffic and its increased carrying capacity. Thus, beginning in the 1860s, the construction of steamships increased, to the detriment of the until-then dominant sailing vessels. Steamships considerably decreased the time required for the voyage, and considerably increased the capacity for transporting emigrants. In a steamship, the crossing took a minimum of one month. During the first half of the century, the voyage might take much longer. This occurred in the case of Faustino Mariñelarena, who overcame all of the obstacles to reach Havana in 1851.[1] The voyage of this Navarrese lasted fifty-nine days. The ship set out on October 10, 1851, and did not arrive in Cuba until December 8. Five days after leaving, it was hit by a storm with strong winds and rain in which "the waves served as a roof for the ship." Some of the passengers had to help, "serving as sailors, drawing the ropes of the sails and rigging." Others said rosaries continuously inside the ship. Two days before reaching Havana, the rudder broke, making navigation extremely dangerous, although in the end the ship went straight. From calamity to calamity, Mariñelarena said that they still had the strength and desire for diversions during the crossing: "When the weather was good, we enjoyed ourselves to the hilt. We had our good music of guitars, flutes, tambourines, and the rest. . . . We absorbed ourselves in long sessions of music, in order to entertain the belly, which was often empty." In general, the poverty of the crossings, the bad condition and scarcity of the food, and the abuses and dishonesty of the ship outfitters and captains were the norm of the nineteenth-century transatlantic journeys. In 1855 and 1856, Nicolás Soraluce tried for six months to organize Basque peasants and send them to America as emigrants. On March 11, 1856, he left Pasaia with his first group of migrants. The food on board consisted of an abundance of potatoes, little meat, a lot of cod, and sardines that rotted at sea. The quality of the food was so poor that for several days the passengers survived on garlic soup.[2]

In addition, sometimes there were great tragedies. One was the shipwreck that occurred off the coast of Uruguay in June 1842. It was the *Leopoldina Rosa*, which had left Bayonne on January 31 of that year with over three hundred passengers; only a few survived.

For several days in a row in 1862, the description of a transatlantic crossing suffered by a Basque emigrant appeared in the newspaper *Euscalduna*. This article was written precisely to dissuade those who wanted to go to America at that time. It was an experience lived in first person by the author and narrated in great detail. At nine o'clock in the morning on February 25, 1858, the man, who had the potential to be a hero, left for Buenos Aires from the port of Pasaia. The 280 emigrant-passengers were piled "like bundles" within the little habitable space of the 230-ton brig in which they were traveling. The passengers began to complain about the discomfort from the very beginning. Of course, these complaints were never heeded. In addition to the lack of accommodations, they suffered from the rocking of the ship. With each storm gust, the beds were flooded—if one could call a sixteen-inch wide mattress over a six-by-four-foot platform, which accommodated six men, a bed. The complaints were never heeded by the captain. But, in addition, the food, "scarce and detestable," consisted of one raw sardine per person and a sip of horrible wine for breakfast. At lunchtime, one portion of vegetables for each twelve people filled the stomachs. At night, again, there was a paltry amount of vegetables, mixed with pork fat (usually rancid). As the discontent increased, the anonymous author described with precision what occurred; in his words:

> Those on board have just rebelled because of the wretched food that they give us, and the agreement that our commissioned recruiter Iraola promised to re-

spect in front of the scribe, obliging him to respect the agreement and everything mentioned in it, has been presented to the captain. The captain responds that he does not have anything to do with either our agreement or Iraola; that he had an agreement with the charterer Apesteguy in France and that he would explain our condition to the latter, adding that he had not even met Iraola until a few days before departing, denying that there was any type of agreement or promise, even verbal, between the two. He has shown us the conditions upon which he agreed with the charterer, written in French and, upon examining them, we see that in effect they are very different from ours; from which it must be deduced that our "disinterested protector" has deceived us in an unscrupulous and thievish way.

The people on board were workers, "simple and ignorant men." They emigrated to America in search of new opportunities, hoping to escape their impoverished state. The majority were piled on the ship because these emigrant transport vessels left port secretly and silently, taking great care to hide their merchandise from the authorities. In 1858, the commissaries, or emigration agents, demanded forty copper reales for expediting passports. They arbitrarily set the number that would travel, according to the tonnage of the vessel. In this way they scoffed at the good faith of the government and the local Basque authorities, overloading the ships and pocketing the difference. The legal procedure for boarding allowed each ship to carry a set number of passengers, depending upon its freight capacity. In each period of history studied, this number varied since, logically, throughout the nineteenth century the capacity of the holds of transatlantic vessels increased. Thus, with the law habitually disrespected, it might occur that (as the passenger above testifies) two hundred mem were crammed into a space forty feet long by twenty-two feet wide by seven feet high. There was always someone who stayed on deck to avoid such crowding, "adapting perfectly well to the rain and the stars." Almost every day, furious disputes broke out between the captain and the passengers, with obvious risks of tragic outcomes; the crew's treatment of the emigrant-passengers was extremely unpleasant. If one wished to improve one's condition on board, one could always bribe the captain or the cook, for example. By paying large sums, passengers could receive better treatment from the heads of the crew. In addition to the inclemencies offered by nature herself, such as the unbearable heat, torrential rains, or hurricanes to which the emigrants were exposed, the poor quality of the food caused suffering. As the days passed, the condition of the food worsened, and it eventually spoiled on each crossing. The following traveler-writer expressed himself clearly: "What causes us the most grief is the rottenness of the water, eager as we are to drink it, and we barely bring it to our lips when the stench makes us back away. In it they cook our less than frugal meals; but in the cabin they serve themselves from the water from the still for all of their needs, so it is not surprising that more than once there has been no drinkable water for the sick."

Digestive illnesses, caused in part because hunger seized the poorly nourished emigrants, were very common. But smallpox also assailed some passengers, causing even more discomfort, if possible. With no doctor or phlebotomist on board, however, and first aid supplies scarce, nobody could be attended by a skilled hand. The remedies were improvised and the anguishes mounted. After ninety-three days of travel and a dozen deaths, the travelers espied the land so greatly longed for:

> The daybreak has pleasantly surprised us. The cry of "Land! Land!" resonating from one end of the ship to the other, has spread such joy among this crowd that, crazy with happiness, they come out to the bridge naked and without even paying attention to gender they hug each other feverishly, repeating the yearned for name of "Land!" It is an island called "Los Lobos" because of the great number of wolves that are said to live there. It is sixteen leagues from Montevideo. When we arrived, there were only cookie crumbs left, which we greedily finished. The rotten unsalted vegetables agreed with our empty stomachs magnificently.

Shortly after this stop they reached the capital, where the suffering continued. The Board of Health of the Port of Buenos Aires quarantined the ship for three days, keeping it under observation for smallpox. After the three days were over, a new life began for these emigrants in the New World.

In 1869, the contract agent Apesteguy chartered one of many expeditions for America that left from Pasaia. The hardships suffered by the emigrants on board followed one after another. The morning's breakfast was one "old" sardine. Lunch was composed of one ladle full of beans per person and hardtack (complete with mold). "The men were so thin that their pants fell down." Chocolate, sugar, and coffee became luxury items. The outfitters had promised a *cuartillo* of wine per person in the contract. The agreement was not kept. Lice infested the emigrants just after they left Pasaia. Not all arrived alive; some died from contagious diseases on the way.

In general, the living conditions on board left much to be desired. Thus, the mattress on which the always crowded passengers slept was of hard straw with a cushion of the same material and a blanket of poor quality. The food, as already indicated, was bad, and medical attention scarce or nonexistent. The cabins in which the emigrants were placed were about three meters high. On the walls of these compartments three canvas cots were placed like stretchers, one above the next. They began in corridors or alleys in which circulation was extremely difficult. In each cabin young people, children, and old people slept together, and separation by sex was sometimes with only a simple curtain. The emigrant passengers did not make the trip alone; they were accompanied by various insects and lice. Thus, the agglomeration of such masses, close contact, the lack of drinkable water, and poor hygiene were the greatest threats to the health of the emigrants. The rooms always smelled bad and the mixture of urine and vomit was insufferable. Dirty clothes were kept in a thick canvas bag, prepared for this purpose, and only those articles absolutely necessary for daily life, such as underwear, stockings, and smelly diapers, could be washed. To maintain minimal hygienic conditions, the passengers should have cleaned themselves regularly; the lack of water, however, often made this impossible. Going below deck only to sleep became the norm, because the interior areas of the ship were not as well ventilated. Washing underwear only once a week was common. Many of the emigrants were natives of towns far from the large ports from which the ships to America set sail. For most, this was their first encounter with a large city, a port, and the sea. On the voyage, these passenger-heroes befriended strangers who chose the same course, with whom they sang popular songs.

Most of the time, the maritime transport companies committed many abuses against their emigrant clients on the transatlantic journey. To begin with, the law regarding stipulations about the capacity of people per boat was rarely complied with. The precise Spanish legislation of the period, examined above, was repeatedly ignored. More emigrants than permitted always went on board, thus making the cargo more profitable.[3] This occurred with French, Spanish, British, and German ships. Mistreatment and physical punishment of "third-class" passengers was also common. Such treatment was administered by captains and sailors longing to ruthlessly "discipline" and largely unsympathetic to the fate of the passengers. Aside from the poor sanitary conditions already mentioned, those in which the Basques and Navarrese traveled to Mexico are an example. In the first steamship that set out for Mexico, after World War I, an epidemic of typhoid broke out. The scant medical attention was responsible for many becoming ill. Many others died, and were simply tossed overboard.[4]

The Public Denunciations

The breaching of many contracts and boarding obligations, the mistreatment of the passengers, and the *ganchos*'[5] eagerness for profit provoked many reactions by the Basque provincial authorities, though these were largely in vain. Thus, as early as 1840, the parliamentarian from Gipuzkoa, Count Monterrón, ordered the printing of a circular that would be spread throughout the province,[6] in which the readers were warned of the magnitude of overseas emigration. The count stated that the number of those who went to Azkoitia in search of passports for travel to America was increasing daily. He saw himself forced to indicate the legal requisites for getting the passport. Few of the applicants arrived with their documents in order. One year later, in the legislature of Segura, the same parliamentarian made clear the enormous potential danger of the Basque emigration to Montevideo (at that time very numerous). But, in addition, he dared to offer suggestions:

With this motive the Honorable Count of Monterrón appeared in front of the Legislature, that he had called the numerous emigration from this country to Montevideo to the attention of the Deputation more than once, and that this could diminish its population in the long run to where the effects would be felt in agriculture, commerce, and the arts. But he has news that an association has been formed to promote agriculture in the Seigneury of Vizcaya; he would suggest the Deputation make an agreement with that association, to see how to make what is left of the youth in the country stay, and to thereby prevent the ills that the emigration to such a distant place can produce over time. Upon hearing this exposition, the Legislature agreed to his recommendation to the Deputation.[7]

In 1852, the bishop of Pamplona published a "Circular in which the system of enticing young people of both sexes to transport them to the American Continent through seductive promises of a stable income and a happy future is reproached as immoral." In 1860, with the intention of warning its mayors of the imminent arrival of a group of agents from Peru, the Deputation of Araba sent them the following circular:

The Deputation has learned through a very authoritative source that Mr. Máximo Navarro has made an offer to the Government of the Republic of Peru to introduce a thousand Spanish colonists into that territory; and that given the ease with which the agents of said Mr. Navarro go to the Basque Provinces, in order that the residents of Alava are not seduced by rosy promises, the Deputation warns His Excellency that it would be wise to impress upon his ministers the inconveniences of becoming associated with a company in which they will certainly be victims of personal ambition; that the offers and contracts attempt to facilitate an emigration whose fate will be as or more unpleasant than that which has befallen English, German, and Asian colonizations on Peruvian soil.

Upon directing this notice to His Excellency, the Deputation verifies it with complete knowledge of the cause, and in the certainty that the zeal that His Excellency has devoted to prevent Alavan emigration if the Peruvian agents arrive to this province will be a special service for which the country will be indebted.

May God protect His Excellency for many years. Vitoria, February 22, 1860.
The Lieutenant Deputy General
The Count of Salazar.[8]

In 1862, all the official bulletins of the Basque Country included among their pages the norms currently in force as to the number of passengers that the boats could carry to Río de la Plata.[9] Beginning on February 14, 1862, the Royal Order of May 6, 1856, directing that ships bound for America could transport equal weights of passengers and freight was abolished. From then on, for the transport of emigrants to the Southern Cone (Argentina, Uruguay, and Chile), lodging was permitted only in ships of the American run, with one emigrant per ton and a half. An important change was instituted in an attempt to avoid abuses by the outfitters and captains: that each vessel would be permitted to accommodate only as many passengers as there were berths. In 1867, the Deputation of Gipuzkoa that met in Tolosa composed another circular, signed by the then-deputy general, the viscount of Santo Domingo. In short, it complained once more about the grave consequences that overseas emigration had for the Basque Provinces:

> Sadly affected by the disagreeable spectacle offered by the growing emigration of the Guipuzcoan youth of both sexes to the distant regions of America, I find it necessary to address my paternal voice to the residents of the country, calling to their attention the ill-fated consequences of this excessive eagerness to blindly abandon native soil, and to the municipal governments, to the illustrious clergy and to all of the individuals that for their knowledge and position are respected and trusted among their neighbors, so that with the legitimate influence of their authority and advice, they might cooperate toward the attainment of my humanitarian objective.

He then continued by painting a paradisiacal picture of the Basque Country, in romantic hues that in some way correspond with reality.

> How lamentable is the confusion of the discontented that thus leave their country! They open their eyes for the first time in what is perhaps the most blessed region of the world: they enjoy here the tenderness of paternal love, games of infancy, the attraction of friendship; and dazzled by the deceiving perspective of a miserable handful of gold, generally unprepared and with no more than the belongings they carry in their arms, leave their happiness, their freedom, their homeland, their family, their friends, never to recover them again, and die crying for them, at the most beautiful period of their life, destroyed by the weather, the work, and the misery.

The solutions came later, full of rhetoric and good intentions mixed with romantic language. Nothing was said about the real problem that caused many of the peasants go to America:

> It is not possible to openly avoid the effects of this deplorable tendency with government measures, but this end could be achieved in great part indirectly, through repeated exhortations that give the simple peasants a true idea of the fate that certainly awaits them overseas.
>
> They should be made to understand through all means possible that for every person from this country that returns from those regions remain a thou-

sand unfortunate ones that cry over their shattered dreams, unable to return to their homeland for lack of resources, because the traffickers that facilitated their emigration are very careful to prevent it even to the point of refunding the price of their passage: that those who speculate with their ignorance and credulity have a clear interest in making their return difficult, in order to exploit their sweat and aptitude for work, while their strength is exhausted; that the habits of liberty, moderate customs, and religious spirit acquired in their native land commonly suffer humiliating and dangerous transformations in America; that the frequent wars, which with rare exceptions overwhelm the former Spanish colonies, now free, contribute to make the plight of our compatriots more agonizing and arduous; that the Basque farmers and workers that come to settle in those lands will be hard pressed to find living conditions similar to the modest welfare and peaceable quiet of our mountains; and that if they are wanting for work here, in the other provinces of our common mother the generous Spain, the sons of this land will find, as they always do, the reception and recompense that their hard work and virtues deserve.

Here, the local institutions are included:

I trust that the City Halls, understanding the importance of these observations, interestedly strive to inculcate their inhabitants and especially the fathers of families, whose young children could not emigrate without their express consent; and if the lack of work contributes to the misfortune that I lament, it would be wise for them dedicate their efforts to promoting, as much as possible, the repairs of need, convenience, and public adornment possible that might facilitate the occupation of working hands.

May God grant that the influx of our joint efforts appease and contain this delirious frenzy that snatches a great part of our spirited youth, causing them to hurl their bodies to the ruinous solitudes of the new world! [10]

The considerable number of emigrants that left the Iberian Peninsula yearly for South America attracted the attention of the government of Alfonso XII. In 1880, the *Official Bulletin* of the province of Bizkaia published a circular with the intention of trying through all means possible to check "these emigrations so damaging for agriculture, industry, and commerce and in which the emigrants, far from finding the fortune that they are looking for, instead see their hopes deceived by the reality of a miserable existence." That same year, the civil governor of Bizkaia, Manuel García Aguilar, believed it necessary to enlighten those who "inspired by illusory profits were going to lend their labors to other countries, that there they did not enjoy at all the happiness hungered for." At least, some of the reports sent by the accredited Spanish consuls in the South American republics advanced such arguments. The governor urged the mayors to impress the inconvenience of emigration upon their "administratees." Even if emigration was inevitable, a lesser evil would be emigration to the island of Cuba where, in principle, future and work were more certain.[11] The same year, in another memo, the comments sounded the same:

> For a long time the constant movement of emigration that exists in various provinces of Spain and that is directed by general rule to the South American republics has been catching the attention of the government. . . .
>
> These currents of emigration not only snatch from agriculture and industry a multitude of useful and vigorous hands, but are also a continuous source of very sad deceptions, and the origin of immoral and shameful speculations. . . . In addition, if it is not possible, except under special circumstances, to impede Spaniards from abandoning their homeland, often seduced by deceptive offers, there are undoubtedly ways of channeling these currents of emigration, directing them to the Spanish provinces that, whether on the seas of the Antilles or on the most remote of the Philippine islands, offers secure incentive, and certain recompenses for hard work and perseverance.[12]

In 1881, José María Gastón, civil governor of Navarre, considered emigration a disgrace that had scourged this province for many years. He tried, unsuccessfully, to cut this evil at its roots or at least make its consequences less damaging. The governor was conscious of the importance of the departure of Navarrese highlanders for Argentina and Uruguay. Although respectful of the civil liberty of emigrating, he contacted the civil and religious authorities of Navarre to try to make the aspirants see the error of choosing to leave the province for a miserable life of illusory riches on the other side of the Atlantic. Gastón expressed himself in his missive to the mayors of Navarre thus:

> I understand well, Mister Mayor, that the means to punish such seductions do not exist in my sphere of action, nor in yours, because representing a government whose motto is "the greatest freedom possible with the most complete order," we cannot impede the exercise of rights granted in writing in the fundamental Code; but we can and should even more energetically and incessantly counter the seductions with our propaganda of good and truth, our loyal advice. . . .
>
> It is imperative that, with the urgency that the case demands, but always respecting the civil liberty of your administratees, you make every directed effort possible that none of the young people of either sex persevere in their intentions of emigration before they and their fathers know what is really behind the promises made them and the clear and sure dangers to which they are exposed.[13]

In 1882, José Colá y Goiti's *Basque and Navarrese Emigration* appeared on the market; a majority of the articles that the author had published previously throughout the Basque press were included in the book. Deputies Gamiz and Laguardia requested that the Deputation of Araba finance the work's publication, which it agreed to do. The Deputations of Bizkaia, Gipuzkoa, and Navarre did the same. The first printing was sold out within one month. Colá y Goiti's great obsession was to maintain a frontal and continuous attack against emigration agents. The book's argument was focused on this criticism of emigration. Its author can be considered the leading exponent of the anti-emigration thesis. This idea appears on every single page of the book.

Also in 1882, the Ministry of Development once again stated its concern about the serious ills of the diaspora. The Deputation of Bizkaia reflected such sentiments in its *Official Bulletin*.[14] Once again, emphasis was placed on the deceptions concerning the "advantages" that awaited the adventurer in America. Nevertheless, the laws could not be excessively coercive since "they would tarnish the respect undoubtedly deserved by the legitimate rights of individual liberty." The lack of work in some Spanish provinces and its excess in others represented a quick, easy solution for checking the heavy migratory outflow. The measures to take were simple. The authorities had to make those without work in their province move to other regions of the country, where useful hands were necessary: "It occurs to our detriment that those hands go looking to other lands or foreign soil for that which without such risk they could obtain in their abandoned homeland." It was even suggested that the railroad companies reduce their fares to transport and place unemployed workers where they were needed. Another measure that they tried to adopt was to distribute basic booklets/brochures or *cartillas* among the general public. These booklets portrayed in simple terms the poverty and deception that tended to destroy Basque emigrants.

A norm was imposed that required provincial authorities (in this case the Basque ones) to watch over the emigration agencies. Such agencies frequently transported the unhappiest overseas with fallacious contracts, painting flattering pictures that almost always vanished as soon as one set foot on American soil. It was suggested that emigration agents be required to live in a fixed residence. That way, they could be located when it was necessary to punish fraudulent and deceptive contracts. And if it was necessary, authorities would bring any necessary lawsuits to trial in the name of emigrants to recompense the damages suffered due to deception. It was demanded that all emigration agencies be licensed in the form mentioned in the law. A new suggestion also appeared in this publication: the urgent need was stated to know how many of the emigrants still outside the country desired to return to their places of origin and lacked sufficient means to do so. It was the task of the provincial and state authorities to send the necessary ships to repatriate those who requested it. The "immoral traffic" of women who, deceived by promises of domestic labor, ended up in American whorehouses was also mentioned. On March 14, 1883, Luis de Villabaso, vice president of the Deputation of Bizkaia, signed another interesting anti-emigratory proclamation:

> By general rule, emigration is considered in all countries to be a serious ill for that country from which the emigrant comes, because its population and richness, which are as great as the sum of intelligence and hands that contribute in it, decrease. The Basque Land should not be excluded from this general rule, however much the love of its natives inclines them, wherever they be, to return to native soil with the fortune that they might have acquired; but to detain, or at least restrain, the currents of emigration from the Basque provinces, is much more convenient as they are almost always directed to the Spanish American republics, almost constantly disturbed by political passions.
>
> Perhaps among those republics there is none that has suffered as much of this disturbance as that which has Montevideo as its capital. A Basque that has remained there for several years and has studied the probabilities of prosperity or ruin that the emigrant has there, has published a book whose object is to make manifest the sad fate that awaits his compatriots that emigrate to the cited republic, and the Deputation of Bizkaia, following the example of her sister provinces par excellence, has acquired examples of this patriotic work.
>
> One of them is sent to you, in order that, along with the parish priest of that location, you might strive to make its contents known to the residents of the same, so that with this knowledge they will learn how pervasive emigration of the youth to the Republic of Uruguay is.

Emigration and its consequences also awakened more than a little interest in Basque and Navarrese professors and intellectuals.[15] Good proof of this is the "Scientific, Literary, and Artistic Competition," which the City Hall of Pamplona organized in 1833, following the models of the "Euskara-Basque Association of Navarre." There were six themes about which works could be submitted. Of these, two were directly related to the issue of migration:

1. To what point the Spanish discovery, conquest, and domination of America was to the glory and good of Spain
2. The pleasantries and excellences of rural life in our mountains, contrasting them to the miseries and degradations that emigration to America offers

All the prizewinners in both categories made anti-emigratory allusions with such suggestive titles as "The Traveler"; "An Emigrant's Song"; "Being Born in the Basque Country and Dying in America"; and "Navarrese Emigration to South America, Its Causes and Consequences."

The Newspaper Campaign Against Emigration

During the entire nineteenth century and the first years of the twentieth, a bona fide newspaper campaign against emigration to America was unleashed on both Basque slopes of the Pyrenees and in Navarre. In 96 percent of the articles, the pens of native writers were sharpened with tenacity against the direct agents of Basque emigration, the *ganchos,* although there was no lack of criticism directed against the local and national authorities or the shipping companies and those hired to transport the emigrants to the other side of the Atlantic (the captains and outfitters). Although the Basque and Navarrese newspaper records are incomplete, the news reports that make reference to Bizkaia have been sufficiently studied,[16] and now the events in Navarre will be examined.[17] Excessive detail will be avoided, as the writings that appear in the Basque local press during the period in question are abundant.[18]

On August 30, 1893, *El Eco de Navarra* alluded to factors like the inefficiency of the successive Spanish governments to explain the massive Navarrese emigration. In this newspaper's opinion, these governments only created obstacles for agriculture, preventing the creation of wealth in the province; this explained the attachment of the peasantry to the land. Similarly, the same periodical (January 29, 1911) referred to the cries for vengeance and justice and the hunger of the residents of an imaginary town from whom the local caciques called in their debts, even when the residents were in the process of abandoning the town. In the same newspaper, a resident of Lezaun (Navarre) narrated the misery and neglect found in the town, which had, in his opinion, made emigration flower; he defined the process as "a present sickness more criminal than war."

In 1913, the *Pensamiento Navarro* maintained that there were towns in this territory in which the peasants were not the owners of the enclosed lands in their municipal jurisdictions, but that these were instead property of the marquis, usurers, and deputies. Nevertheless, a reply in *La Tradición Navarra* claimed that this assertion was untrue, arguing that there were no latifundias in the province, nor a lack of day work, and that the hands that emigration took to America or the big cities were still needed to cultivate the fields of their native territory. On February 8, 1911, the bimonthly illustrated magazine *La Avalancha* made manifest the demographic stagnancy caused by emigration, insisting that the official figures hid the secret departures. To demonstrate this, it made a calculation based on the comparison of natural growth with the evolution between censuses. It thus came to the conclusion that between 1860 and 1900, Navarre had lost 92,334 people through emigration. The article indicated that the migratory depopulation created a need for field hands and placed the blame on the recruiting agents. On May 24, 1911, the heavy migratory outflow was stressed in the same magazine, in spite of the fact that in the first decade of the century, agriculture had been greatly developed through the doubling of vineyards and the appearance of modern machinery on Navarrese farms. And, 47 percent of the territory's land still remained uncultivated. In 1916, Hilario Yaben Yaben wrote a book whose title was significant: *Marriage Contracts in Navarra and Their Influence in Family Stability*. In it, he stated the problems resulting from the excessive demographic pressure on the land, and concluded that emigration was an unavoidable consequence of the very organization of the family and its fertility rate. In the author's opinion, emigration was an important escape valve that prevented social conflict. On April 24, 1919, *El Pueblo Navarro* insisted upon the adventurous character of the emigrants, but also upon the problem of the expansive property in the south and center of the province.

But, undoubtedly, the Navarrese newspapers used a lot of ink against the *ganchos* on various occasions. Here is a sample. On October 14, 1876, *El Eco de Navarra* harshly attacked these recruiters and encouraged the central government to take measures against them. On May 17, 1877, the same newspaper reprinted some paragraphs of a piece from *El Eco de España* (dated April 11 of the same year in Montevideo) in which the precarious situation of the country was made manifest. On December 1, 1880, this periodical reprinted an article from *El Correo Español* of Buenos Aires that spoke of the miserable situation of the Spanish emigrants in Argentina. Two years later, on March 21, it published another letter, sent from Rosario (Argentina) by Juan Cestona; hunger, the spread of disease, and the high infant mortality rate suffered by the emigrants there were all cited. On October 29, 1880, the newspaper *El Arga* published a circular by the Ministry of Governance, directed to the civil governors; it told them to prevent the massive number of departures, citing the news highlighted in other newspapers of the political instability of some American countries. On February 6, 1883, the newspaper *Lau-Buru* published a letter sent from Chile by a Basque in which he reported that the Chilean government planned to colonize inhospitable Araucanian territories with Basques and Navarrese. The letter is interesting because, in opposition to the traditional thesis that Basques and Navarrese were well received in America due to their enterprising and hardworking nature, seriousness, and frugality, the writer told of a negative stereotype. He stated that, in Chile, Basques were seen as largely unsuitable for industry and machine work, superstitious, backward, and an impediment to Spain's progress.

The alarm caused by the demographic regression of the Basque Country appeared frequently in *Lau-Buru*. Thus, on December 2, 1885, this depopulation and the recruitment of young people for America was lamented. On April 10, 1889, *El Liberal Navarro* broke with the general tone, saying that the situation of the South American republics had been greatly exaggerated; it cited the establishing of commercial, industrial, affective, and cultural relations as advantages of emigration. The newspaper maintained that although preventing emigration was impossible, the most important thing was to channel and direct it, helping the emigrants in their decision, as did Belgium. Nevertheless, on August 25, 1896, the same newspaper published "Spaniards, don't go to Brazil," and said "that is a country of death, hunger, prostitution, and misery," at the same time attacking the *ganchos*. On January 1, 1904, *El Pensamiento Navarro* included a letter from Pedro Echeverria from Rosario (Argentina), which said that the Argentine immigrant reception service did nothing to combat the exploitation of the newly arrived.

Two years later, in 1906, the same periodical published letters of clergymen from Buenos Aires criticizing female emigration because women were vulnerable to losing their religious practices, divorce, and abandoning their husbands. On one occasion, *El Pensamiento Navarro* insisted on the possibility of riches and employment in Spain, and that the hands of the American emigration had to be channeled into national necessities. Some newspapers published pamphlets in installments whose central theme was emigration. *El Eco de Navarra* did this beginning on October 27, 1877, with the signature of the writer Julio Nombela and the title "The Basque Americans: Mysteries of Those Who Go to America and Make a Fortune."[19]

This small sample demonstrates the conditions in which Basque emigrants traveled. The evidence indicates that the transport of Basques and Navarrese to the New World was a highly profitable business and that mistreatment had been the order of the day since the sudden upswing of emigration in the 1820s.

Typology of Emigrants and Destinations

To this point, we've seen the labyrinthine, long, and complicated paths traversed by those who decided to undertake the overseas adventure. After dodging bureaucratic obstacles, falling into the *ganchos'* nets, and obtaining money for the voyage, at last it was time to cross the ocean. But what were the backgrounds of these Basque emigrants? From what social group or groups did they come? What age groups emigrated? These factors will now be clarified to shed light on one of the most interesting aspects of the migration phenomenon.

In Araba, as has been established by Ángel María Arrieta,[20] as a rule more men than women emigrated to all destinations. The percentage of men increased when the destination chosen was Cuba, Puerto Rico, or Mexico. In this case, male emigration represented 80 percent, and sometimes even more. Women tended to choose Río de la Plata (especially Argentina) as a destination. According to the data presented by Arrieta, 40 percent of the total Araban female exodus between 1885 and 1895 was to Río de la Plata.

The age group that predominated in emigration to Río de la Plata was between sixteen and twenty-five, decisive years for determining one's future. Nevertheless, Arrieta also shows a significant level of emigration of those fifteen and younger after the institution of obligatory military service in 1876. Fifteen was the age limit to go freely to America, without having to pay the military replacement *quinto* buyout (which amounted to two thousand pesetas). For these adolescents to be able to emigrate, they had to depend upon a family member or well-off ex-neighbor on the other side of the ocean.

As for the civil state of these expatriate Arabans, in most of the cases (around 85 percent) they were unmarried. Nevertheless, Arrieta documents the existence of married couples emigrating—generally without children, although couples with one or more children also made the journey. Married individuals, with or without family members, also did so to be reunited with their spouses in America. There was also no lack of widows who left alone or with a child to live with family, friends, or even other children already established in the New World. Given the argument to this point, it can be affirmed that the nineteenth- and early-twentieth-century Araban emigrant had the following characteristics:

1. Young and unmarried (male in 85 percent of the cases)
2. Coming mostly from a rural background
3. Having family or friends already established in America and, therefore, possessing firsthand information about the world of migration

The following, based on the official statistics, are destinations chosen by the Araban emigrants (following Arrieta's study): of the 510 emigrants from Araba, 70 percent showed a preference for the countries of Río de la Plata, especially Argentina. Nevertheless, Montevideo was initially the main focus of attraction, until the first half of the nineteenth century. Beginning in 1880, Buenos Aires was the main nucleus of reception. Mexico received 9 percent of the nineteenth century Araban emigrants, and the rest headed to Cuba, Puerto Rico, and the Philippines; although it is worth noting that in the case of these last three territories, many replacement soldiers for the colonial wars were counted as emigrants. Other destinations, such as Guatemala or Brazil, were less significant. For the latter republic, Araban emigration was more important during the period of 1889–1891, undoubtedly because of the intense campaign conducted by the *ganchos* in coordination with Brazilian authorities. Venezuela, Chile, Peru, Paraguay, Colombia, and the United States appear as marginal destinations.

The appraisals of Ángel María Arrieta about Araban emigration coincide particularly well with the interpretations of the data concerning the departure of emigrants from this province to Río de la Plata in the nineteenth century.[21] For the period from 1800 to 1900, 1,340 Araban[22] emigrants have been studied. Of those, 69.8 percent settled in Argentina, versus the 30.2 percent that emigrated to Uruguay. Civil status is known for only 42 percent of the emigrants. Of 562 Araban emigrants, the majority were single: 483, or 86 percent, versus 79, or 13.9 percent that were married or widowed. The percentage of men greatly exceeded that of women: 81.9 percent male, 18.1 percent female.

The average age of the Araban emigrants was twenty-four years, and the professions stated at their departure or arrival were, in descending frequency: peasant, farmer, merchant, day laborer, housewife, blacksmith, baker, and dependent.

According to the data cited above, the characteristics of the Araban emigrant to Río de la Plata are similar to those of the Bizkaians and Gipuzkoans. It was a young emigration (a median age of twenty-four), composed mostly of males who were unmarried when they left for America. They were not highly qualified professionals (the majority declared themselves peasants and day laborers), and preferred Argentina to Uruguay as their destination. It was also clear that Araban emigration was much lower than that from Bizkaia and Gipuzkoa.

Various accounts in Navarre, beginning in the 1820s, coincide in indicating that this province's mountainous region has contributed the most to American migration. In 1868, the territory's Deputation sought detailed information "about the important issue of the emigration to America of Highland inhabitants" through a circular issued to the town halls of Lesaca, Vera de Bidasoa, Echalar, Yanci, Aranaz, Goizueta, Arano, Areso, Valle de Bertizarana, and Sumbilla. In 1881, emigration "of alarming proportions" once again became a public concern (this time of the clergy) as evidenced by the circular that the bishop of Pamplona sent to the archpriests of this part of northern Navarre, so that they could inform the parishioners of these towns.[23] Shortly thereafter, the Provincial Congress of Agriculture and Commerce underscored the importance of this mountain emigration, indicating how the scarcity of workers was strongly felt in some districts.[24]

The statistics on emigration and immigration between 1879 and 1883, provided by the Navarrese town halls at the request of the Commission of Social Reforms in 1883, seem to confirm this tendency. Thus, of the 2,903 emigrants that were recorded during those five years, the emigration from the humid Atlantic and Pyrenean valleys regions of Navarre was the highest, with annual rates of 0.57 percent and 0.58 percent, respectively. The pre-Pyrenean basins, with a 0.17 percent annual emigration rate, and the midwestern and mideastern zones, with 0.14 percent and 0.22 percent, respectively, exhibited less significant emigration levels. The Ribera of Estella and the Ribera of Tudela, with 0.04 percent and 0.01 percent, respectively, exhibited migration of little significance. Regarding numbers of emigrants for the period in question (1879–1883), 24 people emigrated from the Ribera of Tudela compared to 454 from the Valley of Baztán: 0.8 percent and 15.6 percent, respectively.

During the nineteenth and early twentieth centuries, 65 percent of Navarrese emigrants headed for the countries of Río de la Plata, and smaller percentages for Cuba, Mexico, Venezuela, and the western United States.[25] Beginning in 1870, Navarrese emigration to Argentina increased considerably, reaching banner volumes from 1880 on. During the second decade of the twentieth century, of 99,039 people that left from Spanish ports between 1923 and 1924, 57,630 disembarked in Buenos Aires. Of that total, 252, or 2.17 percent, were Navarrese. In these years, the ports of Bilbao, Pasaia, and Bordeaux, and to a lesser extent Barcelona, were the leading facilitators of this Navarrese exodus.

Cuba was another significant destination for Navarrese emigration. Traces of Navarre were left there, such as the case of Dionisio Baquedano Arana, who settled on the island in 1882. He founded a coffee-roasting business in Matanzas (Baquedano and Co.) that came to prosper. It was one of the most powerful Cuban businesses at the beginning of the twentieth century, and was still operating in 1954. Bruno Ezquieta Arce, a native of Larraínzar, reached Cuba at the turn of the twentieth century, first working as a wine store clerk; he would later found La Viña (The Vineyard), one of the most important businesses in the entire country, in Havana. Another Navarrese, Prudencio Zabalo Urreaga, stood out at the end of the nineteenth century as an important wholesaler. At the beginning of the twentieth century, the Navarrese presence represented 8.5 percent of Cuba's total population and 90 percent of the foreign white population. Through April 1900, 66,830 people were listed in the General Registry of Spaniards, of which 754 were Navarrese (1.12 percent of the total; 70 percent of them single). They were primarily involved in the business and agricultural sectors. But the Basque and Navarrese colony's importance in Cuba is best manifested by the foundation of the Association of Basque-Navarrese Beneficence in 1878. This organization's main objective was to help the poor and pay for repatriations. It organized its own funeral home and cemetery, reserved exclusively for members who died on the island. In 1887 the Association of Beneficence had 365 members who lived in Havana and 228 in the rest of the provinces.

In the case of Puerto Rico, the first wave of Navarrese emigrants began in the 1840s, in unison with the general immigratory tendency there. It was made up primarily of members of the armed forces and merchants. Beginning in 1850, with the increase in the price of coffee, an incentive was created for the Spanish colony. Members of the armed forces also composed a considerable portion of the Spanish contingent. During the period of 1882–1886, for example, the data of the Geographic and Statistical Institute spoke of 4,737 entries. Regarding the distribution of the emigrants by provinces (using the same sources), Galician, Asturian, and Catalonian emigrant numbers stand out. Next are functionaries who came predominantly from Madrid. Those coming from the Basque Provinces, Navarre, and Santander made up only 10 percent. The majority of them were involved in commerce, indicating that it was a very select emigration. As a whole, Spanish emigrants to Puerto Rico (including the small percentage of Navarrese) tended to devote themselves to the coffee business, colonial administration, and agriculture; these three activities combined for 52 percent of total labor. The remainder were in military-related activities. The Spaniards that arrived in Puerto Rico after the War of Independence (1898) continued to devote themselves to commerce, the railroad and founding industries, and sugar, coffee, and tobacco, which were rapidly expanding due to the significant demand of the North American market. These emigrants tended to fall between sixteen and thirty years of age, and were largely single (78 percent) and male (80 percent).

Navarrese emigration to Chile was not very significant. From 1825 to 1885, the number of Spaniards (males) in Chile did not exceed three thousand; between 1886 and 1907, fifteen thousand Spaniards of both sexes emigrated there. Although by the mid-nineteenth century a great part of Araucanian territory was conquered, it would not be until the 1890s that Navarrese settled (in small numbers) in Chile, devoting themselves primarily to commerce and, in particular, the hardware business.

In Mexico, Navarrese immigration was symbolic, because this country was at the margin of the large mass migrations of the last third of the nineteenth and early twentieth centuries. It was a question of rural emigration trying to attract whole peasant families through farming incentives such as available land, seeds, and equipment. Note that Brazil received 720 Navarrese (18.4 percent of the emigrants) in the period between 1885 and 1895:[26]

Destination Country	No./Percent (%)
Argentina	1,787/45.7
Cuba	1,036/26.5
Brazil	720/18.4
Puerto Rico	121/3.1
Uruguay	109/2.8
Mexico	105/2.8
Colombia	17/0.4
Chile	4/0.1
Venezuela	4/0.1
Peru	3/0.07
USA	1/0.03
Total	3,907/100.0

The years before World War I (1914–1918) were the most significant in terms of the number of Navarrese emigrants: 6,738 between 1911 and 1915. Note the following shifts in emigration to America from 1885 to 1934:[27]

Years	No. Emigrants
1885–1889	2,364
1890–1894	1,367
1911–1915	6,738
1925–1929	2,712
1930–1934	914

After the control of migration following World War I and the stock market crash of 1929, and later following the Spanish Civil War, and as a result of the restrictive legislation of the 1920s and 1930s elsewhere in the Americas, Navarrese headed for the western United States, especially California. In the 1960s, however, this emigration began to decline, with 1970 marking the effective end of Navarrese emigration to America:[28]

Years	No. Emigrants
1940–1944	322
1945–1949	1,026
1950–1954	2,176
1955–1959	1,636
1960–1964	1,061
1965–1969	1,591
1970–1974	690
1975–1979	95

This author has analyzed 2,019 cases of Navarrese emigrants to Río de la Plata during the period of 1800 to 1900. Argentina was the destination of an overwhelming number of these: 1,889 (93.6 percent) versus 130 (6.4 percent) for Uruguay.

By sex, 89.2 percent were men (1,800) versus 10.8 percent women (219). The civil status of 54 percent of the Navarrese is known: 89 percent were single (970), 11 percent were married (120). The professions, listed in decreasing order of importance, were

1. peasant,
2. merchant,
3. cobbler,
4. baker,
5. blacksmith,
6. quarrier,
7. locksmith, and
8. servant.

The profession of peasant was overwhelmingly the most common. By age, Navarrese emigration showed a clear predominance of the those between fifteen and twenty-five, which made up 62 percent of the total. Sample numbers for emigration by place of origin are shown in table 8.1.

It can thus be deduced that the majority of the emigrants came from the mountain area of Navarre and, within this territory, a large number were from the Valley of Baztán. The Navarrese that decided to go to the Río de la Plata chose Argentina over Uruguay, was male and single, a peasant, and between fifteen and twenty-five years old.

TABLE 8.1 *Origins of Navarrese Emigrants to Río de la Plata, 1830–1900*

Place of Origin	No. Emigrants	Percent (%)
Aranaz	135	7.6
Lesaca	129	7.3
Arizcun	127	6.3
Elizondo	121	5.9
Aizaroz	111	5.4
Errazu	109	5.3
Iroz	99	4.9
Irurita	89	4.4
Lecaroz	86	4.2
Vera de Bidasoa	77	3.8
Donamaria	73	3.6
Sumbilla	71	3.5
Arrayoz	70	3.4
Garzain	69	3.4
Ciga	68	3.3
Santesteban	59	2.9
Arbizu	51	2.5
Oronoz	47	2.3
Almandoz	44	2.1
Azpilcueta	41	2.0
Urdax	40	1.9
Goizueta	37	1.8
Pamplona	29	1.4
Garayoa	29	1.4
Elveta	28	1.3
Berroeta	26	1.2
Arano	23	1.1
Cizurquil	19	0.9
Aniz	17	0.8
Maya	16	0.7
Baraibar	14	0.6
Lacunza	13	0.6
Arazuri	11	0.5
Arroniz	10	0.4
Ainzoain	9	0.4

TABLE 8.1 (continued)

Place of Origin	No. Emigrants	Percent (%)
Leiza	7	0.3
Goyaz	7	0.3
Betelu	3	0.1
Corella	2	0.09
Falces	2	0.09
Peralta	1	0.04
Total	2,019	100.00

Source: J. M. Azcona Pastor, 1992, 66.

In Bizkaia, between 1800 and 1810, and taking the towns of Gorliz, Lekeitio, Ondarroa, and Gaminiz as a basis, there were fifteen natives of these places in Mexico, twelve in Venezuela, and eleven in Cuba. Next came Peru with seven,[29] followed by Montevideo with four. Between 1810 and 1826, Cuba was first among the migratory destinations with forty-one people, followed by Mexico (twenty), Venezuela (eight), Peru (six), then Buenos Aires, Montevideo, and Puerto Rico with two each, and Chile, Colombia, Guatemala, and Honduras with one apiece.

Between 1826 and 1850, Cuba was the primary destination (seventy-five emigrants), distantly followed by the United States and Puerto Rico (four each), Mexico (three), and Venezuela (two). As can be seen, the tendency of Bizkaian emigrants to concentrate in the Spanish Antilles increased tremendously, following a pattern begun during the War of Independence. However, reemigration and the departure of Bizkaians from other colonies (for example, Mexico or Peru) to Cuba in the face of the violent turn of events accompanying the outbreak of the War of Secession from Spain must also be noted.

Between 1850 and 1890, Cuba was once again the primary destination of the emigrants from Gorliz, Lekeitio, Ondarroa, and Gaminiz, with 129 settlers. Next came Mexico with eight and Puerto Rico with seven, followed by the United States, Peru, and Montevideo with three each, Buenos Aires and Chile with two, and Venezuela and Honduras with one. Of the total Bizkaians that left Spain between 1860 and 1861, 297 went to Cuba (the primary destination), 235 to Argentina (second), 49 to Montevideo (third), 44 to Mexico (fourth), 24 to Peru (fifth), 21 to Chile (sixth), 11 to Puerto Rico (seventh), and 9 to the United States (eighth).

The majority of the natives of the seigneury that emigrated to America between 1867 and 1881 were under twenty years old (70 percent) and many of them under fourteen.[30] Of the Bizkaian males that went to the New World between these dates, 63 percent were fourteen or under, as opposed to 22 percent of the women. The destination of these emigrants during these fifteen years was South America, Río de la Plata in particular (48 percent), followed by Cuba and Puerto Rico (14 percent combined), and the Philippines (7 percent). The reasons given for emigrating, in descending order of importance, were the following:

1. Make a fortune
2. Summoned by family or friends
3. Devote themselves to commerce
4. Look for work
5. Poor, without resources, in ruins
6. Avoid military recruitment and replacement payment
7. Need to obtain resources
8. Offers from agents of immigration
9. For adventure
10. As a shepherd

The main Basque migration current was directed toward America, especially the wide-open spaces of the Southern Cone. Cuba, Puerto Rico, and the Philippines also attracted Basque natives; for example, one out of every five Bizkaians that decided to emigrate overseas between 1876 and 1881 headed to one of these destinations. This transatlantic diaspora, fundamentally male, took place among the extremely young. Family and neighbor ties with those already established in America could help children make such a long and uncertain voyage. Faced with employment as a miner, factory or shop worker, or clerk for a foreign business, more than a few Basques preferred to try to make their fortune overseas, although they might ultimately end up as industrial workers or cereal cutters in Argentina. This resistance to proletarianization of the semiskilled sector was undoubtedly to the advantage of the receiving countries, but a loss for the region of origin, especially taking into account that the Basque Country was beginning its industrialization process. The Basque Country thus followed the model of other areas of Europe: the beginnings of the industrial revolution coincided with large migratory movements, among them overseas emigration.

For the period between 1800 and 1900, 1,880 cases of emigrants from Bizkaia to Río de la Plata have been studied. The archives of notary protocols of Bilbao, the ecclesiastical archives of Derio, the archives of protocols of Santander, and the general national archives of both Montevideo (Uruguay) and Buenos Aires (Argentina) have been systematically studied. By destinations, 63.29 percent of emigrants headed for Argentina, versus the 36.71 percent of those that went to Uruguay. By civil status, the statistics were divided in the following manner:

Marital Status	No./Percent (%)
Single	1,513/79
Married	330/19
Widowed	37/2

Sex	No./Percent (%)
Men	1,690/89.8
Women	190/10.2

Age	Percent (%)
Under 15	6
15–20	30
21–25	26
26–35	22
36–55	10
56–75	6

Profession	Percent (%)
Peasant	50.1
Day worker	20.2
Merchant	10.4
Sailor	6.2
Carpenter	3.0
Others (seamstress, housewife, baker, etc.)	10.1

By place of origin, the numbers break down as shown in table 8.2

With the different variables analyzed so far, it is time to define the makeup of the Bizkaian emigrant to Río de la Plata. He tended to be a twenty-three-year-old, young, single man who was a peasant. Regarding the place of departure, the emigrants mostly left from areas on or near the coast, not more than twenty kilometers inland. The preferred destination was Argentina.

In the case of Gipuzkoa,[31] during the years 1840, 1841, and 1842, the departure of 1,300 emigrants to the countries of Río de la Plata (Argentina and Uruguay) is recorded. The median age was twenty-two, and the majority were single men. There was also a small but noteworthy number of women who traveled alone or with a brother. The rest of the passengers were married couples, with or without children (the latter being more frequent). There were also married men who left without their wives and, in some cases, married women who left without their husbands. María Pilar Pildain Salazar lists 1,100 Gipuzkoan emigrants for the period from 1852 to 1870, many of whom headed for America after being called by family

TABLE 8.2 *Origins of Bizkaian Emigrants to Río de la Plata, 1800–1900*

Place of Origin	No. Emigrants	Percent (%)
Balmaseda	207	11
Karrantza	169	9
Portugalete	169	9
Somorrostro	169	9
Bilbao	151	8
Galdames	132	7
Santurtzi	113	6
Gernika	94	5
Morga	94	5
Turtzioz	94	5
Mundaka	94	5
Isasti	76	4
Gorliz	57	3
Mendata	57	3
Getxo	38	2
Mungia	38	2
Gaminiz	38	2
Muskiz	18	1
Lekeitio	18	1
Ibarrangelu	18	1
Markina	18	1
Muxika	18	1
Total	1,880	100

Source: Data collected by the author from Basque archives of notary protocols, the archives of protocols of Santander, and the General National Archive (AGN) in Montevideo, Uruguay, and Buenos Aires, Argentina, and General Emigration Administration of both countries.

or friends. Most traveled alone. The main destination points were Buenos Aires, Montevideo, Mexico, Cuba, and Chile. The main motive cited by the majority of these emigrants was "better fortune" given the "fatality or injury of the times" that the emigrants were suffering in their native Gipuzkoa.

Study of the Río de la Plata region[32] yields conclusions that clearly coincide with those of Pildain Salazar. The civil status of Gipuzkoan emigrants to Río de la Plata between 1840 and 1842 was the following. Of a total of 608, 463 (76.2 percent) were single, 138 (22.7 percent) were married, and 7 (1.1 percent) were widowed. Between 1852 and 1900, 1,789 Gipuzkoan emigrants are accounted for, with the following civil statuses: 1,486 (83.1 percent) were single, 266 (14.9 percent) were married, and 37 (2 percent) were widowed. In regard to sex, 79.9 percent were men and 20.1 percent were women.

The professions of those that left the Basque Country from Gipuzkoa were (1) peasant, (2) farmer, (3) merchant, (4) baker, and (5) housewife.

The places of departure are listed in table 8.3. As can be seen, Oñati was the site of most departures, followed by Donostia, Pasaia, Lezo, and Irun.

From the data and tables above, a portrait of the Gipuzkoan emigrant to Río de la Plata can be derived with the following characteristics: single, male, between fifteen and twenty-six years of age, with a preference to emigrate to Argentina over Uruguay, although keeping the latter in mind. The population nuclei with the highest rates of emigration were Oñati, Errezil, and Donostia.

Emigration of Clergy

It can be generally affirmed that the Basque clergy has made a considerable contribution to the American territories during the modern era. We have seen how the Basque and Navarrese churches provided considerable financial support for colonization and evangelization in the New World during the colonial period. During the nineteenth and twentieth centuries this role would come to be the norm, as will be elaborated below in the case of the Navarrese.[33] From 1820 to 1960, the presence of 1,319 Navarrese missionaries is recorded in Spanish America, all males; this number did not include the various clergy members not officially registered prior to the former date. Those studied came largely from the districts of Pamplona and Estella, Yerri, Corella, Caseda, and Olite. The following is a list of the origin of Navarrese missionaries in America from 1850 to 1960:[34]

District	No./Percent (%)
District of Pamplona	366/35.9
Pamplona (capital)	88/8.6
Rest of district	278/27.3

District	No./Percent (%)
District of Estella	294/28.8
District of Olite	65/6.4
District of Sangüesa	183/17.9
District of Tudela	112/11.0
Total	1,020/100.0

They tended to be young missionaries, with a median age of twenty-six, already ordained priests or in the last years of study, who remained in the New World for most of their lives and who would probably die there. The breakdown by destination is as follows:[35]

Country	No.
Venezuela	295
Argentina	245
Peru	192
Colombia	156
Mexico	142
Chile	137
Brazil	132
Puerto Rico	102
United States	101
Ecuador	84
Dominican Republic	84
Panama	51
Bolivia	47
Guatemala	44
Uruguay	43
Paraguay	32
Costa Rica	28
Cuba	20
Nicaragua	19
El Salvador	11
Honduras	5
Canada	2
Haiti	1
Martinique	1
Total	1,974

The sample in the list of Navarrese places of origin shows a clear, direct relationship between the location of the religious institutions and the percentage of mis-

TABLE 8.3 *Origins of Gipuzkoan Emigrants to Río de la Plata, 1852–1900*

Place of Origin	No. Emigrants	Percent (%)
Oñati	161	9.9
Errezil	151	8.9
Donostia	146	8.5
Pasaia	121	6.7
Lezo	109	6.0
Irun	97	5.4
Oiartzun	87	4.8
Tolosa	83	4.6
Altza	83	4.6
Bergara	76	4.2
Astigarraga	70	3.9
Hernani	69	3.8
Azpeitia	61	3.4
Errenteria	55	3.0
Angiozar	50	2.7
Alkiza	41	2.2
Usurbil	39	2.1
Ezkoriatza	29	1.6
Arrasate	29	1.6
Billabona	26	1.4
Hondarribia	26	1.4
Zarautz	18	1.0
Berastegi	15	0.8
Zegama	13	0.7
Asteasu	13	0.7
Urretxu	13	0.7
Zumarraga	13	0.7
Legazpi	13	0.7
Antzuola	10	0.5
Aia	9	0.5
Andoain	9	0.5
Garagartza	8	0.4
Amezketa	7	0.3
Zestoa	7	0.3

TABLE 8.3 (continued)

Place of Origin	No. Emigrants	Percent (%)
Eibar	7	0.3
Soraluze	6	0.3
Getaria	6	0.3
Berrobi	5	0.2
Legorreta	4	0.2
Orio	4	0.2
Total	1,789	100.00

Source: Data collected by the author from Basque archives of notary protocols, the archives of protocols of Santander, and the General National Archive (AGN) in Montevideo, Uruguay, and Buenos Aires, Argentina, and General Emigration Administration of both countries.

sionaries from the surrounding areas. Thus, the main convent of the Franciscans of Navarre (Olite) served as the recruiting post for numerous missionaries of this order. The same can be said of the religious schools of Estella and Irache and of the Jesuit seats in the cities (especially Pamplona). Another significant factor in recruitment was clearly the deep-rooted connections to religion in the family. Thus, in 1980, 9,533 Navarrese families had at least one priest or other member of the clergy, male or female.

It should also be taken into account that the greatest percentage of Navarrese missionaries is found from 1880 onward. The American wars of independence, the Carlist civil wars, and the anticlerical furor of nineteenth-century Spain were important checks on this cassocked migration until that date. From 1880 to 1940, this religious diaspora was on the increase. The trend reversed in the decade of the 1940s as a result of the Spanish Civil War. It reached its zenith in the decade of the 1950s, falling sharply beginning in 1965.

The Order of the Capuchins, whose ecclesiastical province (Navarre-Cantabria-Aragón) has its administrative seat in Pamplona, has contributed the most Navarrese missionaries. From 1890 to 1960, one-fourth of them came from this order. The most common destinations for the Capuchins were Ecuador, Argentina, Chile, the United States, Mexico, Costa Rica, and Nicaragua.

The Augustinian Recoletos played an important role in the evangelization of the Philippines (as is well known), although they also worked extensively in America.

The Navarrese missionaries operated, by order of preference and number, in Brazil, Mexico, Panama, the United States, Venezuela, Colombia, Dominican Republic, Argentina, Peru, Guatemala, Costa Rica, Puerto Rico, Nicaragua, and Chile. These two orders are followed in importance by the Claretians, Jesuits, Escolapios, Dominicans, Discalced Carmelites, Passionists, Paulists, Benedictines, and diocesan priests. During the nineteenth century they devoted themselves to evangelizing Native Americans, and in the twentieth century their work has been more part of the struggle against Latin American social inequality.

The Ports of Departure of the Basque Diaspora

Ángel María Arrieta has documented, in the case of Araba, the close connection between the attraction of emigrants and the greater convenience of overseas emigration at the end of the nineteenth century.[36] As already noted, during the last third of the century, steamship transportation became common, and sailing vessels were a thing of the past. The result was a dramatic shortening of the length of the voyage, along with a considerable increase in the capacity to transport emigrants. Arrieta has analyzed the press of Gasteiz for the period from 1890 to 1895. He has shown through the study of Araban notarial protocols how prices decreased significantly in the early 1880s. Thus, around 1850, a voyage to Río de la Plata in the steerage of a sailing vessel cost between 1,100 and 1,400 copper reales. In 1880, however, a passage to Argentina in third class in a steamship cost from 640 to 700 copper reales. The main shipping companies (in terms of ports of departure and destination) that operated in Gasteiz between 1880 and 1895 are shown in table 8.4.

According to Arrieta's study, the ports used most frequently by Araban emigrants between 1880 and 1895 were Bordeaux, Santander, and Pasaia, due to their proximity and the emigrants' choice of destination. During the first half of the nineteenth century, and even into the 1870s, the Gipuzkoan port of Pasaia undoubtedly played a critical role in channeling Araban emigration.[37] Table 8.5 shows the results of the author's own research into which ports Basques of different provinces embarked from between 1830 and 1900.

It seems logical that the Gipuzkoans emigrated to Río de la Plata via the port of Pasaia, being in the same province. This was followed by Bayonne and Bordeaux, traditional emigration ports. The same happened with the Araban diaspora, which also chose Pasaia as the "waiting room" of emigration. The geographic proximity of the Valley of Baztán to Pasaia as well as Bayonne and Bordeaux worked in favor of these three port cities when it came time to transport Navarrese emigrants. Many Bizkaian natives preferred to leave via Santander, however (especially those from the Enkarterri, due to the proximity), although the French ports of Bordeaux and Bayonne outnumbered the Cantabrian one in passenger volume. Bilbao's docks

TABLE 8.4 *Main Shipping Companies Operating in Gasteiz, 1880–1895*

Company	Port of Departure	Destination
Pacific Steam Navigation Company	Bordeaux/Santander	Montevideo, Buenos Aires/Pernambuco, Bahia, Rio de Janeiro, Talcahuano, Valparaiso
Compañía Transatlántica (until 1880, Antonio López & Co.)	Santander	Havana/Veracruz
Vapores-Correos del Marqués del Campo	Bordeaux/Santander	Pernambuco/Bahia/Rio de Janeiro/Montevideo/Buenos Aires/Valparaiso/Callao/Lima, Colón, Puerto Rico, Havana, and Veracruz
Compañía Transatlántica de Barcelona	Barcelona/Cádiz/Santander/Vigo	Havana/Puerto Rico/New York, Veracruz, Rio de Janeiro, Montévideo, Buenos Aires, Havana, and Mexico City
Compañía Mexicana Transatlántica	Santander	Havana and Veracruz
Compañías Generales Marítimas	Bordeaux/Pasaia/Barcelona and La Coruña	Montévideo and Buenos Aires, Rio de Janeiro
Norddeutscher Lloyd	La Coruña, Villagarcía, Vigo	Montévideo and Buenos Aires, Rio de Janeiro
Compagnie Commerciale de Transports à Vapeur Français	Bordeaux	Buenos Aires, Chile

Source: Data from A. M. Arrieta, 1992, 91–96.

were fourth in receiving Bizkaian emigrants. The important overseas transit between Bizkaia and the French Basque Country played a decisive role in the departure of Bizkaians via Bordeaux and Bayonne. A list of the seventeen main emigrant shipping transport companies to Argentina in 1890 is given in table 8.6.

Appearing on the list are the most prominent companies that operated in Araba,

TABLE 8.5 *Port of Embarkation of Basques, 1830–1900*

Port	Arabans (%)	Bizkaians (%)	Gipuzkoans (%)	Navarrese (%)
Pasaia	30	9	34	42
Bordeaux	26	24	22	17
Bayonne	23	21	29	31
Santander	6	20	—	—
Bilbao	6	12	—	—
Pauillac	5	8	5	—
Donostia	—	—	7	8
Others	4	6	3	2

Source: Data from the General Emigration Administration of Argentina and Uruguay as well as the General National Archive of Montevideo and Buenos Aires.

and the Basque Country in general, during the last third of the nineteenth century. The first ship with French Basque emigrants to reach Buenos Aires, in 1829, was the *Vaillante*, which came from Bordeaux. The following data show the numbers of emigrants sent to Río de la Plata from the French Basque port of Bayonne and Bordeaux between 1862 and 1866:[38]

From Bayonne

Year	No. Ships	No. Emigrants
1862	7	770
1863	8	882
1864	9	935
1865	11	1,046
1866	6	863
Total	41	4,496

From Bordeaux

Year	No. Ships	No. Emigrants
1862	31	925
1863	42	1,296
1864	43	1,443
1865	48	1,563
1866	49	1,517
Total	213	6,744

As can be seen, the quantities of emigrants were truly voluminous; for the five-year period from 1862 to 1866, the significant number of 11,240 people left from the two ports combined.

TABLE 8.6 *Companies Transporting Emigrants to Argentina, 1890*

Company	Adults (over 12)	Children (under 12)	Total
Chargeurs Réunis	14,924	4,083	19,007
Fratelli Lavarello	10,276	2,628	12,904
La Veloce	9,502	2,221	11,723
Navigazione Italiana	5,739	1,289	7,028
Transports Maritimes	5,462	723	6,185
Messageries Maritimes	3,499	575	4,074
Lloyd Norte Alemán	2,883	949	3,832
Transatlántica Española	2,331	460	2,791
Freyssinet y Compañía	2,032	459	2,491
Mala Real Inglesa	1,906	391	2,297
Pacífico de Navegación	1,181	152	1,333
Hamburgo S. Americana	865	173	1,038
Acebal y Díaz	951	70	1,021
Holandesa	541	153	694
Delfino Hermanos	497	69	566
Lamport Holt	389	95	484
Mamus y Dodero	273	45	318
Total	63,251	14,535	77,786

Source: Memoire of the General Immigration Administration; table prepared by its director, Juan A. Alsina, for the 1890 edition.

Chapter Nine

Dramatic Exile

Forced Exit

In the summer of 1937, Franco's troops conquered Gipuzkoa and Bizkaia, the territories that remained faithful to the Spanish Republic founded in 1931, producing a flight and expatriation of the political and military leaders and the civilian population. Javier Rubio (among others) has studied this forced emigration from Spain. Rubio places the number of people that left the Basque-Cantabrian provinces to seek refuge in France after the invasion of the national army at 160,000. Of this total, he affirms that at least half came strictly from the Basque provinces. Based on the account of the then-president of the Basque Government, José Antonio Aguirre y Lecube, Koldo San Sebastián places the number of Basques evacuated during the outburst at 150,000.[1] Whatever the exact figure, it is clear that this dramatic exodus significantly surpassed politically motivated emigration during the nineteenth century.[2] And although many of those who left after the fall of Bilbao in 1937 were repatriated at intervals after the war's end, a significant number ended their disturbing adventures in American republics. Due to proximity, however, they passed through French reception centers and concentration camps. In 1937, the Comité Nationale Catholique d'Accueil aux Basques was formed. Its honorary president was Cardenal Verdier, archbishop of Paris, although the effective and technical presidency was in the hands of Monsignor Mathieu, bishop of Dax.

On December 16, 1938, the French branch of the International League of the Friends of the Basques (Liga Internacional de Amigos de los Vascos, or LIAV) was formed. The league had a representative of the Basque Government, Francisco Javier de Landaburu, on its board of directors. The league's goals were charitable and humanitarian, but also political. It attempted to provide legal support for the measures undertaken by the Basque leaders in exile.

In Great Britain, the National Joint Committee for Spanish Relief was founded, presided over by the duchess of Atholl. Through the section called Basque Children's Trust Ltd., with its seat in London, it evacuated more than four thousand children from the Basque Country in the spring of 1937. Very few of them went directly to America from England; many returned to the Basque Country or traveled to France from where they would embark on a course for the American continent after the German invasion.

For a goodly number of the Basques, exile began the same day as the Civil War, July 18, 1936. But it would not be until December, when General Mola conquered Gipuzkoa, that one could speak of a real exodus. The operation began with 110,000 Gipuzkoan natives, who fled to Bizkaia under fear of possible reprisals. Others chose the adventure of passing through the Pyrenees or crossing the dangerous Gulf of Bizkaia in small fishing boats in search of refuge in France. On March 31, 1937, the final offensive against the Seigneury of Bizkaia began. On April 28, two days after the bombing of Gernika, the then-president of the Basque Government, José Antonio Aguirre, delivered a radio address seeking help for the evacuation of the civilian population. Juan Gracia Colas and Alfredo Espinosa, ministers of social welfare and health, respectively, traveled to France for this reason. They were entrusted with the task of finding refuge and medical care for the exiles. The Basque Government sought the help of the British admiralty to dodge the blockade to which the port of Bilbao was subject. The admiralty responded by sending various destroyers to the Cantabrian coast to transport the civilian population not of military age. France welcomed the refugees by guaranteeing care and aid for them. Some were among the first refugees to arrive in American ports in 1937.

The Basque Government began to think about the possibility of sending delegates to the two Americas to study the possibilities of settling refugees there, though it would not do so until 1938. Until the eve of the German invasion of Poland, José Antonio Aguirre was not in favor of large-scale emigration to America, maybe because of the distant hope that an Allied triumph might put an end to the Franco dictatorship:

> The Government wants to set a criterion. Its position in emigration matters is opposed to emigrations in great number. Neither conviction, nor the circumstances, beyond our control, permit emigrations to this extent.... But the Government respects individual decisions and to this extent supports the petitions of those interested in this action. Those who so desire can also apply to the aid organisms connected to the Republican institutions. We only advise that the Basque Government, as such, has no representation in said organisms.[3]

After the fall of Bilbao, the Basque Government was moved to Santander, followed by hundreds of citizens hoping to find a way to France via the Cantabrian coast. The authorities had two main worries: how the war would unfold and care for the refugees. Eighty thousand Basques were crammed into the city of Santander alone, and eight thousand of them needed medical attention.[4] The impediments to evacuation were formidable, with the sea route blocked by warships, causing José Antonio Aguirre to travel to Valencia to deliberate the situation with the Republican authorities. The objectives of the conversation were the evacuation of the

Basque civilian population stranded in Santander and the transfer of the Basque army to the eastern front.

The decisive participation of the Basque delegation in Great Britain must also be emphasized; it was headed by Juan Lizaso, who was responsible for the evacuation of the civil population. This organization was assisted greatly by Marino de Gamboa, a shipowner from Bilbao entrusted with contacting British outfitters to charter the vessels necessary for the flight. He also bought the ship *Vita*, famous for shipping Republican treasure to Mexico. Finally, after the arduous work of the government, at the beginning of May 1937 the great exodus to France began; it would last until a few days prior to the fall of Asturias in October. The bulk of evacuation was carried out using thirty ships chartered by the Basque Government through its delegations in London and Bordeaux. Sixty-one voyages in vessels converted for passenger transport were carried out. Competent health personnel traveled in them to attend the needy. The ports of destination and the number of refugees are listed as follows:[5]

Port	No. Refugees
Pauillac	84,111
La Pallice	21,635
Sainte Nazaire	9,000
Nantes	1,650
Verdon	350
Total	116,746

At the French ports, all the basic needs of the new arrivals were attended to: currency exchange, distribution of provisions and milk, shipping of luggage, and medical aid to the wounded and sick. Delegations of the Basque Government had been opened for all this in Bordeaux and Bayonne. The delegates played an important intermediary role between the refugees and the French authorities. The exiles were assigned places to live and reception centers right in the ports. The government would maintain a series of shelters and assistance centers (shown in table 9.1) through its own means, independent of those under the control of the French authorities.

In addition, there were centers specializing in aid for child refugees in Great Britain, France, and the Soviet Union. Political parties, unions, and French, British, Belgian, and other aid organizations participated. The attention given to those wounded in war in the continental Basque Country and the work of Doctor Aranguren both also deserve special mention. On August 10, the Basque Government's minister of health, Eliodoro de la Torre, gave Aranguren the order to begin preparations for the evacuation. Two problems had to be overcome: dealing with the

TABLE 9.1 *Principal Shelters of Basque Exiles in France and Belgium, 1937*

Location	Department	No. Refugees
Orthez	Basse-Pyrénées	100
Guethary	Basse-Pyrénées	260
St. Christian	Basse-Pyrénées	620
Dax	Landas	200
Narbonne	Aude	340
Sète	Hérault	300
Pezenas	Hérault	220
Château du Loire	Sarthe	70
Noyon	Oise	180
Châtenay-Malabry	Seine	120
Enghien-les-Bains	Seine (2 shelters)	120
Compans	Seine sur Marne	500
Marcluy-les-Huy	Belgium	100

Source: Iñaki Anasagasti, 1988.

French authorities and finding places to attend to the wounded. Once these initial difficulties were taken care of, the most appropriate hospital locations turned out to be Saint Christaud and La Roserie. Children from Gorliz (Bizkaia) had been in the first; the second was a splendid hotel rented by the Ministry of Social Welfare as a shelter, unused to that point. On August 20, the *Bobie* docked in the port of Bayonne with 360 wounded, accompanied by proper health personnel. Eighty percent of the new arrivals required surgery, and La Roserie was chosen as the center for the worst cases. The medical team was made up of Doctors Aranguren, Garigorta, and Ugalde. One year later, in 1938, the following medical services were available in La Roserie: general surgery, urology, venereology, otorhinolaryngology, general medicine, maternity, and odontology. There were also workshops for rehabilitation and training for invalids such as carpentry, tinwork, orthopedics, shoemaking, electricity, barbering, and tailoring. Primary school classes, introductions to mathematics, French, and Euskara, were also taught.

The splendid evacuation organized by the Basque Government was completely supported by the League of Friends of the Basques recently created in France. In addition, solidarity among the refugees was a constant during the entire period of the exile.

The Basques wanted to apply what José Antonio Aguirre called "Concierto Económico Alimenticio" in Cataluña. Through this plan, they would administer their own rations, thereby avoiding the lack of control and regularity of supplies through the creation of their own hospital infrastructure. On November 15, 1937, the hospital named "Euskadi" began to function in the building ceded by the French Consulate in Barcelona. This center had a capacity of 100 beds and was geared for primary care, since surgery was performed in another clinic organized specifically for that purpose. Another of the hospitals, "Gernika," specialized in pediatrics and had 110 beds. The clinic "Otxandiano" had room for 55 beds and was run by Doctor Arrese, ex-director of the Basurto Hospital in Bilbao. Just outside of the Catalonian capital, near Badalona, there was an antituberculosis sanatorium with 123 beds.

The end of the war was approaching and the fall of Cataluña was imminent, resulting in a mass exodus of 500,000 people to France. In this second exile, the Basques ran a reception service right on the Catalonian border, to which all Spaniards fleeing in defeat arrived. This service was organized by Eliodoro de la Torre, who rented the Hotel Sala in Perpignan. The majority of the refugees of this so-called second exile were interned in concentration camps deemed "reception" camps by the French government. Aid organizations, the Basque Government and the Basque Workers' Union, and the Quakers combined forces to rescue some compatriots from these centers, grouping them according to their specialties and trades. Many remained in France to work. A significant number left for Venezuela, where workers were needed for the operation of oil wells, and other American countries. As can be seen, the Basque evacuation from Cataluña was well organized. The executive council spent one and a half million francs paying for taxis, buses, and trains. It even chartered two boats, the *Danube* and the *Storm*.

Analyzing the entire process that the Basques lived through in their flight from defeat, it can be concluded that the exiles traveled via various routes:

1. From Gipuzkoa to Bizkaia, from Bizkaia to Santander to continue to France, from there to Cataluña, and again to France
2. From the Basque Country to France
3. From the Basque Country to France (for a short period of time) and then Spanish America

It must be remembered that some refugees did not escape through the channels described. Dozens crossed the Pyrenees or the Gulf of Bizkaia alone, and others headed for South America during the first years of the war. The ultimate destination depended on the individual decision of each emigrant. In the wake of the massive Basque presence in France, the Basque Government took regulatory measures. Through a decree in 1939, it tried to force the repatriation of those individuals uninvolved in politics who were in no personal danger. The decree stated the following:

1. From August 15 to September 15, the institutions of the Basque Government will no longer accept persons not of refugee status according to the criteria that have been established.
2. Those currently being subsidized and not meeting such criteria will no longer receive the regular subsidy beginning on the last dates indicated.[6]

With the arrival of the Germans in France and the general mobilization decreed there, the Basques had to decide between remaining in France, and thereby taking part in the history of World War II; returning to the Basque Country, and confronting the authorities of the recently created state; or emigrating to America to await the return of democracy in Spain. Beginning with the first large-scale waves in 1937, the French authorities tried to blunt the Spanish exodus. To put it frankly, it was an exodus that could put France in a compromising position in the wake of the alarming increase of fascist regimes in Europe. Moreover, if it is kept in mind that many Basque Nationalists saw their war as over with the fall of the Northern Front, there were predictions of a massive number of refugees from the Basque Country. The repatriation movement suffered in Cataluña has already been documented. After the end of the war in 1939, the problem of the exiles in France increased. Thousands of Republican civilians and soldiers fled to France through Cataluña to escape reprisal at the war's end. The French authorities, uncomfortable with the relocation of such a numerous Republican population suspected of being sympathetic to, or even strongly supporting, communism, decided to promote the departure of Spaniards to America.

Few nations heeded with enthusiasm the French call to accept refugees from the Iberian Peninsula. Among them, Mexico stands out as accepting the choicest of the Spanish exiles with unusual passion. The Basques were the ones that benefited the most from the refugee policies of some Spanish-American countries such as Colombia, Venezuela, and Argentina. These nations reasoned that their virtues of hard work and morality made expatriate Basques very desirable immigrants.

The Transatlantic Receptions

Argentina was one of the South American countries that most fostered the entry of the Basque exile. The Basque collectivity in Argentina was split at the outbreak of the Civil War. While the more liberal sectors and the nationalists, after some hesitation amid the confusion of the initial reports, positioned themselves with the Republicans, the conservatives of the colony closed ranks with the insurgents. Thus, a self-titled "honorary commission," headed by the aristocrat María Pía de Borbón, passionately devoted itself to raising money for Franco's military headquarters in Burgos. A large, very conservative Basque-Argentine group participated in this organization. Thus, last names as well known in the high spheres of local society as Anchorena, Zanborena, Alzaga, and Uaondo supported this institution financially. In addition, it must be remembered that among the hundreds of emigrants that landed on the shores of Río de la Plata at the end of the nineteenth century were many exiles from the Carlist wars who were very supportive of Franco. They would be the ones to constitute the so-called Basque Nationalist Board in the summer of 1936, a group immediately disqualified by the nationalist sector organized in "Basque Action" (the Basque Nationalist Party in Argentina).

But, in the face of the defeat of the Basque people, the bombing of Gernika, and their misfortune in exile, a group of Basque-Argentines took action. With continuous support from that country's Basque delegation (established in 1938), of diverse political creeds but sharing humanitarian ends, they managed to secure the admission of Basque exiles into the country. The group would receive the unconditional support of the Pro-Basque Immigration Committee, as well as the cooperation of the Basque collectivity and the delegation headed by Minister Ramón María Aldasoro upon their arrival to the shores of Río de la Plata. On August 30, 1939, the Pro-Basque Immigration Committee was formed. After taking several steps, it managed to get two decrees issued favoring the arrival of the exiles in Argentina.

The reception of the Basque exiles by the Republic of Argentina was exceptional, especially considering that country's migration policy in the 1930s. After the grave world economic crisis of 1929, those countries that had been the main recipients of immigrants modified their migration policies to control the flow of foreigners that might aggravate the already catastrophic economic situation. In Argentina, the serious problem of unemployment resulted in the pronouncement of a decree on December 26, 1932, initiating the complete restriction of immigration. It argued that "in defense of the workers rooted in Argentina, it would not be prudent, in the present circumstances, to authorize the entrance into the country of those who do not have a remunerative occupation or subsistence assured."[7] The decree facilitated immigration only for those called by their families or able to produce a work contract.

The request put out by French authorities during the Civil War to accept the Spanish exiles went unheeded by the Argentines, who, claiming economic problems, closed their borders to the Republicans and immigrants by the law of September 30, 1938. Due to the political violence and suffering that broke out in Spain, along with Argentina's sympathies with the Axis powers in the world war, the arrival of the Spanish Republican contingent with "leftist" ideologies was not welcomed by the local authorities. In addition, bureaucratic procedures made entering the country increasingly difficult. Identity papers had to be presented, a certificate of good conduct issued by the commissary of the country of residence, solvency guaranteed by a financial institution, and two years of residence in the country were required. People who did not have close relatives on the other side of the ocean therefore stopped emigrating. If they did have relatives, the discomforts, complications, expenses, and length of time required to expedite the procedure made them think twice about settling in other countries. Thus, there were many Basque exiles who, even though they wanted to go to Argentina, instead decided to head for other countries such as Venezuela or Colombia, where obstacles for the admission of foreigners were less daunting. In spite of such difficulties prior to September 1938, the date the borders were closed, the first exiles arrived. Numerous interviews conducted with the Basque expatriates in Argentina, however, indicate that all of them had relied on close family or had lived in the country previously. These, along with the Basque Delegation, would generate a favorable climate toward the rest of the refugees, most of whom were living in France.

On January 20, 1940, with the signature of President Ortiz and Minister of Agriculture José Padilla, the decree that marked a milestone in the history of Basque emigration to Argentina, as well as an exception in international law, was proclaimed; it was followed by another that amplified it on July 18, 1940.

DECREES OF JANUARY 20 AND JULY 18, 1940 OF THE PRESIDENT AND VICE PRESIDENT OF THE REPUBLIC OF ARGENTINA AUTHORIZING THE ADMISSION OF BASQUE IMMIGRANTS

I. *Authorizing the Admission of Basque Immigrants into the Country*
Buenos Aires, January 20, 1940

Number 53,448. Proceeding 625/1940. In wake of the measures begun by the Pro-Basque Immigration Committee, with the goal that permission be granted to a number of Basque families residing in Spain or France, and. . . .

Considering: That the aims of the Pro-Basque Immigration Committee are to maintain and increase this current of immigration that in the constitution of the country has represented a vigorous contribution to the population and the progress of the nation, due to the qualities of hard work and adaptability to our socioeconomic environment.

That these ends can be reached within the dispositions that regulate the entrance of immigrants into the country, adopting all means necessary to ensure the extreme care demanded concerning good antecedents and aptitudes of the people who enter the Republic.

The President of the Argentine Nation therefore

DECREES

Article 1. The Minister of Agriculture will permit the admission into the country of Basque immigrants, residing in Spain or France, with the documentation that they possess and under the moral and material guarantee in each case, of the Pro-Basque Immigration Committee, or in the absence of which it can be provided by the respective consular officials, regarding the good antecedents and moral and physical aptitudes of the people in whose favor said committee intervenes.

Article 2. Communicate this to the National Register and return its effects to the National Immigration Administration.

Ortiz

José Padilla

II. *Amplifying the Decree number 53,448 in Reference to the Admission of Basque Immigrants into the Country*

Buenos Aires, July 18, 1940

Number 65,384. In wake of this proceeding (5,265/1940), attentive to that sought on folio 1 by the Pro-Basque Immigration Committee and that informed by the Immigration Administration.

The vice president of the Nation of Argentina, exercising executive power,

DECREES

Article 1. Amplifying Decree number 53,448 of the date January 20, 1940, authorizing the Department of Agriculture to permit the admission into the country of Basque immigrants residing in Spain or France, in the following form:

- (a) Comprehending the Basques regardless of origin and place of residence in the benefits that this Decree authorizes.
- (b) The Pro-Basque Immigration Committee can intervene in the regulation of the situation of Basques passing through that find themselves in this country, except in the case of crewmen who have deserted their ships.

Article 2. Communicate, publicize, and give this to the National Register and return its effects to the National Immigration Administration.

Castillo

C. Massini Ezcurra

The demonstrations for and against the measure of January 20, 1940, were not long in coming. Telegrams in favor from the Basque-Argentine collectivity and those from other parts of the world rained down on the committee. For the then-president of the Basque Government-in-Exile, José Antonio Aguirre, the decree meant "solvency, the recognition of honor, as men and as a people, for the Basques. From here the first reaction has been of profound thanks and legitimate pride and enthusiasm."[8]

What is clear is that more than one thousand Basque families were accepted due to President Ortiz Lizardi's measure. The late date of 1940, however, prevented a massive arrival of refugees. The exiles settled from 1937 to 1938 in other American republics; Venezuela, Colombia, and the Dominican Republic were those most favored by the law. In effect, although they had residence and work permits in other countries, they preferred Argentina, either because they had relatives there or because it was the most well developed nation in South America. From 1940 onward, the refugees who were in Europe had to endure very long voyages, German submarines, African concentration camps, and various other vicissitudes that made the sea trips real odysseys. World War II made the journey to South America very difficult. Few ships managed to cross the Atlantic during those years. Moreover, as José Antonio Aguirre explained, "if the war had not begun, the Basque emigratory contribution would have reached considerable proportions. But our compatriots are working in the French war factories and others are taking part in the fighting."[9]

The arrival of President Aguirre, an implicit supporter of the secular Spanish Republic, to Montevideo in 1941, greatly irritated the pro-Franco sectors of Uruguay. Controversy broke out in extended domestic disputes, often producing lifelong enmities. Nevertheless, it can be affirmed that the capital of Uruguay became one of the most important poles of Spanish Republicanism in exile. In April 1943, on the occasion of the anniversary of the Proclamation of the Republic, a multitudinous ceremony was organized there; a large representation of the Basque colony attended. In August 1945, the Committee to Help the Basques was born in Montevideo, with the aim of providing the exiles living in France the emergency assistance necessary to move to Uruguay. The committee was dissolved in August 1946.

Another altruistic undertaking organized by the Basque community in Uruguay was the development of campaigns in support of the clandestine opposition inside the Basque Country and in support of those arrested or convicted by the Franco regime. These also raised funds for the families of the prisoners. Numerous middle-class families contributed to the cause, as did some of the wealthiest residents of the colony, whose fortunes had been amassed since the first waves of immigrants, and sometimes transmitted from generation to generation. The Basque colony in Uruguay was highly supportive of the Bizkaian strikes of 1947 to 1951, encouraging them with written calls to insurrection against the Franco regime.

The Civil War divided the Basque-Chilean population into the sympathizers and the opponents of General Franco. Although the government of Chile did not formalize specific dispositions to favor the entry of the Republican exiles of Basque origin, the direct, precise instructions of both President Aguirre Cerda and high-level functionaries of the Ministry of Exterior Relations (Carlos Errazuriz and Luis Castellón), expedited numerous entrance permits. The first Basques of the exile that saw Chilean soil approached the Pacific by their own means, often thanks to the help of family members, friends, or acquaintances. They tended to use the services of the transatlantic Pacific Steam Navigation Co., which sailed from Liverpool to Valparaiso. The ships used on the route were the *Orduña*, the *Orbit*, the *Oropesa*, and the *Pacific Queen*. The most famous crossing of Republican exiles was undertaken by the *Winnipeg*; more than two thousand refugees left Bordeaux on August 4, 1939, and reached Valparaiso on September 3 that year. The voyage was organized by the then-Chilean consul in Paris, Pablo Neruda.

On May 19, 1941, the Basque Delegation of Chile was created; its first actions were aimed at negotiating with the host country's authorities to guarantee the protection of Basque politicians pursued by either the Franco regime or the Nazi authorities occupying France. To make the delegation's lobbying more effective, in June 1943 the monthly newspaper *Euzkadi* appeared in Santiago; it would remain in circulation until April 1949. *Euzkadi* continued the activity of both *Aurrera,* the first Basque publication in Chile, and its successor *Batasuna,* a Basque magazine dating from 1941. On April 1, 1943, the Basque Democratic Group (Agrupación Democrática Vasca, or ADV) was founded in one of the auditoriums of the Spanish Republican Center of Santiago. Its aim was to unite all Basque anti-fascists. In 1946 the Euzko Etxea of Valparaiso began to function. In 1949, Santiago's Euzko Etxea was built. All these groups tried to unite the Basque colony, which was getting larger day by day. However, frequently antagonistic political ideologies would be the cause of political and emotional internal divisions and discords.

The Basque community in Venezuela would not become significant until the dramatic days of the Civil War. At the beginning of 1938, Jesús María de Leizaola (the Basque Government's minister of justice and culture) met with the European representative of the Venezuelan Institute of Emigration in Paris. After some cordial conversations, they arrived at an agreement allowing Basque emigrants to leave France with indefinite work contracts in hand. The Venezuelan government would assume travel and settling costs. The Venezuelan authorities wanted Catholic refugees, what in their inner conscience meant "people of order." This spurred the protests of the exiled Basque socialists, communists, and, in general, nonbelievers. They rightly saw themselves relegated to a subordinate position when the time came to compose the emigration lists; the Catholic militants of the EAJ invariably received preferential treatment.

The first shipment of exiles would reach Venezuela (La Guaira) on July 14, 1939, on the steamer *Cuba,* which had set sail from the French port of Le Havre with 150 passengers. One month later, the *Flandre* arrived with 200 Basque refugees; the *Bretagne,* with 75, coming from Bordeaux, would reach the Venezuelan coast soon thereafter. From 1939 to 1941, a significant number of Basque Republican refugees arrived in Venezuela via the Dominican Republic. The ships used were from a line that regularly transported Dominican prostitutes to the Venezuelan oil wells to satisfy the sexual demands of the refinery workers.

In 1942, the number of Basque refugees in Venezuela was 2,160. By 1956, it had increased to 10,000. For a long time, the Hotel Zuriñe was the site that housed the new arrivals. In 1940, at the request of several of its tenants, the Basque Association of Mutual Aid was born. It was the first organization of a Basque nature formed in the country. In September 1942, the association already had 218 members, and it began to open delegations outside of the capital. One year later, it was taking care of 640 exiled Basques. In 1940 the first steps were taken for the constitution of the Basque Center of Caracas. The center was finally officially founded in 1942, at the same time that the Emergency Board for Basque Social Welfare appeared. The Board's altruistic mission carried out aid functions other than medical or funerary ones. Also in 1942, the publication *Euzkadi* inundated the Venezuelan newspaper stands. Later, a seemingly endless number of Basque newspapers and magazines arose, product of the exile and exodus from the Basque Country.

The Basque businessman Eugenio de Gamboa y Arrupe arrived in Colombia prior to the Civil War. He was the cousin of the later Jesuit leader of the same name. The vanguard of the exile would cast its eyes on Colombian soil for the first time in 1937, in a small quantity. They grouped around Gamboa y Arrupe, who took charge of organizing the Basque colony. The small collectivity would momentarily escape its monotonous routine politics in 1942, when the President José Antonio Aguirre visited Bogotá. After his visit, the Basque Delegation in Colombia would be founded. Little by little, the exiles there attained notable socioeconomic positions, financing activities of all kinds in benefit of the exiles and the few immigrants that arrived in that little known nation. In 1958 the first Basque Center was built in Bogotá; it would serve as an emotional and personal lodging and shelter for the refugees.

The first wave of new arrivals in the Dominican Republic occurred near the end of 1939, and included (among other politicians) Jesús de Galíndez and Eusebio María de Irujo. Between 1939 and 1940, almost five thousand Basque refugees came to the island. Within ten years, 95 percent of them had emigrated to Venezuela and Mexico. The bad political climate, adverse weather, lack of health care, and miserable infrastructure to receive refugees all contributed to a mass exodus to other destinations. On March 14, 1940, the Basque Delegation of the island was legally and officially founded. Eusebio María de Irujo was the delegate of the Basque Government-in-Exile and Jesús Galíndez the secretary. The Basque colony of Santo Domingo actively provided and supported aid to the Allied cause during World War II within its limited means. The Basque Delegation also organized diverse cultural activities, such as conferences, chats, and the recovery of folklore and traditions. At the end of 1942, the Dominicana Film Company publicly showed a film about President Aguirre's visit to the country. In addition, between 1943 and 1944 the island's only magazine dealing with Basque themes appeared. It was called *Eri*, and only eight issues were published. The activity of Jesús Galíndez (who would later disappear mysteriously) during his Dominican period, marked by his rising cultural and literary career, was noteworthy.

At the beginning of the Civil War, the leadership of the Basque Nationalist party approached some Basque residents in Cuba in search of aid for the Republican cause, naming José Luis de Garay as the delegate of the party's executive commission on the island. The response to this request was lukewarm, however, because of the lack of Basque colonists supporting the Republican cause. The majority of those involved in the Basque Center in fact supported Franco openly.

Mexico took a position in favor of the legitimate government of the Republic from the very beginning. Under the leadership of President Lázaro Cárdenas, the country instituted a process of consolidating some revolutionary goals such as the expropriation of land and the nationalization of oil. In the Basque colony, however, there was not unanimity at the hour of positioning itself on the Civil War. A pro-Franco sector even abandoned the Basque Center (founded in 1907) to organize the Spanish-Basque Center. The first exiles that reached Mexico were children who came mostly from the evacuation of Gipuzkoa. They formed a part of the "children of Morelia," who left Valencia on May 20, 1937. In terms of cultural activity and propaganda, on March 13, 1937, the first issue of *Aberri Aldez* ("In Favor of the Homeland") was published. It was directed by Jesús Aldamiz-Etxeverria Arriandiaga, and the official emblem of the Basque Government appeared on its cover. In addition, from early on, the nationalist newspaper *Euzko-Deya* was distributed in Mexico.

On February 23, 1937, the Pro-Euzkadi Committee was created in New York City. It came to have 238 members, and its main activity was raising funds for the Basque Government; its doors would close on June 1. In 1938, the Basque Delegation in the United States appeared. Its first delegates were Antón de Irala and Ramón de la Sota, who organized the seat in New York. Its mission was to coordinate the activities of the forty thousand Basques who at the time resided in California (twenty-five thousand), Idaho (eight thousand), Oregon, Nevada, and Utah. It tried to inform U.S. society of the uniqueness of the Basque people and sought support to salvage Basque autonomy and the Republic. The presence of President Aguirre in New York would significantly assist the development of these activities.

At the End of the Dream

The two world wars, particularly the second, improved the average income on the American continent. From 1938 to 1949 the increase in income was greater than that of the population. Due to the exhaustion of the currency surplus caused by World War I, the fall of prices in the international markets, and the recession in investments from 1950 to 1960, the income per inhabitant and the spectacular growth of the previous decade was reduced, albeit not in alarming terms. This general growth in economic activities, rooted in World War II and continuing afterward, promoted the arrival of significant waves of Basque emigrants in those destinations experiencing the greatest economic growth.

Thus, the Basque diaspora was directed (always to a lesser extent than early in the century) to Argentina, where the farming and industry sectors made great profits in those years. Salaries were high, and work in industrial sectors easy to find. The same occurred in Uruguay. In Chile, salt, silver, and gold mining generally relied on

Basque workers, although many other Basques were engaged in hardware, general stores, baking, and business in general. Mexico and Venezuela attracted the Basque exodus because of their contributions in oil exploitation. In addition, the increase in their heavy and transformative industries often required specialized work, which was furnished by Basque immigrants. The United States and its important, well-developed farm and ranch activity in the American West continued to lure Basque family members. Other nations such as Colombia and Peru also experienced a good flow of immigrants. Moreover, as has already been shown, well-established Basque colonies existed in all these republics, making integration easier and less unpleasant. Nevertheless, this optimistic scenario was upset beginning with the world oil crisis of 1973. A significant portion of the active American population began to remain at the margin of the economic development that had already begun to show signs of weakening years earlier. The process of the massive displacement of the rural population to the city then began, with unemployment as the common norm of life and with high levels of tension and social violence.

On the other hand, the 1960s were times of economic growth for the Basque Country, where hundreds of factories were founded and where it was easy to find work. As a result, Basque emigration slowed considerably by the mid-1960s. Many small-farm owners preferred combining work in the field with salaried and stable work in some nearby factory to embarking on the uncertain future of an American adventure. All these factors clearly combined to eliminate Basque departures to America almost completely starting in the second half of the 1970s. Only the short trips by New World Basques to visit family or to vacation are worth mentioning. To this end, the Basque Government has created specific programs allowing families divided by the exile or emigration to rediscover their transatlantic counterparts.

Nor can the so-called technical emigration be forgotten. It has catapulted professionals from the industrial and service sectors to American lands to cooperate in joint ventures, or simply to lend their highly qualified services to Iberian-American factories and companies. In the heat of the Marxist revolutionary processes in Cuba, Nicaragua, and El Salvador, and with the proliferation of communist guerrillas in much of South America, a new concept of Basque emigration developed. It consisted of the departure from the Basque Country of altruistic volunteers who, sometimes with a rifle on their shoulder, have assisted in the formation of revolutionary political ideologies in these nations.

Chapter Ten

The Future of the Basque-American Communities

The Conference Meeting

From November 6 to 9, 1995, the World Conference of Basque Collectivities was held in Gasteiz; it was organized by the secretary-general of foreign action of the presidency of the Basque Government. During these days, representatives of the Basque diaspora from all over the planet posed their concerns and proposals about the past, present, and future of the Basques and their descendants on both sides of the Atlantic and Pacific Oceans. The presentation by the anthropologist Professor William A. Douglass made an excellent impression for its sincerity and proposals that looked to the future in regard to the Basque exodus outside of the Basque Country. He began by affirming that the Basque emigration "of oppressed masses" had ended, and noted that the future could still bring new, unforeseen opportunities, although "lacking a constant immigration that makes it profitable, an ethnic community dies." This is especially true, affirmed Douglass, when the immigrant population intermarries with the native, and with time the Basqueness that identifies the individual with the social group is lost. In addition, the language (Euskara), "that has no role outside of the ethnic group as a medium of communication," is also being lost. "Also with time, in the diaspora, the essence of being Basque is being diminished, making present, vital elements mythological." He continued by arguing that the Basques of the diaspora therefore tend to have a very archaic image of their homeland, anchored in a rural, pastoral, and fishing life that was the focus of the farmstead of yore. It is a vision imported prior to World War II, as early as the beginning of the century:

> It was the world left by the young emigrant that later became a parent, grandparent and great-grandparent, always transmitting an increasingly anachronistic vision of Basque reality to their descendants. For those that received these images, the global experience, the importance of having descended from Basques, comes to form a part of their persona, at least once a year on the occasion of the *festival* of the local Basque Center. But it is no longer a fact that informs their daily life. In this pessimistic scenario, Basque identity is dying

with time, not in giant steps and with the sound of trumpets but little by little, leaving neither traces nor remorse.[1]

Douglass believes that the Basque center has good possibilities only if it adapts itself to new realities. In other words, it will not last through the twenty-first century if it is based exclusively on the symbolism of folkloric and nostalgic memories of a bucolic Basque Country or a Happy Arcadia characterized by that first immigratory phase. It is clear that Douglass does not anticipate its complete disappearance, either. But he insists that we are facing a problem of the aging of the Basque diaspora, given the absence of a colonial framework to renovate it or a framework of mass open immigration such as took place in the nineteenth and early twentieth centuries. He therefore proposes utilization of the initiatives of the Basque Government in favor of the Basque-American diaspora and the advances in technology and communication media to show the Basque essence and culture where its protagonists have a real, strong presence.

The Pledges

Throughout the course of the conference and the heated workshops organized there, some interesting proposals were made and methods suggested for the promotion and expansion of Basque culture.[2] Thus, in advance, the Basque Government, through the secretary-general of foreign action will destine a growing amount of economic resources "to partially subsidize the regular activities of the Euskal Etxeak [Basque centers], as well as cultural, folkloric, and linguistic events." A portion of its budgetary resources will also be destined to the maintenance and improvement of the infrastructure of the Basque centers. It will also send funds for publishing, and the printing of appropriate materials will be supported; the Basque Government has also promised to promote the learning of Euskara in America. As for sports, the Administration of Sports of the Basque Government and the Basque Handball Federation promised to contribute to meeting the needs and demands for equipment. They will also send handball teachers to the interested Basque centers, which will serve as the future guarantors of the initiative's continuity. Rural sports will be supported as well, with the initial contribution set at 2 million pesetas. And, to promote the exhibition of such sports throughout the world, the conference expressed its desire that an International Association of Basque Sports be founded. Likewise, the Department of Youth Services will organize stays of young people of the diaspora in work-study programs in the Basque Country, and the precise channels of information will facilitate all host programs, cultural campaigns, and artistic courses that might benefit the young people of the Basque collectivities through the Basque centers abroad.

On the matter of communication and information, the Basque Government promised "to substantially intensify the flow of information about Euskadi and its current institutional, economic, cultural, and social reality," while Basque radio and television (Euskal Irrati Telebista, EITB) announced a plan to begin transmission of one television channel and two radio stations via satellite within between one and two years. This service would initially cover South America, Mexico, Central America, and the southern United States, and then be extended to the rest of the American continent and Europe in the future. The conference considered it opportune to organize a competition once every four years to award a prize to a literary or audiovisual work that has contributed to the diffusion of the realities of the diaspora.

In the field of education, the Basque Government along with the universities and other Basque educational organizations promised to take measures to make the stay and education of undergraduate, graduate, and doctoral students and teachers from the Basque collectivities possible in the Autonomous Community, promoting teacher and student exchange programs. On the matter of tourism and gastronomy, the organization of "Basque weeks" with gastronomic, artistic, cultural, sports, and cinematographic presentations in the Basque centers or with their collaboration was decided upon. The Basque Government will also provide logistic support to the diaspora to bring organized tourist groups to the Basque Country. The installation of foreign companies in the Basque Country was also discussed, and it was affirmed that "all the Basques abroad that wish to establish a company or business in Euskadi will be guaranteed technical and legal support from the corresponding institutions."

In the terrain of social welfare, it was decided to implement a system to extend assistance from the Basque Country to those destitute members of the diaspora in the greatest need, on a trial basis. In addition, the Basque Government promised to take steps to encourage the Basque financial institutions to study the viability of articulating a Voluntary Plan of Social Foresight in the Basque Country specifically for members of the Basque collectivities. Likewise, the Basque institutions will establish lines of assistance to partly defray the displacement costs of those people deciding to definitively return to the Basque Country. Such individuals will qualify for the same level of social welfare services as Basque citizens. The creation of a housing program in the Basque Country for members of the diaspora over sixty-five years old was also studied. In terms of health, the Basque Government promised to guarantee medical and hospital care for members of the Basque collectivities that wished to return to the Basque Country once and for all. Moreover, a doctor of Basque origin of the diaspora will have the right to practice professionally in any Basque hospital having the corresponding specialization if he or she is correspondingly listed as a member in the Registry of Basque centers. In addition, the members of the Basque collectivities who wish to definitively return to the Basque Country and who fulfill the necessary requirements are eligible for subsidized housing with no proof of prior residence.

The Beneficiaries

All these measures, as well as the efforts in diffusing the essence of the culture and behavioral guidelines of the Basques, will be focused on the 129 Euskal Etxeak (Basque centers) that presently exist (as of 1997), distributed throughout sixteen countries: eleven on the American continent, three in Europe, and one in Oceania.

ARGENTINA

The sixty-one Basque centers of Argentina are spread throughout the country. The distribution is presently as follows:

Forty centers with 11,000 members are legally integrated into the Federation of Basque-Argentine Entities (*Federación de Entidades Vasco Argentinas*, FEVA).

Thirteen centers with 1,100 members are in the process of formalizing their institutional situation.

Eight centers with about 550 members are being formed or consolidated and are at the point of being integrated into FEVA.

In addition, Argentina has the Basque-Argentine Cooperation and Development Foundation.

UNITED STATES

The majority of the Euskal Etxeak in the United States are located in the West, and almost all of them are integrated into the North American Basque Organization (NABO). The "Basque clubs," as they are called, are distributed in the following manner:

California: nine Basque centers
Idaho: six centers (including the Boise Basque Museum)
Nevada: five centers
Oregon and Wyoming: two centers each
Washington (state): one Basque center
New York City: two centers

In addition, there are three Basque centers in Florida that are not part of NABO. The United States also has a foundation, the American Basque Foundation (ABF), which has two offices: one in Washington D.C. and the other in Boise, Idaho.

SPAIN

The Spanish state has eight centers, distributed as follows: Madrid (two centers), Barcelona, Valladolid, Valencia, Salou, Fuengirola, and Las Palmas. It also has a federation and a total of 3,400 member families, comprising about 9,000 people.

VENEZUELA

The Basque centers in Venezuela are located in Caracas, Valencia, and Puerto La Cruz. They have a total of 644 member families, comprising more than 2,500 people. Venezuela also has a foundation, the Eguzki Basque-Venezuelan Cooperation Institute.

URUGUAY

The Republic of Uruguay has nine Basque centers distributed throughout its territory: three in Montevideo and the others in Durazno, Minas, Flores, Salto, Lavalleja, and Carmelo. There are a total of 3,500 members. It must be underscored that six new Basque centers have been created between 1990 and 1992.

FRANCE

France has four centers: one each in Paris, Bordeaux, Pau, and Tolouse. There are a total of 4,000 members.

CHILE

Chile has the Euskal Etxea of Santiago with 260 member families and the Basque-Chilean Development Foundation.

MEXICO

Like Chile, Mexico has a Basque Center in its capital, with 203 member families and the Basque-Mexican Development Institute.

OTHER COUNTRIES

Other countries such as Australia, Belgium, Brazil, Canada, El Salvador, Guatemala, Peru, and Puerto Rico have one Basque center, some very recently founded, such as those in Belgium, Puerto Rico, and Canada.

To bolster the development of such activities as those of the Basque centers, the Basque Government now has three laws regulating its relations with the diaspora. Law 8/May 27, 1994, regards relations with the Basque collectivities and centers outside of the Basque Autonomous Community. Decree 318/July 28, 1994, regulates the recognition and registration of the Basque centers located outside of the Basque Autonomous Community. Decree 235/April 11, 1995, regulates the subsidies destined for the Basque centers located outside of the Autonomous Community.

As to how to diffuse the character of the Basque people, at the conference Francisco Igartua prudently proposed to display Basqueness throughout the world with amiability and not arrogance nor aggressiveness, leaving the task of spreading the international image of the positive elements of the Basque Country in the hands of the mass media professionals and politicians. To attain these objectives and counteract the frequent ETA-generated negative images of Basqueness that appear throughout the world, the Basque-Venezuelan journalist Hugo Díaz Milano proposed using the mass media. He highlighted the positive news that occurs on a daily basis in the Basque Country.

The Closing

In the concluding act of the conference discussed in this chapter, in which the challenges for the future of the Basque collectivities outside of the Basque Country were posed, President José Antonio Ardanza echoed the words of Professor Douglass. Ardanza encouraged the representatives of the diaspora to work toward the maintenance and diffusion of the Basque essence throughout the world in the future, while also insisting that the Basque society of today is fully plural and distinct from that which many of the participants of the emigration or exile knew. The representatives of the Basque collectivities abroad made the following final declaration:

> The World Conference of Basque Collectivities, assembled in Vitoria-Gasteiz, made up of representatives of the Basque Collectivities and the Basque centers of Argentina, Australia, Belgium, Canada, Chile, Spain, El Salvador, France, Mexico, Peru, Puerto Rico, Spain, United States of America, Uruguay, and Venezuela, as well as representatives from the Basque Institutions and under the presidency of the Lehendakari of Euskadi,
>
> Proud heirs of the centuries of generations of Basques that abandoned their homeland to settle in new lands but determined to always maintain their original uniqueness and culture.
>
> Conscious of the historical responsibility that they have today in the maintenance and promotion of Basque identity throughout the world.
>
> Moved to prove the strong desires of the Basques of Euskadi to maintain, strengthen, and project their relationship with their brothers abroad into the future.
>
> Enthused by the new framework of collaboration opened by the law of relations with the Basque Collectivities and Basque centers abroad.
>
> DECLARE their solemn, unmistakable, and permanent pledge to the Basque cause.

ASSUME the challenge to keep the Basque centers active and bond the Basque Collectivities around their cultural, linguistic, and ethnic identity in all corners of the World.

REAFFIRM the full vigor and force of the Basque centers as a common house for Basques abroad, a place of meeting and unity for Basques, and essential platform for the projection of Basqueness throughout the world, for which all efforts possible will have to be focused on the maintenance of the current Basque centers and in the creation of new ones.

PROCLAIM their will to accommodate these structures and their activities to the new times with the aim of guaranteeing and bequeathing a network of Basque houses abroad to their children and grandchildren for the twenty-first century.

PLEDGE to work continuously to unite the Basque youths from abroad, giving them a relevant role in the Basque centers, in order to assure the generational transfer and the continuity of the Basque Collectivities abroad as an organized movement.

CONSIDER themselves a critical part of the activity of the Basque Institutions abroad.

INCUR proudly and willingly, the responsibility of representing Euskal Herria in each of these countries, of promoting its institutional, economic, and cultural interests and working toward an increase in the relations between Euskadi and all of them.

HAIL with satisfaction the growing self-governance and the vigorous activity of its Institutions, in which they place their confidence and which they encourage continuing on the path undertaken, especially in the development of Euskadi's own external policies.

CONGRATULATE themselves for the new expectations of collaboration among the Institutions of the Autonomous Basque Community, the Foral Community of Navarra, and Iparralde, and have faith that beginning with respect for the will of their respective citizens and going beyond some determined administrative bodies, they know how to find their many common bonds and assume the transcendental mission with which they are faced to safeguard a heritage and a common store insofar as they are branches of the same ancestral trunk, Euskal Herria.

VOW so that the resolutions adopted during the Conference, especially the Institutional Plan of Action, becomes reality and they establish the bases of a new stage in the relations between the Institutions of Euskadi and the Basque Collectivities abroad.

AND EXPRESS as their final promise, their decided belonging to the Basque People, their vocation for being incorporated into the Euskadi of the twenty-first century, from a geographical distance but a nearness of their hearts and also their minds, an Euskadi in which they have a place and a mission to accomplish: to open the doors of our new World to the Basques.

Vitoria-Gasteiz, November 9, 1995[3]

The die was cast. A new stage of reciprocal hopes and pronounced challenges would be opened at the end of the millennium. Accordingly, and following the trend and the guidelines marked out by the above-mentioned conference, from August 2 to 8, 1996, José Manuel Azcona and Fernando Muru organized the First Seminar on Basque Immigration, History, and Culture in Montevideo, Uruguay. It was a smashing public success and had even greater social repercussions. The event was supported by the Basque Government through its Secretary of Foreign Action (presidency), and in 1997 the experience would be repeated in Santiago, Chile, and Buenos Aires, Argentina, and in 1998 in Venezuela. In 1999 and 2001, José Manuel Azcona gave several lectures in Montevideo (both within academic circles and for the media). He emphasized Basque-American themes, underscoring in particular that Uruguay, in the early nineteenth century, was the first Latin American country to welcome Basque immigration in the post-colonial period.

Appendix 1

TABLE 1.1 *Basque Crew Members on Magellan's Voyage of Circumnavigation*

Name	Place	Position	Ship
Domingo de Urrutia	Lekeitio (Bizkaia)	Master	*Trinidad*
Sebastián de Olarte	Bilbao (Bizkaia)	Sailor	*Trinidad*
Pedro de Olarte	Portugalete (Bizkaia)	Sailor	*San Antonio*
Lope de Ugarte	Segura (Gipuzkoa)	Sailor	*San Antonio*
Juan de Segura	Segura (Gipuzkoa)	Sailor	*San Antonio*
Lorenzo de Iruña	Sorabilla (Gipuzkoa)	Sailor	*Concepción*
Juan de Aguirre	Bermeo (Bizkaia)	Sailor	*Concepción*
Juan Sebastián Elcano	Getaria (Gipuzkoa)	Master	*Concepción*
Juan de Acurio	Bermeo (Bizkaia)	Boatswain	*Concepción*
Juan de Elorriaga	Deba (Gipuzkoa)	Master	*San Antonio*
Martín de Aguirre	Irun (Gipuzkoa)	Cabin boy	*San Antonio*
Juan de Irún Uranzu	Irun (Gipuzkoa)	Cabin boy	*San Antonio*
Pedro Mugartegui	Bermeo (Bizkaia)	Cabin boy	*Concepción*
Juanico el Vizcaíno	(Bizkaia)	Cabin boy	*Victoria*
Martín de Inchaurraga	Bermeo (Bizkaia)	Cabin boy	*Concepción*
Juan de Arratia	Bilbao (Bizkaia)	Cabin boy	*Victoria*
Pedro de Tolosa	Tolosa (Gipuzkoa)	Cabin boy	*Victoria*
Juan de Orue	Mungia (Bizkaia)	Cabin boy	*San Antonio*
Pedro de Basozabal	Mungia (Bizkaia)	Cabin boy	-excluded-
Juan Navarro	Pamplona (Navarre)	Cabin boy	*San Antonio*
Ochoa de Erandio	Erandio (Bizkaia)	Cabin boy	*Victoria*
Pedro de Bilbao	Bilbao (Bizkaia)	Cabin boy	*San Antonio*
Martín de Goytisolo	Bakio (Bizkaia)	Caulker	*Victoria*
Antonio de Basozabal	Bermeo (Bizkaia)	Caulker	*Concepción*
Domingo de Icaza	Deba (Gipuzkoa)	Carpenter	*Concepción*
Pedro Sautua	Bermeo (Bizkaia)	Carpenter	*San Antonio*
Martín Garate	Deba (Gipuzkoa)	Carpenter	*Victoria*
Juan de Menchaca	Bilbao (Bizkaia)	Crossbowman	*San Antonio*
Pedro de Chindurza	Bermeo (Bizkaia)	Page	*Concepción*
Juan de Zubileta	Barakaldo (Bizkaia)	Page	*Victoria*
Juan Ortíz de Gopegui	Bilbao(Bizkaia)	Steward	*San Antonio*
León de Ezpeleta	Bilbao (Bizkaia)	Accountant	*Santiago*
Diego de Peralta	Peralta (Navarre)	Bailiff	*Trinidad*
Pedro de Olabarrieta	Galdakao (Bizkaia)	Barber	*San Antonio*
Martín de Barrena	Orio (Gipuzkoa)	Gallery gunner	*Santiago*
Lope Navarro	Tudela (Navarre)	Sailor	*Santiago*

Source: E. Ruiz de Azua, *Vascongadas y América* (Madrid, 1992), 56, and J. Bilbao Azkarreta, ed., *América y los vascos* (Bilbao, 1992), 84.

TABLE 1.2   *Privateering Recruiters and Vessels in Atlantic Spain, 17th Century*

Region	Recruiters/%	Vessels/%
Province of Gipuzkoa	218/46.8	396/56.0
Donostia	141/30.2	271/38.3
Hondarribia	48/10.3	71/10.0
Seigneury of Bizkaia	59/12.6	77/10.9
Bilbao, Nervión Estuary	33/7.1	50/7.0
Cuatro Villas de la Costa	33/7.1	30/4.2
Laredo, Santoña	24/5.1	22/3.1
Principate of Asturias	25/5.3	36/5.1
Llanes	8/1.7	16/2.2
Kingdom of Galicia	68/14.6	89/12.5
La Coruña	24/5.1	37/5.2
Vigo	26/5.5	27/3.8
Kingdom of Portugal	1/0.2	2/0.3
Kingdom of Andalusia	22/4.7	20/2.8
Unspecified	40/8.6	57/8.0
Total (Atlantic Spain)	466/100	707/100

Source: E. Otero Lana, 1992, 59.

TABLE 1.3 *Basque Positions and Titles in the Bourbon Court, 1721–1799*

Date	Name	Place	Positions/Titles
1721	Esteban de Otazu	Araba	Member of Council of Orders Knight of Santiago
1722	Andrés de Pes	Bizkaia	Sea Admiral and General War Advisor President of Council of the Indies Secretary of State of the Indies and Navy
1723	Jacinto de Arana	Gipuzkoa	Advisor of the Holy Inquisition Bishop of Zamora
1724	Diego Vélez Ladrón de Guevara	Araba	Postmaster General Grandee of Spain Knight of Calatrava
1728	Ventura de Landeta y Horna	Bizkaia	Member of War Council Captain General of the Canaries Knight of Santiago
1731	Andrés de Orbe y Larreátegui	Bizkaia	Governor of Council of Castile Archbishop of Valencia
1734	José de la Quintana	Bizkaia	Advisor to the Indies Secretary of State of the Indies and Navy
1736	Francisco de Aguirre y Salcedo	Araba	Majordomo to the Queen Tutor to the Infante Charles III
1739	José Mª Diego de Guzmán	Araba	Majordomo to His Majesty Postmaster General Grandee of Spain Knight of the Golden Toisón
1741	Tomás de Guzmán Spinola	Gipuzkoa	Head Chaplain of the Royal Reformed Orders Member of Council of Castile Knight of Santiago
1742	Juan de Eulate y Santa Cruz	Araba	Advisor of the Holy Inquisition Bishop of Malaga
1743	Gabriel de Olmedo Aguilar	Bizkaia	Member of the Council and Chamber of Castile
1744	Carlos de Areyzaga	Gipuzkoa	Gentleman of His Majesty's Chamber Assistant Tutor First Stableman to Ferdinand VI Captain General of the Army
1746	Antonio de Pando y Bringas	Bizkaia	Advisor to His Majesty Advisor of Royal Board of Supplies

TABLE 1.3 *(continued)*

Date	Name	Place	Positions/Titles
1747	Miguel Antonio de Zuaznabar	Gipuzkoa	Member of Board of the Treasury Assistant Head Bodyguard
1748	Juan Antonio de Gauna	Araba	Member of Council of the Indies First Stableman to the Queen Knight of Calatrava
1749	Agustín Pablo de Ordeñana	Bizkaia	Member of Board of the Treasury Secretary of War Council Secretary of Council of State
1750	Salvador de Querejazu	Gipuzkoa	Member of Board of the Treasury Accountant General of Assets
1752	Agustín de Montinao y Luyando	Bizkaia	Secretary of the Chamber of Clemency and Justice Secretary of Council of Castile Academician of Language Founder of Academy of History
1753	Andrés de Otamendi	Gipuzkoa	Member of His Majesty's Council Secretary of the Chamber of Clemency and Justice Secretary of Council of Aragon
1758	Tomás de Mello	Bizkaia	Member of His Majesty's Council Secretary of the Chamber of Clemency and Justice
1759	Pedro Colón de Larreátegui	Gipuzkoa	Member of Council of Castile Knight of Alcántara
1764	Nicolás de Mollinedo	Bizkaia	Member of His Majesty's Council Secretary of the Chamber of Clemency and Justice Secretary of State of Castile Knight of Santiago
1765	Esteban José de Abaría e Imaz	Gipuzkoa	Advisor to the Indies
1766	Tomás Ortiz de Landazuri	Araba	Member of His Majesty's Council Accountant General of Council of the Indies Knight of Santiago
1767	Gaspar de Munive	Bizkaia	Advisor to the Indies
1769	Simón de Anda y Salazar	Araba	Member of Council of Castile Governor and Captain General of the Philippines President of the High Court of the Indies

Date	Name	Place	Positions/Titles
1770	Pedro Francisco de Goosens	Bizkaia	Member of Board of the Treasury Treasurer General of the Kingdom
1772	Fco. González de Echavarri	Araba	Captain General of New Spain President of the High Court of Mexico Member of Council of the Indies Knight of Santiago
1776	Fco. de Silva Alvz. de Toledo	Araba	Dean of Council of State Captain General of the Army Director of Academy of Language Knight of the Golden Toisón
1780	Antonio de la Quadra	Bizkaia	Advisor to His Majesty District Attorney of Council of Orders Knight of Santiago
1781	Pablo Antonio de Ondarza	Gipuzkoa	Member of the Hall of Justice on the Board of the Treasury Honorary Member of Council of Castile
1782	Fco. de Viana Sáenz Villaverde	Araba	Minister of Council of the Indies District Attorney of the High Court of Manila Judge of the High Court of Mexico Knight of the Order of Charles III
1783	José Antonio de Armona	Bizkaia	Advisor to His Majesty Intendant of the Army Magistrate of Madrid Knight of the Order of Charles III
1784	Juan José de Eulate	Gipuzkoa	Member of His Majesty's Council Member of the Hall of Justice on the Board of the Treasury Member of the Council of Castile
1786	Manuel Jimenez Bretón	Bizkaia	Member of Board of the Treasury Secretary General of Commerce, Currency, and Mines
1789	Juan Francisco de los Heros	Bizkaia	Advisor to His Majesty District Attorney of the Board of the Treasury Governor of the Council of Castile Knight of the Order of Charles III

TABLE 1.3 *(continued)*

Date	Name	Place	Positions/Titles
1790	Miguel de Otamendi	Bizkaia	Member of Council of Castile Director of the Board of Governers of the National Bank of San Carlos Knight of the Order of Charles III
1799	Juan Ignacio de Ayestarán	Gipuzkoa	Advisor to His Majesty Secretary of State of the Council of Castile Secretary of the Chamber of Clemency and Justice

Source: E. Ruiz de Azúa, 107–10.

Appendix 2

TABLE 2.1 Iron and Steel Exports from the Basque Country to the Americas, 1511–1699, in Quintals*

Year	Iron	Ironworks	Nails	Total
1511	33.75	29.75	—	63.50
1523	10.00	95.00	240.50	345.50
1526	12.00	100.00	28.00	140.00
1534	31.50	—	—	31.50
1542	—	—	24.00	24.00
1545	624.00	383.75	245.50	1,253.25
1557	71.25	196.75	—	268.00
1583	598.00	861.75	550.00	2,009.75
1584	306.50	949.75	340.00	1,596.25
1585	23.00	—	—	23.00
1586	1,453.50	2,807.25	1,356.00	5,616.75
1588	418.00	525.00	281.00	1,224.00
1589	811.50	1,995.75	205.00	3,012.25
1590	2,775.50	3,083.50	1,144.50	7,003.50
1591	—	1,246.50	20.00	1,266.50
1592	7,591.50	4,978.50	2,786.00	15,356.00
1593	4,603.50	4,637.00	2,421.50	11,662.00
1594	5,324.50	3,620.75	2,771.25	11,716.50
1595	2,285.00	1,007.50	1,270.50	4,563.00
1596	20,514.00	7,106.25	2,545.00	30,165.25
1597	8,091.00	5,104.25	1,313.75	14,509.00
1598	3,340.00	7,211.00	3,810.00	14,361.00
1599	4,395.50	5,236.50	933.75	10,565.75
1600	11,003.50	12,618.50	4,408.50	28,030.50
1601	158.75	266.00	271.75	696.50
1602	541.50	655.00	234.50	1,431.00
1603	1,415.00	2,296.50	515.25	4,226.75
1604	2,280.00	1,674.50	1,119.50	5,074.00
1605	6,373.50	3,580.00	787.75	10,741.25
1606	2,237.50	1,612.75	130.25	3,980.50
1607	346.00	78.00	98.25	522.25
1608	7,851.00	2,606.25	423.75	10,881.00
1609	1,905.50	1,979.25	46.75	3,931.50
1610	3,307.50	3,006.00	760.50	7,074.00
1611	—	—	—	—
1612	476.00	869.75	197.00	1,542.75

TABLE 2.1 (*continued*)

Year	Iron	Ironworks	Nails	Total
1613	2,884.00	3,615.00	484.00	6,983.00
1614	318.00	276.00	—	594.00
1615	1,913.00	14.70	477.00	2,404.70
1616	—	139.00	32.50	171.50
1617	—	—	—	—
1618	2,849.50	1,986.50	380.50	5,216.50
1619	3,093.00	1,788.25	523.00	5,404.25
1620	1,430.00	563.75	195.00	2,188.75
1621	2,534.00	1,287.75	332.25	4,154.00
1622	1,328.00	856.50	120.75	2,305.25
1623	—	—	—	—
1624	—	—	123.25	123.25
1625	3,647.00	2,269.00	55.00	5,971.00
1626	1,440.00	433.50	62.00	1,935.50
1627	1,572.00	1,995.00	—	3,567.00
1628	5,306.00	1,631.75	189.00	7,126.75
1629	—	—	—	—
1630	2,275.25	1,365.75	189.00	3,830.00
1631	668.00	301.75	—	969.75
1632	—	—	—	—
1633	1,367.75	2,803.00	242.50	4,413.25
1634	1,754.00	527.65	—	2,281.65
1635	1,315.00	1,220.00	—	2,535.00
1636	300.00	440.00	—	740.00
1637	530.00	489.75	—	1,019.75
1638	1,968.00	622.75	277.00	2,867.75
1639	3,585.00	2,555.00	—	6,140.00
1640	3,154.00	1,774.00	281.75	5,209.75
1641	83.50	43.50	—	127.00
1642	1,464.50	661.75	—	2,126.25
1643	5,716.00	3,143.25	173.00	9,032.25
1644	3,147.00	964.00	—	4,111.00
1645	2,148.50	979.00	81.00	3,208.50
1646	5,728.50	4,523.75	191.00	10,442.75
1647	5,084.00	2,875.50	92.00	8,051.50
1648	608.50	274.50	98.00	981.00
1649	2,930.00	3,646.75	—	6,576.75
1650	4,308.00	1,872.25	383.00	6,563.25
1651	2,236.00	931.50	144.00	3,311.50
1652	186.00	831.50	1.00	1,018.50
1653	—	388.50	9.00	397.50

Appendix 2

Year	Iron	Ironworks	Nails	Total
1654	—	—	—	—
1655	1,695.00	649.50	8.00	2,352.50
1656	1,049.00	—	—	1,049.00
1657	269.50	—	—	269.50
1658	550.00	237.50	—	787.50
1659	322.00	—	40.00	362.00
1660	1,882.00	3,342.50	731.00	5,955.50
1661	1,030.50	263.00	40.00	1,333.50
1662	4,068.00	3,181.50	967.00	8,216.50
1663	39.75	29.50	25.00	94.25
1664	1,466.50	1,630.00	522.00	3,618.50
1665	2,660.25	2,556.00	190.00	5,406.25
1666	17.00	378.50	6.00	401.50
1667	1,613.50	2,066.50	608.00	4,288.00
1668	5,866.50	3,599.00	359.00	9,824.50
1669	3,534.00	2,998.00	374.00	6,906.00
1670	7,756.25	5,960.75	102.00	13,819.00
1671	4,247.00	2,482.50	142.00	6,871.50
1672	2,151.50	3,991.50	1,104.00	7,247.00
1673	8,723.50	2,792.00	65.00	11,580.50
1674	69.50	88.00	—	157.50
1675	13,733.00	4,439.50	90.00	8,262.50
1676	129.00	—	—	129.00
1677	860.00	205.00	51.00	1,116.00
1678	14,388.50	8,771.00	888.00	24,047.50
1679	64.75	—	—	64.75
1680	7,188.75	4,321.00	—	11,509.75
1681	2,499.75	3,311.50	150.00	5,961.25
1682	7,594.25	2,987.00	8.00	10,589.25
1683	1,733.50	247.00	9.00	1,989.50
1684	3,185.00	6,148.00	77.00	9,410.00
1685	—	307.50	—	307.50
1686	—	—	—	—
1687	17,708.50	5,754.50	188.00	23,651.00
1688	560.00	94.00	17.00	71.00
1689	2,530.00	1,462.50	26.00	4,018.50
1690	21,240.50	9,625.25	1,991.00	32,856.75
1691	—	—	—	—
1692	19,326.25	3,727.50	923.00	23,976.75
1693	1,647.75	148.50	108.00	1,904.25
1694	—	—	50.00	50.00

TABLE 2.1 (*continued*)

Year	Iron	Ironworks	Nails	Total
1695	24,168.25	16,998.75	1,124.00	42,291.00
1696	2,815.00	2,117.50	5.00	4,937.50
1697	86.75	—	—	86.75
1698	5,076.00	417.00	43.00	5,536.00
1699	18,594.75	2,578.00	76.00	21,248.75

*An old measure of unit of weight, whose value varied according to geographic regions. In the metric system today, it is equal to 100 kilograms.

Source: L. Garcia Fuentes, 1981, 138–42.

TABLE 2.2 *Iron and Steel Exports from the Basque Country to the Americas, 1700–1799, in Quintals**

Year	Iron	Tools	Nails
1700	2,275.50	78.00	75.00
1701	1,374.50	244.50	147.00
1702	1,604.50	384.50	15.00
1703	894.00	632.50	7.00
1704	150.00	5.00	—
1705	576.00	5,204.50	70.00
1706	11,842.50	12,833.75	51.00
1707	465.00	—	30.00
1708	4,099.00	639.25	70.50
1709	40.00	42.00	—
1710	2,767.00	473.50	100.00
1711	15,523.00	5,021.25	14.00
1712	7,133.00	4,799.00	497.50
1713	4,175.00	1,314.00	103.00
1714	3,869.50	646.00	292.00
1715	18,704.00	4,743.75	655.00
1716	4,509.50	17,881.00	18.00
1717	29,421.00	2,626.50	1,091.75
1718	4,020.00	426.75	—
1719	3,811.00	125.00	267.00
1720	31,640.50	2,011.50	478.50
1721	17,641.00	1,784.50	—
1722	10,357.00	219.00	—
1723	63,987.50	8,950.75	2,248.50
1724	3,719.00	533.50	—
1725	28,618.00	5,881.00	1,029.00
1726	3,546.00	140.00	—
1727	—	—	—
1728	15,234.00	732.00	—
1729	33,622.00	7,715.00	3,392.00
1730	37,888.50	2,378.00	—
1731	10,507.00	395.50	—
1732	42,656.00	10,216.25	2,813.75
1733	9,597.00	1,818.00	—
1734	400.00	—	—
1735	49,930.75	3,697.50	530.50
1736	8,651.00	—	—
1737	31,761.00	451.00	—

TABLE 2.2 (*continued*)

Year	Iron	Tools	Nails
1738	1,203.50	—	—
1739	3,190.00	—	—
1740	6,765.00	1,640.00	—
1741	14,599.50	1,096.00	77.00
1742	14,599.50	353.00	455.75
1743	14,682.00	252.00	8,104.50
1744	17,279.00	830.50	898.50
1745	18,710.00	450.00	—
1746	16,406.00	4,472.00	1,652.00
1747	8,466.00	3,051.00	278.00
1748	—	—	—
1749	30,461.50	3,316.00	2,229.00
1750	37,695.50	3,340.50	2,139.25
1751	35,211.00	2,832.75	2,738.00
1752	24,380.00	8,531.00	1,957.00
1753	28,581.00	4,690.00	2,810.00
1754	38,929.00	1,511.00	730.75
1755	25,406.00	3,744.50	1,301.75
1756	4,725.00	418.00	572.50
1757	48,537.50	8,489.25	3,052.25
1758	13,738.50	5,366.50	586.25
1759	8,134.50	2,692.50	714.50
1760	50,843.00	11,590.00	1,997.00
1761	22,210.00	3,195.00	2,382.00
1762	1,257.00	195.00	275.00
1763	24,276.00	5,315.75	1,503.25
1764	9,618.25	1,228.50	676.50
1765	50,329.00	3,623.25	1,823.50
1766	22,884.75	2,518.50	743.50
1767	27,475.50	2,819.25	705.00
1768	52,439.71	6,350.00	412.50
1769	13,222.00	2,654.00	1,121.50
1770	18,530.00	2,798.00	696.00
1771	9,852.00	2,706.00	682.50
1772	41,742.50	9,474.00	1,753.00
1773	17,086.25	3,624.00	978.00
1774	8,658.00	2,255.00	343.50
1775	7,738.00	5,120.00	1,062.00
1776	35,571.00	9,585.50	769.50
1777	26,795.50	3,407.00	2,471.00
1778	20,892.00	5,560.00	773.25

Year	Iron	Tools	Nails
1779	6,541.00	2,782.00	175.00
1780	—	—	—
1781	—	—	—
1782	19,356.25	2,934.00	3,236.50
1783	15,015.00	1,639.50	3,137.00
1784	2,000.00	—	57.60
1785	39,712.00	6,147.25	9,048.00
1786	31,514.90	4,496.25	3,972.25
1787	32,609.50	9,214.50	3,667.00
1788	49,384.00	11,042.75	3,584.50
1789	60,388.50	8,221.50	4,255.00
1790	47,634.00	1,920.75	2,030.50
1791	73,707.50	11,436.00	7,457.50
1792	79,362.50	16,982.00	6,353.00
1793	52,179.75	20,975.50	2,307.25
1794	33,139.00	5,868.50	1,790.00
1795	28,838.75	5,266.75	1,070.25
1796	10,687.50	767.00	455.75
1797	8,593.50	3,770.00	843.00
1798	1,347.00	—	—
1799	4,712.50	3,974.50	1,994.25

*An old measure of unit of weight, whose value varied according to geographic regions. In the metric system today, it is equal to 100 kilograms.

Source: L. García Fuentes, 1981, 200–202.

TABLE 2.3 *Basque Companies Trading in Iron and Metal Manufactures in Sevilla, 1596–1693*

Year	Partners-Associates	Length	Capital*
1569	Juan García Urupain, Pedro Iturbe, Pedro Pérez Urquizu, and Agustín Iturbe	4 years	11,211,000 m
1571	Juan Martínez Altuna & Domingo de Goiaz	2 years	2,765,631 m
1571	Francisco de Igarza & Miguel Sáenz de Ismendi	3 years	4,000 d
1573	Juan Pérez Alzola & Santiago Arana	—	—
1574	Juan Pérez Olaegui & Co.	—	—
1574	Juan Chavarría, Martín Irigoyen & Co.	—	—
1579	Juan García Arriola, Francisco de Igarza, and Juan Martínez Altuna	4 years	3,750,000 m
1580	Andrés López de Unzueta, Pedro de Eizaguirre, and Domingo Jorge	4 years	6,407,085 m
1580	Juan de Isasi, Andrés de Arrizabalaga, Martín López de Isasi, and Pedro de Ochoa	—	—
1583	Joanes de Irauzqui & Co.	—	—
1589	Juan de Olano & Juan García Arriola	—	—
1589	Martín Ochoa de Saciola & Co.	—	—
1589	Martín López de Isasi & Andrés de Arrizabalaga	—	—
1590	Andrés Ibañez de Lixalde, Martín López de Isasi, Pedro de Eizaguirre and Juan de Irauzqui	—	—
1591	Juan de Basterrolaza, Martín Bidarte & Co.	—	—
1591	Miguel Arregui, Francisco Aguirre & Co.	—	—
1591	Agustín Iturbe & Co.	—	—
1591	Juan Pérez Chavarría & Martín Ibañez de Albístegui	—	—
1591	Martín de Arregui & Co.	—	—
1592	Andrés de Arrizabalaga, Antonio de Larreátegui, Martín Ochoa de Saciola, and Juan González de Aldasolo	—	—
1594	Juan Martínez de Murguía, Martín de Arriola, Pedro de Murguía, and Tomás de Arriola	4 years	15,000 d
1594	Martín Sanz de Goias, Juan Martínez Altuna, Juan García Arriola, and Domingo Sanz de Goias	4 years	11,062,000 m
1596	Andrés Urquizu, Juan Ochoa Iturbe, and Juan Pérez de Zubiaurre	—	—
1598	Juan Aldecoa, Juan Ochoa de Zárate, and Juan Ochoa Arriola	6 years	3,180,820 m
1599	Juan Martínez Loyola, Nicolás Sánchez Aramburu, Juan Martínez Mansoro & Co.	—	—

Year	Partners-Associates	Length	Capital*
1618	Juan de Munibe & Juan Martínez de Loyola	4 years	12,000,000 m
1622	Antonio de Arizaga & Blás de Uria	4 years	1,682,526
1623	Francisco de Chavarría & Bartolomé Gastía	4 years	2,098,080 m
1623	Gaspar de Loyola, Domingo de Atallomendía, and Juan Casanueva Caicuegui	4 years	25,000,000 m
1627	Gaspar de Loyola, Juan Martínez de Loyola, and Juan de Munibe	—	—
1627	Miguel Casadevante Ubilla, Gaspar de Loyola, Juan Caicuegui, and Domingo de Atallomendia	4 years	40,000,000 m
1628	Juana de Idiaquez, Martín de Lasalde, Francisco Buster, and Miguel Urrutia	—	—
1629	Juana de Idiaquez, Antonia de Lasalde, Gregorio de Albizuri, Martín de Lasalde, and Francisco Buster	4 years	19,092,406 m
1630	Francisco Chavarría & Bartolomé Gastía	3 years	2,650,000 m
1630	Antonio López Isasi, Juan de Mallea & Co.	—	—
1631	Martín de Arespacochaga & Francisco Arespacochaga	4 years	—
1650	Ana de Arrate, Martín Iñiguez Recabarren, and Lorenzo Gortiortua	—	2,609,665 m
1650	Pedro de Iturri & Domingo de Lequerica	3 years	250,000 cr
1651	Pedro de Beitia, Domingo de Lequerica, and Pedro Goicoechea	—	288,283 cr
1652	Esteban Zulaibar, Domingo de Lequerica, and Pedro Goicoechea	—	—
1660	Agustín de Urquiza & Domingo de Lequerica	7 years	155,000 r
1665	Diego de Urquiza, Domingo Lariz, and Sebastián Aranz	3 years	225,062 cr
1667	Domingo de Lequerica, Agustín Urquiza, and María de Lequerica	2 years	180,000 cr
1668	Diego de Urquiza, Domingo Lariz, and Tomasa de Maurturua	3 years	351,276 cr
1668	Juan Martínez Irureta, Diego de Urquiza, Domingo Lanz, and Agustín de Arabio	3 years	221,515 cr
1668	Gregorio de Otalora & Ana de Vera	3 years	11,000 d
1670	Sebastián de Arteaga, Manuel de Beña Arteaga, and Pedro de Iturri	3 years	176,948 cr
1670	Agustín de Chaverría, Antonio de Betia, and Domingo de Lequerica	3 years	267,929 cr

TABLE 2.3 *(continued)*

Year	Partners-Associates	Length	Capital*
1681	Diego de Urquizu, Gregorio de Otalora, Domingo Lariz, and Agustín de Arabio	—	447,473 cr
1681	Diego de Urquizu, Domingo Lariz, Sebastián de Arauz, and Simón Zearzola	4 years	675,862 cr
1692	Diego de Urquizu, Domingo Lariz, Sebastián de Arauz, and José de Alceneca	4 years	362,683 cr
1692	Diego de Urquiza, Domingo Lariz, Sebastián de Arauz, and Simón Zearzola	28 mos.	416,000 cr
1693	Gregorio de Otalora, Diego de Urquizu, Domingo Lariz, and Agustín de Arabio	4 years	230,781 cr

*m = *maravedíes*, d = ducats, cr = copper reales, r = reales
Source: L. García Fuentes, 1981, 81–102.

TABLE 2.4 *Ships of the Company of Caracas, 1728–1785*

Ship	Type	Tons
La Esperanza	Brig	104
Ntra. Sra. de Aránzazu (1759)	Sloop	167
Ntra. Sra. de los Dolores (1764)	Navío	454
Ntra. Sra. del Coro (1743)	Navío	550
Ntra. Sra. del Rosario	Frigate	154
San Carlos (I) (1760)	Navío	418
San Carlos (II) (1770)	Navío	506
San Gabriel (1768)	Navío	229
San Ignacio (1765)	Navío	764
San José (1743)	Navío	777
San Judas Tadeo	Frigate	534
San Julián	Navío	520
San Miguel y Santiago	Navío	669
San Pedro y San Pablo	Frigate	700
Santa Raquel	Navío	530
San Vicente Mártir	Frigate	199
Santa Ana (1745)	Navío	640
Santa Lucía	Sloop	67
Santa Teresa de Jesús (1776)	Urca	436
Santiago Apostol (1757)	Navío	224

Source: G. E. Vivas, 1989, 309–50.

TABLE 2.5 *Basque Members of Club of the Vizcayans in the Consulate of Mexico, 1700s*

Name	Position	Name	Position
Tomás Domingo de Acha	Consul and prior	José de los Heros	Consul
Diego de Ágreda	Consul and prior	Tomás Ramón Ibarrola	Consul
Manuel de Aldaco	Consul and prior	Isidro Antonio de Icaza	Consul
Juan Bautista de Aldasoro	Consul and prior	Francisco Iñiguez	—
Miguel Alonso de Hortigosa	Consul and prior	Francisco Ignacio de Iraeta	Consul
Baltasar de Arechavala	—	Pedro de Iriarte	—
José Joaquín de Ariscorreta	Consul and prior	Gabriel de Iturbe	Consul
Juan Bautista Aristoarena	Prior	Vicente de Iturgoyen	—
Juan Martín de Astis	Consul	José Lanzagorta	—
Pedro de Ayzinena	Consul	Manuel de Leguinazával	—
Antonio Bassoco	Consul and prior	Sebastián López de Ortuño	—
Francisco Baso Ibañez	Consul and prior	Manuel de Llantada Ibarra	—
Juan de Castañiza	Consul and prior	Martín de Madariaga	—
Manuel de Cozuela	Consul	Manuel Marco y Zemborain	—
Francisco de Chávarri	Consul and prior	Francisco Antonio Marín	—
Juan Díaz González	Consul and prior	José Martín Chávez	—
Joaquín F. Diez Sollano	—	Ambrosio Meave	Consul and prior
Francisco Diez Sollano	—	Juan Fernando de Meoqui	Consul
José María de Echave	Consul and prior	José de Olloqui	Prior
José Joaquín de Echeverría	—	Antonio de Orizar	—
Juan José de Echeveste	—	Francisco de Ozcoz	—
Sebastián de Eguía	Consul and prior	Francisco Rivero	Consul and prior
José de Eyzaguirre	—	Miguel F. Sánchez Hidalgo	Consul
Juan José de Fagoaga	—	José María de Urquiaga	—
Felipe de Gandiaga	Consul	Manuel de Urquiaga	Consul
Diego García Bravo	Consul	Juan Sierra Uruñela	—
Nicolás Garro	Consul	Antonio Villar y Lanzagorta	—
Juan de Guardiamino	—	Antonio Zavala	—

Source: M. C. Torales Pacheco, 1992, 288–89.

TABLE 2.6 *Number of Members of the Royal Basque Society, 1765–1793*

Year	Spain	America	Europe	Total
1765	32	0	1	33
1766	47	0	3	50
1767	65	0	6	71
1768	73	1	7	81
1769	78	2	7	87
1770	88	2	10	100
1771	142	6	14	162
1772	199	13	13	225
1773	240	213	14	467
1774	294	226	15	535
1775	360	250	26	636
1776	434	333	36	803
1777	511	377	41	929
1778	534	403	49	986
1779	543	468	51	1,062
1780	540	473	52	1,065
1781	556	470	50	1,076
1782	563	448	47	1,058
1783	586	529	47	1,162
1784	612	596	51	1,259
1785	641	601	52	1,294
1786	650	626	58	1,334
1787	663	630	57	1,350
1788	654	672	78	1,404
1789	639	645	79	1,363
1790	639	577	81	1,297
1791	651	572	81	1,304
1792	647	571	79	1,297
1793	639	563	32	1,234

Source: J. Vidal Abarca, 1991, 123–24.

TABLE 2.7 *Number of Members of the Royal Basque Society in the Americas, 1765–1793*

Year	Nueva España	Nueva Granada	Peru	Río de la Plata	Total
1765	0	0	0	0	0
1766	0	0	0	0	0
1767	0	0	0	0	0
1768	0	0	0	1	1
1769	1	0	0	1	2
1770	1	0	0	1	2
1771	3	0	0	3	6
1772	8	1	1	3	13
1773	204	2	2	5	213
1774	204	7	8	7	226
1775	217	11	10	12	250
1776	298	11	12	12	333
1777	337	10	18	12	377
1778	362	10	17	14	403
1779	423	10	22	13	468
1780	425	10	25	13	473
1781	422	9	26	13	470
1782	401	8	25	14	448
1783	450	8	58	13	529
1784	507	8	69	12	596
1785	508	8	73	12	601
1786	529	9	75	13	626
1787	530	9	75	16	630
1788	527	12	114	19	672
1789	491	14	121	19	645
1790	422	14	123	18	577
1791	418	15	119	20	572
1792	417	16	119	19	571
1793	412	15	118	18	563

Source: J. Vidal Abarca, 1991, 136.

TABLE 2.8 *Number of Members of the Royal Basque Society in the Main Cities of the Viceroyalty of Nueva España, 1765–1793*

Year	Mexico	Havana	Manila	Chihuahua
1765	0	0	0	0
1766	0	0	0	0
1767	0	0	0	0
1768	0	0	0	0
1769	0	0	1	0
1770	0	0	1	0
1771	0	1	1	0
1772	2	2	2	0
1773	133	18	2	6
1774	135	17	1	6
1775	136	28	1	6
1776	159	29	0	7
1777	163	28	2	7
1778	165	28	2	6
1779	176	31	28	20
1780	176	31	30	20
1781	174	31	30	20
1782	165	32	31	20
1783	173	35	36	20
1784	182	35	34	31
1785	182	36	32	32
1786	191	46	32	32
1787	186	51	32	32
1788	184	48	32	32
1789	163	47	31	31
1790	127	47	29	26
1791	130	47	22	26
1792	130	46	22	25
1793	128	46	22	23

Source: J. Vidal Abarca, 1991, 128, 141.

TABLE 2.9 *Number of Members of the Royal Basque Society in the Main Cities of the Viceroyalty of Peru, 1765–1793*

Years	Lima	Arequipa	Trujillo	Santiago
1765	0	0	0	0
1766	0	0	0	0
1767	0	0	0	0
1768	0	0	0	0
1769	0	0	0	0
1770	0	0	0	0
1771	0	0	0	0
1772	1	0	0	0
1773	2	0	0	0
1774	6	0	0	2
1775	8	0	0	2
1776	10	0	0	2
1777	15	0	1	2
1778	13	1	1	2
1779	15	1	1	4
1780	18	1	1	4
1781	20	1	1	3
1782	19	1	1	3
1783	50	1	1	4
1784	60	1	2	4
1785	63	2	2	4
1786	65	2	2	4
1787	66	3	2	3
1788	72	27	5	4
1789	74	27	5	5
1790	69	31	7	6
1791	65	31	7	6
1792	65	31	6	6
1793	64	31	6	7

Source: J. Vidal Abarca, 1991, 143.

TABLE 2.10 *Provincial and Local Origin of Basque Emigration to America, First Half of the 18th Century*

	No.
Gipuzkoa	
San Sebastián	14
Tolosa	6
Azpeitia	6
Oñati	5
Oiartzun	4
Legazpi	4
Idiazabal	4
Segura	4
Bergara	3
Ataun	3
Arrasate	3
Amara	2
Antzuola	2
Aretxabaleta	2
Eibar	2
Hondarribia	2
Hernani	2
Pasaia	2
Ordizia	2
Albiztur	1
Amezketa	1
Andoain	1
Araotz	1
Azkoitia	1
Zestoa	1
Elgeta	1
Getaria	1
Irun	1
Jauregi	1
Marin	1
Valle de Oñati	1
Errenderi	1
Gatzaga	1
Villareal	1
Zumarraga	1

TABLE 2.10 *(continued)*

	No.
Unspecified	1
Total	98
Bizkaia	
Bilbao	28
Durango	9
Markina	6
Artzentales	5
Karrantza	5
Turtzioz	3
Alonsotegi	2
Galdames	2
Güeñes	2
Gernika	2
Iurreta	2
Lezama	2
Otxandio	2
Orduña	2
Sopuerta	2
Balmaseda	2
Zornotza	2
Abadiño	1
Zeanuri	1
Zearrotza	1
La Cuadra	1
Elorrio	1
Gordexola	1
La Naja	1
Portugalete	1
Villaverde	1
Zorrotza	1
Unspecified	1
Total	94
Araba	
Vitoria-Gasteiz	8
Aramaio	3
Langraiz Oka	3
Laudio	3
Oquendo	2
Dulantzi	1
Arangiz	1

	No.
Artziniega	1
Arroiabe	1
Aztegieta	1
Aiara	1
Beotegi	1
Espejo	1
Izoria	1
Lagrán	1
Landa	1
Menagarai	1
Menoio	1
Morillas	1
Langara-Gamboa	1
Osma	1
Arespalditza	1
Gesaltza	1
Zollo	1
Zurbao	1
Unspecified	4
Total	45

Source: I. Macías Domínguez, 1996, 36–37.

TABLE 2.11 *Destination of Basque Emigration to America, First Half of the 18th Century*

Viceroyalty	Total/Percent
Nueva España	96/40.67
Peru	64/27.11
Mainland	13/5.50
Antilles	11/4.66
Central America	11/4.66
Río de la Plata	11/4.66
Nueva Granada	8/3.38
Kingdom of Quito	8/3.38
Chile	4/1.69
Philippines	4/1.69

Source: I. Macías Domínguez, 1996, 36–37.

TABLE 2.12 *Sample of American Donations Destined for Religious Buildings in the Basque Country, 1526–1814*

Year	Donor	Amount	Reason	Province
1526	Juan Sebastián Elcano	12 ducats	Maintenance of the Church of San Salvador (Getaria)	Gipuzkoa
1568	Diego de Durana	—	Construction of the chapel of the Church of Purísima Concepción de Arguiñiga (Aiara)	Araba
1574	Juan Ortíz de Zarate	10,000 *maravedíes*	Construction of the chapel of the Church of Santa María (Orduña)	Bizkaia
1575	Juan de Araoz y Uriarte	—	Foundation of the convent, church, and school of San Francisco (Arrasate)	Gipuzkoa
1590	Fra Domingo Alzola y Comportaeta	—	Foundation of the Church of San Comportaeta (Elgoibar)	Gipuzkoa
1643	Juan de la Piedra Verástegui of Magdalena de Burgos	1,586,856 *maravedíes*	Foundation of the Convent Santa Clara (Balmaseda)	Bizkaia
1667	Francisco de Arechederra	—	Major reconstruction of the Church of San Esteban de Irazogorria (Gordexola)	Bizkaia
1668	Martín Saenz de Magunaotalora	800 reales	Restoration of the chapel of San Marcos of the Church of San Pedro de Tabira (Durango)	Bizkaia
1670	Juan Martínez de Gallastegui	—	Foundation of the Hermitage of Santo Cristo de la Piedad (Lekeitio)	Bizkaia
1671	Manuel de Oquendo	—	Foundation of the Convent of the Madres Brigadas (Lasarte)	Gipuzkoa
1673	Andrés de Madariaga	20,000 ducats	Foundation of the Church of the Compañía de Jesús (Bergara)	Gipuzkoa
1675	Francisco Guerrezabal	—	Construction of the chapel of Sacramento and sacristy of the Church of Santa María de Uribarri (Durango)	Bizkaia

TABLE 2.12 *(continued)*

Year	Donor	Amount	Reason	Province
1679	Fra Gabriel de Gallastegui	30,000 reales	Construction of choir loft of the Church of Nuestra Señora de la Asunción (Markina)	Bizkaia
1680	Fra Juan de Luzuriaga	600 pesos	Hermitage of the Purísima Concepción de Ozaeta (Barrundia)	Araba
1682	Diego Fernández del Campo	48,000 reales	Reconstruction of the Church of San Román de Lejarza (Aiara)	Araba
1683	Sister Magdalena del Cristo e Idiaquez	—	Construction of the gateway of the Convent of Santa Clara (Azkoitia)	Gipuzkoa
1686	Diego de Berrio y Landazuri	300 ducats	Reconstruction of the Church of San Pedro de Lendoño de Arriba (Orduña)	Bizkaia
1718	Martín de Basarrate	—	Construction of the bell gable of the Church of Santa María (Amurrio)	Araba
1727	Manuel de Landeta	8,437 reales	Construction of the tower of the Church of San Vicente de Sodupe (Güeñes)	Bizkaia
1734	Compañía Guipuzcoana of Caracas	22,000 pesos	Construction of the Church of Santa María (Donostia)	Gipuzkoa
1738	Tomás Ruiz de Apodaca	—	Painting of the walls and ceiling of the baptistry of the Church of San Martín de Manurga (Zigoitia)	Araba
1743	Luis A. de Foronda y González de Lopidana	3,000 reales	Construction of the tower of the Church of the Navidad de Aztigieta (Gasteiz)	Araba
1743	Martín de Lardizabal y Elorza	—	Reconstruction of the crypts of the Church of Santa María (Segura)	Gipuzkoa
1743	Juan de Ibarrola y Castañiza	39,000 pesos	Reconstruction of the Church of Nuestra Señora of Untzaga (Ukondo)	Araba

Year	Donor	Amount	Reason	Province
1749	Pedro Negrete Sierra	25,000 pesos	Construction of the Church of San Bartolomé de Aldeacueva (Karrantza)	Bizkaia
1759	Agustín de Leiza y Latixera	45,000 pesos & 60,000 reales	Construction of the Church of San Martín (Andoain)	Gipuzkoa
1784	Ignacio de Elola y Beobide	—	Various repairs in the Church of San Esteban (Larraul)	Gipuzkoa
1794	Juan Antonio de Jauregui	20,000 reales	Reconstruction of the façade of the Convent of Nuestra Señora de los Remedios (Artziniega)	Araba
1803	Francisco González de Sarralde	10,000 reales	Addition of cornice and pillars of the Church of San Miguel Arcángel de Antezama (Gasteiz)	Araba
1814	Martín de Asteguieta	100,000 reales	Addition of portico, anteportico, portal, and sacristy of the Church of San Martín de Foronda (Gasteiz)	Araba

Source: Author's compilation based on J. M. González Cembellín, 1993, 75ff.

TABLE 2.13 *Sample of American Donations Destined for Social Welfare Buildings in the Basque Country, 1526–1929*

Year	Donor	Amount	Reason	Province
1526	Juan Sebastián Elcano	2 ducats	Hospital of Getaria	Gipuzkoa
1551	Juan Ibañez de Garagarza	—	Foundation of the Hospital of Azpeitia	Gipuzkoa
1595	Martín de Bañueta	—	Hospital of Amurrio	Araba
1609	Juan de Yría	—	Foundation of the Hospital for poor pilgrims of Alegria	Gipuzkoa
1613	Martín García Jauregui	—	Maintenance of the Hospitals of La Magdalena and San Juan (Segura)	Gipuzkoa
1644	Sancho de Urdanibia	2,000 ducats	Foundation of the Royal Hospital of Urdanibia (Irún)	Gipuzkoa
1670	Diego Ortíz de Cargacha	50 doubloons	Reconstruction of the Hospital of Gordexola	Bizkaia
1734	Ignacio de Guizaburuaga	30,000 reales	Extension of the Hospital of Berriz	Bizkaia
1774	Various Basque-American residents	800 ducats	Construction of the Hospital and House of Mercy of Tolosa	Gipuzkoa
1802	Hilario de Taramona	—	New Hospital of Balmaseda	Bizkaia
1803	Francisco de Areta	4,000 reales	Reconstruction of the Hospital of Eibar	Gipuzkoa
1839	José Martín Viador	400 pesos	Foundation of the Hospital for the poor of Urnieta	Gipuzkoa
1871	José Javier de Uribarren	—	Foundation of the Hospice of Lekeitio	Bizkaia
1885	Romualdo Chávarri y de La Herrera	—	Contribution to the construction of the Hospital-Asylum of Soslaño (Karrantza)	Bizkaia
1929	Domingo de Aguirre Pedro de Aguirre	—	Foundation of the Clinic San Juan de Dios of Santurtzi	Bizkaia

Source: Author's compilation based on J. M. González Cembellín, 1993, 75ff.

TABLE 2.14 *Sample of American Donations Destined for the Promotion of Schools in the Basque Country, 1609–1930*

Year	Donor	Amount	Reason	Province
1609	Juan de Yría	150 ducats	Foundation of the primary school of Alegria	Gipuzkoa
1627	Martín Araoz de Lazarraga, Juan Araoz de Lazarraga	5,300 ducats	Foundation of the School of Francisco de Borja, de la Compañía de Jesús (Oñati)	Gipuzkoa
1643	Juan de la Piedra Verástegui Magdalena de Burgos	—	Foundation of the Preceptory of Magdalena de Burgos Grammar (chair of Latin) in Balmaseda	Bizkaia
1650	Sebastián de Aristiguieta	—	Foundation of the elementary school of Donostia	Gipuzkoa
1682	Juan de Urdanegui Constanza de Luján	10,000 pesos	Foundation of the School of the Compañía de Jesús of Orduña (currently PP. Josefinos)	Bizkaia
1685	Domingo de Cueto	—	Construction of the elementary school of Turtzioz	Bizkaia
1749	Pedro Negrete Sierra	—	Construction of the school of Aldeacueva (Karrantza)	Bizkaia
1760	Francisco García de Rodayega	400 pesos	Foundation of the children's school of Santiago de Bárcena (Gordexola)	Bizkaia
1763	Juan de Ibarrola y Castañiza	4,600 pesos	Construction of the school and house of the master of Okendo (including endowment for master)	Araba
1764	Francisco Martínez de Lejarza	—	Foundation of the school of Güeñes	Bizkaia
1770	Juan de Castañiza y Larrea	—	Foundation of secondary and Latin school (Gordexola)	Bizkaia

TABLE 2.14 *(continued)*

Year	Donor	Amount	Reason	Province
1846	José de Negrete y Falla	—	Construction of the School of San Esteban (Karrantza)	Bizkaia
1862	José Javier de Uribarren	—	Foundation of the Official Nautical School (Lekeitio)	Bizkaia
1869	José Luis Abaroa José Vicente de Labeaga	—	Foundation of the Schools of Labeaga (Urretxu)	Gipuzkoa
1870	Vicente de Zabala	—	Construction of the primary school of Gordexola	Bizkaia
1880	Francisco Antonio Olaguibel	—	Foundation of the schools for poor children of Portugalete	Bizkaia
1887	Pio Bermejillo e Ibarra Angeles Bermejillo	125,000 pesetas	Municipal schools of Balmaseda	Bizkaia
1890	Various Basque settlers	—	Foundation of the National School of Aldeacueva (Karrantza)	Bizkaia
1911	Domingo Mª Aquilino Iturbe	75,000 pesetas	Patronage of the Catholic Schools of Niños del Sagrado Corazón de Jesús (Elgeta)	Gipuzkoa
1912	Eustaquio Balenzategui	40,000 pesetas	Foundation of the Schools of Gabiria (Bergara)	Gipuzkoa
1920	Martín de Mendía y Conde	—	Construction and foundation of the School of Commerce and Academy of Design of Balmaseda	Bizkaia
1929	José Antonio de Guisasola	—	Schools of Deba	Gipuzkoa
1930	José Manuel de Ostolaza	—	Foundation of the school and library of the emigrant of Deba	Gipuzkoa

Source: Author's compilation based on J. M. González Cembellín, 1993, 75ff.

TABLE 2.15 *Sample of American Donations Destined for Infrastructure and Services in the Basque Country, 1638–1892*

Year	Donor	Amount	Reason	Province
1638	Antonio de San Martín y Zamudio, Miguel de Oxirando	400 ducats	Acquisition of the staff of the mayorship of Gordexola	Bizkaia
1675	Simón de la Puente	—	Reconstruction of the Tower of La Puente (Sodupe)	Bizkaia
1714	Francisco de Aguirre y Gomendio	2,000 pesos	Construction of the levee of Carraspio (Lekeitio)	Bizkaia
1800	Manuel de Agote y Bonechea	—	Monument to Juan Sebastián Elcano (Getaria)	Gipuzkoa
1812	Gabriel Patricio Yermo	25,000 duros	Purchase of shoes for the soldiers of Gordexola who fought in the War of Independence	Bizkaia
1814	Martín de Asteguieta	—	Construction of the mill of the parish of San Martín de Foronda (Vitoria-Gasteiz)	Araba
1836	Various Indian emigrants Angeles Bermejillo	3,415 pesos	Help destined to the liberals of Bilbao during the First Carlist War	Bizkaia
1857	José Javier de Uribarren	—	Bringing of water from Tracamai and construction of various fountains (Lekeitio)	Bizkaia
1864	Simón de Labayen Francisco de Labayen	—	Bringing of water to Albiztur	Gipuzkoa
1874	Miguel de Elosegui	—	Repair of the road through Lazkao toward Beasain-Navarre	Gipuzkoa
1880	Various Basque-American emigrants	—	Reform and embellishment of the plaza of San Severino (Balmaseda)	Bizkaia
1880	Romualdo Chávarri y de La Herrera	—	Road improvement Biañez-El Callejo-Paúles (Karrantza)	Bizkaia

TABLE 2.15 *(continued)*

Year	Donor	Amount	Reason	Province
1880	Romualdo Chávarri y de La Herrera	1,000,000 pesetas	Donation to the construction company of the Bilbao-Balmaseda railway for its extension to Karrantza	Bizkaia
1880	Romualdo Chávarri y de La Herrera	—	Construction of the cemetery of Biañez (Karrantza)	Bizkaia
1885	Romualdo Chávarri y de La Herrera	—	Construction of fountain-washing place-drinking trough of Biañez and bringing of corresponding water (Karrantza)	Bizkaia
1890	Manuel Calvo y Aguirre	—	Construction of Gran Hotel of Portugalete	Bizkaia
1890	Basque-Spanish Association of Buenos Aires	5,000 pesetas	Monument to José Mª de Iparraguirre (Urretxu)	Gipuzkoa
1892	Marcos Arena Bermejillo	—	Foundation of the hat factory La Encartada (Balmaseda)	Bizkaia

Source: Author's compilation based on J. M. González Cembellín, 1993, 75ff.

TABLE 2.16 *Sample of American Donations Destined As Furnishings in the Basque Country, 1591–1850*

Year	Donor	Amount	Reason	Province
1591	Clemente Hurtado de Monreal	500 pesos	Adornment of the parish Church of San Martín de Monreal	Navarre
1620	Francisco de Sorarte	—	Canadian kayak given as a votive offering to the Church of Santa María de Itziar (Deba)	Gipuzkoa
1624	Pedro de Otalora	—	Religious furnishing and silver lamp valued at 200 pesos donated to the Church of Olkotz	Navarre
1626	Domingo de Arrieta	—	Silver lamps for the Church of Santa Mª de Begoña (Bilbao)	Bizkaia
1626	Juan Pérez de Irazábal	—	Holy Christ donated to the Church of San Pedro (Bergara)	Gipuzkoa
1631	Antonio Oquendo	—	Royal standard, flag won from the Dutch, and bullet that struck the captainship of Oquendo during the Battle of Pernambuco, donated to the Sanctuary of Nuestra Señora de Arantzazu, along with a silver lamp (Oñati)	Gipuzkoa
1645	Pedro de Medrano María de Altamirano Angeles Bermejillo	100 pesos	Damascene frontals for the main and side altars of the Sanctuary of Nuestra Señora de los Angeles of Toloño (Bastida)	Araba
1653	Manuel de Arroniz	—	Silver lamp and 200 pesos donated to the Hermitage of La Blanca (Lerín)	Navarre
1675	Juan de Cenoz Francisco de Labayen	—	Silver half-moon willed to the chapel of the Virgen del Camino of the Cathedral of Pamplona	Navarre

TABLE 2.16 *(continued)*

Year	Donor	Amount	Reason	Province
1679	Miguel Martínez de Aranibar	—	Silver throne donated to the parish of Santa María de la Asunción y del Manzano (Hondarribia). Stolen by French troops in 1794.	Gipuzkoa
1687	Martín de Urra	—	Three silver lamps, a plate, two small silver jars and two gilded silver boxes for the Virgin, donated to the parish Church of Muniain	Navarre
1690	José Jauregui	—	Silver liturgical piece donated to the Church of San Pedro (Puente la Reina)	Navarre
1691	Juan de Sobera y Zebericha	—	Silver monstrance gilded and enameled with 31 standards and 1.5 ounces given to the Church of San Anton (Bilbao)	Bizkaia
1692	José Royo Alonso	—	Canvas of the Virgin of Guadalupe donated to the Basilica of Portal (Villafranca)	Navarre
1692	Diego García de Olloqui y Polo	—	Linen of the Virgin of Guadalupe donated to the Basilica of Portal (Villafranca)	Navarre
1694	Agustín de Herrado	—	Main lamp of the Sanctuary of the Virgin of Encina (Artziniega)	Araba
1698	Bernabé Ochoa de Chinchetru y López de Iazarraga	—	3,000 gold *panes* for gilding the main retable, a silver lamp, expensive material for the frontal of the retable of the Virgen de la Esclavitud, image of the Inmaculada, gold and silver cloth for a vestment of the Virgin, and	Araba

Year	Donor	Amount	Reason	Province
1698	José Cartagena y Ripa	—	299,200 *maravedíes* donated to the Church of Santa María (Agurain) Silver monstrance of the Virgen de Puy (Estella)	Navarre
1704	Martín de Esnoz	400 pesos	Adornment of the hermitage of San Miguel de Miravalles (Huarte)	Navarre
1712	José Martínez de Ordoñana	—	Silver lamp of 11.5 pounds donated to the Church of San Pedro Apóstol (Gasteiz)	Araba
1725	Baltasar de Murga	—	Altar service (chalice, plate, pitchers, and bells) of the Sanctuary of the Virgen Blanca (Aiara)	Araba
1738	Tomás Ruiz de Apodaca	—	Baptistry grate with picture of Saint John the Baptist and Roman missal donated to the Church of San Martín of Manurga (Zigoitia)	Araba
1741	Ignacio de Segurola José Ignacio de Arzadun	244 escudos	Gilding of main retable of the Church of San Sebastián of Soreasu (Azkoitia)	Gipuzkoa
1741	Guipúzcoana Company of Caracas	4,000 pesos	Statue of San Ignacio de Loyola donated to the Sanctuary of Loyola (Azpeitia)	Gipuzkoa
1746	Juan de Azcarazo	—	Image of the Virgen de la Soledad donated to the Church of San Juan Bautista (Arrasate)	Gipuzkoa
1758	Gregorio de Elejalde	—	Chalice, paten, pitchers, plate, and bell of gilded silver (Arratzu)	Araba
1770	Juan de Castañiza	—	Gilding of retable of Nuestra Señora de Loreto of the Church of San Juan de Molinar (Gordexola)	Bizkaia

TABLE 2.16 *(continued)*

Year	Donor	Amount	Reason	Province
1772	Ambrosio de Meabe	—	Canvas of the Virgen de Guadalupe with Fra Juan de Zumárraga at her feet donated to the Church of Santa María of Uribarri (Durango). Destroyed in 1937 during a bombing.	Bizkaia
1774	Guipúzcoana Company of Caracas	—	Gold main retable of the Church of Santa María (Donostia)	Gipuzkoa
1775	Francisco Antonio de Echevarri	—	Sepulchral stone in the Church of Santa María of Gasteiz	Araba
1776	Miguel de Goiti Domingo de Berrio	5,000 reales	Main retable of the Church of Santa María of Delika (Amurrio)	Araba
1776	Gabriel de Zabala	—	Rosary strung on gold for the Baby Jesus of the altar of Nuestra Señora Del Rosario donated to the Colegiata de Santa María de Zearrotza (Markina)	Bizkaia
1776	Fra Francisco Díaz de Durana	—	Set of ornaments embroidered in gold on silk donated to the Church of San Esteban Protomártir de Durana (Arratzu)	Araba
1780	Antonio Bassoco	500 pesos	Clock for the Church of San Juan de Molinar (Gordexola)	Bizkaia
1790	Mateo de la Cuadra y Ranero	—	Silver crown with jewels for the image of the Virgin donated to the Church of Santa María de Soscaño (Karrantza)	Bizkaia
1794	Lorenzo de Angulo y Guardamino	4,800 reales	Chalice, monstrance, ciborium, and censer	Bizkaia

Year	Donor	Amount	Reason	Province
1800	Manuel Agote y Bonechea	—	Silver chalice with paten and spoon, plate, pitchers, and bell donated to the Sanctuary of Nuestra Señora de Arrate (Eibar)	Gipuzkoa
1803	Francisco Acha Albizuri	—	Chalice with paten and spoon, vinegar bottles and silver handbell donated to the Sanctuary of Señora de Arrate (Eibar)	Gipuzkoa
1850	Lorenzo Carrera	—	Portrait of Alonso de Ercilla donated to the Casa Consistorial of Bermeo	Bizkaia

Source: Author's compilation based on J. M. González Cembellín, 1993, 75ff.

TABLE 2.17 *Sample of American Donations Destined for Pious and Charitable Purposes in the Basque Country and Navarre, 1553–1901*

Year	Donor	Amount	Reason	Province
1553	Nicolás Sáez de Elola	100 ducats/yr.	Endowment of the chair of grammar and house for its preceptor	Gipuzkoa
1568	Diego de Orúe	—	One hundred masses in the Church of Santa María of Delika (Amurrio) for the conversion of the natives of the Indies	Araba
1586	Mencia Ortíz de Urbina	—	Chaplaincy of a daily mass in the Convent of San Francisco of Orduña	Bizkaia
1587	Juan de Mondragón y Ascarretazabal	—	Endowment for poor orphan girls	Gipuzkoa
1594	Juan Pérez de Mendeja	3,000 pesos	Endowment to send two or three children from the town of Bermeo to Salamanca to study	Bizkaia
1594	Fra Pascual Fernández	20 ducats	Annuity for the Hospital of Larraga and endowment for the weddings of the poor girls of this town	Navarre
1595	Gonzalo Remirez de Acedo	3,000 ducats	Creation of a coffer for mercy and endowment to support poor local girls (Tafalla)	Navarre
1606	Pedro de Aguirre y Cortázar	1,550 ducats/yr.	Six chaplaincies (each one with one mass prayed by day and another sung on Sundays and holidays) in the Hospital of the Sanctuary of the Virgin of Estibalitz (Gasteiz)	Araba
1607	Martín de Abaurrea	2,000 ducats	Endowment for two local girls each year, creation of three chairs in art, two in theology, and one master of students in the Convent of Santiago (Pamplona)	Navarre

Year	Donor	Amount	Reason	Province
1608	Pedro Echalaz	4,500 pesos	Annuity for the poor of the Hospital of Pamplona and to buy wheat and make bread for the poor	Navarre
1609	Juan de Yría	200 ducats/yr.	Annuity for the costs of two Franciscan students—Gipuzkoan and preferably from Alegria—in the school of San Buenaventura of Sevilla	Gipuzkoa
1613	Martín García Jaúregui	—	Endowment for poor orphan girls (Segura)	Gipuzkoa
1627	Andrés López de Arcaya	16,200 pesos	Endowment for an orphan girl, bank of mercy for the poor, and endowment for the Hospital of Mendixur (Barrundia)	Araba
1635	Juan de Urrutia	4,000 pesos	Chaplaincy of four masses said per week and one sung the day of Saint John the Baptist in the Church of Santa María (Tolosa)	Gipuzkoa
1635	Martín de Larrasoaña	1,000 pesos	Annuity for the poor of the parishes, prisons, and foundlings of Pamplona	Navarre
1639	Andrés de Aguirre	4,000 reales	Annuity for the wax used during the fiestas of Nuestra Señora in the Basilica of Santa María of Begoña (Bilbao)	Bizkaia
1640	Francisco de Lazcano y Ugarte	2,737 ducats	Endowment for poor girls from Baranbio (Amurrio)	Araba
1643	Juan de la Piedra Verástegui Magdalena de Burgos	—	Endowment for poor girls that professed in the Convent of the Clarisas	Bizkaia

TABLE 2.17 *(continued)*

Year	Donor	Amount	Reason	Province
1657	Domingo Balduz	8,000 reales	Endowment enabling two poor girls to get married each year from his lineage or others from the town of Andosilla	Navarre
1666	Andrés de Achegoyen	809 pesos	Endowment for girls and attention to the poor of the Hospital of San Lázaro (Orduña)	Bizkaia
1667	Miguel de Arazola	200,000 reales	Foundation of a *capellanía*, endowment for girls, salary for four masters (primary school, grammar, philosophy, and moral) and creation of a coffer for mercy of 6,000 *arrobas* of wheat in Tafalla	Navarre
1674	Martín de Alzate	8,000 ducats	Endowment for six poor related girls (Vera de Bidasoa)	Navarre
1685	Mateo Pérez de Garayo / Diego Pérez de Garayo	300 pesos/yr.	Dowry for three girls from the family to marry or join the church, or in their lack, girls from Salvatierra, alms for the local hospitals and hospice and alms for redemption of captives (Agurain)	Araba
1690	Juan de Urrutía Retes	1,000 pesos	Endowment for a primary school master in Llanteno (Aiara)	Araba
1695	Diego de Miquelarena	4,000 pesos	Annuity for two natives of Ezcurra to study for priesthood	Navarre
1712	Francisco de Echezarreta	—	Endowment for the maintenance of the children's school and the study of arts and theology of the Convent of San Agustín (Durango)	Bizkaia

Appendix 2

Year	Donor	Amount	Reason	Province
1713	Juan de Justiz	4,000 pesos	Chaplaincy created in Hondarribia	Gipuzkoa
1724	Francisco de Miñaur Bartolomé de Miñaur	12,900 reales	Chaplaincy of one hundred yearly masses in the Sanctuary of the Virgen de la Encina (Artziniega)	Araba
1743	Juan de Ibarrola y Castañiza	1,000 pesos	Endowment for the lighting of the Sacrament in the Church of Nuestra Señora of Untzaga (Okondo)	Araba
1750	Sebastián de Isusi	—	Endowment for free instruction of Latin grammar in Laudio	Araba
1774	José Martín de Garmendia	—	Endowment for a preceptor of grammar and a children's master (Ordizia)	Gipuzkoa
1779	Juan de Castaños y Perón	1,000 reales	In acknowledgment of his being named mayor of the town of Güeñes, to invite his fellow townspeople to a drink	Bizkaia
1780	Francisco de Echevarri y Ugarte	—	Endowment for the worship of Nuestra Señora de Guadalupe in the Cathedral of Santa María of Gasteiz	Araba
1780	Juan Ignacio Obiaga	800 pesos	Endowment for two children from the town of Soraluze to study theology, law, or canons	Gipuzkoa
1848	Juan José Peña	620,000 reales	Help to the poor of Irun	Gipuzkoa
1887	Romualdo Chávarri y de La Herrera	100,000 pesetas	Creation of the Board of Trustees for the schools of Biañez responsible for providing free primary education to 120 children of Karrantza	Bizkaia

TABLE 2.17 *(continued)*

Year	Donor	Amount	Reason	Province
1892	Romualdo Chávarri y de La Herrera	75,000 pesetas	Chaplaincy of 2,000 yearly masses and the saying of ten Rosaries and one Our Father before and after each mass held in the Church of San Andrés of Biañez (Karrantza)	Bizkaia
1901	Manuel Calvo y Aguirre	—	Endowment for distributing food among the needy of Portugalete	Bizkaia

Source: Author's compilation based on J. M. González Cembellín, 1993, 75ff.

TABLE 2.18 *Noble Descent and Institutional Activity of Central American Basques, First Generation*

Name	Post in Chapter	Year
Juan José González Batres Álvarez de Toledo	Alderman	1688
	Alcalde segundo	1717–18
	Alcalde primero	1735
	Police chief	1742
	Alcalde primero	1743
José Mariano Arribillaga	*Alcalde segundo*	1771
	Alcalde primero	1785
Manuel González Batres Arribillaga	*Alcalde segundo*	1760
	Alcalde primero	1761
José González Batres Arribillaga	*Alcalde segundo*	1769
	Alcalde primero	1780
Juan Fermín de Aycinena	Chapter member	1757
	Alcalde segundo	1759
	Retired alderman	1780
	Alcalde primero	1784
Vicente Aycinena Carrillo	Chapter member	1768
	Alcalde segundo	1794
José Aycinena Carrillo	Chapter member	1792
	Alcalde segundo	1803
	Councilman of the Indies	1810
Pedro José Beltranena Aycinena	*Alcalde segundo*	1783
	Alderman	
Juan Bautista Marticorena	*Alcalde segundo*	1797
	Alcalde primero	1801
	Alcalde primero	1805
Gregorio Urruela	*Alcalde segundo*	1780
	Alcalde primero	1808
J. Tomás Micheo Barreneche	*Alcalde ordinario*	1766
	Alderman-for-life	1771
Pedro Micheo Barreneche	*Alcalde ordinario*	1778
Ventura Delgado de Nájera Mencos	*Alcalde ordinario*	1772
	Alcalde ordinario	1793
Pedro de Ariza Rubio	Local alderman	1790–91
	Alcalde segundo	1802

Source: T. García Giráldez, 1996, 334.

TABLE 2.19 *Noble Lineage and Institutional Activity of Central American Basques, Second Generation*

	Profession	Activity	Post
Alejandro Aycinena y Carrillo	Lawyer	Merchant	Councillor of the Indies / Farm exporter
Pedro Aycinena Piñol	Lawyer	—	Minister of foreign relations / Interim president of the Republic
Miguel Nájera Batres	—	Merchant	Assessor of Popayán
José Llano Nájera	Gentleman	Merchant	Supplementary deputy in the coast guard of the Cortes of Cádiz
Manuel Llano Nájera	Artillery colonel	Merchant	Deputy in the Cortes of Cádiz (1810–13) / Assessor of the Intendancy of León
Gregorio Beltranena Llano	—	—	Vice president of the Republic of Central America / Leader of the Republic in 1821
Pedro Nájera Barrutia	—	—	Accountant of the Royal Bank of Guatemala
Mariano Micheo Arzú	Lawyer, writer	—	—
Cayetano Batres Díaz del Castillo	Lawyer, engineer, magistrate	—	Deputy
Antonio Batres Jauregui	Politician, diplomat, historian, intellectual	—	—
Manuel Arzú Batres	Colonel	—	Administrator of Treasury of Quezaltenango and Antigua
Juan Arzú Batres	Engineer, writer, journalist	—	—
Manuel Matheu Sinibaldi	Plantation owner	Coffee grower	President of the Chamber of Representatives

	Profession	Activity	Post
Antonio Aguirre	Banker	Finances: Bank of the West and Mercantile Farming	—
Miguel González Saravia	General, lawyer	—	Intendant of Nicaragua

Source: T. García Giráldez, 1996, 337.

TABLE 2.20 *Occupations of Basques in Puerto Rico in the 19th Century*

Occupation	No.
Administrators	1
Apprentices	2
Bakers	2
Blacksmiths	1
Bleeders	1
Bricklayers and quarriers	4
Candy makers	3
Carpenters and cabinetmakers	16
Cart manufacturers	1
Ceramists	1
Cigar dealers	1
Clerics	40
Commercial clerks and draftees	119
Contractors	2
Convicts	3
Day laborers	4
Doctors	1
Farmers, *hacendados*, peasants	53
Guards	1
Hardware and other merchants	145
Industrialists	10
Journalists	2
Lawyers	31
Machinists	3
Majordomos of haciendas	15
Mechanics	1
Neighborhood judges and commissaries	2
Natural healers	1
Notaries	1
Public accountants	1
Public employees, war lieutenants, public officials, road foremen, nonworking individuals	25
Professors	6
Proprietors	13
Sailors, pilots, cabin boys, sea captains	34
Soldiers: members of battalions and regiments, army doctors and	154

Occupation	No.
musicians, captains of: guard, civil guard, artillery, and fortification engineers, and governors and captains general	
Scribes	4
Speculators	1
Stokers	1
Sugar manufacturers	2
Tanners and breeders	4
Telegraphers	2
Waiters	1
Writers	1
No profession given	344
Total	1,060

Source: E. Cifre de Loubriel, 1996, 39.

TABLE 2.21 *Basque Workers, Barracas al Norte, 1855 (Buenos Aires)*

Occupation	No.
Blacksmith	4
Bricklayer	1
Butcher	1
Carpenter	26
Cartmaker	6
Clerk	7
Clothes presser	1
Cook	17
Cooper	1
Day laborer	24
Ditch digger	1
Estate farmer	3
Harness maker	1
Meat-salting peon	19
Ovenman	2
Peon	18
Peasant	4
Proprietor	2
Sandalmaker	1
Seamstress	2
Servant	20
Shoemaker	1
Tallow maker	4
Tinsmith	2
Washerwoman	6
Warehouse peon	18

Source: Census forms from Barracas al Norte, Municipal Census of Buenos Aires, 1855.

TABLE 2.22 *Basque Workers,
Barracas al Norte, 1869
(Buenos Aires)*

Occupation	No.
Artisan	1
Baker	2
Barber	1
Blacksmith	6
Bricklayer	7
Broker	1
Butcher	7
Candy maker	2
Carpenter	27
Cart maker	13
Clerk	13
Clothes presser	4
Cook	19
Cooper	5
Dairyman	1
Day laborer	76
Domestic	5
Estanciero	1
Estate farmer	2
Estate farm peon	8
Farmer	1
Financier	1
Foreman	5
Gardener	1
Harness maker	1
Lottery ticket vendor	2
Mattress salesman	1
Meat-salting peon	94
Merchant	28
Musician	1
Oven man	13
Oven peon	2
Pastry chef	1
Patrolman	1
Peon	89
Railroad worker	3
Sailor	4
Sandal maker	7

TABLE 2.22 *(continued)*

Occupation	No.
Sawyer	1
Seamstress	19
Servant	29
Shoemaker	7
Tailor	2
Tanner	6
Teacher	2
Tinsmith	3
Warehouse peon	8
Washerwoman	16
Wool dealer	1

Source: Census forms from Barracas al Norte, First National Census, 1869.

TABLE 2.23 *Basque Emigrants Indebted for Their Passage, Uruguay*

Name	Age	Civil Status	Nationality	Arrival Date	Ship	Debts of Passage
Francisco Abanz	28	Married	Spanish	1842	Corvette *Gabriela*	Debt of 160 *patacones* payable in one year of service to José R. Picabea
Ignacio Agotz	27	Single	Spanish	1842	Corvette *Gabriela*	Debt of 80 *patacones* payable in one year of service to José R. Picabea
Celestino Aguirrea	16	Single	Spanish	1842	Corvette *Gabriela*	Debt of 80 *patacones* payable in one year of service to José R. Picabea
José Alberdi	23	Single	Spanish	1842	Paylebot *Bordelais*	Debt of 80 *patacones* payable in one year of service to José R. Picabea
Joaquín Albiztu	36	Married	Spanish	1842	Paylebot *Bordelais*	Debt of 80 *patacones* payable in one year of service to José R. Picabea
Tomás Amunarris	26	Single	Spanish	1842	Corvette *Gabriela*	Debt of 80 *patacones* payable in one year of service to José R. Picabea
Niceto Antelmo	30	Married	Spanish	1842	Corvette *Gabriela*	Debt of 80 *patacones* payable in one year of service to José R. Picabea
Miguel Arámburu	22	Single	Spanish	1842	Corvette *Gabriela*	Debt of 110 *patacones* payable in one year of service to José R. Picabea
Ramón Arámburu	36	Married	Spanish	1842	Brig *Tres Hermanos*	Debt of 70 *patacones* payable in six months of service to Manuel Cifuentes
Antonio de Aranzadi	20	Single	Spanish	1842	Frigate *Cyrus*	Debt of 70 *patacones* payable in one year of service to Miguel Oyenard
Antonio Arbeloa	23	Single	Spanish	1842	Paylebot *Bordelais*	Debt of 80 *patacones* payable in one year of service to Arizabalo and Puyos

TABLE 2.23 (continued)

Name	Age	Civil Status	Nationality	Arrival Date	Ship	Debts of Passage
Benito Arbulo	22	Single	Spanish	1842	Paylebot *Bordelais*	Debt of 80 *patacones* payable in one year of service to Arizabalo and Puyos
Francisco Arbune	28	Single	Spanish	1842	Paylebot *Bordelais*	Debt of 80 *patacones* payable in one year of service to Arizabalo and Puyos
Francisco Arozarena	44	Married	Spanish	1842	Brig *Tres Hermanos*	Debt of 80 *patacones* payable in six months of service to Manuel Cifuentes
Francisco Arrate	20	Single	Spanish	1842	Corvette *Gabriela*	Debt of 80 *patacones* payable in one year of service to José R. Picabea
Juan Ascue	31	Single	Spanish	1842	Corvette *Gabriela*	Debt of 80 *patacones* payable in one year of service to José R. Picabea
Juan Becheveste	24	Single	Spanish	1842	Corvette *Gabriela*	Debt of 80 *patacones* payable in one year of service to José R. Picabea
Miguel Belascuain	23	—	Spanish	1842	Corvette *Gabriela*	Debt of 80 *patacones* payable in one year of service to José R. Picabea
Simón Berrospi	18	Single	Spanish	1842	Corvette *Gabriela*	Debt of 80 *patacones* payable in one year of service to José R. Picabea
Juan Celayeta	20	Single	Basque/Spanish	1842	Corvette *Gabriela*	Debt of 80 *patacones* payable in one year of service to José R. Picabea
José M. Echarra	30	Married	Spanish	1842	Corvette *Gabriela*	Debt of 80 *patacones* payable in one year of service to José R. Picabea
Cristóbal Echarri	21	Single	Spanish	1842	Corvette *Gabriela*	Debt of 80 *patacones* payable in one year of service to José R. Picabea

Name	Age	Status	Nationality	Year	Ship	Notes
Tomás Echave	41	Married	Spanish	1842	Corvette *Gabriela*	Debt of 80 *patacones* payable in one year of service to José R. Picabea
Francisco Elizalde	34	Married	Spanish	1842	Corvette *Gabriela*	Debt of 80 *patacones* payable in one year of service to José R. Picabea
Fernando Esuain	16	Single	Spanish	1842	Corvette *Gabriela*	Debt of 80 *patacones* payable in one year of service to José R. Picabea
Ceferino Esuain	18	Single	Spanish	1842	Corvette *Gabriela*	Debt of 80 *patacones* payable in one year of service to José R. Picabea
José B. Ezual	24	Single	Spanish	1842	Corvette *Gabriela*	Debt of 80 *patacones* payable in one year of service to José R. Picabea
Miguel Ferreiro	24	Married	Basque/Spanish	1842	Corvette *Gabriela*	Debt of 80 *patacones* payable in one year of service to José R. Picabea
Pantaleón Gainza	34	Single	Spanish	1842	Brig *Tres Hermanos*	Debt of 70 *patacones* payable in six months of service to José R. Picabea
Eugenio Gardoy	20	Single	Spanish	1842	Corvette *Gabriela*	Debt of 80 *patacones* payable in one year of service to José R. Picabea
Domingo Gastelumendi	18	Single	Spanish	1842	Corvette *Gabriela*	Debt of 80 *patacones* payable in one year of service to José R. Picabea
Tiburcio Gimenez	23	Married	Basque/Spanish	1842	Corvette *Gabriela*	Debt of 185 *patacones* payable in one year of service to José R. Picabea
José Goenaga	28	Married	Spanish	1842	Frigate *Marsellesa*	Debt of 80 *patacones* payable in one year of service to Messrs. Rivas brothers
Eugenio Goenaga	18	Single	Spanish	1842	Corvette *Gabriela*	Debt of 80 *patacones* payable in one year of service to José R. Picabea
José M. Gurmendi	35	Single	Spanish	1842	Corvette *Gabriela*	Debt of 80 *patacones* payable in one year of service to José R. Picabea

TABLE 2.23 (continued)

Name	Age	Civil Status	Nationality	Arrival Date	Ship	Debts of Passage
José I. Gurruchaga	24	Single	Spanish	1842	Corvette *Gabriela*	Debt of 80 *patacones* payable in one year of service to José R. Picabea
Manuel Izurco	36	Married	Spanish	1842	Brig *Tres Hermanos*	Debt of 70 *patacones* payable in one year of service to Manuel Cifuentes
Antonio Jauregui	18	Single	Spanish	1842	Corvette *Gabriela*	Debt of 68 *patacones* payable in one year of service to José R. Picabea
Cosme Labayen	31	Single	Navarrese	1842	Bark *Fénix*	Debt of 80 *patacones* payable in one year of service to Messrs. Moral and Zubillaga
José Laredo	20	Single	Basque/Spanish	1842	Corvette *Gabriela*	Debt of 85 *patacones* payable in one year of service to José R. Picabea
Juan A. Labayen	24	Single	Spanish	1842	Corvette *Gabriela*	Debt of 80 *patacones* payable in one year of service to José R. Picabea
José Lopetegui	18	Single	Spanish	1842	Corvette *Gabriela*	Debt of 80 *patacones* payable in one year of service to José R. Picabea
Miguel Marticorena	20	Single	Spanish	1842	Corvette *Gabriela*	Debt of 80 *patacones* payable in one year of service to José R. Picabea
Antonio Mentiozal	21	Single	—	1842	Corvette *Gabriela*	Debt of 120 *patacones* payable in one year of service to José R. Picabea
Juan Múgica	20	Single	Basque/Spanish	1842	Corvette *Gabriela*	Debt of 80 *patacones* payable in one year of service to José R. Picabea
José León Múgica	21	Single	Spanish	1842	Corvette *Gabriela*	Debt of 80 *patacones* payable in one year of service to José R. Picabea

Name	Age	Status	Nationality	Year	Ship	Debt
Javier Múgica	34	Married	Spanish	1842	Corvette *Gabriela*	Debt of 80 *patacones* payable in one year of service to Arizabalo and Puyos
Francisco Noain	25	Single	Navarrese	1842	Bark *Fénix*	Debt of 80 *patacones* payable in one year of service to Messrs. Moral and Zubillaga
Pedro Noboa	31	Single	Basque	1842	Corvette *Gabriela*	Debt of 110 *patacones* payable in one year of service to Diego Noboa
Antonio Ordoqui	24	Single	Navarrese	1842	*Corvette Gabriela*	Debt of 80 *patacones* payable in one year of service to José R. Picabea
Antonio Olazabal	22	Single	Spanish	1842	Corvette *Gabriela*	Debt of 80 *patacones* payable in one year of service to José R. Picabea
Manuel Sarrinaga	21	Single	Basque/Spanish	1842	Paylebot *Bordelais*	Debt of 70 *patacones* payable in one year of service to Bernardo de Olartecoechea
Antonio Satrústegui	23	Single	Spanish	1842	Corvette *Gabriela*	Debt of 80 *patacones* payable in one year of service to José R. Picabea
Ramón Sorozabal	23	Single	Spanish	1842	Corvette *Gabriela*	Debt of 80 *patacones* payable in one year of service to José R. Picabea
Joaquín Tellechea	75	Married	Spanish	1842	Corvette *Gabriela*	Debt of 80 *patacones* payable in one year of service to José R. Picabea
Manuel Urbieta	36	Married	Spanish	1842	Paylebot *Bordelais*	Debt of 150 *patacones* payable in one year of service to Arizabalo and Puyos
Juan F. Urbieta	15	Single	Spanish	1842	Paylebot *Bordelais*	Debt of 155 *patacones* payable in one year of service to Arizabalo and Puyos
Jorge Urbieta	14	Single	Spanish	1842	Paylebot *Bordelais*	Debt of 155 *patacones* payable in one year of service to Arizabalo and Puyos
Ramón Urbieta	13	Single	Spanish	1842	Paylebot *Bordelais*	Debt of 155 *patacones* payable in one year of service to Arizabalo and Puyos

TABLE 2.23 (continued)

Name	Age	Civil Status	Nationality	Arrival Date	Ship	Debts of Passage
Federico Urrutia	21	Single	Spanish	1842	Corvette *Gabriela*	Debt of 112 *patacones* payable in one year of service to José R. Picabea
José A. Urtiaga	—	Single	Basque/Spanish	1842	Bark *Fénix*	Debt of 80 *patacones* payable in one year of service to Messrs. Rivas brothers
Bautista Villabona	21	Single	Navarrese	1842	Bark *Fénix*	Debt of 80 *patacones* payable in one year of service to Messrs. Moral and Zubillaga
Pablo Ybarra	30	Single	—	1842	Bark *Fénix*	Debt of 80 *patacones* payable in one year of service to Messrs. Moral and Zubillaga
José M. Zabaleta	22	Single	Spanish	1842	Frigate *Liria*	Debt of 80 *patacones* payable in one year of service to Messrs. Moral and Zubillaga
Juan Zapiain	25	Married	Spanish	1842	Corvette *Gabriela*	Debt of 80 *patacones* payable in one year of service to José R. Picabea
Juan F. Zeizan	26	Single	Spanish	1842	Corvette *Gabriela*	Debt of 80 *patacones* payable in one year of service to José R. Picabea
Tomás Zubillaga	20	Single	Spanish	1842	Frigate *Liria*	Debt of 80 *patacones* payable in one year of service to Messrs. Moral and Zubillaga

Source: Compiled by the author, based on data in AGN, Montevideo, Montevideo Police Books, 1840–1842.

Notes

PREFACE

1. Translator's note: Basque place-names provide perhaps the most formidable translation challenge, as they are frequently the point of political contention and/or geographic vagueness. Pains have been taken to respect political divisions through the use of terms in the Basque language of Euskara to refer to places within the three-province Basque Autonomous Community comprising Araba, Bizkaia, and Gipuzkoa; Spanish names in Navarre; and French names in Iparralde—aside from this latter term itself, which lacks an exact juridico-administrative referent in French. Of course, a general exception is made for the term "the Basque Country," as it is glossable in English. Indeed, the very term "Basque" is itself polyvalent as both a geographic and cultural reality, a fact that justifiably permits using it to refer to either the three-province autonomous community—and as a gloss for the historically related Spanish term *vascongado/as*— to the four provinces juridically within Spain, or to the totality of the seven provinces. The reproduction of such vagueness is itself unavoidable, as it is woven into the fabric of both the language and the political forms of Basque existence.

CHAPTER 1. THE BASQUE COUNTRY AT THE TIME OF COLUMBUS

1. To learn about the socioeconomic and political situation of the Basque Country at the beginning of the modern era, see Wm. A. Douglass and J. Bilbao, *Amerikanuak: Basques in the New World* (Reno, 1975), 49–67; E. Ruiz de Azúa, *Vascongadas y América* (Madrid, 1992), 17–44; J. Aguirreazkuenaga, ed., *Gran atlas histórico del mundo vasco* (Bilbao, 1994), 113–28; F. García de Cortázar and J. M. Lorenzo Espinosa, *Historia del País Vasco. De los orígenes a nuestros días* (San Sebastián, 1988), 47–64.

2. Although the Basque regions remained subject to the Crown of Castile at the end of the fifteenth century, Castilian royal dominion over the Basque Country continued being indirect. In effect, in contrast to other peninsular regions, the Basques preserved a sufficient level of autonomy to possess political power in their dealings with the Castilian monarchy. In other words, the Basques were not citizens of just any region of Castile; they were citizens of territories that had accepted the Castilian Crown as their sovereign. Although subtle, this is a significant difference. It means that Basque loyalties to Castile depended on the respect of the kingdom's monarchs for local traditions, as specified in the *forua*. This juridical code constituted an autochthonous legal corpus encompassing public and private legal institutions. In the *foral* framework, political

autonomy was guaranteed through two vital dispositions. First, to accede to the throne, a new monarch had to take the "royal oath" in order to be obeyed and recognized as the lord and sovereign of the Basque territories. Every so often, the king was also requested to attend *foral* assemblies in order to renew his oath of respect for the *forua*. Second, the *foral* code recognized the Basque right to the so-called *pase foral*. Basque authorities thus consented to, or refused application of, laws decreed by the Crown in the Basque Country, depending on whether or not these were consistent with the *forua*. Both faculties considerably limited royal power on Basque territory. But, in addition, the *forua* comprised other rights inherent to the natives of Basque territory, among which were the exemption from fiscal taxes in all maritime activities (Law XII), the freedom of Basques to devote themselves to commercial activities (Laws XIV and XVI), the right to a trial with all juridical guarantees (Law XXVI), and exemption from obligatory military service outside of Basque territory (Laws IV and V).

3. Both reasons explain why the Roman Empire showed great interest in Basque mining in ancient times.

4. See the work of Ruiz de Azúa, *Vascongadas y América*, where the author gives an exhaustive account of the antecedents of Basque European commerce before mercantile transit to the Americas began.

5. See García de Cortázar and Lorenzo Espinosa, *Historia del País Vasco*, 1–64, where this matter is addressed at length.

6. Ruiz de Azúa, *Vascongadas y América*, 45–48.

7. H. Sánchez, *Discurso de la fundación y antigüedades de Cádiz y los demás sucesos que por ella an passado (1591) e Historia de la ciudad de Cádiz* (1845), book 4, chapter 4.

8. See in this respect Ruiz de Azúa, *Vascongadas y América*, 44–51; J. Garmendia Arruebarrena, *Cádiz, los vascos y la carrera de Indias* (San Sebastián, 1991); L. García Fuentes, *Sevilla, los vascos y América. Las exportaciones de hierro y manufacturas metálicas en los siglos XVI, XVII y XVIII.* (Bilbao, 1991); J. A. García de Cortazar, *Organización social del espacio en la España medieval. La Corona de Castilla en los siglos VIII a XV* (Barcelona, 1985).

9. Christopher Columbus has been and continues to be one of the most controversial characters in history. In the study of his life and work a series of contradictory theses and even imaginative studies have emerged, giving rise to lively polemic. One of the most debated questions has been his nationality. Diverse claims have been made as a consequence of the reticence of Columbus and his men, who tried at all costs to keep it secret since it was not in keeping with attitudes of the day that such an admiral and viceroy have a humble lineage. In any case, what is certain is that Columbus and his son Hernando took pains that the enigma would remain undeciphered. It is therefore understandable that some hypotheses endow him with French, Portuguese, English, or Swiss nationality. Other researchers have identified him as a Greek corsair in service to France. Other hypotheses also suggest that the discoverer was born in Spain, in Extremadura, Galicia, Cataluña, or the Balearic Islands; some even portray him as a descendant of Jewish stock. Nevertheless, based on reliable documents, the vast majority of Columbian specialists proclaim him a native of Genoa. In this respect, see Luis Arranz, *Cristóbal*

Colón (Madrid, 1986), 8–11; L. Navarro García, ed., *Historia de las Américas* (Sevilla, 1991), 318–20; A. Ballesteros Beretta, "Cristóbal Colón y el descubrimiento de América," in *Historia de América y de los pueblos americanos*, ed. A. Melón y Ruiz de Gordejuela, vols. 4 and 5 (Barcelona, 1945).

10. The power to name three candidates for government posts, from which the monarchs would choose one.

11. And one must understand that, undermining their own political authority, the Catholic Monarchs conceded the Genoa native a dilated and unlimited seigneury in the clear feudal tradition and noble status making him equal to the most noble and highest Castilian families. Supported by distinguished medieval precedents, Columbus managed to have his attributions of admiral and viceroy based on those of the admiral major of Castile, Don Alfonso Enríquez, and the viceroys in Aragón, Andalusia, and Navarre. As if this were not enough, the economic benefits collected in the undertaking would permit him to maintain this noble grandeur in luxury. Moreover, as admiral he would be able to control all maritime activity within his realm, and as viceroy and governor he would exercise the highest jurisdictional and government powers over the new lands discovered or conquered.

12. The vast majority of Basque researchers argue that the nao *Santa María* was a vessel of Basque origin, taking into consideration the fact that Basque shipyards had great experience and technique in the construction of this type of round vessel with a large port. The debate increases, however, when the subject of the origin of its owner, Juan de la Cosa, is broached. No one denies that he was from the north. However, some researchers (Enrique Leguina and Antonio Ballesteros) believe him to be from Santoña (Cantabria), while others (Segundo de Ispizua and Antonio Rumeu) categorically affirm his Bizkaian background. Be that as it may, what is certain is that, referring to his country or place of birth, Queen Isabella called him "Juancho Vizcaíno." In any case, Juan Lakotsa, a Bizkaian from Santoña and a man expert in the tasks of the sea, lived at the end of the fifteenth century with his family in Puerto de Santa María. Like so many others, he had gone there because of his activities as an outfitter and merchant.

13. A treaty between Spain and Portugal whereby the two countries divided the recently discovered world.

14. At the time of this diplomatic jockeying, the Castilian Crown landed the second Columbian expedition. The royal orders were clear: head to sea as soon as possible in order to prevent neighboring Portugal from preempting Spanish colonization of eastern lands. The new undertaking essentially had two objectives. The first was the evangelization of the natives, a mission entrusted to Fra Bernardo Boyl and other clerics, especially Franciscans. The second was the establishment of active commerce with the natives; undertaken uniquely and exclusively through the city of Cádiz, the commercial monopoly remained reserved for the Catholic Monarchs and Columbus himself. In an attempt at copying the Portuguese commercial model, Columbus was to establish a customhouse where all of the goods arriving from the metropolis and the spoils attained on the islands would be lodged. This customhouse would be parallel to another, to be established in Cádiz. Other instructions received by Columbus before leaving for the New World for the second time refer to the political and administrative organization

of the new territories of the Crown and the creation of permanent settlements. These aspects were considered of vital importance in undertaking such a great colonization, never before witnessed in Europe.

15. In spite of the fact that the crew on the second voyage numbered around 1,200 men, the Basque presence was scant. The politico-military circumstances of the epoch caused this low participation. In effect, to carry out this second undertaking it was ordered that part of the fleet be prepared in Bermeo (Bizkaia), under the command of Iñigo de Artieta. The outfitter, Juan de Arbolancha, organized five ships and 820 sailors for the occasion in barely two months. Nevertheless, the Crown's priorities prevented this armada from being integrated into the one that ultimately left for the New World in September 1493. Rather, its mission was to transport the Muslim refugees, headed by the last king of Granada, Boabdil the Younger, from Granada to Africa. The Basques thus lost the opportunity to form a more numerous contingent within the second expedition to the New World.

16. The nucleus of the Basques probably configured itself from the outset as a largely dissident group, perhaps due to their mutual language and background. Leading them was probably the Lekeitio native, "Chanchu," who one year earlier had been boatswain of the ill-fated *Santa María*. It makes sense that the personnel of the fort would scatter in search of personal fortunes and thereby become vulnerable to indigenous attack. In this regard, see J. Bilbao Azkarreta, ed., *América y los vascos. 1492–1992* (Bilbao, 1992), 22.

17. There were the pilot Pedro de Ledesma, the boatswain of the *Vizcaína*; Martín de Fuenterrabía; the cooper Martín de Arrieta; the caulkers Domingo Vizcaínos and Diego de Arana; the carpenter Martín Machín; the sailors Pedro Moya and Martín de Atín; six cabin boys; the page "Chench"; and the trumpeter Gonzalo de Salazar. These were but crewmen from the Basque Country on the fourth voyage of discovery. Six of them would die before reaching Cuba, victims of the hardships that plagued those voyages of frequent no return. The rest followed the admiral on his mission to take possession of the territories beyond the limits of Spanish exploration outlined at Tordesillas.

18. Nevertheless, the poor condition of one of the ships forced the fleet to go to Santo Domingo in spite of the Catholic Monarchs' expressed prohibition against landing there. It is for that reason that they chose to head to Jamaica, to then sail westward and set a southerly course along the entire coast of what they believed to be the Asiatic province of Ciamba—the Cochinchina of the tales of Marco Polo. The admiral believed the strait connecting the Atlantic and Indian Oceans to be at its terminus. The currents pushed him to the island of Guanaja, in the Gulf of Honduras, of which he took possession on August 14. From there, razed by a strong storm that lasted almost a month, they followed the coastline east to the Cape of Gracias a Dios and the present coasts of Honduras, Nicaragua, Costa Rica, and Panama. Along these coasts, Columbus learned that he was in front of an isthmus linking the Atlantic with another ocean and that the region was rich in gold. Later, in Veragua, the natives assured him that he could find gold in even greater abundance. On October 17, Columbus reached the coast, landing at Portobelo on November 2. One week later, the expedition continued its eastward course. It cast anchor at what, perhaps due to the abundance of cornfields, was called Puerto de Bastimientos

(Port of Supplies). On the twenty-sixth of that month the fleet entered Puerto Retrete (currently Puerto Escribano). There, on December 5, Columbus decided to return to Veragua, and so did not reach the Belén River until January 6, 1503. He tried to found a gold mining enterprise in Veragua. He had to cease after three months in the face of the hostile, rebellious native reactions. He was forced to set a course east to Jamaica, the island where the ships ran aground on June 25, 1503.

19. This aspect, extremely important for the Basque, Spanish, and European economy of the modern era, has been the one least studied in Basque historiography.

20. For a more in-depth understanding of the Basque metallurgical industry during the modern era, see L. M. Bilbao and R. Fernández de Pinedo, "Auge y crisis de la siderometalurgia tradicional en el País Vasco (1700–1850)," in *La economía española al final del Antiguo Régimen. Las manufacturas*, eds. G. Anes et al., vol. 2 (Madrid, 1982); J. I. Tellechea Idigoras, "Ferrerías guipuzcoanas a finales del siglo XV," in *Boletín de la Real Sociedad Bascongada de los Amigos del País* 79 (1975): 81–111; J. E. Gelabert, "La producción de hierro en Vizcaya y Guipúzcoa hacia 1620," in *Congreso de historia de Euskalherria* (Vitoria-Gasteiz, 1988); various authors, "La siderurgia vasca," *Ernaroa* (Bilbao) 12 (1996).

21. Regarding the later commerce of the Basques with the New World, see J. Ruiz Rivera, "Los vascos en el Consulado de Cádiz," in *Los Vascos y América. Actas de las Jornadas sobre el comercio vasco en América en el siglo XVIII y la Real Compañía Guipuzcoana de Caracas*, eds. R. Escobedo Mansilla, A. M. Rivera Medina, and A. Chapa Imaz (Bilbao: Laida, D. L., 1988), 143–69.

22. R. Larrañaga, *Síntesis histórica de la armería vasca* (San Sebastián, 1981). This author has documented the existence of 163 master armorers in the Basque regions in the sixteenth century; 370 in the seventeenth; 1,012 in the eighteenth; and 463 in the nineteenth. These figures are sufficiently indicative of the splendor achieved by the Basque arms industry thanks, in large part, to the colonization of the New World.

CHAPTER 2. MASTERY OF THE LAND

1. Translator's note: the term "Vizcayan" is frequently used in historical texts to refer to all Basques.

2. J. Pérez de Tudela y Bueso, *Las armadas de Indias y los orígenes de la política de colonización (1492–1505)* (Madrid, 1956).

3. J. J. Alzugaray, "Vascos emprendedores del siglo XVI en el Nuevo Mundo," in *Los vascos y América. Ideas, hechos, hombres* eds. I. Arana Pérez et al. (Madrid, 1990), 276–77.

4. See Ruiz de Azúa, *Vascongadas y América* (Madrid, 1992), 53–73; Wm. A. Douglass and J. Bilbao, *Amerikanuak: Basques in the New World* (Reno, 1975), 73–115; Bilbao Azkarreta, ed., *América y los vascos. 1492–1992* (Bilbao, 1992), 30–143.

5. G. Fernández de Oviedo y Valdés, *Historia general y natural de las Indias, islas y tierra firme del mar Océano* (Asunción del Paraguay, 1944–1945).

6. S. Ispizua, *Historia de los vascos en el descubrimiento, conquista y civilización de América*, vol. 3 (Bilbao, 1914–1919), 39.

7. E. de Labayru y Goicoechea, *Historia general del Señorío de Bizcaya*, 6 vols. (Bilbao, 1968).

8. Fearing an indigenous attack, Cortés had made a supreme decision: capture Moctezuma. The fact that the Aztec king was in the custody of the Extremaduran conquistador, however, only further incited Moctezuma's subjects. The news from Mexico seemed to indicate to the Spanish authorities in Cuba that the conquest was slipping through their fingers. In order to mitigate the situation, Governor Velázquez sent Pánfilo Narváez with 1,500 men under his command, some of them of Basque origin. Narváez was to take Cortés's place, capture him, and send him to Spain to account for his actions in the presence of the emperor. Upon discovering the plans against him, Cortés left a garrison in Tenochtitlán, commanded by Pedro de Alvaro, and ordered his followers to go to the coast to capture Narváez. The battle was brief. Once Narváez was captured, his men abandoned him and joined Cortés, whose army was suddenly larger than ever.

9. V. Lascurain, "Los grandes caudillos en la conquista de México," in *Boletín del Instituto Americano de Estudios Vascos* (Buenos Aires) 25 (1956): 101–11.

10. Lascurain, "Los grandes caudillos," 110.

11. R. C. West, *The Mining Community in Northern New Spain: The Parral Mining District* (Berkeley, 1949).

12. The contract signed by the Crown and Pizarro authorized the latter to continue the exploration, conquest, and colonization of Peru for two hundred leagues southward. Regarding the Basques that were members of "the Thirteen Famous Ones," Emperor Charles V bestowed upon them the title of Knights of the Golden Spur since, with their status as "Vizcayans," they already held the rank of nobleman.

13. See J. Salazar González and R. Hernández Ponce, *Cuatrocientos años de presencia vasca en Chile* (Departamento de Cultura del Gobierno Vasco/Euskal Etxea [Chile], 1991).

14. The social makeup of half of Valdivia's explorers is known in detail: 42 were of noble origin, 26 Andalusians, 36 Castilians, 17 Extremadurans, 12 Basques, 2 Murcians, 1 Valencian, 1 Asturian, 1 Canary Islander, 2 Germans, 1 black, 1 Portuguese, and 1 Italian. One hundred ten could sign their names. A variety of professions were represented: accountants, teachers, pilots, masons, surgeons, barbers, blacksmiths, tailors, one sexton, and three lay priests. Forty-five had Spanish wives; two, Portuguese; one, an Indian noble; one, a Chilean Indian; one, a Chibcha; and one, a mulatta. Francisco de Aguirre had five legitimate and fifty bastard children. In addition, the first inverse mestizo (from white to Indian) seems to have been born in southern Nuevo Toledo.

15. Bilbao Azkarreta, ed., *América y los vascos*, 123–25.

16. The use of slaves was a common practice on Venezuelan *estancias*, especially during the seventeenth century. The Basque captain Antonio Arraez de Mendoza was one of the main *estancieros* in Bobures Valley. A knight of the Royal Order of Santiago and wealthy property owner, he had more slaves than anyone else in the valley—seventeen in 1656. Francisco de Arrieta also had seven black and two Creole slaves in Bobures.

Pedro Hernández de Galarza, who also lived in that region, had five slaves. Juan Félix de Arrúa and Ambrosio de Izarra, *estancieros* in Chama Valley, both had two black slaves in 1655.

17. Since his arrival in the New World in 1543, Garay had participated in the exploration of northeastern Argentina. He participated in the foundation of Santiago del Estero, the oldest settlement in the country. He also was present during the founding of the cities of Tarija, Santa Cruz de la Sierra, and Santa Fe de la Vera Cruz in 1573, and reached the borders of the Chaco.

18. Bilbao Azkarreta, ed., *América y los vascos*, 76.

19. In 1525, after the first circumnavigation of the planet was successfully completed by Juan Sebastián Elcano, a new expedition to the Spice Islands was organized. Aside from Elcano, several sailors from the Basque Country participated. Among them was the young royal page Andrés de Urdaneta. Just over 20 of the original 450 original crew members returned to the peninsula alive, including Urdaneta and an illegitimate daughter that he had in the Spice Islands. The voyage was a complete failure, although the experience gained by the Gipuzkoan would help him during later expeditions of exploration and conquest in the Americas.

In 1542, when the captain was forty-four years old, he abandoned his military career to enter the Augustinian monastery of the city of Mexico. There, in Nueva España, after various failed expeditions in search of the return passageway from the Spice Islands through the Pacific, his desire to attempt the voyage took shape. Based on both his nautical knowledge and previous experience with that sea, Urdaneta firmly believed himself capable of returning from the Philippines through the Pacific. This reinforced the confidence of Philip II to include him in the expedition organized for that purpose, although the king assigned Juan Pablo de Carrión the task of building the expedition's ships. Guido de Lebesarri, from Bilbao, also participated in this adventure.

20. Douglass and Bilbao, *Amerikanuak*, 84–85.

21. Lope de Aguirre has entered into history as a crazy, extravagant, murderous, cruel, satanic, ingenuous, shameless, blasphemous character. In short, he was a monster worthy of a detailed psychiatric study. Nevertheless, he was also called the "prince of liberty" and the "precursor of American independence" by the nineteenth-century liberators of the Americas. See Ruiz de Azúa, *Vascongadas y América*, 72.

22. See M. Lucena Salmoral, *Piratas, bucaneros, filibusteros y corsarios en América. Perros, mendigos y otros malditos del mar* (Madrid, 1992), 26–33.

23. Stede Bonnet, a landowner from La Barbeda, told his neighbors that he became a pirate "due to inconveniences that he felt in his matrimonial status" (P. Gosse, *The History of Piracy* [New York, 1968], 193).

24. At this point it is important to define what is meant by pirates, corsairs, buccaneers, and freebooters; although they all were part of the same pirate family, their field of action and particular circumstances make them distinct from one another. A pirate undertook armed actions in the sea for economic ends, without state authorization. A corsair acted just like a pirate, but was protected by a state license. The difference between the two is, therefore, so subtle that a pirate that observed the orders of a sovereign became a corsair, while a corsair that disobeyed truces between nations and contin-

ued robbing ships became a pirate in official eyes. Buccaneers were an exclusively American creation, and pirates who operated mostly in the Caribbean were known by this name. Finally, freebooters arose from the fusion of buccaneers and corsairs. They appeared beginning in 1630, and their theater of operations included both the Caribbean Sea and the Pacific Ocean. Both buccaneers and freebooters lacked nationality, and did not distinguish among flags in their seizures.

25. Lucena Salmoral, *Piratas, bucaneros, filibusteros y corsarios*, 269–71.

26. As presently understood, privateering—"the naval undertaking of individuals against the enemies of the state carried out with the permission and under the authority of a belligerent power with the sole object of causing the enemy economic losses and obstructing neutral parties that interact with said enemies"—appeared in Europe at the end of the Middle Ages, as territorial and authoritarian monarchy was created and fortified. Some authors go back as far as the first century B.C. for the beginning of privateering, citing the Mithridatic Wars. It was not prevalent, however, until the end of the Middle Ages. By the fourteenth century, there were numerous instances of reprisal privateering between the English and Bretons during the Hundred Years' War. In both the Atlantic and the Mediterranean, the figure of the merchant-corsair or merchant-pirate (they are difficult to distinguish) existed. In their commercial voyages, these men tried to capture smaller ships that crossed their paths. Henry VIII of England proposed practical solutions to eliminate this cross between piracy and privateering, and to regulate its activity to the extent possible. In a treaty between England, France, and Castile (1420), each of the signatories promised to avoid engaging pirates and to work jointly to eliminate them. No armed ship could set sail without a license and before posting a bond that would guarantee its future good behavior. In spite of the brevity of its positive results, the joint venture set the stage for legalizing the activity of profiteering. See E. Otero Lana, *Los corsarios españoles durante la decadencia de los Austrias. El corso español del Atlántico peninsular en el siglo XVII (1621–1697)* (Madrid, 1992), 41ff.

27. Spanish privateering was regulated by the Crown of Aragón during the fourteenth century, similar to what was happening in other European countries. This Aragonese ordinance is dated 1356. In Castile, both Henry IV and John II supported privateering; in 1487, the Catholic Monarchs signed a document favoring Gipuzkoan seafarers that wanted to practice this profession. In 1525 Juana la Loca and Emperor Charles V legislated in the Cortes of Toledo regarding the authorization of arming their vessels for privateering. This law was also approved in the Cortes of Valladolid in 1598 by Philip III, to be published in 1604.

28. Otero Lana, *Los corsarios españoles*, 53ff.

29. Ibid., 57.

30. The privateering outfitters were those who equipped, armed, supplied, and devoted their vessels to one or more voyages and had a captain or patron to direct seizure expeditions. The outfitters had to meet three conditions in devoting themselves to privateering, which also distinguished them from pirates. They had to have an expressed governmental authorization granting them various types of permission: for private or retaliatory privateering—granted to an individual to retaliate against attacks or damages at the hands of subjects of another country, regardless of whether or not there was

a war with it—"cards or letters of retaliation"; and for privateering in general—only possible in times of war between two countries and waged against the subjects and property of the enemy—"scorecards" were conceded (with the permission to attack the enemy's commerce) and "counter-scorecards" (privateering licenses granted to repel enemy corsairs). These departure cards or privateering permits were given by the Spanish monarch himself or, in the case of the Americas, by his authorized representatives (viceroys, governors, captains general). On the other hand, before obtaining such licenses, one had to pay a deposit that later served as indemnification for possible abuses committed while privateering. Lastly, the captured spoils had to be submitted for judgment and sentencing by a special tribunal under which the right of plunder, so prevalent throughout the pirating and freebooting community, was eliminated.

31. Otero Lana, *Los corsarios españoles*, 99–107.

32. In 1637, when the French Basque province of Labourd was invaded, there were Labourdine sailors in the Northern Squadron; a company of nations was therefore organized to better control them.

33. Otero Lana, *Los corsarios españoles*, 108.

34. Ibid., 109.

35. Lucena Salmoral, *Piratas, bucaneros, filibusteros y corsarios*, 252ff.

36. Ibid., 264ff.

37. See A. Domínguez Ortíz, ed., *Historia de España. Descubrimiento, colonización y emancipación*, vol. 8 (Madrid, 1990), 282ff.

38. The bull *Inter Coetera I* (May 3, 1493) conceded the discovered lands to the Spanish Crown in exchange for the promise of the deployment of missionaries and the conversion of the natives, unless they belonged to another Christian prince. The *Inter Coetera II* set the territorial boundaries of the apostolate in order to avoid contact with the Portuguese jurisdictions. The *Eximia Devotionis* (May 3, 1493) granted the Spanish Crown the same spiritual prerogatives as the Portuguese enjoyed in Africa. With the *Dudam Siquidem* (September 26, 1493), the earlier deferences were expanded.

39. In 1504, Ferdinand the Catholic built the first three American dioceses: Yaguata, Magua, and Baynúa. Beginning in 1508, new episcopal sees were added to these at an accelerated pace. In 1513, one was founded in Santa María de la Antigua del Darién; in 1515, in Jamaica; in Baracoa, or Asunción (Cuba); in 1518, in the Yucatán; in 1521, in Panama; in 1522, in Santiago (Cuba); in 1526, in Tlaxcala; in 1530, Mexico; in 1531, in León (Nicaragua), Coro, and Comayagua; in 1534, in Santa Marta, Cartagena (Colombia), and Guatemala; in 1535, in Oaxaca; in 1536, in Michoacán; in 1537, in Cuzco; in 1539, in Trujillo (Honduras) and Chiapas; in 1541, in Lima; in 1546, in Quito and Popayán; in 1547, in Asunción (Paraguay); and in 1548, in Guadalajara. Sevilla was the metropolitan province to which religious problems posed in the Americas were referred. Nevertheless, the distance and resulting delay in the transmission and resolution of the disputes resulted in the foundation of the archdioceses of Santo Domingo, Mexico City, and Lima in the Americas.

40. The first of these experiences—and also the first failure—was led by the Dominican Fra Pedro de Córdoba. The attempt to gather the natives in isolated missionary territories, an initiative supported by both the Crown and Cardinal Cisneros, collided head

on with the greed of the Spanish traders who came to the region to find pearls and capture natives. Years later, Fra Bartolomé de Las Casas, also a Dominican and a partisan of insulation of natives from the harmful Spanish influence, would gather evidence to support such an initiative. The setting chosen was a remote, jungle region of Guatemala. In 1542, Las Casas received authorization from the Crown to carry out this project, and Spaniards were denied entrance into this territory. Everything suggested unprecedented success. Nevertheless, the opposition of the *encomenderos*, who were thus left without Indians to work their lands, and the raids in search of slaves, provoked indigenous resistance and, with it, the end of the missionary experiment of Las Casas. The third isolationist attempt was directed by the Mexican judge Vasco de Quiroga. Influenced by the utopian theories of Thomas More and his good friend Bishop Zumárraga, he set in motion his famous Indian hospitals in Santa Fe (Mexico) and in the towns of Michoacán surrounding Lake Pátzcuaro. This nearly came to function with an internal system of government very similar to More's utopian republic. Vasco de Quiroga chose a model of evangelization in which the Indians would live according to their traditions. But, not all isolation attempts were failures. At the beginning of the seventeenth century, the Jesuits once again revived the idea of isolation in the missionary enterprise and managed to make it a reality in their Paraguayan Guaraní communities, known as *reducciones*, and in those of California.

41. The Franciscans arrived in the New World with Commander Bobadilla in 1500, initiating a continuous flow that would lead them to found a province called Santa Cruz of the West Indies in Hispaniola in 1505. In 1509, they landed on the mainland, accompanying the governor of Nueva Andalucía, Alonso de Ojeda. They arrived in Mexico in two waves: the first in 1523, and the second one year later. The Order of San Francisco soon branched out to the Yucatán (1547), Central America—Nicaragua (1527) and Guatemala (1541)—the Andean region—Lima (1535), Quito (1538), and Potosí (1547)—and Río de la Plata. The Dominicans disembarked in Hispaniola in 1510 and soon spread throughout the American lands. Like the Franciscans, they had headquarters on that island, which they established in Santa Cruz in 1530. A bull dated July 2, 1532, allowed them to found the province of Santiago, Mexico, while in 1551 they established those of San Vicente (Chiapas) and Guatemala. They were also active in South America from early on—Santa Marta (1529), Coro (1531), Lima (1532), Cartagena, Colombia (1534), and Quito (1540)—demonstrating great missionary zeal. The Order of Saint Augustine began in Mexico in 1533, and its apostolic action was equally notable, although the Augustinians were often accused of excessive luxury and constant extravagance in the decoration of their convents and churches, which, without doubt, were among the greatest examples of Spanish-American art. The presence of the Mercedarians in Hispaniola is documented in 1514—even in 1493, since a friar of this order accompanied Columbus on his second voyage. They accompanied Cortés on his Mexican adventure in 1519, and were with the conquistadors of Peru, Ecuador, and Chile. In 1543, their missionary work was limited to Nicaragua, Santo Domingo, Panama, and Peru. Finally, Jesuit activity in the Americas was approved in 1568 thanks to the support of the viceroy of Peru, Francisco de Toledo. Along with the Franciscans, the Jesuits were the ones who covered

the most territory and successfully developed the isolationist thesis of evangelization in the Guaraní *reducciones* of Paraguay.

42. The Spanish Crown did not oppose the presence of foreigners among the religious personnel that traveled to the Americas. In fact, already in 1493 the passage of foreigners was noticeable, albeit in small numbers, as it was in 1502 with Ovando. The Franciscans frequently included Flemish and other Europeans of their order in their expeditions, unlike the Dominicans and Augustinians, among whom it was rare to find outsiders. Nevertheless, beginning in 1530, non-Spanish natives needed a license from a Spanish superior or authorization from the Council of the Indies if they wanted to go out to Spanish overseas jurisdictions.

43. Christianity appeared among the Basques in the fourth century. Not until the ninth century, however, would it take hold, the result of the early creation of the episcopal see of Pamplona. In the twelfth century, Calahorra was founded as the main Basque diocese, serving almost all of Bizkaia, Araba, and part of Gipuzkoa. Calahorra was outside the Basque Country, however, which provoked permanent conflicts between the episcopal see and the dependent parishes and monasteries. The principal Basque churches and monastic centers had a seigneurial structure in which the *parientes mayores* were the founders and beneficiaries (of tithes and first fruits). The conflict with and desire to escape episcopal control stemmed from this structure, which caused the clergy and feudal lords to join forces. At the same time, the alliance between the clergy and the lords would serve to establish a social differentiation (*belatores, oratorians,* and *laboratores*), which did not prevent the appearance of a low clergy connected to and identifying with popular demands, frequently conspicuous in its participation in opposition movements and its deviations from orthodoxy.

44. M. Lucena Salmoral, and P. E. Pérez-Mallaina Bueno, eds. *Historia de Iberoamérica. Historia moderna,* vol. 2 (Madrid, 1990), 277ff.

45. See Ruiz de Azúa, *Vascongadas y América,* 147–70.

46. The Jesuits began their evangelization of American territories much later than the other religious orders. In fact, the other religious orders were already performing pastoral work in the Americas when Saint Ignatius of Loyola founded the Society of Jesus in 1540. In addition, the Society's first fields of missionary action were in the East Indies, and it did not reach the Americas until well into the sixteenth century, when a great part of the continent was already occupied. The Society's presence is documented in Florida in 1566, in Peru in 1567, in Mexico in 1572, in Ecuador in 1586, and in Chile, from where the Jesuits arrived in Río de la Plata, in 1593. As the remaining orders had been establishing themselves in the Hispanicized cities from the beginning, the Jesuits began their missionary work among the Indians of the interior. With the exception of Central America, they were prevalent throughout the New World; they were especially strong in South America, where they founded a large number of missions. See A. Santos Hernández, "Jesuítas en la América Meridional," in *America (1492–1992). Contribuciones a un centenario* (Madrid, 1988), 43–106.

47. These *reducciones* were well known for their juridical administrative organization. In Paraguay, the Jesuits achieved the difficult isolation that Fra Bartolomé de Las Casas

always envisioned for the natives. Las Casas wanted to have them completely separated from the Spanish civil population and handed over to the religious and civil magisterium of the missionary fathers assigned to instruct them, thus isolating them from the bad examples of Spanish laymen. This was the primary material and spiritual goal of the *reducciones*. Their urban design was centered around the church and mission house, and the profits from confiscated private and communal property were divided among those unable to support themselves. The high authorities that governed the *reducciones* were the very natives that inhabited them, although they, like the entire kingdom, recognized the authority of the king and the governor of the province, paid their tributes, provided military levies to the state, and behaved like authentic subjects of the king. Economically, the *reducciones* maintained their self-sufficiency through the fruits of their agricultural and livestock production. They also had their own justice system, run by the missionaries, and organized military training to defend the Jesuit colonists from Portuguese slave raids. It was therefore normal for the natives to handle firearms; they were taught by some missionary brothers, such as the Bizkaian Pedro de Ledesma, that had been soldiers prior to entering the Society.

48. See Lucena Salmoral, *Piratas, bucaneros, filibusteros y corsarios*, 280–82.

49. See Ruiz de Azúa, *Vascongadas y América*, 140–46.

50. From a purely cultural point of view, the Spanish evangelizing clerics often participated in reproachable actions in carrying out their pastoral mission in the Indies. The destruction of indigenous cultural practices was the price paid for the spread of the Christian faith. Zumárraga participated in some of these measures that, although perhaps surprising by present standards, were common and understandable within the mentality of the sixteenth century. He frequently used Euskara, especially when dealing with members of the Basque colony.

51. See Ruiz de Azúa, *Vascongadas y América*, 140–46.

52. See Domínguez Ortíz, ed., *Historia de España*, 8, no. 37, 305ff.; Lucena Salmoral, *Piratas, bucaneros, filibusteros y corsarios*, 284ff.; and Navarro García, ed., *Historia de las Américas*, 281ff.

53. Ruiz de Azúa, *Vascongadas y América*, 162.

54. In chapter XLVII of the second part of *El Quijote de la Mancha*, Miguel de Cervantes wrote: "Hearing this, Sancho said: 'Who here is my secretary?' And one of those present responded: 'I am, Sir, because I know how to read and write, and I am Vizcayan.' 'With that addition,' said Sancho, 'you could easily be the secretary to the Emperor himself.'" Years later, Ruíz de Alarcón, in his work *Exámen de maridos*, makes one character say: "And as sure as the weather is fickle / it is a rare event / that he who is not Vizcayan / might become a secretary."

55. J. Lynch, *España bajo los Austrias*, vol. 2 (Barcelona, 1973), 34.

56. See H. Kamen, *La España de Carlos II* (Barcelona, 1981), 54; J. A. Escudero, *Los secretarios de Estado, 1474–1724*, vol. 1 (Madrid, 1969); J. Garmendia Arruebarrena, "Los secretarios vascos," in *Boletín de la Real Sociedad Bascongada de Amigos del País* 41, nos. 1–2 (1985): 364–65.

57. G. Anes, *El Antiguo Régimen. Los Borbones* (Madrid, 1976), 295.

58. See Ruiz de Azúa, *Vascongadas y América*, 111–22.

59. The figures given by the historian A. Martínez de Salazar in his work *Presencia alavesa en América y Fílipinas (1700–1825)* (Vitoria-Gasteiz, 1988) about the Arabans—the sector of the Basque population that least frequently chose to emigrate to the New World—in the Indies and the Philippines between 1700 and 1825 illustrate this concentration. According to his estimates, of a total of 556 people, 143 served in the royal administration. Ten were aldermen; 25, mayors; 16, magistrates; 4, officials of the Holy Office; 19, governors; 1, lieutenant governor; 1, captain general; 25, employees of the treasury; 35, justices and attorneys general of the High Court; 2, secretaries of the Council of the Indies; 3, secretaries of the viceroy; and 2, consuls general. One-third of these positions were occupied in Nueva España (6 aldermen, 17 mayors, 2 magistrates, 2 officials of the Holy Office, 4 governors, 5 employees of the treasury, 8 justices and attorneys general, 2 secretaries of the Council of the Indies, and 2 secretaries of the viceroy).

CHAPTER 3. COLONIAL COMMERCE

1. See J. M. Oliva Melgar, "El monopolio de Indias en los siglos XVI y XVII. Plata y mitos en un sistema imperial," *Revista Rabida* (Huelva) 11 (1992): 34–47.

2. It is important to remember that any political and economic theory of the modern era involved a notion of monopoly, and exclusivity was considered a norm of natural law founded in the titles acquired through discovery and conquest. This was even more true in the case of the Spanish Indies, juridically incorporated into the patrimony of the Crown like other provinces and kingdoms of one single monarchy. That axiom was revalidated by the papal bulls of 1493 issued by Alexander VI.

3. See Oliva Melgar, "El monopolio de Indias en los siglos XVI y XVII."

4. Ibid.

5. J. Lynch, *España bajo los Austrias. Imperio y absolutismo, 1516–1598*, vol. 1, (Madrid, 1970), 205–9.

6. Caribbean pirates managed to completely destroy an Indies fleet only three times throughout the Spanish colonial history in America. In 1628, a substantial Dutch armada—composed of 31 vessels, 700 cannons, and 3,000 men—attacked a fleet from Nueva España made up of about 20 vessels off Matanzas, Cuba. The Dutch destroyed the fleet and captured its immense treasure, about 6 million pesos by their own estimate. This disaster, largely due to the lack of information about enemy movements, sent Spanish commander Juan de Benavides to the gallows for negligence. In 1656, an English squadron of Blake's fleet captured the flagship and another galleon from the American mainland fleet when it approached Cádiz, seizing about 2 million pesos. One year later, the same British corsair managed to almost completely sink the Mexican fleet as it was passing through the Canary Islands.

7. See Lynch, *España bajo los Austrias (1516–1700)*, 2 vols., for a more in-depth description of the commercial process with the Americas.

8. See Lynch, *España bajo los Austrias*, vol. 2 (Barcelona, 1973), 230.

9. For various reasons, commerce with America had been organized in large fleets that crossed the Atlantic once a year. Only by taking maximum advantage of the outposts

and natural supply ports could the crossing be made with a minimum of danger. Experience therefore determined a course to America that the fleets followed punctually. When the official documents speak of "the Indies run," they are referring to this imaginary line that American commercial traffic systematically followed. In a wider sense, the relations and commerce with America is known as the "Indies run," both crossing the sea and operating from the seat of the mercantile monopoly.

10. An edict by Emperor Charles V in 1529 opened the way for travel to America from other Spanish ports besides Sevilla, such as Barcelona, Valencia, La Coruña, and Bilbao. This open market policy was never effectively applied, however, partly due to the opposition of the monopolists, partly because the government itself needed the monopolism to effectively monitor the flow of wealth.

11. See E. Schaefer, *El Consejo Real y Supremo de las Indias* (Sevilla, 1935), 377ff.; B. Gildas, "La Casa de Contratación de Sevilla, luego de Cádiz en el siglo XVIII," in *Anuario de Estudios Americanos (AEA)*, vol. 12 (Sevilla, 1955).

12. L. García Fuentes, *Sevilla, los vascos y América. Las exportaciones de hierro y manufacturas metálicas en los siglos XVI, XVII y XVIII* (Bilbao, 1991), 20ff.

13. See Fray G. de la Concepción, *Emporio del Orbe. Cádiz Ilustrada* (Amsterdam, 1960); J. Garmendia Arruabarrena, *Cádiz, los vascos y la Carrera de Indias* (San Sebastián, 1990), 70–71.

14. A. Heredia Herrera, *Catálogo de las consultas del Consejo de Indias (1631–1636)* (Sevilla, 1988), 34, 169.

15. P. E. Pérez-Mallaína Bueno, and B. Torres Ramirez, *La Armada de la Mar del Sur* (Sevilla, 1987), 37.

16. Endowed with various powers, only a few specific matters such as those related to the Inquisition and war were beyond its control.

17. See Schaefer, *El Consejo Real y Supremo de las Indias,* 35ff. Regarding the Council of the Indies, see also A. García Gallo, "La evolución de la organización territorial de las Indias de 1492 a 1824," in *Anuario Histórico Jurídico Ecuatoriano*, vol. 5 (Quito, 1980); J. J. Real Díaz, "El Consejo de Cámara de Indias. Génesis de su fundacion," *Anuario de Estudios Americanos (AEA)*, vol. 19 (Sevilla, 1962).

18. A. Domínguez Ortíz and F. Aguilar Piñal, *El Barroco y la Ilustración* (Sevilla, 1976), 86.

19. Bilbao Azkarreta, ed., *América y los vascos. 1492–1992* (Vitoria-Gasteiz, 1992), 55ff.

20. Guiard y Larrauri, *Historia del Consulado y Casa de Contratación de Bilbao del Comercio de la Villa (1514–1830)* (Bilbao, 1913–1914).

21. See E. Ruiz de Azúa, *Vascongadas y América* (Madrid, 1992), 173–80.

22. García Fuentes, *Sevilla, los vascos y América*, 125ff.

23. Basque foundries experienced a clear period of recovery during the first third of the 1600s in regard to the number of workshops and production. It was only a relative prosperity, however, given the sector's lack of technical advance.

24. See C. Cardell, *La casa de Borbón en España* (Madrid, 1954); V. Palacio Atard, *Los españoles de la Ilustración* (Madrid, 1964); J. Tapia Ocariz, *Carlos III y su época* (Madrid,

1962); S. Zabala, *España bajo los Borbones* (Barcelona, 1955); A. Domínguez Ortíz, *Sociedad y Estado en el siglo XVIII español* (Barcelona, 1976); J. Vicens Vives, ed., *Historia social y económica de España. IV. Los Borbones. El siglo XVIII en España y América* (Barcelona, 1962); A. Domínguez Ortíz, ed., *Historia de España. VII. El Reformismo borbónico. VIII. Descubrimiento, colonización y emancipación de América* (Barcelona, 1989–1990); L. Navarro García, *Hispanoamericanos en el siglo XVIII* (Sevilla, 1975); E. Arcila Farias, *El siglo ilustrado en América. Reformas económicas del siglo XVIII en Nueva España* (Caracas, 1955); G. Cespedes del Castillo, *América hispánica (1492–1898)* (Barcelona, 1983); G. J. Walker, *Política española y comercio colonial (1700–1789)* (Barcelona, 1979); M. Bitar Letayf, *Los economistas españoles del siglo XVIII y sus ideas sobre el comercio con las Indias* (Mexico City, 1975); A. García-Baquero González, *Cádiz y el Atlántico (1717–1778)*, 2 vols. (Sevilla, 1976).

25. In essence, the Project of Galleons and Fleets maintained the Hapsburg traditional sailing scheme of periodic convoys, while also sending individual ships (system of registry), and retaining the form of commercial monopoly centralized in Cádiz. However, the most important changes in fiscal structure would be produced with the consolidation of the so-called right of palm as the main tax, to the detriment of the traditional *almojarifazgo*. The objectives of this legislation were to make mercantile traffic with America more regular and agile, increase the revenue of the Royal Treasury through simplified taxes, and favor national production destined for America.

26. See M. J. Matila Quiza, "Las Compañías privilegiadas en la España del Antiguo Régimen," in *La economía española al final del Antiguo Régimen*, vol. 4 (Madrid, 1982); R. Rico Linaje, *Las Reales Compañías de comercio con América* (Sevilla, 1983). The Basque author that has best studied the Real Compañía Guipuzcoana de Caracas is Montserrat Gárate.

27. M. Briceño Perozo, *Temas de la historia colonial venezolana* (Caracas, 1981). Olavarriaga's cited report also includes precise data about the borders of Venezuela, jurisdictions, the nature of the coasts, fortifications, haciendas and the names of their proprietors, Spanish commerce and smuggling, the state of the Venezuelan Royal Treasury, and other topics.

28. See J. M. Mariluz Urquijo, *Bilbao y Buenos Aires. Proyectos dieciochescos de compañías de comercio* (Buenos Aires, 1981).

29. See L. Diaz Trechuelo, *La Real Compañía de Filipinas* (Sevilla, 1965).

30. See A. Heredia Herrera, *Sevilla y los hombres del comercio (1700–1800)* (Sevilla, 1989).

31. See J. B. Ruiz Rivera, *El Consulado de Cádiz. Matrícula de comerciantes (1739–1823)* (Cádiz, 1988).

32. G. Lohmann Villena, "Los comerciantes vascos en el virreinato peruano" in *Vascos y América. Actas de las Jornadas sobre el comercio vasco con América en el siglo XVIII y la Real Compañía Guipuzcoana de Caracas en el II Centenario de Carlos III*, eds. R. Escobedo Mansilla, A. M. Rivera Medina, and A. Chapa Imaz (Bilbao, 1989), 61.

33. To give an idea of the significance of this amount, it is sufficient to note that, at that time, the viceroy received an annual salary of 60,500 pesos; the director of the

Review Board, 10,000; a judge, 4,860; the head accountant of the Board of Fiscal Inspection, 3,645; a magistrate, between 960 and 1,560; a university professor, between 590 and 1,000; and a captain of escort to the viceroy, 120.

34. See J. M. Mariluz Urquijo, "Proyección y límites del comercio vasco en el Río de la Plata," in *Los vascos y América*, eds. Escobedo Mansilla et al. (Bilbao, 1989), 109–33.

35. The Company of Buenos Aires embraced the slave trade not so much because of the partners' wishes but rather to facilitate obtaining the the Crown's approval. Their lack of knowledge in such commerce obliged them to enter into a partnership with prominent foreign slave firms, especially from London and Guinea.

36. See M. R. Moreno Fraginals, "Importancia del elemento vasco en el siglo XVIII en Cuba," in *Presencia vasca en América* (Vitoria-Gasteiz, 1992), 249ff.

37. See A. Zabala Uriarte, "Las relaciones comerciales en América del Norte," in *Presencia vasca en América*, 313ff.; Zabala Uriarte, "Bilbao y el comercio con el Norte de América en el siglo XVIII. Negocio y burgesía," in *América y los vascos*, ed. Bilbao Azkarreta, 173ff.; see also N. Rueda, *La compañía comercial "Gardoqui e Hijos" (1760–1800)* (Vitoria-Gasteiz, 1992).

38. From the beginning of the seventeenth century, some Basques tended to meet in the convent of San Agustín of Lima, but they never had the legal status of an association. In Potosí, on the other hand, the Basques, mostly wealthy proprietors, met in the church of the Augustinians and managed to found the first official mutual aid society in the New World.

39. See A. Elorza, *La ideología liberal en la Ilustración española* (Madrid, 1970); J. Herrero, *Los orígenes del pensamiento reaccionario español* (Madrid, 1971); A. Mestre Sanchis, *Despotismo e ilustración en España* (Barcelona, 1976); F. Moreno Saez, *La Ilustración española* (Alicante, 1986); J. Sarrailh, *La España ilustrada de la segunda mitad del siglo XVIII* (Madrid, 1979); A. Domínguez Ortíz, *Sociedad y estado en el siglo XVIII español* (Barcelona, 1988); J. Marias, *La España posible en tiempos de Carlos III* (Barcelona, 1988).

40. See Fundación BBV, *La Real Sociedad Bascongada y América* (III Seminario de Historia de la RSBAP) (San Sebastián, 1991).

41. See J. Astigarra Goenaga, "La expansión de la RSBAP por América," in *La Real Sociedad Bascongada y América*, 93–102.

42. "Irurac Bat" means "the three are one" and refers to Gipuzkoa, Bizkaia, and Araba. Other such organizations added Navarre and were named "Laurac Bat," meaning "the four are one."

43. See M. C. Torales, "Los comerciantes de Nueva España socios de RSBAP," in *La Real Sociedad Bascongada y América*, 59–89; J. Arenas Sanchez and J. I. Tellechea Idigoras, "Socios de la RSBAP en Chihuahua (México)," in *La Real Sociedad Bascongada y América*, 149–71.

44. See I. Alvarez Cuartero, *Las Sociedades Económicas de los Amigos del País en Cuba* (Vitoria-Gasteiz, 1992).

45. See M. L. Rodríguez Baena, *La Sociedad Económica de Amigos del País de Manila en el siglo XVIII* (Sevilla, 1966).

CHAPTER 4. BASQUE AMERICANS

1. A. Domínguez Ortíz, ed., *Historia de España. Descubrimiento, colonización y emancipación* (Madrid, 1990), 196.

2. See R. Konetzke, "Legislación sobre inmigración de extranjeros en América durante la época colonial," *Revista Internacional de Sociología* (Mexico) 11–12 (1945): 269–99.

3. The legislation was configured in this regard throughout the sixteenth century. Ferdinand the Catholic thus approved an initiative of Governor Nicolás Ovando in 1504 demanding that married colonists from his territory return to Spain for their wives. And several years later Emperor Charles V made the same demand in order to reestablish the conjugal union in the New World broken temporarily with the man's departure.

4. E. Lemus and R. Márquez, "La emigración española a Ultramar. Los precedentes," in *Historia general de la emigración española a Iberoamérica*, vol. 1 (Madrid: CEDEAL, 1992), 38.

5. J. L. Martínez, *Pasajeros de Indias. Viajes transatlánticos en el siglo XVI* (Madrid, 1983), 33ff.

6. R. Carande, *Carlos V y sus banqueros. La vida económica de España en una fase de su hegemonía (1516–1556)*, 2 vols. (Madrid, 1943), 1:265.

7. Lemus and Márquez, "La emigración española a Ultramar," 44.

8. A. Domínguez Ortíz, *La sociedad española del siglo XVII* (Madrid, 1963), 2:90.

9. See C. Martínez Shaw, *La emigración española a América (1492–1824)* (Colombres, 1984), 40ff.

10. J. Nadal Oller, *La población española. Siglos XVI a XX* (Barcelona, 1986), 28ff.

11. M. Mörner, "La emigración española al Nuevo Mundo antes de 1810. Un informe del estado de la investigación," *Anuario de Estudios Americanos (AEA)* 32 (1975): 88.

12. J. Martínez Cardos, *Las Indias y las Cortes de Castilla durante los siglos XVI y XVII* (Madrid, 1956), 114–15.

13. R. Konetzke, "Las fuentes para la historia demográfica de Hispanoamérica durante la época colonial," *Revista Internacional de Sociología* (Mexico) 3 (1945): 281.

14. Nadal Oller, *La población española*, 121.

15. Ibid., 62.

16. See C. Martínez Shaw, *La emigración española a América (1492–1824)* (Colombres, 1984), 13–26.

17. Mörner, "La emigración española al Nuevo Mundo antes de 1810."

18. Domínguez Ortíz, *La sociedad española en el siglo XVII*, vol. 1.

19. Nadal Oller, *La población española*, 54–64.

20. R. Konetzke, "Las fuentes para la historia demográfica de Hispanoamérica durante la época colonial," *Anuario de Estudios Americanos (AEA)* 5 (1947): 267–323.

21. P. Boyd-Bowman, *Indice geobiográfico de cuarenta mil pobladores españoles en América en el siglo XVI (1493–1519)* (Bogotá, 1964); "La emigración peninsular a América (1520–1539)," *Historia Mexicana* 13, no. 2 (1963); "La procedencia de los españoles de América (1540–1559)," *Historia Mexicana* 16, no. 65 (1967); "La emigración española a América (1560–1579)," in *Studia Hispánica* (1974); and "Patterns of Spanish

Emigration to the Indies until 1600," *Spanish American Historical Review* (1976): 123–48.
22. Nadal Oller, *La población española*, 74.
23. Martínez Shaw, *La emigración española a América*, 91–101.
24. J. I. Rubio Mañe, ed., "Gente de España en la Ciudad de México. Año de 1689," *Bolétin del AGN* (Mexico City) 7, nos. 1–2 (1966).
25. V. Vázquez de Prada and J. B. Amores Carredano, "La emigración de navarros y vascongados al Nuevo Mundo y su repercusión en las comunidades de orígen," in *La emigración española a Ultramar, 1492–1914*, 133–42.
26. See R. Márquez Macías, *La emigración española a América, 1765–1824* (Oviedo, 1995).
27. Martínez Shaw, *La emigración española a América*, 163ff.
28. Ibid, 165ff.
29. Márquez Macías, *La emigración española a América*, 125ff.
30. Ibid., 143ff.
31. J. M. Morales Alvarez, *Los extranjeros con una carta de naturaleza de las Indias durante la segunda mitad del siglo XVIII* (Caracas, 1980). Thus, numerous Basques from Iparralde went to America during this epoch.
32. Márquez Macías, *La emigración española a América*, 143ff.
33. Martínez Shaw, *La emigración española a América*, 182–83.
34. Ibid., 184–85.
35. Vázquez de Prada and Amores Carredano, "La emigración de navarros y vascongados al Nuevo Mundo," in *La emigración española a Ultramar, 1492–1914*, 133–42.
36. I. Macías Domínguez, "La emigración vasca a Indias en la primera mitad del siglo XVIII," in *Álava y América*, eds. R. Escobedo, A. Zaballa, and Ó. Álvarez (Vitoria-Gasteiz, 1996), 27–45.
37. See J. Andrés-Gallego, ed., *Navarra y América* (Madrid, 1992), 21ff.
38. Ibid., 27.
39. Ibid., 26.
40. Ibid., 28.
41. Ibid., 30.
42. Ibid., 43.
43. Ibid., 43–44.
44. Ibid., 33.
45. See J. L. Martínez, *El mundo privado de los emigrantes en Indias* (Mexico City, 1992).
46. Mörner, "La emigración española al Nuevo Mundo antes de 1810," 73ff.
47. Andrés-Gallego, *Navarra y América*, 45–47.
48. G. Lohmann Villena, "Los comerciantes vascos en el virreinato peruano," in *Los vascos y América. Actas de las Jornadas sobre el comercio vasco con América en el siglo XVIII y La Real Compañía Guipuzcoana de Caracas en el Centenario de Carlos III*, eds. R. Escobedo Mansilla, A. Rivera Medina, and A. Chapa Imaz (Bilbao, 1989), 55.
49. J. Friede, "Algunas observaciones sobre la realidad de la emigración española a America en la primera mitad del siglo XVI," *Revista de Indias* 49 (1952): 483.

50. See Martínez, *Pasajeros de Indias*, 31–110; Andrés-Gallego, *Navarra y América*, 57–74; F. López-Rios Fernández, *Historia médica de las navegaciones colombinas, 1492–1504* (Valladolid, 1993), 27–98.

51. See Lemus and Márquez, "La emigración española a Ultramar," 41ff.

52. Pierre Chaunu calculates that around the 1520s, a clerk collected 2.5 ducats a year, a laborer—when he had work—earned 13.5 ducats per year, a mason's assistant 16 ducats, and a master mason 32 ducats. The yearly salaries of sailors, bearing in mind that they received room and board, were slightly higher: in 1543 they ranged from 24 ducats for sailors, to 72 for a master, 84 for a pilot, and around 134 for a captain.

53. Fra Antonio de Guevara, "De las cosas que el mareante se ha de proveer para entrar en la galera," in *Libro de los inventores del arte de marear y de muchos trabajos que se pasan en las galeras* (Valladolid, 1539).

54. Ibid., 27.

55. The caravel and the galleon were the most frequently used ships for trips to the New World from the mid-sixteenth century on, although there were urcas and carracks for commercial traffic and smaller dispatch boats like filibotes, pingues, polacras, tartans, sloops, and pinnaces, in general patches with a capacity of 40 to 200 tons. Such vessels were staffed with a crew of about thirty men and could carry between twenty and thirty passengers on board crowded into approximately twenty-four meters in length by eight in width by four in height. See C. H. Haring, *Comercio y navegación entre España y las Indias en la época de los Habsburgos* (Mexico, 1979), 328–29.

56. Ibid., 330.

57. Eugenio de Salazar, *Disquisiciones náuticas* (1573), in Martínez, *Pasajeros de Indias*, 281ff.

58. Fra Tomás de la Torre, *Diario del viaje de Salamanca a Ciudad Real (México)* (1545), in Martínez, *Pasajeros de Indias*, 235ff.

59. A. Domínguez Ortíz, *El Antiguo Régimen. Los Reyes Católicos y los Austrias* (Madrid, 1981), 80ff.

60. See J. M. González Cembellín, *América en el País Vasco. Inventario de elementos patrimoniales de origen americano en la Comunidad Autónoma Vasca (referencias bibliográficas)* (Vitoria-Gasteiz, 1993), 23–72.

61. In the opinion of the members of the RSBAP, "education of young people should not only be the main objective of society, but the only one, until the Enlightenment is spread and the happy time arrives to properly apply its ideals to particular objectives."

62. Private houses paid for by the emigrants upon their return from American travels would also be included under this heading.

63. González Cembellín, *América en el País Vasco*, 34.

64. Ibid., 35ff.

65. J. A. Barrio Loza and J. R. Valverde Peña, *Platería antigua en Bizkaia* (Bilbao, 1986), 26–29.

66. The reader curious about this type of artistic representation financed with American money can look through the recently published patrimonial inventories in the Basque Country and Navarre. One of the most complete works of bibliographic references is González Cembellín, *América en el País Vasco*.

67. Ibid., 45–47.
68. See A. M. Arrieta, *La emigración alavesa a América en el siglo XIX* (Vitoria-Gasteiz, 1992), 289ff.
69. Andrés-Gallego, *Navarra y América*, 197.
70. Arrieta, *La emigración alavesa a América*, 328.
71. See González Cembellín, *América en el País Vasco*, 67–75.

CHAPTER 5. THE OVERSEAS DESTINATIONS

1. M. Mathes, "Los vascos en la expansión de la frontera de Nueva España en el siglo XVI. La fundación de Nueva Vizcaya y Nuevo México," in *Los vascos y América. Ideas, hechos, hombres*, eds. I. Arana Pérez et al. (Madrid, 1990), 238–46.
2. Ibid., 48.
3. P. Boyd-Bowman, *Indice geobiográfico de más de 56.000 pobladores de la América hispánica. I. 1493–1519* (Mexico City, 1985).
4. I. Rubio Mañé, "Gente de España en la Ciudad de México," *Bolétin del AGN* (Mexico City) 7, nos. 1–2 (1966).
5. B. Hausberger, "La comunidad vasca en Sonora (1640–1767)," (unpublished manuscript, 1993).
6. J. Nadal Oller, *La población española. Siglos XVI al XX* (Barcelona, 1984).
7. Hausberger, "La comunidad vasca en Sonora," 54.
8. See their biographies in Hausberger, "La comunidad vasca en Sonora," 90ff.
9. Hausberger, "La comunidad vasca en Sonora," 53–54.
10. I follow the interesting work of Berd Hausberger, already cited, which also contains a significant number of biographies of Basques in the colonial period of 1640–1767, pp. 77ff.
11. M. C. Torales Pacheco, "Comerciantes vascos en Nueva España en la segunda mitad del siglo XVIII," in *Tercer Seminario*, Madrid, 1987.
12. Torales Pacheco, "Comerciantes vascos en Nueva España," 281.
13. Ibid., 282.
14. E. Luque Alcaide, *La Cofradía de Aránzazu en México (1681–1799)* (Pamplona, 1995). See also J. Garate Arriola and J. I. Tellechea Idigoras, *El Colegio de las Vizcaínas de México y el Real Seminario de Vergara* (Vitoria-Gasteiz, 1992).
15. Archivo Histórico del Colegio de las Vizcaínas. Est. 6, T. 1, V. 2, fol. 2, cited by Luque Alcaide, *La Cofradía de Aránzazu en México*, 37.
16. Luque Alcaide, *La Cofradía de Aránzazu en México*, 79.
17. Ibid., 79.
18. See J. I. Tellechea Idigoras, "El Colegio de las Vizcaínas de la Ciudad de México," in *Los vascos y América*.
19. See J. Gárate, *Los Colegios de las Vizcaínas y Vergara en el siglo XVIII* (Mendoza, 1972); A. Martínez Salazar and K. San Sebastián, *Los vascos en México. Estudio biográfico, histórico y bibliográfico* (Vitoria-Gasteiz, 1992).

20. Luque Alcaide, *La Cofradía de Aránzazu en México*, 98ff.
21. See the complete list in J. Gárate Arriola and J. I. Tellechea Idígoras, *El Colegio de las Vizcaínas de México y el Real Seminario de Vergara* (Vitoria-Gasteiz, 1992), 100–119.
22. Ibid., 120.
23. E. Ruiz de Azúa, *Vascongadas y América* (Madrid, 1992), 291–92.
24. A. Alday Garay, "La emigración del Valle de Baztán a América en el siglo XX" (Ph.D. diss., University of Deusto-Bilbao, 1992).
25. L. Gaarder, "The Basques of Mexico: An Historical and Contemporary Portrait" (Ph.D. diss., University of Utah, 1976).
26. We employ the interesting information in T. García Giráldez, "La formación de redes familiares vascas en Centroamérica," in *Emigración y redes sociales de los vascos en América*, eds. R. Escobedo Mansilla, A. Zaballa Beascoechea, and Ó. Álvarez Gila (Vitoria-Gasteiz, 1996).
27. The founder of the family in Central America, Diego González Batres, was a soldier and nobleman, and had *encomiendas* in Amapal, Escohayguin, and San Miguel (El Salvador). His marriage to a descendent of Jorge de Alvarado, a brother of the provincial governor, conferred upon him the status of descendant of conquistadors and first settlers. He was *alcalde ordinario* in 1720 and alderman of San Miguel; ibid., 333.
28. Ibid., 335.
29. T. García Giráldez, "La formación de redes familares vascas en Centroamérica" in *Emigración y redes sociales*, 338.
30. M. M. Ciudad Suárez,"Presencia vasca en Centroamérica. La provincia dominica de San Vicente. Siglos XVI–XVII," in *Euskal Herria y el Nuevo Mundo. La contribución de los vascos a la formación de las Americas*, eds. R. Escobedo Mansilla, A. Zaballa Beascoechea, and Ó. Álvarez Gila (Vitoria-Gasteiz, 1996), 389.
31. I follow the work of M. M. Ciudad Suárez, ibid., 373ff, 388.
32. In addition to the Spanish and Euskara that they had probably learned in their infancy, these missionaries knew the Mexican language, which they used as an auxiliary aid in their preaching to the natives. For source of missionary data, see "Presencia vasca en Centroamérica. La provincia dominica de San Vicente, siglos XVI–XVII" in *Euskal Herria y el Nuevo Mundo*, 388.
33. J. Luján Muñoz, "Los vascos en el comercio del Reino de Guatemala al final del período colonial," in *Los vascos y América*.
34. We follow the already cited work of Jorge Lujan Muñoz.
35. R. Arrieta Villalobos, "Notas sobre la presencia vasca en Hispanoamérica y Costa Rica," in *Los vascos y América*.
36. Ibid., 22.
37. M. Estornés Lasa, "Topónimos vascos en los países americanos," in *Los vascos y América*.
38. Mons. R. Arrieta Villalobos, "Notas sobre la presencia vasca en Hispanoamérica y Costa Rica," 139–41.
39. Estornés Lasa, "Topónimos vascos en los países americanos," 94–95.

40. See J. Bilbao, *Vascos en Cuba, 1492–1511* (Buenos Aires, 1958).

41. E. Fernández de Pinedo, *La emigración vasca a América, siglos XIX y XX* (Asturias, 1993).

42. Ibid., 29ff.

43. Ibid., 30ff.

44. M. Moreno Fraginals, *El ingenio. Complejo económico social cubano del azúcar*, vol. 2 (Havana, 1978), 59. Pío Baroja well illustrates the black slave trade with Cuba in his work "Los pilotos de altura."

45. See Moreno Fraginal.

46. Ibid., 38–39.

47. Fernández de Pinedo, *La emigración vasca a América, siglos XIX y XX*, 131.

48. J. Bilbao, "Vascos en Cuba," in *América y los vascos. 1492–1992*, ed. J. Bilbao Azkarreta (Bilbao, 1992), 28.

49. Ibid., 29.

50. "Gaspar de Arteaga y Aunaovidao, gobernador de Puerto Rico (1670–1674)," in *Euskal Herria y el Nuevo Mundo*.

51. The Puerto Rican governorship was either the first link in a chain of more desirable future commands or the culmination of a vigorous military career. All the seventeenth-century Puerto Rican governors had extended, impressive military records of the heroic acts. None had experience in civil government. They came from the noble stratum.

52. A. López Cantos, *Juegos, fiestas y diversions en la América española* (Madrid, 1992), 133.

53. Ibid., 135.

54. Note their childishness and lack of seriousness.

55. López Cantos, *Juegos*, 155.

56. The practice of smuggling was very common among the Puerto Ricans since the colony's foundation.

57. B. Sonesson, "La emigración española a Puerto Rico," in *Españoles hacia América*, comp. N. Sánchez-Albornoz (Madrid, 1988), 330.

58. Ibid., 332.

59. Ruiz de Azúa, *Vascongadas y América*, 280.

60. Sonesson, "La emigración española a Puerto Rico," in *Españoles hacia América*, 302.

61. Ibid., 307.

62. Ibid., 305.

63. Ibid., 304.

64. Ibid., 307.

65. Ibid., 306.

66. Ibid., 305.

67. We follow the interesting works of E. Cifré de Loubriel, *La inmigración a Puerto Rico durante el siglo XIX* (San Juan, 1964); *La formación del pueblo puertorriqueño. La contribución de los vascongados, navarros y aragoneses* (San Juan, 1986).

68. This also occurred in the case of Catalonian immigration, which was 92 percent male.

69. Only three lawyers, a fortification engineer, three civil and military doctors, a notary, two journalists, a writer, three professors, forty priests and sisters of mercy, and four clerks have been found.

70. E. Cifré de Loubriel, "Los vascongados y su contribución a la formación del pueblo puertorriqueño," in *Emigración y redes sociales*, 37.

71. There is presently a Basque Center in Puerto Rico structured around the descendants of those dealt with here.

72. F. de Abrisketa, *Presencia vasca en Colombia* (Vitoria-Gasteiz, 1983), 12.

73. Abrisketa, *Presencia vasca en Colombia*. The relations among Basque personalities can be seen in this work by Abrisketa.

74. Ibid., 51ff.

75. Abrisketa, *Presencia vasca en Colombia*.

76. M. E. Martínez Gorroño, "El exilio vasco en Colombia," in *Emigración y redes sociales*.

77. Ibid., 52ff.

78. Ibid., 51ff.

79. In this position, he replaced the country's former president, Mariano Ospina Pérez. He had as important students Mijael Pastiana Borro and Gabriel Betancourt (ibid.).

80. For this reason, he received the Boyacá Cross at the rank of knight.

81. Three members of the Perea-Sasiain family remain in Colombia (his wife and children María Victoria and José). See Martínez Gorroño, "El exilio vasco en Colombia."

82. The production of armaments of the Basque factories was under the jurisdiction of this secretariat.

83. All this data is from Martínez Gorroño, "El exilio vasco en Colombia."

84. He received the Boyacá Cross.

85. He was director of the Institute of Statistics of the Organization of American States in Washington.

86. A monument to Gernika was built, and placed in the park of the same name, in the neighborhood of Palermo. It was designed in bronze by the sculptor Oteiza.

87. K. Hummel, *A Wanted Man: The Basque, El Cojo Gómez in Colombia*, 1989.

88. Presently, his wife and two of their three children are still alive (see Martínez Gorroño, "El exilio vasco en Colombia").

89. He authored two novels: *Joanixio* and *Bizitza garratza da* (see Martínez Gorroño, "El exilio vasco en Colombia," in *Emigración y redes sociales*.

90. The reader will have observed how this book sometimes discusses the use of Euskara among the Basque colony. The Company of Caracas sometimes used it for military purposes. In 1779, the captains of two frigates, belonging to a convoy of the Company of Caracas at the point of being boarded by the English, used Euskara in communication from ship to ship in order to conceal their defense tactics.

91. Between 1730 and 1810, a total of 3,260 Basques reached Venezuela. See M. Mörner, "Inserción del fenómeno vasco en la emigración europea a América," in *Emigración y redes sociales*.

92. Cited by Ruiz de Azúa, *Vascongadas y América*, 286.

93. Ortiz de la Tabla Ducasse, "Presencia vasca en el Ecuador colonial," in *Emigración y redes sociales*.

94. Nevertheless, there were also cases of influential families in colonial Ecuador, such as the Larreas. Without holding honorary titles or posts in the high imperial bureaucracy, they were capable of surviving with notable dignity and reproducing and increasing their family's initial capital. Their importance was more than evident in the 1740s. (See Tomás Herzog in *Emigración y redes sociales*.)

95. Bilbao Azkarreta, ed., *América y los vascos*.

96. J. Cardenal Landazuri, "El tercer concilio provincial de Lima y la evangelización del Nuevo Mundo," in *Los vascos y América*.

97. *Constitución de la Ilustre Hermandad Vascongada de Nuestra Señora de Aránzazu* (Lima: printed by J. María Masia, 1858).

98. C. D. Malamud, "La consolidación de una familia de la oligarquía arequipeña. Los Goyeneche," in *Revista Quinto Centenario* 4 (1982): 49–135.

99. See the work of Eusebio Quiroz Paz-Soldán, "Los vascos en la ciudad de Arequipa," in *Emigración y redes sociales*. The author gives the complete biographies of thirty-three Basques that settled in the city and attained high levels of power, whether military, commercial, or in the colonial administration. The study encompasses the sixteenth, seventeenth, and eighteenth centuries. The individuals that appear are 1. Juan José Aguerrevere (eighteenth), 2. Martín José Albizu y Baquedano (eighteenth), 3. Antonio de Albizuri (eighteenth), 4. Francisco de Arancibia (seventeenth), 5. Juan José Arechavala (eighteenth), 6. Pedro Ignacio de Arrambide (eighteenth), 7. José de Avellaneda Sandoval y Rojas (seventeenth), 8. Juan Francisco Belaunde (eighteenth), 9. Antonio de Butrón y Mújica (seventeenth), 10. Mateo Cossío (eighteenth), 13. Martín de Gareca (seventeenth), 14. Antonio Gómez Butrón de Vergara (seventeenth), 15. Juan Crisóstomo de Goyeneche (eighteenth), 16. Lope de Idiáquez (sixteenth), 17. Martín Jauriondo (seventeenth), 18. Gabriel de Larramendi (eighteenth), 19. Juan Bautista Larramendi (eighteenth), 20. Juan Larrea (sixteenth), 21. Sebastián de Laurtaun (sixteenth), 22. Gabriel López de Dicastillo y Ascona (seventeenth–eighteenth), 23. Juan López de Ricalde (sixteenth), 24. Isidro de Mendinburo (eighteenth), 25. Juanes Navarro (?), 26. Juan de Olazabal y Arteaga (sixteenth), 27. Juan Felipe Portu (eighteenth), 28. José Ruiz de Somocurcio (eighteenth), 29. Juan de San Juan (sixteenth), 30. José Lino Urbicain (eighteenth), 31. Pedro de Verastegui (seventeenth), 32. Miguel de Vergara (sixteenth), 33. Fernando de Yrazabal (seventeenth).

100. Ruiz de Azúa, *Vascongadas y América*, 286.

101. Ibid., 284.

102. R. E. Velázquez, "Presencia vasca en la historia del Paraguay," in *Los vascos y América*.

103. Ibid.

104. J. Salazar González and R. Hernández Ponce, *Cuatrocientos años de presencia vasca en Chile* (Santiago, 1991), 9.

105. Ibid., 8.

106. J. Figueroa Salas, "El informe Villareal," in *Los vascos y América*.

107. Salazar González and Hernández Ponce, *Cuatrocientos años de presencia vasca en Chile*, 40ff.
108. Ibid., 54.
109. A. Edwards, *La fronda aristocrática en Chile* (Santiago, 1928).
110. Population census of the Republic of Chile, 1907, Instituto Nacional de Estadística (INE).
111. M. Camus Argaluza, *La inmigración vasca en Chile. 1880–1990* (Santiago, 1991), 32.
112. Ibid., 23.
113. Ibid., 24.
114. All the data is from Camus Argaluza, 24.
115. Ibid., 28.
116. Ibid., 26–27.
117. It is currently very common in Chile to hear the saying: "The Basques have made two important contributions to humanity: the Society of Jesus and Chile."
118. H. de Charnisay, *L'emigration basco-béarnaise en Amerique* (Biarritz, 1996), 211ff.
119. All the data and information come from J. de Souza-Martins, "La inmigración española en Brasil," in *Españoles hacia América*, 249–69.
120. Lack of knowledge about the country, the foreign language, and the less hospitable conditions in Brazil can explain the reservations of the Basques of Iparralde concerning this territory.

CHAPTER 6. THE HUMAN DELUGE TO RÍO DE LA PLATA

1. See A. M. Cocchi, J. Klaczko, and J. R. Roade, "Una red urbana ordenadora de un espacio vacío. El caso uruguayo," *CIESU* 24 (1997): 37–54. Maps I, II, and III provide graphic evidence of the locations of these early settlements. We also follow José Ramón Pando's lead (*Las migraciones internacionales del Uruguay* [Montevideo, 1982]), with regard to the colonial period.
2. E. M. Narancio, A. R. Fournier, and F. Capurro, "Historia y análisis estadístico." According to Félix de Azara's 1797 census, 17,000 residents remained from the expulsion of the Jesuits decreed by the monarchy in the 1760s. Consistent with the claims of these authors, when the Portuguese took definitive possession of the Banda Oriental missions in 1801, their population did not exceed 7,000.
3. See J. R. Uriarte, *Los baskos en la nación argentina* (Buenos Aires, 1919).
4. L. C. Benvenuto, *Breve historia del Uruguay. Economía y sociedad* (Montevideo, 1967). In 1760, 30,000 hides were exported; in 1780, 300,000. In 1783, 1,500,000 hides were warehoused.
5. O. M. Arbiza, *El aporte vasco al departamento de Artigas* (Montevideo, 1987).
6. Archivo General de la Nación Montevideo (AGN), Montevideo Police, Passport Book, 1829–1832, book no. 934.

7. Ibid.
8. Ibid.
9. Ibid.
10. Ibid.
11. Archivo General de la Nación Montevideo (AGN), Montevideo Police, Passport Book, 1833.
12. A. Lamas, *Los apuntes estadísticos* (Montevideo, 1928).
13. Arsène Isabelle, *Le Patriote Française* on 25 and 26 September 1843.
14. W. Reyes Abadie and A. Vázquez Romero, *Crónica general del Uruguay*, vol. 3 (Montevideo, 1964), 310.
15. Cited by J. A. Oddone, *La emigración europea al Río de la Plata. Motivaciones y proceso de incorporación* (Montevideo, 1966), 15.
16. F. Michel, *Le pays Basque. Sa population, sa langue, ses moeurs, sa littérature et sa musique* (Paris, 1857), 193.
17. We follow the interesting study of Henry de Charnisay, *L'emigration basco-béarnaise en Amerique* (Biarritz: J. & D. Éditions, 1996).
18. "Urban population" refers to places with 2,000 or more inhabitants.
19. The migratory surplus is determined by calculating the difference (during a set period) between the surplus births and deaths, on one hand, and the variations between the legal population and location of residence, on the other.
20. H. de Charnisay, *L'emigration basco-béarnaise en Amerique* (Biarritz, 1996), 113ff.
21. It is made up of the French Basque Country, or Iparralde (Basse-Navarre, Soule, and Labourd) and the region of Béarn.
22. All the figures are from Charnisay, *L'emigration basco-béarnaise en Amerique*, 114–15.
23. Mauricio Azevedo argues that there were 5,900 Basque and Béarnaise men and 1,457 Basque and Béarnaise women between 1832 and 1841. The ratio of four men per one woman was maintained. The emigrants that traveled as families were 27 percent of the total (with a median of two children). The minors that left alone accounted for 31 percent, and the adults that departed alone 42 percent.
24. "Raport du baron Deffandis au ministere des affaires etrangerès," cited by M. Marenales Rossi and G. Bourdé, "L'immigration française et le peuplement de l'Uruguay (1830–1860)," *Cahiers des Ameriques Latines* (Paris) (1977): 20ff.
25. The Iparralde clergy also conducted an active anti-emigration campaign within its territory. It was extremely worried by the departure of Basque youths from the region of the Basses-Pyrénées, especially by the conditions under which they emigrated. But what bothered the clergy from that side of the Pyrenees the most was its loss of influence over its shrinking following. Facing the impossibility of staunching the flow of Basques and Béarnaises from its diocese, the Order of Betharram decided to found a branch in Río de la Plata. The first priests left Bayonne for Buenos Aires in 1856 on the ship *L'Etincelle*. In 1858, this same order built the Church of the Basques in Montevideo; it would come to exert a notable influence throughout the region.

26. J. Quiroga, *Memoria sobre el fomento de la emigración vascongada a la República Oriental del Uruguay*, Comisión Central Directiva de Inmigración, annual report from 1875.

27. Archivo General de la Montevideo (AGM), Montevideo Police, Passport Book, 1829–1832, book no. 1035.

28. It is titled "Algunas reflexiones a partir de los legajos matrimoniales de la catedral de Montevideo del año 1853 y la Guía de Forasteros de 1861" (Montevideo, 1996, unpublished manuscript).

29. To the degree that the port of Montevideo received a subsidy from the French authorities.

30. An interesting study of a married couple and their descendants (nineteenth and twentieth centuries) can be found in A. Abal Oliu, "Bernard Bidegaray Haramboure–Jeanne Beheran Garra, Montevideo" (1983, unpublished manuscript).

31. This affirmation is consistent with the result of the 1843 census done by Andrés Lamas. Of a total of 19,845 inhabitants, 11,431 were native (38.3 percent), 5,328 were French (17.8 percent), and 4,205 were Italian (14.0 percent). The Spaniards would follow.

32. In a magnificent presentation at the First Seminar on Basque History, Culture, and Immigration in Uruguay (Montevideo, August 1996), Martín Ospitaleche showed how the associative impulses of the Basque colony were important throughout the nineteenth century in both Montevideo and the interior.

33. We follow the information of A. Arbillaga Arriola, *Lo que se ha dicho de Iparraguirre* (Bilbao, 1967); L. de Castresana, *Vida y obra de Iparraguirre* (Bilbao, 1971); J. Gárate Arriola, *Iparraguirre* (Bilbao, 1987); F. Grandmontagne, *Los inmigrantes prósperos* (Madrid, 1944); J. M. Salaverria, *Iparraguirre, el último bardo* (Madrid, 1932).

34. AGN, Madrid, Box 5400.

35. AGN, Sección: Periódicos. *El Día*, 1908.

36. Ibid.

37. Ibid.

38. Cited by J. P. Barrán and B. Nahum, *El Uruguay del novecientos* (Montevideo, 1979), 175.

39. Ibid., 177.

40. Ibid., 176.

41. Here we follow the works of C. Martínez Martín, "Destacados vascongados en la consolidación territorial del Tucumán. La frontera del Chaco, 1670–1724," in *Euskal Herria y el Nuevo Mundo. La contribución de los vascos a la formación de las Américas*, eds. R. Escobedo Mansilla, A. Zaballa Beascoechea, and Ó. Álvarez Gila (Vitoria-Gasteiz, 1996); and A. J. Gullón Abao, "La frontera Oriental del Tucumán a principios del siglo XVIII. Las expediciones de Esteban de Urízar y Arespacochaga, 1710–1711," in *Euskal Herria y el Nuevo Mundo*.

42. Some scholars believe that Juan de Garay was born in Burgos, not in Bizkaia.

43. As a random sample, the sections concerning wills from 1790 to 1820 of the Archivo General de la Nación (AGN) of Buenos Aires have been consulted.

44. V. O. Cutolo, *Nuevo diccionario biográfico argentino (1750–1930)* (Buenos Aires,

1975). See also N. L. Siegrist de Gentile, "Familias de origen vasco-navarro y santanderinas en Buenos Aires y sus enlaces con el litoral desde fines del siglo XVIII hasta mediados del XIX," in *Noveno Congreso Nacional y Regional de historia Argentina* (Buenos Aires: Academia de la Historia, 1996).

45. Cutolo, *Nuevo diccionario biográfico argentino*.
46. Ibid.
47. Ibid.
48. Ibid.
49. See C. A. García Belsunce, *Los vascos en Buenos Aires en 1810* (Buenos Aires, 1982).
50. This commission was eliminated by Rosas in August 1830, and restored in 1854. Its aim was to (1) intervene in the event of any disagreement arising between the contractor and the emigrant; and (2) ensure the fulfillment of contracts agreed upon between emigrants and agents in Europe and, later, the ones between emigrants and their employers.
51. The author has determined this by examining various notarized contracts and agreements between *estancieros* and shepherds (AGN, Buenos Aires. Scribe section).
52. It is common to find allusions in the wills to how they began working with extremely limited resources and ended up owning an acceptable family livestock business.
53. Marcelino Iriani, *Los vascos y la inmigración temprana en la provincia de Buenos Aires* (Rosario, 1989), 79.
54. Citado por Marcelino Iriani, *Los vascos y la inmigración temprana en la provincia de Buenos Aires* (Rosario, 1989), 81.
55. Nora Siegrist, "Redes sociales, económicas, espirituales y religiosas de vasco-navarros en Buenos Aires: 1826–1865," in R. Escobedo Mansilla, A. Zaballa Beascoechea, and Ó. Álvarez Gila, eds., *Emigración y redes sociales de los vascos en América* (Vitoria-Gasteiz, 1996).
56. Translator's note: Probably Basse Navarre in France.
57. J. A. Hammerton, *The Real Argentine: Notes and Impressions of a Year in the Argentine and Uruguay* (New York, 1915), cited by Douglass and Bilbao, *Amerikanuak*, 191ff.
58. J. H. Lesca, *Les Basques et les Béarnais dans l'Argentine et l'Uruguay*, 1907, 41.
59. *Annals of the Sociedad Rural Argentina*, 1899, 419.
60. *Annals of the Sociedad Rural Argentina*, 1899.
61. See the interesting study of Óscar Álvarez Gila, entitled "Vascos y Vascongados, luchas ideológicas entre carlistas y nacionalistas en los centros vascos del Río de la Plata (1900–1930)," in *Emigración y redes sociales*.
62. See B. Cava, "El asociacionismo vasco en Argentina. Política cultural," in ibid.
63. Felipe Muguerza, "¿Qué es la Federación de Entidades Vasco Argentinas?" in *The Basque Diaspora, La Diáspora Vasca*, eds. Wm. A. Douglass, C. Urza, L. White, and J. Zulaika (Reno, 1999), 61–77.

CHAPTER 7. FOUNDATIONS OF THE RECENT EXODUS

1. M. Reinhard and A. Armengaud, *Historia de la población mundial* (Barcelona, 1966).

2. Especially when in the Basque Country, due to the mountainous nature of its territory, parcels of terrain were small rather than large.

3. P. Hourmat, "De l'emigration basco-bearnaise du XVIII siécle à nos jours," *Societé des Sciences et Lettres et Arts de Bayonne* (Bayonne) 132 (1976): 227–54.

4. J. A. Oddone, *La emigración europea al Río de la Plata. Motivaciones y proceso de incorporación* (Montevideo, 1966).

5. As during the early Modern Age, more than a few European fortunes were linked to black slave commerce.

6. For example, beginning in 1882, Chile offered, through its immigration agency established in Paris to attract immigrants, free railroad passage from the point of immigrant departure to the closest or chosen port.

7. S. Fernández Gimenez, *Historia de la navegación* (Madrid, 1988).

8. H. Silva, "La política inmigratoria nacional argentina," in *Legislación y política inmigratoria en el Cono Sur*, eds. H. Asdrúbal Silva et al. (Mexico City, 1987).

9. H. Silva et al., *Legislación y política inmigratoria en el Cono Sur* (Mexico City, 1987).

10. Ibid., 420.

11. Ibid., 422.

12. Translator's note: The Spanish verb *enganchar* has a variety of overlapping meanings, including "to hook," "to recruit," and "to inveigle." *Enganchadores,* or *enganchador* agents, therefore, were quite literally those that "hooked" emigrants through persuasion. The *ganchos* worked for them, with this term deriving from the same word.

13. J. J. Arteaga and E. Puiggros, "Legislación y política migratoria en Uruguay," in *Legislación y política inmigratoria en el Cono Sur,* 403–55.

14. Ibid., 407.

15. *La inmigración europea en Chile (1882–1895)* (Santiago, 1896).

16. Oddone, *La emigración europea al Río de la Plata,* 11–12.

17. Archivo General de la Nación (AGN), Buenos Aires, National Government Division (1817–1843), Sala X-1-4-6.

18. Ibid.

19. Ibid.

20. P. Lhande, *La emigración vasca* (San Sebastián, 1971). The first edition was published in 1910.

21. Meaning Euskara and French.

22. Cited by Azcona Pastor, *Los paraísos posibles. Historia de la emigración vasca a Argentina y Uruguay en el siglo XIX* (Bilbao, 1992), 212ff.

23. Historical Archive of Notarial Protocols of Oñati. Scribe Miguel Francisco de Eizmendi. Protocol of Astigarraga, leg. 271, fol. 252.

24. Historical Archive of Notarial Protocols of Oñati. Scribe Joaquín Elósegui. Protocol of San Sebastián, leg. 4 (new), fols. 593–94.

25. M. P. Pildain Salazar, *Ir a América. La emigración vasca a América (Guipúzcoa 1840–1870)* (San Sebastián, 1984), 227–28.

26. Ibid., 228.

27. C. Idoate Ezquieta, *Emigración navarra del Valle del Baztán a América en el siglo XIX. Inventario de documentos* (Pamplona, 1989), 33ff.

28. See Azcona Pastor, *Los paraísos posibles*.

29. AHA, Protocolo de Miguel Angulo (Villanueva de Valdegovia), no. 11,867. Obligación de embarque a Montevideo y Buenos Aires, de Carlos y Romualdo del Castillo y Sobrón, hermanos, naturales y vecinos de Sobrón, y D. Angel Alonso y Angulo que lo es de Villanueva, Villanueva de Valdegovía, April 5, 1870, fols. 378–79.

30. AHA, Protocolo de José de Zumárraga (Vitoria), no. 13,735. Contrata D. Vicente Suso y Bengoa, vecino de Salvatierra, y su fiador D. Fausto Aguirre y Parrigorria [sic], vecino de Arcaute, a Isidro Rico y Gómez, vecino de Buenos Aires y domiciliado accidentalmente en Haro, Vitoria, July 23, 1878, fols. 3,311-3,314.

31. J. Cola y Goiti, "Las emigraciones," *La Concordia* 680 (May 20, 1888).

32. "No vayáis a América," *El Anunciador Vitoriano* 306 (April 2, 1881).

33. *El Anunciador Vitoriano* 144 (March 11, 1880).

34. *La Concordia* 628 (January 18, 1888).

35. J. Cola y Goiti, "Los españoles en el Uruguay," *El Anunciador Vitoriano* 1500 (September 16, 1886).

36. *La inmigración europea en Chile (1882–1895)*.

37. Conyoumdjiam Bergamali and A. Rebolledo Hernández, *Bibliografía sobre el proceso inmigratorio en Chile desde la independencia hasta 1930*, IPGM, vol. 1 (Mexico City, 1984), 122.

38. J. Vicens Vives, ed., *Historia de España y América* (Barcelona, 1961),34.

39. J. M. de Nieva, *Decretos, Leyes y Reales Órdenes del Rey Nuestro Señor Don Fernando VII*, vol. 12 (Madrid, 1928), 32–33.

40. J. M. de Nieva, *Decretos, Leyes y Reales Órdenes de la Reina Dª Isabel*, vol. 19 (Madrid, 1834), 481–82.

41. See J. Nadal Oller, *La población española. Siglos XVI a XX* (Barcelona, 1986).

42. R. Gutiérrez Nieto, *Ley de emigración* (Madrid, 1980), 17.

43. Letter from the Minister in Full Powers in the Argentine Republic, Pablo Soler, to the Minister of the Spanish State, Buenos Aires, October 28, 1914. Historic Archive of the Ministry of Foreign Affairs.

44. Speech of Senator Cavestany in the session held in the Senate on Thursday, May 25, 1916. In BCSE, 1916.

45. Speech of Senator Altamira in the session held in the Senate on Thursday, May 25, 1916. In BCSE, 1916.

46. Address of the Royal Decree of August 10, 1929, by the Minister of Work and Planning, Eduardo Aunós Pérez. In BCSE, 1929, 236.

47. Ibid., 235.

48. Address of the Royal Decree of January 24, 1930, by the Minister of Work and Planning, Eduardo Aunós Pérez. In BCSE, 1930.

49. Ibid.

50. Idoate Ezquieta, *Emigración navarra del Valle de Baztán a América en el siglo XIX* (Pamplona, 1989).

51. A. García-Sanz Marcotegui, "La emigración navarra a América a través de la publicista," in *Historia general de la emigración española a Iberoamérica*, vol. 2 (Madrid, 1992), 44.

52. Ibid., 411ff.

53. Ibid., 419–20.

54. Cited by ibid., 420.

55. García-Sanz Marcotegui, "La emigración navarra a América a través de la publicista," 440.

56. Pildain Salazar, *Ir a América*, 17.

57. M. Ferrer, D. Tejera, and J. F. Acedo, *Historia del tradicionalismo español*, vol. 28 (Sevilla, 1959), 7ff.

58. Ibid., 11–12.

59. A. I. Garaico Echea, *De Vasconia a Buenos Aires* (Buenos Aires, 1965).

60. A. M. Arrieta, *Emigración alavesa a América en el siglo XIX* (Vitoria-Gasteiz, 1992), 97ff.

61. Ibid., 97–98.

62. Cited by A. M. Arrieta, A. M. Barrundia, Expediente General de Quintas, 136.1.

63. García-Sanz Marcotegui, "La emigración navarra a América a través de la publicista," 422.

64. Wm. A. Douglass and J. Bilbao, *Amerikanuak: Basques in the New World* (Reno, 1975), 123–24.

65. Azcona Pastor, *Los paraísos posibles*, 78ff.

66. AMAB, Documental Fund of El Ferrol, leg. 8161.

67. Ibid.

68. In effect, for all the revolutionaries of 1789, that all the citizenry might equally realize armed service was a condition that made all men equal before the law. Prior to that year, army commanders were always noblemen and infantry soldiers came from the peasantry.

69. H. de Charnisay, *L'emigration basco-béarnaise en Amerique* (Biarritz, 1996), 134.

70. All the figures are from Henri de Charnisay.

71. Sometimes they even went so far as to perform amputations on themselves to avoid service, the most common being severing an ear or finger. There were even doctors that performed such operations. Teeth necessary for opening cartridges were also extracted. Lack of teeth meant exemption from military service.

72. P. Lhande, *La emigración vasca*, vol. 1, 27–28.

73. J. Andrés-Gallego et al., *Navarra y América* (Madrid, 1992), 369ff.

74. *Statistic of Emigration and Immigration of Spain* (Madrid, 1891), 15.

75. Wm. A. Douglass and J. Bilbao, *Amerikanuak: Basques in the New World* (Reno, 1975), 128.

CHAPTER 8. THE BUREAUCRACY, THE DREAMED-OF VOYAGE, AND THE TYPOLOGY OF THE EMIGRANT

1. P. Anselmo de Legarda, "De Pamplona a La Habana en 1851," BIAEV 100 (1975): 235–38.
2. J. M. Azcona Pastor, *Los paraísos posibles. Historia de la emigración vasca a Argentina y Uruguay en el siglo XIX* (Bilbao, 1992). See the chapter "Los viajes-martirio."
3. Ibid., 228.
4. J. Andrés-Gallego et al., *Navarra y América* (Madrid, 1992), 351.
5. Translator's note: *Gancho* is the Spanish word for "hook," thereby related to the power of persuasion. *Ganchos* were, therefore, agents that got their hooks into prospective clients, recruiting them for passage to the New World.
6. Collection of Circulars, June 1, 1840, to June 25, 1841, dossier 479, Library of the Foru Aldundia of Gipuzkoa.
7. In the *Boletín Oficial de Vizcaya* (1841): 84.
8. ADFA, DH 135, no. 1, Expediente sobre la adopción de las convenientes disposiciones para evitar la emigración de los habitantes de esta Provincia (de Alava) a la colonización del territorio de la República Peruana halagados por las ofertas que lleguen a dirigirseles por los agentes de D. Máximo Navarro, que ninguna de ellas sea cumplida.
9. In the *Boletín Oficial de Vizcaya* (1862): 84.
10. Collection of Circulars, July 14, 1866, to June 22, 1868, circular no. 30, vol. 479, Library of the Foru Aldundia de Gipuzkoa.
11. In the *Boletín Oficial de Vizcaya* (1880): 537–38.
12. In the *Boletín Oficial de Vizcaya* (1888): 155.
13. *El Navarro* (Pamplona), May 7, 1881.
14. In the *Boletín Oficial de Vizcaya* (1882): 552–53.
15. A. García-Sanz Marcotegui, "La emigración navarra a América a través de la publicista," in *Historia general de la emigración española a Iberoamérica*, vol. 2 (Madrid, 1992), 417–18.
16. Azcona Pastor, *Los paraísos posibles*, 160–62.
17. A. García-Sanz Marcotegui, "La emigración navarra a América a través de la publicista," 419ff.
18. For more on the subject, see Fernando Muru Ronda, "Prensa local y emigración vasca contemporanea," in *Emigración y redes sociales de los vascos en América*, eds. R. Escobedo Mansilla, A. Zaballa Beascoechea, and Ó. Álvarez Gila (Vitoria-Gasteiz, 1996).
19. There was also a current of *bertsolariak* who sang harsh improvised verses against emigration. There were even contests in Iparralde that had Basque emigration to Montevideo as their central theme. Regarding this topic, see Txomin Peillen, "La emigración económica vascofrancesa vista por los bardos populares de Uruguay y de Euskal Herria" (unpublished manuscript). In his doctoral thesis, "Los paraísos posibles," José Manuel Azcona also speaks of these popular anti-emigration bards.
20. A. M. Arrieta, *La Emigración alavesa a América en el siglo XIX* (Vitoria-Gasteiz, 1992), 214–17.

21. Azcona, *Los paraísos posibles*, 62–64.

22. In addition to the archives located in the Autonomous Basque Community, documentation has been searched for in the following places: the Archivo General de la Nación (AGN) in Montevideo, Uruguay; the Uruguayan National Library; General Emigration Administration of the Eastern Republic of Uruguay; Euskal-Erria Basque Center of Montevideo; El Euskaro Español Basque Center of Montevideo; the AGN in Buenos Aires, Argentina; the judicial section of the AGN in Buenos Aires, Argentina; and the Argentine National Library.

23. J. J. Virto, "La emigración de Navarra hacia América en la segunda mitad del siglo XIX," *Estudios de Ciencias Sociales* (Navarre) 4 (1991): 109–24.

24. J. Andrés-Gallego, *Historia contemporanea de Navarra* (Pamplona, 1982), 19.

25. Andrés-Gallego et al., *Navarra y América*, 302ff.

26. Ibid., 337.

27. Ibid., 335.

28. Ibid., 336.

29. According to the work of Álvaro Hilario Pérez de San Román, "Destinos de la emigración bizkaina a América en el siglo XIX," *Ernaroa* 6 (June 1991): 255–70.

30. See Azcona Pastor, *Los paraísos posibles*, 55–59.

31. M. P. Pildain Salazar, *Ir a América. La emigración vasca a América (Guipúzcoa 1840–1870)* (San Sebastián, 1984), 76ff.

32. Azcona Pastor, *Los paraísos posibles*, 59ff.

33. Andrés-Gallego et al., *Navarra y América*, 460ff.

34. Ibid., 461.

35. Ibid., 472.

36. Ibid., 89ff.

37. Azcona Pastor, *Los paraísos posibles*, 131.

38. H. de Charnisay, *L'emigration basco-béarnaise en Amerique* (Biarritz, 1996), 200.

CHAPTER 9. DRAMATIC EXILE

1. K. San Sebastián, *El exilio vasco en América. La acción del gobierno, política, organización, propaganda, económica, cultural, diplomacia* (San Sebastián, 1988).

2. The volume of Basque exiles in particular, and the Spanish in general, after the Civil War was ultimately higher than had occurred previously.

3. San Sebastián, *El exilio vasco en América*.

4. K. San Sebastián, *Crónicas de post-guerra* (Bilbao, 1982).

5. San Sebastián, *El exilio vasco en América*, 10.

6. I. Anasagasti, "El exilio vasco," *Muga* (San Sebastián) 40 (February 1985): 26–57.

7. L. Senkman, "La política migratoria argentina durante la década de los treinta. La selección étnica," in *Jornadas de Inmigración*, Ministerio de Educación y Justicia, Buenos Aires, November 1981.

8. I. Anasagasti Olabeaga, ed., *Homenaje al comité pro-inmigración vasca en Buenos Aires* (San Sebastián: Txertoa, 1988), 82.

9. Ibid., 83.

CHAPTER 10. THE FUTURE OF THE BASQUE-AMERICAN COMMUNITIES

1. Presentation of William A. Douglass, in *Euskaldunak Munduan, Construyendo el futuro* (Vitoria-Gasteiz: Servicio Publicaciones del Gobierno Vasco, 1995), 23–29.
2. Ibid., 36ff.
3. Ibid., 77–78.

Bibliography

Abal Oliu, A. "Bernard Bidegaray Haramboure–Jeanne Beheran Garra, Montevideo." Unpublished manuscript, 1983.
Abrisketa, Francisco de. *Presencia vasca en Colombia.* Vitoria-Gasteiz: Servicio Central de Publicaciones, Gobierno Vasco, 1983.
Aguirreazkuenaga, J., ed. *Gran atlas histórico del mundo vasco.* Bilbao: El Mundo del País Vasco, 1994.
Alday Garay, A. "La emigración del Valle de Baztán a América en el siglo XX." Ph.D. diss., Universidad de Deusto, 1992.
"Algunas reflexiones a partir de los legajos matrimoniales de la catedral de Montevideo del año 1853 y la Guía de forasteros de 1861." Unpublished manuscript. Montevideo, 1996.
Alvarez Cuartero, Izaskun. *Las Sociedades Económicas de los Amigos del País en Cuba.* Vitoria-Gasteiz, 1992.
Álvarez Gila, Óscar. "Vascos y Vascongados. Luchas ideológicas entre carlistas y nacionalistas en los centros vascos del Río de la Plata, 1900–1930." In *Emigración y redes sociales de los vascos en América,* ed. Ronald Escobedo Mansilla et al., 171–92. Vitoria-Gasteiz: Servicio Editorial, Universidad del País Vasco, 1996.
Alzugaray, Juan José. "Vascos emprendedores del siglo XVI en el Nuevo Mundo." In *Los Vascos y América. Ideas, hechos, hombres,* ed. Ignacio Arana Pérez, 269–82. Madrid: Gela/Espasa-Calpe/Argantonio, 1990.
AMAB. Documental Fund of El Ferrol. Leg. 8161.
Anasagasti, Iñaki. "El exilio vasco." *Muga* (San Sebastián) 40 (February 1985): 26–57.
Anasagasti Olabeaga, Iñaki, ed. *Comité Pro-Inmigración Vasca (Buenos Aires).* Departamento de Cultura y Turismo del País Vasco.
———. *Homenaje al comité pro-inmigración vasca en Buenos Aires.* San Sebastián: Txertoa, 1988.
Andrés-Gallego, José. *Historia contemporánea de Navarra.* Pamplona: Ediciones y Libros, 1982.
———, ed. *Navarra y América.* Madrid: Editorial MAPFRE, 1992.
Andrés Lamas, *Los apuntes estadísticos.* Montevideo, 1928.
Anes Alvarez, Gonzalo. *El antiguo régimen. Los Borbones.* Madrid: Alianza Editorial/Alfaguara, 1975.
Annals of the Sociedad Rural Argentina, 1899.

Anselmo de Legarda, P. "De Pamplona a La Habana en 1851." *BIAEV* 100 (1975): 235–38.
El Anunciador Vitoriano. No. 144, March 11, 1880.
———. No. 306, April 2, 1881.
Arana Pérez, Ignacio, ed. *Los vascos y América. Ideas, hechos, hombres*. Gran Enciclopedia de España y América. Madrid: Gela/Espasa-Calpe/Argantonio, 1990.
Arbillaga Arriola, A. *Lo que se ha dicho de Iparraguirre*. Bilbao: Publicaciones de la Junta de Cultura de Vizcaya, 1967.
Arbiza, O. M. *El aporte vasco al departamento de Artigas*. Montevideo: Ediciones de la Plaza, 1987.
Archivo General de la Nación, Montevideo (AGN). Montevideo Police, Passport Book, 1829–1832.
Archivo General de la Nación (AGN). Buenos Aires, National Government Division (1817–1843), Sala X-1-4-6.
Archivo Histórico del Colegio de las Vizcaínas. Est. 6, T. 1, V. 2, fol. 2.
Arcila Farias, E. *El siglo ilustrado en América. Reformas económicas del siglo XVIII en Nueva España*. Caracas, 1955.
Arenas Sanchez, J., and J. I. Tellechea Idígoras. "Socios de la RSBAP en Chihuahua (México)." In *La Real Sociedad Bascongada y América*. San Sebastián, 1991.
Arranz, Luis. *Cristóbal Colón*. Madrid, 1986.
Arrieta, Ángel María. *La emigración alavesa a América en el siglo XIX*. Vitoria-Gasteiz: Servicio Central de Publicaciones, Gobierno Vasco, 1992.
Arrieta, Ángel María, and A. M. Barrundia. Expediente General de Quintas, 136.1.
Arrieta Villalobos, Mons. Román. "Notas sobre la presencia vasca en Hispanoamérica y Costa Rica." In *Los vascos y América. Ideas, hechos, hombres*, ed. Ignacio Arana Pérez, 137–41. Madrid: Gela/Espasa-Calpe/Argantonio, 1990.
Arteaga, J. J., and E. Puiggros. "Legislación y política migratoria en Uruguay." In *Legislación y política inmigratoria en el Cono Sur*, ed. Hernán Asdrúbal Silva et al., 403–55. Mexico City: Instituto Panamericano de Geografía y Historia, 1987.
Astigarraga Goenaga, J. "La expansión de la RSBAP por América." In *La Real Sociedad Bascongada y América*. San Sebastián, 1991.
Azcona Pastor, José Manuel. "En torno a las causas que propiciaron la emigración vasca al Río de la Plata." In *Estudios de Geografía e Historia*. 2 vols. 611–26. Bilbao: Universidad de Deusto, 1988.
———. "Julio de Lazurtegui, algunos de sus proyectos en torno a Iberoamérica." In *II Congreso Mundial Vasco*. Vol. VII. Donostia/San Sebastián: Editorial Txertoa, 1988.
———. "América, el continente olvidado por la *historiografía vasca, Revista de Indias*. Vol. XLIX, no. 187 (September–December), 1989.
———. *Los paraísos posibles. Historia de la emigración vasca a Argentina y Uruguay en el siglo XIX*. Bilbao: Servicio de Publicaciones, Deustuko Unibertsitatea, 1992.

———. "Política migratoria americana en el siglo XIX." In *Estudios de Ciencias Sociales*. 6. UNED-Navarne, 1993.

———. "Las bienandanzas y fortunas de los pastores vascos en Norteamérica." In Ronald Escobedo Mansilla, Ana de Zaballa Beascoechea, and Óscar Álvarez Gila, *Emigración y redes sociales de los vascos en América*. Vitoria-Gasteiz: Servicio Editorial, Universidad del Pais Vasco, 1996.

———. "Cultura vasca contemporánea en los paises del Cono Sur." In William A. Douglass, Carmelo Urza, Linda White, and Joseba Zulaika, *The Basque Diaspora/ La diáspora Vasca*. Reno, Nevada: Basque Studies Program, Occasional Papers Series, No. 7, 1999.

Azcona Pastor, José Manuel, Inés García-Albi Gil de Biedma, and Fernando Muru Ronda. *Historia de la emigración vasca a Argentina en el siglo XX*. Vitoria-Gasteiz: Eusko Jaurlaritza, 1992.

Azcona Pastor, José Manuel, Fernando Muru Ronda, and Inés Garcia-Albi Gil de Biedma. *Historia de la emigración vasca al Uruguay en el siglo XX*. Montevideo: República Oriental del Uruguay, Ministero de Educación y Cultura, Archivo General de la Nación, 1996.

Ballesteros Beretta, Antonio. "Cristóbal Colón y el descubrimiento de América." In *Historia de América y de los pueblos americanos*. Vols. IV and V, Barcelona, 1945.

Barrán, José Pedro, and Benjamín Nahum. *El Uruguay del novecientos*. Montevideo: Ediciones de la Banda Oriental, 1979.

Barrère, E. *Emigration à Montévidéo et à Buenos Ayres*. Pan; Vignancour, 1842.

Barrio Loza, J. A., and J. R. Valverde Peña. *Platería antigua en Bizkaia*. Bilbao, 1986.

Benvenuto, Luis C. *Breve historia del Uruguay. Economía y sociedad*. Montevideo: Arca, 1967.

Bergamali, Conyoumdjiam, and A. Rebolledo Hernández. *Bibliografía sobre el proceso inmigratorio en Chile desde la independencia hasta 1930*. IPGH. Vol. 1. Mexico City, 1984.

Bilbao [Azkarreta], Jon. *Vascos en Cuba, 1492–1511*. Buenos Aires: Editorial Vasca Ekin, 1958.

———. "Vascos en Cuba." In *América y los vascos. 1492–1992*, ed. Jon Bilbao Azkarreta, 27–28. Bilbao: Deia/Eusko Jaurlaritza, Kultura Saila, 1992.

———, ed. *América y los vascos. 1492–1992*. Bilbao: Deia/Eusko Jaurlaritza, Kultura Saila, 1992.

Bilbao, L. M., and R. Fernández de Pinedo. "Auge y crisis de la siderometalurgia tradicional en el País Vasco (1700–1850)." In *La economía española al final del Antiguo Régimen*, ed. Gonzalo Anes Alvarez et al. Vol. 2, *Las manufacturas*. Madrid: Servicio Editorial, Universidad del País Vasco, 1982.

Bitar Letayf, Marcelo. *Los economistas españoles y sus ideas sobre el comercio con las Indias*. Mexico City: Instituto Mexicano de Comercio Exterior, 1975.

Boletín Oficial de Vizcaya. 1841.

———. 1862.

———. 1880.

———. 1882.

———. 1888.

Boyd-Bowman, Peter. "La emigración peninsular a América (1520–1539)." *Historia Mexicana* 13, no. 2, 1963.

———. *Indice geobiográfico de cuarenta mil pobladores españoles de América en el siglo XVI (1493–1519).* Bogotá: Instituto Caro y Cuervo, 1964.

———. "La procedencia de los españoles de América (1540–1559)." *Historia Mexicana* 16, no. 65, 1967.

———. "La emigración española a América (1560–1579)." *Studia Hispánica,* 1974.

———. "Patterns of Spanish Emigration to the Indies until 1600." *Spanish American Historical Review,* 1976: 123–48.

———. *Indice geobiográfico de más de 56 mil pobladores de la América hispánica.* Vol. 1, *1493–1519.* Mexico City: Instituto de Investigaciones Históricas, UNAM: Fondo de Cultura Económica, 1985.

Branaa, Jean-Eric. "Les archives d'un agent d'émigration basque, entre 1945 et 1975 (Émigration des basques du Nord)." In *Emigración y redes sociales de los vascos en América,* ed. Ronald Escobedo Mansilla et al., 241–58. Vitoria-Gasteiz: Servicio Editorial, Universidad del País Vasco, 1996.

Briceño Perozo, Mario. *Temas de historia colonial venezolana.* Caracas: Academia Nacional de la Historia, 1981.

Camus Argaluza, Maite. *La inmigración vasca en Chile. 1880–1990.* Santiago: Eusko Etxea-Chile, 1991.

Carande, Ramón. *Carlos V y sus banqueros. La vida económica de España en una fase de su hegemonía, 1516–1556.* Vol. 1. Madrid: Revista de Occidente, 1943.

Cardell y Pujalte, Carlos. *La casa de Borbón en España. La vida económica de España en una fase de su hegemonía (1516–1556).* Madrid: Agemundo, 1954.

Cardenal Landázuri Ricketts, Mons. Juan. "El tercer concilio provincial de Lima y la evangelización del Nuevo Mundo (1582–1583)." In *Los Vascos y América. Ideas, hechos, hombres,* edited by Ignacio Arana Pérez, 222–25. Madrid: Gela/Espasa-Calpe/Argantonio, 1990.

Castresana, Luis de. *Vida y obra de Iparraguirre.* Bilbao: Editorial La Gran Enciclopedia Vasca, 1971.

Cava Mesa, Begoña. "El asociacionismo vasco en Argentina. Política cultural." In *Emigración y redes sociales de los vascos en América,* ed. Ronald Escobedo Mansilla et al., 137–69. Vitoria-Gasteiz: Servicio Editorial, Universidad del País Vasco, 1996.

Céspedes del Castillo, Guillermo. *América hispánica (1492–1898).* Barcelona, 1983.

Charnisay, Henry de. *L'emigration basco-béarnaise en Amerique.* Biarritz: J. & D. Éditions, 1996.

Cifré de Loubriel, Estela. *La inmigración a Puerto Rico durante el siglo XIX.* San Juan, P.R.: Instituto de Cultura Puertorriqueña, 1964.

———. *La formación del pueblo puertorriqueño. La contribución de los vascongados, navarros y aragoneses.* San Juan, P.R.: Instituto de Cultura Puertorriqueña, 1986.

———. "Los vascongados y su contribución a la formación del pueblo puertorriqueño." In *Emigración y redes sociales de los vascos en América,* ed. Ronald Escobedo Mansilla et al., 31–42. Vitoria-Gasteiz: Servicio Editorial, Universidad del País Vasco, 1996.

Ciudad Suárez, María Milagros. "Presencia vasca en Centroamérica. La provincia dominica de San Vicente, siglos XVI–XVII." In *Euskal Herria y el Nuevo Mundo,* ed. Ronald Escobedo Mansilla et al., 373–89. Vitoria-Gasteiz: Servicio Editorial, Universidad del País Vasco, 1996.

Cocchi, Angel M., Jaime Klaczko, and Juan R. Roade. "Una red urbana ordenadora de un espacio vacío. El caso uruguayo." *CIESU* 24, 1997: 37–54.

Cola y Goiti, J. "Los españoles en el Uruguay." *El Anunciador Vitoriano* 1500. September 16, 1886.

———. "Las emigraciones." *La Concordia* 680. May 20, 1888.

Colección de Circulares desde el 1 de junio de 1840 hasta el 25 junio de 1841. Dossier 479. Library of the Foru Aldundia of Gipuzkoa.

Colección de Circulares desde el 14 de julio de 1866 hasta el 22 de junio de 1868. Circular no. 30, vol. 479. Library of the Diputación Foral de Gipuzkoa.

Concepción, Fray G. de la. *Emporio del Orbe. Cádiz ilustrada.* Amsterdam, 1960.

La Concordia. No. 628, January 18, 1888.

Constitución de la Ilustre Hermandad Vascongada de Nuestra Señora de Aránzazu. Lima: printed by J. María Masia, 1858.

Cutolo, Vicente Osvaldo. *Nuevo diccionario biográfico argentino (1750–1930).* 7 vols. Buenos Aires: Editorial Elche, 1968–85.

Díaz-Trechuelo Spínola, María Lourdes. *La Real Compañía de Filipinas.* Sevilla. Escuela de Estudios Hispano-Americanos de Sevilla, Consejo Superior de Investigaciones Científicas, 1965.

Domínguez Ortíz, Antonio. *La sociedad española en el siglo XVII.* 2 vols. Madrid: Consejo Superior de Investigaciones Científicas, Instituto "Balmes" de Sociología, Departamento de Historia Social, 1963.

———. *El antiguo régimen. Los Reyes Católicos y los Austrias.* 8th ed. Madrid: Alianza Editorial, 1981.

———. *Sociedad y estado en el siglo XVIII español.* Barcelona: Ariel, 1976.

———, ed. *Historia de España.* Vol. 7, *El Reformismo borbónico.* Barcelona: Planeta, 1989–1990.

———, ed. *Historia de España*. Vol. 8, *Descubrimiento, colonización y emancipación de América*. Madrid: Planeta, 1990.

Domínguez Ortíz, Antonio, and Francisco Aguilar Piñal. *El Barroco y la ilustración*. Sevilla: Secretariado de Publicaciones de la Universidad de Sevilla, 1976.

Douglass, William A. "Intervencion de William Douglass." In *Euskaldunak Munduan, construyendo el futuro*. Vitoria-Gasteiz: Gobierno Vasco/Eusko Jaurlaritza, 1996.

Douglass, William A., and Jon Bilbao. *Amerikanuak: Basques in the New World*. Reno: University of Nevada Press, 1975.

Echegaray, Carmelo. Provincia de Vizcaya. In *Geografía general del País Vasco-Navarro*, ed. Francisco Carreras y Candi. Barcelona, 1918.

Edwards, Alberto. *La fronda aristocrática en Chile*. Santiago: Imprenta nacional, 1928.

Elorza, Antonio. *La ideología liberal en la ilustración española*. Madrid: Editorial Tecnos, 1970.

Escobedo Mansilla, Ronald, Ana de Zaballa Beascoechea, and Óscar Álvarez Gila, eds. *Álava y América*. Vitoria-Gasteiz: Diputación Foral de Álava, 1996.

———, eds. *Emigración y redes sociales de los vascos en América*. Vitoria-Gasteiz: Servicio Editorial, Universidad del País Vasco, 1996.

———. *Euskal Herria y el Nuevo Mundo. La contribución de los vascos a la formación de las Américas*. Vitoria-Gasteiz: Servicio Editorial, Universidad del País Vasco, 1996.

Escobedo Mansilla, Ronald, Ana María Rivera Medina, and Alvaro Chapa Imaz, eds. *Los vascos y América. Jornadas sobre el comercio vasco con América en el siglo XVIII y la Real Compañía Guipuzcoana de Caracas*. Bilbao: Laida, 1989.

Escudero, José Antonio. *Los secretarios de Estado y del despacho, 1474–1724*. Vol. 1, *El desarrollo historico de la institución*. Madrid: Instituto de Estudios Administrativos, 1969.

Estornés Lasa, Mariano. "Topónimos vascos en los países americanos." In *Los Vascos y América. Ideas, hechos, hombres*, ed. Ignacio Arana Pérez, 93–97. Madrid: Gela/Espasa-Calpe/Argantonio, 1990.

Fernández de Oviedo y Valdés, Gonzalo. *Historia general y natural de las Indias, islas y tierra firme del mar Océano*. Asunción del Paraguay: Editorial Guaranía, 1944–45.

Fernández de Pinedo, Emiliano. *La emigración vasca a América, siglos XIX y XX*. Colombres, Asturias: Ediciones Jucar, 1993.

Fernández Gimenez, S. *Historia de la navegación*. Madrid, 1988.

Ferrer, Melchor, Domingo Tejera, and José F. Acedo. *Historia del tradicionalismo español*. Vol. 28. Sevilla: Ediciones Trajano, 1959.

Figueroa Salas, Jonás. "El informe Villareal. Los vascos en el desarrollo urbano de Chile en el siglo XVIII." In *Los Vascos y América. Ideas, hechos, hombres*, ed. Ignacio Arana Pérez, 128–36. Madrid: Gela/Espasa-Calpe/Argantonio, 1990.

Friede, J. "Algunas observaciones sobre la realidad de la emigración española a América en la primera mitad del siglo XVI." *Revista de Indias* (Sevilla) no. 49 (1952): 483.

Fundación BBV. *La real sociedad bascongada y América*. III Seminario de Historia de la RSBAP. San Sebastián, 1991.

Gaarder, Lorin R. "The Basques of Mexico: An Historical and Contemporary Portrait." Ph.D. diss., University of Utah, 1976.

Garaico Echea, Abraham Ignacio. *De vasconia a Buenos Aires o la venida de mi madre al Plata (historia de una emigración en el siglo XIX)*. Buenos Aires: Editorial Vasca Ekin, 1965.

Gárate [Arriola], Justo. *Los colegios de las vizcaínas y Vergara en el siglo XVIII*. Mendoza, 1972.

———. *Iparraguirre*. Bilbao, 1987.

Gárate Arriola, Justo, and José Ignacio Tellechea Idígoras. *El Colegio de las Vizcaínas de México y el Real Seminario de Vergara*. Vitoria-Gasteiz: Gobierno Vasco, Secreteria de la Presidencia, 1992.

García-Baquero González, Antonio. *Cádiz y el Atlántico (1717–1778). El comercio colonial español bajo el monopolio gaditano*. 2 vols. Sevilla: Escuela de Estudios Hispano-Americanos, CSIC: Excelentísima Diputación Provincial de Cádiz, 1976.

García Belsunce, César A. *Los Vascos en Buenos Aires en 1810*. Buenos Aires, 1982.

García de Cortázar, Fernando, and José María Lorenzo Espinosa. *Historia del País Vasco. De los orígenes a nuestros días*. San Sebastián: Txertoa, 1988.

García de Cortazar, José Angel. *Organización social del espacio en la España medieval. La Corona de Castilla en los siglos VIII a XV*. Barcelona: Ariel, 1985.

García Fuentes, L. *Sevilla, los vascos y América. Las exportaciones de hierro y manufacturas metálicas en los siglos XVI, XVII y XVIII*. Bilbao: Fundación BBV, en colaboración con Laida, 1991.

García Gallo, A. "La evolución de la organización territorial de las Indias de 1492 a 1824." In *Anuario Histórico Jurídico Ecuatoriano* (Quito) 5, 1980.

García Giráldez, Teresa. "La formación de las redes familiares vascas en Centroamérica, 1750–1850." In *Emigración y redes sociales de los vascos en América*, ed. Ronald Escobedo Mansilla et al., 317–48. Vitoria-Gasteiz: Servicio Editorial, Universidad del País Vasco, 1996.

García-Sanz Marcotegui, A. "La emigración navarra a América a través de la publicista." In *Historia general de la emigración española a Iberoamérica*. Vol. 2. Madrid: Historia 16, 1992.

Garmendia Arruebarrena, J. "Secretarios de Estado." In *Boletín de la Real Sociedad Bascongada de los Amigos del País* (San Sebastián) 41, 1985: 364–65.

———. *Cádiz, los vascos y la carrera de Indias*. San Sebastián: Eusko Ikaskuntza, 1990.

Gelabert, J. E. "La producción de hierro en Vizcaya y Guipúzcoa hacia 1620." In *Congreso de historia de Euskal Herria*. San Sebastián: Txertoa, 1988.

Gildas, B. "La Casa de Contratación de Sevilla, luego de Cádiz en el siglo XVIII." In *Anuario de Estudios Americanos (AEA)* (Sevilla) 12, 1955.

González Cembellín, Juan Manuel. *América en el País Vasco. Inventario de elementos patrimoniales de origen americano en la Comunidad Autónoma Vasca (referencias bibliográficas)*. Vitoria-Gasteiz: Servicio Central de Publicaciones del Gobierno Vasco, 1993.

Gosse, Philip. *The History of Piracy*. New York: Tudor Publishing Co., 1932. Reprint, New York: B. Franklin, 1968.

Grandmontagne, Francisco. *Los inmigrantes prósperos*. Madrid: M. Aguilar, 1944.

Guevara, Antonio de, Fray. "De las cosas que el mareante se ha de proveer para entrar en la galera." In *Libro de los inventores del arte de marear y de muchos trabajos que se pasan en las galeras*. Valladolid, 1539.

Guiard y Larrauri, Teófilo. *Historia del Consulado y Casa de Contratación de Bilbao y del comercio de la villa*. 2 vols. Bilbao, 1913–1914.

Gullón Abao, Alberto J. "La frontera oriental del Tucumán a principios del siglo XVIII. Las expediciones de Esteban de Urízar y Arespacochaga, 1710–1711." In *Euskal Herria y el Nuevo Mundo*, ed. Ronald Escobedo Mansilla et al., 247–61. Vitoria-Gasteiz: Servicio Editorial, Universidad del País Vasco, 1996.

Gutiérrez Nieto, R. *Ley de emigración*. Madrid: Instituto Nacional de Prospectiva, 1980.

Hammerton, John Alexander. *The Real Argentine: Notes and Impressions of a Year in the Argentine and Uruguay*. New York: Dodd, Mead, 1915.

Haring, Clarence Henry. *Comercio y navegación entre España y las Indias en la época de los Habsburgos*. Mexico City: Fondo de Cultura Económica, 1979.

Hausberger, B. "La comunidad vasca en Sonora (1640–1767)." Unpublished manuscript, 1993.

Heredia Herrera, Antonia, ed. *Catálogo de las consultas del Consejo de Indias (1631–1636)*. Sevilla: Diputación Provincial, 1988.

———. *Sevilla y los hombres del comercio (1700–1800)*. Sevilla: Diputación Provincial, 1989.

Herrero, Javier. *Los orígenes del pensamiento reaccionario español*. Madrid: Editorial Cuadernos para el Diálogo, 1971.

Herzog, Tamar. "De la autoridad al poder. Quito, los Larrea y la herencia inmaterial, siglos XVII y XVIII." In *Emigración y redes sociales de los vascos en América*, ed. Ronald Escobedo Mansilla et al., 373–83. Vitoria-Gasteiz: Servicio Editorial, Universidad del País Vasco, 1996.

Historical Archive of Notarial Protocols of Oñati. Scribe Miguel Francisco de Eizmendi. Protocol of Astigarraga, Leg. 271, Fol. 252.

Historical Archive of Notarial Protocols of Oñati. Scribe Joaquín Elósegui. Protocol of San Sebastián, Leg. 4 (new), Fols. 593–94.

Hourmat, Pierre. "De l'emigration basco-bearnaise du XVIII siécle à nos jours." *Societé des Sciences et Lettres et Arts de Bayonne* (Bayonne) 132 (1976): 227–54.

Hummel, Kay. "A Wanted Man: The Basque, El Cojo Gómez en Colombia." In *Essays* in *Basque Social Anthropology and History*, ed. William A. Douglass. Reno: Basque Studies Program, University of Nevada, 1989.

Idoate Ezquieta, Carlos. *Emigración navarra del Valle de Baztán a América en el siglo XIX. Inventario de documentos*. Pamplona: Gobierno de Navarra, Departamento de Educación y Cultura, Dirección General de Cultura, Institución Príncipe de Viana, 1989.

La Inmigración europea en Chile (1882-1895). Santiago, Chile, 1896.

Iriani, Marcelino. *Los vascos y la immigración temprana en Buenos Aires*. Rosario, 1989.

Isabelle, Arsène. *Le Patriote Française*, 26 September 1843.

Ispizua, Segundo de. *Historia de los vascos en el descubrimiento, conquista y civilización de América*. Vol. 3. Bilbao: Impr. J. A. de Lerchundi, 1914-1919.

Kamen, Henry. *La España de Carlos II*. Barcelona: Editorial Crítica, 1981.

Konetzke, R. "Legislación sobre inmigración de extranjeros en América durante la época colonial." *Revista Internacional de Sociología* (Mexico) 3, 1945: 269-99.

———. "Las fuentes para la historia demográfica de Hispanoamérica durante la época colonial." *Anuario de Estudios Americanos (AEA)* (Sevilla) 5: 1947. First published in *Revista Internacional de Sociología* (Mexico) 3: 1945.

Labayru y Goicoechea, Estanislao Jaime de. *Historia General del Señorío de Bizcaya*. 6 vols. Bilbao: La Gran Enciclopedia Vasca, 1968.

Larrañaga, Ramiro. *Síntesis histórica de la armería vasca*. San Sebastián: Caja de Ahorros Provincial de Guipúzcoa, 1981.

Lascurain, V. "Los grandes caudillos en la conquista de México." In *Boletín del Instituto Americano de Estudios Vascos* (Buenos Aires) 25, 1956: 101-11.

Lemus, E., and R. Márquez. "La emigración española a Ultramar. Los precedentes." In *Historia general de la emigración española a Iberoamérica*. Vol. 1. Madrid: CEDEAL, 1992.

Lesca, J. H. *Les Basques et les Béarnais dans l'Argentine et l'Uruguay*. Bordeaux, 1907.

Lhande, Pierre. *La emigración vasca*. 2 vols. Trans. D. Ignacio Basurko Berroa. San Sebastián: Editorial Auñamendi, 1971.

Lohmann Villena, Guillermo. "Los comerciantes vascos en el virreinato peruano." In *Los vascos y América*, ed. Ronald Escobedo Mansilla et al., 53-106. Bilbao: Laida, 1989.

López Cantos, Ángel. *Juegos, fiestas y diversiones en la América española*. Madrid: Editorial MAPFRE, 1992.

———. "Gaspar de Arteaga y Aunaovidao, gobernador de Puerto Rico (1670-1674)." In *Euskal Herria y el Nuevo Mundo*, ed. Ronald Escobedo Mansilla et al., 151-57. Vitoria-Gasteiz: Servicio Editorial, Universidad del País Vasco, 1996.

López-Rios Fernández, Fernando. *Historia médica de las navegaciones colombinas, 1492-1504*. Valladolid: Secretariado de Publicaciones, Universidad de Valladolid, 1993.

Lucena Salmoral, Manuel. *Piratas, bucaneros, filibusteros y corsarios en América. Perros, mendigos y otros malditos del mar.* Madrid: Editorial MAPFRE, 1992.

Lucena Salmoral, Manuel, and Pablo Emilio Pérez-Mallaína Bueno, eds. *Historia de Iberoamérica.* Vol. 2, *Historia Moderna.* Madrid: Sociedad Estatal para la Ejecución de Programas del Quinto Centenario/Cátedra, 1990.

Luján Muñoz, Jorge. "Los vascos en el comercio del Reino de Guatemala al final del período colonial." In *Los Vascos y América. Ideas, hechos, hombres,* ed. Ignacio Arana Pérez, 157–63. Madrid: Gela/Espasa-Calpe/Argantonio, 1990.

Luque Alcaide, Elisa. *La Cofradía de Aránzazu de México (1681–1799).* Pamplona: Ediciones Eunate, 1995.

Lynch, J. *España bajo los Austrias (1516–1700).* 2 vols. Madrid, 1970.

———. *España bajo los Austrias.* Vol. 1, *Imperio y absolutismo (1516–1598).* Madrid, 1970.

———. *España bajo los Austrias.* Vol. 2. Barcelona, 1973.

Macías Domínguez, Isabelo. "La emigración vasca a Indias en la primera mitad del siglo XVIII." In *Álava y América,* ed. Ronald Escobedo Mansilla et al., 27–45. Vitoria-Gasteiz: Diputación Foral de Álava, 1996.

Malamud, Carlos D. "La consolidación de una familia de la oligarquía arequipeña. Los Goyeneche." *Revista Quinto Centenario,* no. 4, 1982: 49–135.

Marenales Rossi, Martha, and G. Bourdé. "L'immigration française et le peuplement de l'Uruguay (1830–1860)." In *Cahiers des Amériques Latines* (Paris), 1977.

Marías, Julián. *La España posible en tiempo de Carlos III.* Barcelona: Planeta, 1988.

Mariluz Urquijo, José María. *Bilbao y Buenos Aires. Proyectos dieciochescos de compañías de comercio.* Buenos Aires: Universidad de Buenos Aires, 1981.

———. "Proyección y límites del comercio vasco en el Río de la Plata." In *Los Vascos y America. Jornadas sobre el comercio vasco con América en el siglo XVIII,* ed. Ronald Escobedo Mansilla et al., 107–33. Bilbao: Laida, 1989.

Márquez Macías, Rosario. *La emigración española a América, 1765–1824.* Oviedo: Servicio de Publicaciones, Universidad de Oviedo, 1995.

Martínez, José Luis. *Pasajeros de Indias. Viajes transatlánticos en el siglo XVI.* Madrid: Alianza Editorial, 1983.

———. *El mundo privado de los emigrantes en Indias.* Mexico City: Fondo de Cultura Económica, 1992.

Martínez Cardós, J. *Las Indias y las Cortes de Castilla durante los siglos XVI y XVII.* Madrid, 1956.

Martínez Gorroño, María Eugenia. "El exilio vasco de 1939 en Colombia. Circustancias y aportaciones más destacables." In *Emigración y redes sociales de los vascos en América,* ed. Ronald Escobedo Mansilla et al., 215–28. Vitoria-Gasteiz: Servicio Editorial, Universidad del País Vasco, 1996.

Martínez Martín, Carmen. "Destacados vascongados en la consolidación territorial del Tucumán. La frontera del Chaco, 1670–1724." In *Euskal Herria y el Nuevo Mundo,* ed. Ronald Escobedo Mansilla et al., 47–72. Vitoria-Gasteiz: Servicio Editorial, Universidad del País Vasco, 1996.

Martínez Salazar, Angel. *Presencia alavesa en América y Filipinas (1700–1825)*. Vitoria-Gasteiz: Diputación Foral de Alava, Servicio de Publicaciones, 1988.

Martínez Salazar, Angel, and Koldo San Sebastián. *Los vascos en México. Estudio biográfico, histórico y bibliográfico*. Vitoria-Gasteiz: Gobierno Vasco, Lehendakaritza, 1992.

Martínez Shaw, Carlos. *La emigración española a América (1492–1824)*. Colombres, Asturias: Archivo de Indianos, 1994.

Mathes, Michael. "Los vascos en la expansión de la frontera norte de Nueva España en el siglo XVI. La fundación de Nueva Vizcaya y Nuevo México." In *Los vascos y América. Ideas, hechos, hombres*, ed. Ignacio Arana Pérez, 238–46. Madrid: Gela/Espasa-Calpe/Argantonio, 1990.

Matila Quiza, M. J. "Las compañías privilegiadas en la España del Antiguo Régimen." In *La economía española al final del Antiguo Régimen*. Vol. 4. Madrid: Servicio Editorial, Universidad del País Vasco, 1982.

Mestre Sanchis, Antonio. *Despotismo e ilustración en España*. Barcelona: Ariel, 1976.

Michel, Francisque. *Le pays Basque. Sa population, sa langue, ses moeurs, sa littérature et sa musique*. Paris: Feirmin Didot frères, fils et cie, 1857.

Morales Alvarez, Juan M. *Los extranjeros con carta de naturaleza de las Indias, durante la segunda mitad del siglo XVIII*. Caracas: Academia Nacional de la Historia, 1980.

Moreno Fraginals, Manuel. *El ingenio. Complejo económico social cubano del azúcar*. Vol. 2. Havana: Editorial de Ciencias Sociales, 1978.

Moreno Fraginals, M. R. "Importancia del elemento vasco en el siglo XVIII en Cuba." In *Presencia vasca en América*. Vitoria-Gasteiz, 1992.

Moreno Saez, F. *La ilustración española*. Alicante, 1986.

Mörner, Magnus. "La emigración española al Nuevo Mundo antes de 1810. Un informe del estado de la investigación." *Anuario de Estudios Americanos (AEA)* (Sevilla) 32, 1975: 73ff.

———. "Inserción del fenómeno vasco en la emigración europea a América." In *Emigración y redes sociales de los vascos en América*, ed. Ronald Escobedo Mansilla et al., 15–30. Vitoria-Gasteiz: Servicio Editorial, Universidad del País Vasco, 1996.

Muguerza, Felipe. "¿Qué es la Federación de Entidades Vasco Argentinas?" In *The Basque Diaspora/La diáspora Vasca*, ed. William A. Douglass, Carmelo Urza, Linda White, and Joseba Zulaika, 61–77. Reno: Basque Studies Program, University of Nevada, 1999.

Muru Ronda, Fernando. "Prensa local y emigración vasca contemporánea (siglos XIX y XX)." In *Emigración y redes sociales de los vascos en América*, ed. Ronald Escobedo Mansilla et al., 193–213. Vitoria-Gasteiz: Servicio Editorial, Universidad del País Vasco, 1996.

Nadal Oller, Jorge. *La población española. Siglos XVI a XX*. Barcelona: Ariel, 1984.

———. *La población española (Siglos XVI a XX)*. Barcelona: Ariel, 1986.
Navarro García, Luis. *Hispanoamérica en el siglo XVIII*. Sevilla: Publicaciones de la Universidad de Sevilla, 1975.
———, ed. *Historia de las Américas*. Sevilla: Alhambra Longman, 1991.
Nieva, Josef María de. *Decretos, Leyes y Reales Órdenes del Rey Nuestro Señor Don Fernando VII*. Vol. 12, 32–33. Madrid, 1928.
———. *Decretos, Leyes y Reales Órdenes de la Reina Dª Isabel*. Vol. 19, 481–82. Madrid, 1834.
"No vayáis a América." *El Anunciador Vitoriano*, no. 306, April 2, 1881.
Oddone, Juan Antonio. *La emigración europea al Río de la Plata. Motivaciones y proceso de incorporación*. Montevideo: Ediciones de la Banda Oriental, 1966.
Oliva Melgar, J. M. "El monopolio de Indias en los siglos XVI y XVII. Plata y mitos en un sistema imperial." *Revista Rábida* (Huelva) no. 11, 1992: 34–47.
Ortiz de la Tabla y Ducasse, Javier. "Presencia vasca en el Ecuador colonial. Linajes y redes de parentesco, s. XVI–XVII." In *Emigración y redes sociales de los vascos en América*, ed. Ronald Escobedo Mansilla et al., 349–71. Vitoria-Gasteiz: Servicio Editorial, Universidad del País Vasco, 1996.
Otero Lana, Enrique. *Los corsarios españoles durante la decadencia de los Austrias. El corso español del Atlántico peninsular en el siglo XVII (1621–1697)*. Madrid: Editorial Naval, 1992.
Palacio Atard, Vicente. *Los españoles de la ilustración*. Madrid: Ediciones Guadarrama, 1964.
Pando, José Ramón. "Las migraciones internacionales del Uruguay." Montevideo, 1982.
Peillen, Txomin. "La emigración económica vascofrancesa vista por los bardos populares de Uruguay y de Euskal Herria." Unpublished manuscript.
Pérez de San Román, Álvaro Hilario. "Destinos de la emigración bizkaina a América en el siglo XIX." *Ernaroa: Revista de Historia de Euskal Herria* (Bilbao) no. 6, June 1991: 255–70.
Pérez de Tudela y Bueso, Juan. *Las armadas de Indias y los orígenes de la política de colonización (1492–1505)*. Madrid: Instituto Gonzalo Fernández de Oviedo, 1956.
Pérez-Mallaína Bueno, Pablo Emilio, and Bibiano Torres Ramírez. *La Armada de la Mar del Sur*. Sevilla: Escuela de Estudios Hispano-Americanos de Sevilla, CSIC, 1987.
Pildain Salazar, María Pilar. *Ir a América. La emigración vasca a América (Guipúzcoa 1840–1870)*. San Sebastián: Grupo Dr. Camino de Historia Donostiarra: Sociedad Guipuzcoana de Ediciones y Publicaciones, 1984.
Protocolo de José de Zumárraga. No. 13,735, Fols. 3,311–3,314. Vitoria, 23 July 1878.
Protocolo de Miguel Angulo. No. 11,867, Fols. 378–79. Villanueva de Valdegovia, 5 April 1870.

Quiroga, J. *Memoria sobre el fomento de la emigración vascongada a la República Oriental del Uruguay.* Comisión Central Directiva de Inmigración. Annual report, 1875.

Quiroz Paz-Soldán, Eusebio. "Los vascos en la ciudad de Arequipa." In *Emigración y redes sociales de los vascos en América,* ed. Ronald Escobedo Mansilla et al., 385–98. Vitoria-Gasteiz: Servicio Editorial, Universidad del País Vasco, 1996.

"Rapport du baron Deffandis au ministere des affaires etrangerès." Cited by Marenales Rossi, M., and G. Bourdé in "L'immigration française et le peuplement de l'Uruguay (1830–1860)." In *Cahiers des Amériques Latines* (Paris), 1977.

Real Díaz, J. J. "El Consejo de Cámara de Indias. Génesis de su fundación." In *Anuario de Estudios Americanos (AEA)* (Sevilla) 19, 1962.

Reinhard, Marcel, and André Armengaud, *Historia de la población mundial.* Barcelona: Ediciones Ariel, 1966.

Reyes Abadie, Washington, and Andrés Vázquez Romero. *Crónica general del Uruguay.* Vol. 3, *El Uruguay republicano.* Montevideo: Ediciones de la Banda Oriental, 1964.

Rico Linaje, R. *Las Reales Compañías de comercio con América.* Sevilla, 1983.

Rodriguez Baena, María Luisa. *La Sociedad Económica de Amigos del País de Manila en el siglo XVIII.* Sevilla: Escuela de Estudios Hispano-Americanos, 1966.

Rubio Mañé, José Ignacio. "Gente de España en la Ciudad de México." *Bolétin del AGN* (Mexico City) 7, nos. 1–2, 1966.

Rueda Soler, Natividad. *La compañía de comercio "Gardoqui e Hijos" (1760–1800).* Vitoria-Gasteiz, 1992.

Ruiz de Azúa, Estíbaliz. *Vascongadas y América.* Madrid: Editorial MAPFRE, 1992.

Ruiz Rivera, J. "Los vascos en el Consulado de Cádiz." In *Vascos y América. Jornadas sobre el comercio vasco en América en el siglo XVIII,* ed. Ronald Escobedo Mansilla et al., 141–69. Bilbao: Laida, 1989.

Ruiz Rivera, J. B. *El Consulado de Cádiz. Matrícula de comerciantes (1739–1823).* Cádiz, 1988.

Salaverria, José María. *Iparraguirre, el último bardo.* Madrid: Espasa-Calpe, 1932.

Salazar, Eugenio de. "Apéndice 3. La mar descrita por los mareados. 1573." In José Luis Martínez, *Pasajeros de Indias.* Madrid: Alianza Editorial, 1983: 279–96.

Salazar González, Julene, and Roberto Hernández Ponce. *Cuatrocientos años de presencia vasca en Chile.* Vitoria: Departamento de Cultura, Gobierno Vasco; Santiago, Chile: Eusko Etxea-Chile, 1991.

Sánchez, H. *Discurso de la fundación y antigüedades de Cádiz y los demás sucesos que por ella an passado (1591) e historia de la ciudad de Cádiz.* Book IV. N.p., 1845.

San Sebastián, Koldo. *Crónicas de post-guerra.* Bilbao: Idatz Ekintza, 1982.

———. *El exilio vasco en América. La acción del gobierno, política, organización, propaganda, economía, cultura, diplomacia.* San Sebastián: Txertoa, 1988.

Santos Hernández, A. "Jesuítas en la América Meridional." In *America (1492–1992). Contribuciones a un centenario.* Madrid, 1988.

Sarrailh, Jean. *La España ilustrada de la segunda mitad del siglo XVIII.* Madrid, 1979.

Schaefer, Ernst. *El consejo real y supremo de las Indias.* Sevilla: Imp. M. Carmona, 1935.

Senkman, Leon. "La política migratoria argentina durante la década de los treinta. La selección étnica." In *Jornadas de Inmigración.* Buenos Aires: Ministerio de Educación y Justicia, November 1981.

"La siderurgia vasca." *Ernaroa: Revista de Historia de Euskal Herria* (Bilbao) 12, 1996.

Siegrist de Gentile, Nora L. "Familias de origen vasco-navarras-santanderinas en Buenos Aires y sus enlaces con el litoral desde fines del siglo XVIII hasta mediados del XIX." In *Noveno Congreso Nacional y Regional de Historia de Argentina.* Buenos Aires: Academia de la Historia, 1996.

Silva, Hernán A. "La política inmigratoria nacional argentina." In *Legislación y política inmigratoria en el Cono Sur de América. Argentina, Brasil, Uruguay,* ed. Hernán Asdrúbal Silva et al. Mexico City: Instituto Panamericano de Geografía e Historia, 1987.

Silva, Hernán Asdrúbal, et al., eds. *Legislación y política inmigratoria en el Cono Sur de América. Argentina, Brasil, Uruguay.* Mexico City: Instituto Panamericano de Geografía e Historia, 1987.

Sonesson, B. "La emigración española a Puerto Rico." In *Españoles hacia América. La emigración en masa, 1880–1930.* Comp. Nicolás Sánchez-Albornoz. Madrid: Alianza Editorial, 1988.

Souza-Martins, José de. "La inmigración española en Brasil." In *Españoles hacia América. La emigración en masa, 1880–1930.* Comp. Nicolás Sánchez-Albornoz. 249–69. Madrid: Alianza Editorial, 1988.

Statistics of Emigration and Immigration of Spain. 1891.

Tapia Ocariz, J. *Carlos III y su época.* Madrid, 1962.

Tellechea Idígoras, José Ignacio. "El Colegio de las Vizcaínas de la Ciudad de México." In *Los vascos y América. Ideas, hechos, hombres,* ed. Ignacio Arana Pérez, 214–21. Madrid: Gela/Espasa-Calpe/Argantonio, 1990.

———. "Ferrerías guipuzcoanas a finales del siglo XV." *Boletín de la Real Sociedad Bascongada de los Amigos del País* 79, 1975.

Torales, M. C. "Los comerciantes de Nueva España socios de RSBAP." In *La Real Sociedad Bascongada y América.* San Sebastián, 1991.

Torales Pacheco, M. C. "Comerciantes vascos en Nueva España en la segunda mitad del siglo XVIII." In *Tercer Seminario de Historia de la Real Sociedad de los Amigos del País,* Documento. La Real Sociedad Bascongada y América. Madrid: Fundación Banco Bilbao Vizcaya, 1992.

Torre, Tomás de la, Fray. "Apéndice 2. Diario del viaje de Salamanca a Ciudad Real: 1544–1545." In José Luis Martínez, *Pasajeros de Indias.* Madrid: Alianza Editorial, 1983.

Uriarte, José R. de. *Los baskos en la nación argentina.* Buenos Aires: José R. de Uriarte, 1919.

Vázquez de Prada, V., and J. B. Amores Carredano. "La emigración de navarros y vascongados al Nuevo Mundo y su repercusión en las comunidades de orígen." In *La emigración española a Ultramar, 1492–1914,* ed. Antonio Eiras Roel, 133–42. Madrid: Tabapress, Grupo Tabacalera, 1991.

Velázquez, Rafael Eladio. "Presencia vasca en la historia de Paraguay." In *Los vascos y América. Ideas, hechos, hombres,* ed. Ignacio Arana Pérez, 187–202. Madrid: Gela/Espasa-Calpe/Argantonio, 1990.

Vicens Vives, Jaime. *Historia de España y América.* 5 vols. Originally titled *Historia social y económica de España,* 1957. Vol. 4, *Los Borbones. El siglo XVIII en España y América.* Barcelona: Editorial Vicens-Vives, 1961.

Virto, J. J. "La emigración de Navarra hacia América en la segunda mitad del siglo XIX." *Notas y Estudios de Ciencias Sociales* (Navarra) 4, 1991: 109–24.

Walker, Geoffrey J. *Política española y comercio colonial (1700–1789).* Barcelona: Editorial Ariel, 1979.

West, Robert Cooper. *The Mining Community in Northern New Spain: The Parral Mining District.* Berkeley: University of California Press, 1949.

Zabala, S. *España bajo los Borbones.* Barcelona, 1955.

Zabala Uriarte, Aingeru. "Bilbao y el comercio con el Norte de América en el siglo XVIII. Negocio y burguesía." In *América y los vascos. Jornadas sobre el comercio vasco con América en el siglo XVIII,* ed. Ronald Escobedo Mansilla et al., 171–202. Bilbao: Laida, 1989.

———. "Las relaciones comerciales en América del Norte." In *Presencia vasca en América.* Vitoria-Gasteiz, 1992.

Index

Abal Oliu, A., 495 n. 30
Abarca y Aznar, Silvestre, 110
Abasolo, Juan, 84
Aberri Aldez (newspaper), 404
ABF. *See* American Basque Foundation
Abrisketa Iraculis, Francisco de, 205–6
Acapulco, 144
Acebal y Díaz transport company, 391
Acoma Pueblo, 165
Acurio, Juan de, 33
administrators, Basque, 67–73
ADV. *See* Agrupación Democrática Vasca
Aesthetic Interpretation of the Augustinian Megalithic Culture (Oteiza), 207
Aginaga, 6
Agorreta, Francisco de, 42
Agreda, María Jesús de, 115
agriculture, 3; Basque contributions in Argentina, 273, 288; European migrations and, 298–99; impact of the New World on, 20–21; vineyards, 292–93, 299. *See also* cattle raising; sheep herders and sheep raising
Agrupación Democrática Vasca (ADV), 423
Aguado, Juan de, 18
Aguirre Acharán, José de, 97, 105
Aguirre Albisua, Pedro de, 120
Aguirre, Andrés de, 47–48
Aguirre, Antonio de, 196
Aguirre, Asensio de, 47
Aguirre, Baltasar, 293
Aguirre Beltrán family, 181
Aguirre Burualde, Martín de, 120, 172
Aguirre, Diego de, 66
Aguirre, Domingo de, 174
Aguirre family, in Guatemala, 184

Aguirre, Felipe de, 95
Aguirre, Francisco de, 41, 43, 45, 217, 478 n. 14
Aguirre, García de, 45
Aguirre, José Antonio, 207, 223
Aguirre, Juan de, 30, 34, 47, 49, 193
Aguirre, Juan Fco., 184
Aguirre, Juan M., 80
Aguirre, Lope de, 37, 49–50, 207, 479 n. 21
Aguirre, Luis de, 184
Aguirre, Pedro de, 39, 174
Aguirre, Tomás de, 42, 69
Aguirre y Aldazabal, Javier María de, 104
Aguirre y Lecube, José Antonio, 392
Aguirre y Parrigorria, Fausto, 331
Agustini, Delmira, 256
Aitamarren, Florentín de, 72
Aizpa, Miguel de, 193
Aizpurua, Nicolás de, 105
Ajanguiz, Juan de, 24
Alava y Sáez de Navarrete, Luis de, 220
Alberdi, Salvador, 271
Alberro, Francisco, 78
Albistur, Domingo de, 83
Albizu, Celestino, 318–19
Albret, Alain d', 6
Albret, Jean d', 1
Alcarazo family, in Costa Rica, 191
Alcayaga, Jacobo de, 72
Alcega, Diego de, 79
Alcega, Juan de, 79
Alcega, Pedro de, 55
Aldaco, Manuel de, 108, 114
Aldama, Domingo, 194
Aldama, Leonardo, 174

Aldama, Miguel, 194
Aldamiz-Etxeverria Arriandiaga, Jesús, 404
Aldana, Hernando de, 38
Aldana, Lorenzo, 71
Aldasoro, Ramón María, 398
Alday, Martín de, 167
Alday y Aspée, Manuel, 221
Aldaz, Juan de, 320
Alegría, Pedro de, 42
Alejos family, 181
Alexander VI (pope), 57, 485 n. 2
Alfinger, Ambrosio, 37
Alfonso, José Luis, 194
Alfonso XII (king of Spain), 367
Alfonso X (king of Castile), 9
Almagro, Diego de, 38, 39, 40–41
almojarifazgo, 487 n. 25
Alonso Niño, Pero, 26
Alonso Pinzón, Martín, 13, 14, 15
Alonso y Angulo, Ángel de, 330
Alquiza, Sancho de, 69
Alsasua, Bartolomé de, 80, 120
Altamirano, Cristóbal, 46, 70
Altolaguirre, Juan Pablo de, 320
Altuna, Francisco, 258
Altuna, Manuel Ignacio de, 117
Alvarado, Jorge de, 493 n. 27
Alvarado, Pedro de, 35
Alvarez de las Asturias Arroyave family, 182
Alvarez de las Asturias family, 184
Alvaro, Pedro de, 478 n. 8
Alzaga, Martín de, 70
Alzate, Martín de, 24
Alzola, Andrés de, 83
Alzola y Compostaeta, Domingo de, 210
Amazon River, 26
American Basque Foundation (ABF), 409
American War of Independence: Basque commerce and, 86; emigration trends and, 135
American West. *See* United States
Amescua, Sebastián de, 42

Amestoy, Juan de, 120
Amézaga, Juan de, 42, 69
Amézaga, Miguel de, 83
Amézqueta, Bartolomé de, 72
Amolaz, Francisco de, 80
Amozarrain, Miguel de, 114
Ampuero, Francisco de, 40
Amuchástegui-Eloizaga family, in Colombia, 204
Amuchástegui, Kepa, 207
Amuchástegui Mújica, Pedro, 205
Amusquibar y Ochoa de Racalde, Mateo de, 102
Añasco, Luis de, 196
Anaya, Carlos, 316
Anaya, Pedro de, 34
Anchía, Domingo de, 13
Anchieta, José de, 61–62, 63, 225
Andagoya, Pascual de, 31, 37, 38
Andalusia, 5, 7–9; banking in, 81; Basque iron companies and, 90–91; colonial commerce and, 76, 77; emigration to Mexico, 165–66; emigration trends, 129, 130, 131, 132, 136, 137. *See also* Cádiz; Sevilla
Anda y López de Armentia, Simón, 121
Andonaegui, José de, 70
Andrea, Alonso, 42
Andriani, Severo, 240
Angertor Denisquet, Lohizune, 83
Angostino, Eugenio Hernández, 345
Angula, Cristóbal, 47
Angulo, Miguel de, 330
Aniceto Padilla, Manuel, 306
animal husbandry. *See* cattle raising; sheep herders and sheep raising
Anselmí, Carmelo, 262
Ansogarlo, Miquelón de, 83
Ansorena de Garayoa, Fernando, 159
Antezana, Pedro de, 186
Anthony of Padua, Saint, 115
Antigua, María de la, 115
Antilles, 30–31, 37, 52, 57, 123, 128, 132, 138, 139. *See also individual countries*

Antonio López and Co., 303, 389
Anza, Juan Bautista, 168
Anzonegui, Juan de, 83
aparcería, 277
Aparicio family, 181
Apeizteguy (emigration agent), 363
Apérregui, Manuel, 80
Apestéguy emigration firm, 334
Apodaca y Eliza, Juan José Ruiz de, 73
Apoitia, Pacífico, 204
Araba: *Basque and Navarrese Emigration* and, 369; Church of Nuestra Señora de la Natividad of Elguea, 155; donations from America and, 160; draft evasion in, 349; eighteenth-century emigration, 140, 485 n. 59; emigration agents and, 330; emigration to Argentina, 272, 286, 287, 288; emigration to Puerto Rico, 201; *foral* system and, 2; origins of emigrants, 438–39; political state prior to Columbus, 1; ports of departure for emigrants, 388–90; public denunciations of emigration, 365; typology of emigrants and emigrant destinations, 373–75
Araba, Pedro de, 18
Araba y Sáenz de Navarrete, Luis Gonzaga de, 71
Aragon: emigrants in Guatemala, 190; emigration trends, 130, 134; privateering and, 480 n. 27
Aragón, Vera de, 46
Aramburu, Pedro de, 81
Aramendía, Domingo de, 46, 70
Arana, Baltasa Antonio de, 268
Arana, Diego de, 12, 13, 15, 17, 70, 212, 476 n. 17
Arana, Francisco de, 49
Arana, Nicolás, 84
Arana, Pedro de, 17, 30, 47, 196
Arancibia y Ormaegui, José Ignacio de, 61
Araneder, Joanes de, 83
Aranguren (Basque doctor), 394, 395

Aranguren y Zubiate, Antonio, 79
Arancibar, Juan de, 159
Aranya Goiri, Sabino de, 292
Aranybar, Joanes de, 83
Araoz, Josefa de, 271
Araucamendi and Brothers, 199
Araucanian Indians, 41
Araucanian, The (Ercilla), 218
Aráuz, Pedro de, 45
Araya, Rodrigo de, 41
Arbarola family, in Costa Rica, 191
Arbide, Nicolás, 175
Arbiza, O. M., 230
Arbolancha, Juan de, 476 n. 15
Arbolancha, Pedro de, 31
Arbolancha, Sebastián de, 40
Arce, Alonso de, 70
Arce family, 181
Arce, José Francisco de, 63
Archer, Juan, 84
architecture, Catholic Church and, 66–67
Arciaga, Diego de, 17
Arciniega, Claudio de, 66
Ardanza, José Antonio, 411
Areatza, 6
Arechaga, Juan de, 193
Aredi, Esteban, 251
Arenas island, 15
Arespacochaga, Martín de, 91
Arestegui, Joanes de, 83
Aresti, Lope, 13
Arga, El (newspaper), 372
Argañaraz y Murguía, Francisco, 70
Argentina: Basque agricultural contributions, 273, 288; Basque Centers in, 409; Basque emigration to, 239–40, 248, 249, 259, 260, 270–72, 276–77, 283, 286–89, 373, 374, 375–76, 377, 378, 380, 381, 382, 384, 385, 387, 397, 398–99, 404; Basque exiles and, 397–400; Basque social and political institutions, 289–92; Basque social, religious, and family networks, 279–80; Bizkaian emigration to, 375, 380;

Carlist militants in, 345; cost of steamship passage to, 388; dairy industry, 283, 284–85; distribution of lands in, 274–75; eighteenth-century colonization, 270–71; emigration agencies and, 312; emigration agents and, 305, 306, 312–14; emigration to Brazil, 225; explorers and conquistadors, 479n. 17; immigration policies, 305–7, 313, 398–400; immigration trends, 239–40; inflation of land values, 282; Pedro Luro and, 280–82; Navarrese emigration to, 368, 372; navigation lines to, 391; nineteenth-century Basque presence in, 270–86; origins of Basque immigrants, 286–89; seventeenth-century colonization of Tucumán region, 267–69; sheep and cattle raising in, 273–74, 276–78, 279–82, 283–86, 293, 299; urban labor by immigrants, 277–79. *See also* Río de la Plata
Argentine Commission of Emigration, 315–16
Argentine Information Office, emigration agents and, 323–30
Argote, Roldán de, 33
Arguena, Juan, 34
Argueta, Hernando de, 34
Arguiñarena, Ignacio, 266
Arias, Cristóbal, 83
Arias de Saavedra, Hernando, 227
Arias, Juan, 12
Arieta e Iturriaga, Juan de, 104
Arisnea, Diego de, 34
Aristarain, Joaquín de, 120
Aristizabal, Joaquín de, 318
Ariza, Alonso de, 39
Arizabala, Antón de, 34
Arizabalo, Santiago, 255
Ariza family, 180, 182, 183
Ariz, Andrés de, 83
Ariza Rubio, Pedro de, 182
Ariza y Rubio family, 181

Arlas, Margarita, 250
Arlegui family, in Costa Rica, 191
Armada family, in Costa Rica, 191
Armada of the Indian Guard, 77
Armada of the South Seas, 79
Armada of Vizcaya, 6
armadas, 11; Basques in, 79; defense of colonial commerce, 76–77; Dutch, 485n. 6; royal, 53, 76, 79, 97
Armendia, Juan, 83
Armentia, Juan de, 39
Armentia, Pedro de, 36
Armona y Murga, Matías de, 109
arms industry, 22, 477n. 22
Arnés de Sopuerta, Andrés del, 34
Arocena y Leandro, Rafael, 175
Arosllozu, Martín de, 120
Arosqueta, Josefa de, 108
Arosqueta, Juan Bautista de, 108
Aróstegui, Antonio de, 68
Arostegui Larrea, Martín de, 110
Arostegui, María Jesús, 110
Aróstegui, Martín de, 61, 79, 98
Arraes, Juan, 13
Arraes, Pedro, 13
Arraez de Mendoza, Antonio, 478n. 16
Arrasate, 3, 22
Arratia, Juan de, 33
Arratia, Pedro de, 72
Arratibel Zafinea, Sebastián de, 110
Arrazabal, Joanot de, 83
Arrazu, Joanes de, 84
Arreche, José A. de, 102
Arreche, Juanot de, 84
Arredondo, José, 79
Arregui, Juan de, 81
Arregui, Miguel de, 67
Arrese (Basque doctor), 417
Arrese y Lardizabal, Joaquín J. de, 101, 102
Arriaga, Antón de, 35
Arriaga, Antonio, 42
Arriaga, Diego de, 30
Arriaga, Juan de, 34

Arriaga, Luis de, 24
Arriaga, Martín de, 42, 72
Arriaga, Miguel, 34
Arriaga, Pablo José de, 66
Arriaga, Pedro de, 42
Arriaga, Pedro José de, 210
Arriaga y Gurbista, Miguel de, 102
Arría, José de, 72
Arriano, Pedro, 196
Arriarán, Amador de, 47
Arriarán, Martín, 18
Arriarán, Pedro, 81
Arriaregari, Oyer de, 83
Arribillaga, Diego, 182
Arribillaga family, in Guatemala, 180, 182, 183, 184, 189
Arribillaga, Francisco, 184
Arribillaga, Juan, 182
Arribillaga, Juana, 182
Arribillaga y Castilla de Portugal, María Josefa, 189
Arribillaga y Montufar, José Agustín de, 189
Arrieta, Ángel María, 349, 373, 374, 388
Arrieta family, in Costa Rica, 191
Arrieta, Francisco de, 68, 478n. 16
Arrieta, Juan, 258
Arrieta, Juanes de, 35
Arrieta, Martín de, 476n. 17
Arrieta, Ramón de, 83
Arriola Balerdi, Martín de, 216
Arriola, Manuel de, 98
Arriola, María de, 49
Arriola, Martín de, 71
Arrizabalaga, Andrés de, 91
Arroyo Grande, Battle of, 233
Arrúa, Juan Felíx de, 479n. 16
Arrupe, Felipe de, 42
Arruti, Fernando, 174
art: Catholic Church and, 65–66; donations of objects from America, 154–56
Art and General Compendium of the Gregorian Chant (Marcos y Mavas), 115

Arteagabeitia, Ramón de, 231
Arteagabeitia, Sergio de, 231
Arteaga de Mendiola, Pedro, 62
Arteaga, Domingo de, 34
Arteaga, Francisco de, 41, 98
Arteaga, Juan de, 42
Arteaga, Luis de, 17
Arteaga, Martín de, 42
Arteaga, Sebastián de, 67
Arteaga y Aunavidad, Gaspar de, 196–199
Arteaga y Avendaño, Juan de, 61
Arteaga y Ochoa, Juan Vincente, 80
Arthum, Daniel, 84
Artieda, Diego de, 191
Artieta, Nicolás de, 31
Artuaga, Martín de, 42
Arzamendia, Andrés de, 44
Arzú y Díaz de Arcaya family, 180, 181, 182
Asarta, José de, 142
Ascensión, Martín de la, 61
Aspine family, in Costa Rica, 191
Aspiruntza, Martín de, 35
Association of Basque-Navarrese Beneficence, 376
Association of Basques of Sevilla, 90
Association of Saint Ignatius of Madrid, 114
Astigarribia, Francisco de, 47
Astrain, Martín de, 142
Astruarena e Iturralde, Pedro de, 97, 105
Asturias, emigration trends, 129, 136, 137
Asuá, Ochoa de, 34
Asunción, 44, 209
Atín, Martín de, 476n. 17
Augustinians, 482n. 41
Aulestia, Cristóbal de, 66
Aurrera (newspaper), 402
Austro-Hungarian Empire, emigration from, 295
Avalancha, La (magazine), 371
Avellanada family, in Costa Rica, 191

Avellaneda, Nicolás de, 307
Avendaño, Juan de, 31, 38
Avendaño, Prudencio de, 42
Avila, Juan de, 115
Avilés, 20
Axpe, Francisco de, 42, 70
Ayala, Diego de, 30, 196
Ayala, Lope de, 41
Ayala, Pedro de, 72
Ayarde, Juan de, 42
Ayardi, Tomás de, 79
Ayau, Pedro, 181
Aycaguez family, in Chile, 224
Aycinena e Irigoyen family, 180, 181, 182
Aycinena e Irigoyen, Juan Fermín de, 188
Aycinena family, in Guatemala, 184, 188
Aycinena y Carrillo, Juan Vicente de, 188
Aycinena, José, 184
Aycinena Larraín, Pedro, 184
Aycinena, Mariano, 184
Aycinena, Pedro de, 173
Aycinena, Vicente, 184
Aycinena, Xabier, 184
Ayeta, 6
Ayolas, Juan de, 44, 216
Azanza, Miguel José de, 73
Azara, Félix de, 229, 497 n. 2
Azarina Muñoz, Gloria, 206
Azcárate Escobedo, Nicolás de, 110
Azcárate Lascurain, Gabriel de, 110
Azcárate, Ramón, 215
Azcona, José Manuel, 413
Azcuénaga e Iturbe, Domingo de, 103
Azevedo, Mauricio, 498 n. 23
Azkoitia, 117
Azócar, Santiago de, 41
azogueros, 208
Azpeitia, 8
Azpeitia, Juan de, 34
Azpeitia, Nicolás, 39
Azpilicueta, Juan de, 63, 224
Azpiroz, Francisco, 347

Aztec Empire, conquest of, 35, 162, 478 n. 8
Azúa Iturgoyen, Tomás de, 220
Azúa, Juan de, 17, 30

Babeque island, 15
Baigorri, Pedro, 70
Balmaseda, 8
Balparda, Esteban, 231
Balparda, Saturnino, 231
Balsa, Juan de, 39
Balzola, Juan de, 35
Banda Oriental, 227–28, 497 n. 2
banking, 81
Baquedano Arana, Dionisio, 376
Baquijano, José de, 121
Baquijano y Urigüen, Juan Bautista de, 103
Baracaldo, Antonio de, 31
Barbero-Muñoz family, in Colombia, 204
Barcelonesa Company, 199
Bardeci, Pedro de, 62
Barjiarena, Juan Francisco, 142
Barón de Berrieza, María Felipa Mencos, 182
Barot, Juan, 251
Barreda y Benavides, María Josefa de, 214
Barrena, Francisco de, 30
Barrenechea y Campo, Andrés, 72
Barrow, Lorenzo, 84
Barrundia Iparraguirre family, 181
Barrutia Echeverría family, 182
Barrutia, Irisarri, 180
Barrutia, Juan de, 30
Barrutia, Luis Fco., 184
Barrutia, Xabier, 184
Barrutia y Olabegoitia family, 181
Barruti, Ignacio Francisco de, 167
Barruti, Juan de, 17
Basabe, Francisco José de, 120
Basagoiti, Antonio de, 175
Basauri, Simón de, 42
Basconia, La (periodical), 290
Basoa, Pedro M., 81

Basori, Pedro Bueno, 172
Basque Action of Argentina, 292, 398
Basque-American communities, William Douglass on the future of, 406–7
Basque and Navarrese Emigration (Colá y Goiti), 369
Basque Association of Mutual Aid (Venezuela), 207, 402
Basque associations, 112–13; in Mexico, 113–16; in Peru, 112–13
Basque Centers: in Argentina, 409; Basque Government's pledge to support, 407; "Basque weeks" and, 408; in Chile, 223, 410; in Colombia, 203; in Cuba, 195; William Douglass on, 406–7; in France, 410; in Guatemala and El Salvador, 192; laws regulating, 410; in Mexico, 176, 177, 178, 404, 410; in Puerto Rico, 495 n. 71; in Spain, 410; in the United States, 409; in Uruguay, 249, 254, 410; in Venezuela, 207, 403, 410
Basque Children's Trust Ltd. (Great Britain), 392
Basque-Chilean Development Foundation, 410
Basque Church, 59–60
"Basque clubs," 409
Basque Country: arms industry, 22, 477 n. 22; Castilian royal dominion and, 473–74 n. 2; Christianity and, 483 n. 43; colonial enterprises and, 7; commerce and, 81–92; connections with emigrants, 152; donations from America and (*see* donations from America); draft evasion in, 349–53; economic activities prior to Columbus, 3–5; effects of emigration on the balance of the sexes, 157; emigration agencies and emigration agents, 305–22; enclosure of the commons, 243; Enlightenment movement and, 117–18; farmsteads, 356–57; *foral* system, 2–3, 473–74 n. 2; idealization of rustic life, 355–56; impact of the Columbian expeditions on, 20–23; industrial revolution and, 296–97, 299; inheritance systems, 141, 353–54; iron industry (*see* iron industry); late-twentieth-century emigration, 405; political dominions prior to Columbus, 1; population density, 7; privateering and, 53, 54, 55, 56, 416; public denunciations of emigration, 364–73; stem family concept, 353; whaling and cod fishing industries, 3, 81–86, 111
Basque delegations: in Argentina, 398; in Chile, 402; in Colombia, 403; in the Dominican Republic, 403; in the U.S., 404
Basque Democratic Group, 402
Basque emigration, 128–45; agreements and contracts by emigration agents, 307–22; American destinations, 132, 140, 387–88, 440; "American relatives" and, 143, 146; to Argentina, 239–40, 248, 249, 259, 260, 270–72, 276–77, 283, 286–89, 373, 374, 375–76, 377, 378, 380, 381, 382, 384, 385, 387, 397, 398–99, 404; balance of the sexes in Basque Country and, 157; to Brazil, 225–26; to Chile, 218–24, 401; clergy and missionaries, 384–88; to Colombia, 202–7, 400, 405; for colonial government administration, 142; connections with places of origin, 152; documents required for, 145–47, 359–60; donations from America, 152–61; draft evasion and, 349–53; eighteenth-century trends, 139, 140–45; emigrants indebted for their passage, 467–72; emigration agencies and, 312–14; family networks and, 143; idealization of rustic life and, 355–56; industrial revolution and, 296–97, 299, 355; inheritance patterns and, 141, 353–54, 357; living conditions on transatlantic passage, 148–51,

360–64; as a male phenomenon, 131, 132; to Mexico, 165–67, 295, 296, 334, 344, 354, 355, 364, 373, 374, 375, 377, 380, 384, 385, 387, 397, 403, 404, 405; migratory chains, 294, 354–55; motivations for, 140–45, 356–57; myths of America and, 357–58; newspaper campaigns against, 371–73; origins of emigrants, 437–39; to Paraguay, 215–18; to Peru, 132, 138, 140, 147, 210–15, 405; ports of departure, 388–91; public denunciations of, 364–70, 504n. 19; to Puerto Rico, 195–202; seventeenth-century trends, 132–33, 137, 141, 145; sixteenth-century trends, 126, 128–29, 131, 132; social class and, 131; Spanish Civil War and, 341; stem family concept and, 353; transatlantic passage, 145–51; twentieth-century economic growth and, 404–5; twentieth-century trends, 343, 405; typology of emigrants and destinations, 373–84; to the United States, 295–99, 334, 405; to Uruguay, 227–67, 374, 377, 378, 381, 382, 385, 405; to Venezuela, 145, 207, 334, 405, 495n. 91; women in, 125, 126, 135–36, 139. *See also* Basque exiles; colonial emigration

Basque exiles: "children of Morelia," 404; forced exit from Spain, 392–97; shelters and hospitals in France, 393–96; transatlantic receptions, 397–404

Basque Government, pledges to promote and expand Basque culture, 407–9

Basque Handball Federation, 407

"Basque Hunters" (Uruguay), 233

Basque inns/hotels, in Chile, 224

Basque-Mexican Development Institute, 410

Basque Nationalist Action of Argentina, 292

Basque Nationalist Board (Argentina), 398

Basque National Party. *See* Partido Nacionalista Vasco

Basque-Navarrese Beneficient Association, 195, 376

Basque Union Association of Mutual Aid (Argentina), 292

"Basque weeks," 408

Basque Youth-Euzko Gaztedija (Chile), 223

Basse Navarre, political state prior to Columbus, 1

Basses-Pyrénées: Basque draft evasion, 350, 352–53; emigration agencies and agents in, 334–35; emigration to California, 240, 249; emigration to Uruguay and America, 237–38, 240–45; nineteenth- and twentieth-century population statistics, 234–40, 241, 242, 243; nineteenth-century economic decline, 303–4; opposition to emigration, 498n. 25; smuggling and, 304. *See also* Iparralde

Basseta, Domingo, 186

Bassoco, Antonio de, 108, 114, 169, 170

Bastarrica family, in Costa Rica, 191

Basterra Nanclares, Judit, 206

Basterra, Restituto, 322–30

Bastidas, Rodrigo de, 26, 27

Basualdo, Juan de, 46, 70

Basurto de Acha, 6

Basurto, Juan de, 31

Batasuna (magazine), 402

Batlle y Ordóñez, José, 257, 259, 262

Batres family, 182, 183, 184

Batres, Josef, 184

Batres Juarros family, 184

Batres Muñoz, José Antonio, 184

Batres Nájera family, 184

Battalion of Volunteers (Uruguay), 233

"Batllism," 257, 260

Baucells, Josef, 190

Bautista de Urquiola, Juan, 72

Bautista Echevarria, Juan, 84

Bayonne, 1, 16, 20, 301, 395

Bazán, Santiago, 41
Baztán, Valley of, 375, 378; emigration agents and companies in, 320–21; emigration to Mexico, 175; impact of the Carlist Wars on emigration, 344; migratory chains, 354
Beauzmont Hotel, De (Montevideo), 251
Becerro, Ricardo, 256
Beckwelt, Pedro, 84
Beginner for All Explanations to Sing Solfeggio in All Keys (Master Jerusalem), 115
Beguiristain, José Ignacio de, 318
Beitia, Antonio José, 120
Beitia y Rentería, José de, 109
Belanzacín, Juan Bautista de, 167
Bell, Alexander Graham, 300
Beltrán de Guzmán, Nuño, 162
Beltranena family, in Guatemala, 184
Beltranena, Manuel, 184
Beltranena, Pedro Josef, 184
Beltranena, Vicente, 184
Beltranena y Aycinena family, 180, 181
Benavides, Juan de, 485 n. 6
Bengoechea, Francisco de, 194
Bengoechea, Sebastián de, 42
Beracoechea family, in Costa Rica, 191
Berástegui, Ojer de, 13
Berchaguren y Yarzo, Francisco Antonio de, 103
Berenguer de Marquina, Félix, 73
Bergara, Antonio de, 39
Bergara, Gaspar de, 40, 41
Bergara, Juan de, 30, 39, 42
Bergara, Martínez de, 41
Bergara, Miguel de, 30
Bergara, Pedro de, 30, 39
Beristain, Miguel, 116
Berlanga, Tomás de, 39
Bermeo, 3, 5, 54
Bernardo de Zamácola, Simón, 62
Berne, Juan de, 193
Beroiz, Antonio de, 55
Berrio, Antonio de, 43

Berrio, Francisco de, 34
Berrio, Hernando de, 17, 30
Berrio, Juan de, 39
Berrio, Pedro de, 34
Berrio y Saldivar, Miguel de, 108
Bertendoa, Jimeno de, 80, 81
bertsolariak, 358, 504 n. 19
Betancourt, Gabriel, 495 n. 79
Beteta, Hernando de, 42
Betharramites, 249
Bidarte, Joanes de, 83
Bilbao, 4–5, 6, 8, 20; American War of Independence and, 86; Company of Buenos Aires and, 96–97, 106–7; departure of Basque emigrants from, 376; eighteenth-century fishing merchants, 84–85; emigration agents and, 323–30; iron industry and, 4; privateering and, 53, 54, 55; shipbuilding industry, 6; shipping industry, 4–5; whaling and cod fishing industries, 83, 84–85, 86
Bilbao, Antonio de, 42
Bilbao, Jon, 233, 350, 355
Bilbao, Juan de, 35
Bilbao, Martín de, 40
Biran, Mathieu de, 83
Bizarrón, José Antonio, 81
Bizkaia: arms industry, 21, 22; *Basque and Navarrese Emigration* and, 369; colony on Hispaniola, 18–19; donations from America and, 154, 156, 160; eighteenth-century emigration, 139–40; emigration to Argentina, 272, 286, 288, 289; emigration to Puerto Rico, 201; emigration to Uruguay, 249; *foral* system and, 2; iron industry and, 3, 4, 21, 86–89; labor strikes, 401; origins of emigrants, 438; political state prior to Columbus, 1; population density, 7; population loss, 23, 250; ports of departure for emigrants, 388; privateering and, 52–53, 54, 55, 416; public denunciations of emigration,

367, 369, 370; shipbuilding industry, 6; tobacco trade and, 111; typology of emigrants and emigrant destinations, 375, 380–84; whaling and cod fishing industries, 3, 82, 83, 85–86, 111
Boabdil the Younger, 10, 476 n. 15
boarding licenses, 128, 135, 359
boarding obligations, 359–60
Board of Navigators, 28
Board of Settlers of the Kingdom of Chile, 220
Bobadilla, Francisco de, 19, 482 n. 41
Bobie (ship), 395
Bobures Valley (Venezuela), 478 n. 16
Bodega y Quadra, Tomás de la, 101, 103
Bogota, 403
Bohío island, 15
Bolívar, Juan, 83
Bolívar, Simón ("the elder"), 42
Bolívar, Simón (the Liberator), 208, 209
Bolivia, 178, 208
Bonnet, Stede, 479 n. 23
Bono de Guecho, Juan, 34
Book for Self-Instruction and with Bass for Accompaniment (Master Jerusalem), 117
Boroa, Diego de, 63
Bordeaux, 313, 314, 315, 316, 322, 331, 332, 335, 347, 350, 351, 376, 388, 389, 390, 394, 401, 402, 410
Borgoña, Juan, 18
Borica y Retegui, Diego de, 73
Boyd-Bowman, Peter, 129, 132, 165, 192, 202, 207
Brazil, 225–26, 303, 324–25, 334
Bretagne (ship), 402
Breve y más compendiosa doctrina christiana en lengua mexicana y castellana, 65
Brevísma relación de la destrucción de las Indias (Las Casas), 64
Brie & Co., 320
Brie, Francisco, 319–20
Brie, Juan Bautista, 233

Brotherhood of Aránzazu of Lima, 112, 113, 170
Brotherhood of Aránzazu, 170–71. *See also* Confraternity of Our Lady of Aránzazu of Mexico
Broussain family, in Chile, 224
Brunel, Isambard K., 302
Bucarelli y Ursúa, Antonio, 120
buccaneers, 479 n. 24
Buenos Aires, 46, 255–56, 270–80, 283–86, 289–92; Araban emigration to, 374; Basque draft evaders in, 353; Basque emigration to, 140, 145; Basque mercantile activities, 96–97, 104–7, 272–73; Basque organizations, 289, 290–92; Basque periodicals, 290; Basque professions and jobs in, 464, 465–66; Charles of Bourbon in, 347; Hotel for Immigrants, 276; immigration laws and, 306; immigration trends, 238, 239–40, 272–73; Navarrese emigration to, 376; nineteenth-century Basque population, 272–73; transatlantic passage to, 361–63
Buhalde family, in Chile, 224
bulls. *See* papal bulls
Burguete, 355
Butrón, Gabriel, 17, 30

Cabarrús, Francisco, 99
Cabeza de Vaca, Alvar Núñez, 44, 216–17
Cabot, John, 82
Cabrera, Alonso, 44, 216
Cabrera y Quintero, Cayetano, 115
Cabrero, Juan, 10
Cádiz, 8, 9, 11; Basque administrators and officials in, 80–81; Basque influence in, 100–101; Basque iron companies and, 90–91; colonial commerce and, 8–9, 25, 77–78; Company of Buenos Aires and, 97–98; emigration and, 127, 131, 135, 138; Guatemalan trade and, 187, 188; House of Trade and, 77, 78; second voyage of Columbus and, 475 n.

14; transfers of American capital and, 152–53
Calahorra, 483 n. 43
Calamet, Francisco, 251
Calatayud, Jerónimo de, 101, 142
Calderón, Mencía, 217
California: explorers and conquistadors in, 27, 48–49; immigration from Iparralde, 240
Camousseigt family, in Chile, 224
Campo Soberón y Larrea, José del, 167
Camuz, Juan de, 47
Canada, 295, 296
Canary Islands, 9, 12, 13, 126, 187, 200, 215
Candelaria, Fort, 44
Canelones (Uruguay), 228
Cano, Melchor, 115
Cantabria, 136, 137
Caonabó, 17
Capitana (ship), 19
Capitulaciones de Santa Fe, 10, 16
Capitulations of Toledo, 38
Capuchins, 387
Caracas, 42, 62, 69, 207, 403. *See also* Royal Guipuzcoan Company of Caracas
caravels, 491 n. 55
Cardel, Martín, 83
Cárdenas, Lázaro, 176, 404
Cardiel y Laguna, José, 63
"cards of retaliation," 481 n. 30
Caribbean Indians, 17
Carlism, in Argentina, 348–49
Carlist Wars: Basque emigration and, 344–49; José María de Iparraguirre and, 254; smuggling and, 304; Uruguayan immigration and, 233, 245
Caroline (ship), 231
Carolini, Vicente, 263
carracks, 491 n. 55
Carranza, Cosme de, 72
Carranza, Francisco Antonio, 269
Carranza, Gómez de, 39

Carranza, Pedro de, 34, 35
Carricarte, E. J., 323
Carrillo y Galvez, Ana María, 188
Carrión, Juan Pablo de, 479 n. 19
Carta de Marear o Mapamudi (De la Cosa), 26
Cartagena, 29
cartography, Juan De la Cosa and, 26
Casabide, Félix, 320
Casabide, Martín, 320
Casa da Inda, 74
Casa de Contratación. *See* House of Trade
Casas y Aragorri, Luis de las, 120
Casaus Arzú, Marta Elena, 180
Caseda, 384
Casenave, Martín, 251
Castañada, Josefa, 271
Castañeda, Francisco de, 39
Castañiza, Juan de, 107, 108, 114, 169, 170
Castañiza, Marquis, 120
Castañiza y Agüero, Ignacio María de, 108
Castaños, Martín de, 79
Castaños y Beisagasti, Juan, 72
Castaños y Beisagasti, Martín, 72
Castellón, Luis, 401
Castex family, in Chile, 224
Castile: Basque iron industry and, 4; Capitulaciones de Santa Fe, 10–11, 16, 24; dominion over the Basque Country, 1, 473–74 n. 2; emigration trends, 129, 130, 132; Navarre and, 1, 2; privateering and, 480 n. 27; War of Succession, 6
Castilla y Portugal family, 183
Castillo, Cánovas del, 346, 351
Castillo, Rafael del, 186
Castillo y Sobrón, Carlos del, 330
Castillo y Sobrón, Romualdo del, 330
Castro Street (Sevilla), 8
Catalonia: emigrants in Guatemala, 187; Puerto Rico and, 200, 202; Spanish Civil War and, 396

Cathedral of Cádiz, 7
Catherine (queen of Navarre), 1–2
Catholic Church: architecture and, 66–67; in the Basque Country, 59–60, 483 n. 43; church-state relations in the Americas, 57–59; dioceses and sees established in America, 481 n. 39; donations from America and, 153–54, 155–57, 160, 441–43; education and, 66; fine arts and, 65–67; key figures in the Americas, 57–65; papal bulls, 57–58, 481 n. 38, 485 n. 2; theater and, 66; treatment of indigenous Americans, 63–65. *See also* missionaries
cattle raising: in Argentina, 273, 274, 275, 277, 280–82, 283, 284–86; in Uruguay, 227–29. *See also* dairy industry, in Argentina
Cauchela, Andrés de, 47
Cayo Rum island, 15
Cazcan Indians, 162
Cebu island, 47–48
Celaya, Hernando de, 31
Central America: Basque family networks and power elites, 178–85; indigo dye industry, 187–89; San Vicente, 185–86. *See also individual countries*
Central Immigration Commission (Argentina), 276
Centre Basque Français (Argentina), 290, 291
Centro Euskaro (Uruguay), 254
Centro Navarro (Argentina), 290, 291
Cepeda y Chamorro, Teresa de, 190
Cerain, Miguel, 83
Cervantes, Miguel de, 484 n. 54
Cestona, Juan, 372
Chaco frontier, 267–69
chain emigration, 294, 354–55
Challa, Ogero de, 83
Challe family, in Chile, 224
Chamorro y Sotomayor family, 180, 181

Chargeurs Réunis transport company, 391
charity: Confraternity of Our Lady of Aránzazu of Mexico and, 169; donations from America for, 156–58, 454–58
Charles III (king of Spain): Argentina and, 270; Juan Fermín de Aycinena e Irigoyen and, 188; College of the Vizcayans and, 114–15; economic reforms and, 98; liberalization of mercantilist trade, 98–100; Mexican mining industry and, 108; Royal Basque Society and, 117–18, 172
Charles II (king of Spain), 54
Charles IV (king of Spain), 270
Charles of Bourbon (Charles VII; Don Carlos), 245, 346, 347
Charles V, 2, 20; Diego de Almagro and, 40; American colonization and, 24; Basque administrators under, 68; Catholic clergy and, 58; church-state relations and, 59; conquest of Peru and, 478 n. 12; Cuba and, 192–93; emigration policy and, 125, 126; liberalization of American commerce, 78, 486 n. 10; Magellan's voyage and, 31–32, 33; married colonists and, 489 n. 3; New World conquests and, 33; privateering and, 480 n. 27
Charles VII. *See* Charles of Bourbon
Charles VIII (king of France), 1
Charnisay, Henry de, 334
Chaunu, Pierre, 75, 491 n. 52
Chavarrieta, Martín de, 79
Chaves Galindo, Alonso de, 79
Chaves, Nufri de, 217
Chazarreta, Miguel de, 79
Chichimec Indians, 164
"children of Morelia," 404
Chile, 497 n. 117; Basque administrators and officials in, 70–71; Basque Centers in, 223, 410; Basque emigration to, 222–23, 405; Basque exiles

and, 401–2; conquistadors and explorers in, 40, 41–42, 218–19; eighteenth-century Basque presence, 219–20; emigration agencies and, 312, 334; Miguel Gómez de Rivero and, 268; immigration policies, 309–12, 334, 501 n. 6; independence of, 221–22; migratory chains and, 354; Navarrese emigration to, 377; nineteenth- and twentieth-century Basque presence, 221–25; seventeenth-century Basque presence, 219
Chindurza, Pedro, 33
Christianity, in the Basque Country, 483 n. 43
Church of Nuestra Señora de la Asunción de La Atalaya (Bermeo, Bizkaia), 155–56
Church of Nuestra Señora de la Asunción (Hondarribia, Gipuzkoa), 156
Church of Nuestra Señora de la Natividad (Elugea, Araba), 155
Church of Nuestra Señora (Lacorzanilla, Araba), 156
Church of Saint Augustine (Cádiz), 8
Church of San Francisco (Lima), 112, 113
Church of San Juan de Molinar (Gordexola, Bizkaia), 156
Church of Santa María del Juncal (Irún, Gipuzkoa), 156
Church of the Basques (Montevideo), 498 n. 25
Church of Virgen de Guadalupe y el Santo Cristo de Zacatecas (Ea, Bizkaia), 156
church-state relations, 58–60. See also Catholic Church
Cibao, 15, 16
Ciamba, 476 n. 18
Cifre de Loubriel, Estela, 201
Cipango, 13
circumnavigation voyages, 31–33, 479 n. 19; Magellan's Basque crew, 415–16

Clement XIII (pope), 114
clergy: opposition to Basque emigration, 498 n. 25. See also missionaries
clerks, salaries of, 491 n. 52
Coast Guard Squadron, 77
cod fishing industry, 82, 83, 84–86, 111
coffee, 175
Cola y Goiti, José, 322, 331, 332
Colba island, 15
cold-storage plants, in Uruguay, 259, 262, 263
College of Basque Pilots of Cádiz, 7
College of Charity, 171
College of Peace, 116
College of Saint Ignatius. See College of the Vizcayans
College of the Vizcayans, 61, 112, 114–16, 171–72
Coloma, Juan de, 10
Colombia: Basque administrators and officials in, 71–72; Basque Centers in, 203, 403; Basque emigration to, 202–3, 405; Basque exiles and, 399, 400, 403; Basque presence and activity in, 202–7; conquistadors and explorers in, 37–38; early expeditions to, 27, 29; Perea-Saisain family in, 495 n. 81; "Santa Cruz" colony, 27
Colón de Larriátegui, Francisco, 79
Colón (French admiral), 6
Colonia del Sacramento, 227, 228, 229, 230, 268, 270
colonial commerce, 20; American War of Independence and, 86; Andalusia and, 7–9; Basque iron industry, 86–92, 421–30; Basque whaling and cod fishing, 81–86, 111; in Cuba, 109–11; decline in, 77; Indies fleet, 74–77, 485 n. 6, 485–86 n. 9, 491 n. 55; "Indies run," 78–81, 486 n. 9; iron companies and, 90–92, 428–30; in Mexico, 107–8; with North America, 111; in Peru, 101–4; in Río de la Plata, 96–97, 104–7; slave trade, 91–92; Spanish

economic monopoly, 74–77; Spanish mercantilism, 92–100
colonial emigration: American destinations, 132, 138, 140; boarding licenses, 145–47; to Cuba, 194; eighteenth-century trends, 134–40; as a male phenomenon, 131, 132, 135–36; to Mexico, 144–45, 165–67, 175–76; motives for, 140–45; to Puerto Rico, 195–202; seventeenth-century trends, 132–35; sixteenth-century trends, 128–32; social class and, 131, 137; Spanish migration policy, 123–28; transatlantic passage, 145–51; women in, 125, 131, 135–36, 139. *See also* Basque emigration
Colonia (Uruguay), 227
Columbian expeditions: Basques in, 12–13, 17, 18, 19, 24, 476nn. 15, 16, 17; Columbus's contract with Castile, 10–11, 16, 24; Columbus's search for backers, 9–10; description of the first voyage, 13–16; fourth voyage, 19–20, 476–77nn. 17, 18; impact on the Basque Country, 20–23; organizing of the first voyage, 11–13; repercussions of the first voyage, 16; second voyage, 17–18, 475–76n. 14, 476n. 15; third voyage, 19
Columbus, Bartolomé, 18–19
Columbus, Christopher: contract with Castile, 10–11, 16, 24; nationality of, 474–75 n. 9; ranks and titles given to, 475 n. 11; search for backers, 9–10. *See also* Columbian expeditions
Columbus, Diego, 192–93
Comité Nationale Catholique d'Accueil aux Basques, 392
Commentaries on the Mining Ordinances (Gamboa), 108
commerce: Basque economy and, 3–5, 20–21, 78, 81–82. *See also* colonial commerce
Commerce, Du, hotel (Montevideo), 251

Committee to Help the Basques (Uruguay), 401
communication: Basque Government's pledge to support, 408; European migrations and, 301–2
Compagnie Commerciale de Transports à Vapeur Français, 389
Compagnie Générale Transatlantique, 302
Compañía Marítima Frutera, 303
Compañía Mexican Transatlántica, 389
Compañías Generales Marítimas, 389
Compañía Transatlántica, 303, 389
Compañía Transatlántica de Barcelona, 389
Compañía Transmediterránea, 303
Compañón, Martíñez de, 62
Compañón y Martínez Bujanda, Baltasar Jaime Martínez, 121
Company of Buenos Aires, 96, 97, 106–7, 488 n. 35
Company of Caracas, 55, 57, 94–96, 97–99, 104–5, 111, 144, 160, 207, 431, 495 n. 89
Company of Honduras, 94
Company of Indigo Harvesters, 187
Complete Method for Singing (Beristain), 116
Compostela, 162
Concepción, 209, 220–21, 224
Concepción (ship), 31
Condeau Camachez family, in Chile, 224
Conderina, Antonio de, 61
Confraternity of Our Lady of Aránzazu of Lima, 121
Confraternity of Our Lady of Aránzazu of Mexico, 61, 114, 115, 116, 119, 169
Confraternity of Sanctity and Charity, 171
Confraternity of the Basque Nation, 5, 7
Confraternity of the Most Holy Christ of Humility and Patience, 8
Confraternity of the Sailors and Pilots of the Passage of the Indies, 76

conquistadors and explorers: in Chile, 40, 41–42, 218–19; in Colombia, 37–38; in Cuba, 192–93; in Ecuador, 40; in Mexico, 34–37, 162–65, 478n. 8; in New Mexico, 48, 162, 165; in Paraguay, 44, 45; in Peru, 37–40, 49–50; in the Philippines, 46–48; in Río de la Plata, 43–46; in Venezuela, 42–43
Conrrard, Plácido, 251
Consulate of Bilbao, 96, 97, 105
Consulate of Cádiz, 97, 101
Consulate of Lima, 97, 101, 104
Consulate of Mexico, 167, 169, 187, 432
Consulate of Sevilla, 76, 80, 89, 100, 101
Consulate of the Merchants of Mexico, 107
Convent of Saint Francis, 7
Copiapó Valley, 40
Coquimbo, 41
Córdoba, Pedro de, 481n. 40
Corella, 384
corn, 20
Coro Euskaro (Argentina), 290
Corporation of Indies' Shippers, 76
Correo de la Plata, El (newspaper), 244
Correo Español, El (newspaper), 255, 372
corsairs, 52, 479n. 24, 485n. 6
Cortabarría, Juan de, 112
Cortabarría, Pedro, 318–19
Cortazar, Julián de, 61
Corterreal brothers, 82
Cortés, Andrés Rodríguez, 159
Cortés, Hernán, 34, 35, 72, 162, 163, 193, 478n. 8
Cortés, Luis de, 164
Cortés Moctezuma, Leonor, 163
Cosmópolis. *See* Villa del Cerro
"Cosmópolis," 308
Costa Rica, 180, 190–92
Cote, Martín de, 31, 40
Cotto, Tomás de, 185
Council of Bayonne, 83
Council of Burgos, 63
Council of Castile, 219

Council of the Indies, 75, 76; Gaspar de Arteaga and, 199; Basques in, 78, 79, 105; boarding licenses and, 145; church-state relations and, 58
Council of Trent, 59
"counter-scorecards," 481n. 30
Courrier de la Plata, Le (newspaper), 244
Cramer Mañecas, Agustín, 110
Crooked Island, 15
Cruz Gainza, Juan, 81
Cruz, Juan de la, 186
Cuba: Basque Centers in, 195; Basque exiles and, 403; Basque mercantile activity in, 109–11; Bizkaian emigration to, 380, 381; Columbus's discovery of, 15; commercial activities and, 193–95; conquest of, 30; conquistadors and explorers in, 192–93; donations to Basque Country from, 160; Marxist revolutionaries and, 405; Navarrese emigration to, 375–76, 377; population growth in, 194; Royal Basque Society and, 120; Royal Company of Honduras and, 97; slave trade and, 194
Cunard, Samuel, 302
Cuzco, 39–40, 62, 66, 67, 71, 210–11, 212

dairy industry, in Argentina, 283, 284–85
Danube (ship), 396
Dávalos Espinosa, José, 114
David, José, 170
Dávila, Pedrarias, 37
Davile de Aguirre, Martín, 83
Deception of the Clerics and the Souls That Deal with Virtue, The (Antigua), 115
Deffontaines, Pierre, 232
De la Cosa, Juan, 11, 12, 15, 17, 26, 28, 29, 475n. 12
De la Cruz Pact, 257
Delfino Hermanos transport company, 391
Delgado de Nájera family, 184

Delgado de Nájera, Ventura, 184
Delgado de Nájera y de la Tovilla, José Tomás, 182
Department of Emigrations (Spain), 337
Description of Perú, Tucumán, Río de la Plata, and Chile (Lizarraga), 209
Deusto, 6, 8
Devern, José, 251
Devotion to the Holy Trinity (Oviedo), 115
Dia, El (newspaper), 260
Díaz, Acevedo, 256, 257
Díaz de Argandoña, Bernardo, 78
Díaz de Armendariz, López, 79
Díaz de Armendariz, Martín, 49
Díaz de Azpeitia, Juan, 34
Díaz de Melgarejo, Ruiz, 227
Díaz de Mena, Arriarán and Martínez, 6
Díaz de Solís, Juan, 28, 33
Díaz, Martín, 255
Díaz, Melchor, 162
Díaz Milano, Hugo, 411
Díaz Saravia, Manuel, 81
Díaz Sasiain family, in Colombia, 204
Diesel, Rudolf, 300
Díez de Armendaríz, Lope, 72
dioceses, established under Ferdinand II, 481 n. 39
Diústegui, Agustín de, 54
Dobarganes, Marcelo, 258
dockyards. *See* shipyards and shipbuilding
Dominicana Film Company, 403
Dominican Republic: Basque emigration and, 334; Basque exiles and, 400, 402, 403; Basque influence and presence in, 196
Dominicans, in San Vicente, 185–86
donations from America: art objects, 154–56; for charity, 156–57, 411–58; distribution by recipients, 157–59; distribution in Basque provinces, 160; for education and schools, 154, 158, 445–46; general benefits from, 152; for poor and orphaned girls, 157–58;

principle objectives of, 160–61; for religious buildings, 153–54, 441–43; for religious furnishings, 156, 449–53; for social welfare buildings, 154, 444; transfers of capital, 152–53; transport services in Spain, 153; for works of infrastructure and services, 447–48
Don Carlos. *See* Charles of Bourbon
Donostia, 8, 20; Company of Caracas and, 94, 95; privateering and, 53
Douglass, William A., 233, 350, 355, 406, 407, 411
Doyharçabal, Bernard, 321
draft evasion, 349–53
Dubrocq brothers, 84
Ducasse family, in Chile, 224
Dudam Siquidem (papal bull), 481 n. 38
Dugarana, Pelen, 83
Duhart family, in Chile, 223, 224
Durango, 22
Dutch armada, 485 n. 6

Ea, 54, 286
Echabarri, Juan de, 79
Echagoyen, Ignacio, 120
Echaide Orcazaguirre, Josefa, 348
Echalar (Navarre), 249
Echandía, Tomás de, 39
Echandi family, in Costa Rica, 191
Echarren, Juan de, 146
Echarren López, Martín, 345
Echarte, Eugenio, 251
Echavarry y Ugarte, Francisco Antonio González de, 73
Echebarnel, Juan Pedro, 321
Echeberry family, in Chile, 224
Echegaray-Barreneche family, in Colombia, 204
Echegaray Barreneche, José María, 204 n. 2
Echegaray, Pedro de, 112
Echegoyen, Salvador, 320
Echenique y Echenique, Pedro Gregorio de, 220

Echeto, Miguel de, 83
Echevarne, Antonio, 321
Echevarria, Domingo, 80
Echevarría, Francisco, 181
Echevarría, Juan de, 42
Echevarría, Martín de, 120
Echevarría, Santiago, 120
Echevarría y Uría, Juan de, 102
Echevarri, Joanes de, 83
Echevarri, Lorenzo de, 55
Echevarri, Marticot de, 83
Echeverria, Pedro, 373
Echeveste, Francisco de, 114
Echo, L' (newspaper), 244
Eco de España, El (newspaper), 372
Eco de Navarra, El (newspaper), 345, 371, 372, 373
Economic Association of Havana, 120
Economic Company of Friends of the Country of Guatemala, 187–88
Ecuador: Basque families in, 496n. 93; Basque presence in, 178; explorers and conquistadors in, 401
Edison, Thomas A., 301
education: Basque Government's pledge to support, 408; Catholic Church and, 66; Confraternity of Our Lady of Aránzazu of Mexico and, 171; donaions from America and, 154, 158, 445–46; Royal Basque Society and, 118–19, 154
Edwards, Alberto, 222
Egoaguirre, Juan de, 67
Egües, Diego de, 79
Eguía, Jerónimo de, 79
Eguia, José, 84
Eguiara y Eguren, Juan José de, 61, 114
Eguía, Sebastián de, 120
Eguino y López de Arregui, Juan, 121
Eguizabal, Bartolomé de, 103
Eguzki Basque-Venezuelan Cooperation Institute, 410
Eguzquiza, Miguel, 83
Eibar, 22

Eibar, Andrés de, 34
Eibar, López Fernández de, 193
Eibar, Pedro de, 193
EITB. *See* Euskal Irrati Telebista
Eizaguirre, Pedro de, 91
Elcano, Juan Sebastián, 479n. 19
Elcano y Balda, Pedro de, 101, 103
Elejalde, Domingo de, 35
El Euskaro, 177
Elexpuru y Larrínaga, Antonio de, 102
Elgueta, Hernando de, 34
Elhuyart, Fausto de, 108, 120
Elissetche family, in Chile, 224
Elizalde y Arretea, Antonio de, 121
Elola y Beobide, Ignacio de, 103
El Olonés, 52
Elormendi, José Joaquín, 317
Elorrio, 8, 22
Elorz, Jesús, 345
Elosu, Adrián, 81
El Salvador: Basque Centers in, 192; Basque family networks, 180; Basque influence, 192; indigo market and, 187; Marxist revolutionaries and, 405
Elzoizaga, Pilar, 205
Emasabel, Bartolomé de, 42, 69
Emergency Board for Basque Social Welfare (Venezuela), 403
Emigración vasco-navarra, La (Cola y Goiti), 322
emigration agencies: agreements and contracts by emigration agents, 314–22; Basque regulation of, 370–71; in Iparralde, 334; in Navarre, 308; structure and foundations of, 312–14
emigration agents, 362; agreements and contracts by, 314–22; American, 330–31; American immigration policies and, 334; Restituto Basterra and E. J. Carricarte, 322–30; criticisms of, 332–35, 371–73; influence of, 331; in Iparralde, 334
emigration policy: boarding licenses, 145–47; changing goals of the Crown

in, 123; of the Enlightenment era, 127–28; evasions of, 126; License of Passengers to America, 123–24; modifications of, 126; peoples prohibited by, 124; populationist theory and, 127; toward non-Spaniards, 124–25; toward women, 125. *See also* Basque emigration; colonial emigration; immigration laws and policies

Emparan, Manuel, 79
Enciso, Bartolomé de, 40
Enciso, Fernández de, 46, 70
Enciso, Martín de, 29
Enea, Ulpiano, 345
enfiteusis, 253
engachadores, 501 n. 12. *See also* emigration agents
England: Basque commerce with, 5; colonial fishing industry and, 86; iron imports, 4, 90; piracy and, 52; privateering and, 480 n. 26
Enkarterri, 388
Enkarterriak, 3
Enlightenment era/movement: Basque Country and, 117; obstructions to, 116–17; Royal Basque Society and, 117–22; Spanish emigration policy and, 127–28; underlying principles and beliefs, 116
Enríquez de Arana, Beatriz, 12
Entre Rios, 305
Epoque, L' (newspaper), 244
Eradication of the Idolatry of the Indians of Peru: Spiritual Exercises (Arriaga), 210
Eraso, Antonio, 80
Eraso, Antonio de, 68
Eraso, Francisco, 80
Eraso, Miguel de, 79
Erauso, Antonio de, 83
Erauso, Catalina de ("the Ensign Nun"), 219
Erauso, Miguel de, 83

Ercaizti Goizueta, Gabriel Francisco de, 110
Ercilla, Alonso de, 218
Ercilla y Zúñiga, Alonso de, 41
Eri (magazine), 403
Ermua, 22
Errazuriz, Carlos, 401
Errázuriz, Carmen, 221
Errea y Eugui, Juan Fermín, 121
Errecabord, Martín, 284
Errenderia, 6
Ersilbengoa y Orbezu, Francisco de, 102
Escalante, Juan Bautista de, 168
Escañuelas, Bartolomé de, 197, 199
Escarza, Juan de, 35
Escobar, Domingo de, 19
Escobedo, Rodrigo de, 12, 14
Espeleta-Sasiain family, in Colombia, 204
Espilla, Juan de, 83
Espinal, 355
Espinosa, Alfredo, 393
Espinosa, Juan, 34
Espinoza y Alegría, José, 352
Espira, Jorge de, 42
Espíritu Santo de Guadalajara, 36
Espíritu Santo (ship), 91
Esquer family, in Chile, 224
Esquivel, Diego de, 31
estancias, 227, 246, 255, 256, 260, 276, 277, 281, 283, 284; slavery and, 478 n. 16
estancieros, 252, 253, 273, 274, 276, 277–78, 286, 478 n. 16
Estella, 375, 384–85, 387
Estigarribia, Juan de, 44
Estomba, José, 258
Estomba, Ventura, 258
Etchegaray family, in Chile, 224
Etchegaray, Ramon, 258
Etcheverry family, in Chile, 224
Etcheverry, Juan, 251
Etcheverry, Louis, 249

Etcheverry, M., 238
Etchevers family, in Chile, 224
Etincelle, L' (ship), 498 n. 25
etxekojaun, 355
European migrations: agricultural revolution and, 294–95; attitude of ancien régime towards, 335; European population growth and, 296, 297, 298–99; historical overview of, 294–96; increase in life expectancy and, 297; industrial revolution and, 296–97; motivations for, 296–302; navigation companies and, 302–3; notions of individual liberty and, 335; Southern Cone immigration policies and, 304–12; Spanish immigration laws and policies, 335–44; transportation and communication advances and, 299–302
Europe, population growth in, 296, 297, 298–99
Euscalduna (newspaper), 361
"Euskadi" hospital, 396
Euskal Echea Association of Mutual Aid (Argentina), 292
Euskal Etxeak. *See* Basque Centers
Euskal Herria (newspaper), 290
Euskal-Herria (Uruguay), 254
Euskal Irrati Telebista (EITB), 408
Euskara: Basque Government's pledge to support, 407; William Douglass on, 406
Euskaria, La (newspaper), 290
Euskaro Center (Havana), 195
Euzkadi (newspaper), 402, 403
Euzkaldunak Denak Bat Association of Mutual Aid (Argentina), 292
Euzko-Deya (newspaper), 404
Euzko Etxea: of Chile, 223; of Santiago, 402; of Valparaiso, 402
exiles. *See* Basque exiles
Eximia Devotionis (papal bull), 481 n. 38
explorers. *See* conquistadors and explorers; navigators

Exponi Nobis (papal bull), 58
Extirpación de la idolatría del Perú (Pablo José de Arraiga), 66
Extremadura, 129, 132
Eyzaguirre Escutasolo, Domingo, 220
Ezcurra, José María de, 271
Ezpeleta, Juan de, 143
Ezquerra, Juan, 17, 30, 186
Ezquiaga, José Ignacio, 200
Ezquiaga, Sobrián, 199
Ezquieta Arce, Bruno, 376
Ezquieta, Idoate, 344

Fagoaga Arosqueta, Francisco, 114
Fagoaga, Francisco, 107–8, 114
Fagoaga, Juan José de, 169, 170
Fajardo, Francisco, 42
Famalbide, Martín de, 79
family networks: in Central America, 178–85; primary and secondary families, 181
Farga, Joanes de, 83
Farming Association of the Basses-Pyrénées, 238
Farming Chamber of Bayonne, 238
Farming Chamber of Oloron, 238
Farming Committee of Orthez, 242
farmsteads: inheritance systems and, 353–54, 357
Federación de Entidades Vasco Argentinas (FEVA), 292, 409
Federation of Basque-Argentine Entities, 292, 409
Federman, Nicolás de, 37
Felipe IV (king of Bizkaia), 208
female emigration, 125, 131, 135–36, 137; newspaper criticism of, 373
Ferdinand III, 9
Ferdinand II: American colonization and, 24–28; Basque administrators and, 67; Catholic dioceses and sees established in America, 481 n. 39; Columbus and, 10, 16, 19; conquest of Cuba and, 30;

emigration policy and, 125, 126; married colonists and, 489n. 3; Navarre and, 1; privateers and, 52–53
Ferdinand VI, 97
Fernández de la Torre, Pedro, 217
Fernández de Recalde, Juan, 211
Fernández de Retana, Ciro, 206
Fernández Orizco, Juan, 80
Fernandina island, 15
Fernando Aldayturriaga, J., 84
Ferrer, Melchor, 346
Ferrón, Juan Martín, 231
FEVA. *See* Federación de Entidades Vasco Argentinas
filibotes, 491n. 55
fine art, donations of objects from America, 154–56
fine arts, Catholic Church and, 65–67
Foix-Albret dynasty, 1
First Carlist War: Basque emigration and, 344, 346; immigration to Uruguay and, 232; José María de Iparraguirre and, 254
First Seminar on Basque Immigration, History, and Culture, 413, 499n. 32
fishing and whaling industries, 3, 82–86, 111
Flanders, 5
Flandre (ship), 402
fleets. *See* armadas; Indies fleet
Flores (Uruguay), 246
Florida, 33
foral system, 2–3, 141, 473–74n. 2
Fort, Martín José, 320
forua, 473–74n. 2
Foru Berria, 2, 21, 36
France: Basque Centers in, 410; Basque commerce with, 5; Basque draft evasion and, 350–51, 352–53; Basque exiles and, 392, 393, 394–97; Basque immigration to Uruguay, 230–40; Carlist Wars and, 346; colonial fishing industry and, 86; emigration from, 296; emigration to Brazil, 226; immigration laws, 335; imports from Río de la Plata, 274; influence on Uruguay, 243–44; mid-nineteenth-century population trends, 234, 236, 237, 240, 241, 243; Navarre and, 1–2; navigation companies, 302; Paraguay and, 218; phylloxera and, 299; piracy and, 51–52
Franciscans, 482–83n. 41, 483n. 42
Francisco de Foix (king of Navarre), 1
Francisco de Leceta, Juan, 81
Francisco de Uribe, José, 114
Franco de Miravalles, Esteban, 39
Franquelin, Guillermo, 55
Fratelli Lavarello transport company, 391
freebooters, 479–80n. 24
French Basques: emigration to Brazil, 226; emigration to California, 240; emigration to the United States, 241, 242; emigration to Uruguay, 230–34, 240, 243–45. *See also* Iparralde; Basses-Pyrénées
French Convention, War against the, 122
French Hospital (Argentina), 289
"French Legion" (Uruguay), 233
Freyssinet y Compañía transport company, 391
Frigorifique, Le (ship), 301
Fructuoso Rivera, José, 233
Fuensaldaña, Jacinto de, 168
Fuenterrabía, Juan de, 34
Fuenterrabía, Martín de, 476n. 17
Fuentes y Arguibel, Isabel, 271
Fuero of Bizkaia, 2, 21
Fuertes de Portu, Juan, 79

Gaarder, Lorin, 176, 177
Gais, Juan, 83
Galarza, Lorenzo, 31
Galbis, Ricardo, 195
Galdemes, Francisco, 40
Galdona, Pedro, 81
Galicia: emigration trends, 129, 132, 136
Galíndez, Jesús, 207, 403
Galindos River, 6

Gallega (ship), 19
galleons, 77, 491 n. 55
Galvez family, 188
Galvez, José de, 109
Gamarra, Domingo, 186
Gamarra, Francisco de, 71
Gamarra, Luis de, 42
Gamarra Urquizu, Pedro, 79
Gamarra y Arriaga, Pedro de, 80
Gamboa, Cristóbal Martín de, 34
Gamboa, Félix, 204 n. 2
Gamboa, Francisco de, 108
Gamboa, Francisco Javier de, 114, 169
Gamboa, Lope de, 80
Gamboa, Marino de, 394
Gamboa, Martín Ruíz de, 70
Gamboa, Pedro de, 41, 47
Gamboa, Pedro Sarmiento de, 210
Gamboa, Sarmiento de, 42
Gamboa y Arrupe, Eugenio de, 203, 403
Gaminiz, 54, 380
Gámiz, Pedro, 19
ganchos, 501 n. 12. See also emigration agents
Garaicoechea, Francisco Javier de, 120
Garalde, Marticot de, 83
Gárate, José de, 114
Garay family, in Costa Rica, 191
Garay, Francisco de, 17, 24, 30
Garay, Iñaki, 207
Garay, José Luis de, 403
Garay, Juan de, 45–46, 70, 270, 479 n. 17, 499 n. 42
Garay, Mariano de, 67
García Aguilar, Manuel, 245, 367
García Belsunce, César, 272, 273
Gracia Colas, Juan, 393
García de Arregui, Juan, 91
García Márquez, Gabriel, 207
García Oñaz, Martín, 70
Garciarena, José de, 319
Garciarena, Martín, 319–20
García San Mamés, Luis, 39
García Sarmiento, Cristóbal, 12

Garibay, Pedro de, 73
Garigorta (Basque doctor), 395
Garnica y Ortiz de Zárate, Bartolina de, 268
Garralda, 355
Garrastegui y Oleaga, Pedro de, 108
Garro, Domingo de, 112
Garro, José de, 70, 219, 268
Gasteiz, 8, 388
Gasteiz, Fernando de, 44
Gasteluzar, Joanes de, 83
Gastón, José María, 368
gastronomy, 408
Gauchegui, Domingo, 83
Gavira, Agustín de, 67
Gavira, Lorenzo de, 164
Gaytán, Luis, 46, 70
Gaytán, Pedro, 46
Gaztelu, Rafael, 345
General Armero (ship), 303
General Immigration Commission (Argentina), 276
Germany, emigration from, 295
"Gernika" hospital, 396
"Gernikako Arbola Cafe," 255
"Gernikako Arbola" (song), 254
Getaria, 3, 8
Gipuzkoa: arms industry, 22; *Basque and Navarrese Emigration* and, 369; Carlist Wars and emigration, 346, 348–49; Company of Caracas and, 94–95; donations from America and, 156, 159; eighteenth-century emigration, 139; emigration to Argentina, 266, 288, 290; emigration to Cuba, 195; emigration to Puerto Rico, 201; Enlightenment movement and, 117; *foral* system and, 2; iron industry and, 3, 21, 87–91; origins of emigrants, 437; political state prior to Columbus, 1; ports of departure for emigrants, 388; privateering and, 54, 416; public denunciations of emigration, 366–67, 369; shipbuilding industry, 6; Spanish Civil

War and, 392; typology of emigrants and emigrant destinations, 382, 384; whaling and cod fishing industries, 3, 82, 83–84, 85–86, 111
Giralt, J., 233
Giujonets, Julián, 251
Gizaburuaga, 250
Goicoa, Bernardo de, 110
Goicoechea, Felipe, 73
Goiri, Juan de, 48
gold: donations from America and, 155; prospectors in California, 240
Gómez-Basterra family, in Colombia, 204
Gomez de la Torre, Ventura, 85
Gómez de Rivero, Miguel, 268
Gómez, J. Antonio, 116
Gómez Lekube, Luis (Cojo Gómez), 206
Gómez Saiz, Paulino, 206
González Batres Arribillaga family, 182
González Batres, Diego, 493 n. 27
González Batres, Juan José, 182
González Batres Muñoz family, 182
González, Ceferino, 204
González de Ayala, Pedro, 39
González de Echávarri, Francisco Antonio, 69
González de Echavarry y Ugarte, Francisco Antonio, 73
González de Legarda, Antonio, 80
González de Mendoza, Pedro, 9, 42, 44
Gónzalez de Urquieta, Juan, 79
González Larrinaga, Bonifacio, 194
González Saravia family, 181
Good Soup Inn (Montevideo), 251
Gorbea y Vadillo, José de, 102
Goríbar, Nicolás de, 67
Gorliz, 380
Gorocica, Domingo de, 83
Gorosizo, Juan Bautista, 321
Gorostizaga, Manuel de, 221
Gorrichu family, in Colombia, 204
Gortari, Juan Bautista, 320
governmental officials and administrators, 67–73

Goxenola, Francisco, 268
Goya, José Ramón de, 120
Goyeneche family, in Peru, 214
Goyeneche, Francisco Javier de, 105
Goyeneche y Aguerrevere, Juan Crisóstomo de, 214
Granada, Luis de, 115
grape vines. *See* vineyards
Great Britain: attacks on the Indies fleet, 485 n. 6; Basque exiles and, 392, 394–95; emigration from, 294–95
Great Colombian Merchant Company, 203
Great Eastern Co., 302
Great Potato Famine, 294
Great War (Uruguay), 233
Grijalba, Juan de, 33
Guacanagarí, 15, 17
Guadalquivir, 74, 77
Guadalupe island, 19
Guanahaní island, 14
Guanajuato, 144
Guaraní Indians, 46, 216
Guaraní Paraguay. *See* Paraguay
Guarionex, 17
Guatemala: Basque administrators and officials, 72; Basque Centers in, 192; Basque family networks and power elites, 180–85; Catholic clergy in, 65; Economic Company of Friends of the Country of, 187–88; groups affecting eighteenth- and nineteenth-century economy, 190; indigo dye industry, 187; major family dynasties in, 188–90; missionaries in, 41, 482 nn. 40, 41; Royal Consulate of, 187
Guatemala Gazette, 188, 189
Guecho, Esteban de, 193
Guendica y Mendieta, Luis, 71
Guernica, Gaspar de, 34
Guernica, Pedro de, 36
Guernica, Santiago de, 48
Guerra, Cristóbal, 26
Guerra, Juan, 186

Guerra, Luis, 26
Guerrico, José Prudencio de, 320
Gerrikagoitia, Honorio, 205
Guetaria, Juan de, 33
Guevara, Diego de, 42
Guevara, Fernando de, 17
Guevara, Hernando de, 19, 27
Guevara, Juan de, 34
Guevara, Pedro de, 47
Guevara, Vasco de, 39
Guevara y Suescun, Nicolás Vélez de, 72
Guiard, Teófilo, 53
Guillétegui y Ubilla, Gabriel, 63
Guinea, Diego de, 34
Guipúzcoano, Rodrigo, 34
Guirior y Portal de Huarte, Manuel de, 121
Gure Echea, 292
Gurochaga, J., 320
Gutierrez Garibay, Juan, 79
Gutiérrez Gómez family, 181
Gutiérrez Nieto, Ricardo, 338
Guzmán, Alvaro de, 38
Guzmán, Fernando de, 50
Guzmán, Nuño de, 36
Gypsies, 124

Haiti, 11, 16
Hamburg Amerika Linie, 302
Hamburgo S. Americana transport company, 391
handball, 407; in Argentina, 272; in Caracas, 207; in Havana, 195
Haritza (newspaper), 290
Hasparren, Harriague d', 293
Havana, 109–10, 189
Haya, Luis de, 48
health care, Basque Government's pledge to support, 408
helix-screw propellers, 300
Henares de Lezama, Diego de, 42, 69
Henares, Diego de, 42
Henry IV (king of Castile), 480n. 27

Henry VIII (king of England), 480n. 26
Heraldo de Navarra, El (newspaper), 345
Heredia, Alonso de, 37
Heredia, Pedro de, 37, 71
Hermenegildo Querejazu, Antonio, 71
Hermitage of Los Remedios (Sesma, Navarre), 156
Hernaiz y Chávarri, Manuel, 199
Hernández de Galarza, Pedro, 479n. 16
Herran, Fermín, 256
Herran, Mario, 62
Herrera y Reissig, Julio, 256
hide-exporting, Uruguay and, 293
Hierro island, 13
Hiribarren family, in Chile, 224
Hispaniola, 18–19, 29; Bizkaian colony on, 24; Catholic missionaries, 482–83n. 41; Columbus's discovery of, 15; non-Spaniards on, 125
Historia del descubrimiento y conquista del Perú (Zárate), 66
Historia eclesiástica indiana (Mendieta), 65, 66
History of the Conquest and Discovery of Peru (Zárate), 210
Hoa, José Pérez de, 83
Holandesa transport company, 391
Hondarribia, 3, 54
Honduras, 94, 180, 192
Honorary Commission of Immigration and Agriculture (Uruguay), 308
hospitals: in Argentina, 289, 291; Catholic missionaries and, 482n. 40; in France for Basque exiles, 395–96; in Uruguay, 265
Hotel for Immigrants (Buenos Aires), 276
Hotel for Immigrants (Uruguay), 261
Hotel Zuriñe (Venezuela), 207, 402
House of Trade, 8, 25; Basque commercial licenses and, 139; Basques in, 78–79, 80–81; boarding licenses and, 145; emigration policy and, 123–24, 126;

Indies economic monopoly and, 75–76, 77; move to Cádiz, 77, 80, 93–94
Hualde, Domingo, 231
Hualde, Juan, 231
Huancavelica mines, 104
Huarte, Gonzalo de, 49
Huelva, 75
Huici, Victoriano de, 159
Hulle & Brothers and Co., 306
Hummel, Kay, 206
Hundred Years' War, 1, 5
Hutton, Felipe de, 42

Ibacaya family, in Costa Rica, 191
Ibaceta, Jacques de, 83
Ibaceta, Pascual de, 41
Ibaibarriaga, Juan de, 42
Ibañez de Hernani, Juan, 193
Ibañez de la Rentería, Antonio, 62
Ibañez de Mendoza, Mateo, 79
Ibañez, Pedro, 80
Ibarburu, Lorenzo, 81
Ibarburu, Martín de, 168
Ibarburu y Galdona, Andrés, 81
Ibarburu y Galdona, Lorenzo Ignacio, 80
Ibargüen family, in Colombia, 204
Ibargüen, José, 204 n. 1
Ibarra, Bernardo de, 18, 24
Ibarra, Carlos de, 79
Ibarra de Ibañez, Juan, 17
Ibarra, Diego de, 79, 163, 164
Ibarra, Domingo de, 45
Ibarra, Esteban de, 68
Ibarra, Francisco de, 36, 67, 163, 164
Ibarra, Ignacio de, 113
Ibarra, José de, 67
Ibarra, Juan de, 42
Ibarra, Martín de, 47, 91
Ibarra, Miguel de, 36, 40, 162, 163
Ibarrarán, J. M., 174
Ibarrola, Martín de, 41
Ibarrola, Rodrigo de, 46, 70
Ibarrola, Tomás Ramón de, 116
Icaza, Antonio de, 170

"Identity Portfolios," 343
Idiaquez, Alonso de, 54
Idiaquez, Juan de, 68
Idiaquez, Lope de, 39
Idiarte Borda, Juan, 257
Igartua, Francisco, 411
Igarza, Juan, 83
Ignacio de Loyola, Martín, 62
Ignacio Orueta, Francisco, 85
Ignacio Urriza, Juan, 110
Ilincheta, José, 120
Illapel, 221
Illareta, Francisco de, 83
Immigration Advisory Commission (Uruguay), 266
immigration boards (Spain), 342
Immigration Commission (Argentina), 273, 306
immigration laws and policies: Argentina, 306–7, 397–400; Brazil, 334; Chile, 309–12, 334, 501 n. 6; emigration agents and, 334; Spain, 336–44, 303; Uruguay, 307–9, 313–14
Inca Empire. *See* Peru
Inchaurraga, Martín de, 33
Inchaurregui, José Santos de, 271
Inchauspe, Andrés, 284
Inchauspe, Pedro, 284
income growth, Basque emigration and, 404–5
Indian hospitals, 482 n. 40
Indians. *See* indigenous Americans, Catholic missionaries and
Indies fleet, 76–77, 485 n. 6, 486 n. 9, 491 n. 55
Indies monopoly, 74–77
"Indies run," 78–81, 486 n. 9
indigenous Americans, Catholic missionaries and, 60–67, 481–83 nn. 40, 41, 483 n. 46, 483–84 nn. 47, 50
indigo dye industry, 187
industrial revolution: in the Basque Country, 4, 346, 348, 355–56; European migrations and, 296–97

Inés, Machín, 30
inheritance systems: Basque emigration and, 141, 353–57; Basque farmsteads and, 353–57
Iñigo de Eraso, Juan, 67
Iñiguez, Juan, 81
Inorai, Marticot de, 83
Inquisition, 58
Inter Coetera I (papal bull), 481 n. 38
Inter Coetera II (papal bull), 481 n. 38
International Association of Basque Sports, 407
International League of the Friends of the Basques, 392
Inza, Jerónimo de, 72
Iparraguire, Martín de, 83
Iparraguirre, José María de, 254–56
Iparraguirre, Martín Barrundia, 190
Iparralde: agricultural exports to Argentina, 292–93; Basque military service and draft evasion, 352–53; colonial fishing industry and, 82, 83, 85; commerce with the New World and, 20; emigrants in Uruguay, 252; emigration agencies and agents in, 334; emigration to Canada, 240; emigration to Chile, 224–25; emigration to Mexico, 176; emigration to the United States, 240; emigration trends, 241, 242, 243; nineteenth-century economic decline, 303–4; opposition to emigration, 498 n. 25; public denunciations of emigration, 504 n. 19; rural depopulation, 238; smuggling and, 304. *See also* Basses-Pyrénées
Ipiñarrieta, Cristóbal de, 68
Irache, 387
Irala, Antón de, 404
Irala, Domingo Martínez de, 44
Irasa, Miguel de, 83
Iraurgui, Juan de, 85
Irauzqui, Juan de, 91
Irazabal, Tristán de, 45, 216
Irazusta Munoa, Juan Antonio, 206

Ircio, Martín de, 34
Ircio, Pedro de, 34, 35
Ireland, 294
Iriarte Ansaño, Juan, 285
Iriarte, Braulio, 177
Iriarte, Esteban de, 83
Iriarte, Oscar, 258
Iribarren, Miguel, 80
Irigoyen family, in Guatemala, 184
Irigoyen, Joanes de, 83
Irisarri family, in Guatemala, 180
Irisarri, Juan Bautista de, 184
Irisarri, Martín de, 189
Irisarri, Santiago de, 95
Irisarri y Larrain family, 181
Irisarri y Larrain, Juan Bautista de, 189
Iriziar, Esteban de, 43
iron companies, 86–92, 428–30
iron industry, 486 n. 23; American markets and, 87–91; exports, 87–90, 91, 421–27; impact of foreign and domestic competition on, 89–90; impact of New World on, 21–22; iron companies and commerce, 89–91, 428–30; overview of, 3–4
Irrintzi (newspaper), 290
Irujo, Eusebio María de, 403
Iruña, Lorenzo de, 33
Irungaray Matheu family, 181
Irurac Bat, 120, 488 n. 42
Isabela island, 15
Isabella I (queen of Castile): American colonization and, 24–25; Basque iron industry and, 4; Basque shipbuilding industry and, 22; Columbus and, 10, 18; Juan de la Cosa and, 475 n. 12; death of, 20; Navarre and, 1
Isarraga, Juan de, 79
Isasaga, Francisco de, 39
Isasi, Alberto de, 78
Isasi, Antonio de, 79
Isasi, Francisco de, 175
Isasi, José, 184
Isasi, Juan de, 91

Isidro, Carlos María, 254
Isleña Marítima (ship), 303
Italy, 238, 295, 341
Iturain, Miguel de, 83
Iturbide, Pedro de, 268
Iturriaga, Juan de, 49
Iturrigaray, José de, 73
Iturri Gaztelu, Domingo de, 79
Izarra, Ambrosio, 479 n. 16
Izarra, Pedro de, 46, 70
Izcue, Juan Francisco, 215

Jalisco, 36
Jamaica, 19, 30, 476–77 n. 18
Jáuregui, Andrés, 120
Jaúregui, Pedro de, 31
Jáuregui y Aldecoa, Agustín de, 121, 220
Jáuregui y Urrutia, José Antonio Fernández de, 73
Javier Izturiz, Cristóbal, 81
Jerónimo Feijóo, Benito, 117
Jesuits. *See* Society of Jesus
Jews, Spanish emigration policy and, 124
Jiménez Bretón, Manuel, 62
Jiménez de Bertendona, Ortún, 40
Jimenez, Ortuño, 35
Jironza Petriz de Cruzat, Domingo, 168
Joaquín de Arrillaga, José, 73
John II (king of Castile), 480 n. 27
José Olazabal, Francisco, 81
Juana Inés de la Cruz, Sor, 61
Juana island, 15
Juanchuteau family, in Chile, 224
Juarez, Benito, 116
Juarros, Manuel J., 184
Julius II (pope), 58

Kadagua River, 6
kalekuak, 355
Katarain, José Vicente, 207
Knight of Santiago, 54

Labezares, Guido de, 47
Labordian family, in Chile, 224

labor, in Uruguay, 256, 262–63
Labourd, 1, 481 n. 32
Lacasse family, in Chile, 224
La Coruña, 20
La Ermita (ship), 221
Laffont (Lafone), Samuel, 308, 316, 317
Lafone, Samuel. *See* Laffont, Samuel
Lakotsa, Juan, 475 n. 12
Lalanne family, in Chile, 224
Lamport Holt transport company, 391
Landaburu, Francisco Javier de, 392
Landa, Gabriel de, 61
Landa, Lope de, 41
Landazuri y Bolivar, Estanislao de, 102
Landeta y Urtuzuastegui, Francisco José de, 108
land inheritance, 141, 353–54, 357
Lapagesse (emigration agent), 335
La Paz, 45
lapikoko, 20
Lardizabal, Domingo Ignacio de, 106
Lardizabal, Juan Antonio, 140
Laredo, 20
Largacha, Diego de, 72
Lariz, Jacinto de, 70
La Roserie, 395
Larrabaster Calzada, Eulogio, 352
Larrabaster y Esquiaga, Juan Luis, 352
Larraegui, Martín de, 83
Larraín Cerda, Juan Francisco, 221
Larraín Vicuña, Santiago, 220
Larralda, María, 285
Larralde, Joanes de, 83
Larralde, Juan, 85
Larrañaga, Juan de, 40
Larrañaga, R., 477 n. 22
Larraspuru, Tomás de, 79
Larrauri, Pedro, 85
Larrauri family, in Colombia, 204
Larrave family, 182
Larrave, Manuel, 184
Larrazabal, Simón de, 190
Larrea family, in Ecuador, 496 n. 94
Larrea, Juan de, 68, 79

Larrea y Amez, Domingo de, 121
Larregui, Sabat de, 83
Larrinaga, Jacinto, 194
Larronde family, in Chile, 224
Lartaun, Sebastián de, 62, 210–11
Larumbe, Ramón, 80
Lasa e Irala, Sebastián de, 110
Lasala, Sabat de, 83
Lascamburu, Juan, 63.
Las Casas, Bartolomé de, 61, 64, 193, 482n. 40, 483–84n. 47
La Serena, 41
Lasserre family, in Chile, 224
Lastarria Dendagorta, Miguel de, 72
Lau-Buru (newspaper), 372
Laurac Bat, 488n. 42
Laurak Bat of Buenos Aires, 256, 289–90, 291, 292
Laurak Bat association (Montevideo), 249
Laurak Bat Association of Mutual Aid (Argentina), 292
Laurak Bat (newspaper), 249
Lavalle y Cortés, José Antonio de, 104
La Veloce transport company, 391
Law of Immigration and Colonization (Argentina), 307
Law of Reformed Emigration (Spain), 339–40
Laws of Burgos, 64
Laws of Emigration (Spain), 336–41
Lazcano, Juan de, 47
Lazcano, Rodrigo de, 31, 38
Lazoaga, Juan Francisco de, 189
Leaequi, Juan de, 98
League of Friends of the Basques (France), 392, 395
Leandro de Viana, Francisco, 69
Lebesarri, Guido de, 479n. 19
Lebrón, Jerónimo, 37
Leclairc, Pedro, 251
Lecuanda y Ezcarraga, José I. de, 102
Ledesma, Pedro de, 18, 29, 63, 476n. 17
Ledesma, Tomé de, 42
Ledesma y Valderrama, Martín, 268

Legarra, Rodrigo, 83
Legaso, Bartolomé de, 68
Legazpia, 3
Legorburu, Antonio de, 80
Leguía, Gregorio de, 80
Leguizamón, Diego de, 42, 69
Leguizamón, Pedro de, 39
Leguizamón, Tristán de, 6
Leiza, 344, 380
Leizaola, Jesús María de, 402
Lekeitio, 3, 5, 8, 54, 380
Lekube, Luis Gómez (Cojo Gómez), 206
Lemus y Aguirre, Juan de, 38
Leopoldina Rosa (ship), 361
Leo X (pope), 58
Leoz y Ripa, Miguel, 85
Lepe, Diego de, 26
Lequeitio, Domingo de, 12
Lequeitio, Juan de, 12
Lerdo de Tejada, Sebastián, 346
Lesser Antilles, 17
Lete, Esteban, 83
Letona, Fernández de, 167
Letona, Juan Fernández de, 167
"letters of retaliation," 480–81n. 30
Levant, emigration trends, 130
Lezama, Hernando de, 34, 35
Lezcano, Juan de, 34
Lhande, Pierre de, 83, 237, 249, 316, 353–54
Lianiz, Manuel, 258
LIAV. *See* Liga Internacional de Amigos de los Vascos
Liberal Navarro, El (newspaper), 372
Licendo y Goicoechea, José de, 190
License of Passengers to America, 123–24
Liendo y Goicoechea, Antonio de, 192
Liendo y Goicoechea family, in Costa Rica, 191
Liga Internacional de Amigos de los Vascos (LIAV), 392
Ligonzat family, in Chile, 224
Ligorio, San Alfonso María de, 115
Lima, 140, 209

limpieza de sangre, 124, 145, 146
Lindolfo Cuestas, Juan, 257
Lisbon, 91
livestock. *See* cattle raising; sheep herders and sheep raising
Lizana, Juan de, 34
Lizardi, Juan de, 63
Lizardi, Ortiz, 400
Lizarraga, Domingo de, 81
Lizarraga, Reginaldo de, 209
Lizarza, Joanes de, 83
Lizarzu, Luis de, 17
Lizaso, Juan, 394
Lizaur, Sancho de, 42
Lizundia, Domingo de, 120
Lizundia y Odria de Echeverría, Domingo de, 109
Llano, Manuel de, 188
Llano Villa Urrutia family, 182
Lloyd Norte Alemán transport company, 391
Loca, Juana la, 480n. 27
Loco, Juan, 83
Lombrana y Foncea, José L., 204
Long Island, 15
Lope de Isasi, Martín, 91
López Cantos, Ángel, 196
López de Arburu, Juan, 72
López de Arcaya, Andrés, 112
López de Arrechulueta, Juan, 42
López de Artunduaga, Dionisio, 79
López de Galazar, Andrés, 38
López de Larburu, Juan, 72
López de Legazpi, Miguel, 47
López de Loys, Leonor, 164
López de Recalde, Juan, 39
López de Ugarte, Juan, 216
López de Zubizarreta, Juan, 79
López Eceiza, Lorenzo, 80
López Izarra, Domingo, 83
López, Joseph, 190
López, Martín, 34, 35, 42
López y López, Antonio, 303
López Zárate, Juan Antonio, 68

Loreilhe (French emigration agent), 314–15
Losada, Juan de, 42
Louis XI (king of France), 1
Louis XIV (king of France), 52
Loyola, Iñigo de, 67
Lugo, Luis de, 37
Luque, Hernando de, 38
Luro, Pedro, 280–82
Luyando, Ulloa de, 80
Luzon Island, 48

Macax, Diego, 29
Machicote, Martín J., 199
Machín, Martín, 476n. 17
Machintoa, Miguel, 320
Maestro, Matías, 66
Magdalena, 29
Magdalena of Navarre, 1–2
Magellan, Ferdinand, 28, 31–33; Basque crew of, 415
Magellan, Strait of, 32
Maguiren, Antonio, 258
Mainguyague family, in Chile, 224
Maisí, Cape, 15
Malamud, Carlos D., 214
Mala Real Inglesa transport company, 391
Maldonado de Armendáriz, Francisco, 42
Mallea, Diego de, 112
Mamus y Dodero transport company, 391
Mange, Juan Mateo, 168
Manila, 48
Manuel Goicoa, José, 71, 79
Manurga y Vera, José de, 79–80
Manzana, 6
Mapil, 6
Mapuche Indians, 40
Marañones, 50
Marconi, Guglielmo, 300
Marcos y Mavas, Francisco, 115
Mariñelarena, Faustino, 360–61

Marítima Unión, 303
maritime industries: colonial enterprises and, 7; commerce with the New World, 20. See also navigation companies; shipping; shipyards and shipbuilding
Marmier, Xavier, 243
Marqués, Ochoa, 46, 70
Márquez de Castañiza, Juan, 61
Marquina, Gaspar de, 39
Marquina, Juanes de, 35
Marquina, Martín de, 39
Marriage Contracts in Navarra and Their Influence in Family Stability (Yaben Yaben), 393
marriages: Basque immigrants and, 252; oral vows and, 157; in Uruguay, 250, 251, 252
Marroquín, Francisco, 65
Martel de Ayala, Gonzalo, 42
Martiartu, Salvador, 194
Marticorena, Juan Bautista, 184, 190
Martínez Alsasua, Francisco, 345
Martínez de Açogue, Juan, 13
Martínez de Aroa, Juan, 35
Martínez de Arraona, Juan, 112
Martínez de Careaga, Juan, 83
Martínez de Irala, Domingo, 44, 70, 215–16, 270
Martínez de Loyola, Juan, 91
Martínez de Ormaechea, Juan, 61
Martínez de Ospina, Francisco, 38
Martínez de Pinillos, Miguel, 303
Martínez de Salazar, A., 485 n. 59
Martínez de Zárate, Francisco, 39
Martínez, Juan, 48, 251
Martínez, Pedro, 143
Martín, Francisco, 12, 34
Martín, Ramos, 34
Marxist revolutionaries, 405
Master Jerusalem, 115
Matías de Elizalde, Antonio, 104
Matías de Elizalde, José, 104
Matienzo, Juan de, 45–46
Matienzo, Sancho de, 31

Matinimó island, 16
Mauricio de Zabala, Bruno, 70
Mayans, Gregorio, 117
mayorazgo system, 9, 67, 141
Mayorga, Martín de, 188
Mayrení, 17
Meabe, Ambrosio de, 114, 120, 167
Mecoalde, Miguel, 56
Medina del Campo, 5
Mediterranean: Basque commerce in, 5; emigration from, 294, 295
Medrano, Galaz de, 44
Mejia Eguiluz, Juan, 196
Melchor de Jovellanos, Gaspar, 117
Mella y Barriola, Francisco Antonio de la, 103
Mena, Francisco, 103
Mendaro, Domingo de, 83
Méndez, José, 258
Mendi, Basco de, 83
Mendiburu y Arzac, Juan Miguel de, 104
Mendieta, Jerónimo de, 65, 66
Mendinueta, Francisco de, 97, 107
Mendiola, Francisco de, 61
Mendiola y Múgica, Francisco Isaac de, 110
Mendívil, Andrés de, 73
Mendoza, Alonso de, 39, 45
Mendoza, Alvaro de, 71
Mendoza, Cristóbal de, 63
Mendoza, Francisco de, 217
Mendoza, González de, 216
Mendoza, Hernando de, 46, 70
Mendoza, Jerónimo de, 163
Mendoza, Pedro de, 215
Mendoza y Ribera, Luis de, 112, 213
Mengolea, Juan de, 79
Meogui, Modesto, 320
Mercado y Villacorta (governor of Tucumán), 268
Mercantile Gazette (newspaper), 215
mercantilism: Bourbon reforms, 92–94; Charles III's liberalization of, 96, 98–

99; major companies in the Americas, 94–98
merino sheep, 305
Meriotegui, José Antonio, 344
Messager de Montevideo, Le (newspaper), 244
Messager Français, Le (newspaper), 244
Messageries Marítimes, 302
Messageries Maritimes, 391
Mexico: Araban emigration to, 373, 374; Basque administrators and officials in, 72–73; Basque associations in, 113–16; Basque Centers in, 176, 177, 179, 404, 410; Basque emigration to, 166–67, 377, 380, 405; Basque exiles and, 396, 404; Basque influence in, 175; Basque mercantile activities, 107–9; Bizkaian emigration to, 380; Catholic clergy in, 61; Catholic missionaries, 518n. 41; Charles of Bourbon and, 364–65; College of the Vizcayans, 174–75; Confraternity of Our Lady of Aránzazu of Mexico, 173–74; conquistadors and explorers in, 34–37, 165, 514n. 8; donations to Basque Country from, 163; early expeditions to, 33–34; foundation of Nueva Vizcaya, 162–67; immigration trends, 146–47, 168–70, 177–78; local Basque fraternal groups, 178–80; mining in, 110, 167–70; missionaries in, 529n. 32; Navarrese emigration to, 398; northern expeditions, 36–37; Royal Basque Society and, 122, 175–76; significance of Mexico City to, 172; Sonora, 170–71; Spanish Civil War and, 179; Treaty of Guadalupe Hidalgo, 297. *See also* Nueva España; Nueva Vizcaya
Mexico City: Basque associations in, 115–18; Basque emigration and, 146–47; census of 1689, 134–35; College of the Vizcayans, 174–75; immigration trends, 134–35, 136, 142, 169; influence of Basques in, 170; local Basque fraternal groups, 179; Royal Basque Society and, 122, 175; Royal Board of the Consulate of, 172–73; significance to Nueva España, 172
Micheo Berrenechea family, 181, 182
Micheo family, in Guatemala, 185
Micheo, Pedro José, 185
migratory chains, 354–55
migratory legislation. *See* immigration laws and policies
migratory surplus, 498n. 19
Miguel, Alvarez de las Asturias, 184
Miguel, Rodrigo, 142
Miner, Marcial, 215
mining: in Basque economy, 3–4; in Bolivia, 210; Huancavelica mines, 106; in Mexico, 110, 166, 170–71; in Nueva España, 36; in Peru, 106; in Sonora, 170–71
Minondo, Juan Martín, 142
Miranda, Martín de, 83
Miranda, Pedro de, 41
Mirandaola, Andrés de, 47
Mirror of Youth (Oviedo), 115
missionaries, 529n. 32; activities in the Americas, 60–64, 518nn. 40, 41, 519n. 46, 520nn. 47, 50; foreigners accompanying, 519n. 42; Navarrese, 407–9; in province of San Vicente, 187–88
Mogrovejo, Toribio de, 62
Moguer, 11
Moniteur, Le (newspaper), 244
Monjaraz, Andrés de, 35
Monjaraz, Gregorio de, 34
Montano, Juan de, 34, 35
Montauser, Bartolomé de, 83
Monterrón (Count), 364–65
Montesinos, Antonio de, 63
Montet, Edouard, 244
Montevideo: Araban emigration to, 395; Basque commercial activities in, 247, 248, 249, 253–54; Basque draft evaders in, 371; Basque emigration to, 234,

247, 395, 400; Basque exiles and, 422; Basque meeting places, 252–53; Basque presence in, 231, 235–36; Basque society in, 250–54; Basque weddings in, 252, 253; Bizkaian emigration to, 400; Charles of Bourbon in, 365–66; Church of the Basques, 535n. 25; Don Carlos and, 247; early-nineteenth-century immigration, 232–33; First Seminar on Basque Immigration, History, and Culture, 434, 535n. 32; founding of, 230, 245; French influence in, 245–46; Great War and, 235; industrial growth in, 263; labor problems, 258; living conditions of immigrants, 265–66; neighborhood for immigrants, 326; population growth in, 326; urban immigration and, 262; working conditions of immigrants, 264–65
Montevideo Cold-Storage Plant, 263
Montezuma, 478n. 8
Mont, Miguel, 190
Montoa y Allende Salazar, Francisco, 156
Montoya, Diego de, 62
Montoya, Pedro de, 186
Montoya, Salvador de, 41
Moors, 124
Morelia, "children of," 404
Moreno, Mariano, 305, 306
More, Thomas, 482n. 40
Morgan, Henry, 52
Morga, Pedro de, 81
Mörner, Magnus, 128
Motrico, Alonso de, 34
Motrico, Diego de, 34
Motrico, Rodrigo de, 31
Motriko, 3
Moya, Pedro, 476n. 17
Mucaras island, 15
Múgica, Ventura de, 70
Múgica y Guevara, Bernardino de, 73
muleteers, 153, 159

Muncharaz, Miguel de, 17
Munguía, Pedro de, 49
Munibe, Andrés, 78
Munibe, Javier María de, 117
Munibe, Juan de, 91
Munibe, Lope de, 112
Munibe, Miguel de, 112
Muñoz, Francisco Joaquín, 316
Murga, Diego de, 94
Murguía, Manuel de, 78
Murguía y Ortíz de Guinea, Pedro Martínez de, 73
Muru, Fernando, 413
Muskiz, 54
Mutiloa, 3
Mutiloa y Anduenza, Juan José de, 70
Múxica, Adrián, 19
Múxica, Alonso de, 79
Muxica, Martín de, 219
Mystical City of God (Agreda), 115

NABO. *See* North American Basque Organization
Nadal, Jordi, 166
Nájera y Mendoza, María, 188
Narváez, Pánfilo de, 193, 478n. 8
Nationalist (Blanco) party (Uruguay), 257
National Joint Committee for Spanish Relief (Great Britain), 392
National Liberation Movement (Uruguay), 267
Native Americans. *See* indigenous Americans, Catholic missionaries and
Navarre: *Basque and Navarrese Emigration* (Goiti), 369; emigration agents and companies in, 338–39; France and, 1–2; incorporation in Castile, 1, 2; missionaries in America, 407–9; public denunciations of emigration, 389–90; signatories of the foundational statutes, 471. *See also* Navarrese emigration
Navarrese Center of Chile, 224

Navarrese emigration: Carlist Wars and, 362–64; clergy and missionaries, 407–9; draft evasion and, 368; eighteenth-century trends, 139, 140–42; late-nineteenth-century trends, 250; to Mexico, 169, 177–78; migratory chains, 375, 376; motives for, 142–47; newspaper campaigns against, 392–94; origins of emigrants, 396–97, 401–2; public denunciations of, 389–90; seventeenth-century trends, 134, 135–36; sixteenth-century trends, 131, 132–33; typology of destinations, 397–99; typology of emigrants, 399–400
Navarro, Antonio, 38, 39, 40
Navarro, Lope, 33
Navarro, Máximo, 365
Navarro, Miguel, 46, 70
Navarro, Pedro, 39, 40
Navidad, fort of, 11, 15, 17
Naviera Vascongada, 303
navigation companies, 320–21; to Argentina, 411; emigration agents and, 341–48; operating in Gasteiz, 410
navigators, 28–34; voyages of circumnavigation, 31–33, 435–36, 515n. 19. *See also* Columbian expeditions; conquistadors and explorers
Navigazione Italiana transport company, 391
Negrete, Pedro, 114
Neruda, Pablo, 401
Nervión River, 6, 84
Netherlands, piracy and, 51–52, 56–57, 485n. 6
New Castile, 129
New Laws, 64
New Mexico, 48, 162, 165
newspapers: in Argentina, 292; of Basque exiles, 423, 424, 425; campaigns against emigration, 392–94; Carlist, 366; in Uruguay, 245, 251

New World explorations: Basques in, 24, 26–28; early navigators, explorers, and conquistadors, 28–51; following Columbus, 24–27. *See also* Columbian expeditions
New York, 302, 314, 347, 404
Nicaragua: Basque family networks, 183; Basque influence, 194; Catholic missionaries, 518n. 41; Marxist revolutionaries and, 426
Nicuesa, Diego de, 28, 29
Nieremberg, Eusebio de, 115
Niña (ship), 12, 13, 16
Niño, Francisco, 12
Niño, Juan, 12
Niño, Peralonso, 12
Noblesa, Ignacio de, 57
Nogués Inn and Cafe (Montevideo), 251
Nombela, Julio, 344, 373
Nombre de Dios, 163
Norddeutscher Lloyd company, 320–21, 410; emigration agents and, 341–48
North American Basque Organization (NABO), 409
Northern Squadron (Spain), 481n. 32
Novales, Isabel de, 159
Nueva Bilbao, 221
Nueva Castilla, 39
Nueva España: Apache Territory, 296–97; Araban immigration, 521n. 59; Basque emigration to, 144, 146–47; Basque mercantile activities, 109–10; Catholic clergy in, 62; College of the Vizcayans, 174–75; conquistadors, 34–37; immigration trends, 139, 142; northern expeditions, 36–37; Royal Basque Society and, 122–23, 175–76, 474; significance of Mexico City, 172. *See also* Mexico
Nueva Galicia, 162
Nueva Granada, 37, 94, 138
Nueva Toledo, 39, 40–41

Nueva Vizcaya: foundation of, 162–67; Sonora, 167–70
Nuñez de Balboa, Vasco, 27, 31

Ocean Armada, 77
Ochandiano, Domingo de, 31, 78
Ochandiano, Martín de, 42
Ochandorena, Martín de, 189
Ocharan y Mollinedo, Francisco de, 104
Ochoa Arriola, Pedro, 83
Ochoa de Eizaguirre, Jerónimo, 44
Ochoa de Irazabal, Martín, 83
Ochoa de Lexalde, Juan de, 34, 35
Ochoa de Salcedo, Lope, 33, 193
Ochoa, Gonzalo de, 34
Ochoa Iurretauría, Juan, 81
Ochoa, Juan de, 30, 34, 83, 186
Ochoa, Pedro de, 35, 91
Office of Immigration (Uruguay), 308
Office of Work (Argentina), 307
Oficialdegui, Marta, 250
O'Higgins, Ambrosio, 71
Ojeda, Alonso de, 26, 27, 28, 29, 482 n. 41
Olabarrieta, Diego de, 70, 217
Olabarrio, Manuel de, 271
Olabeaga, 84
Olaberriaga, Adame de, 44, 216
Olano, Lope de, 17, 18, 28, 29
Olano, Sebastián, 17
Olariaga Echaide, Francisco, 348, 349
Olariaga, Francisco de, 348
Olarte, Carlos, 80
Olarte, Diego de, 34, 112
Olarte, Pedro, 80
Olavarriaga, Pedro de, 94, 95
Olavarrieta, Diego de, 45, 46
Olavide, Pablo de, 117
Olavide y Jaúregui, Pablo Antonio de, 71
Olaya, Alonso de, 38
Old Castile, 129
Olea, Antonio de, 41
Olite, 384, 385, 387
Oller, Francisco de, 348

Oloron, Loumiet d', 194
Oloron, Supervielle d', 293
Oña, Martín de, 78
Oñate, Cristóbal de, 36, 162, 165
Oñate, Juan de, 17, 30, 36, 48, 162, 165
Oñate, Martín de, 193
Oñate Mendizabal, Bernabé de, 69
Oñati, 8, 22
Ondarroa, 3, 54, 380
Oñederra y Alvizu, Santiago de, 221
Oquendo, Antonio de, 79
Orbea, Martín de, 79
Orbegozo y Lequerica, Pedro Ventura de, 104
Orbit (ship), 401
Ordaz, Diego de, 34
Order of Betharram, 498 n. 25
Order of Saint Augustine, 482 n. 41
Order of Santiago, 8
Ordoñez de Loyola, Martín, 70
Ordoñez, Rodrigo, 40
Ordozgoiti, Juan Domingo de, 104
Ordozgoiti, Martín de, 142
Orduña, Alberto de, 39
Orduña, Alonso de, 34
Orduña Barriaga, Francisco de, 72
Orduña, Juan de, 35
Orduña (ship), 401
Oria, 6
Oria, Mateo de, 269
Oriar, Juan de, 79
Oribe, Domingo de, 41
Oribe, Manuel, 233
Orinoco River, 18
Oriondo, Martín, 79
Ormaechea, Pedro de, 112
Oronzúa, Martín de, 71
Oropesa (ship), 401
Ororbiogoitia y Aguirre, Juan de, 103
Orozco, Alberto de, 47
Orozco family, in Colombia, 204
Orozco, Francisco de, 34, 35
Orozco, Jerónimo de, 36

Orozco, Lope de, 72
Orozco Melgar, Juan de, 34
orphans, donations from America for, 157
Orquina, Juan de, 19
Orta, Domingo de la, 40
Ortiz Basualdo, Carmen, 271
Ortiz Basualdo, José de, 271
Ortíz de Bedia, Juan, 112
Ortíz de Bergara, Francisco, 45
Ortiz de Matienzo, Juan, 17
Ortíz de Otálora, Antonio, 80
Ortíz de Rozas, Domingo, 70, 221
Ortiz de Urrutia, Sancho, 42
Ortíz de Zárate, Juan, 39, 45, 46, 70
Ortíz de Zárate, Juana, 46
Ortíz de Zárate, Pedro de, 63
Ortíz de Zárate, Rodrigo, 46, 70
Ortíz de Zuñiga, Iñigo, 39
Ortiz, Domínguez, 128
Ortiz, Josefa, 116
Ortuño, Martín de, 41
Orúe, Diego de, 45, 217
Orúe, Martín de, 217
Ospina, Diego de, 37
Ospina Pérez, Mariano, 495 n. 79
Ospitaleche, Martín, 499 n. 32
Ostolaza, J. M., 174
Otaegui y Ondemar, Juan Ignacio de, 104
Otálora, Bernabé de, 78
Otalora, Juan de, 38
Oteiza de la Solana, 345
Oteiza, Jorge, 206
Oteiza, José María de, 204
Oteiza, Juan, 258
Otondo y Dufurrena, Agustín, 224
Otto, Nikolaus August, 300
"Otxandiano" hospital, 396
Ovando, Nicolás, 489 n. 3
Oviedo, Fernández de, 29
Oviedo, Juan Antonio de, 115
Oyanguren, Luis de, 79
Oyanume, Francisco, 208
Oyarzábal Irigoyen family, 181

Oyarzábal, Juan Pedro, 185
Oyarzábal, Miguel de, 83
Oyhagaray, Joanes de, 83
Ozaeta, Martín de, 42

Pacheco, Jorge, 229
Pacific Ocean, 27, 31
Pacific Queen (ship), 401
Pacific Steam Navigation Co., 389, 401
Pacífico de Navegación transport company, 391
Padilla Estrada, José, 114
Padilla, José, 399
painting, Catholic Church and, 60, 67
Palace of Ituren, 159
Palafoz y Mendoza, Juan de, 115
Palos, 11, 16
Pamplona: Catholic Church in, 519n. 43; missionaries in America, 407, 408; "Scientific, Literary, and Artistic Competition," 391–92
Pamplona, Antonio de, 186
Panama: Basque influence, 194; early expeditions to, 27, 31; piracy and, 53
Panama City, 31
Pane, Ramón, 18
Pantaleón, León, 204, 206
papal bulls, 57–58, 481 n. 38, 485 n. 2
Paraguay, 45; Basque presence in, 215–18; Catholic clergy in, 64; explorers and conquistadors in, 46; French attempt at colonization, 218
Paria, Gulf of, 18
parientes mayores, 54
París, De, hotel (Montevideo), 251
Partido Nacionalista Vasco (PNV), 176
Pasaia, 6, 54, 361
pase foral, 474 n. 2
Passionist priests, 203–4
passports, 359–60, 362, 364
Pastiana Borro, Mijael, 495 n. 79
Patagonian Indians, 32
"paternal consent," 359

Patriote Français, Le (newspaper), 232, 244
Patriotic Seminary of Vergara, 172
Payagua Indians, 216
Paz Alonso y Espinoza, María de la, 189
Peace of Aceguá, 259
Peace of Vienna, 297
Pedrueza, Juan de la, 85
Peninsular and Oriental Line, 302
Pensamiento Navarro, El (newspaper), 345, 371, 373
Perea-Sasiain family, in Colombia, 204, 495 n. 81
Perea Gallaga, Andrés, 205
Peredo, Ángel de, 268
Pérez, Antonio, 68
Pérez de Arceniega, Jerónimo, 36
Pérez de Arteaga, Juan, 34, 35
Pérez de Esquivel, Alonso, 40
Pérez de Gordejuela, Juan, 112
Pérez de Guzmán, Juan, 198
Pérez de Idiaquez, Martín, 83
Pérez de Lazcano, Francisco, 39
Pérez de Lezcano, Martín, 35
Pérez de Luzurriaga, Juan, 79
Pérez de Mallea, Antonio, 42
Pérez de Olazabal, Martín, 79
Pérez de Ortubia, Juan, 33
Pérez de Salazar, Alonso, 70
Pérez de Tolosa, Juan, 69
Pérez de Tudela, Juan, 39
Pérez de Urasandi, Martín, 112
Pérez de Urria, Joaquín, 194
Pérez de Zarrondo, Martín, 49
Pérez, Juan, 10
Peru: Lope de Aguirre and, 50–51; Basque administrators and officials in, 72–73; Basque associations in, 114–15; Basque emigration and, 147, 217, 426; Basque mercantile activities in, 102–6; Basque presence in, 210–15; Catholic clergy in, 62–63; conquistadors and explorers, 38–40, 50–51, 514n. 12; immigration trends, 139, 142; Royal Basque Society and, 123, 475
Philanthropic Immigration Association (Argentina), 276
Philharmonic Instructor, The (Gómez), 116
Philip III (king of Spain), 68, 219
Philip II (king of Spain): Lope de Aguirre and, 50; Basque administrators of, 69; church-state relations and, 59; colonial commerce and, 80; emigration policy and, 127, 129; privateering and, 516n. 27; Third Provincial Council of Lima and, 212; voyages of circumnavigation and, 515n. 19
Philip IV (king of Spain), 56, 68, 72
Philippines: Araban emigration to, 521n. 59; Bizkaian emigration to, 402; explorers and conquistadors in, 47–49; mercantilist trade and, 100–101; Royal Basque Society and, 123
Philip V (king of Spain): economic reforms and, 94; mercantilist trade and, 96, 97, 100; Spanish iron industry and, 91; Esteban de Urizar y Arespacochaga and, 271; War of the Spanish Succession and, 87
phylloxera, 299
Pía de Borbón, María, 397
Pilar Pildain, María, 346
Pildain Salazar, María Pilar, 382
Pimongnet family, in Chile, 224
Pineda, Rafaela Labayru, 182
Pinedo, Emiliano Fernández de, 194
pingues, 491 n. 55
Pinillos, Izquierdo and Co., 303
Pinillos Maritime Company, 265
pinnaces, 491 n. 55
Piñol, José, 190
Piñol Salas family, 181
Piñol y Muñoz, Micaela, 188
Pinos del Puente, 10
Pinta (ship), 12, 13, 14, 15, 16
Pintos, Manuel, 314

Pinzón family, 26
piracy, 77, 152–53, 515n. 24; attacks on Indies fleets, 521n. 6; Stede Bonnet, 515n. 21; Caribbean geography and, 52; history of, 52–53; privateering and, 53–58; reasons for, 51–52
Pizarro, Francisco, 29, 37, 38, 39
Pizarro, Gonzalo, 39
placet regio, 58
Plaza Euskara (Argentina), 290
Plaza y Lazárraga, Manuel de, 79
Plaza y Ubilla, Joaquín de, 120
Plum, Pierres, 47
PNV. *See* Partido Nacionalista Vasco
Poey family, in Chile, 224
polacras, 491n. 55
political emigration, 392
Ponce de León, Juan, 33
populationist theory, 127
Portales Irarrázaval, Diego, 221
Portobelo, 29, 476n. 18
Portugal: competition with Spain, 16–17; Treaty of Tordesillas and, 17; Uruguay and, 229
Portugalete, 8
potato, 20
Potosí, 208, 209, 216, 219, 488n. 38
Prado Beltrán de Guevara, Bernardo de, 38
Pra family, in Chile, 224
Presencia alavesa en América y Fílipinas (1700–1825) (A. Martínez de Salazar), 485n. 59
primary families, 179
privateers, 53–58; Basque outfitters, captains, and home ports, 54, 55, 56, 438–51, 516n. 26; history of, 516n. 26; social origins, 55–56; Spanish ordinances and regulation of, 516n. 27; Spanish recruiters and vessels, 437
Pro-Basque Immigration Committee (Argentina), 398
Pro-Euzkadi Committee (New York), 404
Progres, Le (newspaper), 244

Project for Galleons and Fleets, of Peru and Nueva España, 94
Project of Galleons and Fleets, 487n. 25
Protector of Indians, 64
Puebla de los Angeles, 140
Pueblo Navarro, El (newspaper), 372
Puerta de Salazar, Juan de la, 71
Puerto de Santa María, 11
Puerto Rico, 17, 31; Gaspar de Arteaga and, 198–201; Basque Center in, 531n. 71; Basque influence and presence in, 198–204; Basque professions and jobs in, 498; Bizkaian emigration to, 400, 402; commercial activities, 201–2; governors, 530n. 51; immigration to, 202–4, 397–98; smuggling and, 530n. 56

Querejeta, Angela, 254–55, 256
Quesada, Jiménez de, 37
Quexo, Bono de, 42
Quijote de la Mancha, El (Cervantes), 484n. 54
Quintanilla, Alonso de, 9
Quintero, Cristóbal, 12
Quintero, Juan, 12, 13
Quiroga, Horacio, 256
Quiroga, Julián, 313, 321
Quiroga, Vasco de, 482n. 40
Quiroja, Julián, 245
Quiroz Paz-Soldán, Eusebio, 496n. 99

Rada, Juan de, 39, 40
Rada, Martín de, 47
railways, European migrations and, 299–300, 301
Ramírez de Velasco, Juan, 70
Ramos, Martín, 34
Razquin, Jaime de, 46
Real Compañía Guipúzcoana de Caracas. *See* Royal Guipuzcoan Company of Caracas
Real Sociedad Bascongada de Amigos del País, 62, 117–22, 172–74. *See also*

Royal Basque Society of the Friends of the Country
Rebollo, Manuel, 121
Recacoechea, Domingo, 85
Reconquest, 6, 9
Recopilación de las leyes de los reynos de Indias, 21
reducciones, 482n. 40, 483–84n. 47
refugees. *See* Basque exiles
Regulations of Free Trade, 96, 107
Relectiones de Indios (Vitoria), 64
Relectiones theologicae (Vitoria), 64
religious buildings, donations from America and, 153–54, 441–43
religious furnishings, donations from America and, 156, 449–53
Rentería, Iñigo de, 62
Rentería, Martín de, 36
Rentería, Pedro de, 30, 65
retables, 156
Retama, Fernández de, 167
Retes Mollinedo family, 181
Revolutionary War. *See* American War of Independence
Reyes family, in Costa Rica, 191
Reyles, Carlos, 256
Rezábal, Andrés de, 167
Rezabal y Ugarte, Ignacio José de, 71
Rezola, Matías de, 112
Ribera of Estella, 375
Ribera of Tudela, 375
Ribera, Rafael de, 38
Rico, Gonzalo del, 85
Rico y Gómez, Isidro, 331
right of palm, 487n. 25
Río de la Plata: Araban emigration to, 395, 396; Basque administrators and officials in, 71; Basque emigration to, 147, 395, 396, 403, 404; Basque mercantile activities, 98–99, 106–9; Bizkaian emigration to, 403, 404; Catholic clergy in, 63–64; cost of ocean passage to, 409; emigration agencies and emigration agents, 330–40; explorers and conquistadors in, 43–47; exports to France, 295; Gipuzkoan emigration to, 404–6; immigration trends, 139; national immigration policies, 323–30; Navarrese emigration to, 397, 400, 401–2; Royal Basque Society and, 123. *See also* Argentina; Uruguay
The Rising (ship), 57
Rivadavia, Bernardino, 273, 276, 306
Rivera, Pedro de, 168
Rocha (Uruguay), 228
Rodó, José Enrique, 256
Rodríguez Bermejo, Juan, 9, 14
Rodríguez Campomanes, Pedro, 117
Rodríguez de Vergara, García, 217
Rodriguez, Lorenzo, 172
Rojas, A., 207
Rojas, José, 85
Rojas Urturguren, José Antonio de, 221–22
Rojas y Sandoval, Cristóbal de, 79
Roldán, Francisco, 18
Romá y Asturias, José Mariano, 184
Ronda, Beltrán de la, 83
Rosas, Juan Manuel de, 275
Royal and Supreme Council of the Indies. *See* Council of the Indies
Royal Armada, 76, 79, 97
Royal Basque Society of the Friends of the Country, 63, 119–24, 154, 172, 174, 175–76; number of members, 472–75
Royal Board of the Consulate of Mexico City, 169
Royal Coast Guard (Spain), 57
Royal College of Saint Ignatius of Loyola, 172. *See also* College of the Vizcayans
Royal Company of Havana, 109
Royal Company of Honduras, 97
Royal Company of Our Lady of Zacatecas, 163
Royal Company of the Philippines, 98–99

Royal Consulate of Guatemala, 187
Royal Document of Free Commerce, 228
Royal Guipuzcoan Company of Caracas, 55, 57, 94, 95–96, 97–99, 104–5, 111, 144, 160, 207, 431
Royal Mail Steam Navigation Company, 302
Royal Mail Steamship Company, 302
Royal Patriotic Seminary, 118–19
Rubio, Javier, 392
Ruiz de Echave, Martín, 83
Ruiz de Gama, Sancho, 12
Ruiz de la Peña, Juan, 13
Ruíz de Monjaraz, Martín, 34
Ruiz de Viana, Juan, 34
Ruiz de Zurbano, Francisco Ruiz de Aguirre, 69
Russian Empire, emigration from, 295

Sacred Heart, 203, 205
Sáenz de Martín de Arlucea, Manuel, 71
Sáenz de Villaverde, Juan Antonio de Viana y, 62
Sáenz, Diego de, 186
Sáenz Sáenz, Jenaro, 206
Sáenz, Teodoro Olarte, 192
Sáez de Agorreta, Pietre, 83
Sáez de Arexmendi, Martín, 83
Sáez de Echave, Martín, 83
Sáez de Ibaneta, Martín, 83
Sáez de Lizardi, Martín, 83
Sagasti y Heredia, Mariano, 349–50
Sagastume Artola, José Ignacio, 270
sailors, salaries of, 491 n. 52
Saint Aubin, 6
Saint-Espirit (ship), 83
Saint-Macary family, in Chile, 224–25
Saint Thomas, Bay of, 15
Sainz, Lucas, 258
Sala, Martín, 321
Salazar, Andrés de, 61
Salázar del la Peña family, 181
Salazar, Diego de, 196
Salazar, Gabriel de, 41

Salazar, Gonzalo de, 476 n. 17
Salazar, Juan de, 44
Salazar, Pedro de, 39
Salazar Robles, José Martínez, 70
Salazar, Sancho de, 193
Salcedo, Bartolomé, 17
Salcedo, Felipe de, 47, 48
Salcedo, Fernando de, 35
Salcedo, García de, 38, 39, 40
Salcedo, José García de, 167
Salcedo, Juan de, 38, 48
Salcedo, Manuel de, 215
Salcedo, Miguel de, 70
Salcedo, Rodrigo de, 39
Saldivar, Fernández de, 79
Salinas, Battle of, 39
Salinas de Jaúregui, Antonio, 212
Samayoa Aguinaga family, 181
San Agustín of Lima, 488 n. 38
San Antonio (ship), 31
Sánchez, Antonio de, 34
Sánchez Cotillos, Alonso, 24
Sánchez de Bilbao, Diego, 49
Sánchez de Zamudio, Martín, 29
Sánchez, Florencio, 256
Sánchez, Gabriel, 10
San Esteban del Saltillo convent, 164
San Francisco el Grande, 171
San Francisco Javier (ship), 105, 106
San Ignacio de Loyola (ship), 105
San Ignacio (ship), 57, 95
San Joaquín (ship), 95
San Juan Bautista, 17
San Juan de los Caballeros, 165
San Juan Evangelista (ship), 106
San Juan, Martín de, 34
San Juan (Puerto Rico), 198
San Juan (ship), 47
San Juan y Santa Cruz, Manuel de, 167
San Julián, 32
San Julián Olaso, Joaquín, 345
Sanlúcar de Barrameda, 18, 20, 32, 33
San Lucas (ship), 47
San Mamés, 6

Index

San Miguel de Culiacán, 36, 162
San Nicolás de Ugarte y Portu, 6
San Pablo (ship), 47
San Pedro (ship), 47, 106
San Salvador, 14
San Salvador de Jujuy, 267
San Sebastián, Juan de, 34
San Sebastián, Koldo, 392
Santa Ana (ship), 27
"Santa Cruz" colony, 27
Santa Cruz (ship), 106
Santa Fe, 10
Santa María de la Antigua de Darien, 29
Santa María de la Concepción, 15
Santa María, Felipe de, 186
Santa María (ship), 11–12, 13, 14, 15, 19, 475 n. 12, 476 n. 16
Santander, 376, 381
Santángel, Luis de, 9–10
Santa Rosa (ship), 57
Santaulary, Enrique, 85
Santelices, Juan de, 33
Santelices y la Vía, Manuel Antonio de, 104
Santiago, 41, 402
Santiago del Estero (Argentina), 479 n. 17
Santiago de Tucumán, 269
Santiago (ship), 31
Santo Domingo, 24, 30, 52, 55, 57, 58, 65, 66, 71, 193, 476 n. 18
Santo Domingo (city), 18
Santurtzi, 8
San Vicente (province), 185–86
Sanz, Pedro, 83
São Paulo, 225–26
Sarachaga brothers, 85
Sarasu, Domingo de, 83
Saravia, Aparicio, 257
Saravia y Mollinedo, Nicolás González de, 104
Sardaneta y Legazpi, Vicente Manuel de, 108
Sarmiento de Sotomayor, García, 113
Sarra, Ignacio de, 268
Sarraoa e Iriarte, Juan B. de, 101
Sarría, Agustín, 320
Sarría, Juan de, 42
Sarricolea y Zamudio, Diego Hordoño, 212
Sasiain Aberasturi, Dominga, 205
Sautu, José María de, 271
Savannali (ship), 302
Sayas Espeluca, Pedro de, 46
Scandinavian emigration, 295
scholarships, Spanish immigration laws and, 341–42
schools, 120–21; Catholic, 67; donations from America and, 158, 160–61, 483–84
Schools of Primary Education, 118
"Scientific, Literary, and Artistic Competition" (Pamplona), 370
"scorecards," 481 n. 30
sculpture, Catholic Church and, 67
Sebastián Elcano, Juan, 28, 32, 33
secondary families, 179
Second Carlist War: impact on Basque emigration, 344, 345; Uruguayan immigration and, 245
sees, established under Ferdinand II, 481 n. 39
Segura Zabala, Pedro de, 217
Segure, Michel de, 83
Senegal (ship), 347
Sevilla: Basque administrators and officials in, 81; Basque iron industry and, 91, 92, 463–65; colonial commerce and, 7–8, 20, 75–76, 77, 78; slave trade and, 94; transfers of American capital and, 155
sheep herders and sheep raising: in Argentina, 275–76, 277–78, 279–80, 281, 285, 286, 323; in the United States, 298–300, 303–5, 306–8; in Uruguay, 229–31, 254–55, 323
shipping: in Basque economy, 4–5; commerce with the New World, 20; com-

panies operating in Gasteiz, 410; Indies fleet, 77–78, 521n. 6, 522n. 9, 537n. 55
ships: conditions of transatlantic passage, 150–54, 381–85; cost of ocean passage to Río de la Plata, 409; regulations on numbers of emigrants carried, 387; types used on transatlantic voyages, 527n. 55. *See also* steamships; transatlantic passage
shipwreck, 361
shipyards and shipbuilding: in Basque economy, 6; Basque iron industry and, 86–87; impact of the New World on, 21–22
Sierra de la Plata, 44
Siglo, El (newspaper), 260
silver: donations from America and, 155–56; mines in Nueva España, 36
Sinaloa, 36
slave markets, 91–92
slavery/slave trade: Basque merchants and, 93, 94; Company of Buenos Aires and, 524n. 35; Cuba and, 196; Puerto Rico and, 202; Venezuela and, 43, 514n. 16
sloops, 491n. 55
smallpox, 363
Smith, Juan, 85
smuggling, 494n. 56
social class, colonial emigration and, 131, 146
social welfare: Basque Government's pledge to support, 429–30; College of the Vizcayans and, 174–75; Confraternity of Our Lady of Aránzazu of Mexico and, 173–74; donations from America and, 158–61
Society of Jesus: in Brazil, 227; missionary activities, 518n. 40, 519nn. 41, 46, 520n. 47; in Río de la Plata, 64
Sojo, Juan, 40
Solaluce, Domingo de, 38
Solano, Jerónima, 142
Solano, Juan Jerónimo de, 156

Soloaga, Antonio de, 62
Soloaga y Gil, Antonio de, 213
Somorrostro, 3, 54
Somorrostro, Simón de, 49
Sonora, 162, 164, 167–70
Sopuerta, Diego de, 34
Soraluce, Domingo de, 38
Soraluce, Nicolás, 361
Soraluze, 22
Soriano, 227, 246, 248
Sorricoleta, Diego, 79
Sorozábal, Juan, 81
Sosa family, 181
Sota, Ramón de la, 404
Soule, 1
Spain: Basque Centers in, 431; Basque draft evasion and, 369–70; Basque officials, governors, and functionaries, 68–74; Basque positions and titles in the Bourbon court, 452–55; Bourbon economic reforms, 94–96; Caribbean pirates and, 51–53; church-state relations in the Americas, 58–60; competition with Portugal, 16–17; domestic iron industry, 90–91; emigration from (*see* Basque emigration; colonial emigration); Enlightenment movement in, 119; immigration laws and policies, 354–62; Indies monopoly and, 75–79; migratory policy, 125–30; privateering and, 53–58, 437, 438, 516n. 27; settling of Uruguay, 229–32; Treaty of Tordesillas and, 17
Spanish Association of Mutual Aid (Argentina), 289
Spanish Civil War: Basque emigration and, 362; Chile and, 223; Cuban and, 197; emigration of Basque exiles, 413–25; immigrant Basques in America and, 311; Mexico and, 179; Navarrese missionaries and, 408
Spanish Hospital: Argentina, 289; Uruguay, 265
Spanish Legitimist, The (newspaper), 348

Spanish Succession, War of, 56, 70, 86, 89, 93
Spice Islands, 28, 29, 30, 31, 32, 43, 479 n. 19
Spiritual Exercises (Loyola), 115
sports, 407, 408. See also handball
Statistic of Emigration and Immigration of Spain in the Five-Year Period 1891–1895, 344
steamship companies. See navigation companies
steamships: conditions on transatlantic passages, 381–85; cost of passage to Argentina, 409; technological advances and, 318
steel exports, 421–27
stem families, 353
Storm (ship), 396
Suarade, Miguel de, 83
Suarez, Inés, 41
Suberos, José, 251
Subiza, Juan de, 79
sugarcane, 293
sugar refineries, 87
Susi, Pedro de, 83
Susmiaga, Juan de, 34
Suso y Bengoa, Vicente, 331
Suso y Sorazábal, María Concepción de, 331

Tabla Ducasse, Javier Ortiz de la, 209
Taino Indians, 17
talo, 20
tambos, 266
Tarahumara Indians, 167
tartans, 491 n. 55
technical emigration, 405
telegraphs, 300–301, 302
telephones, 300, 301
television, 408
Tellería y Tapia, Blás Ignacio, 121
Tellier, Charles, 301
Temiño de Bañuelos, Baltasar, 163
Tenochtitlán, 35

Tepeaca, 35, 65
Terra, Gabriel, 263
Terranova, 82, 83, 85, 86, 111
Teso, Miguel de, 196
theater, Catholic Church and, 66
"Thirteen Famous Ones, the," 478 n. 12
Tierra del Fuego, 32
Tirapu, Agustín de, 143
tobacco, 74, 85, 95, 97, 109, 110, 111
Toledo, Francisco de, 482 n. 41
Tolosa, Ignacio de, 63
Tolosa, Juan de, 36, 163, 165
Tolosa, Pedro de, 33
Topographic Commission (Argentina), 275
Tordesillas, Treaty of, 13, 16
Torpehall (ship), 205
Torraeta, Anton de, 34
Torre, Eliodoro de la, 394, 396
Torres, Bartolomé, 12
Torres, Luis de, 12
Torrezábal, Juan de, 72
Torrezar, Ramón, 80
Tortuga, 52
tourism, 408
Tradición Navarra, La (newspaper), 345, 350, 371
Transatlántica Española transport company, 391
Transatlántica Maritime Company, 265
transatlantic passage: advice to passengers, 150; boarding licenses, 147–49; costs of, 149; disembarking, 154; living conditions on ships, 150–54, 381–85; provisions and supplies for, 149–50; World War II and, 422
transportation: European migrations and, 301–2, 302–3
Transports Maritimes transport company, 391
Treaty of Lisbon, 268
Treaty of Utrecht, 86, 137
Treaty of Victory (Cano), 115
Tribunal of Aztec Mining, 108

Tribunal of the Holy Office, 124
Trinidad, 18, 26, 42
Trinidad (ship), 31, 33
trolleys, 300
Trujillo, 39
tuberculosis, 264
Tucumán region (Argentina), 267–69, 271
Tufan Elida (ship), 57
Tuñón y Quirós, Gregorio Alvarez, 168
Tupamaros, 267
typhoid, 364

Ubilla, Andrés de, 61
Udaondo, Juan Bautista de, 271
Ugalde (Basque doctor), 395
Ugalde, Domingo, 231
Ugarte de la Cruz, Juan de, 34
Ugarte, Fernando Arias de, 212
Ugarte, Joanes de, 83
Ugarte, Lope de, 45, 216
Ugarte y Loyola, Jacobo, 73
Ugarte Zubiate, Domingo, 110
Uhagón, Vicente, 244
Uhart-Cize emigration firm, 334
Ulaiz, Felipe de, 72
Ulíbarri, Miguel, 258
Ulloa, Jerónimo de, 80
United States: Apache Territory, 296–97; Basque Centers in, 311, 430; Basque emigration and, 303–6, 352, 426; Basque exiles and, 425; Basque marital practices in, 309; Basque political activities in, 310–11; Basque population in, 301–2; Basque religious involvements and practices, 309–10; Basque sheep herders in, 298–300, 303–5, 306–8; commerce in immigration, 319–20; decline of the American myth for Basques, 306–8; gold prospectors in California, 297–98; immigration laws, 303
Universalis Ecclesiae (papal bull), 58
Urabá, 28

Urbieta, Miguel de, 35
Urbieta, Pedro de, 34
Urbieta, Sebastián de, 193
Urbina Apaloa, Juan de, 79
Urbina, Diego de, 39
urcas, 491 n. 55
Urdaiaga, 6
Urdanegui, Juan de, 79
Urdaneta, Andrés de, 47, 479 n. 19
Urdarribia, Pedro de, 112
Urdiñola, Francisco de, 48, 164
Urdunia, 8
Ureña, Juan de, 39
Uría, Alonso de, 42
Uriarte, Baltasar, 174
Uriarte, Millán de, 349–50
Uribe, Domingo de, 269
Uribe, García de, 83
Uribe, Pedro, 78
Uribe y Salazar, Catalina de, 210
Uriondo y Martínez de Murguía, Joaquín Antonio Pérez de, 71
Uriortúa, Juan M., 80
Urizar, Antonio de, 120
Urizar y Arespacochaga, Esteban de, 269
Urqueta, Sancho de, 42
Urquiza, Justo José de, 276
Urquiza Sánchez de Alba, Santiago de, 121
Urquiza, Sancho de, 42
Urquizu, Francisco de, 61
Urrezti, Pedro de, 6
Urriola, Gonzalo de, 34
Urruela family, in Guatemala, 185
Urruela, Gregorio de, 185
Urruela, José, 185
Urruela, Rafael, 185
Urruela y Angulo family, 180
Urrutia family, in Costa Rica, 191
Urrutia, Francisco, 174
Urrutia, José María, 175, 199
Urrutia, Juan de, 39, 42, 112, 113
Urrutia Mendiburu, Francisco de, 221
Urrutia y Arana, Juan Antonio de, 73

Urrutia y Guerrero, Mateo Cayetano de, 61
Urso, Miguel de, 46, 70
Ursúa, Pedro de, 50
Ursúa y Armendariz, Pedro de, 37
Urtubai, Perocho de, 83
Urtubia, Martín de, 13
Urueba, Juan de, 30
Uruena, Juan de, 196
Uruguay: Araban emigration to, 396; Basque Centers in, 251, 254, 431; Basque commercial activities in, 247–49, 253–54; Basque draft evaders in, 371; Basque emigration to, 232–47, 396, 403, 426; Basque exiles and, 422; Basque marriages in, 252, 253, 254; Basque society in, 250–55; Bizkaian emigration to, 403; Catholic clergy in, 64; Charles of Bourbon in, 365–66; emigration agencies and, 330; emigration agents and, 334–36; emigration from, 228, 262; First Seminar on Basque Immigration, History, and Culture, 434, 535n. 32; French influence in, 245–46; Great War and, 235–36; immigration policies, 326–27, 332; José María de Iparraguirre and, 255–58; living conditions of immigrants, 265–67; modern economic transformation, 261–62, 268; modern population trends, 262; movements of Basque immigrants, 249–50; nineteenth-century immigration, 232–50; Julián Quiroga's assessment of Basques as immigrant-colonists, 339–40; settling of Banda Oriental, 229–32; sheep herders and sheep raising in, 229–31, 254–55, 323; success of Basque immigrants, 254–55; twentieth-century history, 258–67; twentieth-century immigration, 262–64, 267–69; working conditions of immigrants, 264–65. *See also* Montevideo; Río de la Plata

Uruguayan League against Tuberculosis, 264
Usurpi, Martín de, 208
Uztáriz, Juan A., 80
Uztáriz, Martín, 80
Uztáriz y Vertiz Verea, Juan Andrés, 220

Vaca de Castro, Cristóbal, 40
Vaca y Echeverría, Joaquín Cabeza de, 103
Veramendi, Juan de, 66
Vaillante (ship), 390
Valdivia, Pedro de, 41, 478n. 14
Valdivieso, Luis de, 208
Valenciana de Navegación (ship), 303
Valle de Erro, 355
Valle, Manuel Cecilio de, 159
Valparaiso, 401, 402
Vapores Tintoré (ship), 303
Varela, José Pedro, 256
Vasco-Asturiana company, 303
Vasconcelos Berruecso y Cuelleno, Francisco Javier, 108
Vasconia, Iñigo de, 42
Vasconia (newspaper), 290
Vaz Ferreira, María Eugenia, 256
Vedya, Gonzalo de, 26
Veitia Linaje, Juan de, 80
Veitia y Linaje, José de, 68, 78
Velarde y Murga, Joaquín Antonio de, 61
Velasco, Luis de, 163
Velasco, Pedro de, 185
Velasco y Sánchez de Samaniego, José Antonio Manso de, 70
Velasco y Tejada, Manuel, 70
Velasco y Zuñiga, Pedro de, 38
Velázquez de Cuellar, Diego, 30, 193, 478n.8
Vélez de Guevara, Lópe de, 39
Vélez de Mendoza, Alonso, 26
Vélez y Ladrón de Guevara, Cristóbal, 72
Vempraet, Adolfo, 320
Venegas, Francisco Javier de, 108
Venero de Leyva, Andrés Díaz, 72

566 Index

Venezuela: Basque administrators and officials in, 70–71; Basque Centers in, 210, 424, 431; Basque emigration and, 147, 209–10, 352, 426, 532n. 90; Basque exiles and, 420, 421, 423–24; conquistadors and explorers in, 42–43; donations to Basque Country from, 160; early expeditions to, 26; Royal Guipuzcoan Company of Caracas and, 96–97; slavery in, 514n. 16
Veragua, 28
Vera, Jerónimo de, 41
Vera, Juan de, 41
Vera, Marcos, 258
Verástegui, Juan de, 72
Veraza, Miguel de, 34
Verazu, Ochoa de, 34
Vergara, Alonso de, 34
Vergara, Cristóbal de, 196
Vergara, Juan de, 26, 34
Vergara, Martín de, 34
Vergara, Pedro de, 34
Vertiz y Ontañón, Juan José, 167
Vértiz y Salcedo, Juan José, 70
Vespucci, Amerigo, 26
Vial, Ramón Javier de, 220
Viana, Francisco Leandro de, 120
Viana, Leandro de, 172
Viana y Saenz de Villaverde, Francisco Leandro de, 73
Viana y Sáenz de Villaverde, Gregorio de, 71
Viana y Saenz de Villaverde, José Joaquin de, 70
Victoria (ship), 31, 32
Vicuñas, 208
Vidaurre, Antonio de, 62
Viejo, Heredia el, 34
Vildósola, Agustín de, 168
Villabaso, Luis de, 370
Villabona y Zubiaurre, Juan de, 38
Villa del Cerro (Uruguay), 231
Villafranca de Lezcano, Juan, 39
Villalba, Juan de, 36

Villamontes, Ignacio, 258
Villar, Angel de, 349
Villareal, Joaquín de, 220
Villareal report (Chile), 220
Villar, Francisco de, 42
Villarreal, Francisco de, 72
Villar, Sancho de, 42
Villar y Zubiaur, Pedro del, 101
Villate, Manuel, 258
Villaurrutia, Antonio de, 120
Villa Urrutia, Jacobo de, 187, 190
Villaurrutia, Jacobo de, 72
Villavaso, Juan, 85
Villela, Juan de, 71
Villota, Agustín, 80
vineyards: in Argentina, 292–93; phylloxera and, 299
Vita (ship), 394
Viteri family, 181
Vitoria, Francisco de, 64, 65
Vitoria, Tomás de, 186
Vitoria y Pagazaurtundua, Domingo Ignacio de, 73
Vivero, Juan M., 80
Vivero y Aberrucia, Rodrigo de, 109
Vizarrón y Eguiarreta, Juan Antonio de, 114
Vizcaína (ship), 19
Vizcaíno, Cristóbal, 30
Vizcaíno, Gonzalo, 30
Vizcaíno, Juan de, 34
Vizcaíno, Pedro, 17, 30, 34, 38
Vizcaíno, Pérez, 13
Vizcaíno, Santiago, 34
Vizcaíno, Sebastián, 49
Vizcaínos, Domingo, 476n. 17
volume companies. *See* iron companies
Voluntary Plan of Social Foresight, 408

Wanted Man, el Cojo Gómez in Colombia, A (Hummel), 206
War of Granada, 6, 10
War of Succession (Castile), 6
wedding vows, 157

whaling industry, 3, 81–86, 111
widows, College of the Vizcayans and, 171–72
Williman, Claudio, 260
Windward Armada, 77, 79
Winnipeg (ship), 401
women: College of the Vizcayans and, 171–72; in colonial emigration, 125, 126, 133, 135–36, 139
World Conference of Basque Communities: on displaying Basqueness, 432; William Douglass on the future of the Basque diaspora, 427–28; final declaration of, 432–34; pledges by the Basque Government, 428–30
World War II, transatlantic passages and, 401

Yaben Yaben, Hilario, 372
Yáñez Pinzón, Vicente, 28, 33
Yañez, Vicente, 12
yangüeses, 153
Ybarra and Company, 303
Yermo, Gabriel, 169
Yerri, 384
The Young Gentleman (ship), 57
Young William (ship), 57
Ypenza, Ambrosio, 186
Yribarren, Fernando, 258
Yucatán, 33

Zabala, Agustín de, 72
Zabala, Aingeru, 53
Zabala, Andrés de, 112
Zabala, Antón de, 42
Zabala, Bruno Mauricio de, 227, 228, 243
Zabala, Martín de, 72
Zabaleta, Martín, 83
Zabaleta, Pedro de, 72
Zabalo Urreaga, Prudencio, 376
Zacatecan Indians, 163
Zacatecas, 36, 144
Zaldivar, Juan de, 162, 216
Zaldivar, Vicente de, 165
Zaldivar y Pascual, Domingo de, 101
Zaldivia, Martín de, 83
Zaldizar, Juan de, 45
Zamacolada rebellion, 62
Zamácola, Simón Bernardo de, 121
Zamácola y Jáuregui, Juan Diego de, 62
Zamácola y Jáuregui, Juan Domingo de, 121
Zamudio, Francisco de, 39
Zamudio, Juan de, 17, 30, 34, 269
Zamudio, Martín de, 17
Zamudio, Sánchez de, 29
Zañartu Iriarte, Luís Manuel de, 221
Zangroniz, José de, 194
Zangroniz, Juan Bautista de, 194
Zarandia, Juan Bautista de, 69
Zarandona y Chavarría, Juan de, 103
Zárate, Agustín de, 65, 210
Zárate, Fernández de, 46
Zárate, Ortiz de, 217
Zárate, Pedro de, 40
Zárate, Pedro José de, 121
Zárate y Mendieta, Domingo Ortíz de, 45
Zárate y Murga, Diego de, 72
Zarautz, 31
Zárraga Beográn, Francisco de, 54–55
Zarranz, Santiago de, 223
Zavala, Martín de, 194
Zavala y Miranda, José de, 96
Zerain, 3
Zozoya, Nicolás de, 49
Zuaxo, Juanes de, 35
Zuaznabar, José Antonio de, 318
Zuaznabar, Miguel Antonio de, 95, 98
Zuazo, Alonso de, 34, 65
Zuazo, Francisco de, 91
Zuazo, Sancho de, 42
Zuazo, Tomás de, 68
Zuazo y Otalora, Juan de, 72
Zubeldi, Antonio María, 230–31
Zubia, Juan de, 34
Zubiate, José de, 167–68
Zubieta, Juan, 83
Zubieta, Sebastián de, 34

Zubileta, Juan de, 33
Zubillaga, Antonio, 85
Zubirtuaga, Ignacio, 80
Zubizarreta, Domingo de, 42, 72
Zuloaga, Joaquín, 81
Zulueta, Julián de, 194
Zulueta y Amondo, Julián de, 194
Zumarán, Josefa, 231

Zumarán, Ramón de, 231
Zumárraga, José de, 331
Zumarraga, Juan de, 64–65, 484 n. 50
Zúñiga, López de, 219
Zúñiga y Acevedo, Gaspar de, 165
Zurbano, Jerónimo, 39
Zurbano, Juan de, 41
Zuricarai, Joanes de, 83